BSH

27

THE GERMAN CANADIANS
1750—1937

The German Canadians 1750–1937

Immigration, Settlement & Culture

Heinz Lehmann

Translated, Edited & Introduced
by
Gerhard P. Bassler

Jesperson Press
St. John's, Newfoundland
1986

Jesperson Press
26A Flavin Street
St. John's, Newfoundland
A1C 3R9

Text & Cover Design: Alan J. de Gonzague
Typesetting: Jesperson Printing Ltd.
Printing & Binding: Gagne Printing Ltd, Quebec

This book has been published with the help of a grant from the Canadian Federation for the Humanities using funds provided by the Social Sciences and Humanities Research Council of Canada, and with the financial assistance of Multiculturalism Canada.

The publisher acknowledges the assistance of the Cultural Affairs Division of the Department of Culture, Recreation & Youth of the Government of Newfoundland & Labrador which has helped make this publication possible.

Appreciation is expressed to the Canada Council for its assistance in publishing this work.

Cataloguing in Publication Data
Lehmann, Heinz, 1907-1985.
The German Canadians 1750-1937

Bibliography: p.
Includes index.
ISBN 0-920502-76-8

1. German Canadians.   2. Germans—Canada.
3. Canada—Emigration and immigration.
I. Bassler, Gerhard P., 1937—   II. Title.

FC106.G3L43 1986   971'.00431   C86-093949-9
F1035.G3L43 1986

To my very own German Canadians
— Elisabeth, Heidi, Christine & Paul

Table of Contents

List of Tables

List of Illustrations

FOREWORD

"Habent sua fata libelli."

I consider it great luck that amidst a lot of daily teaching and lecturing I was able to complete my book on the Germans in western Canada by the end of 1937, so that the book could be published in March 1939, just in time before the outbreak of World War II. Otherwise my text and notes as well as all the source material on which they were based would most probably have been lost when we were bombed out of our Berlin flat in 1943. And yet all my endeavours seemed to have been in vain when the remainder of the edition, after only about one hundred copies had been sold and only a few had reached Canada, was destroyed in an air raid on Leipzig as early as 1942. My books were completely forgotten for decades.

It is entirely due to the initiative of Professor G.P. Bassler of the Department of History of Memorial University of Newfoundland and the new interest in ethnic minorities and in multiculturalism that the results of my early research work can be published now in an English version. It was his suggestion to combine my two books of 1931 and 1939 and two or three additional papers into the present publication to create a new organic whole. First, the history of German-speaking immigration and settlement is narrated in chronological and geographical order from east to west, and then the religious, secular and cultural life of western Canada's Germans is examined. I am particularly grateful that he shouldered the hard work of translation and that he translated so excellently. I have read the proofs of the whole English version and thus share with him full responsibility for every detail of the present English translation. It was his idea to give a somewhat shortened version on my original publications of the years 1931 to 1939, including the prefaces to both my books, in order to preserve them as historical testimonies of the attitudes of the times. No critic of good will can doubt my endeavours at the time to report objectively and to abstain from ideological propaganda.

I shall be very happy indeed when this English version of my early studies, that took me long years of research in libraries and archives and several months of field studies in Canada, can now appear around my golden wedding anniversary. I take it as a late, but not too late, recognition of my work for the benefit of Canada and the German Canadians.

Tübingen, May 25th, 1985.
Heinz Lehmann

EDITOR-TRANSLATOR'S NOTE

The contents of this edition consist of five publications: Heinz Lehmann's two books of 1931 and 1939 (*Zur Geschichte des Deutschtums in Kanada* and *Das Deutschtum in Westkanada*), two articles on German postwar immigration to eastern Canada—"Das Deutschtum in Ostkanada," *Deutsche Arbeit* 34:12 (1934), 610-613, and 35:1 (1935), 12-17—and the interpretation of his map of western Canada "Zur Karte des Deutschtums in den kanadischen Prärieprovinzen," *Deutsches Archiv für Landes- und Volksforschung*, II: 4 (1938), 859-866. These represent Lehmann's most original and most significant scholarly contributions on this topic.

It was possible to integrate these publications in such a way that they formed chronologically and topically a well-structured book. Chapters I to III consist of the unabridged translation of Lehmann's first book. Chapters IV to VII represent an abridged version of *Kapitel* 2 to 5 and 7 to 11 of Lehmann's second book. In Chapter VIII, parts 1, 3 and 4 contain the gist of *Kapitel* 6, 12 and 13 of the second book; and part 2, a contraction of the articles on the postwar immigration to eastern Canada. The appendix includes statistical tables, mostly taken from *Kapitel* 10 of *Das Deutschtum in Westkanada* and a condensed version of the cartographic article of 1938 with maps (three of which were not published by Lehmann but discussed by him).

My original plan was to publish an unabridged translation of the five publications by Lehmann. But this turned out to be unrealizable, due to the size and bulk of the manuscript. In preparing this abridged edition, I was guided by the desire to preserve for posterity all the historical facts that Lehmann had unearthed and recorded in Canada, as well as by Heinz Lehmann's wishes to streamline his work by deleting dated and repetitive passages. It is hoped that this publication can serve as a starting point for further research, as a tool of reference, and as the documentation of a crucial period in the history of German Canadians.

Considerable research was necessitated in tracing, wherever possible, the authentic terms, paraphrases and quotations of Lehmann's original English-language sources. With few exceptions, all of Lehmann's footnotes were translated and many of them were verified. My own footnotes and comments are, unless otherwise indicated, always clearly prefaced with the words "editor's note." In the footnotes Lehmann's method of citing his sources by their number in the alphabetically arranged bibliography was retained as a useful system of cross reference for this extensive edition. To avoid confusion, the number in parentheses directly following the author's name always denotes the consecutive number under which the source is listed in the bibliography.

Thanks to the new awareness of the ethnic dimension in North American society, I was able to avail myself of the widely used term "ethnic" and its various derivatives in order to render the multiple meaning of the German word *Volkstum* more adequately into English than was possible twenty years ago or earlier. At that time the standard English equivalents used were "racial" and "national," both of which are inaccurate. Depending on the meaning and context, I translated *Volkstum* either as ethnicity, ethnic identity, ethnic cause, ethnic aspirations, ethnic heritage or ethnic community. For the equally difficult term *Deutschtum*, the ugly improvisation of "Germandom"—which appears neither in *Webster's* nor in the *Oxford Universal Dictionary*—was avoided in favor of an equivalent spectrum of translations as for *Volkstum*, such as Germans, German element, German population, German heritage, German identity, etc. For *Auslandsdeutsche*, the translation "Germans in other lands" was considered more meaningful than "Germans abroad." *Kanadadeutsche* are Canadian Germans, while for *Russlanddeutsche* the more widely accepted translation "Germans from Russia" was preferred. The correct English equivalent for *evangelisch* is not "evangelical" which has a fundamentalist connotation in North America, but "Protestant." *Katholik* and *katholisch*, translated as "Catholic" since they often appear in conjunction with "German," always mean Roman Catholic. The term "German," unless defined more clearly, always means German by ethnic descent or origin, and does not necessarily imply German-speaking, or related to Germany by birth or former domicile. The designation "German by origin" refers to the so-called "racial origin" (since 1941 officially renamed "ethnic origin") classification of the Canadian Census. It should not be confused with either the nativity (i.e., place or country of birth), the nationality (i.e., citizenship), the country of origin (i.e., former domicile or residence) or the mother tongue classifications of the Canadian Census, the Canadian immigration agencies, port statistics, etc. The "racial origin" data reflect the responses to the question on the male line of descent, i.e. the paternal ancestry.

For the decision to prepare this edition, for its format and the quality of its translation, I bear full and exclusive responsibility. Without the encouragement of Mr. Myron Momryk of the Multicultural Directorate in Ottawa this project might not have been completed. The generous assistance awarded me by his department facilitated the necessary research, the painstaking labors of translation and the publication of this extensive manuscript in Canada. A Vice President's Research Grant from Memorial University of Newfoundland enabled me to make the personal acquaintance of Heinz Lehmann in Tübingen, Germany, in April 1981, in order to consult with him and obtain his blessings for my undertaking. I am grateful to Heinz Lehmann for offering to proofread the entire manuscript and for authorizing my edition of his original publications. My colleagues William A. Kearns and R. Keyserlingk deserve credit for suggesting editorial and stylistic improvements, and Judy Gibson for her conscientious editorial assistance. The greatest debt I owe, however, to my wife Tonya Kurt Bassler, M.A., who gave me invaluable moral, intellectual and editorial support through all the stages of this project.

Gerhard P. Bassler
St. John's, Newfoundland

HEINZ LEHMANN AND GERMAN-CANADIAN HISTORY

by

Gerhard P. Bassler

Despite the many excellent monographs available on the German ethnic groups in the United States and in other lands, Heinz Lehmann noted in his foreword to volume I of *Zur Geschichte des Deutschtums in Kanada* (1931), "no comprehensive critical account of the history of Canada's Germans has yet been attempted." Among the written manifestations of the German Canadians themselves, Lehmann found only fragmentary, mostly inaccurate sketches about their almost two-hundred-year-old presence in the East. With regard to the more recent history of western Canada's Germans, Lehmann observed that as late as 1939, not even the first beginnings towards a critical record were noticeable. On their behalf he offered the apology that their struggle for the daily bread and the difficulties of organizing the many heterogeneous elements of the largely rural German ethnic community in Canada appeared to have left the German Canadians little time to reflect upon the past contributions of their ethnic group.

Today, looking back on the more than two decades of preoccupation with ethnic studies in North America, the more recent record of official Canadian multiculturalism and a greatly reinforced population of German ethnic descent in Canada with a large proportion of educated representatives, Lehmann's observations still appear to hold true, though not the apology he suggested.

We need today, even more than fifty years ago, an up-to-date historical assessment of the German Canadian identity and of the role of the German element in the economic, political and cultural development of Canada as a counterpart to the growing number of studies on the other Canadian ethnic groups. Most unfortunate is the fact that Lehmann's work has remained largely unknown and inaccessible to Canadian historians as well as to German Canadians. Almost the entire first and only edition of *Das Deutschtum in Westkanada* was destroyed in an air raid on Leipzig in 1942 and, for a long time, only a handful of the original copies existed in North America. Although the book was included in the Peel Bibliography in 1973 as one of the fundamental studies on the history of western Canadian settlement,[1] and thus became available on microfiche in 1977, most researchers into areas of German settlement in Canada remained unaware of Lehmann's work and of the contributions of the settlers of German descent which Lehmann so painstakingly recorded.

However, the main reason for bringing Heinz Lehmann's fifty-year-old work to the attention of Canada is simply the fact that to this day it remains the most comprehensive and scholarly account of the immigration and settlement of the entire ethnic German element in Canada. In spite of a vast new literature on the Mennonites and the Hutterites, the discovery of German settlers in mid-seventeenth century Quebec and the changed perspective of the 1980s, no major aspect of Lehmann's scholarship has been refuted to date. On the whole, our knowledge of German settlement in the Maritimes, Ontario and the Prairie provinces has not been expanded significantly since the 1930s. Lehmann's history is an indispensable compendium of historical scholarship, and a starting point for any new inquiry into the subject, by the mere fact that it is the product of an exhaustive digestion of the principal primary and secondary sources published in English and German and, to a limited extent, even in French up to the 1930s. It is, in addition, based on valuable unpublished first-hand information destroyed by the war. The attempt to be comprehensive, to deal with all the regions of Canada, all the events, groups, personalities, institutions and data of any significance to the history of German Canadians, makes this study also the main reference work on the subject up to the present time.

Lehmann's findings, finally, are still relevant today. He exhaustively documented the fact that from the beginning, the immigrants and settlers of German descent from all over Europe and North America represented not only numerically the second largest ethnic group in western Canada and the third largest ethnic element in Canada, but that they might also properly be considered as one of Canada's founding peoples. Lehmann shows that pioneers of German descent were among the first to colonize large regions in eastern and western Canada, and that the role of ethnic German settlers in the growth and fortunes of Canada was far greater than any English-language study has ever acknowledged. The significance of the historical evidence he unearthed is obvious in the light of long-cherished and still powerful traditions in Canadian historiography.

In the Niagara Peninsula of Ontario, for instance, "the Palatine Germans and other aliens outnumbered the British Anglicans ten—or perhaps twenty—to one" in the early nineteenth century. However, as a consequence of the War of 1812, bilingualism was frowned upon in a British colony and "Germans in the Niagara Peninsula were almost as objectionable as French in Lower Canada." The resulting systematic effort at reeducation not only made "99 percent of the descendants" of these pioneer Germans forget their heritage within two generations, but also led to their deletion from the historical record. "They were left out of all the textbooks. It worked in the Niagara Peninsula."[2]

In Saskatchewan, as recently as the 1930s, more than 15 per cent of the population still acknowledged German as their mother tongue, and no more than 40 per cent of the rural population were of British origin. Here the historical evidence for the prominent role of German settlers in the colonization and development of the province is overwhelming. Yet, even on the occasion of the seventy-fifth anniversary of the province in 1980, professional historians fastidiously passed over the German ethnicity of a large contingent of the pioneers. Little credit is given to the significant contributions made by the non-British majority of Saskatchewan's immigrants to the effort that civilized the prairies.[3] Among prairie historians, one of the dominant themes has been the idea of a unique prairie personality whose roots and life-style have supposedly been British in essence. Treatises on the genesis of prairie society tend to overlook the ethnic background of the colonists from Ontario and the United States, and ignore the statistical fact that during the period 1870 to 1900 about 10 per cent of Ontario's population and, by 1931, as many as 23.1 per cent of the American-born in Saskatchewan were of German descent.[4] In English-Canadian historical accounts, as in public opinion, the German element tends to enter the picture only when the events of the world wars come up for discussion. In view of the perpetuation of this kind of historical image to second and third generation German Canadians, should we be surprised at the rapid withering of Saskatchewan German culture? To be sure, "the hot blast of intolerance directed against it during the two world wars" was an incisive, though perhaps somewhat overrated factor.[5] But is it not, one might wonder in this context, a self-fulfilling prophesy that "western Canada has never produced a frontier myth, a body of lore and legend which defines its traditions," as Heather Robertson put it so poignantly, and that "the Canadian West has been of no account: either we never had a frontier or it was boring. No attention is paid to it."[6]

The challenges which the prevailing schools of contemporary Canadian historiography have posed were as evident to Heinz Lehmann's generation of the 1920s and 1930s as they are to the historian of Canadian multiculturalism in the 1980s. Noting with dismay that the representative works of Canadian historians deliberately or unconsciously ignored and belittled the contributions of German Canadians, Lehmann was determined to correct this deficiency. His eagerness to illuminate the historical role of Canada's German-speaking population as prominently as possible was but the antithesis to the obvious bias of Anglo-Canadian historical writing. To him, "putting the accomplishments of Germans in the opening up of Canada into the proper light,"[7] was overdue.

When Heinz Lehmann decided on a field for his doctoral studies in 1928, he was motivated by a deep concern for the fate of the German minorities in other lands as a result of the First World War. "It was one of the positive consequences of Germany's defeat sanctioned by the Treaty of Versailles," Lehmann recalled in 1983, "that one became aware of the fact (and nursed it among the young generation) that besides the 65 million Germans on the reduced territory of Germany there were many millions of the German people, so-called *Volksdeutsche*, outside Germany. We felt it was our right and duty to maintain spiritual contact with them and to assist them in their struggle for cultural survival." Student trips in 1926 and 1927 to Danzig, West Prussia and South Tyrol (where he was shocked by Mussolini's efforts to italianize even the German inscriptions on old tombstones) made lasting impressions on him.

Attention to Canada was drawn by Lehmann's academic advisor, Wilhelm Dibelius, professor of English studies at the University of Berlin. Having established his international reputation with a two-volume study of *England* (1923), Dibelius planned to undertake a large-scale study of Canada along the lines of André Siegfried's subsequently appearing work *Le Canada, puissance internationale* (1937). During an extended exploratory visit to Canada in the summer of 1928, Dibelius was astonished to find traces of German immigrants and German influences everywhere. Dibelius therefore suggested the history of the Germans in Canada, which had never been researched before, as a topic for Heinz Lehmann's doctoral dissertation. "Neither Dibelius nor I had the slightest idea what a large project I had taken upon myself at twenty-one years of age," Lehmann mused in retrospect.

Heinz Lehmann was born in Berlin in 1907 and died in Tübingen, Germany, in June 1985. The son of a federal civil servant, he studied English, history and political science at the Universities of Berlin, Bonn and London with the intention of embarking on a teaching career at a German secondary school (*Gymnasium*). A scholarship from the German Academic Exchange Service enabled him to study in London from October 1929 to June 1930. There, at the British Museum, the Royal Empire Society and the Record Office, he collected the materials for his dissertation. In the summer of 1931 he was awarded a doctoral degree with the distinction *summa cum laude* for his dissertation on the German element in Canada, part of which was published as vol. 31 in series A (*Kulturhistorische Reihe*) of the Deutsches Ausland-Institut Stuttgart under the title *Zur Geschichte des Deutschtums in Kanada. Band I: Das Deutschtum in Ostkanada* (Stuttgart: Ausland und Heimat Verlags-Aktiengesellschaft, 1931).

After passing his examinations for a teaching position at a German public secondary school, Dr. Lehmann, as a Studienassessor, was given the opportunity to continue his research during a visit to western Canada from May to August 1934. His study trip was funded by the *Volksbund für das Deutschtum im Ausland*, known as VDA, the oldest private non-partisan association supporting German linguistic and cultural retention in other lands. Lehmann's research in Canada was encouraged by a number of religious organizations including the Central Agency of German Mennonites from Russia in Karlsruhe, the Vicar General of the Roman Catholic Order of the Oblates of Mary Immaculate and the Lutheran Churches in North America. His visit to western Canada provided Lehmann with a unique opportunity to examine life in, and the situation of, the German communities in western Canada on the spot. He established personal contact with German Canadians from all walks of life—church leaders, businessmen, politicians, newspaper editors and leaders of cultural organizations. He interviewed hundreds of people. As a result, virtually all the material of any relevance for a history of the German element in western Canada which had been collected by German-Canadian agencies and organizations was put at his disposal. Of particular interest were 128 reports from various districts of German settlement recording their origins and early history. Most of them were handwritten, many of them spelled in the ancestral dialects of the settlers, and one even in Cyrillic script, and included recollections of the last surviving pioneers. Bernhard Bott, editor of the German-language newspaper *Der Courier* in Regina, Saskatchewan, from 1923 to 1934, had obtained these in response to appeals in the form of a questionnaire circulated to the readers of six German-language papers in Canada,[8] and turned all of them over to Lehmann. Together with Lehmann's notes and files, these valuable documents were destroyed in air raids on Berlin during World War II.

In search of an academic career, Lehmann worked as an assistant to Dr. G.A. Rein, professor of overseas history at the University of Hamburg. In return for a one-year stipend from the VDA, he helped organize the Hamburg research center for the study of German ethnic groups overseas (*Forschungsstelle für das Überseedeutschtum*). In order to support his family, he took a part-time teaching position at a Berlin *Gymnasium* and offerd English language courses at the Berlin Hochschule für Politik. In 1936 he was offered a lecturership (*Lehrauftrag*) in the study of the society and government of Great Britain and the Commonwealth at the Orientalisches Seminar in Berlin which in 1940 became the Auslandswissenschaftliche Fakultät of Berlin University.

In the summer of 1938 his pioneering study of the Germans in western Canada was accepted by the Philosophical Faculty of the University of Breslau as a qualifying dissertation for a university professorship (*Habilitationsschrift*). It was published under the title *Das Deutschtum in Westkanada* (Berlin: Junker und Dünnhaupt Verlag, 1939) with a map of the German settlements in western Canada, which broke new ground in the cartography of German settlements in the Canadian Prairie provinces at the time.

Heinz Lehmann was then promoted to the rank of *Dozent* at Berlin University and to *ausserordentlicher Professor* in 1942. In 1943 his third book *Grossbritannien* and in 1944 his fourth book *Kanada und Neufundland* appeared as volumes 27-28 and 31 in the series "Kleine Auslandskunde" by Junker und Dünnhaupt, Berlin. Towards the end of the war he was drafted by the German army to serve as an interpreter. There he contracted typhoid fever and spent the rest of the war in hospital in Tübingen, Germany.

In the first years after the war, when academic preoccupation with overseas problems was taboo in Germany, Bishop Wurm and Prelate Dr. Hartenstein of the Evangelical Church of Württemberg enlisted Lehmann's services in their negotiations with the Allied powers. From 1946 to 1948 he worked in the Ministry of Finance of the Government of Württemberg-Hohenzollern. In 1948-1949 he served for nine months as a secretary of the Conference of the West German Ministers of Education. A public secondary school in Tübingen offered him a teaching position in 1949, and from 1952 onward the University of Tübingen enabled him to resume academic teaching in his old field of specialization, the study of England and the Commonwealth. He held honorary membership in the *Deutsch-Kanadische Gesellschaft* since its foundation in the 1950s. In 1954 he was elected secretary of the newly-founded *Deutsch-Indische Studiengesellschaft*, the oldest private association for the promotion of aid to developing countries, and served in that office until 1965. Most of his postwar publications dealt with India, among them a book on Nehru (1965).[9]

From the time he wrote his doctoral dissertation, Lehmann's patriotic convictions were rooted in a right-of-center conservative *Weltanschauung*, as advocated in 1928 by Gustav Stresemann's German People's Party (DVP), in 1930 by the People's Conservatives of Treviranus, and in 1932 by the German National People's Party (DNVP). These more or less moderate conservatives became increasingly apprehensive of the growing weakness and instability of the Weimar Republic. Without endorsing the National Socialist platform, they eventually came around to the view that the untested Hitler ought to be given a chance in a national front of conservative forces to demonstrate his claim that he was able to improve conditions. Political comments culled from the personal correspondence of the years 1930 to 1935 between Heinz Lehmann and his fiancée, later wife, Dr. phil. Lotte Böckheler express his political attitude at the time: "If Hitler would only recognize the essence of politics, namely balance and compromise! I am sick of his egocentric stupid rhetoric," Lehmann wrote her on November 8, 1932. In a letter of March 3, 1933, Lehmann commented to his wife on the appointment of Hitler as Germany's chancellor with the conservative aristocrat von Papen as vice-chancellor: "You are right, I shall not become a one hundred per cent Nazi. I can't help feeling more in step with the aristocrat than with Hitler and my sympathies are with the entire front." The memoirs of the late Klaus Mehnert provide a unique insight into the mentality of Lehmann's frequently misunderstood and maligned generation.[10] Mehnert and Lehmann, by the way, both historians at Berlin University, became acquainted with each other through the German Academic Exchange Service as recipients of their fellowships in the United States and the United Kingdom respectively.

Bearing in mind that the subject of Germans in other lands was dear to the hearts of all dedicated National Socialists, nothing would have been easier for Lehmann than to steep his study heavily in the postulates of official racial doctrine at great material benefit to himself. Refusing lip service to official views entirely, on the other hand, would almost certainly have meant the termination of his budding academic career. Considering the times and circumstances on the eve of World War II in Germany and the nature of his topic, Lehmann's study of the Germans in western Canada is surprisingly detached from official ideology. In 1939 a reviewer in Germany, representing the official point of view, criticized *Das Deutschtum in Westkanada* for lack of ideological clarity and biological perspective and referred to it as "a rather straightforward descriptive account."[11]

When Heinz Lehmann visited western Canada in 1934, he witnessed a new feeling of ethnic self-confidence and cultural renaissance in many German-Canadian circles and he was fascinated by it. It manifested itself in the call for more German language instruction, the growth of the German-language press, the sprouting of German-Canadian organizations and their coordination on a regional and provincial level. Annually celebrated province-wide cultural festivals, known as German Days (*Deutsche Tage*), rapidly turned into demonstrations of ethnic solidarity among German Canadians. Lehmann was able to document the growth of this new ethnic consciousness and even to quantify it. He noted the increasing proportion of Canadians reporting their ethnic origin as German by comparing the Canadian census reports of 1921, 1931 and 1936. This was particularly striking for the period 1931 to 1936 when there was German emigration from, rather than German immigration to, Canada.

The rise of this ethnic self-assertion, its exact nature and extent, is still awaiting careful and detached examination. Was this a genuine manifestation of a new German ethnic group consciousness, or should it be shrugged off as merely a response to the appeals of the National Socialist movement in Germany? Post-World War II commentators have tended to ignore it and focused on the more tangible efforts of organizations like the *Deutscher Bund Canada*, its functionaries and membership, and the attitude of the press. The anticipation of a better future for Germany and Germans everywhere that accompanied Hitler's assumption of power no doubt reinforced its momentum. But the direct influence of German National Socialism on German Canadians appears to have been insignificant,[12] especially if compared to the impressive manifestations of fascism and anti-Semitism in French-Canadian and English-Canadian circles at the time.[13] It would be difficult indeed to credit all those ordinary German Canadians who had been participating in the celebrations of the so-called German Days from 1928 through the 1930s with sudden pro-Nazi attitudes after 1933.[14]

Heinz Lehmann, who attended the 1934 German Day in Saskatoon, recalled in 1983 that it followed the tradition of those that had preceded it since 1928:

> Many participants came on bad roads from places hundreds of kilometers away, primarily in order to have a reunion with countrymen from the old homeland, but also in order to experience the new feeling of community with so many other Germans and to renew the old demands in an official form. The events in Germany were barely mentioned among the participants. It was only natural that German Canadians would be more interested "in their skins than in their clothes" for few had seen Germany themselves. Yet I experienced a definite mood of general optimism and a determination to fight for the restoration of German language instruction in predominantly German school districts. Experience had taught them that their religious and cultural heritage and their ancestral values could be passed on to their children and their children's children only through the German language in a framework of bilingualism.

The German Day celebrations were, according to Lehmann, the most important expression of the new consciousness of German identity among German Canadians of the most heterogeneous geographical and religious backgrounds, a phenomenon which among German ethnic communities in eastern Europe became known as *volksdeutsches Erwachen*.[15] In Canada it may be attributed to a combination of factors. From the late 1920s the urge for revenge among the victors of the Great War began to give way to a revisionist attitude which manifested itself in historical writing, public opinion, economic policy and international diplomacy, and ultimately benefited Hitler. At the same time, Canada's German-speaking community was rejuvenated by an infusion of new blood as German-speaking immigration reached unprecedented peaks between 1928 and 1930. German Canadians were thus no longer willing to accept the wartime discriminations as justifiable, and they demanded restitution. Especially to Germans from eastern and southeastern Europe who formed the bulk of the German community in the West, the continued closure of their German schools appeared as an undeserved penalty. Conscious of their contribution as pioneers in the opening and civilizing of the West, they had viewed schools in their mother tongue as a part of their pioneering accomplishments, as a religious need and as a self-evident right prior to 1914. Among their countrymen who had stayed in their European homelands and who before the war had been, almost without exception, loyal to their host countries, the *volksdeutsches Erwachen* was a direct reaction to being persecuted as "Germans" during the war and, by the new east European national states, after the war. An outspoken German ethnic consciousness was therefore particularly noticeable among the postwar German immigrants from these areas.

A particular case in point was that of the postwar Mennonite immigrants from Soviet Russia who had experienced religious persecution, expropriation and resettlement in their homeland. Lehmann made the personal acquaintance of their leading representatives, Elders David Toews, Daniel Enns and Jacob H. Janzen in Rosthern, Saskatchewan. They invited him to attend a reunion held in tents on the Abraham P. Klassen farm near Herschel, Saskatchewan, on July 17-18, 1934. Travelling on poor roads, *Russländer* Mennonites with wives and children converged from far and wide, in order to revive old friendships and exchange new experiences. Lehmann's recollections in 1983 reveal that this gathering made an unforgettable impression on him:

> There I experienced a sort of elite of a German ethnic community. Judged by their linguistic articulation and their educational level, these *Russländer*, who immigrated between 1923 and 1929, must all have been lay preachers and teachers, even if now they have to eke out a living as farmers with their families. They were well informed not only about the history of Mennonite emigrations, but also about the entire German community in Russia and about German history in general. In contrast to the earlier Mennonite immigrants, they considered themselves, as a matter of course, members of the German people, for they had been persecuted in Russia as Germans. They embodied, therefore, the *volksdeutsches Erwachen* in its purest form.

Among these postwar ethnic German immigrants, the desire for identification with the wider German community and the search for help, orientation and inspiration from Germany was undeniable. That the perversion of *volksdeutsche* aspirations by the *völkisch* (i.e. ethnic-racist) rhetoric of National Socialist propaganda would strike a responsive chord among some segments of these minorities and immigrants is not surprising and can easily be misinterpreted.[16] Never having been part of the modern German state nor of the modern German nation, they had no other way of perceiving of their cultural identity than as members of a wider German ethnic community, or *Volk*, that shared a common language, culture and descent. The problems arising from the incongruity between *Volk* and *Staat*, between *Kulturnation* and *Staatsnation*, which are a fundamental fact of German history, have often been incomprehensible to the English and French.[17]

The sympathy of German Canadians for the homeland of their cultural heritage and their desire for contacts with it needs as little justification as that of any other ethnic group in Canada, including the British and the French groups, whether German National Socialists made particular efforts to promote such contacts or not. The international atmosphere of grudging respect—if not admiration—for Adolf Hitler's Germany of the mid-1930s was certainly conducive to a resurgence of pride in the German cultural heritage. German Canadians were in no better position to anticipate and judge the true totalitarian objectives of the Nazi regime than such prominent figures as Canada's Prime Minister William Lyon Mackenzie King and the British prime ministers from David Lloyd George to Winston Churchill.[18] That Hitler's regime would be capable of abusing and perverting every decent German aspiration, value and tradition and of flouting the international standards of civilized behavior came as much as a shock to the people of German descent in Canada as to the British and French appeasers and admirers of Hitler.

For today's generation of German-speaking people, it is difficult to understand the acute concern for the linguistic and cultural survival of the German ethnic group in Canada which stands out as a leitmotiv in Lehmann's studies. This concern reflected public preoccupation in post-World War I Germany with the German-speaking enclaves outside its borders. *Volkstumsarbeit*, as this preoccupation was known, was almost a national obsession in Weimar Germany, from the political left to the right.[19] It was a response to the loss of the war, to Allied implementation of national self-determination at the expense of the ethnic German population in post-world War I Europe and to the above-mentioned *volksdeutsches Erwachen*. There was a widespread feeling of solidarity in Germany with the undeserved fate of the German minorities in the succession states of the former Habsburg and Romanov empires and in the territories detached from Germany by the Treaty of Versailles.[20] Public concern in Germany was nourished by the constant arrival in the 1920s of ethnic German refugees, such as the Mennonites from Soviet Russia, and by the new trend among the young generation of ethnic Germans to study at universities in Germany. A host of institutions and periodicals—such as the above-mentioned nonpartisan VDA that funded Lehmann's field work in Canada and its journal *Deutsche Arbeit*, the Deutsches Ausland-Institut, and its publications, the encyclopedic project of the *Handwörterbuch des Grenz- und Auslanddeutschtums*, all of which published some of Lehmann's writings, as well as a vast literature of every kind—thrived on this preoccupation.[21]

To appreciate Heinz Lehmann's engaged attitude, we should also remember that the wartime discrimination against Canadians of German descent did not reach its climax until after the end of World War I, with traumatic effects on the German-Canadian community lasting much longer. Robert England remembered that "the difficulty of making contacts with a non-English community in the years immediately after the war led some of us to believe that racial group settlements were undesirable and that such settlements became suspect of being subversive of national unity and unprogressive in agriculture."[22] Deep apprehensions were prompted by the all-out English-Canadian efforts to assimilate or stigmatize the "dangerous foreigners,"[23] as exemplified in J. T. M. Anderson's campaign for "The Education of the New Canadian" and Reverend Captain Wellington Bridgeman's demand that all "Huns" and "Austro-Huns" be dispossessed and deported for the benefit of English-Canadian war veterans.[24]

Lehmann hoped for a future where recognition would be accorded to the contributions of Canada's Germans and to the fact that the preservation of their ethnic heritage is of benefit to Canada. In 1936 he wrote

> Perhaps, as improbable as it may sound today, the idea will become accepted in North America someday that it is to the benefit of the country to leave ethnic minorities in peace and to grant them cultural autonomy, an idea which has been implemented in at least a few European countries so far.[25]

The somewhat uneven treatment accorded to Germans in eastern and western Canada in Lehmann's two books may require some explanation, since both books sprang from the grand design of his doctoral dissertation on the history of German Canadians from the Atlantic to the Pacific coasts. In his book on the Germans in eastern Canada, the focus was on German-speaking immigration and settlement. In the volume on western Canada, the religious, secular, and cultural life and the statistics of ethnic retention were singled out for separate analysis. The different format of the second volume was in part due to the adoption of a more sophisticated methodological frame of reference. But it was also conditioned by the contemporary notion of what constituted an ethnic group, and the resulting realization that German Canadians in the West did not fit the same criteria as those in the East. For Heinz Lehmann and his generation, the centuries-old, linguistically virtually assimilated, German element in eastern Canada had essentially become history by the end of the First World War. With the loss of its objective criteria of ethnicity, namely language and cultural aspirations, it had ceased to be a genuine ethnic group. The subjective acknowledgement by linguistically assimilated German Canadians of their German ethnic descent as manifested in the census reports was considered a transitional phenomenon, and their subjective assimilation as simply a matter of time.

In western Canada, on the other hand, the ethnic heritage of the much larger population of German descent was still very much alive, as evidenced by the extent to which German was spoken. It challenged the critical observer to a separate examination of its cultural conditions, institutions, manifestations and identity. Heinz Lehmann realized that, in spite of the obvious vitality of the German heritage in the West and the manifestations of its revival from the wartime depression, it was, short of a miracle, bound to succumb eventually to the irresistible forces of the anglophone environment as well. While he was impressed by the impact that the German postwar immigration and the initial glamour of the Third Reich had on the revitalization of German ethnicity in Canada, he showed an equally acute awareness of the negative effects that the Depression had on the material conditions and cultural life of the rural German community and on the individual settler. These observations of the unique economic, cultural and political conditions in western Canada in the 1930s and the reflections about their meaning have also become history by now.

Students of the German-Canadian ethnic scene have always been plagued by the question whether the German Canadians actually do constitute one identifiable ethnic group that is united by more than the coincidence of their German mother tongue. Lehmann observed the fact that German Canadians appear to consist of a number of separate religious, national and regional minorities that tend to identify with the characteristics that separate them as much as with those that unite them. He exposed theological and cultural rifts not only among various German-Canadian groups, but also within them. These rifts were shown to be sometimes aggravated, sometimes superseded by ethnic conflicts between newcomers and first-generation Canadian Germans (as Lehmann called the latter), as well as with the partially assimilated later-generation German Canadians. Basic to any understanding of Canada's German community was for Lehmann the historical and psychological gulf separating the fully-anglicized Germans of Lunenburg County, Nova Scotia, from the nearly-assimilated German element of Waterloo County, Ontario, and both of these from the young and ethnically "genuine" German groups in western Canada.

Lehmann showed German Canadians of the pre- and post-World War I era to be an ethnic community *sui generis* by the mere fact that in western Canada, where in the 1930s three-quarters of German Canadians lived, at least 70 per cent of the German population came from the rural areas of eastern Europe and Russia, and Mennonites constituted western Canada's second largest religious group of Germans. Also significant was his observation that nearly 20 per cent of western Canadian Germans immigrated via the United States, and no more than 12 per cent came from the urbanized environment of Germany. Canada's German element could thus be understood neither as an extension of overseas emigration from Germany nor as a replica of the German-American community.

The main thrust of Lehmann's findings, however, is in his presentation of persuasive historical evidence that different German-Canadian groups were part of one larger community. Firstly, their common German cultural heritage, although at times obscured by the inadequacies of the Canadian census and by barriers of different educational, religious and geographical backgrounds, enabled them to interact and associate easily. Lehmann's analysis of the formation of German settlements in western Canada revealed that German-speaking immigrants of the same denominational background desired to associate regardless of their former homelands or places of origin. There were no settlements consisting exclusively of Germans from Russia, Romania,

Poland, Hungary, Austria or Germany. Yet in eastern Canada the Mennonites, widely regarded as a separate religious minority, are known
to have pioneered the largest and most viable areas of settlement for
Germans of every denominational and geographical background. Lehmann showed that the Mennonite colonies at the Grand River and
in the Niagara District of Ontario, launched in the first decade of the
nineteenth-century, attracted almost the entire immigration from Germany from the 1830s to the 1850s. Had the Grand River colony not
been there, Lehmann argued, the large nineteenth century German
community of the Kitchener-Waterloo area would not have formed,
and the immigrants from Germany would have dissipated.

Secondly, the divisive denominational structure, while preventing
German Canadians from forming a united front in defense of their
common interests, was also in many instances the very reason for the
retention of the cultural heritage that they all shared. Because the church
had been the only vehicle of social and cultural organization for many
German-speaking immigrants in the Old World, it continued to be so
in the new pioneer environment of Canada. The degree of ethnic maintenance was thus to Lehmann, in more than one way, a function of
the continuation of denominational integrity and separation.

Thirdly, the crucial historical role of the Mennonites in any definition of German-Canadian identity is, according to Lehmann, evident
in their cultural contributions. The manifestations of German-Canadian
culture are more indebted to their genuinely German customs, folklore and folklife, their educational efforts and achievements, and their
German arts and crafts, than to those of any other German-Canadian
group. Lehmann stressed the fact that Mennonites were responsible
for the budding of an indigenous German-Canadian literature, and,
after the First World War, for the resurgence of the first widespread
feeling of ethnic identity among German Canadians from coast to coast.

Like his mentor Dibelius, Lehmann was personally acquainted with
C.A. Dawson of McGill University and his research on German com-
munities in western Canada. They exchanged ideas on their closely
related, parallel projects—*Das Deutschtum in Westkanada* (1939) and
Group Settlement: Ethnic Communities in Western Canada (1936). However,
"Dawson selects signs of culture penetration while Lehmann focuses
on evidence of culture preservation," as Dawson's collaborator Albert
Moellmann put it.[26]

By today's criteria of North American immigration historiography,
Lehmann's work might be classified as a sophisticated example of the

so-called "gift of immigrants approach."[27] The model of this kind of approach is A.B. Faust's monumental history of *The German Element in the United States*.[28] This type of historical writing attempts to bring out the contributions of immigrants to the host society in a more systematic and critical fashion than the filial-pietous type of literature. The "gift of immigrants approach," however, tends to be more biographically oriented and is not, as a rule, concerned with the structural analysis of the wider social, economic and cultural context that has become the hallmark of the best of the post-World War II ethnic and immigration studies. Lehmann, one might argue, accomplished on a smaller scale for the German Canadians what A.B. Faust did for the German Americans. While the encyclopedic reconstruction of all the relevant German contributions to American life distinguished Faust's work of 1909, Lehmann's study thirty years later of western Canada's German element went methodologically beyond that. Here we find an early model of a structural analysis of the historical evolution of the German-Canadian community, the push and pull of its migrations, its settlement patterns, intra-group relations, religious and secular institutions and manifestations of cultural identity. Except for the high quality of recent research on the Mennonites and Hutterites, few studies on German Canadians have updated Lehmann's approach along the lines pursued by scholarship on German Americans.

The following, by no means exhaustive, review of research on the topic and period covered by Lehmann is intended to indicate in what instances our knowledge of specific events, aspects, groups or regions has been expanded since 1939. One may argue about the significance of the legends that Germans were among the very first documented discoverers and early explorers of North America. The Icelandic sagas identify a German by the name of Tykir, the alleged foster father of Leif Eiriksson and a member of the Norse expedition of 1001, as the first German to set foot on North America—probably in northern Newfoundland. The sagas credit him with discovering wild grapevines there, with being the first European to get drunk in North America and with suggesting the name of Vinland for the newly discovered land.[29] Equally difficult to verify is the German identity of two skippers in the Danish service, named Diedrich Pining and Hans Pothorst, and the claim that they rediscovered Newfoundland and Labrador on their mysterious expedition from Iceland to the land of the Baccalos (codfish) in the mid 1470s, i.e. more than two decades before John Cabot landed there in 1497.[30] What is certain is that a German put foot on

Newfoundland as early as 1583.[31]

Of unquestionable relevance to the history of the German presence in Canada was the detection in recent years of Swiss and German settlers in Quebec a century prior to the arrival of the boat *Anne* in Halifax harbour in 1750. In 1955, Claude de Bonnault, and in 1976, E.H. Bovay uncovered evidence that German Swiss had arrived in Acadia as early as 1604 and that Germans had settled on the Ile d'Orléans as early as 1633.[32] By 1664 some German settlers apparently lived in and around Quebec, as de Bonnault and W.H. Debor discovered in old Quebec parish records and registries of deeds.[33] Some of these Germans arrived as Lutherans and converted to Roman Catholicism in New France. They came from the Moselle River valley, from Speyer, Breisach and Vienna. More recently, Cornelius J. Jaenen noted that, prior to the revocation of the Edict of Nantes in 1685, not only French Catholics and Protestants immigrated to New France but that the number of non-French people—Scots, Irish, Germans, Basques, Italians, Jews and New Englanders—assimilated into the original French-Canadian community is remarkable.[34]

De Bonnault and Debor drew attention to the fact that in the English-French struggle for the control of North America, both sides enlisted the services of Swiss and German soldiers and officers. From 1721 to the siege and conquest of Louisbourg in 1745 by General Waldo's Palatines, Swiss-German troops of the Karrer regiment were among the garrison of the fortress. In General Wolfe's attack on the fortress of Quebec in 1759, German and Swiss were among his commanding officers. One of them, Friedrich Haldimand, later to be Governor General of Canada. Their troops, too, consisted of many Germans, mostly Palatines, in the Royal American Regiment. In 1755 General Baron von Dieskau from Saxony was supreme commander of the French forces.[35] In the French command at the time as well as in certain Quebec industries such as mining, there were apparently many more Germans, as sources brought to my attention by my colleague William A. Kearns suggest.[36] In the eighteenth and early nineteenth century settlement of Vaudreuil and Soulanges west of the Ile de Montréal, German names occur rather frequently, as R.L. Séguin showed.[37] We owe it to Jean-Pierre Wilhelmy's painstaking research that more than thirteen hundred family names in Quebec are traceable to the settling of German mercenaries there after the American War of Independence.[38]

To the work of German missionaries of the Moravian church among the Eskimos in Labrador, Lehmann devoted only one brief footnote because their activity was not then part of Canada. W.H. Whiteley sketched the 1752 foundation of the Labrador mission by Mecklenburg native Johann Christian Ehrhardt at a site on the coast that he named Hoffenthal (now Hopedale).[39] According to James Hiller, forty-seven of the sixty-four missionaries arriving before 1810 can be identified as of German nationality.[40] Hedwig Brueckner examined their theology and missionary efforts on the basis of their late eighteenth-century records.[41] From the beginning, these missionaries acted as educators and teachers in the broadest sense of the word, whether as preachers, traders, artisans, scientists, doctors, linguists, or simply as ordinary people. Reviewing their work, Alfred Ratz pointed out that "with little or no bloodshed they succeeded in preserving a Stone Age people in danger of being decimated, if not exterminated, by other Europeans who happened to be engaged in a struggle for territorial and economic gain that took little account of the natives' needs." Some scholars, such as Shmuel Ben-Dor and Carol Brice-Bennett, have taken a more critical view of the Moravian legacy in Labrador and regretted the loss of indigenous Inuit beliefs and culture.[42]

Despite the fairly extensive English-Canadian literature dealing with the Hudson's Bay Company and the Red River Colony, little note has been taken of the party of 180 Swiss settlers that Lord Selkirk recruited in 1820. Were it not for the posthumous fame of the Swiss-German artist Peter Rindisbacher, who emigrated from Switzerland as a member of that party, we would have little to add to Lehmann's account of these colonists.[43]

Considerable attention, however, has been lavished on the Lunenburg Germans, their folklore and folk customs, their dialect, their school and church life, their heritage and immigration, as well as the naming of Lunenburg.[44] The most extensive and detailed study of "the foreign Protestants" as W.R. Bell called these almost exclusively ethnic German immigrants in the title of his book,[45] showed no awareness of Heinz Lehmann's treatment of that subject. Bell, who meticulously researched the founding and early years of the Lunenburg settlement, went to great lengths to put forward his allegedly new theory on the origin of the name of Lunenburg, when in fact Lehmann had already suggested that same explanation much earlier. Interesting leads for taking a fresh look at the German cultural heritage in Lunenburg have been suggested by David Artiss.[46]

The picture that Lehmann sketched of the development of Ontario's German-speaking community has been confirmed and embellished in

many respects by the largest number of studies undertaken, during the
last forty-five years, on any area of German settlement in Canada. These
studies have focused in particular on (1) German immigration and settlement in eastern and southwestern Ontario in the eighteenth and
early nineteenth centuries, (2) the nineteenth century history of the
German community of the Kitchener-Waterloo area, (3) the prominent
role of German settlers in the founding of Toronto, and (4) the social
and cultural life of the Mennonites. In the first category there are numerous monographs on German troops and biographies of officers and
soldiers who operated and settled in Upper Canada before, during and
after the American War of Independence. In these the remarkable role
of Baron Friedrich von Riedesel, whose memoirs were republished in
1968, stands out prominently. This literature reveals that during the
years 1776-1783 German mercenaries and Loyalists appear to have outnumbered English troops, and that the defense of Canada was dependent on Germans. The so-called "Hessians" garrisoned Canada's towns
and forts and were in action in every major battlefield.[47]

Furthermore, we have accounts of the Pennsylvania-German migration around the end of the eighteenth century, of German immigration to Ontario, of the origins and early history of German Lutheran
congregations in eastern Canada, as well as the memoirs of the first
German pastor on Upper Canadian soil, the Reverend Schwerdtfeger.[48] Acknowledging Lehmann's research as its starting point, Gottlieb Leibbrandt's history of the German Canadians of Waterloo County
from 1800 to 1875 deserves to be singled out as the most informative
and richly documented regional history of any German-Canadian community. Its many biographical sketches of leading personalities and discussions of various aspects of community life, such as the press, the
schools, the churches and the arts as well as of public, social and economic life, add many new facets to Lehmann's story.[49] Thanks also to
the *Reports* of the Waterloo Historical Society, the publications by Uttley,
Kalbfleisch, Moyer, Tiessen, English and McLaughlin, and the new editions of Ezra E. Eby's *Biographical History* of 1895 and 1896 and *The
Gordon C. Eby Diaries*, we know more today about German Canadians
of this area than of any other in Canada.[50] The credit for gaining public recognition of William Moll-Berczy and his 180 German settlers as
co-founders of Toronto in 1794 belongs to the research of John Andre
and the public relations effort of the Historical Society of Mecklenburg Upper Canada. Based on meticulous investigations in European
and North American archives, Andre was able to establish the true

identity of the man known to Lehmann under the assumed name of Wilhelm Berczy as Johann Albrecht Ulrich Moll, born in Wallerstein near Nördlingen in 1744.[51] Jean R. Burnet's assumption that in the genesis of Upper Canadian society a German element entered the picture only in the form of the sects of the Tunkers, Moravians and Mennonites is thus no longer tenable. Peter Hessel's study of German mass migration to the Ottawa valley informs us about the largest government scheme of settling Germans in Canada prior to the opening of the prairies, and Brenda Lee-Whiting traced the migration experience and cultural legacy of the German settlers of Renfrew County.[52]

The Mennonites have become the most thoroughly documented and most frequently reexamined group of German Canadians.[53] Recent publications have focused on their distinctly German art, culture and folklore,[54] their escape from Soviet Russia [55] and their problems of adaptation and identity.[56] Frank H. Epp's judicious and comprehensive account of the endemic dilemmas of fundamentalism, separation and adaptation have made his impeccably researched two-volume history the standard work on the topic to date.[57] Amish Mennonites have told the story of the separate culture of the Amish of Ontario.[58] The Mennonites of western Canada have been perceptively portrayed in the highly acclaimed monograph by E.K. Francis.[59] Francis appears to have drawn on Lehmann, whom he identifies as a folklorist, in various instances, such as his characterization of the Old Colony village settlement pattern.[60] Regrettably, he does not clearly acknowledge his indebtedness to Lehmann. Following C. Henry Smith (1927), C.A. Dawson (1936) considered the Manitoba Mennonite village layout an adaptation of the Russian and Polish farm village, while it reminded Robert England (1936) of the manorial system known in England and on the Continent.[61] The credit for identifying it as a type of medieval German street village known as *Gewanndorf* and the arrangement of their field holdings as *Gewannflur*, must, as far as I could ascertain, go to Heinz Lehmann. From Francis, who discussed at length the meaning of these terms, they have spread into the anglophone literature without Lehmann ever being cited as the source.[62] Some of the most interesting glimpses of early Mennonite life in the East and West Reserves are to be found in the local histories of their communities, such as those of Grunthal, Blumenort, Reinland, Winkler and Steinbach, and congregations such as the Bergthaler.[63]

Das Deutschtum in Westkanada has inspired one doctoral and two masters' theses, which have added much color and detail to Lehmann's

account. Arthur Grenke's painstakingly researched doctoral thesis
informs us about every aspect of the social organization and residential patterns of Winnipeg's German community from 1872 to 1919. He
traces its institutions, associational life, press, politics and wartime
experience, within the context of Winnipeg's role as a gateway for
immigration to western Canada and as a stopover for German settlement in the West. The methodologically exemplary scholarship of this
thesis could make it a model for the study of other urban ethnic communities in Canada.[64] Edmund Heier examined the immigration and
settlement of Catholic and Lutheran German immigrants from Tsarist
and Soviet Russia.[65] Kurt Tischler took a fresh look at the language
problem of the Germans in Saskatchewan from 1900 to 1930.[66]

On the whole, the historical analysis of Saskatchewan's large German community has not progressed significantly beyond Lehmann's
fifty-year-old findings. Canadian Plains research appears to have been
preoccupied with socio-political protest movements and the geographical
and economic determinants of the Prairie region.[67] The literature on
the German immigrants from Russia concentrates, with few exceptions,
on their Russian and German origins.[68] There are only scattered references to the political impact of the German element before 1939.[69]
Several works review the record of German Catholic and Lutheran
churches and parishes.[70] In a comparison of ethnic retention among
seven bloc settlements in Saskatchewan, Alan B. Anderson found German Catholics the least eager to preserve their identity, with the most
significant loss occurring in the first and second generations.[71] For
occasional first-hand glimpses of the lives and experiences of ethnic
German settlers we have to turn to local histories of the districts of
German settlement, many of them compiled by amateur historians to
commemorate Saskatchewan's seventy-fifth anniversary. Yet even the
family histories of Germans from eastern Europe, which fill most of
the pages of these publications, manifest a striking urge to conceal their
German ethnic background.[72] A few memoirs by German pioneers
suggest a store of untapped source materials.[73] The trailblazing role of
German settlers in western Canada in initiating the migration of Ukrainians to the prairies is documented in Czumer's recollections.[74]

The Hutterite way of life and agricultural economy has, next to that
of the Mennonites, become one of the best explored aspects of German ethnicity. This is due to the exceptional interest in western Canada's
closed Hutterite communities by politicians, sociologists, demographers,
economists, geographers, folklorists, psychologists, linguists and

historians.[75]

An exhaustive bibliography on German Albertans was recently compiled by Alexander Malycky.[76] When Howard Palmer earlier reviewed the state of research into Alberta's German element, he noted that the anglophone student is hampered by the fact that most of the literature is in German.[77]

Lehmann's work is least informed about the history of the German element in British Columbia. This deficiency was corrected by Bruce Ramsay. He traced the presence of colonists of German descent back to the distinguished career of Dr. John Sebastian Helmcken, who was a physician, magistrate and member of the first legislative assembly on Vancouver Island from 1850 to 1865. We learn that, as early as 1861, residents of Victoria formed a *Germania Sing Verein* which lasted apparently right up to the outbreak of the First World War. Ramsay's slim but rewardingly informative historical account is, unfortunately, without any bibliographic references.[78] So are the chapters dealing with German Canadians under the headings of "Germans," "Austrians," "Swiss" and "Mennonites" in the centennial history of British Columbia's ethnic groups, edited by John Norris.[79] Dorothy Blakey Smith prepared a careful edition of the memoirs of Helmcken.[80] In 1982 Peter Liddell published a bibliography of the Germans in British Columbia.[81]

The impact of the First World War and of German National Socialism on German Canadians has so far received scholarly attention mostly in articles and in unpublished Ph.D. and M.A. theses. These have looked at specific aspects, such as the suppression of the German language press in 1918,[82] the experiences of the Mennonites,[83] and the role of the *Deutscher Bund Canada*.[84] Episodes of anti-German sentiment and activities have been treated in regional studies of Canadian nativism.[85]

The lack of studies on pre-World War II Canadian Jews of German origin may be due to the fact that, with a few notable exceptions, they appear to have played a very small part in German-Canadian as well as in Canadian Jewish life, in contrast to their prominent role in the United States. Statistical data show that in 1931 only 388 German-born, and 2,678 Austrian-born, Jews lived in Canada, that the number of German-born Jews had declined from 965 since 1911, and that from 1931 to 1938 no more than seventy-nine Jews born in Germany, and thirty-nine born in Austria, were admitted to Canada. Jews born in Germany formed 0.38 per cent of all Jewish immigrants to Canada from 1926 to 1931, and their percentage increased only to 1.75 per cent for the period 1931 to 1938. Although a higher percentage of Cana-

dian Jews born in Germany spoke the language of their country of birth
than Canadian Jews born in most other countries, except for Scandinavia, as many as 86 per cent of the German-born, and 92 per cent
of the Austrian-born Jews, claimed Yiddish as their mother tongue in
1931. While Irving Abella and Harold Troper have provided a penetrat-
ing analysis of why so few German Jews were admitted to Canada during the 1930s and 1940s, and Eric Koch recorded the odyssey of
internment during World War II, the story of the internment of German Jews as enemy aliens in Canada during World War I and their
subsequent return to Germany or emigration to the United States is
still untold.[86] Events like the celebration of a splendid *Goethefest* in
Winnipeg on March 22, 1932, attended by leading Canadian Jews and
distinguished German Canadians[87] suggest German-Jewish inter-
ethnic social and cultural contacts in Canada before 1933 about which
little is known today.

Three recent publications attempt to review the entire scope of the
German-Canadian experience from different perspectives. The focus
of K.M. McLaughlin's 20-page booklet is on the five waves of German
immigration and settlement in Canada from 1750 to the 1950s, and
on the ease with which each wave was assimilated into the mainstream
of Canadian life. Rudolf A. Helling's 150-page research report provides
an insightful, but uneven and sketchy, socio-economic survey of
German-Canadian history. To Michael Bird and Terry Kobayashi, finally,
we owe an impressive introduction to the legacy of folk and decorative
arts produced by the most diverse groups of settlers of German descent in Canada from the mid-eighteenth century.[88]

Migrations of Germans from Switzerland and Austria to Canada
have received as much if not more attention from professional historians
than the immigration of Germans from Germany and Russia.[89]
Hedges' monograph of 1939, which was unfortunately unavailable to
Lehmann for his book on the Germans in western Canada, is still a
basic source for the collaboration between the Canadian government,
the railways and the church boards in bringing considerable numbers
of ethnic Germans, especially Mennonites, to Canada in the 1920s and
1930s.[90] The escape of some five hundred Social Democratic Sudeten
German refugees to Canada on the eve of World War II was described
by A. Amstatter and Fritz Wieden.[91]

George K. Epp and Hartmut Froeschle have reexamined the form
and content of Canada's indigenous German literature from its beginnings.[92] The discussions about the forces that shaped this literature,

as well as the interactions between German-speaking Europe and Canada, are continuing in the pages of the German-Canadian Year-book and the German Canadian Studies Annals. W. Riedel's edition of *Literary Perspectives of German-speaking Canadians* examines the reaction of the migration experiences of major writers in their Canadian writings.[93]

Last but not least, Lehmann's research deserves some of the credit for the essay on "the cultural contribution of the German ethnic group to Canada" prepared by H.W. Debor for the editors of Book IV of the official report of the Royal Commission on Bilingualism and Bicultural-ism in 1970. Book IV inspired the Canadian government to initiate the current policy of multiculturalism.

NOTES

All translations from German-language sources into English are my own, unless indicated otherwise.

[1] Bruce Bradon Peel, comp., *A Bibliography of the Prairie Provinces to 1953 with Biographic Index* (2nd ed., Toronto, 1973), 406, 486.

[2] Ivan Groh, "The Swiss-Palatine-German-Pennsylvania-'Dutch' Pioneers of the Niagara Peninsula," Conrad Grebel College Library and Archives, as quoted in Frank H. Epp, *Mennonites in Canada, 1920-1940: A People's Struggle for Survival* (Toronto, 1982), 6-9.

[3] Typical of the treatment of western Canada's Germans in historical accounts is T.D. Regehr, *Remembering Saskatchewan: A History of Rural Saskatchewan* (Saskatoon, 1979), which was planned as part of Saskatchewan's seventy-fifth anniversary celebrations. In this slim, attractively illustrated and richly documented review of the gist of western Canadian historiography, the many German-speaking pioneers (whose German ethnicity was easily identifiable before 1914) are referred to only as "Russian Mennonites" and "other East Europeans." The non-British settlers in general, and the Mennonites in particular, are portrayed as an economically necessary (though in every other respect undesirable) element.

[4] Concerning the genesis of Prairie society see W.L. Morton, "A Century of Plain and Parkland," in Richard Allen, ed., *A Region of the Mind: Interpreting the Western Canadian Plains* (Regina, 1973), 165-180, and J.E. Rae, "The Roots of Prairie Society," in David P. Gagan, ed., *Prairie Perspectives: Papers of the Western Canadian Studies Conference* (Toronto, 1970), 48-51. In Ontario 9.8 per cent in

1870-71 and 1880-81, and 9.3. per cent in 1901, of the total population were German by origin, according to the Canadian census. The percentage of Germans in the American population was 10.5 in 1900, according to Kathleen Neils Conzen in Stephen Thernstrom, ed., *Harvard Encyclopedia of American Ethnic Groups* (Cambridge, Mass., and London, 1980), 406. For the proportion of Germans among Saskatchewan's American-born population see R.H. Coats and M.C. MacLean, *The American-Born in Canada: A Statistical Interpretation* (Toronto, 1943), 115.

[5] Zenon Poharecky, "The Changing Role of Ethnocultural Organizations in Saskatchewan: Case Studies with Statistical Data Cast in Historical Perspective," in Martin L. Kovacs, ed., *Ethnic Canadians: Culture and Education* (Regina, 1978), 199. See also Russell Doern, "Stereotypes aren't for real. German-Canadians continue to suffer from discrimination," *Maclean's*, October 6, 1980.

[6] Heather Robertson, *Grass Roots* (Toronto, 1973), 35.

[7] Heinz Lehmann, *Das Deutschtum in Westkanada*, (Berlin, 1939), 9.

[8] Bernhard Bott, "Ein Beitrag zur deutschen Siedlungsgeschichte Westkanadas," *Die Getreuen*, XII (1935), 156-158. The questionnaire which was printed in *Der Courier* (Regina), *Der Nordwesten* (Winnipeg), *St. Petersbote* (Muenster, Sask.), *Die Post* (Steinbach, Man.), *Der Bote* (Rosthern, Sask.) and in *Mennonitische Rundschau* (Winnipeg) posed the following eighteen questions:
1. What were the origins and name of the settlement?
2. What were the origins and migrations of the settlers prior to their settlement in Canada?
3. Did daughter colonies branch off from the mother colony?
4. What was the number of Germans by descent?
5. What were the church congregations and their denominations?
6. What was the year of foundation of the congregation, its ministers and development?
7. Was it a German or bilingual ministry?
8. Was there German school instruction?
9. Were teachers of German descent or not?
10. What were the religious and secular associations, German libraries, circulation of German-language press?
11. What was the representation of the German element in municipal, church, town and city councils and on school boards?
12. What were the economic conditions?
13. What was the new influx of postwar immigrants?
14. What were the chances for expansion of the settlement?
15. What were the German settlements in the surrounding area and the names of these settlements?
16. Other information?
17. Have accounts about the history of the respective settlements been published?
18. Has the settlement produced representatives of intellectual occupations?

[9] Heinz Lehmann, *Nehru: Baumeister des neuen Indien* (Zürich, Göttingen, Frankfurt, 1965).

[10] Klaus Mehnert, *Ein Deutscher in der Welt: Erinnerungen 1906-1981* (Stuttgart, 1981). For the experiences that Lehmann and Mehnert shared concerning the roots of postwar nationalism among young intellectuals, see pp. 83-86, 91-93. For their attitude toward Hitler see pp. 106f. The Berlin rally described on pp. 106f. was Lehmann's only personal encounter with Hitler, and Lehmann had exactly the same impressions as Mehnert.

[11] Carl-Heinz Pfeffer, "Zur Erforschung des kanadischen Deutschtums," *Deutsches Archiv für Landes- und Volksforschung,* III (1939), 693-694.

[12] See Jonathan Wagner, *Brothers Beyond the Sea: National Socialism in Canada* (Waterloo, Ont., 1981).

[13] Lita-Rose Betcherman, *The Swastika and the Maple Leaf: Fascist Movements in Canada During the Thirties* (Toronto, 1975). David Rome, *Clouds in the Thirties: On Antisemitism in Canada 1929-1939,* sections 1 to 13 (Montreal, 1977-1981). I. Abella and H. Troper, *None Is Too Many: Canada and the Jews of Europe, 1933-1948* (Toronto, 1983).

[14] Interview with Franz Straubinger, January 14, 1981. He helped organize various German Days in Saskatchewan and Ontario and confirmed that National Socialists played no prominent role in these celebrations until after 1936. See also G.P. Bassler, "Franz Straubinger and the Deutsche Arbeitsgemeinschaft Ontario," *German-Canadian Yearbook,* VIII (1984), 225-234.

[15] Martin Broszat, "Die völkische Ideologie und der Nationalsozialismus," *Deutsche Rundschau,* 89:1 (January 1958), 60.

[16] See Jonathan F. Wagner, "Transferred Crisis: German Volkisch Thought among Russian Mennonite Immigrants to Western Canada," *Canadian Review of Studies in Nationalism,* I:2 (Spring 1974), 202-220.

[17] For the standard definition of *Volk* as distinct from linguistic community, race, society, nation and state see Max Hildebert Boehm, *Das eigenständige Volk: Volkstheoretische Grundlagen der Ethnopolitik und Geisteswissenschaften* (Göttingen, 1932), and *Das eigenständige Volk in der Krise der Gegenwart* (Wien-Stuttgart, 1971). The arguments of this Baltic German, which clashed with the theory and practice of National Socialist racism, are derived from the concrete experiences of ethnic German minorities and linguistic enclaves outside the borders of Germany. See also Hermann Ullmann, *Pioniere Europas: Die volksdeutsche Bewegung und ihre Lehren* (Munich, 1956), and Eugen Lemberg, *Nationalismus,* 2 vols. (Reinbek, 1964). For a discussion of *Kulturnation* versus *Staatsnation* see Friedrich Meinecke, *Weltbürgertum und Nationalstaat* (Munich, 1908).

[18] For David Lloyd George and William Lyon Mackenzie King's embarrassingly candid praises of Hitler and his Third Reich see Thomas Jones, *Lloyd George* (Cambridge, Mass., 1951) and James Eayrs, *In Defence of Canada* (Toronto, 1965).

In 1935, and as late as November 1938, Churchill is reported to have publicly spoken of Hitler with admiration. See Hans Rothfels, *The German Opposition to Hitler: An Appraisal* (Chicago, 1962), 25.

[19] Ernst Ritter, "Die deutsche Volkstumsarbeit in der Zeit zwischen den Weltkriegen," *Zeitschrift für Kulturaustausch*, 31:2 (1981), 183-195. Max Hildebert Boehm, "Die Reorganisation der Deutschtumsarbeit nach dem ersten Weltkrieg," *Ostdeutsche Wissenschaft: Jahrbuch des Ostdeutschen Kulturrates*, V (1958), 1-34.

[20] Ernst Ritter, *op. cit.*, 185 and Rudolf Aschenauer, *Die Auslandsdeutschen. 100 Jahre Volkstumsarbeit. Leistung und Schicksal* (Berg, 1981), 69, cite a speech by VDA chairman Franz von Reichenau in late 1918 which aptly expressed the situation:

> The old edifice of the larger German state, the *Reich*, has collapsed. With it the forms of the German and Austrian states, in which 82 million of the 100 million Germans in the world have lived before, have broken up. Laid bare with one blow and without the curtains of the state, the notion of the German *Volk* stands in a new, unaccustomed, light before us. In the same moment as we lose our state, we win our *Volk*. In other words, it becomes a live certainty and realization for us that besides the community of the Reich which has united us with our fellow citizens, there exists a community of blood and descent which unites us with our fellow ethnic Germans.

[21] Ernst Ritter, *Das Deutsche Ausland-Institut in Stuttgart, 1917-1945: Ein Beispiel deutscher Volkstumsarbeit zwischen den Weltkriegen* (Wiesbaden, 1976), 18-53. Friedrich Carl Badendieck, *Volk unter Völkern: Aus der Geschichte deutscher Schutzarbeit* (Bad Godesberg, 1967). Heinz Lehmann was chief author of the article "Kanada" in *Handwörterbuch des Grenz- und Auslanddeutschtums*, vol. III (Breslau, 1938), 250-279. Preoccupation in the interwar period by a European nation with its ethnic minorities outside its borders was not confined to Germany. For Italy and Poland see Richard Pfalz, *Das Auslanditalienertum seit dem Friedensschluss und seine kulturelle Bedeutung: Ein Beispiel moderner Auswanderungspolitik* (Münster, 1933) and H. Radecki with B. Heydenkorn, *A Member of a Distinguished Family: The Polish Group in Canada* (Toronto, 1976), 68.

[22] Robert England, *The Colonization of Western Canada: A Case Study of Contemporary Land Settlement 1896-1934* (London, 1936), 167.

[23] Donald Avery, *'Dangerous Foreigners:' European Immigrant Workers and Labor Radicalism in Canada, 1896-1932* (Toronto, 1979).

[24] J.T.M. Anderson, *The Education of the New Canadian: A Treatise on Canada's Greatest Educational Problem* (Toronto, 1918). Rev. Capt. Wellington Bridgeman, *Breaking Prairie Sod* (Toronto, 1920).

[25] Heinz Lehmann, "Der Kampf um die deutsche Schule in Westkanada," *Deutsche Arbeit*, 36:2 (February 1936), 78.

[26] Albert Moellmann, unpublished manuscript (Waterloo College, dated June

28, 1939) reviewing Lehmann's books, in the possession of the estate of the late Heinz Lehmann.

[27] Kathleen Neils Conzen in Günter Moltmann, "Die deutsche Auswanderung in überseeische Gebiete: Forschungsstand und Forschungsprobleme," *Der Archivar: Mitteilungsblatt für Deutsches Archivwesen.* 32:1 (February 1979), 62.

[28] A.B. Faust, *The German Element in the United States with Special Reference to its Political, Moral, Social and Educational Influence*, 2 vols. (Boston and New York, 1909).

[29] Helge Ingstadt, *Westward to Vinland* (London, 1969). M. Magnusson and H. Palsson, eds., *The Vinland Sagas: The Norse Discovery of America* (Hammondsworth, 1965). Samuel Eliot Morrison, *The European Discovery of America: The Northerly Voyages A.D. 500-1600* (New York, 1971). David B.Quinn, *North America From Earliest Discovery to First Settlements: The Norse Voyages to 1612* (New York, 1975).

[30] *Ibid.*, Armin M. Brandt, *Bau deinen Altar auf fremder Erde: Die Deutschen in Amerika. 300 Jahre Germantown* (Stuttgart, 1983), 31-36. Lawrence M. Larson, "Did John Scolvus Visit Labrador and Newfoundland In or About 1476?" in J. R. Smallwood, ed., *The Book of Newfoundland*, vol. VI (St. John's, 1975).

[31] David B. Quinn, ed., *The Voyages and Colonizing Enterprises of Sir Humphrey Gilbert*, vol. I (London, 1940), 87, 404, 416.

[32] E. H. Bovay, *Le Canada et les Suisses 1604-1974* (Fribourg, 1976). Claude de Bonnault, "Les Suisses au Canada," *Le Bulletin des recherches historiques*, (Quebec), 61 (1955), 51-70.

[33] H.W. Debor, *1664-1964: Die Deutschen in der Provinz Quebec* (Montreal, 1963), 5.

[34] Cornelius J. Jaenen, "Ethnic Studies: An Integral Part of Canadian Studies," in W. Isajiw, ed., *Identities: The Impact of Ethnicity on Canadian Society* (Toronto, 1973), xiv.

[35] The standard account of Dieskau's role in 1755 is in F. Parkman, *Montcalm and Wolfe* (Boston, 1884). See also Irvin Cooper, "Three German Military Officers in Canada," *German-Canadian Yearbook*, IV (1978), 57f. As to Haldimand, see Ivor C.E. Luethy, "General Sir Frederick Haldimand: A Swiss Governor General of Canada (1777-1784)," *Canadian Ethnic Studies*, III (1971), 63-75, and E.H. Bovay, *Le Canada et les Suisses 1604-1574* (Fribourg, 1976).

[36] See for example H.R. Casgrain, ed., *Collection des manuscrits du Maréchal de Lévis*, 12 vols. (Montreal, 1889-1895), vol. V, 247, vol. III, 178, and "General Murray's Report of the State of the Government of Quebec in Canada, June 5th, 1762," in Adam Shortt and Arthur G. Doughty, *Documents Relating to the Constitutional History of Canada, 1759-1791* (Ottawa, 1907).

[37] Robert L. Séguin, "L' apport germanique dans le peuplement de Vaudreuil et Soulanger," *Le Bulletin des recherches historiques* (Quebec), 61 (1957), 42-58.

[38] Jean Pierre Wilhelmy, *Les mercenaires allemands au Québec du XVIIIe siècle et leur apport à la population* (Beloeil, Quebec, 1984).

[39] William H. Whiteley, "The Establishment of the Moravian Mission in Labrador and British Policy, 1763-83," *The Canadian Historical Review*, XXXIII (March 1964), 29-50, and "The Moravian Missionaries and the Labrador Eskimos in the Eighteenth Century," *Church History*, XXXV:1 (March 1966), 3-19.

[40] James K. Hiller, "The Foundation and the Early Years of the Moravian Mission in Labrador 1752-1805," unpublished M.A. thesis, Memorial University of Newfoundland, 1967; and "Moravian Land Holdings on the Labrador Coast: A Brief History," in Carol Brice-Bennett, ed., *Our Footprints Are Everywhere* (Nain, Labrador, 1977), 83-94.

[41] Hedwig E. Brueckner, "Religiöse Einstellung der frühen Herrnhuter und Wirken ihrer ersten Missionare in Labrador, dargestellt und kommentiert auf Grund ihrer Aufzeichnungen aus dem späten 18. Jahrhundert," 2 parts, unpublished M.A. thesis, Memorial University of Newfoundland, 1975.

[42] Alfred Ratz, "Frühe Kulturarbeit deutscher Herrnhuter in Labrador," *German-Canadian Yearbook*, III (1975), 50-69. Shmuel Ben-Dor, *Makkovik: Eskimos and Settlers in a Labrador Community: A Contrastive Study in Adaptation* (St. John's, 1966). Carol Brice-Bennett, "Two Opinions: Inuit and Moravian Missionaries in Labrador 1804-1860," unpublished M.A. thesis, Memorial University of Newfoundland, 1981.

[43] Alwin M. Josephy, *The Artist was a Young Man: The Life Story of Peter Rindisbacher* (Fort Worth, 1970). Karl J. R. Arndt, "The Peter Rindisbacher Family on the Red River in Rupert's Land: Their Hardships and Call for Help from Rapp's Harmony Society," *German-Canadian Yearbook*, I (1973), 95-106. Karl Meuli, "Peter Rindisbacher, der Indianermaler aus dem Emmental," *Beiträge zur Volkskunde* (Basel, 1960), 140-174. See also George F. Stanley, "Documents Relating to the Swiss Immigration to Red River in 1821," *The Canadian Historical Review*, XXII (1941), 42-50. F.H.N. Davidson, "His Majesty's Regiment de Meuron," *The Army Quarterly* (London), XXXIII (1937), 58-72. John D.P. Martin, "The Regiment de Watteville: Its Settlement and Service in Upper Canada," *Ontario Historical Society, Papers and Records*, 53 (1960), 17-30. John P. Pritchett, *The Red River Valley 1811-1849: A Regional Study* (New Haven, 1942).

[44] Ursula Bohlmann, "The Germans: The Protestant Buffer," in Douglas F. Campbell, ed., *Banked Fires — The Ethnics of Nova Scotia* (Port Credit, Ont., 1978), 183-211. Laurie Lacey, ed., *Lunenburg County Folklore and Oral History: Project '77* (Ottawa, 1979). Helen Creighton, *Folklore of Lunenburg County* (Ottawa, 1950). Christine Ullmann, "German Folksongs of Lunenburg County, N.S.," *German-Canadian Yearbook*, V (1979), 143-155. Murray B. Emeneau, "The Dialect of Lunenburg, Nova Scotia," *Language*, 11 (1935), 140-147; 16 (1940), 214-215. H.

Rex Wilson, "The Dialect of Lunenburg County, Nova Scotia: A Study of the English of the County, with Reference to its Sources, Preservation of Relics, and Vestiges of Bilingualism," unpublished Ph.D. thesis, University of Michigan, 1958. Manfred Richter, "Die deutsche Mundart von Lunenburg County, Nova Scotia: ein Ueberblick," *German-Canadian Studies Annals*, II (1978), 19-28. J. A. Flett, *The Story of St. Andrew's Presbyterian Church, Lunenburg, N.S.* (N.p., 1970). Udo Sautter, "Ein deutscher Geistlicher in Neuschottland: Johann Adam Moschell (1795-1849)," *German-Canadian Yearbook*, I (1973), 153-159, and "Die Lunenburg-Deutschen," *German Canadian Studies Annals*, I (1976), 69-85. Lunenburg Hospital Society, Ladies Auxiliary, *Dutch Oven: A Cook Book of Coveted Traditional Recipes from the Kitchens of Lunenburg* (Lunenburg, 1953). Franklin Russell, "The Art of Lunenburg Cooking — and Eating," *Maclean's*, March 28, 1959, 26-27, 51-52. Gertrud Waseem, "German Settlements in Nova Scotia," in Peter G. Liddell, ed., *German Canadian Studies: Critical Approaches* (Vancouver, 1983), 56-64. For additional materials see *German-Canadian Yearbook*, vols. I, III, IV and VII.

[45] Winthrop Pickard Bell, *The 'Foreign Protestants' and the Settlement of Nova Scotia: The History of a Piece of Arrested British Colonial Policy in the Eighteenth Century* (Toronto, 1961).

[46] David Artiss, "German Cultural Heritage Studies in Atlantic Canada," in Rainer L. Hempel, ed., *Proceedings of the Atlantic University Teachers of German Conference 1979 at Mount Allison University, Sackville, New Brunswick* (Sackville, 1979), 72-82.

[47] See Lothar Zimmermann's introduction to his edition of *Vertrauliche Briefe aus Canada und Neuengland vom J. 1777 und 1778 aus Hrn. Prof. Schlözers Briefwechsel* (Toronto, 1981), 18, and the comprehensive bibliography on "German troops in North America 1776-1783" that he appended to this edition. Compare also the older exhaustive bibliography by Emil Meynen, *Bibliographie des Deutschtums der kolonialzeitlichen Einwanderung in Nordamerika* (Leipzig, 1937). On Riedesel see Mrs. General Riedesel, *Letters and Journals Relating to the War of the American Revolution and the Capture of the German Troops at Saratoga*, translated from the original German by William L. Stone (Albany, 1867. Reprint: New York, 1968). Marvin L. Brown, ed., *Baroness von Riedesel and the American Revolution: Journal and Correspondence of a Tour of Duty 1776-1783* (Chapel Hill, 1965). Louise Hall Tharp, *The Baroness and the General* (Boston, 1962). Anna K. Hess, "A Voyage of Duty: the Riedesels in America," *German-Canadian Yearbook*, I (1973), 131-139. Additional items not listed in Zimmermann's bibliography include: Karl J. R. Arndt, "The German Occupation of Quebec in 1776," *Journal of German-American Studies*, XIII (1978), 107-111, and "Die Reise der Braunschweigischen Hulfstruppen nach Quebec im Jahre 1776 und die Folgen," *German Canadian Studies Annals*, II (1978), 1-3. Marion Gilroy, ed., *Loyalists and Land Settlements in Nova Scotia* (Halifax, 1937). E.C. Wright, *The Loyalists of New Brunswick* (Ottawa, 1955). Samuel S. Smith, *The Battle of Trenton* (Monmouth Beach, N.J.), 1965. Mary Beacock Fryer, *Loyalist Spy: The Experiences of Captain John Walden Meyers during the American Revolution* (Brockville, Ont., 1974). Lothar Zimmermann, "It's a Long Way to Quebec: An Episode Relating to the North American Campaign of the Knyphausen Regiment," *German-Canadian Yearbook*,

VI (1981), 28-41. Nick and Helma Mika, *United Empire Loyalists: Pioneers of Upper Canada* (Belleville, Ont., 1976). E.A. Cruikshank, ed., *The Settlement of the United Empire Loyalists on The Upper St. Lawrence and Bay of Quinte in 1784: A Documentary Record* (Toronto, 1934).

⁴⁸ G. Heintz, "German Immigration into Upper Canada and Ontario from 1783 to the Present Day," unpublished M.A. thesis, Queen's University, 1938. Mabel Dunham, *Grand River* (Toronto, 1945). G. Elmore Raeman, *The Trail of the Black Walnut* (Toronto, 1957). Hazel Mae Schwerdtfeger, *Memoirs of Reverend J. Samuel Schwerdtfeger: The Saint of St. Lawrence Seaway* (New York, 1961). Carl Cronmiller, *A History of the Lutheran Church in Canada*, vol. I (N.p., 1961). Frank Malinsky, *Grace and Blessing: A History of the Ontario District of the Lutheran Church—Missouri Synod* (Elmira, Ont., 1954).

⁴⁹ Gottlieb Leibbrandt, *Little Paradise: Aus Geschichte und Leben der Deutschkanadier in der County Waterloo, Ontario, 1800-1975* (Kitchener, 1977), and its English translation *Little Paradise: The Saga of the German Canadians of Waterloo County, Ontario, 1800-1975* (Kitchener, 1980). See also "100 Jahre Concordia," in *Concordia Club Nachrichten Nr. 57. Jubliäums-Ausgabe* (Kitchener, 1973), 1-98, bilingual edition, and "Deutsche Ortsgründungen und Ortsnamen in der Grafschaft Waterloo," *German-Canadian Yearbook*, I (1973), 119-129.

⁵⁰ W.V. Uttley, *A History of Kitchener* (Waterloo, Ont., 1937). H.K. Kalbfleisch, *History of the Pioneer German Language Press of Ontario, 1835-1918* (Toronto, 1968). Bill Moyer, *Kitchener: Yesterday Revisited: An Illustrated History* (Burlington, Ont., 1979). Paul Tiessen, ed., *Berlin, Canada: A Self-Portrait of Kitchener, Ontario Before World War One* (St. Jacobs, Ont., 1979). John English and Kenneth McLaughlin, *Kitchener: An Illustrated History* (Waterloo, 1983). Ezra A. Eby, *A Biographical History of Early Settlers and their Descendants in Waterloo Township*, edited by Eldon D. Weber (Kitchener, 1971, 1978). James M. Nyce, ed., *The Gordon C. Eby Diaries, 1911-13: Chronicle of a Mennonite Farmer* (Toronto, 1982).

⁵¹ John Andre, *William Berczy: Co-Founder of Toronto* (Toronto, 1967). John Andre, *Infant Toronto as Simcoe's Folly* (Toronto, 1971). Florence M. Burns, *William Berczy* (In Don Mills, Ont., 1977). Beate Riedle, "William Moll-Berczys 'l'Art enchanteur' und die kanadische Siedlungspolitik," *German Canadian Studies Annals*, III (1980), 164-176. Isabel Champion, *Markham 1793-1900* (Markham, Ont., 1979).

⁵² Jean R. Burnet, *Ethnic Groups in Upper Canada* (Toronto, 1972). Peter Hessel, *Destination: Ottawa Valley* (Ottawa, 1984). Brenda Lee-Whiting, *Harvest of Stones: The German Settlement of Renfrew County* (Toronto, 1985).

⁵³ See the following bibliographies: Donovan E. Smucker, ed., *The Sociology of Canadian Mennonites, Hutterites and Amish: A Bibliography with Annotations* (Waterloo, Ont., 1977). Victor G. Wiebe, *Alberta-Saskatchewan Mennonite and Hutterite Bibliography 1962-1981* (Saskatoon, 1981). Lawrence Klippenstein, "Canadian Mennonite Writings," *German-Canadian Yearbook*, VI (1981), 284-293. Lawrence Klippenstein, *Mennonitengeschichte und Literatur: Eine Buecherliste* (Winnipeg, 1981).

[54] Jacob Janzen, *Tales from the Mennonite History* (Waterloo, Ont., 1945). Mary Ann Horst, *My Old Order Mennonite Heritage* (Kitchener, 1970). Blodwen Davies, *A String of Amber: The Heritage of the Mennonites* (Vancouver, 1973). Isaac R. Horst, *Up the Conestogo* (Mt. Forest, Ont., 1979). Allan M. Buehler, *The Pennsylvania German Dialect and the Life of an Old Order Mennonite* (Cambridge, Ont., 1977). Mary Ann Horst, *Pennsylvania Dutch Fun, Folklore and Cooking* (Kitchener, 1974). Edna Staebler, *Food that Really Schmecks* (Toronto, 1968), and *Sauerkraut and Enterprise* (Toronto, 1969). Nancy Lou Patterson, "Mennonite Folk Art of Waterloo County," *Ontario History*, 60 (1968), 81-104. Nancy Lou Gellermann Patterson, *Swiss German and Dutch German Mennonite Traditional Art in the Waterloo Region, Ontario* (Ottawa, 1979). Michael S. Bird, *Ontario Fraktur: A Pennsylvania-German Folk Tradition in Early Canada* (Toronto, 1977). L.M. Nykor and P.D. Musson, *Mennonite Furniture: The Ontario Tradition in York County* (Toronto, 1977). Rolf Wilhelm Brednich, *Mennonite Folklife and Folklore: A Preliminary Report* (Ottawa, 1977) and *The Bible and the Plough: The Lives of a Hutterite Minister and a Mennonite Farmer* (Ottawa, 1981).

[55] John B. Toews, *Lost Fatherland: The Story of the Mennonite Emigration from Soviet Russia 1921-1927* (Scottsdale, Pa., 1967). Frank H. Epp, *Mennonite Exodus: The Rescue and Resettlement of the Russian Mennonites Since the Communist Revolution* (Altona, Man., 1962).

[56] John W. Friesen, "Characteristics of Mennonite Identity: A Survey of Mennonite and Non-Mennonite Views," *Canadian Ethnic Studies*, III:1 (1971), 25-41. F.H. Epp, "Problems of Mennonite Identity: A Historical Study," in Leo Driedger, ed., *The Canadian Ethnic Mosaic* (Toronto, 1978), 281-294. A. Sawatzki, "The Mennonites of Alberta and their Assimilation," unpublished M.A. thesis, University of Alberta, 1964. H. Paetkau, "A Struggle for Survival: The Russian Mennonite Immigrants in Ontario, 1924-1939," unpublished M.A. thesis, University of Waterloo, Ont., 1977. L. Driedger, "A Sect in Modern Society: A Case Study of the Old Colony Mennonites in Saskatchewan," unpublished M.A. thesis, University of Chicago, 1955.

[57] Frank H. Epp, *Mennonites in Canada, 1786-1920: The History of a Separate People* (Toronto, 1974), and *Mennonites in Canada, 1920-1940: A People's Struggle for Survival* (Toronto, 1982).

[58] Orland Gingerich, *The Amish of Canada* (Waterloo, Ont., 1972). Compare also Dorothy Sauder, ed., *Sesquicentennial of the Amish Mennonites of Ontario* (N.p., 1972).

[59] E.K. Francis, *In Search of Utopia: The Mennonites in Manitoba* (Altona, Man., 1955). See also John H. Warkentin, "The Mennonite Settlement of Southern Manitoba," unpublished Ph.D. thesis, University of Toronto, 1960. Gerhard Lohrenz, *The Mennonites of Western Canada: Their Origin, and Background, and the Brief History of Their Settling and Progress Here in Canada* (Winnipeg, 1974). Lawrence Klippenstein and Julius G. Toews, eds., *Mennonite Memories: Settling in Western Canada* (Winnipeg, 1977), with good bibliography.

⁶⁰ E.K. Francis, "A Bibliography of the Mennonites of Manitoba," *The Mennonite Quarterly Review*, XXVII:3 (July 1953), 238.

⁶¹ C. Henry Smith, *The Coming of the Russian Mennonites: An Episode in the Settling of the Last Frontier, 1874-1884* (Berne, Ind., 1927). C.A. Dawson, *Group Settlement: Ethnic Communities in Western Canada* (Toronto, 1936), 110. Robert England, *op. cit.*, 234.

⁶² See for example John Warkentin, "Mennonite Agricultural Settlements in Southern Manitoba," *Geographic Review*, XLIX:3 (1959), 342-368. C.J. Tracie, "Ethnicity and the Prairie Environment: Patterns of Old Colony Mennonite and Doukhobor Settlement," in Richard Allen, ed., *Man and Nature on the Prairies* (Regina, 1976), 47f. Richard J. Friesen, "Saskatchewan Mennonite Settlements: The Modification of an Old World Settlement Pattern," *Canadian Ethnic Studies*, IX:2 (1977), 72-90.

⁶³ Frank Brown, *A History of the Town of Winkler, Manitoba* (Winkler, 1973). Abe Warkentin, ed., *Reflections on our Heritage: A History of Steinbach and the R.M. of Hanover from 1874* (Steinbach, 1974). J. Friesen et al., eds., *Grunthal History 1874-1974* (Grunthal, Man., 1974). Peter D. Zacharias, *Reinland: An Experience in Community* (Reinland, 1976). Orlando Friesen and Irma Neudorf, eds., *The History of the Friedensfeld School District* (Winnipeg, 1976). Karl Fast, ed., *Fiftieth Anniversary of the Mennonite Settlement in North Kildonan* (Winnipeg, 1978). R. Loewen, *Blumenort: A Mennonite Community in Transition, 1874-1982* (Blumenort, 1982). Henry J. Gerbrandt, *Adventure in Faith: The Background in Europe and the Development in Canada of the Bergthaler Mennonite Church of Manitoba* (Altona, Man., 1970).

⁶⁴ Arthur Grenke, "The Formation and Early Development of an Urban Ethnic Community: A Case Study of the Germans in Winnipeg, 1872-1919," unpublished Ph.D. thesis, University of Manitoba, 1975, and "Settling the West: The German Experience to 1914," *Archivist/L'archiviste*, XII:4 (1985), 10-12.

⁶⁵ Edmund Heier, "A Study of the German Lutheran and Catholic Immigrants in Canada, Formerly Residing in Tsarist and Soviet Russia," unpublished M.A. thesis, University of British Columbia, 1955. By the same author, "The Immigration of the Russo-German Catholics and Lutherans into Canada," *Canadian Slavonic Papers*, IV (1959), 160-175, and "Russo-German Place Names in Russia and North America", *Names*, IX:4 (1961), 260-268.

⁶⁶ Kurt Tischler, "The German-Canadians in Saskatchewan with Particular Reference to the Language Problem 1900-1930," unpublished M.A. thesis, University of Saskatchewan, 1978.

⁶⁷ See Richard Allen, ed., *A Region of the Mind: Interpreting the Western Canadian Plains* (Regina, 1973). For a good review of the extent of geographic research on German ethnicity see Hansgeorg Schlichtmann, "Ethnic Themes in Geographical Research on Western Canada," *Canadian Ethnic Studies*, IX:2 (1977), 9-41. Gerald Friesen, *The Canadian Prairies: A History* (Toronto, 1984), perhaps the

most outstanding synthesis of the recent historiography of that region, at least identifies a German community in western Canada 1870-1940, in his 500-page work.

[68] See e.g. Edmund Heier, *op. cit.* Adam Giesinger, *From Catherine to Khrushchev: The Story of Russia's Germans* (Winnipeg, 1974). Joseph S. Height, *Memories of the Black Sea Germans: Highlights of their History and Heritage* (N.p., 1979). Fred C. Koch, *The Volga Germans in Russia and the Americas, From 1763 to the Present* (University Park, Pa., 1977). George P. Aberle, *From the Steppes to the Prairies* (Bismarck, N.D., 1963). Fred W. Gross, *The Pastor: The Life of an Immigrant* (Philadelphia, 1973). A. Becker, "St. Joseph's Colony, Balgonie," *Saskatchewan History*, XX:1 (1967), 1-18, "The Germans in Western Canada: A Vanishing People," *Canadian Catholic Historical Association Study Sessions*, 42 (1975), 29-49, and "The Germans from Russia in Saskatchewan and Alberta," *German-Canadian Yearbook*, III (1976), 106-119. For additional publications see Marie Miller Olson, comp., *A Bibliography on the Germans from Russia. Material Found in the New York Public Library* (Lincoln, Neb., 1976), and Emma S. Haynes, comp., *Bibliography of the AHSGR* (American Historical Society of Germans from Russia), *Archives and Historical Library, Greeley, Colorado* (Lincoln, Neb., 1981). The most comprehensive bibliography is by Karl Stumpp, *Das Schrifttum über das Deutschtum in Russland. Eine Bibliographie.* 5th expanded edition (Stuttgart, 1980).

[69] Seymour Martin Lipset, *Agrarian Socialism: The Cooperative Commonwealth Federation in Saskatchewan: A Study in Political Sociology* (Berkeley, 1950. 2nd ed., Garden City, N.Y., 1968). Norman Ward and Duff Stafford, eds., *Politics in Saskatchewan* (Don Mills, Ont , 1968). D. Flanagan, "Ethnic Voting in Alberta Provincial Elections, 1921-1971," *Canadian Ethnic Studies*, III (December 1971), 139-164. J. W. Brennan, "A Political History of Saskatchewan, 1905-1929," unpublished Ph.D. thesis, University of Alberta, 1976.

[70] Pater A. Zimmermann, *Zum fünfzigjährigen Jubiläum: Die römisch-katholische Pfarrei St. Joseph bei Balgonie, Saskatchewan* (N.p., 1936). Rev. P. Windschiegl, *Fifty Golden Years* (Muenster, 1953). J.G.F. Judt, *The History of the Canada District of the American Lutheran Church*, unpublished M.Th. thesis, University of Saskatchewan, 1946. C. Kleiner, *Festschrift zur Feier des Goldenen Jubiläums der Evangelisch-Lutherischen Synode von Manitoba und anderen Provinzen 1897-1947* (N.p., n.d.). Ernest G. Goos, *Pioneering for Christ in Western Canada: The Story of the Evangelical Lutheran Synod of Manitoba and Other Provinces: Synod's Golden Jubilee, 1897-1947* (N.p., 1948). Paul E. Wiegner, *The Origin and Development of the Manitoba-Saskatchewan District of the Lutheran Church-Missouri Synod.* 35th Anniversary Booklet (N.p., 1957). Clinton O. White, "Language, Religion, Schools and Politics among German-American Catholic Settlers in St. Peter's Colony, Saskatchewan, 1903-1916," *Canadian Catholic Historical Association Study Sessions*, 45 (1978), 81-89, and "Education among German Catholic Settlers in Saskatchewan, 1903-1918: A Reinterpretation," *Canadian Ethnic Studies*, XVI:1 (1984), 78-97.

[71] Alan B. Anderson, "Assimilation in the Bloc Settlements of North-Central Saskatchewan: A Comparative Study of Identity Change Among Seven Ethno-Religious Groups in a Canadian Prairie Region," unpublished Ph.D. thesis,

University of Saskatchewan, 1972. See also his articles "Ethnic Identity in Saskatchewan Bloc Settlements: A Sociological Appraisal," in Howard Palmer, ed., *The Settlement of the West* (Calgary, 1977), 187-225, "Linguistic Trends among Saskatchewan Ethnic Groups," in Martin L. Kovacs, ed., *Ethnic Canadians: Culture and Education* (Regina, 1978), 63-86, and "German Settlement in Saskatchewan," in Martin L. Kovacs, ed., *Roots and Realities Among Eastern and Central Europeans* (Edmonton, 1983), 175-221.

[72] R.W. Grant, *The Humboldt Story, 1903-1953* (Humboldt, 1954). *Memories of Muenster's 70 Progressive Years, 1903-1973* (Muenster, 1973). Gilbert Johnson, *Seventy-Five Years: A History of Langenburg School District No. 105, 1887-1962* (Langenburg, Sask., 1963), and *A History of Langenburg 1887-1962* (Langenburg, Sask., 1972). Irene Adams and Gilbert Johnson, *Walk Back Through Time: A History of Langenburg and District* (Langenburg, Sask., 1980). Grosswerder and District New Horizon Heritage Group, comp., *Prairie Legacy: Grosswerder and Surrounding Districts* (North Battleford, 1980). Holdfast History and Heritage Committee, comp., *Holdfast: History and Heritage* (Melfort, Sask., 1980). Qu'Appelle Historical Society, comp., *Qu'Appelle: Footprints to Progress* (Qu'Appelle, 1980). Raymore and District Historical Society, comp., *From Prairie Wool to Golden Grain: Raymore and District 1904-1979* (Raymore, 1980). Sister M. Philippine, *50 Golden Years: Tramping Lake, 1905-1955* (Tramping Lake School District, 1955). *Richmound's Heritage: A History of Richmound and District 1910-1978* (Richmound, 1978). June Gale, ed., *Pioneers and Progress: The History of Southey and District* (Southey, 1980). Paul W. Riegert, *2005 Memories: A History of the Hamburg School District No. 2005* (Laird, Sask., 1980).

[73] Karl Götz, *Brüder über Land und Meer: Schicksale und Geschichten der Ausgewanderten* (Bodman, 1970), and *Die Heimstätter: Ein deutsches Schicksal in Kanada* (Leipzig, 1944). Hugo Meilicke, *Leaves from the Life of a Pioneer: Being the Autobiography of Sometime Senator Emil Julius Meilicke* (N.p., 1948). Anna Friesen and Victor Carl Friesen, *The Mulberry Tree* (Winnipeg, 1983). Karl A. Peter and Franziska Peter, "The Kurtenbach Letters: An Autobiographical Description of Pioneer Life in Saskatchewan Around the Turn of the Century," *Canadian Ethnic Studies*, XI:2 (1979), 89-96. Perry A. Mazone, "An Immigrant Family in Saskatchewan, 1903-1943," *Canadian Ethnic Studies*, XII:3 (1980), 131-139. A.S. Bowman, *Homestead Days and Early Settlement of the Waterloo District South West of Guernsey, Saskatchewan* (Rosthern, Sask., 1951).

[74] William A. Czumer, *Recollections About the Life of the First Ukrainian Settlers in Canada* (Edmonton, 1981).

[75] For a survey of the literature on the Hutterites in Canada see the bibliographies by D. E. Smucker, *op. cit.*; Hansgeorg Schlichtmann, *op. cit.*; V.G. Wiebe, *op. cit.*; and John Ryan, *The Agricultural Economy of Manitoba Hutterite Colonies* (Toronto, 1977). In addition compare Michael Holzach, *Das vergessene Volk. Ein Jahr bei den deutschen Hutterern in Kanada* (Hamburg, 1980); Herfried Scheer, "Die Mundart der hutterischen Brüder: ein Spiegel ihrer Geschichte," *German Canadian Studies Annals*, I (1976), 56-68; John Horsch, *The Hutterite Brethren, 1528-1931: A Story of Martyrdom and Loyalty* (Cayley, Alta., 1977). Robert

J. Macdonald, "Hutterite Education in Alberta: A Test Case in Assimilation, 1920-70," in A. W. Rasporich, ed., *Western Canada Past and Present* (Calgary, 1975), 133-149; John W. Bennett, "Change and Transition in Hutterian Society," in *ibid.*, 120-132; Karl Peter, "The Instability of the Community of Goods in the Social History of the Hutterites," in *ibid.*, 99-119; Karl Peter, "The Decline of Hutterite Population Growth," *Canadian Ethnic Studies*, XII:3 (1980), 97-110, 118-123; Edward D. Boldt and Lance W. Roberts, "The Decline of Hutterite Population Growth: Causes and Consequences—A Comment," *ibid.*, 111-117; S. and E. Schludermann, "Personality Development in Hutterite Communal Society," in Leo Driedger, ed., *The Canadian Ethnic Mosaic: A Quest for Identity* (Toronto, 1978), 169-187.

[76] Alexander Malycky, "The German-Albertans: A Bibliography," parts 1 and 2, *German-Canadian Yearbook*, VI (1981), 311-344, and VII(1983), 239-325.

[77] Howard Palmer, *Land of the Second Chance: A History of Ethnic Groups in Southern Alberta* (Lethbridge, 1972), 268f., 272.

[78] Bruce Ramsay, *A History of the German-Canadians in British Columbia* (Winnipeg, 1958).

[79] John Norris, ed., *Strangers Entertained: A History of the Ethnic Groups of British Columbia* (Vancouver, 1971).

[80] Dorothy Blakey Smith, ed., *The Reminiscences of Dr. John Sebastian Helmcken* (Vancouver, 1975).

[81] Peter G. Liddell, comp., *A Bibliography of the Germans in British Columbia* (Vancouver, 1982).

[82] Arthur Grenke, *op. cit.*, chapter IX. Barbara Wilson, "Loyalty in Question," in *Ontario and the First World War* (Toronto, 1971). Werner A. Bausenhart, "The Ontario German Language Press and its Suppression by Order-in-Council in 1918," *Canadian Ethnic Studies*, IV:1-2 (1972), 35-48. W. Entz, "The Suppression of the German Language Press in September 1918 (with special reference to the secular German language papers in western Canada)," *Canadian Ethnic Studies*, VIII:2 (1976), 56-70.

[83] F.H. Epp, "An Analysis of Germanism and National Socialism in the Immigrant Press of a Canadian Minority Group, the Mennonites, in the 1930s," unpublished Ph.D. thesis, University of Minnesota, 1965. H. Paetkau, *op. cit.*; A. Sawatzki, *op. cit.*; E.K. Francis, *op. cit.*; F.H. Epp, *Mennonite Exodus, op. cit.*; J.F. Wagner, "Transferred Crisis...," *op. cit.*; David Warren Fransen, "Canadian Mennonites and Conscientious Objection in World War II," unpublished M.A. thesis, University of Waterloo, Ont., 1977.

[84] Watson Kirkconnell, *Canada, Europe and Hitler* (London, 1940). John Offenbeck, "The Nazi Movement and German Canadians 1933-1939," unpublished M.A. thesis, University of Western Ontario, 1970. Jonathan F.

Wagner, "Deutscher Bund Canada 1934-9," *The Canadian Historical Review*, LVIII:2 (June 1977), 176-200; "Nazi Membership in Canada: A Profile," *Social History*, XIV:27 (1981), 233-8; "Heim ins Reich. The Story of Loon River's Nazis," *Saskatchewan History*, XXIX (1976), 41-50; *Brothers Beyond the Sea: National Socialism in Canada* (Waterloo, 1981).

[85] Howard Palmer, "Nativism in Alberta, 1925-1930," *Historical Papers 1974* (Ottawa, 1974), 183-212; *Patterns of Prejudice: A History of Nativism in Alberta* (Toronto, 1982). Tracy Reynolds, "A Case Study in Attitudes Towards Enemy Aliens in British Columbia 1914-1919," unpublished M.A. thesis, University of British Columbia, 1973. J.A. Boudreau,"The Enemy Alien Problem in Canada, 1914-21," unpublished Ph.D. thesis, University of California, 1965. M.F. Smeltzer, "Saskatchewan Opinion on Immigration from 1920-1939," unpublished M.A. thesis, University of Saskatchewan, 1946. Morris Mott, "The Foreign Peril: Nativism in Winnipeg, 1916-1923," unpublished M.A. thesis, University of Manitoba, 1970. W.E. Calderwood, "The Rise and Fall of the Ku Klux Klan in Saskatchewan," unpublished M.A. thesis, University of Saskatchewan, 1968. Jean Burnet, *Next Year Country: A Study of Rural Social Organization in Alberta* (Toronto, 1951). Internment operations 1913-1918 are described in Desmond Morton, *The Canadian General Sir William Otter* (Toronto, 1974). J.A. Boudreau, "Interning Canada's 'Enemy Aliens', 1914-1919," *Canada*, II:1 (1974), 15-28. David J. Carter, *Behind Canadian Barbed Wire: Alien and German Prisoners of War Camps in Canada, 1914-1946* (Calgary, 1980).

[86] B.G. Sack, *History of the Jews in Canada* (Montreal, 1965). Stephen A. Speisman, *The Jews of Toronto: A History to 1937* (Toronto, 1979). Irving Abella and Harold Troper, *None Is Too Many: Canada and the Jews of Europe 1933-1948* (Toronto, 1982). Eric Koch, *Deemed Suspect: A Wartime Blunder* (Toronto, 1980). For the statistical data see Louis Rosenberg, *Canada's Jews: A Social and Economic Study of the Jews in Canada* (Montreal, 1939).

[87] Watson Kirkconnell, *A Slice of Canada: Memoirs* (Toronto, 1967), 265.

[88] K.M. McLaughlin, *The Germans in Canada* (Ottawa, 1985), published by the Canadian Historical Association as Booklet No. 11 in the series *Canada's Ethnic Groups*. Rudolf A. Helling, *A Socio-Economic History of German-Canadians: They, Too, Founded Canada. A Research Report* by Rudolf A. Helling, Jack Thiessen, Fritz Wieden, Elizabeth and Kurt Wangenheim, Karl Heeb, edited by Bernd Hamm (Wiesbaden, 1984), published by *Vierteljahreshefte für Sozial- und Wirtschaftsgeschichte* as Beiheft No. 75. Michael Bird and Terry Kobayashi, *A Splendid Harvest: Germanic Folk and Decorative Arts in Canada* (Toronto, 1981).

[89] Virtually all post-World War II studies of the history of German overseas migration focus on the emigration of German citizens from Germany to the United States. See G.P. Bassler, "German Overseas Migration to North America in the Nineteenth and Twentieth Centuries: Recent German Research from a Canadian Perspective," *German-Canadian Yearbook*, VII (1983), 8-21. Information on German migration to Canada from the United States is equally scarce. See Marcus Lee Hansen, *The Mingling of the Canadian and American Peoples* (New

Haven, 1940); R.H. Coats and M.C. MacLean, The American-Born in Canada: A Statistical Interpretation (Toronto, 1943). Harold Troper's *Only Farmers Need Apply: Official Canadian Government Encouragement of Immigration from the United States, 1896-1911* (Toronto, 1972), although well researched, barely touches on the large contingent of German-American immigrants. For Swiss migration to Canada see E.H. Bovay, *op. cit.*, Claude de Bonnault, *op. cit.*, Roxroy West, "Canadian Immigration Agents and Swiss Immigration," M.A. thesis, University of Ottawa, 1978, and Leo Schelbert, *Einführung in die schweizerische Auswanderungsgeschichte der Neuzeit* (Zurich, 1976).

On Austrian migration to Canada see Johann Chmelnar, "Die Auswanderung aus den im Reichsrat vertretenen Königreichen und Ländern in den Jahren 1905-1914," unpublished Ph.D. thesis, University of Vienna, 1972, and "The Austrian Emigration 1900-1914," in D. Fleming and B. Bailyn, eds., *Perspectives in American History*, vol. VII (Cambridge, Mass., 1974), 275-378.

[90] James B. Hedges, Building the Canadian West: The Land and Colonization Policy of the Canadian Pacific Railway (New York, 1939).

[91] Andrew Amstatter, *Tomslake: History of the Sudeten Germans in Canada* (Saanichton, B.C., 1978). Fritz Wieden, *The Sudeten Germans* (Toronto, 1979).

[92] Heinz Kloss, ed., *Ahornblätter. Anthologie deutschkanadischer Dichtung* (Würzburg, 1961); "Bemerkungen zur deutschkanadischen Literatur," *German-Canadian Yearbook*, III (1976), 188-192. Hartmut Froeschle, "Die deutschkanadische Literatur: Umfang und Problemstellungen," *German Canadian Studies Annals*, I (1976), 18-30; "Gibt es eine deutschkanadische Literatur?" *German-Canadian Yearbook*, III (1976), 174-187; *Drei Frühe deutschkanadische Dichter: Eugen Funcken, Heinrich Rembe, Emil Querner* (Toronto, 1978); *Nachrichten aus Ontario: Deutschsprachige Literatur in Kanada* (Hildesheim, New York, 1981). William DeFehr, Gerhard Ens, George Epp, Helen Janzen, Peter Klassen, Lloyd Siemens and Jack Thiessen, eds., *Harvest: Anthology of Mennonite Writings in Canada, 1874-1974* (Winnipeg, 1974). George K. Epp, ed., *Unter dem Nordlicht: Anthologie des deutschen Schrifttums der Mennoniten in Canada* (Winnipeg, 1977); "Dialekt und Hochdeutsch im Schrifttum der Mennoniten," *German Canadian Studies Annals*, II (1978), 71-81; "Der mennonitische Beitrag zur deutschkanadischen Literatur," *German-Canadian Yearbook*, VI (1981), 140-148. Hermann Boeschenstein, "Betrachtungen zur deutschkanadischen Literatur," *German Canadian Studies Annals*, I (1976), 1-17. Clive H. Cardinal and A. Malycky, "German-Canadian Creative Literature: A Preliminary Check List of Authors and Pseudonyms," *Canadian Ethnic Studies*, I:1 (1969), 31-37. Clive H. Cardinal, "Studies on German-Canadian Creative Literature: First Supplement," *Canadian Ethnic Studies*, V:1-2 (1976), 91-93. William R. Gilby, "Imprints of German-Canadian Creative Literature: First Supplement," *Canadian Ethnic Studies*, V: 1-2 (1976), 85-90.

[93] Walter E. Riedel, ed., *The Old World and the New: Literary Perspectives of German-speaking Canadians* (Toronto, 1984).

[94] Herbert Wilhelm Debor, "The Cultural Contribution of the German Ethnic Group to Canada," one of ten unpublished cultural essays commissioned

by the Royal Commission on Bilingualism and Biculturalism in order to assess
the contributions of certain of the other ethnic groups to Canadian life
(Montreal, 1965), copy in the National Library, Ottawa. *Report of the Royal
Commission on Bilingualism and Biculturalism, Book IV: The Contribution of the
Other Ethnic Groups* (Ottawa, 1970).

PREFACE

Preface to the Original Edition of
Das Deutschtum in Ostkanada

This study represents the major part of my doctoral dissertation accepted by the Faculty of Philosophy of the University of Berlin in the summer of 1931. The topic was first suggested to me in 1928 by Professor Wilhelm Dibelius and Professor Paul Traeger, who continued to be of great support in my research by their willingness to help at any time in procuring materials, and by their generous advice. I am especially grateful to them for assisting me in obtaining a scholarship from the Academic Exchange Service which enabled me to study in London from October 1929 to June 1930. There I was able to collect the English-Canadian source materials which are essential for this study, and are not to be found anywhere else in comparable completeness. I would also like to express my deeply felt gratitude to the Academic Exchange Service and its director Dr. Morsbach for my year in England.

Professor Dibelius was unfortunately not able to see the completion of this study to which he so much looked forward as a supplement to his own large scale research project on Canada. He passed away suddenly in January 1931. In his place, Professor W. Vogel and Professor F. Hartung assumed the responsibility for approving my finished dissertation in the most accommodating manner. I also want again to thank them.

For the time being, economic reasons compel me to have published only this first volume of my comprehensive study of the German element in Canada. But I also hope to be able to improve and amplify still further my account of the German element in western Canada as a result of a projected study trip to Canada in a few years.

I am much obliged to the *Deutsches Ausland-Institut* which has made possible the publication of this study as a part of its series on cultural history. Futhermore, I wish to acknowledge my indebtedness to the directors of the Royal Empire Society, 18 Northumberland Avenue, London, the *Auswanderer-Beratungsstelle des Evangelischen Hauptvereins*, Berlin, the *Reichsverband für das katholische Auslandsdeutschtum*, Berlin, and the central office of the *Verein für das Deutschtum im Ausland*, Berlin, for granting me generous access to their libraries and archives.

We already have a wealth of monographs on the most diverse areas of German settlement outside the boundaries of Germany, many of which were written by distinguished Germans living in other lands, such as the classic on the German element in the United States by A.B. Faust. Yet a comprehensive critical account of the history of Canada's German element has never been attempted. The literature of the German Canadians themselves contains, apart from the *Annual Reports* of the Waterloo Historical Society which are only relevant to local history, only fragmentary and mostly very inaccurate references to their own history in such publications as calendars, occasional anniversary pamphlets and in the newspapers. There is no doubt that Canada's 180 year old German element deserves not only an historical account but also the interest of all those who care in the least for the fate of ethnic Germans in other lands.

Canada as a whole constitutes a country with one of the richest accumulations of ethnic groups. Similarly, its German element represents one of the most colorful mixtures in the world in terms of its places of origin and denominations, that have been integrated into a new ethnic community of German descent. All the regions of Germany and every German element in other European lands have sent sons and daughters to Canada. Sects about whom little or nothing is remembered in Germany, such as the Mennonites, the Amish and the Hutterites have been able to save their particular ways of life in Canada. The various German elements which are very interesting from the viewpoint of cultural history, particularly those who came to Canada during the last sixty years from the German colonies in Russia and the eastern border provinces of the old Dual Monarchy (Galicia, Bukovina, Transylvania, Hungary), remind us of all the more or less unfortunate phases of the German emigration movement since the seventeenth century.

Particularly noteworthy is the fate of the German Canadians, however, inasmuch as it is typical of the chances of a survival of German ethnicity in countries of the British colonial empire, which are still important destinations for German emigrants.

May the realization of the historical role, by no means insignificant, that Canada's Germans played in the overall development of the country become a source of new strength in their efforts to preserve their ethnic heritage! This would be the most rewarding justification of my work.

Berlin-Neuköln, in the autumn of 1931
H. Lehmann

Preface to the Original Edition of *Das Deutschtum in Westkanada*

A comprehensive account of the German element in western Canada, its past and present, has so far not been able to get beyond the very first beginnings. Their struggle for their daily bread and their absorption in practical efforts on behalf of their ethnic group have left the leaders of the German community in western Canada no time for a more comprehensive endeavor at self-reflection. The present book attempts to close this gap, and provide an overdue account of the significant contributions of ethnic Germans to the development of western Canada, for which perhaps in the very near future the currently available sources will no longer be accessible. This book should, above all—I expressed the same wish in 1931 when my study on the German element in eastern Canada appeared—familiarize the descendants of our people over there with their own historical accomplishments, reinforce their ethnic consciousness and give them new strength in their efforts for the preservation of their ethnic identity. May the Germans in Canada receive kindly this study by a citizen of Germany. It is the result of a three month study trip to western Canada (May to August 1934) and a preoccupation with the subject matter for a period of more than nine years; it was undertaken more or less at their behest, since the leaders of the German organizations turned over to me all the materials available for a history of settlement explicitly for the purpose of interpretation and publication.

The delay in the completion of the account, which was necessitated for professional reasons, also had its advantages, inasmuch as Canadian scholarship has been more strongly preoccupied in the last years with settlement and with economic and sociological problems, and I would have very much regretted not being able to utilize their results and to evaluate them critically. It is, for instance, urgently necessary to undertake a fundamental correction from the German point of view of the findings of those Anglo-Canadian scholars associated with the Canadian Pioneer Problems Committee. The German share in the development of the Canadian West was greater and still is much greater than that of any other non-British ethnic group. In spite of this, the German contribution is deliberately or unconsciously ignored or certainly belittled. Tuckermann had already pointed this out[1] and mentioned that, for example, in H.A. Kennedy's *Book of the West* (Toronto, 1925) there is no reference to German settlers at all while Ukrainians, Doukhobors and other ethnic groups of immigrants are dealt with in detail, and even the extremely minute number of immigrants from the Channel Islands and the Isle of Man are given loving consideration. In this omission there appears to be system. Even Isaiah Bowman, President of the American Geographical Society, does not mention Germans anywhere in his book *The Pioneer Fringe* (New York, 1931), which has become a basis for more recent works of American and Canadian historians on western Canada.[2] D.A. McArthur, Professor of History at Queens University in Kingston, Ontario, and deputy chairman of the Canadian Pioneer Problems Committee, also makes no reference at all to Germans in his essay "Immigration and Colonization in Western Canada, 1900-1930."[3] Robert England, too, as well as C.A. Dawson and his school, consistently separate in their works the Mennonites from the rest of the German element, nowhere do justice to the accomplishments of the entire German element, and especially treat the question of assimilation from a point of view which should not remain unchallenged. In view of this attitude of representative Canadian scholars, it has become even more necessary to put the accomplishments of Germans in the development of Canada into the proper light.

I gratefully acknowledge the generous assistance that was given me from many quarters, and without which I could never have accomplished my task. First I have to thank the directors of the *Volksbund für das Deutschtum im Ausland* for the research scholarship which enabled me to visit western Canada. Futhermore I am greatly indebted to all those who helped me by word and deed in Canada, above all the former German consul for western Canada, Dr. Seelheim, who is now the consul general in Yokohama, and the editor of the *Deutsche Zeitung für Canada*, Mr. Bernhard Bott in Winnipeg. Mr. Bott undertook the most important spade work several years ago by calling on the readers of the German-language newspapers to collect materials about the various German settlements. He kindly made the 128 responses which he received available to me for my study. In addition, I have to thank the directors of the various Canadian German organizations who have smoothed the way for me, such as the officers of the *Deutscher Bund Canada*. With gratitude I recall the long and informative conversation with Cabinet Minister Dr. Uhrich in Regina, Saskatchewan. I also found generous support among the representatives of the churches. On the Lutheran side these were President Hartig and the former President D. Ruccius in Winnipeg (Manitoba Synod), President Fritz in Regina (Canada District of the American Lutheran Church) and professors Schwermann and Baepler in Edmonton at the Concordia College of the Missouri Synod. Among the Mennonites, my work was supported above all by Elder Toews and Mr. D. Enns in Rosthern, Saskatchewan, and Elder J. Janzen in Waterloo, Ontario. On the Roman Catholic side, I am greatly obliged to the General Secretary of the Order of the Oblates of Mary Immaculate, Rev. Dr. Pietsch, who introduced me to the Oblates serving in western Canada. Among these I recall with particular gratitude Fathers Hilland, Schäfer, Krist, Böning and Schaller. I owe valuable particulars about the German Baptists to the Reverend Bloedow in Winnipeg.

Numerous fellow Germans from all walks of life whom it is not possible to thank here individually have told me of their fates and about their experiences. They have not only given me their advice and help for this study, but have also extended to me an unexpected and most delightful German hospitality. The month of my visit on the western Canadian prairies thus also belong to the richest time of deeply felt human contacts in my life.

Finally, I am indebted to Professor C.R. Hennings in Freiburg i. Br., Professor Walter Kuhn in Breslau, Dozent Dr. Meynen in Berlin and Dr. A. Möllmann in Waterloo, Ontario, for the valuable suggestions they gave me in the course of several exchanges of ideas.

The following study was accepted in the summer of 1938 by the Hohe Philosophische Fakultät of the University of Breslau as fulfilling the requirements of a *Habilitationsschrift*. I am particularly happy that it is able to appear in print as a publication of the Hochschule für Politik where I have had the honor to teach since 1933. My sincere thanks are due the director of its *Forschungsabteilung*, Professor Dr. Fritz Berber, for this and for the awarding of a substantial publication grant. My map of the German element in the Prairie provinces which is attached to the book appeared originally in the fourth issue of *Deutsches Archiv für Landes- und Volksforschung* II (1938) with an extensive explanatory comment. I take this opportunity to thank sincerely the editor of the *Deutsches Archiv*, Dr. habil. Meynen, for his permission to make this map available for my book.

Last but not least, cordial thanks go to my father for the maps that he sketched of St. Peter's colony and the layout of the field strips of Rosengart and, above all, to my dear wife. Not only did she help me read the proofs and share the laborious task of compiling the index, but, by her sympathetic concern and constant encouragement, she decisively supported the work over the years in all its stages. The book is therefore dedicated to her.

Berlin, in the autumn of 1938
Heinz Lehmann

Footnotes

[1] W. Tuckermann, "Das Deutschtum in Kanada," in *Aus Sozial- und Wirtschaftsgeschichte. Gedächtnisschrift für Georg von Below* (Stuttgart, 1928), 339 ff.

[2] I. Bowman, *The Pioneer Fringe*, "The pioneers of today include . . . tens of thousands of settlers of many sects and nationalities in the Canadian North-West, among others Icelanders, Scandinavians and Ukrainians, Doukhobors, Hutterians and Mennonites" (p. 2); "Racial groups such as Italians, Poles, Scandinavians and Russians are scattered through the Canadian North-West" (p. 20).

[3] D.A. McArthur in *Pioneer Settlement: Co-operative Studies by Twenty-Six Authors* (New York, 1932), 23: "(By 1900) the Doukhobors . . . in addition to the Ukrainians and an infiltration of Danes, Poles and Austrians — constituted the chief European Continental elements in the population of Western Canada."

CHAPTER I

German Migrations to the Territory of Present-Day Canada Prior to Confederation

1. German Military Assistance in the Conquest of Canada

The decisive triumph of the English over the French in their struggle for control over the North American continent in the eighteenth century must primarily be attributed to the more liberal design of their policy of colonization. The French had aimed at giving their colonies a social and religious structure completely identical to that of the motherland. Only French of the orthodox Catholic faith were admitted as settlers, no Protestants and no foreigners. In the New World the bulk of the settlers could only become tenants on a seigniory, thereby again entering a relationship of dependence on a landlord. Thus the number of emigrants to "La Nouvelle France," as they called Canada, remained much smaller than would have been necessary for a French expansion of power from there. The English, on the other hand, had realized that the first prerequisite for the acquisition and retention of colonial territory was people, and they arrived at a practice of colonization diametrically opposite to that of the French. All the undesirable elements at home, be they Irish, dissenters or even criminals, were packed off to the colonies. There, however, they promised them full economic freedom. Emigrants of foreign nations, too, were given land to own without reservation, as long as they professed their allegiance to the British flag. In this way the English tied the innumerable waves of German emigrants, who had been streaming into North America since the end of the seventeenth century, entirely to the British interest. These unassuming Germans, after having barely escaped with their lives from the constant devastations of war, famine and religious persecution in their southwest German homelands, even had to be grateful to the English for giving them refuge in their colonies. The English, in turn, knew how to utilize the military efficiency and labor of the Germans.

In the English-French wars over Canada, Germans were used repeatedly as soldiers as early as 1711. The huge exodus from the Palatinate in 1709 had brought some 2,200 Palatines to New York State in 1710, where they were to be settled in the northwest as border guards against Indians and French, and where free land was promised them in the Mohawk Valley and along the Schoharie River. At first, however, these emigrants were detained at the upper Hudson, south of Catskill, in a temporary colony where they were supposed to pay off the expenses of their passage by manufacturing tar and pitch.[1] In this forced labor camp the Palatines were subjected to unimaginable suffering, so that in 1711 it was easy for the English to press three hundred of them into service for a military campaign against Canada.[2] The ambitious strategy of advancing with a greatly superior force, simultaneously attacking Quebec by sea and Montreal by land, failed due to the incompetence of the English admiral. Under heavy losses, he allowed his fleet to run aground in the St. Lawrence River so that the entire enterprise had to be called off.[3]

When hostilities resumed in 1743 after thirty years of peace, German settlers again defended English interests in the struggle for Canada. A general by the name of Waldo, son of a rich Bostonian merchant descended from the Prussian family von Waldow, had enticed Germans to his estates in Maine.[4] The terrors of the War of the Austrian Succession drove about three hundred Palatines to accept his offer. Although many of them went back home, or moved on to Pennsylvania when Waldo's agents made them wait in Cologne and at the Dutch border, most of them did arrive in Maine in 1742 and founded the settlement of Waldoburg on the Medomak River.[5] Led by the agent Zuberbühler, who had recruited them in Europe,[6] and their schoolmaster Ulmer, almost all these settlers with their families followed Waldo's call to take part in the siege and capture of the French fortress of Louisbourg on Cape Breton Island. Outside the walls of the conquered fortress they founded a new settlement in 1745 called Waldoburg. It was the first German settlement on Canadian soil. In 1748, however, it had to be abandoned when, by the Treaty of Aix-la-Chapelle,

Cape Breton Island, including Louisbourg, was returned to the French.[7] The Germans then returned to Maine.

Militarily, the most important German contribution to the English cause was the armed assistance of a regiment raised by the English for the decisive battle for Canada in 1755, from Germans and Swiss in Maryland and Pennsylvania[8]. Initially it manned the forts and block-houses all the way from Philadelphia to Detroit. Later, however, the regiment took a prominent part in the final conquest of Louisbourg in 1758, fought gloriously under Wolfe in the battle at Quebec in 1760, and thereafter was among the first garrisons in the conquered fortresses of Canada.

2. The First German Immigrants

Germans not only participated in the conquest of Canada, they became even more manifestly the most valuable assistants of the English in the retention and development of the newly acquired territories. As settlers, Germans followed close on the heels of Englishmen every-where and, in many places, even preceded them.

Canada, in the narrower sense the present-day Province of Que-bec, which at the time of conquest in 1763 had a purely French popu-lation of nearly 65,000, could offer few attractions to the English and the German colonists. Since the French Canadians retained their own judicial system, under which the individual New Englander could not and would not feel at home, the French character of Quebec has remained virtually intact to this day, in spite of English rule.

The situation was different with regard to the vast, still virtually unexplored, adjoining territories. Acadia, now the Maritime Provinces of Nova Scotia and New Brunswick (except for Cape Breton Island with Louisbourg), had belonged to England since the Treaty of Utrecht in 1713. Yet the constant guerilla warfare in these territories, which were sparsely populated by a mixture of French, natives and half-breeds, made their systematic colonization unthinkable. The Treaty of Aix-la-Chapelle of 1748 confirmed England's possession of these lands, with the exception of Louisbourg, which as the point strategically command-ing the St. Lawrence River was again awarded to the French. This became the incentive for the construction of a harbor to compete with Louisbourg. Its site on the southeastern coast of Nova Scotia was to be the starting point for the colonization of the hinterland.

In 1749 Halifax was founded. Because of the political importance of this undertaking the English government itself decided to take charge of the colonization, a rather unique phenomenon in the history of the English colonial empire. In the years 1750-52, in response to British recruiting efforts, not only several thousand Irish and English arrived from the British Isles and the New England colonies, but also about two thousand Germans. These were settled in Lunenburg and Halifax. They marked the real beginning of the history of German settlement in Canada.[9] Thus, even before the political contest over the Maritime Provinces was decided (the English took undisputed possession only during the course of the Seven Years' War in 1758), German settlements existed in Nova Scotia. After the expulsion of the Acadians in 1755 there were hardly any settlers left, and the mere existence of these German colonies provided support for England's cause.

Between 1760 and 1776, that is, from the victorious termination of the colonial war with France to the beginning of the American War of Independence, clever propaganda lured thousands of farmers from the New England colonies to Nova Scotia. Among these were also several hundred Germans from Pennsylvania, the first German Americans on Canadian soil.[10]

3. German "Loyalists" and "Hessians"

The development sketched up to this point, however, appears to have been merely a prelude. Modern Canada was not really born until the year 1783. England's confinement to its Canadian possessions at the end of the War of Independence, and the serious threats to which even these were exposed, made it an urgent duty of British colonial policy to launch settlements loyal to England in the still unpopulated parts of Canada. These were to function as a bulwark against the young independent American nation, and simultaneously as a counterweight against Quebec which, though kept together under British rule, was purely French. The English were provided with the means to recuperate by the very fanaticism of the independent states, when all those who during the war had fought on the English side against the troops of the Revolution, or had otherwise openly sided with England, were punished with confiscation of their property and expelled from the country. The English government seized the opportunity, and promised land in Canada as compensation to all those expelled on account of their loyalty to England. Thus about forty-five thousand so-called United Empire Loyalists were available at the end of the war for a large-scale colonization and administration of the territories still under English rule. About half of these settled in Nova Scotia and New Brunswick, the rest moved up the St. Lawrence River and colonized the southern-most tip of Canada, the peninsula of Ontario southwest of the French area of settlement. The Loyalists came to form the basic stock of the English-Canadian population, who deeply hated the Americans and clearly let them know that a peaceful extension of their territory to the north was out of the question.

Germans were involved in two ways in the history of those years so fundamental to present-day Canada. First, there were among the Loyalists expelled from the independent states a not insignificant per-centage of German Americans. Secondly, moreover, a large number of the approximately thirty thousand German mercenaries, who had been sold by German rulers to England for the War of Independence, settled permanently in Canada after the end of the war. These had been fighting Washington's troops from Canadian territory as the base of their operations for seven years.

German-American historians, including A.B. Faust, estimated the number of German Loyalists to be extremely low, or even denied their existence altogether. That, however, is incorrect. The percentage of "Tories" among the Germans was, no doubt, lower than among the British. England was not their mother country, and most of them led the tough life of pioneers, with little prospect of upward social mobil-ity in English society, which made them particularly susceptible to the notion of independence. In Pennsylvania, for example, the German colonists, who formed about one-third of the total population, were particularly enthusiastic for the cause of independence.[11] Even non-conformist religious groups such as the Mennonites willingly raised taxes for the armies of the Revolution, despite their opposition to military service.[12] In New York State, however, the citadel of Loyalism,[13] Ger-mans, especially those from the Palatine colonies on the middle Hud-son (Dutchess County), on the Mohawk and on the Schoharie, had not uniformly backed the revolutionaries.[14]

The fact that the wealthy and influential Sir John Johnson, who lived in the vicinity of the Germans at the Mohawk and the Scho-harie and who was himself the son of a German mother,[15] was a dedicated Tory,[16] was not without its effect on their attitude. His father Sir William Johnson, an Irishman, had distinguished himself by his personal adroitness in winning over the Mohawk Indians to England's side in the war for Canada.[17] When civil war threatened to erupt, Sir John, who managed to treat the Indians just as intelligently as had his father (by now deceased), succeeded in keeping them on the King's side. For the Germans in his vicinity, identification with the cause of the Revolution was fraught with grave danger, for it meant expecting the cruel raids of the Mohawks. Since, in addition, they were very far removed from the mainstream of political events, a great many colonists from this area opted in favour of Sir John Johnson and the Tories.

At the beginning of the war Sir John had attempted to venture a strike against "treason and disloyalty" from Johnstown. However, he and his followers had to seek refuge in Canada as early as the spring of 1776.[18] Here he became famous as the founder and leader of the 84th Royal New York Regiment, the so-called "Royal Greens" who were feared for their heavy raids into the territory of their former countrymen. Sir John's German neighbors formed the bulk of the daring Royal Greens,[19] whose casualties in the bloody fratricides must have been considerable.[20] After peace was restored the survivors did not dare to return to their old property. Their estates had already been confiscated by law on October 22, 1779,[21] and no one would have been safe from the rage of their assaulted former countrymen. Therefore Sir John with his regiment, like thousands of other Loyalists, had to ask for the assignment of land in Canada. His German followers, who under these circumstances had to emigrate to Canada, had been recruited from Schoharie County in particular, predominantly from the villages of New Rheinbeck, New Durlach and Breakabeen.[22] The assumption of Pierce[23] must be correct that more than one thousand German Loyalists with their families took up residence in Ontario alone. There we find them in present-day Dundas and Stormont Counties, at the Bay of Quinte west of Kingston and near Queenston at the Niagara. Moreover, we encounter German Loyalists in the Maritime provinces and at the southern border of Quebec.[24] How many in all, however, who found a new home in Canada after 1783, cannot be exactly determined.

There is similar uncertainty about the number of "Hessians" remaining in Canada. The troops of German mercenaries were generally known by this name, since their main contingent consisted of Hessians. Although much has been written about the disgraceful trade in sold-

iers by German princely rulers, the question of how many of the survivors stayed in America has barely ever been touched on.

Probably somewhat more than one-third of the 11,853 men—who
according to Schlözer's Staats-Anzeigen of 1784[25] failed to return to
their German homeland—died in combat or as a result of climatic diseases, overexertion and deprivations. About seven thousand survivors
were left behind in America after the end of the war.[26] We should not
be surprised that such a large number stayed there, more or less voluntarily, at that time. The German princes themselves were eager to dis-
band their troops if at all possible while they were still in North
America.[27] The English as well as the American governments, at the
same time, attempted to retain as many "Hessians" as possible in the
country as settlers.[28]

At the end of the war most of these German troops stood on Union
territory, some combat-ready in the coastal towns that were still in
English hands, some in American prisoner of war camps, from which
many had already escaped in order to become farm hands. It seems
likely that whoever was discharged, willingly or unwillingly, from his
unit before its return to Europe would not have minded settling even
on the territory of his former enemy, whom he had never really fought
out of conviction anyway. It is safe to assume that few Hessians cared
to be transferred from American ports to Nova Scotia, as the English
government had urged them to do.[29] Most of the German troops stationed in Canada in 1782-83, on the other hand, accepted land grants
there after their discharge.

Thus, two-thirds of the seven thousand German soldiers staying
in America, as calculated above, may have sought their new homes
in the newly independent states of New York, Pennsylvania, Maryland,
Virginia, North and South Carolina,[30] and up to twenty-five hundred
men in Canada.[31] There we find them after 1783 as craftsmen or
farmers in the small towns or townships on the St. Lawrence River
in Quebec, in Annapolis County in Nova Scotia, along the lower St.
John River in New Brunswick and in Prince Edward County,
Ontario.[32]

4. The Mennonite Immigration from Pennsylvania

The tide of emigrants heading for Canada, in 1783, was not to ebb away soon. In a few years large tracts of Nova Scotia, New Brunswick and Ontario had been transformed from impenetrable virgin forests to flourishing cultivated land. A surprisingly rapid development was experienced by Ontario, which as early as 1791 was raised to the level of the independent province of "Upper Canada" in order to free its Loyalist settlers from future tutelage by the French of Lower Canada, who, by that time numbered almost 120,000.[33]

Canadian historians have, not without reason, attached the label of "late Loyalists" to those immigrants who continued to arrive in groups both small and large from the American states for a few more decades to come. They distinguish among three groups of Loyalists:[34]

1. those driven away during the war who had taken up arms against the revolutionaries,

2. those expelled after the end of the war, because their sympathies for England were known or suspected,

3. all those who out of dissatisfaction with the new course of events in the independent states, or simply from land hunger, migrated voluntarily to Canada, even after 1800.

We noted above that a considerable number of Germans had belonged to the first two groups. A particularly strong German element, however, was to be found in the third group of voluntarily emigrating "Loyalists." These were the nonconformist German denominations opposed to military service. From 1786, when they first settled in present-day Lincoln County, Ontario, near the Niagara Falls,[35] until the second decade of the nineteenth century, Mennonites moved in large numbers from Pennsylvania to Ontario.

The oppressions in their homelands had driven the Mennonites and the related German denominations, who traced their origins to the Anabaptist movement of the sixteenth century, to emigrate early in their history. Some of them went to eastern Europe, groups which will be considered later in the context of the settlement of the Canadian Prairies. Others emigrated directly to North America. Through their relations with English Independents [Congregationalists], these groups, towards the end of the seventeenth century, had come into contact with William Penn, who opened his colony of Pennsylvania as much to his German as to his English fellow believers. Starting in

1683, wealthy Mennonite individuals came over from western Germany and Holland and settled Germantown, today a suburb of Philadelphia, and adjacent Montgomery County.[36] In 1709 the mass emigration began of Mennonites, mostly very poor, who had been expelled from their homes and land in Switzerland and the Palatinate. Emigration from the latter was especially heavy during the years 1717 and 1726. Mennonites settled mainly in Lancaster County, from where they spread over the entire southeastern part of Pennsylvania. Here they lived in close contact with other noncomformist religious communities of German origin, such as the Schwenckfelders and Tunkers[Dunkards]. From among the latter some Tunkers appear to have migrated to Canada as well.[37]

At the outbreak of the War of Independence the conscientious objection of the sects to military service was reluctantly acknowledged. Although the Mennonites paid their war taxes faithfully, their lack of participation in other respects was resented during the general flush of victory at the end of the war. The Mennonites had to fear revocation of their privilege of exemption from military duty in the future. Their quite justifiable mistrust of the new authorities in this matter became the occasion for the emigration of those first small groups of Mennonites from Bucks County, Pennsylvania, who headed for the country of all the sympathizers of the old system, namely Upper Canada.

In the background, however, were economic considerations which soon played the main role. In Pennsylvania the Mennonites had created from scratch, as they had everywhere else, flourishing colonies in a few decades by their exemplary economic methods. As did all genuine farmers, they strove to invest their wealth in ever-growing land holdings. In Pennsylvania, however, due to the rapid increase of population following the War of Independence, cheap land was no longer available within a wide radius of their villages. Further economic growth was blocked for them. In order to ensure that even the younger sons would inherit a halfway viable farming operation, they had to sell their cultivated but small holdings, take up cheap virgin land somewhere else and put their proven abilities as pioneers to the test again.[38]

The desire of the Mennonites to preserve the fellowship they had practiced in Pennsylvania for centuries led to the attempt in 1795 to acquire a large coherent tract of six townships in Ontario through direct negotiations with the Canadian government. There a new closed daughter colony based on their Pennsylvanian model was to be launched.[39] The departure of individual Mennonite families for Ontario began even though the governor of Upper Canada, John Graves Simcoe, refused to agree to the proposed deal. Starting in 1796 these families settled in the Niagara district in the present-day Welland, Lincoln and Haldimand Counties. From 1800 on they settled on the middle Grand River in what was later Waterloo, and from 1803 on in Markham and Whitchurch Townships in York County, and in adjoining Ontario County.[40] Apart from these there was only one other group of Mennonites in Ontario; they had settled in present-day Lincoln County as early as 1786. Therefore instead of one large bloc settlement, three smaller ones were formed. The tide of emigration from Pennsylvania, which only gradually ebbed away in the 1820s and appears to have brought well over two thousand Mennonites to Ontario, resulted in an almost equal growth in all three colonies. The most homogeneous colony was the one on the Grand River. There wealthy Mennonites had been forced by a curious fraud to make a virtue of necessity and purchase for a very high sum the huge area of what would become Waterloo and Woolwich Townships in 1805 and 1807.[41] What they did not succeed in negotiating with Simcoe in 1795, they now managed to obtain through a private purchase. A large area from which all strangers could be excluded was available for the young generation of Mennonites. It was primarily this purchase which set in motion the exodus from Pennsylvania, and made the Grand River district the most attractive of the three young colonies.

The Mennonites were certainly not the only Germans in the first three or four decades of the nineteenth century who migrated to Ontario hungry for land. Some others appear to have come from New York, the home of the Palatine Loyalist immigrants of 1784,[42] but most, like the Mennonites, came from Pennsylvania. We can trace them everywhere in southwestern Ontario, in the Niagara district, in Wentworth, Halton, Norfolk, Oxford, Elgin, Middlesex and in the extreme southwest.[43] Hundreds, even thousands of German Americans seem to have come to southwestern Ontario in the early years of its colonization, yet they were scattered in groups of varied size, like squatters who occupy land as they see fit over a wide area without in the least considering the formation of closed German colonies. Thus, of all the German-American immigrants of those decades who are significant in our history, only the Mennonites created viable settlements in their desire for concentration and seclusion from strangers. These colonies— and that applied particularly to Waterloo, but also to their communities in the Niagara district—were already developed sufficiently by 1830 to enable them to attract almost all of the new immigration from Germany from its very beginning. The dissipation of this German element from Germany was thus prevented in western Ontario, and the basis was formed for the development of relatively large areas with German majorities. Not just the German Americans generally, but specifically the Mennonites, were thus the trailblazers for immigrants from Germany. Had they not been there from as early as 1800, it is highly unlikely that so many Germans from Europe would have settled in southwestern Ontario as farmers or craftsmen.

5. The Immigration from Germany to Ontario from about 1830

Apart from three quite significant instances, no immigrants had ever come directly from Germany to Canada until 1820.[44] Only from the beginning of the 1820s could the first occasional immigrants from Germany be traced in southwestern Ontario.[45] They must all have come there by way of New York.

With the end of the European Wars of Liberation [from Napoleon], German emigration to North America reached new dimensions and became a steady phenomenon. The emigration in the eighteeth century, by contrast, had brought Germans across the ocean at irregular intervals in times of distress. The economic crisis which struck after the Wars of Liberation weighed especially heavily upon the small farmers and agricultural laborers, who after 1817 had begun to leave their homeland by the thousands. Emigrants came in particular from southwestern and western Germany, just as in the eighteenth century. Here the partition of peasant holdings due to the lack of a right of entail or primogeniture (*Anerbenrecht*) and the resulting continuous division of inheritances was furthest advanced, and consequently farming was most uneconomical.[46] After the peak years of 1817 and 1818 the volume of emigration remained constant at a medium level. It increased strongly again around the mid-1840s due to the potato blight and bad wheat harvests, and after 1848 due to the political disappointment and economic stagnations resulting from political events.

German emigration to Canada has so far been treated only as an appendix to that of the United States. No doubt the United States attracted the bulk of the emigrants from Germany as well as from the

British Isles. Canada was still far from being able to offer attractions
similar to those of the great neighboring country. Lord Durham had
pointed this out openly in his epoch-making report of 1839.[47] In its
economic development Canada lagged far behind the United States.
The population was still thinly spread, communications were undeve-
loped, and road and canal construction neglected. Paper money was
unpopular, so that wages were still predominantly paid in goods. Large
cities comparable to the American ones were virtually non-existent.
The United States could, therefore, in fact offer the European emigrant
a much greater variety of opportunities for getting ahead.

Yet economic backwardness did not play the most important role
in the neglect of Canada as a goal for emigrants, since for the individual
emigrant the conditions for colonization in Canada were rather more
favorable than in the Union.[48] The main reason was simply that at
the beginning of our epoch of emigration there were no districts of
closed German settlement in Canada except for southwestern Ontario,
whose natural development might have attracted new emigrants every
year, in contrast to almost all the regions of the Union. There was a
general ignorance in Germany regarding Canadian conditions and
related to this were apprehensions about the climate. This was compounded in some instances by a strong political prejudice around the
middle of the nineteenth century that it would be better to live in the
mighty free republic rather than in the English crown colony. These
factors made it impossible for the Canadian government, despite all
its efforts, to divert a share of the German mass migration to North
America into the Canadian provinces, a share in proportion to the
size of the cultivable land. Nevertheless, the migration from Germany
to Canada was not as trifling as has hitherto been assumed.

The immigration from Germany which had begun timidly in the
1820s came into full swing around the mid-1830s.[49] Simultaneously,
the number of Mennonites and other German Americans immigrating to Ontario declined decisively.[50] For the following four decades
until the end of the 1870s and only for this period, the bulk of the
German immigrants to British North America came directly from Germany. Later, during the opening up of the Canadian prairies, Germans
from other parts of Europe as well as German Americans formed by
far the largest proportion of German immigrants.

The immigrants from Germany, small farmers and craftsmen by occupation, turned almost exclusively to southwestern Ontario. In the
nineteenth century the Maritime provinces attracted no more

immigrants because of their remoteness from the customary shipping routes. The only exceptions to the above observation were German craftsmen looking for employment in Montreal, as well as East German farmers who had land allotted to them in the Ottawa district after the late 1850s.

The German immigration to the southwestern tip of Ontario should actually be viewed as merely an offshoot of the great British-German-Scandinavian emigration movement to the American midwestern and northwestern States.

Two important overland routes used by thousands of German immigrants to the American West over the years were:

1. the route from Quebec[51] up the St. Lawrence River across to Detroit, and

2. the route from New York up the Hudson, either to a port on Lake Ontario (Oswego, Sackett's Harbour) and by boat across to Ontario, or up the Erie Canal to Buffalo and across the Niagara (i.e., later on across the Suspension Bridge) to Ontario and also via Detroit to the West.

Both routes, as we can see, touched the southern tip of Ontario. Here some of the German immigrants stayed behind. They were afraid to continue the difficult trip across the continent with the majority, and they considered the economic opportunities in western Ontario, for good reasons, to be as favorable as on the American prairies.[52] The stream of German emigration to the American West was barely noticeably weakened by this diversion.

Of the two routes to the western States and to Ontario, by far the more important one for the German emigration was always the one via New York. Even for the British emigration, Quebec was never as important as New York, in spite of the pains the English government may have taken to promote the Quebec route. The land routes from Quebec and from New York to the point where they converged in western Ontario were of approximately equal distance and difficulty, and were always equally expensive for the emigrants. Yet conditions for the passage to Quebec were considerably less favorable from almost all European ports. The connections to New York from everywhere were indisputably more frequent, faster and far more comfortable, and that turned the scale for the bulk of the emigrants.[53]

Quebec attained some sort of monopoly as a port of immigration only for francophone Quebec and for the Ottawa district and the eastern counties of Ontario, areas that were virtually out of question for German immigration. Direct emigration from Germany via Quebec did not begin until 1846, after a stream of German immigrants had been moving for a period of more than ten years via New York to western Ontario, and by way of western Ontario on to the western States.[54] Even then the Quebec route was able to secure for itself only a relatively small number of the German emigrants to Ontario and into the Union.

Although the Canadian government was very accommodating and even employed a German interpreter at Quebec, it failed to make the Quebec route popular among the Germans.[55] All the German emigration guides that have come to my attention did, in fact, recommend the trip via New York even to those who wanted to settle in Canada.[56] Perhaps rightly so. Emigrants departing from Bremen and Hamburg for Quebec had only sailing ships to choose from, while for the passage to New York they could use steamships, with weekly departures alternating between Bremen and Hamburg after 1860. Had not the American Civil War (1861-1865) deterred some from the New York route, the route via Quebec would certainly have been used only by completely destitute emigrants. A steamship connection was apparently not considered profitable, while sailing ships, requiring about fifty days from Hamburg and Bremen to Quebec, could simply not compete with the steamships to New York under normal circumstances. In 1871 the shipping connection from Germany to Canada was therefore discontinued.

At first glance, the figures [see Table I.1] reveal that for German emigrants, even more than for the simultaneous British emigration, this Quebec route via Canada to the American Northwest was only a secondary one. Around the mid-1840s German emigration had suddenly swelled to such an unexpected volume that the main route to New York could not accommodate all the emigrants. There was therefore good reason in 1846 to hope that a somewhat cheaper, though in fact longer, second shipping connection would be able to attract some of the poorer emigrants for some time to come. Still, in the early years virtually all the German emigrants moved on to the Union. Only in the 1850s, when German emigration to all parts of the world was at an all-time high, and thousands moved to the American continent, even via Quebec, could the Canadian provinces secure for themselves a larger proportion of the German settlers they sought, though never more than half of them. The increase in numbers after 1861 is related to the American Civil War, which made the route via New York appear to many to be too dangerous. However, it does not necessarily follow that in

Table I.1

Direct German Emigration from Hamburg and Bremen to Quebec

Year	German emigrants to Canada[57]	German immigrants (accord. to Canadian Immigration Reports)			Of these immigrants via Quebec (accord. to Canadian Immigration Reports)	
		directly from Bremen-Hamburg	via English ports (Liverpool)	total	moved on to U.S.A.	stayed in Canada
1846	—	896	158	1,054	c.800	c.200
1847	7,352	7,437				
1848	1,322	1,395	?	?	almost all (1847-1849)	almost none (1847-1849)
1849	315	436				
1850	593	594				
1851	647	645	?	?	majority (1850-1852)	minority 1850-1852
1852	4,648	5,159	70-80	5,229-39		
1853	2,367	2,400	735	3,135	half	c.1,600
1854	5,302	5,688	5,371	10,959	majority	c.3,000
1855	3,168	3,597	218	3,815	three-quarters	c.1,000
1856	3,626	4,537	117	4,654	barely half	c.2,400
1857	4,208	4,961	?		?	1,987
1858	902	922	?		?	?
1859	968	964	136	1,100	majority	300-400
1860	534	533	192	725	barely half	c.400
1861	1,983	1,951	103	2,054	982	1,072
1862	2,216	2,407	109	2,516	?	?
1863	3,082	3,019	28	3,047	two-thirds	c.1,000
1864	2,147	2,066	196	2,262		
1865	1,412	1,308	788	2,096		
1866	3,398	3,330	683	4,013	?	?
1867	5,591	4,800	474	5,274	(1864-1869)	(1864-1869)
1868	4,342	4,204	864	5,068		
1869	1,082	1,073	886	1,959		
1870	408	411	184	595	c.350	c.250

those years more Germans migrated to Canada via Quebec, although Canada experienced a temporary economic boom as a supplier of grain and lumber to the northern American states. For this period, unfortunately, the data about the numbers of Germans actually staying in Canada are least reliable.

In the 1850s, when the Quebec route reached the peak of its demand in Germany, it was used primarily by very poor emigrants. These were frequently the local paupers who, with the support of their communities or their states, were sent the cheapest way to America. They had to put up with being packed in large numbers into relatively small sailing boats with unsatisfactory sanitary arrangements.[58] On the average, one-quarter of all the German immigrants and passers-through had to be financially supported upon their arrival at Quebec by the Canadian authorities.[59] Their inability to raise sufficient funds for the continuation of their trip to their intended destination in the northwestern states of the Union may frequently have been the reason for their remaining on Canadian soil.[60] According to the calculations of the Canadian authorities (see above statistical tables), about ten thousand to twelve thousand actually settled in Canada between 1850 and 1857. Apart from several hundred craftsmen who found work in Montreal, Toronto or Hamilton, all of them were engaged as farmers or agricultural laborers in western Ontario, in Waterloo, Perth and in Bruce and Grey Counties, which had just recently been opened to immigration.[61]

For the much more important immigration route by way of New York and the American border we unfortunately have no comparable data until 1862. We are, however, able to calculate the approximate volume of immigration on the basis of its reflections in the census reports.

Until 1848, at least twelve thousand natives of Germany migrated via New York to southwestern Ontario. Of these, according to the Census of 1848, about nine thousand resided in Waterloo, more than 1,500 in Perth and Huron and more than one thousand in the Niagara district. The rest were scattered elsewhere.[62] At that time a total of about twenty-five thousand farmers of German descent appear to have lived in western Ontario and about fifteen thousand in eastern Ontario.[63] According to the 1871 Census, which in contrast to all previous Canadian census reports asked for the first time not only for the birthplace but also the "racial origin," with Canada and the United States excluded as countries of origin, 158,608 Germans by origin were recorded in Ontario. Of these, 41,743 lived in eastern Ontario, 115,189 in southwestern Ontario and 676 in New Ontario (i.e., the area north of Lake Superior and Georgian Bay), if divided according to my geographical criteria applied in chapters II and III.

Apart from the German immigration to the Ottawa district, the 1871 Census figure for eastern Ontario may be interpreted as a result of the natural population growth in the older German-American settlements along the St. Lawrence and at the Bay of Quinte. The census figure for southwestern Ontario, however, even if we assume a threefold natural increase in the twenty-two years between 1848 and 1870, is quite inconceivable without assuming a further immigration of thirty thousand to forty thousand Germans during this period. Only ten thousand to twelve thousand of these entered the country via Quebec, as we saw. Between 1848 and 1860, the peak years of German immigration, fifteen thousand to twenty thousand citizens of Germany alone appear to have come to western Ontario by way of the New York route. For decades it had been the more frequently used, faster and more comfortable route and thus was preferred by all but the most destitute immigrants. The data of the immigration agent in Hamilton provide a reliable clue for this. According to these, 1,916 and 1,032 respectively of the Germans immigrating in the years 1857 and 1885 at the Niagara by way of New York and the Suspension Bridge stayed in southwestern Ontario.[64] Regular statistical data are available from the immigration agency in Hamilton, which intercepted almost the entire immigration across the American border, unfortunately only from 1862 on. The route via New York was then interrupted by the Civil War, and German immigration was already slackening [see Table I.2].

According to these statistics, six thousand of the German immigrants coming by way of New York settled in western Ontario in the 1860s.[66] Although the direct shipping connection from German ports to Quebec lost any significance after 1871, the immigration to southwestern Ontario via New York continued, as can be seen from the Hamilton statistics. To a certain extent it even lasted until the [First] World War, although it was, of course, vastly overshadowed after the 1880s by the German immigration to the Prairie provinces.

Table I.2

Year	Route of arrival		Total	Destination		
	Quebec– St. Lawrence	New York– Suspension Bridge		U.S.A.	Ontario	Manitoba
1857	–	–	14,679	–	1,916	
1858	–	–	9,689	–	1,032	
1862	188	3,132	3,320	2,767	553	
1863	143	7,135	7,278	6,588	690	
1864	125	7,375	7,500	6,601	899	
1865	16	8,947	8,963	8,443	520	
1866	333	10,848	11,181	10,667	514	
1867	–	–	–	–	–	
1868	–	–	–	–	594	
1869	3	10,611	10,614	10,007	607	
1870	4	7,913	7,917	7,549	368	
1871	4	9,547	9,551	9,182	369	
1872	25	27,680	27,705	26,637	1,054	
1873	15	25,581	25,896	24,899	997	
1874	33	18,343	18,376	17,802	574	
1875	85	7,004	7,129	6,456	675	
1876	43	6,517	6,560	5,907	653	
1877	29	2,683	2,712	2,040	672	
1878	59	4,025	4,084	3,488	580	16
1879	175	5,453	5,628	4,491	1,098	39
1880	102	20,785	20,887	19,720	969	198
1881	82	32,241	32,323	31,266	850	207
1882	32	36,972	37,004	36,059	584	361
1883	7	27,606	27,613	26,388	735	490
1884	32	23,776	23,808	22,489	846	473
1885	7	9,028	9,035	8,176	759	151[65]
1886	7	18,801	18,808	17,744	702	440[65]
1887	15	24,412	24,427	23,373	790	367[65]
1888	22	27,759	27,781	26,568	749	496[65]
1889	10	20,444	20,454	19,797	400	257
1890	18	16,683	16,701	15,988	398	315
1891	8	16,602	16,610	15,929	415	266

6. German Pioneers in Western Canada's Oldest Settlement: Lord Selkirk's Colony

For two whole centuries, from 1670 to 1869, a trading company had ruled the vast territory comprising the present-day Prairie provinces. When, around the middle of the seventeenth century, the French began to consolidate their colony, *La Nouvelle France*, which forms the foundation of the present-day Province of Quebec, on the St. Lawrence, England tried to get a foothold on the soil of present-day Canada. The English came from the north, from Hudson's Bay, mainly to take part in the profitable fur trade. In 1670 the Hudson's Bay Company was founded, and Prince Rupert of the Palatinate, who was related to the English royal house, was made its first governor. His name still survives in the names of the town of Prince Rupert, B.C., and in Rupert's Land. As long as the trading company had the rights of a sovereign ruler, the territory between the Canadian Shield and the Rocky Mountains was kept virtually free of settlers, since the hunting of valuable furbearing animals, especially the beaver, was not to be interfered with by permanent settlers. In addition, the lack of waterways in an east-west direction made the opening of the prairies virtually impossible prior to the advent of the railways. Thus the few small forts and posts of the trappers remained the only white settlements.

As long as the Hudson's Bay Company ruled, only a single attempt at colonization was made. German-speaking people had been involved in this very first episode of agricultural development of western Canada, the colonization experiment of Lord Selkirk. This venture at settlement, which hurried far in advance of historical developments, therefore deserves a brief exposition.

Around 1810, the Scottish Lord Selkirk, who was then governor of the Hudson's Bay Company, had decided to establish a large agricultural settlement with his own money in western Canada, to ease the social misery in Scotland, Ireland and elsewhere. For this purpose he obtained land from his company on the Red River, in present-day Manitoba, comprising an area of forty thousand square kilometers—an indication of the fantastic scale of his plans. He proceeded with the recruiting of emigrants without an exact knowledge of the geographic conditions. As early as 1811, the first transport was ready to leave for the Selkirk colony. By 1815 about three hundred Scots had come over via the northern trade route through Hudson's Bay, and were allotted their homesteads on the Red River.[67] For their protection a fort was erected, which later became known as Fort Garry and can still be seen outside Winnipeg today.

Meanwhile, a second trading company, which was founded in Canada, contested the rights of the London-based Hudson's Bay Company to the large western Canadian hunting grounds. In 1783 the North West Company was founded in Montreal by Americans who had supported the cause of England during the War of Independence and who, as Loyalists, were compelled to go to Canada after the war. This company also claimed hunting rights in the entire American Northwest. The competition between the two trading companies degenerated at times into open warfare between their factories. The new settlers were immediately drawn into these struggles. Basically the hunters and traders of both companies were hostile towards the settlers. In particular, however, the "Nor'-Westers" tried to expel the settlers before they could get a firm foothold. They persuaded most of the settlers to leave for Ontario and inflicted a grave bloodbath among the remaining ones in the summer of 1816.

Lord Selkirk, however, did not yet give up his plan. He was on his way to his colony when in Montreal he received the news of the bloody raid. At that moment two regiments were being disbanded in Montreal and Kingston, Ontario. They had been hired by the English to fight in Spain against Napoleon and then from 1812 to 1815, had been used in the war against the United States for the protection of Canada. They were named after their colonels, de Meuron and von Wattenwil, and were composed mainly of German soldiers as well as Swiss and some Italians.[68] From these two regiments Selkirk enlisted about one hundred men as a bodyguard for himself and as guards for his colony. The British government had offered land to officers and men in eastern Canada in order not to have to transport them back to Europe. But Lord Selkirk could offer them the prospect of new military employment and sufficient pay, and therefore had no trouble forming a new military force from among their ranks.[69] Eighty men of the de Meuron Regiment followed him from Montreal. They were led by four officers: captains Matthey and D'Orsonnens, and second lieutenants Fauché and Friedrich von Grafenried (Graffenreith), the last of whom left an account of his Canadian period of service.[70] In Kingston they were joined by twenty men from the von Wattenwil Regiment. The journey to the Red River was long and difficult. Quarters were taken up for the winter at the Kaministiquia River opposite Fort William at a spot called Point de Meuron ever since.[71] The destination was finally reached in June 1817. After brief engagements, order was restored, the dispersed and imprisoned farmers were brought back and the colony was rebuilt.

The officers and men received their land near the small forts so that they could reassemble there anytime in the event of danger. They took up residence at a small tributary of the Red River, the present-day Seine, which at that time was named "German Creek" for the German and German-Swiss soldiers.[72] The entire colony, however, received the name St. Boniface in memory of the patron saint of the Germans, Winfried Bonifatius. The name was given by the first two French-Canadian clergy who, as the story goes, had come out to the Red River in 1818, at the request of Catholics among the German officers.[73] The name has been retained to this day for the northern suburb of Winnipeg without its predominantly French-Canadian population being aware of the German origin of the name.

Colonies of soldiers have never been very successful anywhere, and at the Red River the soldiers were not suitable as settlers either. As long as they were needed for military protection, and the Hudson's Bay Company as well as the Scottish settlers provided their livelihood, life in the wilderness was tolerable. In 1821, however, a union between the North West Company and the Hudson's Bay Company came about, the hostilities against the Selkirk colony ceased and the "de Meurons" lost their *raison d'être*. When, from then on, they were treated like the other farmers, life soon became intolerable for them.

In the meantime new settlers had arrived. Lord Selkirk, who had left his colony again by September 1817, undertook the recruiting of new immigrants immediately upon his return to Europe, this time in Switzerland. There, wives, particularly for the soldiers, and as many settlers of the Reformed faith as possible were to be recruited.[74] A Swiss by the name of Chetlain who had accompanied Lord Selkirk on his return trip from the Red River wrote for this purpose a very rosy, totally misleading, description of the conditions which appeared in 1819, in German and French, published in Berne by Burgdorfsche Buchhandlung under the attractive title:

> Clear and impartial description of the extensive and fertile land holdings of Lord Selkirk on the Red River in British North America including a description of the Killdonan, New Switzerland and St. Peter colonies founded ibidem since the year 1813. Printed and published for the better understanding of those desirous of emigrating.

On the basis of this pamphlet and the promotion of Colonel May, retired from the von Wattenwil Regiment, about two hundred persons could be enlisted in 1820 in the cantons of Basel, Bern, Fribourg, Solothurn, Neuburg, Geneva and Waadt as well as in neighboring Alsace and the Franche Comté. Most of them adhered to the Reformed and Lutheran denominations. They were assembled in Rheinfelden near Basel, and travelled down the Rhine under the leadership of May. Not until the fall of 1821 did they reach their distant destination along the customary route via Hudson's Bay, which is open only during the late summer.[75] Their arrival at the Red River caused a lot of excitement, as most of the former soldiers were unmarried and immediately began to fight for the marriageable daughters of the newcomers. At first only families who had grown-up daughters could count on a warm accommodation. New sons-in-law and brothers-in-law placed their cottages at the disposal of these families. The others had to put up their tents outside the fortifications until the settlers moved to Pembina within the present-day American border for their annual quarters during the winter. There the Hudson's Bay Company had large storage facilities and solid dwellings.

Selkirk's oldest colonists, the Scots, were unhappy with their new neighbors. They had to share their supplies with them and got little help from the newcomers who were mostly cooks, musicians, watchmakers, etc. and knew nothing about agriculture. The Swiss had been promised parcels of eighty-eight acres (which is only half the size of the later homesteads on the prairies) as well as free seed grain, stable and draft animals and farming tools. Yet they were to repay these advances after three years, and in addition pay a small purchase price of five shillings for the lot. In all this, obviously no one had worried about the market where the settlers would sell their products and thus earn the money necessary for the repayment. It turned out that in the long run these terms could not be fulfilled. All in all, the emigrants found themselves deceived in their exaggerated expectations and were soon as unhappy as the former soldiers. Yet even experienced farmers might have despaired in the Selkirk colony. Swarms of grasshoppers, severe summer frosts, buffalo herds, cattle epidemics, belated arrival of the seed grain, etc. destroyed their hopes year after year.

In the spring of 1822 the first five Swiss families refused to return from Pembina to St. Boniface.[76] They followed the Red River to the south, and finally settled at the confluence of the Minnesota and Mississippi where St. Paul is situated today. Within several years, they had become wealthy cattle ranchers. They were the first settlers in what is now the State of Minnesota. In 1823 another thirteen families left Selkirk's colony and travelled, under indescribable hardships, on trails and along rivers that no white man had ever before navigated, thousands of miles south to St. Louis. From there they headed further northeast for La Pointe, where they settled in the area of the present-day town of Galena in the northwestern corner of the State of Illinois, and found work in the nearby lead mines. Another group of ten families turned towards Ontario where in Hay Township (in the far west on Lake Huron) they founded the settlements of Bern and Zurich. The leaders of this group were Christian Hay, after whom the township was named, Georg Hess and Johann Rotermühl. When in the spring of 1826 on top of all the other bad luck, the Red River rose unusually high above its banks and destroyed all the previous efforts, almost all the remaining German-speaking settlers left the Selkirk colony, former soldiers and emigrants alike, numbering 243 in all, and followed their countrymen to La Pointe. There the majority settled again as farmers while some worked in the mines. The first attempt of people of German descent to make western Canada their new home thus ended in hunger and misery and the eventual departure of all of them. The 1849 Census recorded only two families at the Red River settlement whose heads had been born in Switzerland.[77]

Lord Selkirk's ambitious colonization experiment had therefore virtually collapsed, as similar colonial ventures overseas by highranking and idealistic personalities had done before. The promoter did not lack the noble will to personal sacrifice, which made him spend a large fortune for the realization of his cherished dream, but rather lacked an adequate knowledge of the climatic and economic conditions. Otherwise he would not have attempted to launch a colony without regard to markets and with the most unsuitable settlers imaginable, in such a godforsaken place which, at a time prior to the invention of railways and prior to the colonization of the American Midwest, was completely unconquerable. The colonists, on the other hand, whom Lord Selkirk wanted to save from the economic misery of the beginning industrial age and to lead to a better future, were plunged even deeper into privation and misery through his ambitious, but still entirely premature, venture at colonization. Thanks to the endurance and modest needs of a few Scottish and French-Canadian families, the colony continued to exist. In the 1830s and 1840s it even grew and managed to supply at least the company trading posts, increasing in number, with the necessary grain.

The fates of these first German settlers in western Canada were, by the way, recorded on canvas by a young painter named Peter Rindisbacher, who belonged to the 1821 group of arrivals. In forty watercolor paintings he recorded for posterity the ups and downs of the great journey and of pioneer life in the wilderness. His pictures are in the public archives of Canada and are frequently reproduced in textbooks. Like the others, Rindisbacher migrated with his family in 1826 to the States, where he died in St. Louis, not yet twenty-eight years old, immortalized, however, through the work of his hands.[78]

CHAPTER II

Pioneers and Colonizers in the Maritimes, Quebec and Eastern Ontario

1. The Immigration from Germany in the 1750s

The history of the German element in Canada begins with the arrival of German immigrants in Halifax in 1750. Contrary to previous practice, the British government did not leave it up to private initiative to secure settlers for the founding of Halifax but instead commissioned official agents to recruit Protestants in the British Isles and on the Continent.[1] In charge of recruitment on the Continent was merchant John Dick in Rotterdam[2] and his sub-agent Köhler in Frankfurt am Main. The latter translated the official English prospectus into German and had it disseminated under the title *Historische und geographische Beschreibung von Neu-Schottland . . .* (Frankfurt and Leipzig, 1750). In it political dissatisfaction was very skillfully taken into account, and conditions in and around Halifax were painted unscrupulously in the brightest colors, when in fact no preparations at all were made to accommodate large numbers of immigrants, as the subsequent events would bring to light.[3]

In the late summer of 1750, the first three hundred Germans who responded to Köhler's promises arrived in Halifax, much earlier than had been expected. The governor was at a loss as to how to accommodate them for the winter and supply them with food.[4] The disappointment of the new arrivals was immense because what they expected was cleared land, ready for cultivation. Instead they found themselves in a garrison on whose soldiery they became dependent. What they expected least of all, however, was the constant siege of Halifax by Indians, making it impossible to set foot outside the palisades without military protection and to consider any kind of regular agricultural activity in the foreseeable future. Immediately after their debarkation, even before they reached Halifax itself, the Germans were subjected to the first raid and had to leave behind a number of dead.[5] The camp which was quickly improvised for them had to be guarded constantly against the Indians by soldiers. Added to the insecurity of their external conditions and the complete uncertainty about their future were deprivations and illnesses of all kinds, and on top of it poor treatment by their protectors who saw in these Germans, from whom they had expected help, only an intolerable burden. Only a few of the immigrants appear to have really been fit for the colonist's life awaiting them. Dick and his men did not care in the least about their suitability and also sent along many old and frail people. Many of them did not survive their first severe winter in Nova Scotia.[6]

The situation became even more difficult when about one thousand additional immigrants arrived in Halifax in the spring of 1751 and a like number arrived in 1752. This time, however, there were younger and stronger persons.[7] The immigrants came from Hanover, Brunswick-Lüneburg, the Palatinate, the upper Rhine, Switzerland and a small number from Montbéliard County, which explains the small French-speaking minority in the later Lunenburg settlement.[8] The Indians were still a serious threat. Even after the Treaty of Aix-La-Chapelle in 1748, the French had not given up all hope of reconquering Acadia, which they had lost in 1713. They kept on trying, therefore, to thwart the establishment of larger English settlements by inciting the natives.[9] Thus the two thousand German immigrants of 1751 and 1752 also had to be accommodated in the small fortress as well as circumstances permitted.[10]

All the German immigrants were obligated to repay their passage and that of their families in the form of labor. The governor could therefore put them to work immediately on the construction of fortifications and roads, without giving them any time to improve the completely inadequate supplies and accommodation facilities of their families.[11]

In 1752 the Indians of Halifax were finally induced to cease hostilities.[12] Now the original plan, to settle the German emigrants in a special colony, could at last be carried out. Of the approximately two thousand Germans, 1,453 left their provisional barracks in Halifax on

May 28, 1753 and sailed under military guard and the personal guidance of Colonel Ch. Lawrence, later to be governor, in fourteen small sailboats along the coast southwest as far as Merliguesh (or Merligash) Bay where they arrived on June 7.[13] Here they founded the community of Lunenburg, which in the years to follow became the base for a predominantly German colonization of the wider area around it. Those who stayed behind in Halifax settled permanently in the north of the city, where they formed a closed German sector. The two German communities in Halifax and Lunenburg had very few links from the beginning. They went their own ways almost entirely.

In 1755 and the following years, when Britain proceeded with the cruel expulsion of the entire French population of Acadia, the partially German population of Halifax and the exclusively German community of Lunenburg were the only settlements left in Nova Scotia for several years.[14] The attempt to bring in new English settlers immediately was frustrated by the new war with France and the hostilities with the Indians. Only after the fall of Louisbourg and Quebec was the struggle for North America decided forever in Britain's favor. As a result of this the Indians had also concluded peace in Halifax in 1760.[15] Now the British colonization of Nova Scotia and New Brunswick could begin. The latter had also been definitely conquered by 1758, and until 1784 was administered from Halifax as a part of Nova Scotia. Thanks to a skillful propaganda campaign which was primarily the work of a certain imaginative and adventurous Colonel McNutt, both provinces, as a result of immigration from Ireland and the New England States, acquired a sizable basic stock of British settlers.[16] Part of the immigration from New England consisted of a few hundred Pennsylvania-Germans, some of whom also came in response to McNutt's efforts and settled in small groups in all the newly-arising townships of Nova Scotia, and on Chignecto Bay in New Brunswick in present-day Albert County.[17]

In 1766-67 the British authorities carried out the first census in Nova Scotia which, in contrast to all the later enumerations of the population in Canada until 1871, asked the settlers for their nationality. The result showed that in the territory of present-day Nova Scotia there were 1,838 Germans (1,417 in Lunenburg, 264 in Halifax and 157 in the remaining townships), and 108 Germans in Moncton and Hopewell townships in present-day New Brunswick.[18] The immigration of Pennsylvania-Germans which is therefore clearly proven for 1765 and 1766, must have continued on a limited scale until the War of Independence, just like the immigration from the older colonies in general.[19]

After the unpleasant experiences of the years 1750 to 1752[20] there was no more immigration from Germany to Nova Scotia until the end of the 1760s. The economic troubles in the wake of the Seven Years' War, however, drove another wave of several hundred Germans to Nova Scotia.[21] Thereafter no noticeable immigration seems to have taken place from Germany. Throughout the nineteenth century the large German emigration to America bypassed the Canadian Maritime Provinces except for insignificant splinters.

For the Germans in Nova Scotia, the only influx from outside came in the wake of the War of Independence in the form of German mercenaries who were allotted land in Annapolis County and New Brunswick after the war,[22] and in the form of Loyalists of German descent from Pennsylvania and New York. Most of the latter, however, moved to Ontario. Nova Scotia was, by and large, the destination only of Loyalists from New York City, who had belonged to the upper class and may have provided some cultural revitalization for the German colonies in Halifax and Lunenburg.[23] Following the years 1783-84, the German settlements, particularly Lunenburg, still had enough strength to expand by founding daughter colonies. But this development came to an end by the third decade of the nineteenth century at the latest. By then the period of stagnation and steady loss of the ethnic heritage had set in.[24]

2. The Germans in Lunenburg County

At the beginning of June 1753 the 1,453 colonists, mostly Germans, landed in Merligash Bay. Within a short time they launched the new settlement, which was named Lunenburg, under the direction and protection of the military and according to the model of the fortress of Halifax. The county's historian attributed the origin of this name to the fact that many of the settlers came from the region in Lower Saxony in Germany known as Lüneburg, which then became anglicized to Lunenburg.[25] But it is more likely that Governor Hopson conferred this name upon the township in honor of the English royal house of Hanover and its Guelph dynastic dominions in northwestern Germany, in much the same way as New Brunswick got its name in 1784 and four districts in Upper Canada were named Hesse, Nassau, Mecklenburg and Lunenburg in 1788.[26] The town, fortified with palisades and log houses, formed the center of the settlement. It served as a rallying place in times of danger. Under normal circumstances, however, the settlers lived on their farms, scattered in a wide area around the fortified town.[27] In spite of its protection by regular troops and the arming of all the colonists, the settlement could not become fully viable. Until peace was formally concluded in 1760, the Lunenburgers were constantly harassed by the Indians. Although they dared not attack the entire settlement, individual farms could not be protected against their sudden raids by the fortified core of the settlement. Lunenburg was therefore unable to grow as long as there was war. Until 1758 the settlers declined in number in spite of their high birth rate.[28] Yet, the moment external security had been established after 1760, the Lunenburg farmers made rapid economic progress due to the fertility of the soil, and their number increased steadily, though slowly at the beginning.[29]

As Nova Scotia filled up with thousands of New Englanders including settlers of German descent here and there, Lunenburg hardly got any new immigrants.[30] Only in 1765 did a fairly large group of new German immigrants settle in their neighborhood. A certain Joseph Pernette, an officer of German descent in the English service according to concurring sources, received along with other discharged officers a large piece of land for settlement on the La Have River. He settled Germans on it almost exclusively.[31] Only a very few of the German Loyalists seem to have settled in Lunenburg. An interesting document is the official land patent for all the settlers of Lunenburg Township of 1784. Except for a few English and French names (of the immigrants from Switzerland and Montbéliard) it shows that seven-eighths of the surnames were undeniably German.[32]

There were three natural directions in which the German population of Lunenburg could expand: to the northeast, to the southwest along the Atlantic coast and up the La Have River into the interior of the country. Prior to 1766, the first German families had begun to move on along the coast in each direction and had settled in the adjoining townships of New Dublin in the southwest and Chester in the northeast, where British settlers had already established themselves. In the following decade more and more Lunenburg families migrated to these two townships, which eventually had a German majority as large as Lunenburg itself, and which were later united with Lunenburg Township to form Lunenburg County.[33]

The expansion of the German element to the southwest reached as far as present-day Queens County where the community of West Berlin can be found. One of the more important German settlements in New Dublin was Voglers Cove. Its first inhabitants were the two families of Conrad and Vogler. Its German population, as in other places in Lunenburg County, abandoned farming entirely and, under the influence of the geographic conditions, turned to shipbuilding.[34] The name of Voglers Cove, by the way, shows the typical connection of a German surname with an English geographical designation, as can be found rather frequently in Canada.[35]

The opening up of the immediate hinterland which is part of Lunenburg Township today, as well as the gradual penetration of Chester and New Dublin Townships by German settlers, cannot be documented in detail. As in all agricultural colonizations of this kind, it was entirely the result of the personal initiative of individual families who, without any elaborate plans, cleared and cultivated a piece of fertile ground in the interior of the still untouched land. By their example they drew other settlers after them, until sooner or later, almost accidentally, a village community formed. By 1780 the German colonists advanced as far as Mahone Bay and Indian Point.[36] By the beginning of the nineteenth century the communities of Bridgewater and New Germany[37] emerged at the La Have River and gradually, step by step, almost the entire area of present-day Lunenburg County was occupied by settlers of German descent.[38]

The bond of unity among the settlements scattered in an ever-growing radius around the small town of Lunenburg, the old parent settlement, was maintained for decades by the regular gathering of all the German settlers, at least from as far as Bridgewater and Mahone Bay, for German church services in Lunenburg.[39] The cohesion among the German colonists and the preservation of their ethnic heritage for at least a century was here, as everywhere among Germans in foreign countries, largely due to the church.

As long as possession of the Maritime Provinces had not been definitely secured from France, the British government admitted only Protestants as a matter of principle. At first almost all the Germans were Lutherans. Not long after the founding of Lunenburg they formed a congregation, without, however, having a church and a pastor of their own before 1772.[40] Until then they were served by priests of the Anglican Church, who in spite of their efforts did not succeed in alienating the Germans from their Lutheran faith and thus accelerating their ethnic assimilation.[41] Where persuasion would not succeed, pressure was tried. When the Lutherans founded a school and acquired a teacher from Germany in 1760, the Anglican Church as the spiritual authority demanded that the language of instruction be mainly English and eventually managed to have the school closed.[42] It is safe to assume that the Anglicans were primarily interested in making denominational life difficult for the Lutherans, for even decades later there were no objections to German instruction as such in and around Lunenburg. It is, however, interesting to note that as early as 1760 the British instinctively applied the most effective means in disputes with foreign ethnic groups, namely the closure of the foreign-language schools. This made the desire for a German Lutheran pastor of their own even more urgent. In 1772 Zion's Lutheran Church in Lunenburg was completed and the first German pastor, Friedrich Schultz, arrived. He remained until 1782. His successors were: Pastor Johann Gottlieb Schmeisser (1782-1806), Pastor Ferdinand Conrad Temme (1808-1832) and Pastor Carl Ernst Cossmann (1835-1897), who after 1877 had the help of English-speaking assistant pastors.[43] For quite some time all the Germans in the neighborhood came to the services in Lunenburg. In the nineteenth century the Lunenburg pastors in turn preached in the small communities nearby. Pastor Cossmann even held services in Halifax at intervals.[44]

As the language of church services, German was retained for a longer period of time than it was as the language of everyday life, which had become English by the middle of the nineteenth century due to the influence of English officials and merchants.[45] Apart from a religious-conservative desire to retain their German church services and their German Bible, the only book that they read, the farmers were not the least interested in putting up with economic disadvantages in return for the maintenance of their native language. The era of national consciousness had not yet arrived.

Although Pastor Cossmann preached in German until his death and was apparently understood without difficulty by the older generation, the calling of English assistant pastors in 1877 marked the definite beginning of the English period for the Lutheran congregation in Lunenburg.[46] After the fall of this last bulwark of German identity— German language instruction appears to have long been discontinued by then—the population of Lunenburg County could no longer be characterized ethnically as a German community, although they were, of course, aware of their German descent, which is manifest in almost all the surnames, and they continued to report themselves as being of German origin in the census after 1871. Even after the World War, in the 1921 Census, more than half the population of the county still reported their origin as German.[47]

3. Germans in Halifax and Other Parts of Nova Scotia

After Lunenburg, the second most important German colony in Nova Scotia was the one in Halifax. Only about three-quarters of the German immigrants of 1750-52 had moved on to Lunenburg in the spring of 1753. The rest stayed behind and formed a neighborhood of their own in the north of the city, clearly delimited from the Irish and English residential areas. It was generally known as "Dutch Town."[48] Their ignorance of the English language, their Lutheran faith and their common plight kept the Germans isolated from others, yet closely united among themselves. The immediate establishment of a burial fund, which existed until 1761, may be taken as proof of the cohesion and self-sufficiency of the German community in the early period.[49] It appears that shortly after their arrival, when all the German immigrants in Halifax were still together, a Lutheran congregation was formed under the direction of the zealous schoolmaster Johann Jorpel. In the absence of a pastor, Jorpel himself held services in the schoolhouse.[50] In 1756 work was started to transform the schoolhouse, which stood at the corner of the present Gerrish and Brunswick Streets, into a church. In 1761 the new edifice was dedicated as St. George's Church. It was the first Lutheran church on Canadian soil.[51] Teacher Jorpel held the first confirmation in it on October 4, 1761.[52] He unfortunately died in the same year. Now, having a church, the new settlers did not succeed in obtaining a pastor for it no matter how many pleas they sent to Pastor H.M. Mühlenberg in Pennsylvania.[53] The Anglicans of St. Paul's, on the other hand, became more and more interested in the German Lutherans.[54] They knew that according to British law anyone, including the Germans, belonged to the one Anglican congregation in Halifax and saw no need to argue with the Germans about this.[55] With the very natural ulterior motive of winning the German Lutherans over to Anglicanism, Dr. Breynton, the rector of St. Paul's, offered to conduct the service from time to time in St. George's as well. He was willing to carry out all those duties which required special priestly consecration, such as baptisms, marriages and funerals. The regular church services however, were still being held by the schoolmaster, who was now Master Hagelsieb.[56]

By the 1760s the German population in the city had declined to between 250 and 270.[57] Soon after the outbreak of the American War of Independence, however, a new German element moved in. German mercenary troops, among whom was the poet Johann Gottfried Seume, were stationed in Halifax.[58] Upon their discharge at the end of the war many of these "Hessians" appear to have stayed in the city and increased its German colony noticeably.[59] It is certain also that quite a few Loyalists came to Halifax. The most important newcomer was Pastor Hausihl, who had to leave New York City with a part of his congregation and who became the first and only German minister for the Lutherans in Halifax.[60] Apparently his small new congregation could not support him in the way he desired.[61] In order, therefore, to qualify as a missionary for the subsidies of the Society for the Propagation of the Gospel, he had himself ordained as an Anglican chaplain in 1785, without ceasing to be the Lutheran pastor for his congregation. Almost imperceptibly he led them from their native faith to the Anglican confession, which was not very different with regard to dogma. Neither he nor the congregation realized that absorption by the Church of England might jeopardize their German ethnic heritage. After Hausihl's death in 1799 the point was reached where St. George's congregation could officially be declared Anglican, and all the possessions of the German Lutheran congregation became the property of the Church of England. In his "Notes on the Early History of St. George's Church, Halifax" (1891), F. Partridge argues that the German congregation had already abandoned Lutheranism on their own as a result of Breynton's influence and the services rendered to them by other Anglican clergy, before Pastor Hausihl's conversion got things moving. In 1784 "the congregation was no longer Lutheran, though still German." For the seizure in 1800, which to the men of the Church of England apparently also meant the confiscation of the real estate and the valuable altar pieces of the German congregation, the following justification was presented: "The congregation was by this time (1800) more than half English, and those who still retained their German predilections, were inclined to the English Church, which alone had cared for their souls during a period of half a century." This should only be accepted with great caution. Surely, over the period of sixteen years things had not changed in the Lutheran congregation to the point where the German character of the majority was open to question.[62]

Through the early loss of their own church life, the Germans in Halifax became anglicized even faster than those in Lunenburg, although in Halifax German as a language of everyday life was probably not abandoned until the 1830s or 1840s. Since then, only the occasional German surnames are to be found in Halifax. The long used designation of "Dutch Town" for the original German sector of the city and various German street names are reminiscent of the role which a fair-sized German colony had played for almost a century since the founding of the city. In 1764 the Germans asked the governor for permission to name their suburb Göttingen. The request was granted. The name, however, was not in use very long for the entire suburb. Only one of the major streets is called Gottingen Street to this day. The Germans named their main street Brunswick Street which is still its name today. These designations clearly indicate the northwest German origin of the immigrants of 1750-52. Additional clues about the original German inhabitants are manifest in the names of Jacob Street, Lochmann (possibly 'Lohmann?') Street, Bauer Street, Artz Street, Veith Street and Dresden Row. All of these were named after the families of well-to-do residents or their places of origin.[63]

German newspapers did not exist in Halifax or anywhere else in the Maritime Provinces. However, we have evidence from as early as the eighteenth century that German newspapers published in the United States, such as the *Philadelphia Staatsbote*, were read here.[64]

About the history of the other German settlements we have virtually no sources. All we know is that in 1765 hundreds of farmers of German descent came from the old English colonies, particularly from Pennsylvania, and began to set up small German colonies, that at the end of the 1760s several hundred immigrants from Germany became settlers, and that after the War of Independence several hundred German mercenaries and German Loyalists settled here and there.

In Annapolis County all these German elements can be verified. The first German families were found in Grenville Township in 1765. They came from New York, Massachusetts and other New England states.[65] Three or four years later some of the immigrants from the Palatinate and from Swabia arrived in Annapolis.[66] Most important numerically, however, were the two large parallel settlements established by Waldeck and Hessian troops in Clements Township starting in 1783.[67] All the settlements of the "Hessians" have withstood anglicization least, since all the soldiers had gone to America young and single, and marriage with English girls became the rule as early as the first generation. It would seem therefore that after fifty or sixty years only the surnames in Clements Township were reminders of the original German settlers. Rogers, though, compares the area around Clementsport with Lunenburg and characterizes it as "rather German."[68] According to the racial origin map in the *Atlas of Canada* (1915) which presents the results of the 1911 Census, there were no majorities of Germans or descendants of Germans left in Annapolis County.

Such majorities are, however, evident in all the districts of Lunenburg County and the western tip of Halifax County at St. Margaret's Bay, the southern tip of Kings County and in two localities in Queens County, all of which have to be considered as the natural offshoots of the German community of Lunenburg. Other majorities of residents of German descent were found in 1911 only in the center of Shelburne County, which after 1783 had experienced the largest immigration of Loyalists, in Hants County somewhat south of Windsor and in three coastal districts of Halifax County.[69] In conclusion we list the numbers of those who reported themselves as German by origin in Nova Scotia according to five census reports between 1871 and 1921:

Table II.1

	1871	1881	1901	1911	1921
Lunenburg	16,612	20,102	22,709	22,837	17,867
Halifax City	1,469	2,147	7,402	7,246	1,546
Halifax County	6,418	8,165			
rest of Nova Scotia	7,443	9,651	10,909	8,761	7,633
total	31,942	40,065	41,020	38,844	27,046
total population	387,800	440,572	459,574	492,338	523,837
German percentage	8%	9%	9%	8%	5%

After 1871 the Canadian census asked for the "racial origin" whereby "Canadian" or "American" were excluded as nationalities. In many cases only family tradition and name determined with what origin one identified. How little, in particular, the numbers of "Germans by origin" in Nova Scotia permit us to infer about the existence of a live German ethnic community is proven by the fact that in 1921, only 410 persons were still able to speak their German mother tongue. And these were

probably the few immigrants of the preceding decades.[70] The decline
in the number between 1911 and 1921 may be interpreted merely as
a desire to abandon an old, faded tradition by long-ago anglicized
farmers of German descent. The English war propaganda may, on top
of this, have made them ashamed of their German descent.

4. German Pioneers in New Brunswick

The two provinces of Prince Edward Island and New Brunswick,
which were separated in 1769 and 1784 respectively from Nova Scotia,
play only a minor role in our considerations. In P.E.I. there have always
been no more than a few German families, who have never lived in
any closed major settlements. The fact might be mentioned that the
American ambassador of many years in Berlin, J.B. Shurman, is the
descendant of a distinguished, originally German family in Bedeque,
P.E.I.

The share of the Germans in the development of New Brunswick,
which is spatially the largest of the three Canadian Maritime Provinces,
is almost as unclear and insignificant as their role on small Prince
Edward Island. Germans, however, were among the first pioneers here,
too. In 1765 and 1766 a colonial association settled the first Pennsylvania-
Germans—the 1767 Census registered 108 of them—in the newly laid-
out Monckton and Hopewell Townships (the present Moncton and
Hillsborough Townships).[71] By 1776 their number appeared to have
increased due to an influx of Germans from the New England colonies. At first, the settlement of Germantown was founded in 1765 at
the shore of the northern part of the Bay of Fundy on the site of the
abandoned Acadian settlement of Shepody, which is now called
Shepody Bay and was then known for some time as "German Creek"
after its coastal residents.[72] In the same year, several dozen German
families went up the Petitcodiac and founded Moncton.[73] Shortly
thereafter other Germans established the settlement of Coverdale on
the opposite bank.[74] As a result of new immigration and as daughter
colonies of these three German settlements, Hillsborough,[75] Salisbury,[76] and somewhat further down the river, Petitcodiac,[77] were
founded in the following decades. In time, the entire river district was
occupied by the descendants of the Pennsylvania-Germans from the
original Monckton and Hopewell Townships.[78] The names of the set-

tlements of Lutz Mountain (Westmoreland County) and Memel (Albert County) suggest a role of predominantly German settlers in their foundation.[79]

Whether and for how long these German colonists, who gradually scattered over most of present-day Albert County and adjacent districts in Westmoreland County, ever led a cultural life of their own, is unknown. They apparently never formed specific church congregations and probably had no schools of their own either. While British immigration continued on a modest scale, a later influx of Germans is improbable. In the course of the nineteenth century the farmers of German descent were absorbed by the British majority. According to the 1871 Census 1,079 persons in Albert County reported themselves as German by origin (636 of these in Hillsborough and 255 in Coverdale) and 457 in Westmoreland County (133 of these in Moncton and 253 in Salisbury). In the 1881 Census, which showed the largest population of German descent in New Brunswick, these numbers increased somewhat, only to decrease very rapidly since then in proportion to the total population. The awareness of German descent became increasingly blurred and seems to have been virtually lost by now.

Not much can be said about the remaining German settlements of New Brunswick. Franz von Loeher, who in the mid-1840s estimated the number of Germans in New Brunswick to be five thousand, wrote: "In New Brunswick one can find Germans here and there, but rarely in large settlements, most of them on the John's River and in St. John." The contemporary German population in Saint John and on the St. John River dated back to the years when all the settlements in this area originated, i.e. the years immediately following the American War of Independence. Among the mass of Loyalists who settled on the St. John River at that time,[80] we have to assume a large number of German-American refugees and probably most of the twelve hundred Brunswick mercenaries. The latter were discharged in 1783 and settled in New Brunswick, which was then still part of Nova Scotia.[81]

It is safe to assume that most of the Germans to be found here and there in the immense forest region of New Brunswick in the nineteenth century traced their origins to the German colonists on the lower St. John River.[82] A direct immigration from Germany appears to have been highly unlikely at any time. Any German immigration appears equally unlikely from the United States after 1785.[83]

According to the 1871 Census 4,478 persons out of a total population of 285,594, or 1.6 per cent, reported themselves as German by origin. Their distribution was as follows:

In the Petitcodiac River area (Albert and Westmoreland Counties)	1,536
On the lower St. John River (City of Saint John, Kings and Queens Counties)	2,006
York and Carleton Counties[84]	563
Remaining counties	373
Total	4,478

In the 1881 Census the number of persons of German descent increased to 6,310 even though there is no evidence of any German immigration in the interval. This may be proof for the assumption that the German tradition was still alive and that German as a language of everyday life and the German Bible were still in use. Thereafter, however, the number of those who declared their German descent declined absolutely and rapidly in proportion to the increasing total population. In 1901 there were 3,816; in 1911, 3,144; after the World War, in 1921, however, a mere 1,698 in all of New Brunswick. For the past forty or fifty years German no longer seems to have been spoken, even within the family. According to the 1921 Census only 135 persons could speak German.

In summing up, one cannot escape the conclusion that in the Maritime Provinces the German element, which dates back to the eighteenth century, is extinct today. After a few more decades perhaps not even the memory will survive of the quiet, stubborn pioneer effort and active participation in the opening up of Nova Scotia and New Brunswick to which thousands of Germans devoted themselves over the course of time.

5. The German Element in Quebec

The German element in the two Canadian core provinces of Quebec and Ontario is not quite as old as in Nova Scotia and in New Brunswick. The first German colonists cannot be traced here until immediately after the end of the American War of Independence. They were either German Loyalists or disbanded German mercenaries.[85]

During the war years 1777-83, the fortified places at the St. Lawrence between Montreal and Quebec had been used as bases of operations and as winter quarters by most of the German regiments of mercenaries. Some were even turned into permanent garrisons by them.

By the end of the war quite a few German soldiers had married French Canadians.[86] It is therefore only natural that a considerable number of the approximately 2,500 discharged German mercenaries who settled on Canadian soil after the end of the war[87] stayed as craftsmen in the small towns on the St. Lawrence or scattered as farmhands in the adjacent seigniories. Through their mixed marriages they were rapidly absorbed by the francophone community. Only individual German family names that have been preserved in a few communities of the Province of Quebec to this day, although on occasion with French spelling, still bear witness to them.[88]

The tide of Loyalist refugees passed by Quebec. The English colonial government allotted them land only in Ontario and in the Maritime Provinces. The Loyalists themselves had no desire to settle among the French Canadians of Quebec. Apart from all the ethnic and religious incompatibilities, the old French civil law, which England had to guarantee to the French Canadians explicitly in the Quebec Act of 1774, was repugnant to the American farmers. They demanded freehold property which they were accustomed to, and did not want to enter a relationship of dependence as holders of a hereditary lease no matter how lenient. A Loyalist colony was nevertheless set up in the Province of Quebec which should be of interest to us.

In the fall of 1783, Sorel, on the St. Lawrence, was designated as the temporary rallying place for all the Loyalists who were to be settled in the spring of 1784 in the area that later became Ontario.[89] Those who did not get to Sorel by boat from the towns on the American coast, travelled there the shortest way by land, i.e. up the Hudson, along the western shore of Lake Champlain and down the Richelieu to Sorel. This was the land route which the Loyalists chose from the interior of the State of New York. A large group of those who dreaded the hardships and uncertainties of the long march to Upper Canada bought land amidst the charming scenery of the hill country on the Missisquoi Bay, at the northeastern tip of Lake Champlain, immediately after crossing the Canadian border. They settled there despite the explicit request of the Canadian Governor Haldimand, who feared that Loyalist settlements too close to the border might lead to renewed frictions with the Americans.[90] It turned out that most of the Loyalists who founded the first villages at Missisquoi Bay were of German descent.[91] They were Palatines and some Irish Germans from the Mohawk, Schoharie and the middle Hudson (Dutchess County).[92]

We have a document dating from the spring of 1785, which is quite revealing, signed by some of those Germans at Missisquoi Bay. The colonial Government, which would not tolerate their wilful land purchase but wanted to compel them to take up land in Ontario, had withdrawn subsidies of provisions, clothes and equipment which were normally granted to all Loyalists. In response, those affected thereupon directed a sharply-worded memorandum to the Governor of Quebec, in which they stressed their loyal views and their losses during the war and stated that they had settled at Missisquoi Bay long before Haldimand had allotted any land to Loyalists. Finally, they requested the continued delivery of the still urgently needed subsidies.[93]

The petition is signed by Christian Wehr, Conrad Best, Christian Maver, John Ruiter, Adam Deal, John Cole, Ludwig Streit, George Feller, Josamiad Drow, Lodwik Strit Junr., Jacob Thomas, Philip Ruiter, John Van Vorst, James Henderson and Alexr. Taylor.

Most of these are obviously German. In the petition itself the arrangement of words, the desire to capitalize everything that is important and certain spelling mistakes lead one to conclude that its authors were Germans who were still far from using English as their everyday language. We do not know whether the petition was crowned with success. It is certain, however, that these farmers fought their way through the first most difficult years and did not give up their property at the Missisquoi Bay. By and by they spread over most of the townships of present-day Missisquoi County as well as over some adjacent townships.[94]

When in the decades after 1800, the Eastern Townships acquired their large English population, the German element probably also received reinforcements from the United States. It is unlikely that the number of persons of German descent indicated in later enumerations were all descended from the small groups of Germans who, after 1783, were among the first pioneers of the hilly border region at the northern end of Lake Champlain.[95]

In 1847 Loeher reported: "In Williamsburg as well as in the Mississippi [sic] district to which the towns of Durham, Stanstädt (now Stanstead) and Friedrichsburg belong, there are some German communities which emigrated from Pennsylvania during the War of Liberation."[96]

This remains unfortunately the only vague allusion for those years to the German hamlets and villages in southern Quebec at the Vermont border.

According to the Census reports of 1871, 1881 and 1901, decreasing totals of 2,967, 2,408 and 666 persons respectively declared themselves to be of German descent in the four counties in question.[97] Judging by these reports, the recollection of descent from German settlers must still have been alive around 1870. However, it began to fade and disappeared almost entirely in the 1880s and 1890s. When around the turn of this century Noyes made his inquiries, the German ethnic identity of this one part of the population had already become an obscure historical matter. With regard to their everyday language, this German ethnic splinter in the Eastern Townships appears to have been anglicized by as early as the middle of the nineteenth century.

The only other closed settlements of German farmers in the Province of Quebec emerged on the left bank of the Ottawa River north of the town of Buckingham in present-day Labelle County, and north of Shawville in Pontiac County, simultaneously with the numerous German settlements on the right bank of the Ottawa River in Renfrew County, Ontario.[98] As early as the 1840s the settlement of large areas on the left (Quebec) bank by German farmers was considered.[99] These plans, however, did not become reality until the 1860s when cheap and good land became scarce in southwestern Ontario (with Berlin [now Kitchener] as its center), which had previously been the destination of German immigrants. Then their interest was very much directed to the Ottawa Valley due to the opening up of new townships in Renfrew County after 1857.

In August 1861 the first two to three hundred German farmers settled in Bowman Township at the Lièvre north of Buckingham.[100] In the course of the following years another few hundred took up land in their neighborhood. Eventually sizeable German groups could be found in the townships of Bowman, Villeneuve, Portland, Mulgrave, Derry and some adjacent townships. Due to their exemplary farming operations, to which a revealing report by a Canadian government official in 1887 explicitly attested, [101] the German farmers soon mastered all the difficulties and did materially better than the representatives of any other nationality. They maintained their own schools with instruction in German and English from the beginning and in spite of, or rather because of, their isolation, appear to have preserved the German language and German ways until the [First] World War, if not to the 1920s.[102]

The census showed the following to be German by origin:

in	1871	1881	1901	1911	1921
Ottawa County	528	699			
renamed Labelle County			597	714	673

The second small group of German farms on the east bank of the Ottawa were situated further down the river in Pontiac County, twenty-five kilometers north of Shawville with Thorne Township as their center.[103] The first seven German families seem to have come there in 1865.[104] Additional families followed. The largest number came in 1868, when German immigration to the Ottawa area reached its peak.[105] The sources tell us nothing unusual about the development of these German settlements. It appears that their economic and linguistic conditions were like those of the Germans in Labelle County.[106] In 1875 a Lutheran congregation was formed in Thorne Centre, which has been called Ladysmith since 1902. It has enjoyed the service of a German pastor without interruption until this day.[107] According to the census reports in Pontiac County, (Thorne Centre and adjacent districts), persons declaring themselves as German by origin numbered: 233 (1870-71); 426 (1880-81); 577 (1901); 592 (1911); and 586 (1921).

With these we have exhausted the number of distinctly German colonies in the province of Quebec, although the census shows a few Germans (as farmhands and farmers) scattered over all the counties in Quebec, as in all the other Canadian provinces. It is unlikely that entire seigniories fell into German hands and that therefore large numbers of Germans had been induced to come and live in the center of the French area of settlement, as Bromme reported in two instances for the 1840s.[108]

A regular, though very small, immigration from Germany can be documented only for the cities of Quebec and Montreal where, every year since the beginning of the direct immigration in 1846, German craftsmen, particularly mechanics, have settled.[109] Since the disbanding of the "Hessians," perhaps even earlier, Montreal apparently had a German colony of merchants and craftsmen, some of whom had soon become prosperous. Loeher reported in 1847[110] that "there are about thirty German families in Montreal who all belonged to the prosperous middle classes. Together with an approximately equal number of German descendants they founded a society in 1835 to support the German immigrants by word and deed. This society is very active." In 1853 a German Lutheran congregation was formed in Montreal, namely St. John's congregation, which joined the Canada Synod, and still exists today.[111] Since 1870 the number of Germans in Montreal has been fluctuating between one thousand and two thousand, according to the census.

6. The German United Empire Loyalist Colonies at the St. Lawrence and the Bay of Quinte

The two oldest permanent non-Indian settlements in eastern Ontario were the Loyalist colonies at the St. Lawrence in present-day Dundas and Stormont Counties and at the Bay of Quinte, the richly structured stretch of shore of the present-day Frontenac, Lennox, Addington and Prince Edward Counties. Both of these colonies are important in our context since German Loyalists, particularly from New York State, played a leading role in their formation and development

Here the first townships were surveyed hastily in 1783, five at the Bay of Quinte west of the old military station of Cataraqui (later the town of Kingston) and four further east on the St. Lawrence, in order to procure employment for the expelled Loyalists, and allot them new land as quickly as possible as a replacement for the property they had left behind in the enemy country. Meanwhile the Loyalists who were destined to be settled there were assembled by regiment in Sorel,[112] where in the fall of 1783 they joined their wives and children who also had to flee the young American States as refugees.[113] In the early summer of 1784, going up the St. Lawrence by boat, they reached their destinations.

The four townships of Williamsburg, Matilda, Osnabruck and Cornwall surveyed on the St. Lawrence were assigned to the 1st Battalion of the New York Loyalist regiment, recruited by Sir John Johnson, which disembarked on June 20, 1784.[114] The majority of Johnson's regiment, however—almost the entire 1st Battalion—was composed of Palatine farmers from the Mohawk and Schoharie.[115] Germans therefore became the first European settlers in eastern Ontario. The Scots and English in Johnson's 1st Battalion received their land in Cornwall and

Osnabruck (Stormont County). Yet here, too, Germans were in the majority. Williamsburg and Matilda (Dundas County) were wholly German.[116] The number of Loyalists settled in the four townships has been handed down to us in the form of an inventory of October 1784, which was held to determine the quantity of supplies of provisions, seed grain and equipment required by each settlement.[117] According to it we find:

In	Men	Women	Children	Servants	Acres Cleared
Cornwall	215	87	214	1	101½
Osnabruck	50	7	14	4	30
Williamsburg	93	33	76	1	101¾
Matilda	75	33	64	5	56½
Total	433	160	368	11	289¾

Each Loyalist received, apart from the special allowances for his family, one hundred acres on the riverfront and two hundred acres of the hinterland.[118] Since the ground was apparently easy to clear and the soil was good, as was proven by the amount of cultivated land after the short period of three months, the Palatines were content. Being used to the hard work of pioneers, they managed again to support themselves from the proceeds of their own land, and gradually achieved prosperity. After three or four years the Germans were eager to build their own church in Williamsburg, which was dedicated as Zion's Church in 1789.[119] Most of the German Loyalists were Lutherans, some were Reformed, using the church of the Lutherans, with whom they lived in harmony.[120] The first Lutheran minister was the Reverend Samuel Schwerdtfeger, who came to Williamsburg in 1790. He also preached among the Germans of the other three townships, and founded Lutheran congregations.[121] After his departure the Reverend Fr. A. Meyer ministered to the German Lutherans of Dundas and Stormont between 1803 and 1807. He had previously served at the Bay of Quinte.[122] He was succeeded by the Reverend Wiegand (also spelled Weigand or Wigant) who had also earlier been ministering at the Bay of Quinte.[123] Wiegand, however, secretly joined the Church of England in 1811 and tried, on instruction of his superiors (although in vain), to take his Lutheran congregation with him into the Anglican church.[124]

The Church of England thus attempted to attain its objective among the German colonists of Williamsburg and vicinity in the same manner that a few years earlier had proven so successful with the German Lutherans of Halifax.[125] While in both instances the congregations themselves clung stubbornly to their Lutheranism, the Anglicans managed to win over their ministers. The small congregations of colonists could maintain their pastor only with difficulty. For the sake of a regular Anglican subsidy, these ministers acceded to the proposition of conversion as far as their own persons were concerned and tried to initiate the conversion of their congregations. In the absence of any ethnic perspective the Lutheran pastors viewed the transition into the Anglican camp as a purely religious matter, without considering the inevitable risk of exposing their congregation to the loss of their German ethnic identity. They also did not seem to see through the Church's designs on the material possessions of the German congregations, which may have been justified by the English view that the pastor, not the congregation, had the right to dispose of the church property. There is no doubt that the practices of the Anglican Church did much to promote the absorption of the German colonists into the English-speaking community.

When the Lutherans in Williamsburg and vicinity dissociated themselves from the Reverend Wiegand and again called the Reverend Meyer, who arrived in the winter of 1814-15, the Reverend Wiegand, backed by the Anglican Church with all its rights as a state church, took recourse to force.[126] He barred the church to all who did not recognize the thirty-nine articles of the Church of England. By way of compromise, the Lutherans managed to be able to conduct services in their own church at least every two weeks. All hope was lost, however, when in 1817 the Reverend Meyer was won over by the Anglicans as well.[127] Since the Anglican Church now openly impounded the Lutheran church, the parsonage and the church property, the calling of a new minister was rendered immensely difficult for the German colonists.[128] Another Lutheran clergyman, the Reverend Hermann Hayunga, was not obtained until 1826.[129] With no Lutheran service, the only thing that made the German colonists retain their mother tongue was now lacking. During this decade without a pastor, they started to use English as their everyday language. Until then the use of their native German language had not been questioned, in spite of the immigration of English-speaking settlers in the meantime.[130] Around 1825, however, some of the younger generation tried to switch over to English, thus forcing the Reverend Hayunga to be the first one preaching alternately in German and English. By the end of his ministry—he remained in

Williamsburg until 1837—the development had already progressed to the point where most members of the congregation understood English and he could confine himself exclusively to English services.[131] His successors preached only in English.[132]

Although the colonists of Williamsburg and vicinity lost their German identity after three generations, their Lutheranism has survived to this day, a development which we are able to observe in Lunenburg, N.S., as in many other formerly German Lutheran, now merely Lutheran congregations in Canada. To this day one pastor of the Lutheran Canada Synod serves in Williamsburg, and one in Morrisburg.[133]

According to the 1871 Census, 8,688 persons, or 23 per cent of a total population of 37,764 in the present-day Dundas and Stormont Counties, still reported themselves as German by origin. With the total population slowly rising, their number had increased to 9,794 by 1881. In 1901 there were still 9,409 of them, to be followed by a rapid decrease in the last two census reports.[134] These figures refute Croil's contention of 1861 that, together with their mother tongue, the Germans in the four Loyalist townships at the St. Lawrence had also lost all their remaining ethnic characteristics by that time. Instead, German as a language spoken in the family and the use of the German Bible appear to have been retained for a longer period of time. The general glorification of the United Empire Loyalists in Canada may have helped much to keep alive the tradition of descending from German Loyalists, even among the farmers of Dundas and Stormont, at a time when their German identity had long since become questionable.

All the four townships on the St. Lawrence had been made available to the 1st Battalion of Johnson's New York regiment, as we saw. The 2nd Battalion and the remaining Loyalist groups who were sent from Sorel to Ontario in 1784 had their land allotted in the five townships surveyed at the Bay of Quinte: in Kingston, Ernesttown, Fredericksburg, Adolphustown and Marysburgh.

Kingston, in present-day Frontenac County, the most eastern of the townships beginning at Fort Cataraqui (which is today the town of Kingston), was occupied by Loyalists from New York City who had come by boat to Canada under the leadership of a Captain Grass.[135] Few Germans appear to have been among them, although several German names can be found among the owners of the first allotments.[136]

More important to us, however, are the two townships adjoining to the west, Ernesttown and Fredericksburg, that were allotted to Johnson's 2nd Battalion under Sir John himself, and under Colonel Rogers.

Comprising 477 men at the time, according to an old list,[137] the 2nd Battalion did not consist predominantly of Palatines as did the 1st, yet they still made up more than half the men.[138] The Palatines and Scots from the Mohawk, whom we have to imagine as weatherbeaten farmers and not as professional soldiers, went about clearing the virgin forest with a grim determination. Like their comrades at Williamsburg, they again quickly achieved a certain level of prosperity, especially since Ernesttown admittedly had the best soil of all the new townships in Ontario.[139] Probably many an old friend and neighbor of the Loyalists from the villages in New York joined them and settled among them in the first years.[140] By 1811, at any rate, Ernesttown had as many as 2,300 inhabitants, and had thus become the most populous township in Ontario.[141]

We get an indication of the development of the German element in these townships only from the history of the Lutheran congregations. Around 1800, the German Lutherans in Ernesttown erected St. Peter's Church, and in Fredericksburg, Ebenezer Church, two simple wooden structures. The "stone church" in Camden East Township in present-day Napanee community, situated further inland, was built somewhat later.[142] The first two were always served together by one pastor, who chose Ernesttown, or Bath, as it was later called, for his residence. From there, besides the congregations in Fredericksburg and Napanee, he also served the small church in Marysburgh in Prince Edward County,[143] and the German congregations in Camden and Richmond Townships, who never managed to acquire a church of their own. The parish register of the main congregation in Bath (Ernesttown) has unfortunately been lost, yet we have the one of the smaller Ebenezer congregation in Fredericksburg,[144] which besides baptismal and marriage registers also contains lists of communicants. It does give us, therefore, certain insights, although, for example, not even a complete list of all the German pastors has been handed down to us.[145]

The first German clergyman to preach at the Bay of Quinte was Pastor Meyer. He ministered to the Germans in Marysburgh, perhaps even before 1790, and left in 1804 for Williamsburg.[146] The first preacher among the Germans in Ernesttown and Fredericksburg was the Reverend Wigant. He initiated the construction of the two wooden churches there, also preached in Marysburgh after Meyer's departure, and in 1807 finally left to succeed Meyer in Williamsburg.[147] About the pastors of the following two decades nothing specific is known.[148] From 1826 to 1831 the various German Lutheran congregations at the Bay were served by a Pastor Guenther. He was succeeded until 1833 by Reverend Kilmer, until 1840 by Reverend La Dow and until 1850 by Reverend Plato.[149]

In comparison to conditions in the German congregations on the St. Lawrence, it can be assumed that the transition from German to English in the language of the church and of everyday life took place during the course of the 1830s. In contrast to those congregations, however, the loss of the German services also meant the loss of Lutheranism at the Bay of Quinte. In the 1840s most of the former Lutherans joined the Methodists.[150] Over the course of time the three Lutheran churches were formally turned over to the Methodists, the church in Fredericksburg as late as 1879.[151]

Adolphustown, the smallest of the townships surveyed at the Bay of Quinte in 1783, was, in contrast to the others, taken over by a group of "civil Loyalists" who had fought for England's rights without arms, under the leadership of a Captain Van Alstine. They came from the southern counties of New York State such as Dutchess County,[152] the probable place of origin of the few German families in Adolphustown.[153]

Marysburgh, the fifth and last of the Loyalist townships at the Bay, was situated somewhat apart from the others. It comprised the various necks of land in the east of bay-rich Prince Edward Peninsula. In 1784 the last major group of officers and non-commissioned officers of the Johnson regiment settled here.[154] We presume up to half of them were Palatines.[155] The main part of Marysburgh, however, had been reserved for the so-called "Hessians" in order to make good the promise made to them by the English government. In 1785 a large group of discharged soldiers did, in fact, arrive in Marysburgh after some hesitation in Quebec. Here, however, bitter distress and disappointment awaited them.[156] In contrast to the farmer-soldiers from New York, these German professional soldiers faced an entirely new situation which they could not master. They lacked any experience necessary for the clearing and cultivation of the virgin forest land and probably also the robust physique that such work demanded. The loneliness of the virgin forest, which the others had been used to for a lifetime, oppressed them. Finally, they were also not treated as well as the Loyalists with regard to land grants and the supply of provisions. The latter tended to look down upon them, especially since the neighbourhood consisted mainly of officers, some of whom had previously been well-to-do landlords, and drew a clear line of social distinction.[157]

Thus the German soldiers were unhappy and made no headway. When, earlier than for the Loyalists, subsidies of provisions were withdrawn for good after two years,[158] they were far from being able to support themselves. The crop failure of 1787, which affected all the young colonies, hit the Hessians especially hard. The threatening famine transformed their growing disappointment into sheer despair. Had they not been completely without means, all the Hessians would certainly have turned their backs on Ontario at that time. The circumstances enabled only a few to do this.[159] After more years of severe privations they managed finally, but much later than the Loyalists, to make a living as farmers on their land.[160]

Perhaps even before 1790, but certainly soon thereafter, the German Loyalists and the Hessians in Marysburgh came together for Pastor Meyer's Lutheran services. He had a small wooden church erected on the land of the Schmidt family.[161] Later the little congregation was served by the pastor in Ernesttown.

Unfortunately we are not as well informed about the townships at the Bay of Quinte, settled somewhat later, as about these first five of 1784. It is certain, however, that by 1800 the remaining townships of Prince Edward County as well as a few additional ones on the opposite mainland had already been settled by so-called "Late Loyalists" who, hungry for land, had followed their friends from the U.S.A. Among these we have to presume a large number of Germans.[162] Whether, however, German immigrants supplemented these in the nineteenth century is uncertain.

By 1870 the German element at the Bay had advanced beyond a broad tract along the shore from Kingston to Cramahe Township in East Northumberland County (west of Brighton), and appeared as colonists, especially further inland. When the 1871 Census for the first time inquired about the racial origin of the population, 24,890 Germans by origin, which is 17 per cent of a total population of 144,476, were registered in the six counties of Frontenac, Addington, Lennox, Hastings, East Northumberland and Prince Edward. In 1881 in the same districts as many as 26,857 Germans by origin were counted among a population of 153,312, again equal to 17 per cent. The highest percentages of Germans were registered, as was to be expected, in Ernesttown, Fredericksburg and the townships inland of, and adjoining, Camden and Richmond as well as in Prince Edward County.

Here, too, just as in the smaller German Loyalist colony of Dundas and Stormont, the tradition of descending from United Empire Loyalists had kept the memory of their German origins alive, when the process of anglicization had long been completed in their language of everyday life. With the lack of any new German immigration from outside, this appears to have happened in the third generation, well before 1870. The high percentages of Germans by origin in the two census reports of 1871 and 1881 can, on the other hand, only be understood if we assume that at least among the older generation in the family, German was still spoken, and the German family Bible, the strongest bond with the past, was still read. The later rapidly declining figures however, merely reflect tradition[163] which was almost entirely abandoned during the World War.

Among the first Germans at the Bay of Quinte, by the way, were a number of Moravians.[164] Until 1795 one of them, by the name of Bininger, was active as a teacher in the nearby village of the Mohawk Indians, who had also come as Loyalists to settle on Canadian soil as recently as 1784.[165]

7. Settlement in the Ottawa Valley

As far as can be ascertained, few of the above-described German-American colonies of Loyalists received any German immigration worth mentioning after 1800. Nor were any additional major German settlements established in eastern Ontario in the first half of the nineteenth century. Only in the 1850s, when land became scarcer and more expensive in southwestern Ontario (the main destination of German immigration), was the Canadian government able to divert part of the British and the German immigration to these districts. As an incentive, large tracts of free land on the upper Ottawa were put aside for settlement. Due to the remoteness and rugged climate of the upper Ottawa Valley, earlier attempts at settlement, beginning in the 1820s, had not been entirely successful. Only now did they begin to make some headway. The German immigrants who, starting in 1857[166], were proceeding to the Ottawa Valley, were allotted land mainly in Renfrew County. Here the largest district of German settlement in eastern Ontario developed. It is still the most important one today.

By 1860 as many as ninety-five families were cultivating their own ground at that location. All of them had come from the Neumark, Pomerania and West Prussia.[167] About one-third of them were

Kashubs, who barely mastered German, from the area around Berendt and Karthaus in the government district of Danzig. The Canadian Reports on Immigration, therefore, at one time called them "Prussians" to distinguish them from the rest of the "Germans" but most referred to them, erroneously, simply as "Poles." The total number of immigrants from Germany to Renfrew County is estimated to be 150 families, or 900 persons, by 1860.[168] At that time about fifty families did not yet farm their own land, but appear to have worked on the farms of friends or on road construction.

Even the relatively few German immigrants of the first four years were not settled in one closed colony, but rather in three areas quite distant from each other: in the north of the county in Alice Township not far from Pembroke, in the west in Wilberforce, Algona, Grattan and Sebastopol Townships in the Eganville area, and in the southeast around the village of Renfrew and at the Opeongo. Almost all the Kashubs settled here in the south.[169] The core for the three districts of German settlements in Renfrew had thus been created by that time.

In the following decade German immigration to Renfrew County reached its climax. Apparently enticed by quite irresponsible propaganda of the official Canadian agencies, approximately four thousand Germans tried to make Renfrew their new home between 1861 and 1870.[170] Many of them were destined to be bitterly disappointed.

The land made available free of charge for settlement had mostly poor, rocky or sandy soil. British immigration so far had, not without good reason, passed it by. At that time the German farmer was known all over North America as the best pioneer, due to his perseverance and frugality, particularly on difficult terrain. The Canadian government therefore tried through intensified advertising in Germany to attract as many German settlers as possible, especially for Renfrew, and with good results.[171] Yet under the prevailing soil and climatic conditions even the Germans failed in large part.[172]

They fared worst in the north of the county. Here many had to abandon their land and their efforts, despite all kinds of experiments at cultivation, and turn, penniless, to the United States after they had used up the small operating capital that they had brought over from Germany. Disappointed colonists who are unable to meet the demands made on their physical strength and will power and who throw in the towel prematurely are, of course, to be found in every attempt at colonization. Such despair and desire to flee as seized hold of the Germans in Renfrew County in the 1860s, however, is unique in the history of

German-Canadian settlement. About half of the German farmers left the County at that time. According to the statistics of German immigration after 1857, we might expect about five thousand Germans in Renfrew around 1870. Yet the 1870-71 Census in fact accounted for only 2,318 Germans.

When German immigration suddenly declined sharply in 1865 as a result of the impact of the departure of the immigrants who had foundered, the immigration agency in Ottawa in its official report hurried to refute the rumors that, without exception, the Germans in Renfrew were not doing well and that they had departed in large numbers.[173] Actually the situation of those who stuck it out in Renfrew thus far did become more hopeful as a result of good crops. The memory of the first failures, nevertheless, remained alive for a long time.[174] The cessation of the direct emigrant traffic by boat between Hamburg-Bremen and Quebec in 1871 made a large-scale German immigration to the Ottawa Valley impossible. Yet in the 1870s an additional 1,694 new German immigrants passed through the Ottawa agency, probably mostly relatives and friends of those already in the Ottawa Valley.

From the end of the 1860s even the German settlements in Renfrew enjoyed a fairly regular development, so that 4,831 Germans by origin could be counted there in 1880-81. Yet conditions in the Ottawa were still anything but rosy. As soon as the Canadian prairies and northern Ontario were opened up for settlement, a migration from the Ottawa to these areas became noticeable. At the same time, those Germans who stayed behind made greater efforts than before to fill the vacant farms in their neighborhood with their friends and relatives from Germany.[175] Immigration to the Ottawa Valley thus began again to increase, and 3,409 German newcomers were counted from 1881 to 1891. When the Canadian prairies became the focus of immigration at the beginning of the 1890s, it no longer seemed to be worthwhile after 1892 even to register the immigration to the Ottawa Valley. The number of Germans barely increased from that time on. Their sons now also followed the tide to the West. The census registered in Renfrew County:

1901	9,041 Germans by origin
1911	9,463 Germans by origin
1921	9,429 Germans by origin

According to map 24 of the *Atlas of Canada* of 1915, which depicts the results of the 1911 Census, Germans were in the majority in a broad stretch of land from around Petawawa in the north to the Arnprior-Eganville railway line, as well as south of Eganville and from Golden Lake in a narrower coherent tract of settlement to the southwest corner of the county.[176] In the southeast around the community of Renfrew the Irish element was already predominant at that time.

It is significant that the number registered in 1911 did not decline after the World War, whereas elsewhere in Ontario the numbers for 1921 reached an unnaturally low level as Germans no longer dared to admit their identity under the impact of the wartime oppressions.

The center of the German settlements is still in the north in Alice, Wilberforce and Algona Townships to this day. In the north, in Pembroke, the only small German newspaper on the Ottawa River, the *Deutsche Post*, appeared until 1914.[177] The only change since 1900 among the Germans of this area has been the transformation of a population consisting exclusively of farmers into one that is found increasingly in the towns of Pembroke, Arnprior, Eganville, etc.

Until 1914 the Germans all over Renfrew County appear to have had their own private schools, in which German was taught in addition to English, the language of instruction.[178] The World War abruptly ended this development as it did almost everywhere in Canada.

Except for the Catholic Kashubs, most of the immigrants from Germany were Protestants. Usually they formed local parishes soon after their arrival.[179] According to the 1911 Census 5,504 of the 9,453 Germans by origin still called themselves Lutheran. It appears that in the meantime some had joined the Methodists and Presbyterians.

At this point a few observations about the spiritual care among the German-Canadian Protestants would be in order. Canada was seen as a natural missionary field by the various Protestant synods in the United States. The churches in Germany, which had been providing invaluable services to Germans in other lands such as Brazil, never attempted to supply pastors to Canada from Germany. If the Lutheran Canada Synod, which separated in 1861 from the German-American Pittsburg Synod, had not constantly drawn a part of their clergy from the number of missionaries trained at the Theological Seminary in Kropp (Schleswig) no pastors from Germany would have served over here at all. The German-American ministers, however, who themselves often knew little about Germany, and in many instances had been anglicized to a high degree, could not play the same role with regard to preserving the German heritage of their congregations as the clergy from Germany were able to do among different groups of Germans

in other lands. This fact should, of course, in no way minimize the
self-sacrifice of innumerable German-American pastors for the preservation of the inherited faith and ethnic traditions among their German-
Canadian congregations. In eastern Canada, mainly in Ontario, Protestant ministers of German descent constituted virtually the only clergy
of the above-mentioned Canada Synod, as well as of the strictly Lutheran Missouri Synod and the dogmatically less rigorous so-called Evangelical Church. On the Canadian prairies it is the Manitoba Synod
(the sister organization of the Lutheran Canada Synod in eastern
Canada), the Missouri Synod and the Lutheran Ohio Synod, plus a
number of less dogmatic churches who send their clergy to the German congregations.[180]

Today there are three German Lutheran pastors in Renfrew County
(two from the Missouri, one from the Canada Synod) in Pembroke,
two in Eganville (one from the Missouri, one from the Canada Synod),
and one each in Petawawa and Rankin (from the Canada Synod) and
in Palmer Rapids and Golden Lake (from the Missouri Synod). In addition to these, the Evangelical Church maintains two pastors in Pembroke and one each in Arnprior and Golden Lake.[181] All of these also
serve as itinerant preachers for the scattered German groups in the wider
area around them.

In the city of Ottawa itself, the stopover for all German immigrants
to the Ottawa district, a German colony also developed in the 1860s.
As in Montreal, it founded a German Society in 1872 for the support
of German immigrants.[182] The German colony was still small at that
time (1871: 179; 1881: 340 Germans), but it grew with the rising importance of Ottawa as the capital of the Dominion, to 1,248 by 1901, 1,482
by 1911 and even to 2,005 persons by 1921. The present German clergy
consists of two pastors of the Lutheran Missouri Synod, whose parishes maintain two fully certified private schools for the German
children.[183]

Finally, the small German villages should be mentioned, which developed in the adjacent Denbigh and Abinger Townships of Addington
County, and the Miller and Clarendon Townships of Frontenac County
simultaneously with, but independently of, the German settlements
in Renfrew.[184] Being only in casual contact with the larger villages in
Renfrew through the itinerant Lutheran pastor, the numerically weak
Germans in this remote district have been entirely anglicized by their
neighbors in the meantime.

CHAPTER III

Little Germanies in Nineteenth-Century Southwestern Ontario

1. The Niagara District

In the western part of the province, just as in eastern Ontario, the history of the German element begins with the oldest permanent settlement as such. The Loyalist regiment under Colonel Butler (Butler's Rangers), which like Johnson's regiment contained quite a few Palatines from the State of New York,[1] had its fixed quarters in Fort Niagara during the war. In order to reduce his dependence on the contingencies of the shipment of provisions, Butler as early as 1780 ordered some of his farmer-soldiers who had become disabled to settle with their families on the opposite, Canadian bank of the Niagara and to supply the garrison with grain.[2] By 1783, forty-six families lived in the young settlement, ten of whom had undoubtedly German names.[3] The soil turned out to be of such high quality on this site that the great majority of Butler's officers and men, with many Palatines among them, also chose to settle there after their discharge in June 1784.[4] The settlement, which numbered 620 persons, including women and children,[5] was named Queenston as a counterpart to Kingston which was established simultaneously on the Bay of Quinte.[6]

Queenston did not remain the only colony at the Niagara for long. Since it was the Canadian district closest to Pennsylvania, respectable young colonies of fleeing Loyalists and voluntary emigrants from the American states were soon to be found in the entire Niagara district. Among these, the first Germans that we know about were a group of

○○○
○○○   areas originally settled
○○○   predominantly by Germans

Mennonites from Bucks County, Pennsylvania, who settled in 1786 at Twenty Mile Creek in Louth and Clinton Townships in present-day Lincoln County.[7] According to a note by a contemporary traveller on the Moravians (with whom the Mennonites were frequently confused) in the Niagara district, a large immigration was expected as early as 1791.[8] Yet the large Mennonite migrations from Pennsylvania to Ontario did not begin until the turn of the century. Governor Simcoe (1791-1796) encouraged immigration from the United States, and expressly guaranteed exemption from military service to Quakers and Mennonites, whose exemption privilege was threatened there.[9] Yet when, in the spring of 1795, two agents from Pennsylvania requested the allotment of six adjoining townships, most likely in the Niagara district, for a large-scale settlement of Pennsylvania-Mennonites who had been considering the idea of emigrating since the end of the war, he reneged.[10] Excessively large closed colonies occupied by settlers of foreign descent were to be avoided.

What would not succeed collectively was tried individually. From 1796 on we find German families from Pennsylvania, predominantly Mennonites it seems,[11] scattered in the townships of Bertie, Humberstone, Wainfleet and Willoughby, where many of the Loyalist officers were beginning to divide their large estates of free land into individual farms and sell them.[12]

The Mennonites, who had been settling in Louth and Clinton since 1786, received a new influx of friends from Bucks County in 1799 and 1800.[13] This marked the beginning of the regular Mennonite immigration to Ontario which, after 1805, received a quite unexpected boost as a result of a favorable land purchase at the Grand River (Waterloo and Woolwich).[14] Meanwhile, the Mennonite colonies which developed in the Niagara district did not serve merely as a resting place and stopover for the coreligionists migrating to the Grand River,[15] but they themselves continued for decades to attract large groups of new immigrants, Mennonites and other Pennsylvania-Germans. It was not until that time that these colonies acquired their large German population. New villages were appearing in various townships of the Niagara district. Around 1820, according to Gourlay's incomplete records,[16] there were—apart from Clinton and Louth where Jacob Moyer, elected elder (bishop) in 1807,[17] was preaching—additional Mennonite preachers and congregations in the townships of Humberstone, Crowland and Thorold (in present-day Welland County), Grimsby and Caistor (in present-day Lincoln County) and even in Canboro on the lower Grand River (in Haldimand County).[18] By the end of the 1820s the Mennonites appeared to have advanced across the Grand River as far as the townships of Dunn, Rainham, Cayuga and Walpole in Haldimand County; they were not to be found further west at Lake Erie. Then, however, the Mennonite immigration was declining considerably, while simultaneously, starting around 1830, the first new immigrants coming directly from Germany could be traced in the Niagara district. We pointed out before that the immigrants from Germany settled initially only where German-speaking Mennonite settlements already existed. Here among fellow Germans in the Niagara district, and to an even greater degree in Waterloo, getting accustomed to the new conditions appeared easier.

In the three decades before 1860 at least 2,500 immigrants from Germany settled in the Niagara district.[19] Several hundred appear to have joined them in the 1860s and 1870s. They scattered in small groups across all the townships. In particular they settled in the border districts of Welland County immediately after entering Canadian territory—almost all of them came via New York—or in the districts on the lower Grand River, primarily in Rainham and Cayuga, which had been opened to settlement shortly before 1830. At first, Catholic immigrants from western and southern Germany appear to have predominated; soon however the Lutherans increased in proportion, as in Waterloo.[20] By the mid-1840s the German colonies, in which Mennonites, Pennsylvania-German Lutherans as well as Lutheran and Catholic immigrants from Germany had settled side by side, had grown quite respectably. Loeher reported that at that time "Clinton, Louth, St. Catherines, Niagara were very heavily populated with Germans, and Rainham, Stonybridge, Black Creek (Welland) and Jordan (Lincoln) represented the names of small German settlements (1847)."[21] Due to their extremely high birth rate—with their proverbial large families the Mennonites were, numerically speaking, still the leading element—and as a result of constant German immigration from the United States and Germany, the population of German descent in the Niagara district numbered 20,159 by 1870. Consequently it formed more than one-quarter of the total population.[22]

At that time Germans had the absolute majority in the townships of Bertie and Humberstone (and almost in Willoughby) in Welland County, in the townships of Clinton and Louth in Lincoln County, in the townships of Gainsborough and Canboro in Monck County and in the townships of Rainham and South Cayuga in Haldimand

County.[23] In most of the others they formed significant majorities. The influx had reached its peak.

By 1881 their number had increased only to 22,665, which means a splintering away and weakening had already begun. The main reason for this was the lack of German ministers to help retain the particular German denomination of the congregations, and thus their ethnic heritage as well. In contrast to the Germans in Waterloo and in the Huron district, those in the Niagara district had obviously been neglected, although their ethnic heritage was particularly jeopardized because of their wider spatial dispersal. They should therefore have required even more attention. When the few German Catholic priests of Waterloo County, because of the growing size of their own parishes, discontinued their visits to the German Catholics in the Niagara district after the beginning of the 1860s,[24] these people were compelled to join the neighboring Irish congregations. Many Lutherans, on the other hand, due to the lack of pastors of their own, joined the Methodists and Presbyterians. Of particular importance, however, is the fact that the Mennonites, as their younger generations grew up, could retain only a small part of their inherited denominational customs with all their anachronisms. With their adaptation to the dominant English civilization, their German identity would be lost as well.[25] Thus, by 1871 and 1881 the followers of the two specifically German denominations, the Mennonites and Lutherans, together comprised a mere quarter of all those who reported themselves as German by origin.

In the constantly growing population the number of Germans did not increase after 1881, nor did the number of those who in the census identified themselves as German by origin decline noticeably. In 1901 there were 19,611, in 1911 there were still 19,329 of them.[26] The people of German descent still have an absolute majority in the townships of Bertie, Humberstone, Willoughby (Welland) and Rainham (Haldimand).[27] The undiminished retention of the German tradition, if not of German ethnic identity, made sense only if the German language was still spoken at home to a certain extent. Whether German language instruction in the public and private schools among the Germans in the Niagara district was partially responsible for delaying the process of anglicization is not quite clear. In the early years German schools had existed here too.[28] The school laws of Ontario, which were quite generous to the French and German minorities,[29] would have permitted sufficient German instruction until 1890, if not until the World War. Yet this freedom, which was not even fully utilized by the Germans in Waterloo, was even less likely taken advantage of here and English schools were probably the rule.

Of German newspapers there was only the weekly *Deutscher Telegraph* which started publication in Welland in 1885 but did not survive beyond 1905.[30]

After the World War, 10,090 still called themselves German by origin in the Niagara district, according to the 1921 Census.[31] The situation of these last defenders of the German heritage, if they should at all nourish the desire for a cultural life of their own, is hopeless. Their absorption by the English is not far off. The few German clergymen who still work among them in 1930, two Lutheran pastors in Port Colborne (one Missouri Synod, one Canada Synod) and one each in St. Catherines, Humberstone and Fisherville near Rainham (Missouri Synod), as well as the two pastors of the Evangelical Church in Selkirk near Rainham and Attercliffe (Canboro Township)[32] discontinued services exclusively in German a long time ago.

2. Waterloo County

Here we are dealing with the core area of the Germans in Ontario. From the very beginning, as we saw, Germans participated in the opening up of the young province. More important, however, is the fact that Germans were also the first to penetrate decisively into the interior of the country. Until 1800, large settlements had remained confined to the shore districts of Lake Ontario and Lake Erie, the banks of the St. Lawrence and the Niagara. Dundas near Hamilton extended the farthest to the northwest. From this point in 1800, two Mennonite families advanced in true pioneer spirit and under great difficulties—they had to cross a large area of swamp—to the Grand River, thus laying the foundation for the German stronghold in Ontario, Waterloo County.[33]

After the end of the war in 1783 the area of the Grand River from its source to its mouth had been granted to the "Six Nations," i.e. the Indians who had fought on the English side under their Chief Brant, and who were not permitted to return to their land in New York State. At that time the Grand River district was one of the most densely forested terrains of Canada and rather useless for the primitive agricul-

Waterloo County

ture of the Indians. The Mohawks were therefore not satisfied. In order to get his hands on some money, Brant soon tried to sell parts of the land. His people were supposed to withdraw deeper into the virgin forests.[34] The government, however, had reasons for wanting the Indians to lease their land but not to sell it. It wanted to prevent the exploitation of the Indians by land speculators and, on the other hand, not to hinder colonization of the area in view of the unforeseen rapid population increase, while retaining some influence of its own.[35] It was eventually agreed that three officials of the colonial government should sell the large southern part of the reservation on behalf of the Indians, and administer the proceeds. Out of this the sustenance of the Indians, whose way of earning their living was no longer viable under the changed circumstances, would be defrayed. However, in 1798 only that which later became Waterloo Township could be sold to three newly-rich speculators by the names of Beasley, Wilson and Rousseau. According to the terms of the sale, part of the purchase sum was a mortgage administered with the government officials as trustees.[33] Beasley took it upon himself to procure settlers for the land purchased. But just as everyone had cheated the Indians with the purchase of land until the Colonial Government intervened, so Beasley tried to do in the sale to a few Mennonites. Respect for the law has never been very great in young colonies, especially when one is in the middle of the virgin forest far from any authority. Only this can make one understand how Beasley who, as a member of the provincial legislature was in danger of losing a certain reputation, could sell the land to the Mennonites who were strong in faith but inexperienced in worldly matters, without saying one word about his two co-owners or the mortgage.[37]

About twenty Mennonite families had already settled on their apparently indisputable property at the Grand River,[38] when in 1803 one of them accidentally learned in York (Toronto) of the mortgage which was still on the land, and thus of Beasley's fraud. Great consternation and discouragement![39] Eventually, by an agreement, the sixty thousand acres of present day Waterloo Township were to be acquired by the Mennonites with full title, provided they could repay the mortgage. In their distress the Mennonites turned to their wealthier Pennsylvanian brethren, and the money was actually raised. To assist their friends, and convinced of the quality of the soil, the Mennonites of Lancaster County set up a company which bought the land for £10,000 in June 1805.[40] Only then did Mennonites come in large numbers,

and not only those who had a share in the purchase and who in spite
of the high total price had gotten a cheap deal and now wanted to
take possession of their land. The unusual purchase had made the Grand
River district famous among Mennonites all over Pennsylvania, and
their covered wagons kept converging on Ontario from all parts of the
state.[41] In the final analysis, it was Beasley's fraudulent scheme which
became the immediate cause of the rapid and almost exclusively German settlement of the central Grand River Valley.

In 1807 the Mennonites set up a second company and purchased
a large tract adjoining it, almost as large, namely present-day Woolwich Township.[42] What they failed to achieve in negotiations with
Simcoe in 1795 they now obtained anyway through purchase. They
occupied a large coherent area for the establishment of a closed Mennonite colony whose acreage was sufficient to meet the needs of even
their children and children's children. The second purchase demonstrated clearly the land hunger of the wholly agriculturally-oriented
Mennonites. Without hesitation, they secured for themselves an area
that they would be able to cultivate only after decades. The individual
family head calculated the same way. He, too, bought as much land
as he could in order to be able to divide it up among sons and grand-
sons or to be able to sell it profitably as its value went up. This is the
reason why, by the beginning of the 1820s, almost all the land in Waterloo and Woolwich was divided up and the formerly substantial immigration of Mennonites declined. Unlike the later, much poorer immigrants
from Germany, the Mennonites were not content with smaller lots of
land.[43] Yet they kept arriving on a smaller scale until 1835, and even
beyond that time.

Not much can be said about the first years of settlement. When
war broke out again with the United States in 1812, the English colonial
government was prudent enough not to provoke the Mennonites by
expecting military services from them, although the younger Mennonites, because of Canada's manpower shortage, had to be used as
wagon drivers.[44] Otherwise the war passed them by without any lasting effects. Surrounded on all sides by virgin forest, they lived in complete seclusion from the outside world for the time being. The political
events of the day remained unknown to them. Apart from their religious activities, they cared only for their farms with which they succeeded here, as everywhere, in an exemplary way. They lived under
a kind of theocracy. Their spiritual head was the young bishop Benjamin Eby.

Eby, born in 1785, had come over with several relatives and friends from Lancaster County (Hammer Creek, Warwick Township) in 1807. The small hamlet that they founded was named Ebytown after its largest family.[45] Because Eby, who was elected preacher in 1809 and elder in 1812, had his estate there,[46] Ebytown became the center of the entire township. In 1826 it was named Berlin.[47] It grow slowly, became the county seat of Waterloo County in 1852, and the cultural center of the Germans in western Ontario in general.

Around 1820, 858 persons lived on 138 farmsteads in Waterloo County.[48] The time when the Mennonites were entirely among themselves, and their community could be characterized as a kind of theocracy, came to an end. The settlement by Scots of Dumfries Township, adjoining to the south, began. Some of these Scottish settlers would also settle in Waterloo in the years to come. From 1820 on, the first immigrants from Germany, mostly craftsmen, appeared in the larger villages of Berlin, Waterloo and Preston.[49] It was a strange coincidence that the first large group of immigrants from Germany who acquired land in the neighborhood of Waterloo Township, was also Mennonite, namely the Amish.

The Amish, named according to their founder Jacob Amman from Bern, formed the most conservative group among the Mennonites. Opposed to all material luxuries as traps of the devil, they refused even to wear buttons. This became the main mark of distinction. As the incorruptible *Haftler* (i.e., those using hooks and eyes), they contrasted themselves with the majority of the Mennonites as the *Knöpfler* (button-wearers), whom they suspected of worldly aspirations. As true Mennonites, the Amish remained constantly on the move. From Switzerland, their original homeland, they had moved to the Alsace and to the Palatinate. From there they all came to join the Mennonites in Pennsylvania in the years after 1820. Our group, led by their elder Christian Nachtsinger, or Naffziger as most sources spell his name, believed that they would obtain better conditions in the vicinity of their coreligionists in western Ontario. After negotiations with the Canadian government, a large coherent tract in Wilmot Township west of Waterloo in the area of the settlement later to be New Hamburg was allotted to them. Here they settled in 1823.[50] So they became the first settlers of Wilmot, which together with Wellesley Township, that was not yet surveyed, was to be settled by many new immigrants from Germany during the following decade.

The Mennonites of Waterloo and Woolwich had realized for quite some time, albeit reluctantly, that the natural development of their two townships was seriously hampered by the shortage of labor.[51] As long as the influx of mostly wealthy Mennonites had continued, who bought more property than they could farm for some time to come, this shortage became more and more acute. In spite of this, Scots and English were consistently excluded for linguistic reasons. When in the 1820s, however, immigrants from Germany arrived in western Ontario, the Mennonites attempted to draw them to their highly developed farms as day laborers, or at least as neighbors in Waterloo and Woolwich, by selling them small and cheap parcels of land. They hoped by this to increase the value of their otherwise exemplary farms. The immigrants, at the same time, were motivated by the natural desire for the greater economic and cultural security afforded by the company of fellow Germans whose language they shared. The historical significance of the Mennonite colony at the Grand River, as indicated in chapter I, lies in its ability to attract the considerable immigration from Germany from the very beginning. Only by isolating themselves from British immigrants, which the Mennonites were able to do as the owners of the entire tract of land until the 1850s, were the colonists able to establish the prerequisites for a large closed area of German settlement. There would not have been such a large number of Germans available for the settlement of the Huron Tract either[52], had not the two Mennonite townships at the Grand River and the steadily growing German colonies in their neighborhood constantly attracted new German immigrants. Here, as farmhands, they could earn, within a few years, some money which would enable them to take up cheap virgin land further northwest.

In order to avoid getting stuck as a day laborer and small craftsman among the Mennonites, it was advisable, after acquiring the necessary agricultural experience on the Mennonite farms, to purchase one's land in Wilmot and Wellesley Townships immediately to the west.[53] Wilmot and Wellesley, which after 1850 were united with Waterloo and Woolwich and with North Dumfries Township that was settled by Scots, soon, like the two Mennonite townships themselves, had a predominantly German population as well.

By 1848 more than nine thousand German immigrants from Germany lived in these four townships, while more than fifteen hundred had moved on to the Huron Tract and taken up farming mainly in Perth County.[54]

Until then the German immigrants from Europe were mostly

Catholics from southwestern Germany and Alsace. After the 1850s, the immigrants from the Lutheran regions of central and northern Germany definitely formed the largest numbers. From the beginning, Catholics and Lutherans settled side by side in all four German townships of Waterloo County, although from the early years there were also denominationally separated group settlements. Thus, Catholics are found in large numbers particularly in the northeast of Waterloo Township, in New Germany and vicinity, west of Berlin between Rummelhart and St. Agatha (Wilmot) and in a wide area around this settlement.[55] The Lutherans had formed their own congregations by the end of the 1840s in Preston, Waterloo (Waterloo Township), New Hamburg, Phillipsburg, Mannheim (Wilmot Township) and Heidelberg (Woolwich Township).[56]

In the years after 1848 when the total emigration from Germany reached its peak due to the political and economic consequences of revolution, German immigration to the Waterloo district continued unabated, and perhaps was even stronger.[57] Thus a certain congestion occurred by as early as the mid-1850s. The new immigrant had difficulty finding employment. This is proven by the success that the Canadian immigration agencies finally had in diverting some German immigrants to Renfrew County.[58]

The glut was bound to occur in view of the constant influx since the purely rural and agricultural character of the area had not yet changed. In Waterloo and Woolwich, development was artificially held back by the Mennonites, who opposed the creation of large towns on principle and would not release their land for that purpose.[59] Even Berlin was still a village of only 750 inhabitants by 1850.[60] Only its promotion to county seat in 1852 provided the incentive for a more rapid development. The German immigrants from Germany, to be sure, had introduced the first economic diversification. Besides having their own farms, they continued to practice their crafts or trades and worked as shoemakers, tailors, masons, innkeepers, small merchants, etc., in the surrounding area.[61] Yet their activities were entirely confined to the context of the rural village economy. The Mennonites, by contrast, had produced all the necessities of life on their own farms.

For these small settlers, who besides the occasional work in their old trade were also largely dependent on employment as farmhands in the summer and as forest workers in the winter, the situation became more difficult with the continuing influx of newcomers. The introduction of the first agricultural machines and the disappearance of the forest made their labor increasingly expendable as well. Therefore, not only did migration into the region come to a halt but, on the contrary, since there was no small town in Waterloo County capable of development, a strong outward migration from Waterloo took place. The newly opened districts at the Saugeen in the north of the Huron Tract in the later Bruce and Grey Counties were the goal of this emigration from the end of the 1850s to the end of the 1860s. This diminished the German population in Waterloo by thousands.[62] The "Saugeen Fever" seized far more German small farmers than had been compelled to migrate as a result of the economic development. The gaps which thus developed could not be filled again by new German immigrants. They, by the way, came in much smaller numbers to western Ontario in the 1860s and appeared now to go directly to Grey and Bruce Counties.[63] At the same time, an increasing number of Scots, English and Irish penetrated the four formerly predominantly German townships of Waterloo, Woolwich, Wellesley[64] and Wilmot, reducing, according to the 1870-71 Census, the number of Germans to slightly more than two-thirds of the total population.[65]

In the 1870s the population of Waterloo grew only minimally.[66] Its surplus was still migrating to Grey and Bruce Counties or to the United States.[67] Only after 1880 did the population begin to increase more rapidly. After the county was connected to the railway line, industry developed and agriculture was strengthened by access to new markets. By 1901 the number of Germans who were still primarily engaged in agriculture, as compared to the British, who were mostly businessmen or industrial workers, had increased to three-quarters of the total population in the four main townships, excluding the Scottish North Dumfries.[68]

In the industrial development of Waterloo, German entrepreneurship also played a part. Due to the lack of communications, development remained on a modest scale.[69] Hamilton surpassed Berlin by far, for instance. As the largest town in the county, Berlin still had barely fifteen thousand inhabitants by 1911.

The most well-known German businessman who came from Waterloo County was Sir Adam Beck (born in 1857 in Baden, Wilmot Township; died in 1925). He and his fellow Germans, Snider, Breithaupt and Detweiler, were the first to plan the utilization of the enormous resources of Ontario's hydro power for the production of energy. He created the monopoly of the Hydro-Electric Power Commission of Ontario, and thereby prevented the supply of electric energy from becoming a purely capitalistic enterprise. He is, in fact, the only German in Canada who has made history. He became famous as the "hydro power king" and, in recognition for his services to the Canadian economy, was knighted by King George V in 1914.[70]

With regard to the preservation of their ethnic heritage, the Germans of Waterloo distinguished themselves from all other districts of German settlement in the old Canadian east in two significant respects: their successful advocacy of German instruction, even in public schools, and their creation of an active German-language press.

There were no standard guidelines regarding school attendance in Ontario until 1850. As everywhere in the province, Mennonites, German Catholics and Lutherans had established separate schools in Waterloo, for religious rather than national reasons, wherever they could gather sufficient numbers of pupils. Three Acts from the early 1850s recognized all religious separate schools as equivalent to the public schools, with the same guidelines applying to the language question as in the public non-denominational schools.[71]

For the latter, which, as in all the English-speaking countries, were administered by a board of local taxpayers, the 1851 Act provided, with regard to the teachers' qualifications, that a knowledge of French or German could be substituted for a knowledge of English.[72] That meant that in all the areas where Germans represented the majority of the taxpayers, unilingual German teachers could be employed, and German could be used as the language of instruction as a matter of course. This may actually have been the practice even before 1851 here and there in Waterloo County and in other German districts. But cases are also known, as for instance in South Easthope (Perth County) in 1848, where the German teacher was no longer paid from the funds set aside for school purposes on the grounds that he was a foreigner, and German schoolbooks were suppressed.[73] Such incidents were no longer possible after 1851.

Despite their freedom to choose German teachers, a right which was expressly confirmed again in 1858 and 1870,[74] the Germans, in contrast to the French, almost always desired, for economic reasons, that their children learn sufficient English in addition to their mother tongue even when frequently only German could be taught due to a lack of bilingual teachers.[75] When the Germans of Waterloo County were also granted, in response to their request, a special inspector for their schools in 1872, their national self-determination in school issues was in fact complete.[76] Bilingual instruction with increasing emphasis on English nevertheless remained the rule.[77]

When, however, the principle of nationality came to dominate European political thought, the days of this generous policy towards minorities in Ontario were numbered as well. While the School Act of 1890 did not yet make English the only language of instruction, as the Liberals demanded at the time, it did become a compulsory subject in all schools. In areas with a French or German majority, French or German could be added as supplementary subjects, with one of these languages being permitted only in the primary grades and, only if absolutely essential, as a language of instruction in the other subjects.[78]

While the French, who were backed by the Province of Quebec, fought for many years with the government over the language question, the Germans did not raise any serious objections against the incisive changes of 1890. Many of their schools had for some time voluntarily moved towards conditions of instruction that were similar to those now required by law.[79] Isolated as they were, the language could not become a question of political power for them. In addition, many German parents welcomed a stronger emphasis on English, since they considered the use of German in the family as sufficient for the purpose of learning the mother tongue. In response to pressure from English teachers, increasingly fewer people sent their children to the still-permitted German classes, a development which the foundation of German school associations in places like Berlin and Waterloo was partly able to reverse at the beginning of this century.[80]

The general anglicization could by that time, however, no longer be halted. The loss of German schooling after 1890 very soon made English the language of everyday life among the young generation, and relegated German to the language spoken at home. The daily half-hour of German in German supplementary classes of course, made no difference.[81] The beginning of the defection from their ethnic heritage became manifest for the first time in the relative decline of the number of "Germans by origin" in the 1911 Census.[82] The World War, with its hate propaganda against everything German, brought this development to a head and completely undermined the German heritage. In Canada this propaganda was immediately put into the service of the long-pursued efforts towards assimilation, and was therefore bound to hit hardest the German stronghold in Waterloo County. The German population, whose loyalty to Canada no one could seriously doubt, was systematically intimidated through acts of mob violence, and economically harmed in a most serious manner. They had to put up without protest with the scornful renaming of their main town Berlin as Kitchener, they had to suspend publication of the last German newspaper in Ontario and finally had to renounce the hour of German instruction left to them in public schools.[83] The most depressing spectacle, however, was provided by a certain segment that had already become so completely anglicized that, in response to British war propaganda, they volunteered as soldiers, many of them sealing their loyalty to Canada on the battlefields of France with their deaths, while fighting against the land of their ancestors.[84]

According to the 1921 Census, which fully reflected the impact of the catastrophic World War, 34,637 people still called themselves German by origin in Waterloo County. Yet, in relation to the considerably increased total population, this meant a decisive decline.[85] More important, however, was the fact that in Kitchener, as everywhere in Ontario, only slightly more than half the Germans by origin indicated that they were still able to speak their German mother tongue besides English.[86] Since there is no hope of a reopening of German school classes, it might take no more than twenty or thirty years till the German language is replaced everywhere, even in the family, by English.

About the German newspapers in Waterloo County we have only incomplete information. Until the World War these appeared in increasingly large numbers, even though in small and usually weekly editions. They had subscribers within a wide area including the Germans of the other counties of southwestern Ontario.

The first German-language newspaper that was printed in Canada appeared in Berlin as early as August 27, 1835 under the title of *Canada Museum und Allgemeine Zeitung.*[87]

It was printed partly in English, but for the most part in German, and was read by German farmers in a wide area.[88] In 1839 the second paper appeared, *Der Morgenstern*, in the small neighboring town of Waterloo.[89] They merged in 1841 and were published in a larger format under the name *Der Deutsche Canadier.*[90] Besides this newspaper, which was published in Berlin, the *Hamburger Beobachter* was launched in 1848 in New Hamburg, was renamed *Neu-Hamburger Neutrale* in 1852 and appeared weekly after 1854 as *Canadisches Volksblatt*. Furthermore, there is *Der Canadische Bauernfreund* which appeared in 1849 in Preston, then the largest town in Waterloo County. This paper was moved to Waterloo in 1854.[91] Replacing *Der Deutsche Canadier*, the *Berliner Journal* was founded in December 1859 in Berlin.[92] In 1875 it had a circulation of 1,620[93] which later increased. In the course of time it absorbed a number of smaller papers, including the two oldest, the *Canadisches Volksblatt* in New Hamburg and *Der Canadische Bauernfreund* in Waterloo, in 1909. During the World War it appeared under the plain name of *Journal* as the last significant German paper in Ontario. When it was prohibited in 1918 it reappeared transformed into the English-language *Ontario Journal*.[94]

The following additional newspapers existed for a short time: (1) the *Anzeiger*, launched in Elmira in 1870 with a circulation of only about three hundred (no trace of it appears after 1888),[95] (2) the *Deutsche Zeitung*, founded in Berlin in 1891, which due to a decline in subscribers merged shortly before the war with the *Journal*[96], and (3) five Lutheran parish papers. One of these appeared under the name of *Canadischer Evangelist* at the beginning of the 1870s in Preston.[97] The remaining four were published in Berlin as *Lutherisches Volksblatt* (founded in 1871, bi-monthly, folded before 1905),[98] *Evangeliums Panier* (founded 1879 by Detweiler, bi-weekly),[99] which appeared to continue after 1890 as *Evangeliums Bote*[100] and *Lutherischer Friedensbote* (founded 1884, appeared monthly, verified for 1895, but folded before 1905).[101]

No matter how petit bourgeois and provincial was the character of these newspapers, they did fulfill their duty to report about events in Germany and so at least kept the interest in the homeland alive to a certain extent.[102] It is deeply regrettable that after the wartime experiences no one in Waterloo was able to muster the courage and inner strength, and many did not even appear any longer to feel the urge, to launch a newspaper again for the Germans of Ontario. In western Canada, by contrast, such papers have been launched in increasing numbers, particularly since the war. The cultivation of any cultural relations, which undoubtedly still exist, with the German fatherland has become very difficult if not impossible in eastern Canada.

In conclusion, a few words about church life. This has always been important in the preservation of the German ethnic heritage, since the foundation of German separate schools went hand in hand with the formation of church congregations of Mennonites, Lutherans and Catholics. Even later, when English was made the language of instruction by law for all nondenominational as well as separate schools, supplementary classes were set up among the Mennonites and in many Lutheran congregations on Saturdays and Sundays, or during vacations under the direction of the clergy. Some of them still exist today. For the German minorities, interest in their church and in their ethnic heritage is unconsciously and closely associated.

This is especially true for the Mennonites who cannot imagine a church service in anything but their Palatine dialect. Their congregations, numbering about 850 Mennonites in 1820, and reinforced in 1823 by several hundred Amish,[103] increased in Waterloo to about five thousand members by 1860 in spite of constant small migrations to the Huron Tract. Suddenly, however, there was stagnation. Since then, only a few of the younger generation have retained their parents' faith, with its anachronistic views and old-fashioned customs.[104] Only since the beginning of the twentieth century has the number of Mennonites gone up again, which is due to the anglophone campaigns for linguistic assimilation in the schools and in public. Before this, most of the Mennonites who kept to the faith of their forefathers had also held on strongly to the German language for religious reasons. Now, the opposite occurred, and uniting to defend their German identity strengthened their religious cohesion, resulting in an increase of their numbers to 7,130 by 1921. Today, of course, they can all speak English. Yet the Mennonites of Waterloo, who today comprise more than half of all the Mennonites in Ontario,[106] represent that group of Germans which to this day desires most eagerly to retain their German traditions.

The majority of the Lutherans came between 1848 and 1860, although the first Lutheran congregations can be traced back to 1834.[107] The number of Lutherans, as with the Mennonites, did not grow in proportion to the increase of the total German population. Indifference which the immigrants brought with them from liberal mid-nineteenth century Germany towards church problems in general, a shortage of pastors, and the splintering into several conflicting Lutheran synods, are responsible for the fact that the number of Lutherans barely increased by the beginning of the twentieth century.[108] While the Mennonites lost members to other sects, particularly to the Baptists, the Lutherans lost theirs primarily to the Methodists and Presbyterians, due to the similarity of their church services.[109] Since the turn of the century, however, the Lutherans have been more strongly allied for the same reasons of defense of their ethnic identity as the Mennonites, with the result of an increase in their numbers from 15,281 in 1911 to 16,236 in 1921. Today fifteen pastors of German descent in the Lutheran Canada Synod are serving in the county: three in Berlin-Kitchener, and one each in Waterloo, Preston, St. Jacobs, Heidelberg, New Hamburg, New Dundee, Linwood, Hespeler, Phillipsburg, Conestoga, Elmira and Galt. There are four pastors of the Lutheran Missouri Synod in Berlin-Kitchener, New Hamburg, Elmira and Wellesley, as well as nine pastors of the Evangelical Church[110] (two in Berlin-Kitchener, three in Waterloo, two in New Hamburg and one each in St. Jacobs and Elmira.)[111] Among these church bodies the Canada Synod, which as mentioned above always obtained some of its pastors from the Seminary for Missionaries in Kropp (Schleswig), has best preserved the German tradition,[112] especially in its rural congregations. Its St. Matthew's congregation in Berlin remained the only Lutheran congregation to retain German as the exclusive language of the church service until the World War.[113] Today, English has become the predominant language of the church services almost everywhere in Waterloo County. Yet to this day, in a very large number of congregations, German school classes are still being held on Saturdays and Sundays or in the summer vacations under the direction of the pastor. The pastors, in an almost hopeless situation, are thus still working for the retention of the German ethnic heritage with an admirable spirit of sacrifice. It is almost certain that the circle of those Germans, who by 1921 still knew their mother tongue, is roughly the same as the group of about seven thousand Mennonites and the approximately sixteen thousand Lutherans.[114] Only those who remained affiliated to these specifically German religious communities have, for the time being, escaped complete anglicization.

Initially, the Catholics, who until 1848 were more numerous than the Lutherans and Mennonites, had only priests of German descent in Waterloo.[115] As a result of emigration to the Saugeen starting in the 1850s their number declined considerably, while Irish and other English-speaking Catholics were constantly coming in, so that by and by the initially wholly German character of their congregations changed fundamentally. This exposed the German Catholics in Waterloo to the danger which German Catholic minorities faced, due to the supranational structure of their church, in all the countries that have Catholics among their dominant ethnic group. The priests, even if they were of German descent, were not permitted to cultivate particular ethnic groups at the expense of the unity of their congregation. The decisive anglicization of the German Catholics thus set in as early as the end of the nineteenth century. Today's priests, even if they have German names, and particularly the congregations themselves, as for example the New Germany parish, must be considered English-Canadian.

3. The Huron Tract

The so-called Huron Tract, that huge area of virgin forest to the west and north of the present Waterloo and Wellington Counties up to Lake Huron, had been turned over in 1825 to the Canada Land Company, which was headed by John Galt. In order to facilitate an early settlement, Galt had a road cut right across the virgin forest in 1828 which touched Lake Huron near the present-day town of Goderich.

By using a shrewd sales method, according to which no cash was required for the purchase of a piece of ground, but rather a commitment of labor by the individual, the company was able to get settlers quickly for its new territory.[116] The area was first opened up in a westerly direction as far as Lake Huron. By 1840 Perth and Huron Counties had a population of more than five thousand, by 1848 more than twenty thousand, and in 1851 nearly thirty-five thousand.[117] The mainstream of the newcomers then turned to the north into Bruce and Grey Counties.

One should not be surprised that, especially in the first years, German farmers played a prominent part in the opening up of the Huron Tract. Even later, when the vast majority of the immigrants were British, Germans kept arriving in such large numbers that fair-sized districts of closed German settlement arose over the entire area. The reason for this was simply the existence, in the immediate proximity of the Huron Tract, of the German settlements of Waterloo County, which as early as the 1830s and 1840s had become quite respectable in size. These constantly attracted new waves of German immigrants who, however, used them only as way stations for the acquisition of the necessary agricultural know-how and of a small operating capital until they could take up their own land in the far cheaper Huron Tract. For decades Waterloo County served as a reservoir of people for the German colonies in Perth, Huron, Bruce and Grey Counties.

Among the German settlements of Perth County, those near the border of Waterloo County were naturally the largest and most homogeneous ones. As the first settler of Perth,[118] the German-Swiss Sebastian Freyvogel took up residence at Christmas 1829 on the road that Galt had built in South Easthope Township, immediately adjacent to Wilmot.[119] On behalf of the Canada Land Company he erected an inn, which was to provide the first shelter for the expected immigrants.[120] By 1832 such a large number of German families had settled in his neighborhood, which was later named Sebastopol, that they formed a Lutheran congregation. It was served on a regular basis by Pastor Horn.[121] Starting in 1833 German Catholics also arrived in South Easthope.[122] In the south of the township, furthermore, Amish from nearby Wilmot settled.[123] Except for a few Scots who settled on the Huron road between Shakespeare and Stratford, all of South Easthope was colonized by Germans.[124] By 1840 it had a population of 389.[125] In 1842 the first school was set up, not surprisingly with a German teacher,[126] and by 1850 it was fully occupied.[127]

In the 1830s, when the settlement of Perth was still confined essentially to the tracts of land situated along the main road to Goderich, the German farmers seem to have formed the majority in most of the townships. At any rate, they were among the first pioneers in every settlement. When, however, in the wake of constantly increasing immigration, the land further away from the main road was settled, the Germans retained their numerical superiority only in South Easthope. In North Easthope, Ellice, Logan and Mornington Townships situated north of the Goderich road they formed minorities of quite respectable size. In the southern part of the county, in the townships of Downie, Fullarton, Hibbert and Blanchard, however, only relatively small German colonies developed.

Most of the Germans came to North Easthope between 1840 and 1850.[128] They settled immediately adjacent to the German settlements of Wilmot and Wellesley (Waterloo County). From 1868 on they maintained a German Lutheran church.[129]

The first settler of Ellice was the Bavarian Andreas Seebach, who took up land in 1830 at the highest point of Perth County, which was named Seebach's Hill after him. For the time being, all the Germans who followed him settled along the main road to Goderich. There, in 1835, at a site later named Sebringville after a German American, they founded the first Lutheran church, which like the one in South Easthope and in a few other early congregations, was served by a Reverend Horn.[130] The lands of Ellice situated further inland were also taken up largely by Germans in the 1840s.[131] Here the exclusively German towns of Rostock, the main settlement in the township, and Wartburg arose. Lutheran churches have been maintained in Wartburg since 1856, in Rostock since 1862.[132] The settlements of Brunner and Kuhryville were named after German pioneers. In the latter instance, as in others, the French ending of *-ville* in the naming of places in the early period is noticeable. The Germans of Ellice, in particular, appear to have distinguished themselves from their British neighbors by the lavish and pretentious layout of their farmsteads.[133]

Germans settled in Logan Township, particularly around the present-day sites of Brodhagen and Mitchell.[134] In Mornington Township they were found especially near Milverton.[135]

In the townships bordering to the south on the Huron road, namely, Downie, Fullarton, and Hibbert, Germans were also among the first pioneers in the 1830s. But later the influx of Germans ceased entirely. They were therefore to be found only near the main road, on those very sites where settlement had begun.[136] Blanchard Township at the southern end of Perth never had more than a few Germans.[137]

Summing up, we may quote Johnston: "This county was most fortunate in being located by people of British origin and Germans. A better class of bushmen could not be obtained from any other nationalities, and results afford ample evidence for the fact."[138]

According to the 1851 Census, there were 1,688 persons born in Germany who lived in the Huron Tract: 1,485 in Perth and 203 in Huron.[139] To these must be added several hundreds of German Americans, Mennonites and others. The few immigrants from Germany who were counted in Huron County at that time resided mostly in Hay and Stephen Townships. In Hay, ten German-Swiss families had settled as early as 1823. They had earlier sought their fortunes in vain in Selkirk's Red River colony in Manitoba, and named the district in Huron after their leader Christian Hay.[140] Here they founded the settlements of Zurich and Bern, and thus became perhaps the first permanent settlers in the entire Huron Tract. In the neighborhood of their colony which had grown in the meantime, several hundred Germans from Germany, and German Americans, among them Mennonites, settled about 1850. They did not come along the shore of Lake Huron as the first German-Swiss settlers did, but with the general stream of immigrants from the east, from Waterloo to Hay and adjacent Stephen Township.[141]

From the mid-1850s the German colonies that had developed in Perth and Huron Counties received no more reinforcements from new immigrations. In the townships surveyed so far, the land had already been taken up and the general immigration took a new turn to the north into the virgin forest region at the Saugeen, about whose fertility the most favorable stories were spread. The Germans in Waterloo who, as we saw, experienced a dismal lack of employment opportunities at that time, were gripped by a veritable emigration ecstasy as a result of the propagandistic portrayal of the paradise discovered at the

Saugeen. Starting in 1855 they moved by the hundreds and thousands to Grey and Bruce Counties. The new wave of migration was destined to lead to the settlement of the townships of Elma and Wallace north of Perth, Howick in Huron County and Marysburgh and Minto in Wellington County, all of which were along the route. German farmers have been there ever since.[142] From the first, however, the majority of the immigrants, and of the Germans in particular, proceeded further north.

It is interesting to observe how the Germans from nearby Waterloo County, in true pioneer spirit, were the first to take up land in the adjoining townships and set a permanent stamp upon them. This was the case in the opening up of Grey and Bruce Counties, just as it had been in the settlement of Perth County. Large-scale British immigration, on the other hand, began only later when the way had already been prepared by German pioneers. Due to its superiority in numbers however, the British character was impressed on all the remaining townships, and thereby on the county as a whole. In Grey and Bruce Counties, the Germans formed an absolute majority only in the two most southern townships, Carrick (Bruce) and Normanby (Grey). In the townships bordering to the north and adjacent to each other, Brant, Culross, Greenock (Bruce), Bentinck and Sullivan (Grey) they formed minorities of respectable size. The area of German settlement was therefore essentially large enough to retain its character as a German linguistic enclave to this day in spite of some assimilation.

The first Germans came to Carrick and Normanby at the beginning of the 1850s.[143] The majority followed between 1855 and 1870. In the course of the 1870s, the immigration from Waterloo and directly from Germany was again on the wane. According to the census the number of Germans in Bruce and Grey Counties rose to 6,400 and 4,702 respectively in 1871, and even to 9,627 and 6,992 respectively by 1881.[144] Their dreams, at least in part, came true. Most of the Germans had become quite wealthy farmers in the north.[145] The distinctive agricultural character of the German settlements has not changed to this day. Even the major settlements in which the religious life of the Germans has been concentrated, such as Hanover, Ayton, Neustadt, Desboro, Alsfeldt (Grey County), Mildmay, Walkerton, Elmwood and Chesley,[146] are to be characterized as no more than large villages or hamlets. The adherence to the farmer's way of life and the seclusion from the outside world that goes with it are the very reasons for the survival of the German language. In spite of English language instruction since 1900 in the schools in the southern parts of Bruce and Grey, German is still the everyday language in many places, especially around Ayton and Neustadt. Here the stranger is recognized by his use of English, as might also be the case only here and there in eastern Canada among the Germans along the Ottawa.

A survey of the numbers of persons of German descent in the four counties according to the various census reports is as follows:

County	1881	1901	1911	1921
Perth	10,131	11,540[147]	12,223	11,508
Huron	6,567	6,193[148]	5,954	4,948
Bruce	9,627	11,526	10,516	8,644
Grey	6,992	7,926	7,999	6,805

According to this, the anglicization of Germans and rejection of their heritage began in Huron County, where Germans settled together in large numbers only in Hay and Stephen Townships; otherwise, however, they were scattered into ethnic fragments over a huge area. The somewhat earlier decline of the number of Germans in Bruce County than in Grey County may be attributed to the fact that the Germans in Bruce County were predominantly Catholics, while those in Grey County were predominantly Protestants. The Catholics found much less support for the preservation of their ethnic heritage within their ecclesiastical organization, which lumped them together with the Irish, who happened to be very numerous, particularly in Bruce County. The ethnic situation was most favorable in the colonies in Perth, which together with Waterloo formed a uniform district of German settlement. The number of Germans grew steadily, in spite of a stagnation and even decline in the total population of Perth after 1881, while the younger generation joined the general migration to the urban centers, especially to Stratford, since the turn of the century.[149] The number of persons of German descent as shown in the 1921 Census dropped somewhat for the first time only due to the pressures caused by the World War.

With regard to the language question and the religious life, the same situation applied by and large to the German colonists in the four counties mentioned, as we were able to observe for Waterloo County. The same school conditions helped English to gain ground as a language of everyday life among the Germans here as well. Here, too, the war reduced German to the level of a family language which, apart from a few areas in Grey and Bruce, is only used in the home. The Protestant Synods are even more prominent in the very active church life of the area than in Waterloo. Everywhere their pastors held Saturday and Sunday German schools and continue, in part, to do so to this day. The Mennonites are less numerous, while the Catholic congregations lost their exclusive German character and their German priests some time ago.[150]

According to the list of German clergy in *Der Nordwesten-Kalender* for 1929, German Protestant pastors were still serving in the following settlements:

Perth County: (Canada Synod) Stratford, Tavistock, Listowel, Gadshill, Milverton and Bornholm; (Missouri Synod) Stratford, Wartburg, Mitchell and Gowanstown; (Evangelical Church) Tavistock, Shakespeare, Listowel, Milverton, Sebringville and Gowanstown.

Huron County: (Canada Synod) Zurich, Auburn; (Missouri Synod) Dashwood; (Evangelical Church) Zurich, Auburn, Dashwood and Crediton.

Bruce County: (Canada Synod) Walkerton, Chesley, Wiarton; (Evangelical Church) Mildmay-Walkerton, Elmwood, Chesley and Port Elgin. (The congregation there is very old. "Some of the first settlers in Port Elgin (Saugeen Township) were Germans from Waterloo."[151])

Grey County: (Canada Synod) Neustadt-Ayton, Hanover; (Missouri Synod) Ayton-Alsfeldt, Desborough; (Evangelical Church) Hanover, Ayton-Alsfeldt.

In addition, the Buffalo Synod, a small Lutheran Synod which was founded in 1845 by Prussian emigrants in Buffalo and which has only few footholds in Ontario, maintains pastors of German descent in Walkerton (Bruce County) and Neustadt and Hanover (Grey County).

Finally we will list the various German newspapers that were launched in Perth, Bruce and Grey Counties. All of these small local papers successfully competed in their neighborhood with the "major" German newspapers in Waterloo County, and helped to prevent on their part the rise of one big German paper which might have become possibly the mouthpiece, for instance in school questions, of all the Germans in southwest Ontario. In 1863 Jacob Teuscher launched *Der Canadische Kolonist* in Stratford (Perth County).[152] It appeared weekly until 1906, when it was bought by the owners of the *Berliner Journal* and was amalgamated with it.[153] In the 1870s, perhaps its heyday, it had a circulation of 1,024.[154] In Perth County were also published temporarily *Die Wespe* in Wartburg around 1870, [155] the *Perth Volks-freund* in Listowel in the 1880s,[156] and the *Lutherisches Volksblatt* which in the 1890s, perhaps only temporarily, was moved from Berlin to Sebringville.[157]

For the Germans in Grey and Bruce Counties, the *Wächter am Saugeen* appeared in Neustadt starting in 1868, and the *Ontario-Glocke* in Walkerton starting in 1869, each with an edition of five hundred copies.[158] In 1878 the *Ontario-Glocke* was bought up by the *Berliner Journal*.[159] However, it continued to appear independently in Walkerton until the beginning of the twentieth century.[160] The *Wächter am Saugeen* was probably also bought by the *Berliner Journal* at that time. It folded, at any rate, in 1878.[161] Finally we ascertained that in Ayton a German newspaper appeared temporarily under the name *Die Fama*.[162]

4. The Remaining Counties Adjoining Waterloo

The growth of the German settlements in Waterloo was not inhibited by county borders. From as early as the 1830s on, as we saw, German farmers continued to move westward to the Huron Tract. In the same manner German colonies came into existence in the districts bordering on Waterloo to the south, east and north, starting in the 1830s.

Initially emigration was heaviest to the neighboring townships of Blenheim and East Zorra in the south which belonged to Oxford County. As early as 1846 these made a distinctly German impression on Loeher.[163] It was the destination for Catholics and Lutherans and particularly a large number of Mennonites, mostly Amish, from nearby Wilmot.[164] At that time, the scattered remaining German farmers in Oxford County, who lived primarily in Oxford and Norwich Townships and thus formed a bridge to the Germans of Norfolk County, were German Americans like the latter. They appear to have come over long before at the beginning of the nineteenth century, simultaneously with the Quakers and other settlers from the United States. The outstanding difference of this group of German Americans from the Germans of Blenheim and East Zorra was in the religious affiliations, which they reported in 1871 with barely a typical German denomination among them. Among 2,137 Germans by origin in Oxford and Norwich Townships only twenty-one called themselves Lutherans! They never had an organized church of their own. As early as the 1870s the number of Germans in these two townships began to dwindle noticeably, while among the Germans in East Zorra and Blenheim the growing anglicization became numerically evident only in the twentieth century. These were not scattered settlers like the others, but belonged, even though as an outpost, to the German core area of Waterloo whose fate they shared in school and language issues.[165]

Brant County, separated from the German districts of Waterloo County by the Scottish population of North Dumfries, is mentioned in this context only for the sake of completeness. Its population of German farmers, which is thinly and equally spread over all the townships, appears to have been the result not of immigration from Waterloo County but rather from German settlements in the Niagara district and from Norfolk and Wentworth.[166] Only the development of a German colony in the industrial town of Brantford since the 1880s is noteworthy. A German pastor of the Canada Synod still has a ministry there to this day.

Wentworth County forms the connecting link between the Niagara district and Waterloo County. Even the first Mennonites who came to Waterloo County moved from the villages of their brethren in Louth and Clinton along the shore to Dundas, from where they headed through the swamp of Beverly to the Grand River. All those who migrated from the United States to Waterloo County before the railways were built had to take the route through Wentworth. It is therefore only natural that some of the Mennonites and other German-American immigrants settled in Wentworth.[167] In 1871, 5,727 German farmers were counted among the 31,000 inhabitants of the rural districts of Wentworth. They professed themselves Methodists, Presbyterians, and so on, just like the German Americans in Oxford County,[168] without having developed their own German-oriented religious life. Like the German Loyalists at the Bay of Quinte and in Dundas, they appear to have been strongly anglicized by that time. Their number has declined steadily since then.[169]

A major German colony developed independently from about 1850 in Hamilton from German farming settlements in the surrounding area, which next to Toronto had become the largest commercial center in Ontario by that time. Ever since the first main railway lines were in operation, all the immigrants from the direction of Quebec-Montreal, and from New York across the Suspension Bridge at the Niagara, converged on Hamilton, whether they wanted to remain in western Ontario or move on to the American Midwest. For this reason, since the 1840s, the Canadian immigration agency conducted its statistical checks at this point.[170] It was to be expected that some of the German immigrants who passed through Hamilton annually in large hordes sought and found employment as skilled laborers in this thriving city.[171] As early as 1858 the first German Lutheran congregation was formed[172] and a German Catholic paper named *Katholisches Wochenblatt* began to appear in the city in the same year.[173] In 1871, 1,309 Germans were counted in the city. At that time the two papers *Canadische Volkszeitung* and *Der Deutsche in Canada* were published in Hamilton and were probably read outside Hamilton among the Germans of western Ontario as well. Nothing is known about them later on.[174] By 1911 the German colony had slowly increased to 4,103 persons. In the city, however, anglicization among the Germans was furthest advanced, with the result that in 1921, after the war, a mere 2,944 declared themselves as German by origin. To this day one pastor of the Lutheran Canada Synod and one of the Evangelical Association are serving in Hamilton.[175]

Wellington County, which is settled by the British, got its relatively few Germans exclusively from Waterloo County. They are most densely settled in Puslinch, Guelph, Pilkington and Peel Townships, which are directly adjacent to the German core area. They have been found everywhere in this area since the 1830s.[176] The wave of emigrants to the Saugeen district brought large numbers of German farmers into Marysburgh, Minto and Arthur Townships as well.[177] They settled in all the remaining parts of the county.[178] In Wellington the number of Germans increased from 3,114 in 1871 to 4,941 in 1911, with the German colony in the county seat of Guelph primarily benefiting from the increase.[179] In 1921, after the World War, however, only 3,913 Germans by origin were counted in Wellington.

To the extent that distance permitted, the Germans of Wellington joined the congregations of their coreligionists in Waterloo. They did not develop their own churches. By 1930 there was a pastor of German descent only in Morriston (Puslinch Township); he is maintained by the Evangelical Association.[180]

5. York County and the Surrounding Counties

When in 1793 Governor Simcoe moved the government and parliament of the young Province of Ontario (Upper Canada) to the small port town of York (the present-day Toronto) he tried to settle the still-uninhabited hinterland of the "provincial capital" as fast as possible. The first to follow his invitation to settle in present-day York County were Germans from Germany, a group of about sixty families numbering about 350 persons who had emigrated from Hamburg in 1792 under the leadership of a Wilhelm Berczy[181] to the Genesee Valley in New York State. There they had been severely disappointed in their expectations, and therefore gladly heeded Simcoe's call in the spring of 1794.[182] They were offered Markham Township, an immense territory of 64,000 acres about thirty kilometers north of Toronto.[183] In order to get there they had to cut their own way through the virgin forest. This temporary trail to the German colony was widened by Simcoe in the following years under the name of Yonge Street and continued to the present-day Lake Simcoe.[184] The German emigrants had to commit themselves from the outset by contract for six years to Berczy as the authorized agent of an emigrants' company in the colony that was to be founded.[185] In turn the apparently well-endowed company, true to its promise, arranged in generous fashion for the first inventory, and built schools and grain and saw mills. It even provided from the beginning for a Lutheran minister.[186] As with so many of the early private attempts at launching a colony, Berczy's enterprise was founded in the spirit of commercial speculation combined with true idealism. The prospect of pecuniary gain, however, turned out to be an illusion. Berczy directed the enterprise on the spot, probably on behalf of a few other wealthy men. He may also have financed most of it himself. At any rate, he appears to have spent a fortune of 600,000 Marks [$150,000], on both his first abortive project in the Genesee Valley and later on the generous support he provided for Markham.[187] The money was not wasted entirely. Since the soil was unusually fertile,[188] Markham developed into a true model settlement. The "German mills" of Markham became known in the entire province.[189]

Berczy and his company had planned the establishment of a large German colony and probably intended to bring over more German emigrants from time to time. This must be inferred not only from the financial scale of the entire enterprise, but also from Simcoe's expectations, because he had had an unusually large area put aside for them for settlement. It took Berczy's 250 people years to cultivate barely one-quarter of Markham, and since no new immigrants from Germany were to be seen, Berczy's rights to the still unsettled tracts of Markham were cancelled in 1803, and the township was opened to new immigrants in the same year.[190]

It was perhaps not so strange that these were Germans too, namely Mennonites from Pennsylvania. They were a group on their way to the Grand River who upon learning of Beasley's scandalous fraud, [191] preferred to take up their land in Markham, which had just been made available for further colonization and where other Germans had already proven so successful.[192] They thus became the founders of a third area of Mennonite settlement which developed independently from those in the Niagara district and in Waterloo. Until the 1820s it attracted its share of the general Mennonite immigration, and when in 1820 a Mennonite Provincial Conference was formed, the Markham colony enjoyed equality of status with the other colonies.[193] The Mennonites settled next to the colonists from Germany in the parts of Markham Township situated off Yonge Street and south of adjoining Whitchurch Township.[194] Berczy's colony could not expand further eastward, but only to the west across Yonge Street, so a sizable German Lutheran daughter colony developed in Vaughan Township by the first half of the nineteenth century. In Vaughan, as in the remaining townships of York County, we have to assume scattered German elements here and there.[195]

We know little about the church life of the Germans in York. The Lutherans[196] of Markham and Vaughan suffered from the same shortage of pastors as all the other German Lutheran congregations in Ontario. When the Reverend Liebig, who had accompanied them from Germany[197] left Markham in the winter of 1796-97,[198] they were confronted at this early point with the difficult question of finding a successor. Only around 1800 did they get a new pastor, by the name of Andrich. However, he was drowned in a flood in 1805. The Reverend Joh. Dietrich Petersen arrived only after the ministry had long been vacant. Around 1819 he had the first three small Lutheran churches erected. Up to that time services had been held in the schools. Following the well-proven pattern of Halifax and Williamsburg,[199] the Church of England approached Petersen with the offer of converting his congregation to Anglicanism in return for financial support. Although he promised it, only his successor, the Reverend Mayerhoffer, who arrived in 1829, partly achieved it.[200] At any rate, the inroads made by the Anglican church appear not to have been as severe among the Germans in York as, for instance, in Dundas. From 1833 to 1840 they succeeded in obtaining the Reverend Jacob Hüttner, an outspokenly German and outspokenly Lutheran minister. In the 1840s the Germans were left again without a pastor. When in 1850 the Pittsburg Synod[201] began to take the German Lutherans in Ontario under its wing, and sent the German-speaking Pastor Diehl to Markham and Vaughan, he was compelled to preach in English.[202]

The renunciation of the German mother tongue which occurred here in the third generation appeared, in view of the relative homogeneity of the German settlement, to be attributable less to inter-marriage than to the deliberate intention of the Germans themselves. For economic reasons, such as the desire to improve sales of their merchandise at the nearby Toronto market, they may have wanted to learn the language of the country as fast as possible. Even the conservative Mennonites were no exception here.[203] After 1871 their number declined steadily in the rural districts of York.[204]

In Toronto the situation was different. Here a German colony developed from the 1840s[205] as a result of the immigration of skilled workers from Germany, just as in Hamilton. As early as 1851 they formed a Lutheran congregation.[206] After the 1870s the population of Toronto grew rapidly so that the 1911 Census counted 8,766 Germans by origin in Toronto. Only slightly more than half of these, however, dared to identify themselves as Germans after the war.[207] These Germans were engaged as craftsmen and small businessmen in various branches of industry. Only in the manufacturing of musical instruments, however, did they seem to have an indisputable monopoly.[208]

We are only scantily informed about the Germans in counties bordering on York. In the two southernmost townships of Ontario County, Pickering and Whitby, the first Germans, mostly Mennonites, settled soon after 1800, at the same time as their coreligionists and friends took up residence in nearby Markham and Whitchurch.[209] Later, when land there became scarce, a large number of Mennonites from the latter two townships moved across the county borders to Ontario into Pickering and Uxbridge Townships. From Pickering and Uxbridge, their main settlements, they scattered and settled in decreasing numbers northward and eastward. In 1871, 1,723 Germans by origin were counted in the county. This number had increased by the turn of the century, which may be attributable to a continued emigration from Markham and vicinity.[210] The ethnic identity, moreover, of these

Pennsylvania-German descendants had long become just as problematical as among those in neighboring York. They had been completely anglicized even before the war. By 1921 a mere 336 persons in the entire county remembered their German descent.[211]

In Simcoe County the first ten German families are supposed to have settled in Nottawasaga Township in 1834.[212] They appear to have been Mennonites from York County, who for years drew other coreligionists after them so that a German colony of reasonable size existed by 1871 around the community of Collingwood.[213] Farmers of German descent also lived in all the remaining townships of the county at that time. They too came primarily from the German settlements in York, and only a small proportion was the result of a direct immigration from Europe.[214] They appear to have become anglicized, like the Germans in York and Ontario, long before the war. They never developed a church life of their own.

No more than a scattered few German farmers ever lived in Peel County.[215] In Halton County they were found in larger numbers only in Nelson and Trafalgar Townships along the shore.[216] Their presence probably goes back to the beginnings of colonization, like that of the German Americans in nearby Wentworth County. They probably also came over from the United States, beginning in 1810. They apparently never had an ecclesiastical organization on Canadian soil which could have reminded them of their German heritage.[217]

6. Germans in Other Parts of Southwestern Ontario and in New Ontario

In Norfolk County, no less than 5,384 Germans by origin were counted in 1871. The ancestors of most of them had come over from the American States between about 1800 and 1830, and were probably among the first pioneers in all the townships.[218] The later immigration from Germany must not have been very large.[219] We know of only one closed colony of Germans from Germany, which was founded by eighty Lutheran families from Württemberg in Middleton Township in 1847.[220]

The German Americans appear to have been assimilated very early here and, due to its scattered settlement, the German element from Germany had been assimilated by about 1900. In 1921 a mere 1,453 persons acknowledged their German descent in all of Norfolk.[221]

The situation was similar in Elgin and Middlesex Counties, where in 1871 a few hundred German farmers could be found in each of the townships. They were especially numerous in Bayham and Malahide (Elgin) at Lake Erie. Their places of origin were predominantly in Pennsylvania and other American states.[222] Against this mass of German Americans who, except for a few Mennonites, had lost their ancestral faith long ago, a single major colony of Lutherans from Germany stood out in Aldborough Township (Elgin).[223] The anglicization of these German farmers took place decades ago. Since 1900 their number has been declining decisively, according to the census reports.[224] Only in the town of London did the number of German craftsmen and industrial workers increase further until the World War.[225]

The first Germans in Kent County were a few Moravian missionaries, who had fled from Ohio with a tribe of peaceful Delaware Indians around 1792. They found refuge from the persecutions of other Indian tribes with their protegés in British territory, where they received present-day Orford Township as their land for settlement. Here on the Thames they founded Moraviantown.[226] When in the 1830s the English Government forced the Delaware Indians to sell a large part of their reservation in return for an annual rent, in order not to delay the continuing colonization by Europeans, many of the Indians left once more for the American Northwest, again under the guidance of one of their German missionaries.[227]

With the stream of white immigrants, hundreds of German-American farmers also came to Kent, Lambton and Essex Counties at the southwestern tip of Ontario, starting presumably in the 1830s and probably largely from Pennsylvania, Ohio and Michigan. Around 1845, however, Loeher encountered very few Germans here in the west.[228] In 1871, on the other hand, 6,568 inhabitants of German origin were counted; in 1881 there were 9,662 in the three counties combined.[229] Most of them were scattered settlers and, as in Elgin and Middlesex, in a powerless minority. In Kent County they were more numerous in the town of Chatham, and around it in the townships of Chatham and Camden, Harwich and Raleigh and in Orford; in Lambton County, particularly in Warwick, Enniskillen and Sombra Townships,[231] and in Essex County on the southern shore in southern Colchester, Gosfield and Mersea Townships in the communities of Kingsfield and Leamington. The number of those reporting their German origin for the census enumerations in Kent and Lambton Counties began to decline from as early as 1881. Their number in Essex County, on the other hand, continued to increase until 1911, due to immigration from Detroit which appeared primarily to have augmented the German colony in the town of Windsor. The extent of anglicization here was revealed only by the postwar census.

The Germans appear to have had neither their own clergy nor their own schools in any of the counties dealt with in this last section, except for London (Middlesex), Rhineland and Delhi (Norfolk). No obstacle, therefore, stood in the way of their anglicization. Today the German element is extinct all over southwestern Ontario.

The significance of New Ontario in the context of our subject is in inverse proportion to its vast spatial dimensions. Compact colonies of several hundred Germans developed only in Muskoka County in the townships of Draper, Ryde, Oakley, etc., in the center of the county,[232] and in Parry Sound County, south of Lake Nipissing in the townships of Nipissing, Gurd, Himsworth, Chapman, etc.[233] In Muskoka they dated back to the 1860s, in Parry Sound to the 1870s.

The huge area north of Lake Huron and Lake Superior received a mixed population of all European nationalities after about 1880 as a result of the construction of the transcontinental railways. It is still very thinly spread to this day and its German element is infinitesimal. Most of the Germans live in scattered isolation on their farmsteads that they have wrested from the virgin forest, cut off from all communication with fellow Germans. A few hundred also live as miners in such young mining towns as North Bay (Nipissing County) as well as in the relatively old towns of Sault Ste. Marie (Algoma), Port Arthur, and Fort William, which originated as trading posts of the fur trading companies.[234] In 1911 less than ten thousand Germans were counted among a population of more than 260,000 in all of New Ontario.[235] The attractions of the climatically and economically more advantageous Prairie provinces prevented the scattering of a still larger number of Germans in northern Ontario. Even most of the younger generation of the German farmers in Old Ontario preferred to buy their new land in Manitoba, Saskatchewan or Alberta than to have land allotted free of charge in northern Ontario. An exception are the German farmers in the Ottawa Valley, never very fortunate economically, many of whose sons took up homesteads in the north of the province.[236]

Only in rare cases do the Germans appear to have been strong enough in a school district to enforce the appointment of a bilingual teacher.[237] Since the war all possibilities for German instruction have disappeared. In a few years the Germans will be completely absorbed.

Protestant pastors of German descent served or are still serving in Arnstein and Magnetawan (Parry Sound), North Bay (Nipissing), Massey and Sault Ste. Marie (Algoma) and North Cobalt (Timiskaming).[238]

Finally the numbers of Germans by origin for all of Ontario will be compared with the numbers of the total population of the province according to the different census reports:

Table III.1

	1870-71	1880-81	1901	1911	1921
Germans by origin	158,608	188,394	203,319	192,320	130,545
total population	1,620,851	1,926,922	2,182,947	2,527,292	2,933,662
percentage	9.8	9.8	9.3	7.6	4.4

It can be seen that in 1871 and 1881 the German element still formed almost 10 per cent of the population. In 1901 a decline first becomes noticeable. Since then the percentage has dropped by more than half.

CHAPTER IV

From the Russian Steppes
to the Prairie Frontier

1. The Opening of the West

After the founding of Lord Selkirk's colony, more than half a century elapsed before the systematic colonization of western Canada actually began. Not before the rights of the Hudson's Bay Company over
the Northwest Territories had been taken over in 1869 by the government of the new Canadian Confederation was the way open for settlement. British Columbia's condition for joining Confederation in 1871
had been the construction of a railway line connecting Vancouver with
eastern Canada. This had prompted the transfer of the Prairie territory to the new Dominion of Canada. In response to the rebellion of
the semi-nomadic métis at the Red River led by Louis Riel against the
new order, and to forestall American designs on the prairies north of
the 49th parallel, the Province of Manitoba was created in 1870. The
remaining area was left under the direct administration of the federal
government in Ottawa as the so-called Northwest Territories.

The railway project, and the consequent extension of federal govern-
mental authority over the prairies of the West was, as we saw, primarily politically motivated. In 1870 no one had expected that the
construction of the railway would result in the opening up and settlement of the prairies on the scale on which it actually did subsequently
happen. The agricultural possibilities of the prairie had been investigated
since 1856. Yet the lack of trees on the prairie had erroneously been
taken as evidence of poor, infertile soils and of drought conditions.

It was assumed that the dry belt extended much further north than was actually the case. Experts at the time considered only the zone of mixed forest and prairie—the park belt—to be fit for agricultural use. But due to the great and almost insurmountable distances from all markets, to the danger of frost and the shortage of timber, any major colonization was considered impossible even there.

Yet the federal government was determined to do everything to encourage the opening of the West. The Dominion Land Act of 1872 provided for a free homestead the size of a quarter section [160 acres or 64.4 hectares] to which any male immigrant of twenty-one years of age or over would be entitled under certain conditions. The number of applicants, however, remained minimal at first. They dared to settle only in river valleys. Besides Winnipeg-St. Boniface at the confluence of the Assiniboine and Red Rivers, there were in 1870 only the beginnings of small settlements in Portage la Prairie, Prince Albert and Edmonton. No one dared to do without the water from wells and rivers and without the nearby forests. Neither in Ontario nor in Quebec, from where the first few immigrants came, had this been advisable or even necessary. Then between 1874 and 1879, about seven thousand German Mennonites from South Russia were persuaded to become settlers in Manitoba. They had been used to the steppe, and became the first to take the decisive step of settling on the open prairie. Their example, and the construction of a railway from Winnipeg to Minneapolis-St. Paul (and thus to Chicago) in 1878, marked a decisive turning point. These developments, as well as completion of the Canadian Pacific Railway in 1882, planned since 1870, from eastern Canada across the Canadian Shield to Winnipeg, brought large numbers of immigrants to western Canada for the first time. Colonization, nevertheless, did not make significant headway, not even after the completion of the C.P.R. line in 1885 across the Rocky Mountains to Vancouver, partly because the line had been laid too far south through the dry belt out of ignorance of the agricultural possibilities. In those early years of colonization, the departures of disappointed settlers for the Dakotas and Minnesota often outnumbered the new arrivals. That began to change only around the turn of the century when, in the northwestern United States, cheap virgin land began to become scarce and, simultaneously, the Liberal government of Laurier who had come to office in 1896 turned with new vigor to the policy of immigration. Only then were the climatically preferred northern parts of Saskatchewan and Alberta opened up with the help of the Grand Trunk and the Canadian Northern Railway. The railway network was rapidly extended, and soon took on the form of a large fan, with the Winnipeg-Fort William (at Lake Superior) line as its handle. In addition, after about 1900, western Canada's economic growth was determined by a steady lowering of shipping and railway transport costs, and by a steady rise since 1896 of the world market price for wheat, after prices had been constantly declining for some time. These factors made Canada more and more competitive on the world market, and only then really suitable for large-scale immigration.

This is why the main immigration took place between 1900 and 1914. The most important countries of origin of the immigrants were Great Britain, the United States, the rural regions of eastern and southeastern Europe, from where the large majority of German immigrants came as we shall see, and Scandinavia. So there was formed on the prairies a colorful blend of peoples who through most strenuous effort, transformed the steppe into a flourishing wheatland. Immigration reached its climax in 1913, with a total of 402,432 immigrants, 150,000 of whom came from Great Britain, 140,000 from the United States and the rest from the European continent, mainly from eastern Europe. The World War brought immigration from Europe to an abrupt end. Economic growth and settlement, on the other hand, were even accelerated by the war, since Canada was expected to meet as far as possible the enormous requirements of the Allied powers for wheat. As a result, Canadian wheat prices soared and agriculture experienced, especially after the bumper crop of 1915, a boom never seen before or since. This rapid upswing lasted without interruption until 1920. All the good arable land at that time, especially if it was accessible, for the most part was put to the plough. Within the time span of one-quarter century, western Canada had been transformed from a desert to one of the wealthiest granaries of the world. On the whole, Canada had become the economically strongest Dominion within the British Empire.

Around the turn of the century settlement was still confined to the valleys of the Red River, the Assiniboine, the Souris and the Qu'Appelle. There were more or less isolated settlements as well along the C.P.R. main line (Winnipeg-Regina-Medicine Hat-Calgary) and its branch lines Calgary-Edmonton, Calgary-MacLeod, Dunmore Junction-Lethbridge and Regina-Saskatoon-Prince Albert, as well as along a few additional newly-built private lines in Manitoba.

Only one decade later the park belt, as well as the semi-humid prairie with its tall grass and rich dark-brown soils, were occupied for the most part by thousands of new immigrants. After 1908 settlement began to advance into the dry belt. At the same time, the first settlers moved into the forest zone, and occasionally even to the faraway Peace River district, which is as much as four hundred kilometers northwest of Edmonton and which was not connected with the railway until 1916. Until 1920, settlement in the dry belt and in the forest zone [see Appendix, map 6] advanced step by step.

The economic boom of the war years was followed by the inevitable crash. Falling wheat prices, and bad harvests on top of that from 1920 to 1923, led to the first retrograde movement in the settlement process. Some farmers began to leave the dry belt. Census Division No. 3 in southeastern Alberta northwest of Medicine Hat, for instance, lost more than half its population between 1921 and 1926. The forest zone in the north, too, lost some of its pioneers. The heaviest exodus took place from the area between the large lakes in Manitoba and the Peace River. In 1925, however, a new economic upswing began, and with it again began an expansion of the area of settlement. Now the conquest of the forest zone began in earnest. The Peace River district and the area north of North Battleford in Saskatchewan now became the destination of the land-hungry farmers' sons from the prairie, as well as of new immigrants. In 1923 there was a gradual resumption of immigration. Between 1926 and 1929 it again increased considerably without, however, approaching the volume of the prewar immigration. Its highest number was 167,722 in 1929, compared to 402,432 in 1913. The number of 400,000 immigrants from central, eastern and southeastern Europe quoted by R. England for the postwar period 1924-1930,[1] was proportionately higher than before the war. As before the war, these immigrants were particularly important for western Canada since they, rather than the immigrating British, made up the real settlers who stayed on the land. The British availed themselves of the opportunities of upward mobility which were not open to the average non-British immigrant. While the British therefore tended to dominate the civil service and industries of the growing prairie towns, the fate of the Canadian West was ultimately in the hands of the majority of non-British immigrants who cultivated the land. According to Robert England, who viewed the rapid colonization of western Canada and the development of its resources in terms of Britain's strategic anticipation of the World War, western Canada's German settlers in this way, even unwittingly, contributed to Britain's strength in her conflict with the country of their ethnic origin.[2]

2. Canadian Immigration Policy

According to Section 95 of the British North America Act of 1867, which is Canada's constitution, jurisdiction over immigration has been reserved for the federal government. The individual provinces may make laws in relation to immigration in their own territories. These laws, however, may not be in conflict with any act of the Parliament of Canada and may be suspended by Ottawa at any time. The fact that the promotion and regulation of immigration was primarily entrusted to the federal government was quite in accordance with the great significance of immigration for the future of all of Canada. In the postwar years a special ministry was even established in Ottawa to deal with questions of immigration and settlement. The federal law that provided the basis for the settlement of the West was the Dominion Land Act of 1872 (35th Victoria, Cap. 23). It established the great lure for the land-hungry peasant emigrants in the form of the free homestead grant measuring a quarter section (i.e. 160 acres or 64.4 hectares). Each adult male immigrant was entitled to apply for it by the payment of a mere ten dollar entry fee. The homestead became his after a period of three years, provided he had resided on it for a few months each year, cultivated a specified part of the land and erected domiciles and fences. The patenting of a homestead, however, required the immigrant to be a British subject, or at least to declare his intention of becoming naturalized. Before the war, this was possible after three years; since then, after five years of residence in Canada. If a family immigrated with several adult sons, they could thus immediately obtain considerable land holdings according to this law. Each homesteader, in addition, had a certain right of preemption to a second adjoining quarter section which he could acquire for a payment of only 480 dollars (three dollars per acre) and by fulfilling the same requirements of cultivation applying to his own homestead. For a period of time there appears to have existed a further opportunity of purchasing another half section for four hundred to six hundred dollars, as long as the settler cultivated at least fifty acres of virgin land within the first three years.[3] There was no better way to lure real farmers than by such a generous offer of cheap virgin land. Besides, the soil of this homestead land was of good quality, at least until the World War, although initially it was less favorably situated as far as communications were concerned than the land that the railway companies, above all the Canadian Pacific, offered for sale at low rates as well.

Originally the C.P.R. became owners of almost every second section of a township it opened up. With the proceeds from the sale of these sections, the loans raised for the railway construction were to be serviced and repaid. Similar arrangements were made with railway companies that were formed later. Hence they developed a twofold interest in the largest possible immigration; this was the only way for them to sell their land and count on an increase in the amount of freight. As long as free grants of good quality homestead land were still available, however, the railways were only able to sell their land if it was close to already completed or firmly planned railway lines. Most homestead grants were at a distance of fifty kilometers or more from the most recently completed railway station, and settlers often had to wait for many more years for a railway connection. But that did not bother most of the immigrants. Their state of destitution left them no choice but to apply for a homestead grant and, with the optimism typical of all colonists, they put their trust into the future of the growing country.

By the end of the 1890s, the volume of immigration was still considerably below the expectations of the Canadian government. As long as cheap virgin land was still available on the northwestern prairies of the United States, western Canada, because of its less favorable climate and its even worse system of communications, could not be very attractive. Many of the settlers, who were often recruited with great difficulty, after some time headed south across the American border. In some of the early years this emigration even surpassed immigration.

This was the situation when, in 1897, the relatively young Clifford Sifton from Manitoba became Minister of the Interior in Wilfrid Laurier's new Liberal federal government. He began to conduct Canadian immigration policy energetically and systematically, and thus created the prerequisites for the great immigration during the period 1900 to 1914.[4]

Up to that time a certain amount of unspecified fertile farmland had been reserved for the railway companies as compensation for their construction projects, although they had not yet had to make the final selection of their land. Thereby the colonization of large areas of the West had been critically hampered. Sifton now decreed that the railways had to go ahead immediately with the selection of the land granted to them, and that henceforth they should get their compensation in a different form and no longer through land grants.[5] Only in this way did favorably situated areas again become available to the government for the granting of free homesteads. At the same time, greater efforts were being made to be much more obliging to the immigrants in every respect. The bureaucratic red tape in the allotment of land grants was eliminated, and the issuing of the final patent for the homestead was made easier. This was of the greatest psychological importance for keeping the immigrants content, especially in the first difficult years. Furthermore, the formation of group settlements was promoted as before, which was of particular importance for the non-British immigrants. This was done because a large homogeneous community of settlers would simplify administrative duties with regard to the distribution of seed grains, servicing cattle, provisions, and land surveys, and because the bond of religious and economic community of such groups would make it much easier for them to endure the problems of the difficult early years in the new environment of the prairie or the bush. The greater initial economic successes of such group settlements, in turn, would benefit the government's promotional efforts. However, in view of the desirability of assimilating the non-British ethnic groups in the future, no unusually large spaces for settlement were ever put aside for any specific ethnic group.

The most important innovation in Canadian immigration policy, however, was the much greater care taken than before in the proper selection of immigrants in their European places of origin. To accomplish that, a network of agents was necessary which would actually screen the prospective emigrants as to their farming qualifications. Sifton realized that only land-hungry farmers used to hardships, and with low cultural expectations, would take root in western Canada. Yet open emigration propaganda and the selection of suitable emigrants by Canadian agents was impossible in any European country. Even the visit of the general agent for immigration who was the Canadian High Commissioner in London, Lord Strathcona, to Hamburg in 1898 for negotiations with some shipowners provoked a protest of the German government to the English government.[6] In 1899 Sifton hit upon the expedient of creating an organization of booking agents for shipping companies under the disguise of a North Atlantic Trading Company. For a bonus of five dollars per peasant emigrant, two dollars for each member of his family, and with the help of the existing booking offices of their companies, these agents took over the soliciting and selecting of suitable emigrants for Canada. The names of the individual agents were kept secret.[7]

First of all, efforts were made to promote the immigration of agricultural laborers from Great Britain, especially from northern England

and Scotland, and of farmers from the United States. Peasants desirous of emigrating were also to be found in the Ukraine, in Volhynia, Galicia and other regions of western Russia and the Habsburg Monarchy, from where the great majority of the German immigrants came. For all these continental emigrants, Hamburg was the most important port of embarkation. Sifton, who considered the economic development of western Canada to be his main challenge, and who was not so worried about the potential difficulty of assimilating these immigrants, drew members of the most diverse peoples of eastern and southeastern Europe into the country, as long as they promised to become good farmers. He expressed great satisfaction with these immigrants that he acquired with the help of the North Atlantic Trading Company.[8]

From as early as Sifton's time, therefore, Canadian immigration policy has been dominated by the principle of selection. The Immigration Act of 1910 makes this quite clear. It summarized and expanded the regulations issued up to then. To prevent the shipping companies from contravening the clandestine instructions of the Canadian Ministry of the Interior by bringing over undesirable immigrants anyway, they were held responsible for shipping back, free of charge, immigrants that were rejected. Immigrants brought to Canada by shipping companies who did not accept this obligation were denied entry from the outset.[9] A case in point is Section 37(c) of the Immigration Act, a veritable catchall section, by which any immigrant could be refused admission if need be.[10] Anyone with a physical, mental or moral defect would, as a matter of course, be prohibited from landing.[11] Special provisions applied to Asians, who had already settled in large numbers in British Columbia. Due to racial and economic considerations, they were now also included among the prohibited classes of immigrants.

With regard to immigrants from Europe, however, their presumed qualifications as farmers played the decisive role in their selection until the World War. Only after the war were they selected according to political, national and cultural criteria as well. In Canada, just as in the United States, doubts about the ability to assimilate the East, Southeast and South European immigrants were beginning to grow. The effects of the war psychosis were also still felt to the extent that immigration from the countries of the Central Powers remained prohibited until 1923. Only the territories taken from Germany, Austria and Hungary by the peace treaties were graciously excluded from this prohibition. Immigration from northern and western Europe, and particularly from Great Britain and the British Dominions as well as from the United

States, on the other hand, was declared especially desirable now. Until 1931 a distinction was made between three categories of immigrants from Europe:

(1) those from the British Empire and the United States

(2) those from the so-called "preferred countries" of France, Belgium, the Netherlands, Switzerland, Scandinavia and

(3) those from all the remaining European countries.

Whereas only farmers, agricultural laborers and their dependents as well as female domestic servants were admitted from countries of the last category, immigrants of non-agricultural occupations were allowed entry from most English-speaking countries and also from the so-called preferred countries. Germany was included among the latter in 1927 at the instigation of the German-Canadian Minister W.D. Euler in the Dominion government in Ottawa. Such immigrants were admitted, however, only subject to proof that they had a permanent occupation in Canada or at least 150 dollars in cash, which was considered sufficient for subsistence until employment was obtained. The inclusion of Germany among the preferred countries in 1927 regrettably resulted in a rapid surge of immigrants from Germany from 1927 to 1930, who succumbed to the enticements of the Canadian immigration propaganda and emigrated to western Canada without the necessary agricultural experience. Many of these latter immigrants were bound to be buried under the ruins of the approaching economic collapse.

Otherwise the distinction between the "preferred" and "non-preferred" countries meant little, because the immigrants who were sought because of their easy assimilability, namely those from northern and western Europe, turned up in even fewer numbers after the war than before. These few, furthermore, were no longer eager to accept the fate of settlers in western Canada under conditions that were much too primitive from the standpoint of western European civilization. Only the farmer from eastern and southeastern Europe, who was subjected to political and economic pressures, tended to be willing and able to invest his energy in a new effort to raise the productivity of the land and to put down roots. However, because the economic development of the West urgently demanded new immigrants, the arrival of a sufficient number of industrious farmers and farm laborers was welcomed, even from eastern and southeastern Europe. Thus the immigrants, including Germans, were again recruited essentially from the same places of origin as in the prewar era.

Responsibility for the entire immigration from the so-called non-preferred countries was turned over to the two big railway companies, the privately-owned Canadian Pacific Railway (C.P.R.) and the publicly-owned Canadian National Railway (C.N.R.), on September 1, 1925.[12] We mentioned above that from the outset the railways were most interested in the largest possible immigration. Now, in the postwar years, however, free homesteads with good soil and with adequate access to communications were no longer available. The land belonging to the railways could therefore more easily be sold to immigrants on an instalment plan than before. Prior to 1925, the railways had already received some concessions from the government for the transportation of immigrants classified as agriculturists, and they had created special departments for handling the business of immigration and settlement. The C.P.R. used, in addition, a subsidiary company called the Canada Colonization Association.[13] Their enormous financial resources enabled the railway companies to carry out quite an effective advertising campaign in Europe. The promotional literature promised extensive land at a low cost to the immigrant, without the need of initial fertilization, and, after ten to twenty years of hard work and adjustment, a carefree life in his old age and sufficient holdings to pass on to the children. All these things were bound to impress destitute farm laborers and small peasants, especially in such an unstable time as the postwar years.

In Canada the immigration departments of the railways began to collaborate with the church organizations of the prewar immigrants. The latter had a keen interest of their own in replenishing their congregations with new immigrants from the old homeland. They still had good personal contacts to these places that facilitated the recruiting of immigrants by the railways. Thus German Canadians began to form Catholic, Lutheran and Baptist boards of immigration with the C.P.R. and after 1929, also with the C.N.R. in Winnipeg, which were sponsored by the Association of German-Canadian Catholics (*Volksverein deutsch-canadischer Katholiken*), the three Lutheran Synods collectively and the German Baptist Church. The Mennonites had also established a board of immigration as early as 1923 in Rosthern, Saskatchewan, which cooperated mainly with the C.P.R., later also with the C.N.R. All these organizations have rendered outstanding services, especially in the rescue of German refugees from Soviet Russia. Without the faithful cooperation of the German-Canadian church organizations with the two railways, most of the totally impoverished Germans from eastern Europe would never have had available the necessary credit to emigrate to Canada. The fact that these ecclesiastical agencies directed the

German postwar immigrants predominantly into the agricultural districts where Germans of the same denomination had settled who could help them to adapt, was also important.

For the railways, on the other hand, the business interest always had priority. This meant that the activities of the immigration boards of the churches, especially those that procured employment and farm land, became strongly commercialized as well. Many a German immigrant got the impression upon his arrival in Montreal or Winnipeg that the priest or pastor who looked after him within the framework of one of the boards, was a better businessman than a clergyman. There can be no doubt that the optimism about the economic opportunities, espoused in particular by these boards of immigration, was entirely out of order.

Under the impact of slumping wheat sales after 1929, the superficial optimism which had been entertained everywhere turned suddenly to pessimism. In August 1930, the Dominion government delegated the responsibility of decisions concerning the volume of immigration to the provinces. This was tantamount to immediate closure of immigration. The now meaningless distinction between "preferred" and "nonpreferred" countries was suspended, and the admittance of emigrants was newly regulated by the Order in Council of March 21, 1931 (PC 695),[14] which is still in force. It restricted immigration to:

(1) British subjects and United States citizens with proof of sufficient means to maintain themselves until employment could be secured,

(2) the wife and unmarried children under eighteen years of age of any legal resident of Canada who was in a position to care for them,

(3) agriculturists having sufficient means to farm in Canada (as a rule one thousand dollars was required).

This last provision was further restricted by the requirement that the provinces had to give their explicit assent. Saskatchewan did not do so until January 1, 1934. Since 1930 immigration to western Canada has, in fact, been limited to the wives and minor children of the heads of families who immigrated before 1930. Otherwise immigration has now more or less come to a standstill, as could be expected in view of the continuing economic crisis, regardless of the drastically restrictive immigration legislation.

3. The German Exodus to Western Canada, 1874 to 1914: Places of Origin and Reasons for Emigration

The first large group of immigrants induced by the homestead law of 1872 and by special invitation of the Government of Manitoba to settle on the Canadian prairie in 1874 and in the following years, was approximately seven thousand German Mennonites from South Russia. They were the heralds of the large German immigration from the areas of German settlement in eastern and southeastern Europe. In the following decades their surplus population in the old country and their vitality would give rise to a new permanent German community on the other side of the ocean in faraway western Canada. More than two-thirds of the German population of western Canada came from the colonies of German farmers in old Russia, Austria-Hungary and Romania. This fundamental fact must always be kept in mind in all our considerations. The last third consisted of, for the most part, German farmers from the American Midwest, and only about 12 per cent immigrated directly from Germany.

It has already been pointed out that the climatic and economic conditions, and the psychologically depressing isolation on the prairie and in the bush, did not make western Canada particularly inviting for the average immigrant from western Europe. This also applied to the immigrant from Germany, at least since the 1890s. The attractions were all the greater for the immigrants from the German settlements of eastern Europe. They still represented in its purest form the type of colonizing, land-hungry German peasant who was strongly impressed by the generous offer of virtually free farmland. They were accustomed to the hard life of a colonist, and their cultural expectations were still as easily satisfied as those of their ancestors who had left Germany around the turn of the eighteenth century. Only men and women of such caliber were able to cope with the hardships of the first years in western Canada, to make the prairie their home and to put down roots there. The coincidence of the new worldwide publicity given to the enormous successes of western Canadian wheat farming with the urgent desire of the Germans in the east European colonies to emigrate, was decisive. To all the prospective emigrants, western Canada was played up as "the last best West of America."

The emigration of German colonists from Russia, the Habsburg Monarchy and Romania beginning in the 1870s and especially in the

1890s, had economic and ethno-political causes everywhere. The high birth rate of the colonists resulted in a land shortage in most parent colonies as early as the second generation. In spite of the founding of daughter colonies within the boundaries of various ethnic enclaves, the formation of a class of day laborers with little or no land in the German villages was irreversible. Among this class the restless eagerness to migrate, which had already driven their ancestors to leave Germany, could easily erupt again, given the prospects for economic improvement. The immediate cause that touched off the overseas emigration, however, was almost everywhere ethno-political in nature. It was the abolition of the political, religious and economic privileges originally granted to these Germans or, to put it differently, the efforts of the Russian, Polish (in Galicia), Hungarian and Romanian host societies in general to assimilate their German minorities. This can be observed everywhere, although for the individual peasant emigrant, who had no distinct ethnic consciousness, these ethno-political causes may have been superseded by economic ones.

A comprehensive account of the great German migration overseas from eastern Europe is still lacking, due to a shortage of sources. Among the German community in western Canada, at the same time, the memories of the origins and the history of their immigration are beginning to fade. A deeper understanding of the German-Canadian community, however, is only made possible by a certain knowledge of its east European origins. For these reasons the various places of origin and the causes of emigration prevailing there shall be dealt with in more detail.

a. Russia

i. The Black Sea area

The largest and once most flourishing area of German settlement in eastern Europe is situated in the coastal region of the Black Sea in the Russian provinces (Governments) of Bessarabia, Kherson, Ekaterinoslav, Tauria and the area of the Don River. After conquering the Crimea (1783) the Russian Tsarina Catherine II, and later her grandson Tsar Alexander I, invited Germans to come and colonize the newly-annexed, almost desolate provinces. Their accomplishments as farmers were exemplary. In a few decades they transformed the South Russian steppe into the granary of Europe. Among the first German settlements was Khortitsa (Chortitza), founded in 1790 by German Mennonites from West Prussia, and the home of a large number of the Mennonites settling in Manitoba in the years after 1874. The main immigration to South Russia took place between 1804 and 1809 and in the 1820s, but new colonies were still launched for latecomers from Germany as late as the 1850s.[15] Altogether about ten thousand families of German emigrants, numbering fifty thousand to sixty thousand people, were settled in 209 villages.[16] The splendid economic growth, the high birth rate and the special rights of land ownership led to the continuous launching of daughter colonies until large parts of the Black Sea coastal region were dotted with German villages. By the eve of the World War, the number of Germans had increased to about 600,000, of whom two-fifths were Catholics, two-fifths were Lutherans and one-fifth were Mennonites.[17] Even though in the three provinces of Kherson, Ekaterinoslav and Tauria they formed only 6 per cent of the peasant population, which was composed primarily of Ukrainians but included Great Russians, Tartars, Bulgarians, etc., the Germans owned 20 per cent of the land, and as much as 28.5 per cent of the arable acreage.[18]

All the regions of Germany were represented among the colonists of South Russia, although southwestern Germany (Württemberg, Palatinate, Baden, Alsace) furnished the largest proportion of the emigrants. This observation seems to apply to all the larger German settlements in eastern Europe, as well as the fact that a large number of these emigrants did not come directly from their German homelands, but had in many cases been separated from their native soil for an entire generation. They settled permanently only after attempts in other regions had failed. Thus many families of emigrants from southwestern Germany who eventually settled in South Russia had lived before in the colonies founded in West Prussia by Frederick the Great, or in central Poland, in Volhynia and near St. Petersburg. Some also came from the young German colonies in Galicia, Bukovina and Banat.[19]

Similar stages of migration before permanent settlement can be traced for a large percentage of the first settlers in all the German ethnic enclaves in eastern and southeastern Europe which, because they are places of origin of the German-Canadian population, belong to the context of our considerations. This may be one of the main reasons why the German colonists of southeastern Europe later on also continued to display a peculiarly restless desire to migrate, and why they lost their allegiances to their old homelands particularly quickly.

The desire to migrate, and the restlessness of the first generations in the new country, of course, may be attributed to the initial lack of any strong emotional ties to the new homeland. Kuhn defines the gradual development of a feeling of belonging to a new homeland this way: "It is only a feeling of being reconciled and acquainted with the new country, no deep inner bond, no love which knows homesickness. People living in linguistic enclaves develop such deep allegiances only much later, only after several generations of settlement."[20] As soon as prospects of economic or other improvements of the situation beckon, the country of two or three generations' residence is abandoned much more lightheartedly than if an emigrant were to leave his ancestral homeland.

How fast and how thoroughly the ties to Germany were broken is attested to by the fact that, as early as the the second generation, the colonists in South Russia had only vague recollections of the German homeland of their parents, such as Prussia or Württemberg, and that a German traveller was forced to conclude as early as 1858 that Germany seemed to be completely forgotten by the colonists.[21] In spite of this, they clung stubbornly and with a strong pride to their German ethnic identity within their Slavic environment. They were able to do so because they enjoyed a status that was privileged in every respect.

In order to induce as many German peasants as possible to emigrate to Russia, Tsar Alexander I, as had Catherine II before him, promised them by the decree of February 20, 1804, thirty to eighty dessiatins of land (one dessiatin equals 2.7 acres or 1.09 hectares), exemption from taxation for ten years and from military service for all time, freedom of religion and complete administrative autonomy. Such an offer could not fail to make an impression, especially in southwestern Germany which was politically divided and badly governed. There, a shortage of land and high taxes, long military service and the lack of religious and political freedom weighed heavily upon the people, whose land was devastated by the Napoleonic Wars. The privileges, however, which once had been promised as bait to the German immigrants and their descendants "for all eternity" by the Russian government, were taken away with one blow from all the German colonists in 1871. The decisive turning point in the destiny of the Germans in Russia had arrived.

In 1861, the abolition of serfdom in the Russian villages had already brought the colonists closer to the life led by the Slavs. Now, in 1871, the colonists were placed under general Russian administration. The Odessa-based German Guardians Committee (*Fürsorge-Komität*), created in 1818 as the supreme administrative authority for the German villages in South Russia, was abolished. Among its explicit tasks, according to the decree authorizing its creation, was the protection of the privileges of the colonists. Even though the local self-administration remained untouched, the decisions of the communities no longer required the confirmation of the sympathetic Guardians Committee, but the approval of the less kindly-disposed Russian governors instead, who were at best corruptible. At first the consequences of subjugation to the general administration were not so clearly noticeable in community, church and school matters that the colonists suffered. But the German villages were very deeply disturbed by the suspension in 1874 of the old privilege of exemption from military service. This was the reason for the first wave of emigration overseas of German farmers from Russia in the mid-1870s. At that time the first Germans left South Russia, Poland-Volhynia and the Volga for Brazil, Argentina, the United States and Canada.

The introduction of general conscription into the Russian army for the sons of the German colonists affected the Mennonites most acutely. For them non-resistance is one of their most important articles of faith, by which they are distinguished from other Protestants, and for the sake of which they undertook the emigration to South Russia. Now emigration again appeared to them the only way out of their predicament. The Russian government, however, did not want to lose the Mennonites who were economically the most successful of the colonists. It was finally willing to concede that in peacetime, Mennonites had only to satisfy a kind of alternative labor service, and in time of war they were to serve as medics. In April 1874, the aide-de-camp of the Tsar, the jovial General von Totleben, was sent to the South Russian Mennonite villages. He succeeded, on the basis of this compromise, to convince the majority to stay. Yet several groups, distinguished by their religious conservatism, had justifiably lost their faith in the sincerity of the Russian government towards the colonists, and prepared to emigrate. Close to eighteen thousand Mennonites emigrated to North America between 1874 and 1879. Most of them settled in Kansas, Nebraska and the Dakotas (U.S.A.); some seven thousand, however, settled in southern Manitoba. These came from Chortitza and its three daughter colonies of Bergtal, Fürstenland and Barsenko.[22] A source reveals the fate of the abandoned villages, those of the Mennonites of the Bergtal Volost [administrative district]. There, the villagers of Bergtal, Schönfeld, Schöntal, Heubuden and Friedrichsfeld, sold their land, including the houses, for nineteen rubles per dessiatin. The first four colonies were bought by other German (Catholic) colonists, Friedrichsfeld by Russians.[23]

The emigration of the 1870s remained an episode. Around 1890, however, the emigration from all the areas of German settlement in Russia resumed with new vigor, not to end until the World War. The coincidence of economic and ethno-political causes was pointed out above. Shortages of land as a result of the indivisibility of the farms[24] had always led to the emigration of the younger sons from the old villages. Farmers by nature, they would look for new land of their own in the steppes, where enough cheap land was available to rent and later to purchase. In this way daughter colonies were formed regularly until the World War. At the same time property distinctions had grown in the villages. The landless class became an element of social unrest in which emigration fever, once it had erupted, remained at a high pitch for years. When the anti-German attitude of Russian domestic policy began suddenly to affect each German village around 1890, only the direction of the emigrants changed. They no longer looked for new land exclusively in near and distant provinces of Russia, but more and more migrated overseas. From there, as early as the 1870s, but even more so later on, the successful emigrants sent their encouraging letters to their old villages. The significance of these letters on the decision by individual families to emigrate overseas cannot be rated highly enough.

The policy which had led to the destruction of all the old privileges of the German colonists in 1871 increasingly threatened the autonomous cultural life of the German colonies under the impact of the Pan-Russian nationalist tendencies of the 1880s. In 1891 the German village schools were deprived of their autonomous administration by the communities, and Russian was made the chief language of instruction. The building of new churches was made difficult. Integration into the Russian Zemstvo administration brought serious disadvantages everywhere in the climate of growing antipathy between Russians and Germans. In order to curb the powerful economic expansion of the German farmers in Russia, all colonists who by 1887 had not acquired Russian citizenship, lost the right to buy and cultivate land. In 1892 the Minister of the Interior, Durnovo, even proposed forbidding German colonists who were Russian citizens to purchase land unless they joined the Orthodox Church.[25] The general prohibition against emigration from Russia, on the other hand, was explicitly suspended for German colonists.[26] Having brought civilization to the steppes, the Germans were now free to go. In every way, it was unpleasant for them to remain in the country where large areas had been transformed from a desert to flourishing farmland through the work of their hands. No wonder literally thousands of colonists among the younger generation tried to shake the dust of Russia off their feet.

The great economic successes of the Mennonites in southern Manitoba, above all, directed the attention of prospective emigrants from South Russia to western Canada. Starting in 1890, not only new Mennonites,[27] but also Catholics and Lutherans from the Black Sea region, came over, predominantly to Saskatchewan. At that time an immigrant recruiting office was opened in Odessa, which advertised the advantages of western Canada and procured the necessary papers for prospective emigrants. The tickets, which cost 109 rubles per adult from Odessa to Winnipeg, were sold by the Odessa representative of the Mistler Agency in Bremen.[28]

In 1891, with the founding of Rosthern colony in northern Saskatchewan, the foundation was laid for the second area of German Mennonite settlement in western Canada. It was filled up with newcomers from Russia, and even from Manitoba, in the following ten to twelve years. After 1893, sporadic additional Mennonite settlements were formed in Alberta (Didsbury, Beiseker, etc.) and after 1905 in a third rather closed settlement district in southern Saskatchewan (Morse, Herbert, Swift Current), partly as a result of new immigrations from Russia, partly as daughter colonies of the Manitoba Mennonites. Except for one group, which immigrated in 1894 directly from the lowlands (Werder) of Danzig to Tiefengrund near Rosthern, all the Mennonites of western Canada came from the Black Sea region. In a few very isolated cases they originated from the daughter colonies of the latter in central Russia. They brought with them to Canada their typically sonorous place names, which reflect the picturesque scenery, such as Hochfeld, Waldheim, Schöndorf, Rosenfeld and Neuhorst.

The German Catholics from South Russia, who can be traced in Saskatchewan since 1886, founded the colonies of St. Peter and Josephstal near Balgonie, Neu-Kronau, Davin, Vibank, Odessa and Kendal, all of them southeast of Regina. Considerable numbers also settled in the provincial capital, which still had a distinctly rural character. The successes of the first emigrants were so encouraging that reinforcements, especially from the Catholic colonies of South Russia, were particularly numerous. Allan, Seltz, Holdfast, Claybank, Spring Valley and many other German Catholic colonies in Saskatchewan can be traced to immigration from the Black Sea region. In the handwritten settlement reports collected by Bernhard Bott which serve as our primary source for this and related information, the names of almost all the major German Catholic colonies at the Black Sea appear. Mentioned particularly are the colonies of the Odessa district: Kleinliebental, Mariental, Josephstal, Franzfeld, Selz, Kandel, Baden, Mannheim, Elsass, Landau, Speyer, Katharinental, Karlsruhe, Sulz, Rastatt, Kronau-Kotschubei, München; furthermore the Catholic colonies at the Sea of Azov, such as Grosswerder, and the colonies of Rosenthal in the Crimea and Krasna in Bessarabia.[29]

The first group of Lutherans from the Black Sea region settled in the Hoffnungsthal colony near Langenburg in Saskatchewan in 1889. They came from Bessarabia, as did most of the Lutherans. No Lutherans can be traced to the other provinces of South Russia. Protestant Germans from Bessarabia settled not only in the Winnipeg suburb of Elmwood, but also in Melville, Kipling, and Zorra since about 1904 and, since 1908, in the dry belt (St. Boswells, McEachern, Eatonia, Cosine, Bateman) as well.

ii. *Volhynia and Central Poland*

Restlessness and the desire to migrate have not been greater among any other German ethnic group in eastern Europe than among the group from Poland-Volhynia. In a report from the 1860s we read:[30]

> All German colonists have a strange inclination to migrate. They like to buy land where forests are available, where they can cut down the wood, sell it and after having cleared part of their land, move on again. Often only the fourth or the fifth settler cultivates the entire field and then ekes out his modest living. When all the land is under cultivation and the colony is fully developed, many tend to stay for a longer period and make themselves at home as comfortably as possible. However, it takes only a minor occasion, such as the slight and vague prospect of an easier way to make a living, and they sell all their goods and chattels and take off. This happened frequently in recent years when young and old set out to establish new homes in western and southern Russia and on the Volga.

Here, too, the situation of the German farmers had always been the least satisfactory, especially of those who had been attracted as tenants and laborers to the estates of Polish landlords in densely-populated areas in the first half of the nineteenth century. Nowhere did they receive any chartered privileges like the colonists in South Russia and on the Volga. Frequently, after working hard to clear woodland, they were cheated out of the fruits of their labor by the owners, who would not renew their leases. Closed areas of German settlement were formed only in Volhynia. These German colonies were founded by German farmers from Poland between 1864 and 1875 on Polish landed property.[31] According to the first general Russian census of 1897, 171,331 Germans lived in Volhynia.

The political and economic repression by the Russian government was aimed primarily at this youngest and weakest of the German ethnic enclaves in Russia, and with particular harshness. Volhynia was considered a politically unreliable and militarily endangered area. In the event of a Russian-German war it was feared that the villages of the German colonists would facilitate the advance of the enemy. Since the 1880s it was therefore argued that they should be prevented from spreading any further in the western border provinces. The law of 1887, which forbade the purchase and leasing of land to people without Russian citizenship, primarily affected the Germans in Volhynia, who frequently out of indifference had not acquired Russian citizenship, even though they had forfeited German citizenship long before. Laws of 1888 and 1892 altogether prohibited the purchase of land in the border provinces by persons of German ethnic stock, or made land purchase subject to a special permit. This so-called *Bodensperre* (land embargo) was probably the main trigger for emigration. As early as November 1890, an article in the first German-Canadian weekly newspaper *Der Nordwesten*, launched in Winnipeg only one year before, dealt in detail with Volhynia and the fate of the Germans, whose eyes were already focused on western Canada as their goal of emigration at that time.[32] According to the article, the Germans farmed 20 per cent of the land in the province of Volhynia, 17 per cent in the province of Podolia and 18 per cent in the province of Kiev. A prohibition against the export of rye stimulated emigration even more. Finally in 1890, Russian was proclaimed to be the main language of instruction in all schools. The teachers were given only four months to learn Russian, although there were, for example, in Rovno District, 32 German schools compared to only 15 Russian schools, and in Zytomir District 83 German schools compared to only 28 Russian schools. Church life, too, was made difficult for the Germans. These measures at least partly accomplished their objectives. Starting in 1890, numerous German families emigrated from all the colonies. From some colonies everyone left together. The emigrants went mainly to western Canada, but also to the United States, Courland and Bosnia.[33]

In this way, in all three Prairie provinces were formed numerous small, more or less closed settlements of Germans from Volhynia which, until the World War, were constantly replenished by newcomers from back home. Strangely enough, the first colonies were founded in 1892 in the most western province of Alberta; during the course of the 1890s Germans from Volhynia settled in the colonies of Wetaskiwin, Brightview, Leduc, Nisku, Bashaw, Ellerslie, Brüderheim, Brüderfeld, New Sarepta, Peace Hill and Golden Spike. In present-day Saskatchewan they can be traced back to 1894 in and around Regina, Rosthern, Yorkton, Langenburg, Lampman, Yellow Grass, Lang, Kipling, Lemberg, Lipton, Mossbank, etc. Germans from Volhynia were also among the first ones to move into the dry belt in 1908 (St. Boswells, Morse). Starting in 1898 colonies of Volhynians were also formed in Manitoba, for instance in the vicinity of the Mennonites in Emerson, Gretna, Morris, Brown, Morden and Friedensfeld near Steinbach, as well as east of Winnipeg near Beauséjour, Goldenbay, Greenbay, Grünwald and Thalberg, and in the north near Waldersee, Grahamdale, Moosehorn and Camper.

Except for the Moravian Brethren, who in 1894 founded the colonies of Brüderheim, Brüderfeld and New Sarepta near Edmonton, Alberta, almost all the Germans from Volhynia were Lutheran Protestants.

Germans from central Poland (Warsaw, Lodz, etc.) settled in Alberta in Lutherhorst-Ellerslie, Rosenthal-Leduc and Hay Lakes; in Saskatchewan they settled in Cudsworth, Brightholme, Silvergrove, Herbert, St. Boswells and Kelstern. They, too, were Protestants without exception.

iii. The Volga Colonies

From the Volga region, the oldest and most homogeneous district of German settlement in Russia, the number of emigrants to western Canada was less than from the Black Sea and Volhynia. Nonetheless, Volga-Germans were here as early as 1893 when a large group of families from the village of Jagodnaja Poljana settled in Calgary.

Founded in the period 1764 to 1776, the Volga colonies had their heyday in the first half of the nineteenth century. In contrast to the later established German villages in Russia, they had adopted the *mir*-system. According to this, the land belonged to the community, and was redistributed about every twelve years among the families on the basis of the number of male members. This resulted in unusually large families, since more sons meant more acreage and it kept the younger sons from emigrating in search of a trade. The villages thus grew by leaps and bounds and often became communities of ten thousand or more. The number of German colonists, which in 1775 totalled about twenty-three thousand, increased by 1910 to over 550,000, about four-fifths of whom were Protestants and one-fifth Catholics. The *mir*, however, had another graver consequence. No farmer on the Volga cared to improve the land, because after some time he had to surrender it again. The continuous exhaustion of the soil gradually reduced its yield to a critical point. The economic decline, accelerated by the introduction of the excise tax which ruined the hitherto profitable cultivation of tobacco, therefore became evident after the 1870s. Thus, a shortage of land, decrease of the crop yields and the pressure of higher taxes were the economic prerequisites for the overseas emigration from the Volga. Here, too, the impetus was the suspension of the colonists' privileges in 1871, and the introduction of general conscription in 1874. At that time the first Volga-Germans left for Brazil and the United States. The intensification of the anti-German tendencies of Russian domestic policy around 1890 coincided with years of the severest famine for the Volga-Germans, due to four consecutive crop failures. Bonwetsch called the years 1889 to 1892 "the most dreadful ones experienced by the colonies since the founding years. They would have perished miserably if help had not arrived from all parts of Russia as well as for the first time from the old German homeland."[34] Schmid wrote: "The effect of the crop failures was so desperate that the entire Volga region, the Caucasus and South Russia were overrun by the poor famine-stricken people from Saratov and Samara and entire families had even been reduced to beggary.[35]

The frightful material distress, which entirely overshadowed the beginning ethno-political plight of the Volga-Germans, again led temporarily to a large overseas emigration. Yet the exodus did not reach the proportions one might have expected in the light of the total economic situation of the Volga colonies after 1890, due to the claim of each male to a portion of the communal land. Nonetheless, the letters of the emigrants who had built for themselves a new existence in North or South America continued to encourage individual families and young people to emigrate.[36]

In western Canada the first Germans from the Volga settled, as already indicated, in Calgary-Riverside in 1893. Volga-German colonists also settled in the vicinity of Trochu, Beiseker and Duffield in Alberta, near Grünwald in Manitoba, near Stoughton, Togo and Runnymede in Saskatchewan, since 1906 in the Catholic St. Joseph's colony and since 1910 in the dry belt in the Province of Saskatchewan.

The handwritten community reports mention Norka, Jagodnaja Poljana, Kolb, Preuss, Brabander, Schilling and Alexanderdorf as places of origin. Besides Lutherans and Catholics and a few Mennonites, sects such as the Adventists also came from the Volga. They settled mainly in the dry belt which in the meantime had become western Canada's refuge for sects.

b. Austria-Hungary

i. Galicia

Next to Germans from Russia, German farmers from Galicia formed the largest number of Germans immigrating to western Canada after 1889.

The German presence in Galicia dates, in part, back to the Middle Ages. In our context, however, only the more recent German settlements are of interest. These were mainly east of the San in eastern Galicia, inhabited by Ukrainians, and date back to the years after 1783. They were founded after the annexation of Galicia by Austria (1772) under Emperor Joseph II. The immigrants at that time came predominantly from southwestern Germany and in particular from the Palatinate. Altogether about thirteen thousand immigrants arrived from southwestern Germany with an additional two thousand Sudeten Germans (from Egerland and the Bohemian Forest) and nine hundred Silesians.[37] The villages founded by them thrived, and established numerous daughter colonies in the course of the nineteenth century. By 1890 the German population of Galicia had increased to more than seventy-five thousand (by 1930 it was sixty thousand).[38] Then a considerable emigration took place here as well.

For the emigration of the Germans from Galicia, as for those from Russia, economic and ethno-political causes coincided. The country was already relatively densely populated. Yet there was no industry worth mentioning that could have absorbed the surplus rural population. For this reason, Ukrainians and Poles by the thousands also had to look for new homes across the ocean. The situation of the Germans, however, was aggravated by the fact that in 1867 the government in Vienna had granted Galicia political privileges comparable to those of Hungary, and thereby had surrendered matters of domestic policy to the Poles. When they began to oppress the resident Germans, the government in Vienna did nothing to prevent it.

The abolition of the ecclesiastical supervision of education by the *Reichsvolksschulgesetz* (Imperial Public School Act) of 1869, and the introduction of state control over the schools in all of Austria meant that in Galicia the schools came under Polish administration. The old parochial schools in the German villages were relegated to the status of private schools and lost their claim to state subsidies. As a result, the German schools had to close in the smaller villages, which could not afford to maintain private schools. By 1908 there were only 115 German schools left in 220 German settlements.[39] The German Protestants continued to cling stubbornly to their parochial schools, because state control and thus subordination to a Polish Catholic authority meant not only a threat to their ethnic, but also to their religious identity. The German Catholics, on the other hand, were more inclined to give up their private schools and to put their trust in the contractually recognized continuation of German-language instruction. Nevertheless, state control over the schools always meant eventual polonization as well. In Catholic parishes the ethno-political situation was more critical anyway due to the almost exclusive appointment of Poles as priests. They deliberately pursued the polonization of their parishes. The German secondary schools in the towns, furthermore, disappeared almost entirely. The individual German experienced ethnic discrimination, particularly in the increasing restrictions imposed by the Polish authorities on the purchase of land, and the ill treatment accorded to the non-Polish speaking German in government offices and in court.

The emigration from the German villages began in the 1880s and, according to Zöckler, was directed mainly to western Canada.[40] In 1889 the first Germans from Galicia settled in the colonies of Hoffnungstal, near Langenburg, in Saskatchewan as well as in Josephsberg, near Dunmore, in southern Alberta. In 1890 Germans from Galicia founded Landestreu near Langenburg, and Neudorf. Neudorf, in particular, and the slightly younger neighboring colony of Lemberg, became stopovers for most of the immigrants from Galicia who arrived later, in especially large numbers in the years 1900 to 1908. In addition to the above-mentioned places, we find Germans from Galicia also in Regina, Edenwold, Melville, Kendal, Zorra near Langenburg, Oakshela as well as in the dry belt in Saskatchewan, and also in Edmonton, Stony Plain, Spruce Grove, Golden Spike and Josephsburg in Alberta.

According to my inquiries in Lemberg and Neudorf, in Stony Plain and Josephsburg, as well as according to the handwritten community reports, most of the immigrants can be traced to the districts of Drohobycz and Stryj,[41] primarily to the communities of Josephsberg,[42] Neudorf, Gassendorf, Bolechow (Drohobycz District), Gelsendorf, Duliby and the town of Stryj (Stryj District). Places of origin also mentioned were: Kaiserdorf (Zambor District), Alt-Jazow and München-thal (Yavorov District), Hartfeld, Ottenhausen, Weissenberg, Ebenau (Grodek District), Landestreu, Neu-Kalusz (Kalusz District) and Kamionka Strumilowa.

Almost all the immigrants from Galicia were Lutherans. Only a few small groups professed the Reformed faith and Catholicism.

ii. Bukovina

From Bukovina (meaning "the land of the beech trees"), the emigration of sons of German farmers was relatively large after 1890 and was directed predominantly to western Canada.[43]

Just as in Galicia and southern Hungary, Emperor Joseph II planned the founding of many German villages in Bukovina, which he had acquired from the Turks in 1775. The local authorities, however, insisted that there was no room in Bukovina for German colonization on a major scale. The project therefore never got past its beginnings. In 1782, twenty-two Catholic German families from Banat were settled in Czernowitz and several villages nearby. In 1787, seventy-four mainly Protestant German families, who had been waiting in vain for the allocation of land in Galicia, were settled between Czernowitz and Suczawa, also in close proximity to already existing small Romanian communities.[44] These farm colonies launched at that time were known as "the Swabian villages of the plain," in contrast to the colonies of German miners, glass-workers, artisans, etc., launched simultaneously and later. From these small beginnings the number of Germans in the "Swabian villages" grew rapidly by natural increase, and German minorities developed in the neighboring Romanian and Ukrainian villages. In the German villages small-scale farming prevailed from the beginning. Field crops were supplemented by fruit and vegetable growing and by beekeeping, and was from the outset combined with practicing trade. The economic situation was never rosy. The apparently very active promotion of emigration seems therefore to have fallen on fertile soil in German as well as in Romanian and Ukrainian villages. At times there was even a veritable emigration fever. For the Germans the situation was aggravated also by the lack of German instruction for the children in village communities which had a majority of residents who did not speak German. Even though German was more widely used in Bukovina than in Galicia as an official language, and Czernowitz had a German university, school conditions were favorable for Germans only in the cities.

The Germans from Bukovina settled almost exclusively in Saskatchewan. They began to arrive in Edenwold and vicinity (Zehner, Arat), as well as Vibank, in 1890, and in Mariahilf-Grayson, Kennell-Craven, Markinch, Claybank, Spring Valley and Silton in 1900. Association based on place of origin was rather well retained in these settlements.

As places of origin, virtually all the Swabian villages founded in 1787 between Czernowitz and Suczawa were mentioned by the Protestant majority, such as Fratautz, Satulmare, Badeutz, St. Onufry, Arbora, Tereblestie, Ilischestie and Itzkany, as well as the cities of Czernowitz, Radautz and Suczawa. The Catholic minority which settled in Mariahilf colony near Grayson came from Czernowitz and the nearby villages of Rosch, Moladia, Derelui and Cuszur Mare.

iii. Banat

German farmers from Banat in southern Hungary also began to emigrate to western Canada prior to 1900, but a little later than from Russia, Galicia and Bukovina.

The German element in Banat, which dated back to the beginning of the eighteenth century, had grown to more than 450,000 souls by 1900, due to a strong natural increase and continuing immigration. Meanwhile in the German villages of Banat marked distinctions of property had developed. Since the acquisition of cheap new land had become impossible, and migration to the towns was equally out of the question due to the lack of industries capable of growth, the poorer Banat Swabians had no choice but to emigrate. In 1911 Kaindl could state that 10 to 20 per cent of the Banat Swabians had already gone to America.[45] But here, too, it was not only due to economic reasons that a growing proportion of Banat Germans had to try their luck beyond the boundaries of Hungary. Autonomous in domestic affairs since 1867, Hungary very soon began to embark on a systematic policy of magyarization of the Germans living within its boundaries. In 1879 the Magyar language was made compulsory in all the schools. The next step was the complete magyarization of the public school system. The magyarization of names, the impossibility of upward social mobility without magyarization, the use of Magyar in the courts and the administration—all this was bound to increase dissatisfaction. The early magyarization of the educated class was indirectly responsible for the emigration to America. The Banat Swabians therefore lost their natural intellectual leaders. They might have been able to keep the German surplus population there, benefiting the whole community by their business expertise, or helping people to organize themselves in acquiring land. Consequently the ethno-political plight should not be overlooked as a cause for the emigration of the Banat Swabians, although as far as the individual emigrant was concerned it may have played a minor role in contrast to his tangible economic worries. The Banat German who after thirty-seven years in Canada put down on paper the reasons that drove him and his friends from 1895 on from Zichydorf in Banat (today Mariolana, Yugoslavia) across the sea, therefore remembers only the economic attractions western Canada had to offer him. His account, nevertheless, provides a valuable insight into the causes and origins of that rather considerable emigration, as well as the material conditions of the emigrants from Banat. So far these have not been statistically enumerated, and so have almost entirely eluded scholarly analysis and gone unnoticed.[46] On top of that they are typical of the emigration from the areas of German settlement in eastern and southeastern Europe in general, which went virtually unnoticed and continued to grow almost solely by way of personal solicitation. The account shall therefore be reproduced in its original form:[47]

> The news about the death of Mr. Johann Bolen from Regina rekindles in me, as probably in all the old Zichydorf pioneers, the memory of old times which were so important for so many of our countrymen. With the passing of Johann Bolen the last survivor of the three families departs who, thirty-seven years ago, were the first ones from the community of Zichydorf and the surrounding area to go to Canada.
>
> Among the various communities of farmers the urge to emigrate had always been strong in the 1880s and 1890s because there was not enough land for the growing population. Thus, in the winter

months, in many communities associations were formed and delegations elected to approach the various governments in Hungary, Serbia, Bulgaria and Romania with the request for land for new settlements of German farmers. But all those efforts to find a good area for settlement and hence the guarantee for a better and more secure existence for those wanting to emigrate from Banat and for their children remained unsuccessful.

In 1895, however, news came of a large area in Canada open for settlement. The Bolen brothers managed to contact by letter a Mr. Nickel who had settled in St. Joseph's colony near Balgonie. Inspired by this correspondence, the brothers Johann and Peter Bolen with their families and their parents Johann and Katharina Bolen decided to sell their belongings and bid farewell forever to their beautiful homeland of Hungary. Indeed that was no easy parting for families in those days, to go into the wide world into an uncertain future, without much money, in response to a letter from an unknown man. But to the brave belongs the world, the would-be-emigrant brothers said. The very hope of obtaining a free homestead of 160 acres was the great attraction for them. On the day of their departure they were accompanied to the station by a large crowd of people from the village who wanted to bid the emigrants farewell, they supposed forever.

But the future turned out differently for many of those who saw them off. The families arrived happily and well in Canada and settled temporarily near Balgonie. They found that their trusted agent had written them nothing but the truth, and they were very satisfied with the conditions and the prospects for a better existence. Of course they reported all their impressions back home to their brother and sisters, to relatives, friends and acquaintances and it did not take very long before several families decided to follow these first emigrants. In the years from 1897 to 1914, an emigration movement led to the departure of almost half the original inhabitants of Zichydorf, resulting in their settlement in Canada, the United States and in a few instances, also in South America.[48] The stream of emigration spread in wider and wider circles all over southern Hungary until it was stopped by the outbreak of the war in 1914.

The settlers who arrived during this period in Canada were mostly so-called *Kleinhäusler* [literally: small householders] from the farming villages. They raised the funds necessary to ship their families and their most essential possessions across, in most cases, by the sale of their belongings. But there was seldom enough money left for a new start. This did not appear to be a great obstacle at that time. Full of courage and the desire to work, well versed in every kind of farm duty and prepared for all sorts of privations, these settlers were adequately equipped for everything that awaited them in the New World. We can testify that these were true settlers, that they overcame all difficulties and obstacles; each in his own way managed to carve out his own existence, whether as a farmer on the Canadian prairies, or as a craftsman, professional, business-man or worker in town. Almost all the settlers improved their stan-dard of living considerably in comparison to conditions back home. Many have even reached a level of prosperity — hopefully forever — which is in no way comparable to the fate that would have awaited them or their children and children's children in the old homeland.

Yes, it is true, we are having bad times here too right now. But the old pioneers remember well the bad times over there, where for the poor man the best times were no good. Thus it happened that a great many from Zichydorf who bade farewell forever to the first emigrants upon their departure, could greet them again in the new homecountry after only a few years. Fellow countrymen from Banat, let's remember therefore, on the occasion of the death of one of the first pioneers, the men and women who formed the vanguard that opened this new area of settlement in Canada for us. Here we can earn our daily bread in relative calm and peace, and under much more favorable conditions than in the old homeland.

Banat Swabians who began to arrive in western Canada from the end of the 1890s, like all the German Catholic immigrants, settled almost exclusively in Saskatchewan. They can be found in Regina, Vibank, Kendal, Fort Qu'Appelle, Indian Head, Holdfast, Quinton-Raymore, Horizon and near Swift Current. Besides Zichydorf, Sechenfeld, Glo-gon and Gross-Zsam are mentioned as places of origin.

iv. Other Areas of the Habsburg Monarchy

From the remaining areas of German settlement in the Habsburg Monarchy there was also some emigration to western Canada where, however, these could be identified only in isolated instances. The emigra-tion from the German villages in Batschka (Bacska) and the rest of Hungary was mainly caused by the shortage of land and the high mort-gages on the farmers' properties. Added to this as the immediate cause was crop failures. It is also worth noting that according to Hungarian statistics, the emigration reached its peak in the years 1905 to 1907 when, with Apponyi's public school legislation of 1907, the tide of magyari-zation rolled over the last German schools.[49] Only Transylvania, con-trary to frequently expressed assumptions, seems not to have sent emigrants to settle in western Canada. Among Transylvania-Saxons, though, emigration had also begun in the 1880s, and by 1900 as many as twenty thousand of these Saxons had settled in America.[50] From German Austria as well as from Bohemia, Moravia, Zips and other German ethnic enclaves within the Habsburg state, only a few emigrants went to western Canada prior to the war. There is evidence of a greater emigration from these areas, as from Germany, only after the war.

c. Romania (Dobrudja)

Beginning as early as 1885 a surprisingly large emigration to western Canada took place from the German villages in Romanian Dobrudja. Those German colonies had been formed by the emigration of German colonists from South Russia, especially from Bessarabia. The oldest colonies date back to the 1840s and the early 1850s, the younger ones to the period after 1873, when the introduction of universal conscription led to the first mass emigration among the Germans in Russia.[51] The Turkish authorities cared only to collect the taxes, but otherwise left the colonists to manage their own affairs as they pleased. When, however, in 1878 Dobrudja came to Romania, the Germans no longer remained unmolested. Romanian mayors who, of course, could not understand German, and were primarily out for their own personal gain, were imposed on their villages. They made life miserable for the farmers. New regulations requiring documentary proof of the acquisition of real estate caused great irritation. Under Turkish rule no one was very particular about this. "Some farmers who had occupied their farms for decades and cultivated their land as undisputedly their own, were suddenly expelled because they had no papers, or simply because they had neglected to have it registered in their own names after purchasing it from a legitimate former owner. Wealthy farmers were suddenly reduced to poverty. They lacked the means and also the faith in a just outcome of legal proceedings."[52]

Before the last immigrants from Russia began to feel really at home, therefore, emigration resumed. About its causes and beginnings, the following is reported:[53]

> The rapid natural increase, if allowed to develop unchecked, would have resulted in a tremendous growth of the individual colonies. In reality, however, this did not happen anywhere . . . Soon limits were set to the expansion of the villages and their population. After the Romanian land survey had established the extent of the colonies' holdings, most of them could obtain no more land outside

the boundaries drawn. This is the first and one of the main causes
for the considerable resumption of migration from Dobrudja. It
set in about the time of the surveys, only a few years after the
Romanian takeover, and has not ceased since. There were other
reasons too. For many Baptists, religious separation from the other
members of the community provided the impetus. Above all,
however, it was the deterioration of the situation of the German
colonists, brought about by the conduct of the new rulers. The
first emigration appears to have taken place in 1882. A letter from
Cataloi of June 25, 1883, tells of seven families who had left there
for Dakota the previous year, and of many more who were tempted
to follow them had it not been for a Romanian law. According
to this, the emigrants were not permitted to sell immovable
property, such as houses, farms and land, but merely their port-
able belongings. By 1884 the desire to leave appeared to have
become widespread. The introduction in the Dobrudja of military
service in 1883, as well as the deteriorating siutation of the farmers
due to the unusual drought of 1884, may have been contributing
factors. The *Deutsche Kolonialzeitung* reported about 600 families
who had been compelled to leave their homes and farms at that
time in order to migrate again . . . North and South Dakota were
their primary destinations. A number of Protestant colonists
headed for Canada, and considerable number of Catholics for
Argentina.

From the Dakotas, a sizeable number continued their migration to
western Canada. The first group of Germans from Dobrudja can be
identified in western Canada in 1885. They were Baptists from the village of Tulcea, who founded the colony of Neu-Tulcea which later became
Edenwold in Saskatchewan. Arrivals after 1890 were predominantly
of Germans from Bukovina.

When in the years after 1890 German colonists from Russia began
to emigrate in larger numbers than before, many of them tried their
luck in Dobrudja. But Romanians in the meantime had also become
more hostile towards foreign elements. The German farmers who might
have made good colonizers in still sparsely populated Dobrudja, met
with ill will and snubs everywhere. Romanian citizenship, which could
be obtained only after a ten-year residence in the country, was now
a prerequisite for acquiring real estate. Until they qualified for citizenship, land would be reserved for new immigrants that they could lease
for the time being in the new villages they had built. But the promises
to reserve and allot land after ten years were only very rarely kept. All
kinds of subterfuges were used to postpone the conveyance of property,
and to reduce the promised acreage.[54] If the legitimate claims of the

German immigrants were recognized at all, it was only after considerable fighting and wrangling. The overwhelming majority of German farmers who arrived after 1890 were no longer able to acquire any land of their own in Dobrudja. One can imagine what an impression the Canadian homestead legislation must have made under these circumstances. Sooner or later the Germans lost their patience and emigrated. Entire villages, after flourishing briefly, thus vanished again. For most of those arriving after 1890, the sojourn in Dobrudja became merely a shorter or longer stopover on their way from Russia to the northwest of the United States and to western Canada. They frequently reached the last stop only after another interval of several years in the Dakotas.

The immigration of Germans from Romania (i.e., almost exclusively from Dobrudja) to western Canada continued until the World War. They came from the older German villages of Tulcea, Ciucurova, Cataloi and Caramurat, as well as from numerous younger villages which were for the most part temporary settlements. In western Canada we find them in Edenwold, Balgonie, Josephsthal, Kronau, Davin and in a number of other settlements in Saskatchewan, and particularly in the dry belt around St. Boswells, Kelstern, Morse, Blumenfeld and Bergfeld. Here, too, only a few have been able to stay after the frightening period of drought and most have had to migrate again. Probably no other small group of ethnic Germans has been knocked around so much by fate as those farmers who once settled temporarily in Dobrudja. This was no doubt mainly due to the bitter disappointments with which their truly modest expectations had been met time and again in a foreign country. But it was also due to the inner restlessness typical of the Germans in eastern Europe once they had turned their backs on their German motherland. Adam Kühn, the leader of the first German immigrants to Dobrudja, and founder of the village of Atmagea (1848) once expressed this unrest to his pastor with these words: "You know, pastor, once a German has left his homeland he cannot find peace anywhere. We Germans are like that: once we have bread, we want muffins."[55]

d. Germany

In spite of all the efforts on the part of Canada, immigration from Germany remained relatively small.

When the opening of the West began in the 1880s, emigration from

Germany reached its peak. Between 1881 and 1890, 1,342,423 persons emigrated from Germany, 1,237,136 (i.e., 88.8 per cent) of whom went to the United States.[56] The Canadian authorities hoped to be able to divert a major proportion of this German mass emigration going to its neighbor into its own sparsely populated West, and invited a number of personalities from Germany to come on tours of inspection. Their reports were then publicized and used for propaganda purposes.[57]

One of them was the president of the German Colonial League, Prince von Hohenlohe-Langenburg. In 1883 he undertook such a tour, and praised western Canada highly in a letter to the Canadian High Commissioner in London, Sir Charles Tupper. He compared its economic opportunities favorably with those of the United States and referred to western Canada as the preferred land of emigration for Germans as long as Germany had no colonies of her own.[58] This letter played an important role in early Canadian promotional literature. One of the oldest German settlements in the Northwest Territory was named Hohenlohe in honor of the prince, and its railway station was named Langenburg. Also in 1885, when the colony of Hohenlohe-Langenburg was founded, a second German colony was founded and named Neu-Elsass (Strassburg). It became the destination of emigrants from all parts of Germany.[59] But on the whole, immigration from Germany in no way came up to expectations and the promotional effort. The United States continued to snatch up the largest part of the German emigration. For decades hundreds of thousands of emigrants had gone there, with the result that the most effective way of recruiting emigrants, which was through the letters of relatives and acquaintances who had been successful, continued to attract German emigrants primarily to the United States. The prairies offered, no doubt, great attractions to the Germans from Russia who were used to the steppe, but not to those from Germany. In the American Midwest, too, Germans from Germany preferred the areas with forests and lakes (Wisconsin, etc.), which resembled the physical environment of their homeland, to the treeless prairie as in the Dakotas. The climatic and economic conditions of western Canada appeared too strange to the emigrant from Germany, and therefore too hard to endure. The high level of economic and cultural development of densely populated Germany had also given rise to much greater demands and expectations of the rural population. The German farmers from eastern Europe, by contrast, were able to reduce their everyday needs considerably, in accordance with the inevitable exigencies of emigration and resettlement, and could thus put up more easily with conditions in western Canada. Western Canada's development, finally, was still in its infancy, and suffered serious economic setbacks and so could not in any way bear comparison with the neighboring country during the period when the tide of mass emigration from Germany continued undiminished (until 1893). When around the turn of the century, the production of wheat began to flourish in western Canada, the volume of emigration from Germany had already declined considerably. Germany's rapid industrial development was by and large now able to absorb the surplus rural population.

Canadian immigration propaganda in Germany was therefore doomed to failure, in spite of the great importance that was attached to the immigration of Germans, particularly since 1897, when Sifton instilled new vigor into immigration policy. Mr. Smart, then Deputy Minister of the Interior under Sifton, wrote to Mr. Preston, the Commissioner of Immigration, on July 18, 1900: "We are especially anxious to bring persons of German origin." In another letter to Preston on August 26, 1901, he wrote: "I will be glad if you will let me know what has been the result of the efforts of the North Atlantic Trading Company insofar as its work in Germany is concerned. I may say that after two years, the department is a little disappointed in not seeing greater results from the efforts of the company in Germany and also in Scandinavia. There is no class of people that Canadians are so willing to welcome as German settlers. and it seems too bad that some good commencement cannot be made in connection with the people of this nationality."[60]

The rapid economic growth of the Prairie provinces and British Columbia in the new century did attract emigrants from Germany, nonetheless. There were not only farm laborers, but also craftsmen and tradesmen. They settled in small prairie towns, usually after spending some time on the homestead. There were also quite a few from the upper middle classes, most of whom had suffered economic or social bankruptcy at home. The majority had been living in the United States for some time before moving to western Canada. Yet nowhere did the immigrants from Germany form exclusive settlements of their own. Instead, they spread among the many German settlements founded by Germans from eastern Europe.

Information about immigrants born in Germany can only be derived from the census. Immigration statistics do not distinguish between citizenship and ethnic descent. In 1901 the number of western Canadians born in Germany was reported to be 5,933, in 1911 it was 21,295.

They were distributed as follows:

	1901	1911
Manitoba	2,285	3,839
Saskatchewan	2,170	8,300
Alberta		6,102
British Columbia	1,478	3,054
Total	5,933	21,295

Among the total German population in western Canada, which was 151,900 according to the 1911 Census, those born in Germany thus formed about 14 per cent. Since the actual total of Germans, however, was higher due to the fact that German immigrants from other lands tended to report their former citizenship when asked for their ethnic origin, the Germans from Germany may, in fact, have formed only 12 per cent.

e. The United States

German immigration from the United States began in the early 1890s.[61] After 1903 its volume increased strongly and reached its climax around 1909 to 1910. With regard to this German immigration, one must differentiate between those born in the American Midwest as the descendants of German immigrants, and those who themselves had immigrated to the United States only a few years before. For the latter, therefore, the States had served only as a brief stopover for the purpose of gathering experience on the American continent. These differ, except for their statistical classification, in no way from those who immigrated to Canada directly. The farmer planning to emigrate from eastern Europe reached his decision on whether he should go first to the United States or Canada, solely on the basis of whether the relatives or friends who induced him to emigrate, lived in Dakota, Kansas, etc., or in Manitoba, Saskatchewan or Alberta. After the 1890s, cheap land in the prairie regions of the American Northwest began to become scarce, just as the settlement of western Canada started under favorable conditions. It was therefore an easy decision for the latest arrivals in the United States to move on to western Canada, after a more or less brief apprenticeship at the original destination of their emigration. We may include them without further ado among the groups of emigrants already dealt with.

Only those who were born there or who had lived for a generation in the United States and had become American citizens are to be considered as a special German-American group. Among these, too, the first and second generation of Germans from Russia by far outnumbered the others. Following the true farmer's ambition to own as much land as possible, many who had already attained wealth in the States abandoned their developed holdings in exchange for a greater acreage of virgin land in the Canadian Prairie provinces. Thus, to mention just one example among many others, the *Dakota Freie Presse* of March 10, 1910, reported the story of a German from the Black Sea, who in 1909 sold his homestead land in North Dakota, acquired 1,280 acres of land near Morse, Saskatchewan, and moved there with his steam plough in 1910 in order to cultivate his new land.[62] The sole criterion for the move of all these immigrants across the border was to acquire as much cheap virgin land as possible with high fertility and low taxes. Even though these Russian Germans from the United States may have become somewhat Americanized in their economic views, they still shared the same cultural standards and the same outlook on life as those who immigrated to western Canada directly from eastern Europe.

The other group of German-American immigrants, those from the midwestern States of Illinois, Indiana, Michigan, Missouri, Iowa and Minnesota, traced their ethnic origins to their emigration from Germany around the middle of the nineteenth century. They combined the old European farmer's ambition for large land holdings with the new profit-oriented outlook of the American businessman. Several well-to-do German Americans of the second generation started growing wheat in western Canada as a big business, in systematic capitalist fashion. In 1901, for example, a former German senator from the State of Minnesota set up a giant farm near Dundurn, Saskatchewan, on which he harvested forty-five thousand bushels of wheat in 1905. Another German, a former elected representative from Minnesota, established a similarly huge farm in his neighborhood and managed to cultivate as much as five thousand acres of virgin land after only two years.[63]

From the beginning, German immigrants, next to British and Scandinavian immigrants, have formed the major portion of the immigration from the United States, more than 15 per cent by my estimates. According to the Canadian Census of 1921, which shows an artificially low number of Germans due to the impact of the war psychosis, forty thousand people acknowledged their German descent among a total of 374,024 American-born persons then residing in Canada.[64] To the great regret of the Canadian immigration officials, the World War suddenly interrupted this very welcome German-American immigration.[65]

The Germans from the United States appear to have preferred Alberta. Here they settled in the south as well as in a wide radius around Edmonton, especially along the Red Deer-Wetaskiwin-Leduc-Edmonton railway line. In Saskatchewan they are particularly numerous in the Catholic St. Peter's colony, as well as near Alameda and in the Yorkton district. Moreover, they are scattered over the entire West.

f. Ontario, Switzerland and Other German-Speaking Areas

It would be strange, indeed, had the German farmers in eastern Canada not been seized by the tide of immigration to the West as well. From an early date Ontario-Germans of the second generation left for the Prairie provinces. They came from the area of Berlin-Waterloo on the Ontario peninsula, as well as from the settlements of Renfrew County near the Ottawa River.[66] They shared the same purely economic motives as the Germans from the United States. They wanted to exchange their small developed holdings in a land in which they had not yet entirely put down roots, for much larger tracts of fertile virgin land. As early as 1879, the first itinerant pastor of the Lutheran Missouri Synod was able to visit German Lutherans in Manitoba from the area of Berlin, Ontario. They had also named their new settlement Berlin, but soon abandoned it, and moved on to the United States disappointed.[67] In Alberta, too, Ontario-Germans settled early, for instance in Pincher Creek since 1882, and somewhat later in Edmonton and vicinity (Spruce Grove, etc.). In general, Ontario-Germans can be found scattered in settlements all over western Canada, since the 1880s in Manitoba for instance in Alcester, and Boissevain. Beginning in 1891, individual German Mennonite families from the area of Berlin-Waterloo went to Alberta (High River, Aldersyde, Carstairs near Didsbury, and Acadia Valley near the Saskatchewan border). Others settled near Guernsey, Saskatchewan, starting in 1905.[68]

Since the young generation of Ontario-Germans were already Canadian citizens and had attended schools recognized by the state, it was easier from the outset for them to move up socially. Soon quite a few Ontario-Germans advanced to higher positions, and they could be found particularly among the immigration and colonization agents. The best known Ontario-German in western Canada today is the Minister of Public Health, Dr. Uhrich, in Regina, Saskatchewan.

To be added to the spectrum of German-speaking immigrants from Europe are the Swiss Germans. The oldest Swiss-German colony was founded near Whitewood, Saskatchewan, in 1886 at the initiative of Court President Saanen in Bern Canton, and a Dr. Meyer from Paris.[69]

Another exclusive Swiss-German colony is the settlement of Blumenau in Alberta, founded in 1903 and now known as Stettler. Everywhere the Swiss Germans seem to have taken up dairying and the production of cheese. On the whole, however, the immigration from Switzerland always remained small. According to the Census of 1921, there were 3,479 persons born in Switzerland in all of Canada, 2,810 (i.e., 80 per cent) of whom were German-speaking.[70] According to the 1931 Census, there was a total of 3,560 persons from Switzerland in the three Prairie provinces and in British Columbia. Among these we may assume an equally high percentage of German-speaking persons.

Also in the 1890s, individual German families from South America migrated to western Canada.[71] In addition, Germans from all the remaining smaller areas of German settlement in the world found their way to western Canada.

On the basis of the materials available to me I would like to venture the following estimates of the German prewar immigration to western Canada by their areas of origin.

Table IV.1

Germans from Russia (Black Sea area, Volhynia, Volga area)	44%
Germans from Romania (Dobrudja, indirectly also from Russia)	6%
Germans from Austria-Hungary (Galicia, Bukovina, Banat, etc.)	18%
Germans from Germany	12%
Germans from the United States (second to fourth generations)	18%
Germans from Ontario, Switzerland and other German-speaking areas	2%
Total	100%

The postwar immigration was very similar in character, as we shall see. The composition of the German-Canadian population in terms of its areas of origin has therefore remained virtually unchanged.

CHAPTER V

Trailblazers of Western Immigration and Settlement

1. The Prewar Immigration

The first German immigrants who came to western Canada in large numbers were, as we saw, German Mennonites from Russia who settled in southern Manitoba in the years 1874 to 1879.[1] In the summer of 1871, the abolition of the colonists' privileges was announced by the Russian government. Merchant Cornelius Janzen in Berdyansk, who for a while had been Prussian consul in that port city of the Black Sea, immediately approached the Canadian government via the Colonial Secretary in London, inquiring about the conditions for an immigration of his Mennonite brethren to Canada. In 1872 Wilhelm Hespeler, a German Canadian residing in Winnipeg who later was to play a crucial role in the settlement of the Mennonites, was commissioned by the government of Manitoba to visit the Mennonite settlements in South Russia, and as far as possible make arrangements on the spot for their emigration to Canada.[2] Thereupon the Mennonites sent several small groups of "scouts" to North America, to find suitable virgin land in Manitoba and at the frontier of settlement in the United States (Dakota, Nebraska, Kansas, Texas).

Like Joshua and Caleb in the Bible, such scouts actually always preceded the first settlers. These emissaries had a good eye for suitable land, although there was, of course, no scientific method to their selection. They tended to choose solely according to the criterion of whether the land in question was similar to the land known to be of good quality at home. The farmer from Germany used to forests and pastureland, just like the British, French and French Canadians, would not have ventured out into the treeless prairie. What was required were immigrants who knew the fertility of the grass-steppes from their own experience. This is the reason why Germans from Russia were destined to pioneer the opening of the Canadian prairie as well as large parts of the prairie belt in the United States.

The Mennonite emissaries were favorably impressed when, upon Hespeler's initiative, they were handed a sealed document from the Manitoba Ministry of Agriculture promising that all their special requests of a religious and other nature would be granted: exemption from military service, closed settlements with administrative autonomy, use of the German language in their own private schools and a cheap passage (only thirty dollars per person from Hamburg to Winnipeg).[3] The delegates Jacob Peters and Heinrich Wiebe from the Bergthaler congregation, as well as David Klassen and Cornelius Toews from the *Kleine Gemeinde* in Borsenko, who visited Manitoba under the guidance of Mennonite Jakob Schantz from Waterloo, Ontario,[4] thereupon decided to recommend to their congregations the emigration to Manitoba. To the remaining delegates, emigrating to the totally untested Manitoba prairie appeared too great a risk to take, particularly because of its still utter inaccessibility, in spite of the favorable offer of the Canadian government. They recommended to their congregations emigration to the United States, although the States refused to grant them any privileges.[5] The Canadian government was so eager to have the Mennonite immigrants that it was even willing to loan them the sum of $96,400 against a guarantee given by the Mennonites of Ontario, for the acquisition of livestock, tools, machines, etc. By as early as 1891 this loan was repaid in the full amount of $130,386.58 (interest included).[6] This showed the rapid economic success of the Mennonites as well as their meticulous honesty in business matters, which greatly astonished the parliamentarians in Manitoba. It bore fruit later when as a result of this favorable experience, the Canadian government granted the Mennonites another large credit, even after the war, which made possible the rescue of more than twenty thousand of their brethren from Soviet Russia.

The first group of immigrants travelled from South Russia via Warsaw-Hamburg-Quebec-Berlin, Ontario, then across Lake Superior to Duluth and on to Moosehead, Minnesota. Finally, since there was as yet no railway to Winnipeg, the steamer *International* of the Hudson's Bay Company took them to a place twenty miles south of Winnipeg. They landed near the present-day community of Niverville, where they made their first encampment. From 1874 to 1879 the Canadian authorities in Quebec counted a total of 6,902 Mennonite immigrants,[7] namely:

Table V.1

year	immigrants	year	immigrants
1874 1,532		1877 183	
1875 3,258		1878 323	
1876 1,358		1879 248	

The first contingent arrived in Manitoba on July 31, 1874. Three church groups took part in the emigration:(1) the *Kleine Gemeinde* of Borsenko, from which sixty families arrived in 1874; (2) the Bergthalers, all of whom left their homeland, 1,400 in 1874 and the rest in the next two years; (3) the Old Colony group (*Altkolonier*) or so-called *Grossfürstenländer*, who had moved from Chortitza in 1864 to the private estate of a Grand Duke (*Grossfürst*) near Melitopol in Tauria. Most of them began their emigration to Manitoba in 1875 under the guidance of their elder (bishop) Johann Wiebe.[8] Bergthaler and *Altkolonier* immigrants were about equal in numbers. Under the direction of Hespeler, the Mennonites were settled on two closed tracts of land west and east of the Red River. A small separate colony was formed between the two large settlements on the Scratching River near present-day Morris. There was virtually no return migration to Russia.[9] By the time of the 1881 Census, the Mennonites in Manitoba numbered as many as 7,776 persons among a total white population of about twelve thousand. Besides these, there were 876 Germans by origin in the province, largely from Ontario. Of these Germans, no more than 220 were born in Germany.

The great accomplishment of the German Mennonites from Russia as pioneers has won repeated recognition among the British as well. The Mennonites earned the distinction of being the first to demonstrate the agricultural possibilities of the open prairie even in such northern latitudes. It was their achievement that created the necessary prerequisite for the opening up of western Canada.[10]

There has, however, been much less inclination so far to acknowledge the significant contributions of the non-Mennonite Germans in the opening up of western Canada. German farmers from eastern Europe were the first ones there, after the British, as early as the second half of the 1880s. They came, as we saw, predominantly from the areas where Ukrainian was the native language, i.e., from the Ukraine proper, from Volhynia, eastern Galicia and Bukovina. Their successes not only continued to draw new German immigrants into the country, but also made them the vanguard of the Ukrainians, who today form the next largest proportion, after the Germans, of western Canada's non-British population.[11]

The large immigration of farmers from the United States beginning in 1891 was also initiated by German settlers. The Anglo-American and Scandinavian components in this immigration attained significance only towards the end of the 1890s. Germans thus proved to be the trailblazers of the settlement of western Canada, in the true sense of the word.

The quantification of German immigration has its difficulties. German data on emigration and Canadian port statistics do not at all, or do not clearly, distinguish between eastern and western Canada as a destination of immigration. They take no account whatsoever of immigration via American ports. The number of those who subsequently moved on to the United States cannot be statistically ascertained. The most useful statistics are those of the local immigration agency in Winnipeg (until 1883 in Emerson, Manitoba) which were transmitted to the government and then published in the *Sessional Papers*. Its figures, however, appear to be too low throughout, in view of the fact that the German immigrants were predominantly Germans from areas outside Germany whose ethnic descent tended to be frequently confused with their former citizenship. German immigrants from the United States, moreover, in many cases did not go through Winnipeg, but came by train via North Portal-Moose Jaw or Coutts-Lethbridge, or also by wagon through several other border crossings to western Canada. Concerning the low figures for the early years, it should be kept in mind that immigration was small, on the whole, until the turn of the century. Germans, nevertheless, always formed at least 10 to 15 per cent, in 1893 even one-third, of all the immigrants to western Canada.

Table V.2
German Immigrants to Western Canada 1881 to 1903
(according to the Winnipeg statistics, until 1883 in Emerson)

year	# of immigrants	year	# of immigrants
1881	80	1893	2,626
1882	319	1894	1,904
1883	247	1895	869
1884	231	1896	990
1885	192	1897	520
1886	312	1898	998
1887	356	1899	1,691
1888	458	1900 (until June 30)	1,250
1889	1,043	1900—01	2,251
1890	894	1901—02	5,647
1891	1,312	1902—03	12,367
1892	2,764	1903—04	—

For the budget year 1903-04, unfortunately no accurate figures are available. For the period July 1904 to March 1915 we have the records of Canadian authorities on the destination of the German immigrants from Europe—those who disembarked in Canadian ports as well as of those who immigrated via American ports. Here, too, the chief source of error is the probably frequent confusion of German ethnic descent with Russian, Austro-Hungarian or Romanian citizenship. In addition, Germans who had become American immigrants are missing entirely.

Table V.3
German Immigrants from Europe Giving Western Canada as Their Destination 1904 to 1915

Year	To the Prairie Provinces	To British Columbia	To Western Canada (total)
1904/05 (July-June)	2,134	24	2,158
1905/06	1,229	52	1,281
1906/07 (July-March)	1,844	34	1,878
1907/08 (April-March)	1,692	151	1,843
1908/09	1,063	117	1,180
1909/10	1,071	134	1,205
1910/11	1,816	206	2,022
1911/12	4,400	180	4,580
1912/13	4,275	238	4,513
1913/14	4,724	260	4,984
1914/15	1,933	94	2,027

For the German immigration from the United States we have statistical clues only for the years 1908 to 1915. Starting in 1908, American statistics recorded the departure of aliens to Canada.[12] The number of Germans who moved on to Canada after a more or less brief sojourn in the United States is, of course, also much too low, since most of these Germans did not have German, but Russian or Austro-Hungarian citizenship.

Table V.4

Departure of German Aliens from the U.S.A. for Canada
(Eastern and Western Canada) 1908 to 1915

year	immigrants	year	immigrants
1908/09 3,445		1912/13 2,374	
1909/10 1,296		1913/14 1,208	
1910/11 1,999		1914/15 301	
1911/12 2,556			

We can get a better idea about the growth of the German population from occasional inventories of the German settlements (until 1896) and from the census than from the immigration statistics.

Apart from the 110 small villages that the German Mennonites from Russia had founded in southern Manitoba, a large number of additional German settlements had been formed by 1896 (i.e., before the promotion of emigration by Sifton in the Laurier government began to take effect.) These oldest colonies are listed in the order of their foundation. The date indicates merely the beginning of the settlement, since it takes from four to five years on an average until all the homesteads have been taken up in a new district.

1884/85:	Neu-Elsass, later Strassburg, in Sask.
1885:	Neu Tulcea, later Edenwold, Sask.
	Hohenlohe, later Langenburg, Sask.
1886:	Josephstal near Balgonie, Sask.
1887:	Ebenezer near Yorkton, Sask.
1888:	South Qu'Appelle, Sask.
1889:	Landshut near Langenburg, Sask.
1890:	St. Peter near Balgonie, and Davin, Sask.
	Landestreu and Riverdale near Langenburg, Sask.

	Neudorf and Wolseley, Sask.

Neudorf and Wolseley, Sask.
The first Germans settled in Regina in that year.

1891: Tupper and Waldersee, Man.
Hoffnungstal and Beresina near Langenburg, Sask.
Stony Plain and Spruce Grove, Alta.
Rosthern, Sask.

1892: Wilhelmshöhe near Yorkton, Sask.
Longlaketon, Sask., settled by immigrants from Strassburg.
Neu-Kronau, Sask.
Yellow Grass, Sask.
Boucher on the Carrot River near Prince Albert, Sask.
Heimthal and Lutherhort near Ellerslie, Alta.
Wetaskiwin, Alta.
Josephsberg (Beaver Hills, Fort Saskatchewan), Alta.

1893: Langenau near Ebenezer, Sask.
Leduc, Alta.

1894: Holstein (Tenby), Man.
Lipton, Sask.
Leech Lake near Yorkton, Sask.
Waldheim and Tiefengrund near Rosthern, Sask.
Brüderheim, Alta.
Brüderfeld (Strathcona), Alta.
Lacombe, Alta.

1896: Oldenburg—Whitemouth, Man.
Friedensthal and Ridgeville, Man.
Russell, Man.

The last official inventory of the German settlements and their development is dated October 31, 1896 and reproduced below.[13] According to it there were 35,777 persons of German descent in the settlements, apart from individual farmers living in scattered locations, and this was at a time when the same statistical survey counted a mere 1,447 Slavic and Hungarian settlers in all of western Canada (see Table V.5)

After the change of government in 1897, when immigration policy was revitalized by Sifton and soon began to show concrete results, there was no more time for statistical surveys of new settlements. On the basis of other materials available, we can at least trace the main events of the history of German immigration.

Between 1897 and 1901 the colonies already in existence filled up. In those years an extensive area of German settlement developed, particularly around Neudorf and Lemberg in Saskatchewan. There were new districts of German farmers in Manitoba in the area of Broken-

Table V.5

Name of Colony	Name of nearest		Location of Township and Range	Number of		Acreage under cultivation	Number owned of		
	Railway Station	Post Office		Families	Persons		Horses	Cattle	Sheep
Mennoniten-Siedlungen in Süd-Manitoba	Gretna, Altona, Rosenfeld, Plum Coulà, Morris, Niverville	do.	Tp. 1, Rg. 1 östl. u. Rg. 1—5 westl. 1. Mer. Tp. 2—3, Rg. 1—5 westl. 1. Mer. Tp. 4, Rg. 6 östl. u. Tp. 5, Rg. 5—6 östl. 1. Mer. Tp. 6, Rg. 5—6 östl. u. Tp. 7, Rg. 4—6 östl. 1. Mer. Tp. 5, Rg. 1 östl. u. Tp. 6, Rg. 1 westl. 1. Mer.	2000	24 000	235 160	11 230	20 362	2 500
Holstein	Gladstone	Tenby	Tp. 17—19, Rg. 12 westl. 1. Mer.	40	180	600	80	250	60
	Lake Dauphin	Oak Nook	Tp. 26, Rg. 21 " 1. "	15	70	—	—	—	—
Gilbert Plains	do.	Gilbert Plains	Tp. 24—25, Rg. 23 " 1. "	12	42	200	30	70	—
Brokenhead	Beausejour	Brokenhead	Tp. 14—15, Rg. 7—8 östl. 1. "	25	—	—	—	50	—
Oldenburg	Whitemouth	Whitemouth	Tp. 12, Rg. 11 " 1. "	20	63	20	18	50	—
	Morris	Morris	Tp. 6—7, Rg. 1 westl. 1. "	30	110	500	80	250	80
	McGregor	McGregor	Tp. 11, Rg. 10—11 " 1. "	9	22	600	35	70	—
	Holland	Holland	Tp. 8, Rg. 11 " 1. "	5	18	100	15	40	—
Ridgeville	Emerson	Ridgeville	Tp. 1—2, Rg. 3—4 östl. 1. "	30	125	450	80	280	—
	Russell	Russell	Tp. 22, Rg. 28—29 westl. 1. "	10	43	220	25	70	—
Alcester	Boissevain	Alcester	Tp. 5, Rg. 19 " 1. "	12	40	1 000	50	80	—
Hohenlohe	Langenburg	Langenburg	Tp. 21—22, Rg. 30—31 u. Tp. 20, Rg. 31 westl. 1. Mer.	60	320	1 800	200	800	—
Landshut	do.	do.	Tp. 21, Rg. 32 westl. 1. Mer.	25	110	1 000	30	400	—
Beresina	do.	do.	Tp. 22—24, Rg. 31—33; Tp. 20, Rg. 32;	40	220	1 200	80	450	400
	do.	Redpath	Tp. 21, Rg. 33 westl. 1. Mer.	10	48	450	6	180	—
Landestreu	do.	Langenburg	Tp. 33, Rg. 30 westl. 1. Mer.	30	130	900	12	350	—
Hoffenthal	do.	do.	Tp. 22, Rg. 30 " 1. "	12	40	350	8	120	—
Ebenezer	Yorkton	Ebenezer	Tp. 27—28, Rg. 4—5; Tp. 29, Rg. 4; Tp. 28, Rg. 3 westl. 2. Mer.	150	740	5 000	800	3 200	1 000
Sheho Lake	do.	Sheho Lake	Tp. 30, Rg. 9—10 westl. 2. Mer.	25	90	600	120	350	—
Theodore	do.	Theodore	Tp. 28, Rg. 7 " 2. "	10	48	180	24	100	—

Gemeinde	Bezirk	Post office	Lage						
Josephsberg	Grenfell	Heyde	Tp. 17—19a, Rg. 7—9 westl. 2. Mer.	45	215	1 600	100	550	—
Neudorf	do.	Neudorf	Tp. 19—21, Rg. 7—10 " 2. "	250	1 200	5 000	600	1 400	—
	Wolseley	Pheasant Forks	Tp. 17—18, Rg. 9 " 2. "	35	150	1 000	80	600	—
Ft. Qu'Appelle	Qu'Appelle	Ft. Qu'Appelle	Tp. 25, Rg. 15 " 2. "	10	48	200	18	70	400
Edenwald	Balgonie	Edenwald	Tp. 18—20, Rg. 15—18 " 2. "	265	1 200	6 000	600	1 500	100
New Kronau	do.	Davin	Tp. 15, Rg. 17 " 2. "	30	180	1 000	80	300	100
Davin	do.	do.	Tp. 16, Rg. 17 " 2. "	30	130	900	60	250	50
St. Joseph, St. Peter	do.	St. Peter	Tp. 15—17, Rg. 16—17 " 2. "	150	800	3 000	320	1 200	300
Regina	Regina	Regina	Tp. 15—16, Rg. 18 " 2. "	40	180	850	100	500	—
Yellow Grass	Yellow Grass	Yellow Grass	Tp. 10, Rg. 18—19 " 2. "	15	70	150	60	300	100
Longlaketon	Lumsden	Longlaketon	Tp. 21—22, Rg. 21 " 2. "	20	75	400	50	200	100
Straßburg	do.	Straßburg	Tp. 24, Rg. 21—22; Tp. 23, Rg. 22 westl. 2. Mer.	32	210	2 000	70	350	300
Rosthern, Tiefengrund	Rosthern	Rosthern	Tp. 41—43, Rg. 2—4 westl. 3. Mer. Tp. 42, Rg. 5 " 3. "	150	800	3 200	400	2 000	—
Boucher, &c.	Prince Albert	Boucher	Nördlich u. südöstlich von Prince Albert	50	220	1 000	160	700	—
Moosejaw	Moosejaw	Moosejaw	Tp. 17, Rg. 25 westl. 3. Mer.	15	65	800	70	170	1 500
Josephsberg	Dunmore	Dunmore	Tp. 9—10, Rg. 4 " 4. "	15	70	300	300	1 000	—
Seven Persons	Seven Persons	Seven Persons	Tp. 10—11, Rg. 7 " 4. "	10	45	150	25	100	—
Gleichen	Gleichen	Gleichen	Tp. 23, Rg. 22 " 4. "	10	55	180	25	90	—
Lacombe	Lacombe	Lacombe	Tp. 40—41, Rg. 27 " 4. "	20	75	325	30	150	—
Leduc	Leduc	Leduc	Tp. 40—50, Rg. 24—26 " 4. "	135	650	2 300	200	700	—
Wetaskiwin, Red Deer Lake, Bears Hill, &c.	Wetaskiwin	Wetaskiwin	Tp. 45—46, Rg. 23—24 und Rg. 10—20; Tp. 46—47, Rg. 25; Tp. 43—44, Rg. 22; Tp. 47, Rg. 20—21; Tp. 50, Rg. 19; Tp. 48, Rg. 20; alle westl. 4. Mer.	275	1 350	3 500	600	4 000	1 500
Rabbit Hills	Edmonton	S. Edmonton	Tp. 51, Rg. 24—25 westl. 4. Mer.	40	180	1 200	95	500	—
Indian Reserve (Brüderfeld)	do.	do.	Tp. 52, Rg. 23—24 " 4. "	50	210	1 000	100	475	500
Stony Plains	do.	Stony Plains	Tp. 52—53, Rg. 27—28 " 4. " Tp. 52, Rg. 1 " 5. "	100	525	3 200	280	1 500	500
Beaver Hills	do.	Beaver Hills	Tp. 54—55, Rg. 21 " 4. "	75	330	2 400	200	1 200	—
Brüderheim	do.	Ft. Saskatchew'n	Tp. 55, Rg. 20 " 4. "	18	100	400	40	120	—
Egg Lake	do.	Morrin	Tp. 56, Rg. 26 " 4. "	20	95	350	50	180	—

143

head, Beauséjour, Brunkild and Plumas, as well as in the southeastern corner of Saskatchewan near Alameda, Estevan and Lampman. In British Columbia, German Americans had settled at the Upper and Lower Arrow Lakes.

The Census of 1901 counted as many as 52,000 Germans by origin in western Canada:

Table V.6

From the 1901 Census[15]

Province	Total Population	German by Origin	German Percentage
Manitoba	225,211	27,265	10.7%
Saskatchewan	91,279	11,743	12.9%
Alberta	73,022	7,836	10.7%
Total Prairie Provinces	419,512	46,844	11.2%
British Columbia	178,657	5,807	3.2%
Total Western Canada	598,169	52,651	8.8%

The greatest activity in the launching of German colonies took place in the first decade of the new century. German immigrants concentrated more strongly than before in the present-day Province of Saskatchewan. In 1902 the settlement of the German St. Peter's colony was begun, as well as St. Pius colony (Stoetzel colony) south of Grenfell. Additional German Catholic colonies were formed in 1903 near Allan, in 1904 near Holdfast, in 1905 at Tramping Lake (St. Joseph's colony) and in Wolfsheim-Quinton-Raymore. The Mennonites, apart from appearing in a wide radius around Rosthern, began to settle in 1903 near Herbert and in 1904 near Swift Current. New Lutheran colonies developed, for instance from 1904 in and around Melville, between 1902 and 1907 at the Kirkella railway near Southey, Earl Grey, Markinch and Lipton. In the years 1908 to 1910 the thrust into the dry belt began. The German settlements south of the Swift Current-Herbert-Morse railway line and in the so-called Happy Land were started at that time.

In Alberta a German Catholic colony was founded at Spring Lake in 1903 and in the same year, the German-Swiss colony of Blumenau (now Stettler). German immigration continued to move predominantly into a wide area around Edmonton.

In British Columbia, the first settlements at Lake Okanagan and in the Fraser Valley were formed in this decade.

The Census of 1911 showed that the German population of western Canada had almost tripled since 1901. The record immigration of this decade also increased the proportion of the German element among the total population of Saskatchewan.

Table V.7

From the 1911 Census

Province	Total Population	German by Origin	German Percentage
Manitoba	461,394	34,530	7.5%
Saskatchewan	492,432	68,628	14.0%
Alberta	374,663	36,862	9.9%
Total Prairie Provinces	1,328,489	140,020	10.5%
British Columbia	392,480	11,880	3.0%
Total Western Canada	1,720,969	151,900	8.8%

The number of Germans should, in fact, be somewhat higher than that recorded by the census. We must assume that a number of Germans from Russia undoubtedly reported themselves as Russian (due to their former citizenship) instead of as German when asked for their ethnic origin. In contrast to the postwar years, though, the Mennonites still fully acknowledged their German ethnic descent at that time.

Between 1911 and 1914 the number of German immigrants increased still further. These were directed almost entirely into the already existing settlements, and the founding of new ones was rare. In Manitoba the only new German districts were near Mooseharn, Camper and Grahamdale (1911) and in Friedfeld near Shevlin (1913), and in Saskatchewan the colony of Cornfeld near Eatonia (1912).

The German emigration from eastern Europe was typically a family migration. For the most part, emigrants were young couples and their first children born in the old homeland. If single young men went across the ocean, it was only in order to escape military service and to have their brides from back home follow them as soon as possible, so that they could start their families in the new country. Most emigrants had only a little money. Frequently their passage was paid by relatives or friends who were already in North America. This was indicative of their strong ties of family and kinship. Occasionally their passage was also advanced by Canadian agencies, just as they were able to buy their first inventory on credit. Yet in general, it took only a few years until even the poorest immigrants stood on their own feet economically, as long as they were healthy and hard-working. There were plenty of opportunities at the time for the homesteader to supplement his income. Between seeding and harvest time he could earn money at railway and road construction sites until his own homestead could support him. Many worked first as farmhands in more fully developed German settlements, particularly among the Mennonites in southern Manitoba. Only the German immigrants from the United States tended to have sufficient means and were able to devote their whole energy from the outset to their own homesteads. Many of them were even wealthy.

In Canada, settlement was arranged mainly by the private railway and colonization companies. In order to make things easier at the beginning, these companies tried to create ethnically and denominationally homogeneous districts. Larger coherent areas of German settlement could however only come into existence if the Germans, as the Mennonites and Catholics managed to do, organized their own immigration and founded their own colonization companies. These were able to have a large closed area reserved for themselves by purchasing the railway land in each township. In every township only the even-numbered sections (Nos. 2-36) were given away by the government as homestead land. The railway or colonization companies which opened up the area were granted all the odd-numbered sections. From the sale of these the construction of railways and related expenses had to be defrayed.

Subsequent emigration to the United States, for instance to Montana and Oregon, rarely occurred. The increasing Canadian immigration of German origin recorded by American statistics from 1907 on[16] probably referred mainly to German Canadians from eastern Canada. Like the English Canadians and the French Canadians of the East, these seemed irresistibly attracted to the large American cities nearby. The farmers from western Canada, on the other hand, would not look in the American Northwest for a better future as long as the settlement of the Canadian Prairie provinces continued to expand so encouragingly. Only from the outbreak of war in August 1914 until the spring of 1917, when the United States joined the war against Germany, did a noticeable emigration of Germans take place from western Canada. However, only recent immigrants left who had not yet been naturalized, but still retained their German and Austrian citizenship, about eight thousand altogether. An outspoken anti-German attitude became manifest only in large cities, such as Winnipeg and Vancouver, with the result that Germans were deprived of their jobs, and these unemployed Germans with their families were even temporarily interned in camps.[17] In the rural areas the Germans were left almost unmolested, and there was no reason to emigrate, since due to the war the western Canadian wheat farmer experienced an unexpected economic boom.

2. The Postwar Immigration

The World War interrupted the entire immigration to western Canada for almost a decade. During the war only one German-speaking group immigrated, namely about two thousand Hutterites.

The Hutterites, like the Mennonites, originated as a part of the Anabaptist movement of the sixteenth century, and differ from them only by the economic communism of their *Bruderhofe* (communal farms of brethren). They trace their origins to Jacob Huter, who was burned at the stake as a heretic in Innsbruck in 1536. Driven from Tyrol to Moravia, then to Hungary, Transylvania and South Russia (Hutertal near Melitopol, etc.), they emigrated, like the Mennonites, from there to North America in 1874 because of the suspension of their privilege of exemption from military service. They settled in South Dakota.

As early as 1899 the first Hutterites immigrated from Yankton, S.D., to western Canada, where they established a *Bruderhof* near Dominion City, Manitoba.[18] After the United States entered the World War, the Hutterites, as conscientious objectors who also spoke German, had to suffer particularly from the hatred of 150-per-cent Americans. For their refusal to pay war taxes, they were punished with forcible collection and the confiscation of their property.

The Hutterites even had to mourn two martyrs. They were the vic-

tims of cruel treatment in American military detention camps.[19] A
German Mennonite from Russia, looking back on those years in the
United States, recently gave the following account:[20]

> The last war demonstrated the practical application of American
> liberty most appropriately. Newspapers, particularly the largest
> dailies of the West, the *Chicago Tribune* and the *Kansas City Star*,
> were inciting in the bloodthirstiest manner and whipping up
> intolerance and gangster instincts. In Inola, Oklahoma, two Men-
> nonite churches were burnt. In other places churches were sullied
> inside and outside with tar, yellow paint, etc., and so were the pri-
> vate homes of many well-to-do Mennonites. In Oklahoma a
> preacher was hung from a telephone pole. Honest men, grand-
> fathers, fathers and respectable people were suddenly attacked in
> the middle of the night, usually between midnight and 2:00 a.m.,
> by a gang of Klansmen, dragged out of their beds, their homes
> ransacked from top to bottom, the people beaten or otherwise
> cruelly mistreated, and finally besmeared with tar, yellow paint or
> phenol, and feathered. Around their necks were put nooses with
> which they were raised and lowered. "Will you sign up for war
> bonds? Will you send your son to fight against the Huns?" etc.,
> etc. Government officials entered the homes by day to extort funds
> for the war. Former President Theodore Roosevelt ranted and raved
> against them and demanded they be placed on minesweepers. In
> "rehabilitation centers" such as Fort Alcatraz, Fort Leavenworth
> and in many camps, the glorified American liberty was practiced
> in such a manner as to cause the early deaths of brethren Joseph
> and Michael Hofer from this "rehabilitation."

This was the situation which existed when the Hutterites decided
to turn their backs on the United States forever. After lengthy negotiations, the provincial governments of Manitoba and Alberta guaranteed to acknowledge their religious principle of non-resistance, and in
the summer of 1918 the emigration of two thousand Hutterites was
able to begin. About one-quarter of them settled near Elie, west of Winnipeg in Manitoba, and the remaining three-quarters not far from
MacLeod (Cardston, Woolford, Raley, Magrath, Raymond, Maybutt,
New Dayton) near Lethbridge in Alberta. At the same time a group
of Mennonites migrated from Oklahoma to Laird in Saskatchewan.

The immigration of German-speaking conscientious objectors in the
last year of the war aroused a storm of indignation in Canada. Hatred
fostered by war propaganda now turned against the long-established
Mennonites, who were even physically attacked by returning war veterans. The Great War Veterans' Association took up the battle against

the religious communities of conscientious objectors, and recommended that they all be expelled if possible, since economically, linguistically and culturally they represented nothing but state a within the state anyway. At the least, however, they urged that the recently immigrated Hutterites should be deported and any further immigration of non-resisters be prohibited. Under the pressure of this agitation, an Order-in-Council was passed on June 9, 1919 prohibiting the immigration of conscientious objectors. The immigration of citizens of the formerly hostile Central Powers was also prohibited. Both of these discriminatory Orders-in-Council were rescinded in 1923, and German immigration resumed.

The German postwar immigration from 1923 to 1930 was recruited, just as before the war, predominantly from the east and southeast European areas of German settlement. The same economic and ethno-political reasons that had propelled the prewar emigration across the ocean had become even more effective after the war. All the German ethnic groups in eastern Europe had to experience in the flesh that the World War, as the Russian Prime Minister Goremykin put it at the outbreak of the war, was being led not just against Germany (*Germaniya*) but against everything German (*Germanstvo*). Tsarist Russia hoped to destroy the latter, economically and politically, in its own country. First on the agenda was the prohibition of the German language and the right of assembly of Germans. Partial expropriation was decreed on February 2, 1915, and on December 15, 1915, the last and complete expropriation law was promulgated. It made all German land holdings subject to expropriation under conditions that equalled theft. All the property of the German element in Russia was to be liquidated by the spring of 1917. Any chance to purchase land again, or even merely to lease it, was blocked by prohibitions. The German colonists were also not permitted to leave Russia, but instead were to be dispersed among the Russians in order to work for them. The Germans in Russia had lost their homes and their country. The Russian Revolution of 1917, while leaving the expropriation laws unenforced, inflicted even worse sufferings upon the Germans in Russia. Their ordeals in Soviet Russia are too well known to require more detailed elaboration.[21] Looting, murder, desecration, requisitioning of all the grain supplies, and intolerable levies marked the path of the Communist revolution in the German villages. Then came the famine of 1921. The flight of the German farmers began. What the German Catholics and Protestants by and large lacked, unfortunately, the German Mennonites had preserved

through all the storms of the Revolution: an organization still functioning relatively well. It could now take charge of the emigration in
order to prevent it from assuming the character of a chaotic flight, as
among the other German groups. Thus, among the German emigrants
from Soviet Russia who found their way to Canada, the German Mennonites occupied by far the most prominent place. As grave as the economic consequences of Communism were—the abolition of
independent farming, the redistribution of the land and the unbeara-
bly high levies—even these were not perceived as the main reason for
emigration. What made life unbearable for most German farmers in
the Soviet state was the struggle of Communism against the religious
and moral foundations of their lives, the destruction of the family and
of the church. Better emigrate than leave the education of the children to the collective! This is what a Mennonite farmer wrote in a letter to a relative in America about the opposition to the Soviet
government into which they were driven, with emigration as the only
way out:[22]

> We never disobeyed the authorities except that we cannot aban-
> don our religion. Up to that point we can surrender ourselves to
> communism, i.e. to share our small property with others and to
> work collectively. But to join the conventicle of the godless that
> is beyond our powers, then we have to flee if possible.

Again and again the Germans from Russia justified their flight from
the Soviet state with these words: "We are looking for a new homeland
where we can live among the faithful; we must get away from this land
of the godless!"[23]

Very soon the leaders of the German colonists realized how much
they should believe in the promise of the Soviet Russian government
to the non-Russian peoples of the Soviet Union:[24]

> We were not supposed to have any freedom to be economically
> autonomous, nor to be free to develop our cultural uniqueness.
> Instead we were to be turned into the same kinds of proletarians
> to which many national minorities have in part already been, and
> still are, being converted to this day.

Unfortunately only a very small number of those who wanted to
emigrate from Russia were able to do so. No more than a total of 21,000
Mennonites found their way to Canada. Yet these form the most closely
knit and largest group of Germans that were able to emigrate from Soviet
Russia to Canada. From among the Lutheran and Catholic Germans

barely more than ten thousand made it safely to Canada. The complete impoverishment of the German farmers in Russia made the idea of emigrating without outside help impossible. Furthermore, Russian citizens found it very difficult to leave Soviet Russia and to gain entry into other countries. These difficulties arose from the initial diplomatic non-recognition of Soviet Russia. The Mennonite emigrants to Canada provide the best illustration of all these difficulties.[25]

As early as 1920 the Mennonites of Russia had sent a delegation, consisting of A.A. Friesen, B.H. Unruh, C.H. Warkentin and J. Esau, to North America to investigate the possibilities of emigration. They recommended Canada as the preferred destination. Yet at first the Canadian Order-in-Council prohibiting the immigration of conscientious objectors stood in the way. This obstacle was removed in 1923 when the Liberal government of Mackenzie King came to power in Ottawa. But then the cholera epidemic in South Russia was a new reason to block admission. Canadian doctors, who were supposed to examine the state of health of the prospective emigrants before their departure, were refused entry by the Russian government because a Russian trade delegation had been refused entry into Canada at that time. The government in Moscow also refused to readmit to Russia those emigrants turned down by Canadian doctors in Hamburg. All these difficulties would have been insurmountable had not the German government opened Lechfeld, near Augsburg, as a transit camp for the emigrants. It thereby enabled fellow Germans from Russia to stay in Germany until they had fully recuperated and received their Canadian entry visa. Prof. Lic. B.H. Unruh, now in Karlsruhe, and B. Fast, now in Sardis, B.C., as mediators between the Mennonites in Soviet Russia, the German government and the Mennonite Board of Colonization, deserve much credit for the rescue of the German Mennonite refugees.

In the summer of 1923, the emigration was able to begin. On the Canadian side it was organized by the Canadian Mennonite Board of Colonization in Rosthern, Saskatchewan, under the direction of Elder David Toews. The Canadian government made it a condition that for the time being the new immigrants would have to find accommodation among the resident Mennonites, that they would be settled as farmers and that all the Mennonites were collectively responsible for physically and mentally disabled persons. The Mennonites who immigrated between 1874 and 1879 had, as we recall, received a loan of close to $100,000 against a guarantee put up by their coreligionists already residing in Ontario, the punctual repayment of which had firmly established the reputation of the Mennonites' absolute honesty. Now, the Canadian Pacific Railway granted the Canadian Mennonite Board of Colonization another much higher loan for the passage and settlement of the refugees from Soviet Russia. This loan was bonded by the old established Mennonites in Canada. By 1930, of the $1,924,727 advanced by the C.P.R., $884,000 had been repaid.[26]

When the immigration got underway—the first transport arrived in Rosthern on July 21, 1923—as many as twenty-eight thousand Mennonites had made application to emigrate.[27] Yet only a total of 17,519 Mennonites were able to immigrate to Canada from July 1923 to April 1927, largely because, until 1925, the C.P.R. was allowed to bring in only a limited number of immigrant families from the so-called "non-preferred countries," which included Russia. Also, the credits of the railways were not to be claimed all at one time. Most of the immigrants came from the large Mennonite colonies in the Ukraine, but also from smaller areas of Mennonite settlement in Russia, from Siberia, from the Urals, etc., also from the Terek region in northern Caucasia where they had to leave behind their famous orchards.[28]

The severance of diplomatic relations between Great Britain and Soviet Russia became a new and serious obstacle for immigration after 1927. This was compounded by the new Canadian requirement in 1927 of valid passports as a prerequisite for admission. In Russia, however, passports were prohibitively expensive, and could be obtained only with great difficulty. The German government was prepared at least to issue personal identification cards to emigrating Germans from Russia, provided the Canadian Mennonite Board of Colonization would guarantee not to hold Germany liable for the return fare in the event of a person's deportation from Canada. This was not acceptable to the Canadian government, because it insisted that the Board of Colonization in Rosthern had already assumed more financial guarantees to the government and the C.P.R. than it could fulfill. Negotiations meant that valuable time was lost in the rescue of Germans from Russia.

Among the Germans in Russia, however, the desire to emigrate became more and more urgent. Beginning in late 1928, the Soviet government issued a series of new agricultural decrees aimed at the "elimination of the kulaks," i.e., the class of independent large farmers. The confrontation of Bolshevism with the old rural economy had entered its final stage. In June 1929 the state decreed that huge amounts of grain be raised. How to obtain it was left to the individual villages. If the farmer did not deliver what was demanded from him—frequently more than his entire crop—his house, inventory and land were impounded. At that time more than six thousand German refugees from all parts of Russia gathered in Moscow, desperately demanding exit visas, which they eventually received through the mediation of the German ambassador. They found temporary accommodation in Germany in the refugee camps of Hammerstein (East Prussia), Prenzlau and Mölln.

Unfortunately only 1,123 Mennonites and a small number of Lutherans from the six thousand inmates of these camps could immigrate to Canada. In the Province of Saskatchewan, which was the preferred destination of the immigrants up to that time, a Conservative government under the former public school teacher Anderson had taken office. During the World War he had become known for the outspoken hostility against non-British immigrants, expressed in his book *The Education of the New Canadian* (Toronto, 1918). Now, as Premier, he immediately opposed any further immigration of German Mennonites particularly, and of German immigrants in general. Anderson combined Anglo-Canadian chauvinism and antipathy against the Germans with utter naiveté about Soviet Russia. Elder Toews, the head of the Mennonite Board, provides a typical account of how he had to struggle before Anderson's cabinet for permission for continued immigration into Canada:[29]

> In Regina I had to present the matter before the entire cabinet. They seemed ignorant of the serious conditions in Russia. Instead they talked about the "thriving progress of Russia's agriculture" and an excerpt from a newspaper was recited, according to which whole trainloads full of foodstuff arrived in Moscow and Russians were at a loss about what to do with it. Apparently no credence was given to my accounts about the real conditions in Russia. Although the prospect was held out that in the spring, close relatives would be allowed to immigrate to their next of kin in Saskatchewan, it was pointed out that a general immigration had to be rejected for the time being.

Following the recommendation of the Saskatchewan government, the federal government in Ottawa refused the immigration of the Mennonites in the winter of 1929. Only the railway companies were each allowed to bring two hundred poor families into the country from the "non-preferred" states, in accordance with an old agreement. The C.P.R. used the entire quota allotted to it to bring another 958 Mennonite refugees, who were awaiting their departure from Germany, over to western Canada. The C.N.R., which still had obligations towards the Cunard line, was not able to do this but nevertheless brought over thirty families (165 persons).

Under the impact of the world economic crisis and the sudden drop in the price of wheat, Canada prohibited any further immigration except for the closest kin of resident immigrants. A majority of those German refugees from Russia who were stranded in camps in Germany had to seek refuge in Brazil and Paraguay. According to statistics of the Mennonite Board in Rosthern, a total of 20,171 Mennonites immigrated to Canada with the help of the C.P.R.:

Table V.8

Contingent	Year	Number of Persons
1st	1923	2,759
2nd	1924	5,048
3rd	1925	3,772
4th	1926	5,940
5th	1927	847
6th	1928	511
7th	1929	1,014
8th	1930	269
9th	1931	5
10th	1932	6
Total		20,171

The C.N.R. brought over an additional seven to eight hundred Mennonites, so that the total number of postwar Mennonite immigrants is about 21,000. Of these 2,200 to 2,300 went to Ontario, while 18,700 to 18,800 settled in western Canada.

In spite of the great efforts of the Catholic and Lutheran German immigration boards in Winnipeg, the number of Germans from Russia belonging to these two denominations who managed to find refuge in western Canada in the postwar years barely exceeded ten thousand. Unlike the smaller but more closely-knit group of Mennonites, Lutherans and Catholics lacked a comprehensive organization inside Russia itself at that time. Generally speaking, we have to conclude that unfortunately the most favorable time for the emigration of Germans from Soviet Russia in the first postwar years until 1927 was far from fully utilized.

Although the Germans in Russia no doubt suffered most, the conditions of the Germans in eastern Europe deteriorated markedly everywhere after the World War. The desire to emigrate across the ocean, therefore, grew even stronger than in the prewar period. Again the number of German emigrants from Volhynia and central Poland, Galicia and Banat was particularly high, just as it had been before the war. All these areas had been theatres of war. The German settlements, especially in Volhynia and Galicia, which now belonged to the new Polish state, had suffered terribly. In Volhynia the German farmers had to bear the full brunt of Russian expropriation laws and some had to endure compulsory resettlement to Siberia. When the German army occupied the land, the Volhynia-Germans were sent as agricultural laborers to estates in Germany. Returning after the war, they found it difficult to rebuild their old villages. It is no wonder that many families preferred to follow their relatives and friends who had found a new and apparently much better homeland in western Canada. Similar conditions prevailed in Galicia and central Poland. The Germans in Banat were particularly hard hit. Before the war they were driven to North America in large numbers, due to the lack of economic opportunities. Now Banat was partitioned among Yugoslavia, Romania and Hungary without any regard to economic ties. Many villages were cut off from their old markets and were in distress. As a result, Germans from the Yugoslavian Banat, the Voivodina, for instance, emigrated in larger numbers after the end of the war than representatives of the other ethnic groups. In 1929 alone 3,844 Germans, or 0.76 per cent of the German population of Yugoslavia, emigrated. From Voivodina the proportion of emigrants was as high as 0.95 per cent of the Germans living there — that is in one year![30] These emigrating Swabians also preferred to go where their relatives and friends appear to have made their fortunes before the war, namely western Canada. In the years 1927 to 1931, 14,377 Germans from Romania and Yugoslavia immigrated to Canada, and 2,115 from Hungary. Virtually all of these appear to have come from Banat. In the same period 8,293 German immigrants came from Poland (Volhynia, central Poland, Galicia).[31]

The destruction of the Habsburg Monarchy also took a heavy toll in the core lands of the old state, German Austria, and brought about increased emigration from there as well. Although Austria, unlike Germany, was not treated as a "preferred country" by the Canadian immigration authorities, 5,015 German Austrians, which is 18.2 per cent of the emigrants, went to Canada in the period from 1926 to 1933.[32] According to information from the director of the Migration Bureau in Vienna, about four thousand of these were still living in Canada by 1933. Most of them, however, were no longer engaged in agriculture, but as industrial workers, small tradesmen and clerks in the cities.

Some Sudeten Germans, who had experienced severe economic and political discrimination in Czechoslovakia, emigrated to Canada. From 1926 to 1932, they numbered 1,633 persons, according to Czech statistics, which is 10.3 per cent of all the German emigrants from Czechoslovakia.[33]

Finally emigration from Germany increased again due to the economic crisis of the postwar years, the reduction of Germany's territory, and inflation. Canada became the second most preferred destination of German emigrants. It was still far behind the United States, which attracted about fifty thousand emigrants from Germany annually, while four to five thousand German citizens went to Canada annually between 1927, and 1930. Germany's share of the total German immigration to Canada has never been larger than after 1927 when Germany was included among the "preferred countries," and immigration did not have to be restricted to agricultural occupations. According to Canadian statistics 19,361 immigrants (24.7 per cent) of all the German immigrants came from Germany itself between 1927 and 1931. German statistics show the following figures for the postwar emigration to Canada:

Table V.9

Year	Emigrants	Year	Emigrants
1922	3	1927	4,515
1923	768	1928	4,144
1924	2,221	1929	4,625
1925	994	1930	4,631
1926	1,388	1931	440
Total			**23,729**

As is indicated by the Canadian statistics on those born in Germany, by no means all of these 23,729 Germans from Germany stayed in Canada. The 1921 Census shows their number to be 25,266, and in the Census of 1931 it is 39,163. This means that in those ten years the number of immigrants who had been born in Germany increased by just 14,000; while among the resident immigrants from Germany, a loss due to death or emigration of no more than five thousand may be assumed since 1921. The official gazette states the following reasons:[34]

> Many Germans who could not obtain a visa for the United States in Germany went to Canada with the intention of proceeding to the United States. Immediately upon their arrival, they had their names placed on the waiting list of a United States consulate in Canada and usually left, after a ten to twelve month waiting period, for the United States. This movement ceased in the fall of 1930 after the United States imposed a virtual closure on all immigration as well.

Thus Germany's share of the total German immigration after the war was in reality not much larger than in the prewar era.

The composition of the German postwar immigration, based on place of origin, also resembled the prewar immigration because, again, about 18 per cent of the German immigrants came from the United States. This was due not only to indignation about the shameful conduct of American public opinion towards their fellow citizens of German descent, but also to the economic enticement of cheap virgin land in the Peace River district and in other parts of western Canada. These factors induced about 14,300 Germans from the United States to move to Canada as late as 1927 to 1931.

Canadian statistics do not distinguish clearly between the citizenship and the ethnic identity of the immigrants until 1927. Thereafter more exact information is available about the countries of origin of the German immigrants. The following statistics may not be free from errors—a correction of the number of Germans from Germany was made above—but they are nevertheless an important prop for our investigation (see Table V.10).

For the entire German postwar immigration, Canadian statistics give the following figures[35] (see Table V.11).

According to these statistics, about eighty-five thousand of the total of 90,705 German postwar immigrants appeared to have come to Canada between 1926 and 1931 alone. However, these figures are not reliable until 1926-27, when ethnic identity instead of citizenship became the criterion. First of all, until 1925 inclusive, the Mennonites are missing.

Table V.10

Countries of Origin of German Immigrants — 1927-1931

Germany	19,361	24.7%
Russia and the Ukraine	10,586	13.6%
Romania, Yugoslavia....................	14,377	18.5%
Hungary	2,115	2.7%
Poland	8,293	10.6%
Austria...............................	4,753	6.1%
Czechoslovakia........................	1,516	2.0%
Switzerland	794	1.0%
United States	14,299	18.4%
Other................................	1,869	2.4%
Total	**77,963**	**100.0%**

Table V.11

German Postwar Immigration 1919-1935

Year	Immigrants	Year	Immigrants
1919........................1		1928 17,964	
1920........................12		1929...................17,919	
1921.......................137		1930 13,544	
1922.......................178		1931 2,389	
1923.......................216		1932 1,842	
1924 1,769		1933 1,213	
1925 2,215		1934......................945	
1926 13,791		1935......................725	
1927 15,845			
Total			**90,705**

They were listed as Russian citizens and, as indicated above, numbered more than 11,500 between 1923 and 1925. Secondly, the Swiss who, particularly in those years, immigrated in relatively large numbers (1923: 1,585; 1924: 680; 1925: 418), are missing. Seventy to 80 per cent of these Swiss should be considered as German Swiss. Finally, the majority of the German immigrants from Russia, Romania, Yugoslavia, Hungary, Czechoslovakia and Austria are missing. Their number, however, was still insignificant in those early postwar years. Altogether, we may conclude that German postwar immigration to Canada amounted to slightly more than one hundred thousand persons.

The German immigrants arriving in Canadian ports in the decade 1922 to 1931—these formed about three-quarters of the total number of German arrivals—are classified according to sex and occupation as follows:

Table V.12

Category	1922-26	1927-31	total (1922-1931)	percentage
total	11,734	61,472	73,206	
men	4,621	31,720	36,341	49.7%
women	3,630	15,795	19,425	26.5%
children	3,483	13,957	17,440	23.8%
farmers, farm laborers	8,741	42,699	51,440	70.3%
female domestic servants	1,367	6,152	7,519	10.3%
craftsmen, skilled industrial workers	102	2,370	2,472	3.4%
tradesmen, clerks	49	1,078	1,127	1.5%
unskilled workers	101	712	813	1.1%
miners	20	20	40	0.05%
independent and other occupations	1,354	8,441	9,795	13.0%

The German immigration was thus distinctly agricultural in character. If the 11,500 German Mennonite immigrants from Russia of the years 1923-1925 were included, the proportion of agricultural immigrants would increase to as much as 86 per cent. By and large, German immigration from outside Germany was almost exclusively agricultural, while the groups of tradesmen and clerks, craftsmen and skilled industrial workers, as well as of independent and other occupations, consisted essentially of immigrants from Germany. The Canadian government was quite appreciative of the German agricultural immigration. To remonstrances from Englishmen that Canada favored German immigrants at the expense of the British, the Canadian Minister of Agriculture replied during his visit to England in 1929:[36] "Why don't you send us Englishmen! They don't come and if they come they won't stay. Only the Germans stay on the land and are good for what has to be done—farm chores!"

The final question to be answered concerns the number of German immigrants to Canada who actually settled in western Canada.

The 73,206 German immigrants who between 1922 and 1931 entered Canada via Canadian ports gave the following regions as their destination:

Table V.13

	1922-26		1927-31	
Maritime Provinces	39	(0.3%)	234	(0.4%)
Quebec, Ontario	1,762	(15.0%)	11,085	(18.0%)
Prairie Provinces	9,808	(83.6%)	49,185	(80.0%)
British Columbia	125	(1.1%)	968	(1.6%)
Total	**11,734 (100.0%)**		**61,472 (100.0%)**	

We may therefore assume that of the total German postwar immigration of more than one hundred thousand persons, 80 to 85 per cent (80,000 to 85,000 persons) went initially to western Canada (i.e., the Prairie provinces and British Columbia). Among the agricultural immigration of Germans from outside Germany, the proportion of those migrating to the Prairie provinces was probably over 90 per cent. After Germany's recognition as a "preferred country" in 1927, the Prairie provinces' share of German immigrants from Germany dropped, due to the strong increase in the proportion of urban occupations (craftsmen and industrial workers, tradesmen and clerks, etc.) who looked for employment primarily in the cities of the East, such as Montreal, Toronto, Hamilton, Berlin-Kitchener, and London. Furthermore, the number of immigrants from Germany who considered Canada merely a stopover for the United States was relatively large, as pointed out above. But some of the Germans from eastern Europe also chose this route in order to proceed to the U.S.A. Thus, of the 80,000 to 85,000 Germans who immigrated to western Canada in the postwar years, only about seventy thousand actually settled there.

In western Canada, the postwar immigrants were at first looked after by the immigration boards of the churches who cooperated with the railways (see chapter IV, part 2). They directed the immigrants of their own denomination, first of all, to jobs as farmhands on German-owned farms in one of their parishes, and later advised on the purchase of their homesteads. In procuring jobs and land, the church boards provided invaluable services to the new immigrants who as "greenhorns" would otherwise have easily been at the mercy of exploitation. On occasion, however, immigrants had the impression, at times certainly correctly, but more often unjustly, that by arranging for work and land even the clergy tried to make money off them.

The terrible disappointment experienced by the new immigrants after the economic collapse of western Canada caused them to blame the immigration boards for their misfortunes, although these boards were just as unprepared for the development of events after 1929 as were the Canadian government and the railway companies. In all fairness, one may blame the clergy on these boards mainly for the fact that they shared the superficial optimism about the future of western Canada with other agencies participating in the promotion of immigration. Motivated by the understandable desire to fill up their parishes over here, the clergy strongly promoted immigration to western Canada through their connections with the old homeland. This was done even though, as we know today, the German postwar immigration could be justified neither on economic nor on ethno-political grounds.

Denominationally, the majority of the German postwar immigrants to western Canada were Catholics (30,000 to 35,000) who came from Banat, from the Catholic parts of Germany, from Austria, the Sudetenland and the United States. The most homogeneous group were the approximately 18,700 German Mennonites from Russia. The number of German Lutheran immigrants (from Germany, Volhynia, Poland, Galicia) is estimated to be about fifteen thousand.[37] Added to these must be some small religious groups, especially several thousand Baptists.

Very few new German settlements were started after the war, since postwar immigrants were directed to already existing communities by the church agencies. In Saskatchewan new colonies were established only near Wapella (1924-1925, Germans from Poland), and in the northwest of the province near St. Walburg (Loon Lake, Loon River, St. Boniface colony at the Beaver River), as well as near Nipawin and Tisdale (east of Prince Albert) and near Lashburn. In Alberta the German immigrants preferred the area around Barrhead and Flatbush northwest of Edmonton, near Edson and Rosevear west of Edmonton, as well as around Thorsby and Warburg southwest of Edmonton. Above all, however, they went to the Peace River district, in the far northwest of the province, a district that had played a special role in the promotion of immigration.

Just as in southern Manitoba German Mennonites from Russia had set an encouraging example for the settlement of the entire prairies, one lone German, the "wheat king" Hermann Trelle, established the reputation of the faraway Peace River district after 1926. By his example he directed tens of thousands of farmers into this area of settlement, formerly the most northerly one still suitable for wheat growing on the North American continent. The beginnings of its settlement date back to the prewar years. Yet the long distances from the remaining areas of western Canadian settlement (400 kilometers beyond Edmonton) did not appear to make settlement economically justifiable, and the settlers abandoned the Peace River in growing numbers in the postwar years, especially in 1924 and 1925. Then came Trelle with his outstanding strains of wheat grown in Wembley in the Peace River district. Year after year these earned him the title of "wheat king" at competitions among wheat growers in America, and directed the attention of the Canadian public back to the Peace River. It was Trelle's wheat which drew new immigrants to the far north of Alberta after 1926.[38] As a result, quite a few small German settlements have appeared since then, north of the Peace River near Grimshaw, Berwyn, Fairview (Friedensthal colony) and Hines Creek, and at the Battle River in the far north, also south of the Peace River in and around Northmark, Sexsmith, Grande Prairie, Wembley, Hythe, etc.

The immigrating Mennonites were initially directed to the villages and districts that were vacated in 1922 and 1926 by the departure of some of the old-established Mennonites. The suspension in 1916 of the school privilege granted to them in 1873 (see chapter VIII) and the generally hostile frame of mind towards the Mennonites in the postwar years drove a large segment of the two most conservative groups among them, the so-called Old Colony and the Sommerfelders, to emigrate again and forced them to face all the uncertainties of a new beginning on foreign soil. In 1920 more than 5,500 Old Colony Mennonites—3,200 to 3,300 from southern Manitoba, 1,500 from the area of Swift Current and five hundred from the area of Hague, Saskatchewan—went to the State of Chihuahua in Mexico. In 1926, 1,765 Sommerfelders—1,500 from Manitoba and the rest from Saskatchewan—moved to the Chaco of Paraguay, where they came to much grief as a result of the war between Paraguay and Bolivia.[39] Since, however, the emigrants needed cash, while the immigrants from Soviet Russia arrived completely penniless, the idea of having the immigrants take over the old Mennonite farmsteads succeeded only in a few exceptional cases. From an ethno-political point of view this would have been, no doubt, the most advantageous arrangement. In the existing circumstances, the Mennonite Board in Rosthern, which organized the immigration and settlement, was in favor of purchasing virgin land. In this way the immigrants would have to go least into debt.[40] However, after having worked for some time as farmhands for their old-established coreligionists, they preferred to buy developed farms, which were offered to them in large numbers without a down payment. The high wages and the difficulty of getting any helpers caused many big farmers in the postwar years to rid themselves of their land. The immigrants tended to buy these big farms, on which up to thirty families could settle together. The former owners preferred to sell their land without any down payments to the German Mennonites from Russia, who properly enjoyed the best reputation as industrious farmers, rather than wait for scanty enquiries by interested buyers with money. The former owners even sank additional money into their land for the erection of houses, stables, etc. Most of the sales contracts were set up for a period of fifteen years. The debts were to be repaid with half the crop and a number of Mennonites did, in fact, pay off their mortgages after as short a time as five years. After 1929, however, due to the price slump, even the Mennonites were no longer able to make debt and interest payments (at 6 to 6½ per cent) by using crop surpluses. Many sales contracts, therefore, had to be revoked. Even then most of the Mennonites were left on their farms no longer as owners but as tenants. Some groups bought their land from the C.P.R., which offered it at a price of $7 to $17 per acre, with a $25 down payment, and repayment in thirty annual installments, with the first four years exempt from payments.

Of the 18,700 to 18,800 Mennonites who chose Canada for their new homeland after 1923, about eight thousand went to Manitoba, and the same to Saskatchewan, two thousand to Alberta and seven to eight hundred to British Columbia. A detailed survey of where and in what numbers they settled in the various Prairie provinces can be found in chapter VI.

Since 1931 German immigration has ceased almost entirely, as pointed out at the end of chapter IV, part 2. The few Germans who emigrated to Canada since then took up residence exclusively in eastern Canada (Nova Scotia, New Brunswick, Ontario) except, of course, for those women and children who followed their husbands and fathers to the homesteads they had earlier established in western Canada. For economic, as well as serious ethno-political reasons, the experiences of recent years have made western Canada no longer a destination of German emigrants. The only exceptions would be cases where Germans from lands other than Germany seek refuge at any price from the most serious economic, moral and political distress. Indicative of the severe plight of the Sudeten Germans in the Czech state were the negotiations undertaken in 1936 for the emigration of ten thousand Sudeten Germans to western Canada. This emigration, however, did not materialize.[41]

3. Homesteading

The testimonies of German pioneers illustrate the everyday life of the individual settler and enable the historian to trace the general experience of western settlement. This experience ranges from the troubles and privations in the pioneer years and the ways settlers gradually gained a footing, to the point where they reached a certain, although often only modest, level of prosperity until their ultimate relapse into primitive conditions due to crop failures and economic depression.

Most of the German immigrants, particularly those from eastern Europe, were farm laborers. The hopelessness of substantially improving their economic situation in the old homeland and of leaving their children some land that they could call their own had been their main reason for emigrating. The proceeds from the sale of their belongings in their homeland often barely covered the travel expenses for large families. Their destitution thus complicated the already difficult start even more. It is generally agreed that the money the immigrants brought with them from Europe did them no good anyway. The advice to put their money for the time being into the bank, and to work hard at first and take a look around in the country, often came too late, after speculators had already relieved them of their money. Many had to start by purchasing their first farm inventory, costing on the average from $700 to $800, on credit. Credit, however, was easy to obtain through the railways. To pay it off, on the other hand, often took several years. Immigrants from the United States had the easiest start since they tended to bring furniture, utensils and livestock with them.

The free homestead of 160 acres (64.4 hectares) for an entry fee of only ten dollars was the bait that had lured the immigrants. Many newcomers pictured themselves as rich farmers as soon as the homesteads were registered in their names in the immigration office. But difficulties beset the settler even before he got to see his homestead. As a rule, it was located at a distance of several kilometers from the railway, which did not precede settlement, but at best followed it a few years later. The settlers chose locations where lines were planned or already in the process of being laid. At times, however, anticipated railway construction failed to materialize or the line was suddenly laid several miles further away. As a result the good prospects for the economic development of a district were hampered, for wheat is not worth growing, even in good times, if it has to be hauled to a railway more than twenty-five kilometers away.

At best, therefore, the railway might be expected shortly in the vicinity of the area to be settled. For the time being it was not yet there, and the settler had to cover the last fifty to 150 miles by oxcart across the open prairie. Over this distance all the provisions, livestock feed, seed grains, lumber, furniture, tools and, in cases of illness, any medicine needed, had to be brought by cart. That meant heavy additional expenditure in time and energy in the first years, when the settler needed every minute of his labor to break the ground and to build his house and barn. Anyone who has not gone through this himself—not even the sons and daughters of the first settlers are, as a rule, capable of doing this work—cannot really imagine the hardships of the pioneer years. They made the greatest demands on one's labor, will power and endurance and meant years of daily exertion to the limit of one's physical and emotional strength. Now let's hear the German settlers themselves (in their handwritten community reports).

Ambros Hoedel from Czernowitz, who in 1898 together with other German fellow countrymen from Bukovina settled in Mariahilf colony

(Killaley-Grayson) in Saskatchewan, writes:

> The feelings of the new arrivals differed greatly; some were coura-
> geous and hopeful, others were discouraged and despairing. But
> it was done. No one could think of going back. Poverty had driven
> them over here and the trip had impoverished them even more.
> With a few exceptions they had little or no money at all. The
> wealthier ones stayed back home in that beautiful country. We
> named our settlement Mariahilf [meaning "Mary help"] because
> never before had we been in need of Mary's help as badly as in
> those days. We soon made peace, even friends, with the bushes
> and sloughs, for the bushes supplied us with lumber and firewood
> and the slough with water for every purpose. Form and style of
> the first habitations differed greatly. The building site was usually
> selected near the shelter of bush not far from a large slough. Two
> or three usually helped each other with the construction and stayed
> together until something was built for each of them. One built
> himself a mud hut, the other a loghouse. Anyone who could cover
> his house with shingles was rich. Whoever could not afford this
> luxury used sod or thatch for roofing. The cooking stove was made
> of two or three rocks. Meat was supplied by everything that could
> be reached with a gun. Whoever had any money left could buy
> provisions for a while, otherwise he had to borrow from the others
> until he had accommodated his family and could look for a way
> to earn money. The mill in Grenfell loaned only a limited amount
> of flour for a short period of time. Until 1904, Grenfell was the
> closest town, twenty-two to twenty-eight miles (thirty-five to forty-
> five kilometers) away. We had very little credit with its merchants.
> For cultivating equipment, oxen and horses, we had to pay very
> high prices in order to have them only temporarily at our disposal.
> Yet we needed them in order to cultivate and harvest the land,
> so that we could eke out an existence with our families. Some of
> us bought our first draft animals and tools, plow and carts collec-
> tively. After receiving the patent (after three years) the farm was
> mortgaged immediately and, depending on how far the borrowed
> money reached, old debts were paid off in the false hope that the
> worst was over now. It was hope which was always relayed back
> to the old homeland and enticed new emigrants.

The wife of a German farmer from Russia, Frau Ullrich, tells about
the beginnings of the settlement of Eigenheim near Young in Saskatchewan (1905):

> With how much hope did we leave the old homeland, and how
> disappointed were we now. Far and wide no human habitation,
> nothing but bush! The prairie had burned shortly before and
> looked completely black with many large rocks on it. Only a very

small spot was not burned. There the poor cattle could find some feed until the new green had grown. Then it was time for construction. Most of us built with sod. Soil was mixed with water and prairie grass and the sod bricks stacked one on top of the other. In order to get shingles for the roofs we had to drive sixty miles to the north (almost one hundred kilometers). Some went together and followed the survey marks, finally got there after two days, bought shingles, doors and windows and whatever they needed for subsistence. Everything was cheap to buy, even though it was two to three days before a party returned from a trip. Since it rained a lot during the first summer not much could be done in the field, yet there was no time to rest as the makeshift living quarters had to be readied before the onset of winter. Potatoes, flour, etc. had to be procured, also lumber for smaller buildings and firewood in the nearby bush. On each trip to the bush half a dozen bush rabbits had to lose their lives. In the spring much time was spent driving around in search for seed grain. In spite of this, some from every family plowed furrow after furrow day after day, so that finally at the beginning of the second year each family had prepared thirty to thirty-five acres [which is an exceptional amount,—H. Lehmann] for seeding. In the new year construction of our house progressed no faster, for our entire family had to work at first on other farms, since travel debts had to be paid off. These amounted to about $200 and the daily wage for adults was only one dollar, and ten dollars a month for children. On November 12th we finally moved into our new home and were thus under our own roof! What a great feeling that was for someone who had brought nothing to work with but his hands.

Father Funke, who as the local clergyman since 1904 had witnessed the beginnings of the Catholic settlement of Wolfsheim (Quinton-Raymore) gave the following vivid account:[42]

> The virgin prairie land has to be broken first and left fallow for one year before seeding can begin. Then the bush must be cleared in many places, the rocks removed from the land, sufficient pasture fenced off for the cattle, etc. Added to this are the periodic prairie fires in the spring and fall, against which the farmer has to be on guard day and night. Then the horses get lost and the poor settler, whose entire fortune is at stake here, has to ride around for days and weeks, often in an eighty kilometer radius, to find them again. Provisions which are not produced on the farm, clothes, machines, furnishings have to be picked up at the railway station seventy kilometers away. Mail arrives once a week. In short, if beginning at all is difficult, the beginnings on the farm are doubly so. This is the way it is here in Wolfsheim. The houses which we enter consist entirely of sod pieces which are stacked on top of

each other like tiles and are plastered with clay. The floor consists of stamped clay, the roof is made of clay as well. Inside there are usually only two rooms, the bedroom and the kitchen, no matter how large the family. There are no upstairs, no steps, etc. Other houses are built from braided twigs. Every farmer lives alone on his homestead, one-half to one and three-quarters and even more kilometers away from his neighbor. Only occasionally do three or four gather in the corners of their land and thus form a little "village" where the father, with his sons and sons-in-law, leads a truly patriarchal life. Otherwise the usual farmer's lot is loneliness — and hard work. His food consists of bread, potatoes, eggs and milk, at least during the summer; sometimes also some pork. If he wants different meat he takes his gun and shoots a rabbit or wild duck which are abundant in the bush and sloughs.

Retired farmer Eberhard, who now lives in the small town of Leipzig, gave me the following story about his first year in the young colony of Leipzig near the Tramping Lake (St. Joseph's) colony while I had a little chat with him. He had at first moved alone to the new homestead and left his family behind in the United States. Between April and June 1906 he had to make thirteen trips by oxcart to the next railway station of Battleford (about one hundred kilometers) in order to get all his equipment, seed grain, stove, lumber, tools, livestock feed, provisions, etc. to the homestead. Each trip took four to six days. In the intervals, which were necessary to give the oxen some rest, the barn was built and the most essential first farm work was done. The sod pieces from which barn and house were built had to be hauled from a distance of one and a half kilometers from the shore of the lake, since the grass sod on the homestead itself was too dry. Yet even the sod-house needed wooden posts in the corners and a wooden roof. On the completely treeless prairie the lumber from poplars, however, could only be obtained at a site more than sixty kilometers away. Wood from the shore of the lake was too green and wet and barely good for firewood. The well, in whose construction the neighbors cooperated, had to be dug thirty-five meters deep. The right spot was found only after eight futile excavations. Meanwhile arrangements had to be made for breaking of the ground. In order not to overstrain the oxen in the midday heat, plowing was done from 2:00 a.m. to 10:00 a.m. and from 4:00 p.m. to midnight. The homesteaders could not afford any regular sleep at night for weeks, but at the end of the year twenty to twenty-five acres of prairie land had finally been broken for seeding the following year. Plowing of virgin prairie land took enormous exertion, and required strong teams of animals, while most of the settlers tended to have only weak draft animals fed on prairie grass. In the late summer some hay had to be cut at the lower-lying lake shore. Then fire trenches had to be dug around the small premises, as a protection against prairie fires in the dry days of fall. The severe Canadian winter was particularly hard to bear in those primitive circumstances. Eggs and bread baked by the lonely settler were almost the only nourishment. Every morning water for man and animals had to be hauled from the lake after the one-meter-thick ice cover had been chopped through. In the cellar the water froze too, thereby absorbing the entire frost so that at least some potatoes and wine could be stored. When in the first winter the food shortage was at its worst, officers of the R.C.M.P. fortunately brought the most essential items on horseback. The cold was so fierce that for weeks a farmer never took off his overcoat and fur cap, wrapped himself in three featherbeds simultaneously by night and still had to scrape the ice from his moustache each morning. A carter who was once accommodated in the same single bed, left behind him horse lice for the rest of the winter. Anything that was not clinched and riveted outside disappeared. Foxes even ate the children's shoes in those winter months. A social get-together with the neighbors was impossible. A joint celebration which was nevertheless attempted on Christmas Day, cost farmer Eberhard hours of roaming in the dark and cold as he kept missing his house due to the lack of points of orientation. When spring finally came in April, the seeding had to be done by hand and had to be harrowed under immediately to protect it from gophers, which were a veritable pest in those pioneer days, as well as from crows.

In the second year, after the family had arrived, life became more tolerable. The half dozen smoke streamers rising on the horizon stirred among the neighbors the feeling of belonging together and the first discussions about the establishment of a school district and a church could begin. Only after church and school had been set up did the German settler have the feeling of having progressed beyond the point of merely surviving. He began to experience greater security and to assert himself socially. Yet work on the land remained terribly hard and the standard of living primitive and monotonous. For years there was no rest for husband, wife and children. The women suffered most. There was never a reprieve from household and farm chores, and at times they even had to work in the fields while the men were forced to earn necessary cash at railway and road construction sites, or as farm-hands in distant older settlements. Yet in order to spare women at least the field work, a group of four men frequently would ask a fifth man to stay home and break the ground for all of them while they left their homesteads during the summer months to earn money. The women suffered no doubt most from loneliness. While men were busy in the fields beginning at dawn and frequently could not come home even for their noon break because of the long distances, women felt completely deserted amidst their household chores. Many a settler moved to town (e.g. Regina) or returned to his old homeland because his wife could not stand the lonely life on the homestead.

The accounts so far dealt with homesteading in the park belt and on the open prairie, where the immigrants of the prewar era primarily settled. Even more difficult, perhaps, was homesteading in the forest, where clearing poplars sapped most of a person's energy and where reclamation of an acreage large enough to support the family took many more years than in areas where prairie ground was available. Therefore, in the prewar era, few homesteads were taken up in the boreal forest when there was still good land in the prairie or park belt. In the forest, the same primitive standard of living initially prevailed, except for the availability of firewood and lumber and the interruption of the monotonous menu with game and berries. Instead of sod houses, the living quarters here were made from freshly hewn, mostly very thin, poplar boughs. These were no warmer than the sod houses. Except for vegetables and potatoes, the farmer here did not even raise enough feed for cow and horse in the first three years. Forest fires and fierce storms always threatened to destroy the results of laborious beginnings. Often, homesteads passed through several hands. After an initial enthusiasm, the first owner became discouraged, as did perhaps the second and third, and only the fourth one who took over a large piece of cleared land, stuck it out and took root. In the bush, as well as on the prairie, it usually took six to seven years of very hard work and privations before the farmer had time to replace his first provisional shelter with a reasonably comfortable house built from lumber.

In the first years every settler accomplished truly heroic deeds in the wide expanses of western Canada. Only in association with people of like mind, and with the same ethnic and religious background, could the difficulties of the pioneer years be mastered. Even the Canadian authorities recognized the need for ethnically and denominationally homogeneous settlement of the various farm districts as an indispensable prerequisite for prosperity. It is no wonder that among German immigrants those from Germany had the most difficulties coping with the pioneer years. The higher the cultural expectations and standards of civilization that the immigrants and their wives brought with them from their homelands, the harder life on the homestead must have been for them. Even the German colonist from Russia needed all his energy and willpower to succeed in western Canada, and he still continued to suffer from homesickness. The pioneer's lowered standard of living must have been especially hard to swallow for the immigrant from the educated upper middle class of Germany. In the postwar years, far too many of them tried to establish new homes in the forest zone of Saskatchewan or Alberta. They had to give up too much culturally in order ever to be fully satisfied with the new living conditions. We shall come back to this in our discussion of the fate of the postwar immigrants.

4. The Economic Development

The privations of the first years were willingly borne by the large majority of the German settlers in hopes of a better future. The virgin soil of the prairie actually produced remarkably large yields in good years, and when the projected railway was in fact run near the settlement and prices remained adequate, the homesteader could hope soon to be free from debt, provided he was industrious, thrifty and persistent. He could hope eventually to reach a comfortable level of prosperity, and to leave to each of his children, however numerous, their own landed property.

Soon, however, it became obvious that one could not count on at least an average crop every year. Farming, especially wheat growing, which was practiced far too exclusively in most cases, remained risky. Periods of drought lasting too long in the summer, hail, early frosts, snow before the wheat was harvested, wheat blights, gophers, cutworms, etc., were only the most common of many "Egyptian plagues" that could destroy the crops. The growing preference given to the exclusive growth of wheat over mixed farming, which could much better guarantee the family's own needs, was therefore all the riskier. Yet the lack of pastureland on the dry open prairie made exclusive wheat growing almost the only possible form of operation. Mixed farming also required a larger starting capital, more labor and more experience with the climate. The beginner's preference for exclusive wheat growing is therefore understandable. But it was a mistake that the farmer, even though he conquered the pioneer stage, allowed himself to be drawn by the economic boom more and more into large-scale wheat farming. Another reason for failures was the frequent selection of mediocre land by the European immigrants. They might still have cultivated such soil successfully in their homelands, but were unable to do so over here due to the climate and the lack of communications. In addition, there was too much experimenting without sufficient experience by Canadian authorities in matters of colonization. Farmers were sent, for instance, into southwestern Saskatchewan's dry belt, most of which should never have been settled at all.

From the outset there were therefore various reasons for an economic fiasco. The fabulous yields which the prairie could produce in favorable years, without any fertilizers at first, made one forget the uncertainties and branded western Canada in the eyes of the farmers themselves as the land of unlimited economic opportunities. Prosperity actually came to the wheat farmers in the war year 1915, when record crops were harvested in all of western Canada and the Allies were prepared to pay any price due to the war. With a war price of $2.50 per bushel of wheat, the first big harvest was sufficient in most cases to free the farmers from their debts. From the proceeds of the following harvests they went right ahead to purchase more land, to improve the inventory and to build new houses. Prices remained quite high until 1923, and after a temporary slump, prosperity returned in 1925 and was to last until 1929. The bountiful year of 1925 brought a very good harvest, with equally good prices of $1.50 to $1.70 per bushel of wheat. As much as the farmers were entitled to enjoy the boom after their difficult pioneer years, there was a risky side to this development. Since every good harvest brought large surpluses, the farmer tended to lose his head in a euphoria of blind optimism and immediately buy new land at high prices, mostly more than he could pay for, since land was offered only in quarter sections (160 acres). The average size of the farm increased from the original quarter section to half and three-quarter sections. No money was put aside. On the contrary, the farmer's indebtedness rapidly grew again as a result of unwise land purchases. Every farmer became a land speculator. The entire western Canadian agriculture became one giant, feverish speculative enterprise. Yet credit seemed inexhaustible: the next harvest would mean a new flow of cash. After a good harvest, not only good land, but also cars, trucks, tractors, combines, pianos, electric washing machines, radios, toasters and all sorts of luxuries were bought, and families treated themselves on occasion to a winter excursion to California, or even to Europe.

This development, however, had to come to an abrupt end as soon as its foundation collapsed, namely Europe's need of Canadian wheat, and its willingness to pay high prices of one dollar to a dollar and forty cents to the producer. Public authorities and the Canadian press were much to blame for the extent to which the stagnating market could affect the individual farmer. In speeches and articles by politicians and economists, the farmer was constantly assured that he was prosperous, that his purchasing power was unimpaired, and that his share of the national income amounted to so-and-so many thousand dollars. The farmers, including the German Canadian ones, believed this and kept on buying on credit until after the next harvest. Then the entire credit system collapsed with an enormous crash.

Since 1930 the farmer in western Canada has been thrown back to the prewar level. His prospects for the future have even become considerably less attractive, at least on the open prairie, than they were at that time. The climatic and geographical limits of development have become clearly visible. The return on the land has already considerably declined as a result of the exhaustion of the soil. Large areas in southern Saskatchewan and southeastern Alberta have proven in the long run to be unsuitable for agriculture. For many years there has been insufficient precipitation. The layer of humus, gradually pulverized by cultivation continues to disappear, and dust storms that destroy a young crop in a few hours are increasing in frequency and severity. In the south, crop failure follows crop failure. The cultivated acreage of the three Prairie provinces with a yield of less than five bushels per acre was:[43]

1931	9,178,000 acres
1932	7,876,000 acres
1933	11,435,000 acres
1934	8,642,000 acres

Crop failures were accompanied by very low prices between 1930 and 1935, and hence by an increasingly heavy burden of repayment obligations. Relief measures of the governments such as work programs, food and supply of clothing could barely fend off stark poverty. In many areas of the south, farmers were fighting desperately to keep their property, which they had been fertilizing for twenty-five years with their own sweat, and yet they could see the futility of this struggle. The only way out, chosen by more and more families, was the abandonment of the old farm and resettlement further to the north. Just as individual scouts once preceded the immigration from Europe, German farmers living in closed bloc settlements were again sending out experienced men to the north to look for suitable areas of new settlement in the bush. Once again one could see the old covered wagons drawn by teams of four horses, in which the settlers were slowly moving hundreds of kilometers to the north. Often they had to rely on the charity of people along the road. But they seemed to be driven by a colonizing spirit not yet dead, even after having been separated for generations, perhaps 150 years, from their old homeland. Now, after Poland, South Russia, Romania and the Dakotas, they could add southern Saskatchewan or southern Alberta as way stations on their trek.

The farmers of the so-called parkland, the transitional zone between the forest and the prairie, where fortunately most of the German settlements are situated, still fared the best of all by 1937. Here a return to mixed farming was possible. The objective of mixed farming is first of all the self-sufficiency of the family. In that respect it is not dependent on the marketing of its products. From the perspective of the mid-1930s it appears to be the only possible mode of farming for western Canada in the foreseeable future. Here too the conversion from wheat farming, preferred almost exclusively up to 1929, was not easy. The German farmers here were also deeply in debt due to purchases of land and machinery. Yet at least there were few crop failures, and rising prices since 1935 helped farmers to improve their conditions gradually. By 1937 it looked as if the prosperity of the war and postwar years, however, would not return here either. But as a consequence of the necessary conversion to a more diversified mode of farming, farmers were at least able to continue to enjoy a secure, though modest, existence.

Conversion to mixed farming was obviously easier for Germans than, for instance, the British. It is true, the German allowed himself to be drawn into the fast pace of the postwar years, and saw his ideal in the large producer of wheat. Initially, however, true to his German heritage of farming, he had developed in Canada a more versatile mode of farming, oriented to self-sufficiency, to which he at least could revert without too much difficulty. By and large the German remained a farmer over here as well. The American and English Canadian farmer tends not to have a close relationship to the soil, but treats it as an object of speculation. He concentrates on exploiting instead of fertilizing it. He tailors his operation in accordance with prevailing business trends, and does not mind trading his present farm for another one that promises higher profits. For that reason he invests little money and aesthetic considerations into his buildings. The German, by contrast, has a much more personal relationship to the land that he cultivates and preserves, in Canada as in Europe. English Canadians have stressed repeatedly that the German clings stubbornly to his homestead, which he will try to enlarge, if possible, but seldom abandons. He is intent on building a solid and aesthetically pleasing house, on carefully increasing his inventory. He anticipates the need for fertilizers to preserve the yield of his soil. On occasion he lays out a small experimental farm, on which he tries out new strains of feed plants as a variation in the rotation of crops. In Dawson's sociological study on the Peace River district,[44] four types of settlers are distinguished in each new area of settlement: first, the "chronic pioneer" who, full of inner unrest, keeps giving up his developed farm in order to start from scratch in a new area (like Father Chapdelaine in Louis Hémon's *Maria Chapdelaine*); secondly, the "ne'er-do-well;" thirdly, the "exploiter" who considers his farm property as an investment for the future, who works as little as possible on his land and prefers to look after a business, such as the post office or the telegraph station, and keeps coming up with new ways to do better than the others. Finally, there is the "builder," the quiet farmer and worker who knows how to wait for the fruits of his labor. He will eventually be successful and without him no settlement would succeed. There is no doubt that the overwhelming majority of German immigrants belong to this last and best type, and that western Canada owes its colonization in large part to its German element.

The number of Germans who joined the clearly noticeable migration from the farm to the towns was also much smaller than among the British. As a result the German proportion of the rural population, which provided the mainstay of the entire western Canadian economy, continued to grow. Until 1937, thanks to their farming mentality, the Germans, just like the Slavic immigrants, have proven to be more resistant to crises than the British. It is also worth noting the comparison of living expenditures between German and English-Canadian families made by the above-mentioned English-Canadian sociologist Dawson.[45] The lower household operating costs of the Germans are in part attributed to the more economical practices of German housewives. They spend less cash on eating and drinking, and derive a larger proportion of their menu from their own farms. By the mid-1930s just about everyone had gone back to the old frugality. The immigrants who had turned over their properties to their children were retiring in traditionally modest fashion as small pensioners in nearby towns.

The economic contributions of German settlers to western Canada, to which the relatively flourishing German settlements of the 1930s bear testimony, were manifested mostly in the large share of prizes that individual German and entire German settlements won in agricultural competitions. Among wheat growers, Hermann Trelle from Wembley, Alberta took first place. He was awarded the title of "wheat king" as many as four times, the last time in 1933 at the World's Grain Show in Regina. In the great 1936 Winter Exhibition of Toronto, he was awarded first prize for every variety of spring wheat except durum. In 1933 he shared first place in Regina with Westphalia-born Friedrich Paschetag from Goodfair, Saskatchewan. In Toronto, H.J. Neufeld from Codette, Saskatchewan, was awarded fifth place in the group for Marquis spring wheat. Alexander P. Kinzel from Hague, Saskatchewan, made a special name for himself as a cattle breeder. He owned the best Holstein herd in western Canada, which won the Silver Cup in 1931. His best cows produced 18,052 pounds of milk and 723.6 pounds of butter, while the average yield of his herd was around 17,000 pounds of milk and 582 pounds of butter.

In the Canadian National Railways Community Progress Competition in 1930, 1931 and 1932 among the non-British communities, German settlements were also the most successful prize winners. The level of agricultural development, social institutions and community life, handicrafts, schools and interest in cultural activities of the settlers were judged.[46] Prizes were awarded (see Table V.14, p. 177).

5. The Fate of the Postwar Immigrants

The fate of the postwar immigrants constitutes a special chapter. They had barely been able to gain a foothold when they were caught in the whirlpool of the economic collapse and sucked down by it. Even in the years of prosperity up to 1929, starting out was more difficult for new immigrants than before the war. Homesteads were available only in the boreal forest, and in areas with bad communications. Here, at best, self-sufficiency for one's own family could be expected after

Table V.14

Prizes Awarded to German Prairie Settlements in Canadian National Railway Community Progress Competitions, 1930-1932

1930:		
Manitoba:		
Hanover (near Steinbach) . . . . . 90% German Mennonites	2nd prize
Rhineland (near Gretna) . . . . . 100% German Mennonites	3rd prize
Saskatchewan:		
Edenwold . . . . .75% Germans	1st prize
Laird . . . . 100% German Mennonites	2nd prize
1931:		
Manitoba:		
Rhineland . . . . 100% German Mennonites	1st prize
Hanover . . . . 90% German Mennonites	3rd prize
Saskatchewan:		
Laird . . . . 100% German Mennonites	1st prize
Annaheim (St.Peter) . . . . 90% Germans	3rd prize
1932:		
Manitoba:		
Hanover . . . . 90% German Mennonites	1st prize
Saskatchewan:		
Warman . . . . .100% German Mennonites	1st prize
Annaheim (St.Peter) . . . . 90% Germans	2nd prize
Alberta:		
Montgomery (Wetaskiwin) . . . . 25% Germans	1st prize
Liberty (near Leduc) . . . . .30-40% Germans	2nd prize

one decade of the hardest work, but hardly any profitable marketing of products. Therefore the purchase of farms in areas of well-established settlement was preferred. These were available in large numbers, with long-term mortgages but at very high prices. The terms of the sales contracts varied. Virgin land sold by the C.P.R. cost eight to sixteen dollars per acre. In most cases one-tenth had to be paid down, and the rest was mortgaged at 6 per cent interest, with payments of at least one per cent annually beginning in the second year. Occasionally the first plowing and seeding were even undertaken by the railway company in order to help at the start. But such extra expenses had to be mostly repaid within the first ten years. For example: a farm of 160 acres was sold at a price of twelve dollars per acre for a total of $1,920. The downpayment was $192 and the annual interest and amortization more than $120, and that for many years to come. The house and the first inventory (cow, horses, wagon, clearing tools, breaking plow, stove, provisions, fencing wire) required an extra $1,000 to $2,000, for part of which the farmer also had to obtain credit. He therefore started out with a large burden of debt, which he could only hope to pay off with good crops and stable prices. Even greater was the indebtedness on established farms, for which prices of $25 to $60 per acre were the going rate. Mostly there was very little or no down payment at all, but debts were incurred on the basis of half-crop payments (for principal and interest) instead. Only if the economic conditions remained constantly favorable could the settlers ever hope to be freed from the burden of debt. Then came the sudden fall in prices on top of severe crop failures in many areas. Settlers who were trying to get started were unable to continue to meet their obligations. Many had to return their farms to the previous owners and lost everything. Those who managed to stay afloat saw little hope of ever achieving a relatively comfortable prosperity, as had been their dream when they made up their minds to emigrate. The debt will be a burden to them for the rest of their lives, in spite of legal provisions for assistance.

The worst fate befell those who immigrated between 1928 and 1930. Like all newcomers, they initially worked for some time as farmhands and were then no longer able to acquire their own farms. Most of them had been attracted by the much too favorable reports about high wages in Canada. They earned a daily wage of eight dollars, which was paid to a few skilled farm workers only in exceptional cases and only appeared to be the going rate of pay in the few weeks of the harvest. Many came only with the intention of earning an adequate amount as agricultural laborers in order to acquire some land of their own back in the old homeland. The arduous farm work over here, which required not only exceptional health, physical strength and the determination to work but also experience, provided the first disappointment. Rates of daily pay of one to two dollars, plus subsistence, were certainly attractive for unskilled newcomers, but only small savings could be accumulated at this rate. Then, however, came the whirlwind of the crisis. In 1929 and 1930 many farmhands never received their hard-earned wages, because the farmer simply could not pay any more. In the 1930s only very few could afford to keep hired labor. Starving, in rags, without accommodation and financial resources of any kind, the unemployed immigrants began to traverse the whole of Canada from east to west in search of work. Many of them eventually ended up in Montreal, Toronto, Vancouver and other cities. Here they found accommodation in immigrant ghettos in the eastern parts of these cities in overcrowded, wretched mass quarters, scraping for their living as casual workers. Others went to logging camps in the northern wilderness, or chose the immensely strenuous work of laying railway track, which only few can endure for any period of time. Immigrants were seldom hired for road construction, the only relief work available in western Canada, since preference was given to native residents and heads of families. If they applied they were in danger of being deported. No one was eager to be sent back forcibly to his homeland after having left only a few years before with much ado, and the determination to return only when rich. In the worst years between 1931 and 1933, therefore, a very large number had to be kept alive by friends or church organizations. Some had to rely on municipal soup kitchens for their two daily meals and on begging. In the mid-1930s most of them found some kind of work in the gold mines, paper mills and fish processing plants of British Columbia. As a result of all the bitter experiences of the 1930s, however, and detached from allegiance to their old homelands, they frequently turned Communist and rejected their German heritage. Others continued to scrape through as farmhands at the lowest wages.[47] A few found their way to Germany. To follow them may well have been the most ardent desire of all those German emigrants whose character and spirit were not broken. It may even have been the wish of those who just managed to take up a homestead or a farm on credit just in time, and who were not exposed to the ordeal of being knocked around in the worst years of the crisis. The general plight of the farmers in post-war Germany had driven them out, all those orderly, industrious, young families who, full of courage, energy and longing for a new future, wanted to build a better German home for themselves and their children. Their fate became never-ending intensive physical labor, combined with bitterest poverty, and the endurance of a life virtually barren of any culture, which must have been deeply resented particularly by many of the educated middle class emigrants from postwar Germany. In short, it was a feeling of frightful abandonment, coupled with psychic distress as great as material privations. In the 1930s the difficulties for any beginner on the prairie and in the bush were much harder to endure, due to the lack of economic prospects for improvement, and the expectations of a higher civilization among the postwar immigrants. Here are some typical entries from the diary of the young wife of a German farmer who settled with her husband in northern Saskatchewan in 1929:[48]

> We live in a small shack of the kind that serves homesteaders as a habitation. The whole is one large room six by eight meters, well plastered and warm. Along one of the long walls there are two broad bunks made of spring mattresses brought with us, hay and blankets. On the opposite side the kitchen stove and primitive racks to put buckets and dishes on. In the middle of the room a large roughly hewn table. Opposite the front wall the lightly built, typically Canadian barrel stove. Day and night it is fed thick, knotty wood chunks which burn with a crackling sound. On the walls shelves are everywhere, on which the strangest objects have to get along with each other.

> The homesteader's account looks something like this: In the first year crops from twenty acres of newly broken ground, in the second year crops from as many as fifty acres. In order to satisfy one's own grain and potato needs, land is leased at higher or lower rates, depending on the harvest prospects and the humidity of the soil. If the winter brings much snow which means a high amount of moisture for the soil, the owner anticipates a good harvest for himself and will not lease. The older German settlers help the young ones with all they have. They help not only with their rich experience which everyone offers so eagerly and proudly, but also with housing and food, horses and machines, their own labor and their friendship, which makes us endure everything more easily. They really only offer their friendship in order to make it easier for the recipient, to help him getting started. To many back home it would be most embarrassing to find out about these things. It is wonderful what brotherly help they offer each other out here.

It was becoming increasingly obvious that in those times of distress, homesteading required such enormous efforts and privations that the farmer's cultural aspirations were in danger of being entirely drowned by preoccupation with farming chores. Ties to the ethnic heritage were thus bound to get lost under the stress of the material plight. Who could afford the subscription to a German-language newspaper, who could attend a German Day celebration in Saskatoon, Regina or Edmonton hundreds of kilometers away? Social contacts among German neighbors also suffered under the crushing workload of each individual. The women particularly sacrificed themselves. They were in charge of the house, the farmyard, the garden and the raising of children, and female domestic servants could not be obtained anywhere. How hard it was, for instance, to do a big laundry, for which a woman had to gather wood from far and wide and crank up the water from a well fifteen meters deep and more. We were told that anyone who was able to return to Germany was envied greatly by the others:

> Only our children make life meaningful here. What would be the point of this crazy drudgery and the painful deprivation of all culture, if we did not keep in mind the future of those who succeed us? The first generation here will certainly never rise above the most primitive beginnings.

> Christmas is near. We are homesick. We remember what it used to be like. What will the future bring? It is painful to recall the images of Germany, home, children's paradise, because we know by now that we will never be at home here. We certainly did not leave in order to be able to return as rich people after a few years. We only wanted a future somewhere, and because the fatherland rejected our generation we had to go abroad. We left without suspecting that we gave up something for which we would have to mourn for the rest of our lives.[49]

It is worth noting that Germans who were educated were somehow able to endure the hardships more easily than others:

> It seems that the mustering of all the physical resources alone is not sufficient. Only spiritual discipline can exert all the energies beyond the ordinary capacity for work. The educated ones can thus more easily adapt their needs to the totality of the particular situation. They don't take everything as seriously as the others who always believe that things could not go on like this or that, or that this or that situation had simply become unbearable. Experience shows, furthermore, that people used to hygiene and housekeeping are kept from degenerating by the habit of this necessity. There are farmers from rural backgrounds here who have reached the point of differing in no way from their cattle.[50]

Finally some generally valid experiences pertaining to the economic situation. We want to single out the danger, which in the 1930s was greater than ever, of making one's existence solely dependent on wheat crops:

> Dairy farming would be good, but the delivery system is not yet organized and the same is true for eggs. One should raise cattle. That seems to be the only hope for getting ahead. But it would mean three to four times as much work.[51]

> No one has any cash. In order to pay for threshing we had to sell wheat for 19 cents a bushel last fall (1931). Everything is done by barter. Recently I paid 196 eggs in the store and 10 cents to boot, for a birch-broom. A 350-pound pig brought six dollars. Hemmerich worked with five horses for four weeks for a Swede for $29 because we needed money to pay our winter's bill with the general store for sugar, soap, spices and kerosene. Everything else we female settlers produce ourselves...Everyone slaves to the very limit of his abilities and yet the end result is no more than mere survival.[52]

Hunting and trapping were indispensable sidelines for the homesteader in the 1930s. Many young Germans in places such as Lesser Slave Lake led the lives of trappers entirely, for whom the homestead provided only the necessary shelter. The plight of most German postwar immigrants would have been much worse still if they had not received clothes, linen, even some cash for the whole family, from helpful relatives and friends in Germany. Only the unquestioning generosity of friends in the old homeland kept them from having to go on relief. If it had been possible to sell everything at a halfway reasonable price, which was however out of the question in those days, most postwar immigrants from Germany would probably have reapplied for their German citizenship and returned home on the next steamship.

In British Columbia, which in the 1930s became the promised land for many impoverished Germans from the Prairie provinces, the situation was not much better. Mrs. Ilse Schreiber reported this about her trip in 1937:[53]

> On my way back I talked to many Germans in the rich fruit-growing valleys of British Columbia, mainly women who were busy harvesting the early fruit. Hard work here too and small pay. Two to three dollars for a day from 4:00 a.m. until dusk. And whoever made that much was already broken in at the conveyer belt in the canneries, or outside in the constant sultry heat which is very bad for the heart.

The German women I met there had hands that looked like they were poisoned by fruit acid, dirt and saline solutions. They worked with suppurating finger nails and half broken backs, partly crawling, partly squatting on the steep slopes. They could not even find relief at night on the hard bunks of the narrow cabins in which they lived.

This is how most postwar immigrants were doomed in western Canada. It could no longer be a destination for any immigration. The established German element in western Canada could therefore no longer count on any reinforcements, even if the Canadian government had relaxed its prohibition on immigration. Western Canada's Germans were on their own as far as the future of their ethnic identity was concerned.

CHAPTER VI

Settlement Patterns in Western Canada

On the western Canadian prairies the scattered farmstead is the prevailing form of settlement. In the three provinces of Manitoba, Saskatchewan and Alberta there are no closed rural communities—villages in the European sense—apart from a few exceptions. Even the villages established by the German Mennonites from Russia have for the most part gradually been abandoned, since the North American homestead system is tailored to the single farm. If reference is made in the following chapter to a specific settlement, it almost always only means a number of single farms grouped around a small townlike center within a wide radius of several kilometers. This "town" or "village" is somewhat younger than the farm district itself. It comes into existence when someone opens the first general store, for the newly-settled farmers in the area, and is usually located near a railway station. The grain elevators near the station, as well as one or several churches, mark it from a long distance across the prairies as the center of the entire district. Next to the general store which carries everything a farmer might need, a post office, a filling station, a hardware store, a drug store, a small hotel, a bank and the office of a real estate agent eventually appear. Soon there are a dozen or so wooden houses with large empty spaces between them which are proudly referred to as "streets." Since the streets are not paved, elevated planks serve as sidewalks to prevent pedestrians from getting stuck in mud and snow. Later, old settlers from the vicin-

184

ity who have turned over their farms to their children move to such a town to retire. Six days of the week nothing happens in the town. Only the arrival of, perhaps, one train a week passing through brings a certain change. Saturday night, however, is the climax of the whole week when the farmers from the entire surrounding area meet in the stores, make their purchases, do their business, take out loans, get information and their mail and, above all, have a social get-together.

Usually the small town and the entire district acquire their names from the first little post office at the railway station. To help ease the hardships of the pioneer years for each individual farmer, the government as well as the railway and settlement companies have tried to place settlers of the same ethnic background and denomination together. Homogeneously settled farm districts nevertheless have seldom come into existence. In the small town, there are usually some people of British or other ethnic background.

While the smallest units of settlement frequently lack homogeneity, larger closed settlements of one ethnic group have been formed even less often. Of the German immigrants, only the Mennonites and Catholics have established several large bloc settlements. In general the German settlers are confined to a large number of settlements of varying size, i.e., farm districts, several of which may have sprung up along a railway line not far from each other. They are separated by similar districts of other ethnic groups and so do not form closed German colonies. A map of western Canada's nationalities would look like a large, colorful mosaic.

When farm districts were opened up by Germans, great importance was attached to the uniformity of religious beliefs, in order to make it easier for clergy to serve their parishioners. Thus in one place Lutherans joined Lutherans, in another Catholics joined Catholics or Mennonites teamed up with Mennonites, following the example of the denominationally uniform German colonies in eastern Europe. The places of origin seldom provided a rallying criterion. Instead German Lutherans from Galicia, Volhynia, Bukovina, northern Germany and the United States and German Catholics from South Russia, Banat, from the Volga, from Bavaria and western Germany came together to form new homogeneous settlements. The denominational aspect was of such importance in the settlement of the Germans that it forms the basic criterion for my description of the individual German settlements which follows.

Our historical survey of these settlements is based on the following sources: the official reports of the Canadian immigration agents which have been published in the Canadian *Sessional Papers*, old issues of the newspaper *Der Nordwesten*, anniversary publications and other printed reports on the history of the individual colonies, the lists of the clergy and other statistics of the various churches, several handwritten parish registers, 128 handwritten reports from individual German settlements (sent in to the editor of *Der Courier*, in response to an inquiry among his readers in 1932-33) and, finally, my own observations and inquiries on the spot. All this material is of course very uneven in the amount and type of information contained. Also, it was not possible to obtain information on every single settlement.

1. Manitoba

a. *The Mennonite Settlements in Southern Manitoba*

The oldest and largest area of German settlement in Manitoba was established by German immigrants from Russia between 1874 and 1879. They founded two large colonies and one small one at that time:

1. The so-called East Reserve—the term "Reserve" instead of "Reservation" was used by Canada's German Mennonites themselves—east of the Red River in the municipality of Hanover, between Niverville and Giroux. Twelve townships had originally been reserved of which, however, only eight were actually permanently settled.

2. The so-called West Reserve, west of the Red River in the municipality of Rhineland between Emerson and Morden, comprised seventeen townships.

3. The small colony on the Scratching River near the Red River close to the present-day community of Morris, with only two villages, Rosenhof and Rosenort.

The East Reserve had a greater influx of settlers at first. There, two of the three congregations of immigrants settled, the Bergthaler and the Kleine Gemeinde, while the less numerous Old Colony group took up land in the West Reserve. In 1877, seven hundred families numbering about 3,500 persons were counted in the thirty-eight villages of the East Reserve, and 476 families with 2,576 persons in the twenty-five villages of the West Reserve.[1] Beginning in 1878, however, the East Reserve, which due to new immigrations had increased by six to forty-four villages in that year,[2] suffered from severe flooding. In addition the ground turned out to be too stony or sandy in some parts. Almost half of the approximately seven hundred families therefore moved during 1880 and 1881 from the East to the West Reserve, where they settled east of the present-day Gretna-Rosenfeld railway line.[3]

As some of the immigrants' old diaries, kept by their families, testify, the first years were extremely difficult.[4] The climate was particularly hard to endure in the absence of any previous experience. The Mennonites provided the government with the first experiment ever of a larger colony on the prairie. The cattle especially suffered severely from cold and the lack of feed. Barely half of the stock survived the first winter. Many immigrants were near despair, and regretted their decision to trade Russia for inhospitable Manitoba.[5]

Nevertheless, these German Mennonites overcame their initial difficulties relatively quickly, and as early as the 1880s managed to turn their farming operations into model farms in the fullest sense of the word, as the government could boast in its promotion of immigration. They owed this success solely to their ability to stick firmly together as neighbors, rooted in their strong sense of religious community, and their retention of the traditional village form of settlement.

Settlement in villages facilitated cooperation in construction and the cultivation of the fields, the loan of animals and equipment, and the building of common sawmills and flour mills, churches and schools. In each case eight to thirty-two families, who according to the Land Act were entitled to from two to eight sections of land, built their houses side by side along a wide village street serving as the community center, designated one-quarter of their jointly farmed holdings as common pasture (*Allmende*), and distributed the remaining three-quarters for individual cultivation. The arable land was divided in such a manner that each householder received a strip of land (*Gewann*) in each quarter section, so that all fared equally well as to quality of land and distance from the village, just as in the old open-field type of German village known as *Gewanndorf*. The

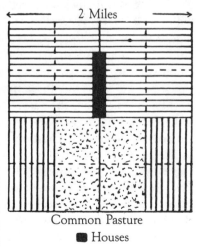

ROSENGART

← ——— 2 Miles ——— →

Common Pasture

■ Houses

preceding sketch of the arrangement of the land (*Flur*) belonging to the village of Rosengart in the West Reserve may serve as an illustration.[6]

By the end of 1877 the following villages had been founded in the West Reserve: Hoffnungsfeld, Eichenfeld, Schanzenfeld, Grünfeld, Ebenfeld, Reinland, Hochfeld, Rosenthal, Waldheim, Neuendorf, Neuenburg, Blumengart, Blumenstein, Krohnsthal, Chortitz, Osterwick, Schönfeld, Schönwiese, Rosenort, Rosengart, Schöndorf, Rosenfeld, Neuhorst, Blumenhorst, Blumenfeld.[7] In the East Reserve, the following villages were founded at a similarly early date: Steinbach, Hochstadt, Chortitz, Bergfeld, Bergthal, Grünthal, Gnadenfeld, Neuanlage, Schönsee, Blumenort, Blumenhof and Blumengart.[8]

A total of 110 villages was established. They are scattered irregularly over the East and West Reserves, and carry without exception the names that are also characteristic of the Mennonite villages in South Russia.

As much as the village system proved itself in the first years of colonization, its drawbacks also soon became manifest. The size of the acreage belonging to each householder (160 acres) made the distances to the various field strips too inconvenient for the farmer. Thus, by as early as the end of the 1880s, individual villages, first along the periphery of the two Reserves, began to redivide the jointly farmed land into the original quarter sections, to which individual families then moved. The single farm settlement suggested by the homestead system was to become the rule in western Canada as in the American Northwest. It gradually displaced the village settlement, even among the conservative Mennonites, who initially considered villages as natural. Between 1890 and 1905 most of the villages were dissolved.[9] Since then additional villages have been abandoned, as the following map of the West Reserve shows.

In the East Reserve the village economy had been entirely given up before the war. Only in Steinbach, which as the commercial center of the settlements has the character of a small town, did the old residential community survive. There are still twenty-two villages in the West Reserve: Neubergthal, Gnadenfeld, Silberfeld, Edenburg, Alt-Altona, Altbergthal (east of the line Plum Coulée-Gretna), which belong to the Bergthaler and Sommerfelder Mennonites; in addition, the Old Colony villages (from east to west) Blumenort, Kronsthal, Rosenort, Neuhorst, Rosengart, Gnadenthal, Schönwiese, Blumengart, Reinland, Friedensruh, Reinfeld, Neuenburg, Hochfeld, Blumenfeld, Schanzenfeld and Osterwick.

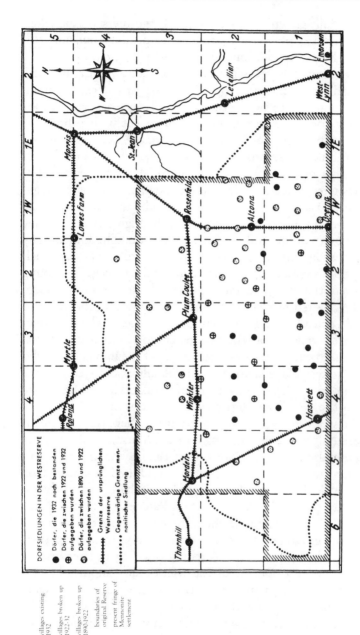

Village settlements in the West Reserve, Manitoba. Source: C. A. Dawson, *Group Settlement: Ethnic Communities in Western Canada* (Toronto, 1936), p. 1116.

The stately, fully grown trees of the old village centers, on the otherwise virtually treeless prairie, mark from a far distance not only still existing, but also many old, long abandoned village sites.

By the Census of 1881 the scant seven thousand Mennonites who immigrated had already increased to 7,775. By the early 1890s they numbered eleven thousand to twelve thousand. The acreage reserved for them was now completely taken up. In 1898 about twelve thousand persons lived in the sixty-five German villages of the West Reserve, and about three thousand persons in the East Reserve.[10] Until the World War, the number of Mennonites in southern Manitoba remained at approximately fifteen thousand. Their excess population went to daughter colonies in Saskatchewan. After one decade, the land originally reserved was no longer sufficient because of the high birth rate. They were farmers by tradition and religious conviction. The Old Colony went as far as excommunicating those who moved to small towns, such as Morden and Rosenfeld that sprang up along the railway. The young generation were therefore reluctant to go to the towns as craftsmen, and instead requested new land. As a result, unrest and the desire to emigrate again spread among the Mennonite villages.[11] The Canadian government was afraid to lose the new generation of its best colonists to the Dakotas, to which in those years many of the immigrants, who had come to western Canada under great difficulties, defected. In 1889 it therefore proposed the establishment of a second large Mennonite settlement in the Northwest Territories. This took shape after 1891, in the area between the North and South Saskatchewan Rivers north of Saskatoon. Not only the young sons of the Manitoba Mennonites went there, but also new coreligionists from Russia who arrived beginning in 1891, as well as Mennonites from the United States. In 1903 young Mennonites began to migrate from Manitoba to the southwest of what would become the Province of Saskatchewan, into the area of Herbert and Swift Current. To these three new areas of settlement the Old Colony group and the Sommerfelders also transferred their village system, which, however, was relinquished again later on.

The economic development of the Mennonite colonies has no parallel in western Canada and can only be compared to the equally rapid growth and prosperity of the German colonies in South Russia. For the Mennonites in Manitoba it was not only due to the advantage of having a head start with their oldest and largest settlement on the prairies, but above all to the industry, thrift, community spirit and agricultural experience of these immigrants on virgin prairie lands, that made their colonies admirable model settlements of the entire West. We must always keep in mind that many of them came over from Russia virtually destitute, for even among the Mennonites the wealthier ones would be more reluctant to emigrate. As early as 1877, when the Governor-General Lord Dufferin visited the East Reserve in the third year of its existence, the young settlement made on him an unusually favorable impression of solid economic development.[12]

The West Reserve especially, with its soil of heavy clay, where wheat growing was about to become predominant, manifested an extraordinary development, since early on it became a junction of several railway lines. It quickly acquired a reputation as the most prosperous farm district of Manitoba. A report in the paper *Der Nordwesten* of July 15, 1897 emphasized the particularly lively construction activity, handsome farmyards and buildings, beautiful trees along the village streets, well-cared-for orchards and the hedges in front of the houses. The commercial center of the West Reserve became Gretna, "Manitoba's German capital," where numerous non-Mennonite Germans from Russia had settled as well. In the winter of 1896-97 the thirty-five German Catholic families of Gretna built their own church.[13]

In the East Reserve, which is situated in the park belt and has lighter soils but a good deal of pastureland, mixed farming, with particular emphasis on dairying, developed. As early as the 1890s there were large cheese factories in Steinbach, Hochstadt, Blumenort, Grünthal and Grünfeld.[14] The rapid growth of Winnipeg brought tangible economic benefits to the entire colony, when the burgeoning provincial capital became a nearby market for dairy products.

From 1890 on the Mennonites preferred to attract German immigrants from Russia as farmhands on their farms, which were by then highly developed. They could in this way acquire their first experience in Canadian agriculture before taking up farming themselves. In this manner the Mennonite colonies became way stations for many German settlers in the West, but nothing more. Almost all the German Catholics from Gretna, Altona, Winkler and Morden, for instance, proceeded on to Saskatchewan after a few years.[15] Some groups stayed as settlers, craftsmen or merchants. Beginning in the 1890s, therefore, German Lutheran congregations developed in Steinbach, Friedensfeld, Rosenfeld, Morris, Friedensthal near Emerson and Brunkild; a congregation of German Baptists was established in Morris as well. The first settlers of Brunkild came from Königsberg and Gilgenburg in East Prussia in 1895. Later Germans from Galicia, Russia and the United

States joined them. Today this congregation has 250 to three hundred members. Friedensthal was founded in 1896 and has about 250 members today. In the small Mennonite towns a number of English-Canadian businessmen and officials took up residence.

Manitoba's Mennonite settlements continued to develop steadily along these lines until the end of the World War. The renunciation of the school privilege and agitation against the conscientious objection of the Mennonites stirred up in all the Mennonite villages the desire to leave what now suddenly seemed to be a very inhospitable country. In the end, only some of the Mennonites acted on this desire. From the West Reserve 3,200 to 3,300 Old Colony Mennonites moved to Mexico in 1922. In 1926 about 1,200 Sommerfelders and others from the East Reserve and about 150 from the West Reserve moved to Paraguay, led by their elder Martin C. Friesen from Niverville.

The loss of people through emigration was partially offset by the arrival of Mennonite refugees from Soviet Russia. Of the Mennonite postwar immigrants to Manitoba (totalling 2,073 families or about eight thousand persons), about six hundred families were settled in the West Reserve and about 120 families in the East Reserve. That means that almost two-thirds of the new arrivals did not make the old colonies of their religious brethren their new home.[16] The 1931 Census showed 30,352 Mennonites in Manitoba. Of these eight thousand to ten thousand were postwar immigrants, and twenty thousand to 22,000 were there before the war. Approximately fourteen thousand of them live in the West Reserve, about 4,500 in the East Reserve, 120 families with 760 persons live in Rosenhof-Rosenort near Morris, and the remainder in small daughter colonies as well as in Winnipeg and surroundings.

In the West Reserve the urban center is no longer Gretna, as around the turn of the century, but Winkler. Here, as in the other small towns, the influences of the English-Canadian environment were more noticeable. In its rectangular layout, with its elevators, hotel, bank, tennis courts and baseball fields, Winkler is no different from any other small Canadian prairie town. On the other hand, Low German is almost all that can be heard in the streets and the herdsman can be seen driving the cattle to the common pasture at seven in the morning. Of the inhabitants 81 per cent are Mennonites. The rest consist of several German Lutheran families, three English-Canadian families, three Jewish businessmen and one Chinese restaurant owner. In Plum Coulée 87 per cent of the inhabitants are Mennonites today, although they formed only one third of the population initially. Here as elsewhere, the advance of urbanization is clearly noticeable.[17] Gretna's population is 85 per cent Mennonite. Altona, the administrative center of the two Mennonite savings and loans institutions, the so-called *Waisenamt*, is as much as 90 per cent Mennonite.

In the remaining villages the open-field system (*Gewannflursystem*) was completely abandoned in the postwar years after some of the inhabitants had moved away. Today only quarter- and half-sections are being cultivated, even though the village as a residential community is still preserved in twenty-two villages as pointed out above. In his economic methods the Mennonite has always been most progressive: tractors, modern threshing machines and so on have been in use from the beginning. With an average size in 1926 of 190 acres, farms have remained relatively small, since the village system did not favor the development of a big operation.[18] On the other hand, Mennonites have always been able to be self-sufficient on their own farms and have not specialized in exclusive wheat growing. This had made the transition to mixed farming in the recent years of crisis easier for them. Besides wheat and flax, barley, oats and potatoes are increasingly grown. Dairy farming also has begun to play a larger role in the West Reserve, as has long been the case in the East Reserve. Worth mentioning is a special industry producing equipment for apiculture in Steinbach. The small, somewhat remotely situated colony of Rosenort-Rosenhof boasts of a cooperative petroleum refinery. An indication about the most common Mennonite family names in southern Manitoba is found in the telephone directory of Steinbach.[19]

The denominationally-related Hutterites tried to establish their first communal farm in Canada near Dominion City not far from Emerson in 1899, but apparently returned shortly thereafter to South Dakota. They did not reemigrate to western Canada until 1918, when they founded eight communal farms near Elie west of Winnipeg; the names James Valley, Bon Homme, Mill Town, Huron, Rosedale, Maxwell, Barrickman and Iberville call to mind their former homes in South Dakota. In 1922 came a group of stragglers, who founded the ninth communal farm of Rosengart, near Plum Coulée, on the land of the Old Colony Mennonites who had emigrated to Mexico. All the Hutterite immigrants to Manitoba belonged to the congregation of the *Schmiedeleut* whose colonies had been situated near Bon Homme, S.D.[20]

b. The Remaining Rural German Settlements

There are no German Catholic settlements in Manitoba at all. Besides the Mennonites, there are only German Lutheran and a few German Baptist congregations. The Lutheran colonies, amidst the large homogeneous Mennonite settlements of Steinbach, Friedensfeld, Rosenfeld, Morris, Brunkild and Friedensthal were already mentioned. In addition, German settlements developed east of Winnipeg in the vicinity of Beauséjour, Greenbay and Goldenbay, with a total of three hundred persons, and in Brokenhead, Grünwald (110 persons), Thalberg (600 persons), Jack Fish Lake, etc., and also still further to the east on both sides of the Whitemouth River in Whitemouth, Oldenburg and Winnipeg Falls (about ninety Lutheran and twenty Baptist families). In 1931 a total of 3,729 Germans and 1,134 persons of Austrian origin were counted in Census Division No. 5. Here the first settlers were Germans from Volhynia in 1896. Later these were joined by Germans from Galicia, Russia and eastern Germany. In the seclusion of their forest settlements, the Germans on the Whitemouth River should be able to preserve their ethnic heritage for a relatively long time. Parishioners in Beauséjour, Thalberg and Whitemouth each have one German Lutheran pastor. In Whitemouth there are also a German Baptist and a German Adventist congregation.

Northwest of Winnipeg, settlements of German farmers sprang up between Camper and St. Martin along the railway line to Gypsumville, especially in Moosehorn which is exclusively German, in Neuheim (Post Office Moosehorn), and in Grahamdale, in dense bush and on land which is rocky or swampy in parts. The colonists have nevertheless been quite successful so far. Colonization began between 1911 and 1914, but considerable immigration to this area, particularly of Germans from Volhynia, continued after the war. A German Lutheran pastor in Grahamdale ministers to about four hundred parishioners in the area. About 2,500 Germans appear to be residing in the vicinity of the above-mentioned railway line.

West of Lake Manitoba, and not far from the Gladstone-Dauphin railway line, there is a German settlement of at least two hundred German Lutheran families. In 1931 a total of 1,156 Germans by origin and 585 Austrians lived in Census Division No. 10. The main settlement is Waldersee, with Glenella as its closest railway station, and eighty families comprising five hundred persons.[21] Waldersee was founded in 1891 by fifteen German families from Galicia. After 1896, more German families arrived from East Prussia, Posen, Volhynia and the Crimea. These were joined by new immigrants from East Prussia, Posen and Austria after the war. The originally dense growth of poplars has been entirely cleared in the meantime. Economic growth has been good despite mediocre soils. In 1896 the Lutheran congregation was founded. Since 1902 the local pastor has also been serving parishioners in the vicinity. Church services are still held exclusively in German. Besides confirmation classes in German, the pastor gives German language instruction each Saturday—in July and August as much as three times a week—to the children. There are also Germans in the six neighboring districts, as follows: thirty families in Glenella (eleven kilometers west of Waldersee), twenty families in Amaranth (twenty-four kilometers to the east, near Lake Manitoba), about ten families in Grass River (eleven kilometers to the southeast), twenty-five families in Tupper (thirteen kilometers to the south, Post Office Plumas) since 1891, about twenty families in Plumas (nineteen kilometers to the south) and nine German families in Tenby (thirteen kilometers to the southwest). The inhabitants of Plumas-Tenby at first named their settlement Holstein. Plumas, like Waldersee, has a German Lutheran pastor.

Finally, Germans have settled in some districts near the Saskatchewan border. In 1913 the German Lutheran settlement of Friedfeld near Shevlin (Post Office Roblin) along the Dauphin-Kamsack railway line, was founded by Germans from Volhynia. Today it numbers 280 Germans. A German farm district with several hundred families was founded twenty-four kilometers to the south at Inglis, which today has two Lutheran pastors and one Adventist minister. Near Grandview there are two small groups of German settlers, one of which came in 1900 from Minnesota, while the other group came from South Russia (Friedrichsfeld in the Molotschna), Volhynia, Germany and Romania, in part as late as the postwar period. In Census Division No. 14, 1,037 Germans by origin and 637 Austrians were counted.

Ontario-Germans have settled near Seeburn, Alcester, Boissevain, and other communities.

After the war several groups of German immigrants settled in the Dauphin district, for instance near Ochre River and Ste. Rose du Lac, as well as further to the north near Swan River and Minitonas. In Ste. Rose du Lac and Minitonas there are German Baptists from Volhynia, with two ministers, whereas the Lutheran settlers are served by a pastor from Swan River and one from Dauphin.

Close to Winnipeg, near historic Fort Garry, one hundred Catholic immigrants, half of whom came from the Black Forest and the other half from Westphalia, founded the much-talked-about colony of Little Britain in the spring of 1927. Led by the young lawyer, Dr. Fritz Schneider from Freiburg in Breisgau, they tried to set up a co-operative venture on 3,124 acres of land that they had purchased. It failed due to internal dissension, which in the years of the Depression accelerated the move to single-family farming. After a few good initial years the settlers, like all the new immigrants, suffered greatly from the sudden fall in prices beginning in 1929, especially since they were still heavily indebted to the former owners of their land. In spite of this, economic conditions seem to be improving in recent years due, above all, to the proximity of Winnipeg, with its large urban market for milk products and the settlers' conversion to exclusive dairy farming. Their produce, too, is in great demand.

c. The Germans in Winnipeg

Winnipeg is a commercial metropolis, the grain exchange and the only large city of the western Canadian prairies, numbering 218,785 inhabitants and close to a quarter of a million with its suburbs. It had been the great gateway for immigration to the Canadian West since the 1880s. Winnipeg's growth from a remote village to a metropolis (241 inhabitants in 1871; 7,985 in 1881; 25,639 in 1891; 42,340 in 1901; 136,035 in 1911) in less than forty years is unparalleled. Each year, this flourishing city was able to offer employment to thousands of newcomers from every country of the world. Even during the winter, work was available for them so that they could save money for their first purchases for their own homesteads. From Winnipeg, they were also easily able to hire themselves out during the summer months as farmhands in the country, in order to acquire the western Canadian farming experience necessary before taking up land themselves. Most German immigrants in western Canada stayed at least temporarily in Winnipeg, and some have taken up permanent residence in the city as craftsmen or tradesmen. Beginning in the mid-1880s a gradually growing German colony was thus formed in the city. In 1901 2,283 Germans were counted; in 1905 there were about 6,500; and according to the Census of 1911 there were 7,957. In 1912 an article in the *Winnipeg Free Press* recorded a number as high as twelve thousand to fourteen thousand.[22] Today the German colony in Winnipeg totals almost fifteen thousand persons. The Census of 1931 registered 13,209 Germans by origin, to which 1,566 Austrians as well as several hundred Mennonites, who are recorded in the census as of Dutch origin, have to be added. As early as 1884, the first German club, the *Deutsche Vereinigung*, was founded in the city. In accordance with Winnipeg's special character as a stopover, it assumed the responsibility of procuring employment and advising German newcomers, free of charge, in the purchase of land.[23] After the war the churches' immigrant information agencies, except for that of the Mennonites, were located in Winnipeg. In 1912 there were, besides the *Deutsche Vereinigung* with its two hundred members, the *Deutsch-Oesterreichisch-Ungarischer Verein* with two hundred members, the *Deutsch-Ungarischer Verein* with 150 members and the *Deutscher Klub Helvetia* with fifty members.[24]

Here the strongest organizations of the Germans, however, were just as in the farm districts—their parishes. The oldest German church of Winnipeg is the Baptist church on the corner of Alexander and Fountain Streets, which was dedicated in November 1890.[25] It was followed by the dedication on December 6, 1891 of Trinity Lutheran Church at Henry Avenue and Fountain Street; its congregation had been founded in 1888. It was destroyed in a fire on Boxing Day, 1904, and the church was not rebuilt on the old site, but in the new northern part of the city (north of the C.P.R. tracks) on Dufferin Avenue. Its dedication in October 1905, however, led to a splitting of the Lutheran congregation.[26] The German Catholic church of St. Joseph's parish was opened on October 8, 1905. German Oblates served in it from the beginning. As on the prairies, the German Catholic clergy in Winnipeg provided for the formation of a homogeneous parish by purchasing a large lot in the suburbs through a society founded for this purpose, and selling it piece by piece to German Catholic immigrants. In this manner they succeeded in creating a small closed German Catholic sector around St. Joseph's church.[27]

Before the war there were seventeen German clergy ministering in the city: eight Lutherans, three Catholics, two of the Evangelical Synod of North America, one Reformed, one Baptist and one preacher of the Evangelical Association. There were six German parochial schools with a total of 786 students, and in all parishes there was an active social life in the respective men's and women's associations.[28] Today Winnipeg has thirteen German churches: seven Lutheran, two Mennonite, one Catholic, one Reformed, one Baptist and one church of the Evangelical Association, plus several additional houses of worship. In 1927 there were 4,600 German Lutherans, eleven hundred German Catholics, five hundred German Mennonites, 581 German Baptists, 440 German Reformed and 275 German members of the Evangelical Association in the city.[29] Most congregations still operate their own schools, mainly in the form of evening or Saturday schools, in which the clergy or special teachers give German language instruction. The official Winnipeg residence of the German professional consul for western Canada also constitutes a certain focal point for the German community.

Brandon's four hundred persons of German descent form the only other German urban community in Manitoba. They are served by a German Lutheran pastor who also looks after German parishioners in the vicinity.

2. Saskatchewan

a. *The Mennonite Settlements*

The oldest and largest district of Mennonite settlement in Saskatchewan is north of Saskatoon, between the North and South Saskatchewan Rivers. It is made accessible by three lines of the Canadian National Railway (C.N.R.). According to the 1911 Census, Germans formed a majority in a contiguous area of forty-two townships.

Around 1890, when virgin land had become scarce in southern Manitoba, and the young generation of Mennonites threatened to emigrate to the United States, the Canadian authorities in association with the C.P.R., which had just completed the Regina-Saskatoon branch line, succeeded in directing the attention of the Mennonites to the area between the two Saskatchewan Rivers. The Mennonites, who had proven themselves in Manitoba so splendidly as the vanguard of colonization, were again sent ahead in order to demonstrate practically the agricultural productivity of the northern latitudes of Saskatchewan, where continuous success in the production of wheat was still considered dubious. The Mennonites were thus to serve again as trailblazers for a general immigration.

Gerhard Ens, one of the most energetic promoters of the entire settlement district of Rosthern, and later the elected member of the provincial legislature for the district, left us a very vivid description of the arrival of the first large group of immigrants in Rosthern, which is characteristic of the beginnings of a settlement in western Canada:

On April 24, 1932, forty years had passed since the first large group of German Mennonites arrived in Rosthern. We comprised a total of forty families. Our first impression reminded us strongly of the story of the creation in the Bible. Desolate and empty was the earth. Not a tree, not a shrub, no grass far and wide. A prairie fire had destroyed everything. The ground was black. There were no building materials nearby. Yet we looked with high spirits and courage into the future. The station did not yet have a building. The railway cars which carried our baggage, livestock and equipment were left on a side-track while the train departed in a northerly direction. Immediately the cars were cleared and converted to living quarters. Tables, chairs, cooking stoves were put up. Meanwhile the little ones had gathered some firewood and soon smoke was rising happily from each car. The fragrance of fried German bacon filled the air with its lovely aroma. The first meal in Rosthern was probably the most delicious one of my life. Soon our town, thus begun, was deep asleep. Here and there a coyote howled. The next morning the train returned from the north. We were afraid that our cars would be picked up again but this was fortunately not the case. We then decided to hitch up five teams of oxen so that some of us could go and search for a suitable homestead. There were no roads, only surveyor's marks for orientation. Deciphering these was not easy. "Help yourselves" was the motto of the government. After several miles, we reached a poplar forest which some of us liked particularly well. We continued our trip along the Saskatchewan River into a deep valley, where we found shelter with a rancher by the name of Diehl. We were very grateful for this, for it began to snow heavily. The next day we returned. We had found good land everywhere. The following day three of us drove to Prince Albert to purchase building materials. We found these in a sawmill that belonged to a German by the name of Penner, who was very helpful. The mill was very primitive; length and thickness of the boards did not matter. I erected the first store and my lumber was in great demand. Everywhere there was hammering and sawing. Thus the town of Rosthern sprang up almost overnight. For the time being, I remained with my wife and our four little children in the railway car until there was enough lumber left for me as well. Eventually we could build our own house measuring eighteen by eighteen feet. After eight months in Canada this was our first home.

By 1893 as many as seventy families had settled on their homesteads in the two new settlements of Rosthern and Waldheim (twenty to twenty-four kilometers west of Rosthern). Most of them were Mennonites, but there were also some German Lutherans from Russia, who later formed a number of congregations of their own within the area of settlement, which was predominantly Mennonite. In 1894 a group of Mennonites arrived from Germany. They came from Rosenort, near Tiegenhof, in the Danzig lowlands of West Prussia. Led by their elder, Peter Regier, they founded the colony of Tiefengrund (twelve to sixteen kilometers north of Waldheim, near what is now Laird). In 1895 the settlement near Hague was started where Elder Wiebe had arranged for the reservation of some land for his Rosenorter Mennonite congregation.[30]

The initial years were extremely difficult for the new colonies. Time and again, as the reward for all the pain of the colonists' existence, early frosts or other unforeseen difficulties ruined the hopes for a good harvest. As a result of this, the Mennonite settlement remained for years, over a wide area, the only large experiment in colonization.[31] While the Mennonites had to pay dearly for their experiences with new soil and climatic conditions, which were to benefit future immigrants, their common bond of unity and spirit of mutual assistance proved themselves in this situation. Repeatedly they received grain, flour and money from their brethren in Manitoba, and so managed to survive the years of distress. Finally, in 1897, they could harvest their first bumper crop. Since then there has been continued economic growth without major reverses, and the Rosthern district, as the immigration authorities had desired, did in fact become as much a model district for northern Saskatchewan as the West Reserve was for southern Manitoba.

By 1896, 125 Mennonite and twenty-five Lutheran German families totalling eight hundred persons had settled in and around Rosthern.[32] By 1897 it had grown to 250 families.[33] After the first good crop, immigration increased considerably, due also largely to Gerhard Ens' successful promotion of this new district in 1898 among the Mennonites in Kansas and South Dakota. After 1899, the number of immigrants from the Mennonite colonies in the United States grew substantially.[34] Until that time most of the Mennonites had come either from Manitoba, or directly from South Russia.

Between 1900 and 1904, immigration reached its climax. Many immigrants from Minnesota, the Dakotas, Nebraska and Kansas, who themselves or whose parents had been in America for barely twenty-five years, had already become quite prosperous. The immigrants of 1899, for instance, are reported to have brought a total of $269,350 with them to the Rosthern district.[35] The immigrants from the United States settled mainly in Dalmeny, Hepburn, Waldheim and Laird.[36]

After 1905 immigration decreased. The interest of the Mennonite immigrants was now directed toward colonies newly forming near Herbert and Swift Current.

Without granting the Mennonites rights of preemption in their respective townships, the area north of Saskatoon between the two rivers became an almost closed German settlement district. In the 1890s immigration officials continued to allot homesteads to the Mennonites and other German immigrants in this district, while British and other immigrants, who were still very sparsely represented in northern Saskatchewan at that time, were assigned to other areas.

In 1901 there were 4,332 persons of German descent living in northern Saskatchewan, 3,683 of whom were Mennonites. By 1911 the Mennonite German settlement district had already spread beyond the two rivers to the east and west, and German majorities were recorded in forty-two adjoining townships.[37] At that time there were more than eight thousand Mennonites and about eight hundred Lutheran Germans from Russia in the district.

According to the Census of 1931, 12,708 Mennonites were counted in this closed settlement of northern Saskatchewan. Compulsory school attendance for the children in English-language public schools, and the contempt with which their principle of non-resistance had been treated, induced eight hundred Old Colony Mennonites from the area around Hague, and several hundred Sommerfelders, to emigrate together with their coreligionists from Manitoba in 1922 and 1926. This loss was, however, more than offset by the arrival of Mennonite immigrants from Soviet Russia. The German Lutherans, who are mostly from Volhynia and the Volga, today number about 1,200. Two pastors in Rosthern look after their spiritual needs and those of their daughter congregations in Stony Hill (since 1902) and Bergheim (since 1906). There is a pastor in Rabbit Lake and one in Radisson, and a minister of the Evangelical Association in Rosthern.

Economic development, after initial years of hardship, has been as pointed out above, surprisingly favorable.[38] The colony is situated in the park belt, the zone of transition between the prairie and the forest, which is ideally suited for mixed farming. In spite of this, wheat is grown almost exclusively, since the wheat harvested in Rosthern and surroundings is among the best in all of Canada. The German farmers have thus become prosperous, as the stately churches and homes reveal at first glance. As early as 1903, Father Dörfler, the chief founder of St. Peter's colony, estimated the value per property of some of the Mennonites there at twenty thousand to thirty thousand dollars.[39] The high profits of farmers here, as elsewhere, induced them to speculative land purchases, resulting in very large farms on the average, but also in mortgages that were much too high when the depression started, thus upsetting all previous economic calculations. However, since the natural conditions encourage mixed farming, and the area had never suffered from drought, and industriousness and frugality have continued to be the virtues of the German farmer, the future of this German Mennonite settlement district in the north of the province seemed secure. It has been among the economically most thriving farm districts of the West.

When Rosthern district was settled in the 1890s, the Mennonites in Manitoba were just beginning to dissolve their village communities and adapt to the prevailing system of single farmsteads. In Saskatchewan, the Mennonites therefore settled from the beginning primarily on single farms. Only the Old Colony group established villages near Warman and Hague with open-field type division of the arable land into equal strips (*Gewannflur*) and common pasturing (*Allmende*). There were seventeen villages at the beginning of the war, some of which still exist today. These have names that keep recurring among the Mennonites: Osterwick, Kronsthal, Blumenheim (founded 1901), Rheinland (1894), Neuanlage (1894), Rosenfeld, Blumenthal (1898), Hochfeld, Chortitz, Grünthal (1897), Schönwiese, Grünfeld, Neuhorst, Edenburg, Olgafeld, Hochstadt and Reinfeld.[40]

Large Mennonite colonies have also developed in the southwest of the province, near Herbert and Swift Current.

In the Herbert area, which the Mennonite Johann P. Wiebe named after his infant son Herbert (who is now mayor of the community), the first farms were taken up in 1903. By 1905 as many as a hundred families had settled in the vicinity.[41] Most of them had come from Russia after 1900, and had worked as farmhands with friends and relatives in Manitoba up to that time. They had "worked out" (*ausgearbeitet*), as they put it. A number of families also came from Kansas, Minnesota, and other states. Coincidental with the beginnings of the farm district of Herbert, which has one hundred families today, the colonies of Main Centre (northwest of Herbert, two hundred families), Grünfarm (to the south, fifty families), Gouldtown (in the north, thirty-five families) and Waldeck were founded. One of their first settlements was given the ambiguous name of Steinreich [i.e. land rich in rocks or in wealth]. Further west near Swift Current, the Old Bergthaler Mennonites founded their first settlement in 1904. Soon various other Mennonite groups moved into the area, especially in 1905 and 1906.[42] At that time the Mennonite colonies south of Swift Current near the present stations of Dunhelm, Wymark and Blumenhof were established. Again, a large number of Old Colony Mennonites were among them. Thus a total of fifteen new villages were founded by 1914: Rosenhof, Rosenfeld, Reinfeld, Rosenbach, Rosenort, Neuendorf, Blumenhof, Schönfeld, Chortitz, Reinland, Schanzenfeld, Blumenort, Schönwiese, Springfeld, Gnadenthal.[43]

After 1908 Mennonite settlements spread into the dry belt south of Herbert, especially near Flowing Well. Here too they were the spearhead of colonization. Today, however, after experience with periods of drought, one would be inclined to argue that colonization of the dry belt was a mistake. Distinguished leaders among the Mennonites, such as Nebraska State Senator Peter Janzen from Janzen, Nebraska, and the mayor of Gretna, Erdmann Penner, had cautioned their people at the time against settling in the dry belt, and instead offered financial assistance for the foundation of a larger colony in the Quill Lakes district. Yet the bumper crops of high-quality gluten wheat which were achieved in the first years with the help of abundant precipitation, seemed to justify the colonization of the dry belt, and held out much greater attractions for the Mennonites than the modest beginnings in the park belt near Quill Lakes. The Census of 1911 recorded as many as 4,598 Mennonites in a wide area around Herbert and Swift Current (in the Moose Jaw district). The departure of about fifteen hundred Old Colony Mennonites and several hundred Sommerfelders after the war was offset by new arrivals from Soviet Russia. According to the Census of 1931 there were about thirty-five hundred Mennonites in and around Herbert, mainly in the municipalities of Coulée, (No. 136) and Excelsior (No. 166), fifteen hundred in and around Swift Current, and 8,231 Mennonites in the entire southwestern part of the province (Census Divisions No. 7 and 8). The recent years of drought have already triggered a partial emigration. In 1934, for example, a number of Mennonites left Herbert for Foam Lake near Yorkton, Saskatchewan, where cheap wooded land was offered to them, although in the midst of a Slavic population.

A planned third district of Mennonite settlement near Quill Lakes, where the Saskatchewan Valley Company had reserved twenty townships for the Mennonites around 1905, did not materialize. Only southwest of Lanigan (as far as Drake and Guernsey) there are about one thousand Mennonites in closed settlement. At Jansen (named after the above mentioned Senator Janzen) and Esk near Big Quill Lake there are no more than one hundred and fifty Mennonites today. Scattered in similar small groups, Mennonites can be found in many more districts of the province. About eighteen hundred families of the postwar Mennonite immigrants—approximately eight thousand persons—settled in Saskatchewan.[44]

b. The German Catholic Settlements

i. St. Peter's Colony

Comprising fifty townships, the colony is the most compact district of German Catholic settlement in western Canada. It is situated in the park belt of northern Saskatchewan on rolling hills, has mostly light loamy soils and ideal conditions for mixed farming but also for exclusive wheat growing. Of the two earlier accounts one, an anniversary publication of 1928, is essentially a brief history of the individual parishes,[45] and the other a sociological study by Dawson.[46]

The colony owes its origins to the farsighted colonization policy of the Catholic clergy. When, around the turn of the century, German Americans from the midwestern and northwestern states began to emigrate, the attention of the Benedictines in Collegeville, Minnesota was drawn to the new mission field. Following the practice of the Catholic clergy in America, the stream of German Catholic emigrants was to be directed into one large closed settlement in order to better preserve their faith and ethnic heritage. Benedictines from the monastery of Cluny, Illinois, who were looking for a new field of activity, sent out Father Bruno Dörfler to select a suitable site for a colony. In preparation for the emigration of German Catholics to the new colony, the Catholic Settlement Society was formed with high school teacher F. Lange in St. Paul, Minnesota as its president. He prepared the launching of an advertising campaign with leaflets and public notices in German-American newspapers. Simultaneously the German American Land Company was created with Messrs. Haskamp and Hoeschen as directors which was to purchase all the odd-numbered sections of the district in question at once and then resell them piecemeal to German farmers intending to resettle. With three company representatives from Stearns County, Minnesota, Father Dörfler travelled through western Canada by train and wagon in August 1902. When this scouting group, under the leadership of Gerhard Ens, reached the Rosthern district and viewed the Hoodoo Plains they agreed that here was the most suitable spot for the planned colony. The German American Land Company immediately bought 108,000 acres from the North Saskatchewan Land Company at $4.50 per acre, paying fifty cents per acre cash. It thereby acquired the rights to all the odd-numbered sections as well as to the even-numbered sections (which were to be distributed by the government free of charge for homesteading) in the sought-after thirty-eight, later fifty, townships. In return for the rights to this area comprising 4,647 square kilometers, the company was only obligated to settle five hundred colonists on the land annually during the next three years.[47]

The first group of twenty-six emigrants assembled by Lange's settlement society in the United States arrived in the new colony as early as October 11, 1902. Until the opening of the Saskatoon-Dauphin railway line in the fall of 1904 the new colony, which the Benedictines had named St. Peter, could best be reached via Rosthern, which was forty kilometers away. Settlement therefore began in the northwestern part of the colony near what would later be the community of Leofeld which was closest to Rosthern. The monastery, however, was deliberately built further to the east at Muenster in 1903, on the railway line which was then under construction. With the completion of the railway, the hub of the colony soon moved to its natural center. Humboldt became the commercial, Muenster the spiritual center of the colony.

By December 1902, more than one thousand persons had already applied for homesteads. After one year the company had brought in six hundred families and could apply for two thousand homestead patents from the Canadian authorities.[48] By 1904 an area as large as twenty thousand to twenty-five thousand acres was under cultivation. By 1906 all free homesteads were occupied, and the land company could start to dispose of the land it had bought. In 1911 it had only twenty thousand acres left. By the outbreak of the war, the good land was almost entirely taken up.

The settlers came mainly from Minnesota, the Dakotas, Wisconsin and Kansas, as well as from some other midwestern states. Many were second generation immigrants. Their parents had emigrated to America between 1860 and 1880. Most of these German Americans brought their livestock, their machinery and their household effects with them. The fathers first went alone to the homesteads and, after one year, had their families follow them. German Catholic families also came from South Russia and from Banat. About ten per cent of the settlers came directly from Germany, particularly during 1905-06.

After the usual privations and reverses of the first years the settlers were, on the whole, quite successful. Here too, there was increasing specialization in the profitable growth of wheat. The transition to mixed farming posed no particular problems. With their experimental farm at Muenster, the Benedictines stimulated and promoted agriculture in the entire colony. The single farmstead is the rule. Only around the churches, which often gave the farm district its name, small, town-like centers sprang up. Next to the stations of the gradually completed railways, however, new "towns" overshadowing the old church hamlets have arisen. The railway became, as everywhere, the stimulator of economic development. Humboldt as a small railway junction soon surpassed the somewhat remote seat of spiritual leadership, Muenster, and became the commercial center of the entire St. Peter's colony.[49] In Humboldt, as in the small towns along the railway, many English Canadians settled. Lately, however, due to migration from the surrounding districts, the German element in the towns has increased faster than the English Canadian element.[50]

In 1911, according to the Census, there were six thousand Germans in St. Peter's colony. Eight of the fifty townships located on the periphery of the colony had majorities of non-German settlers while, on the other hand, in various adjoining townships the German element was predominant, as in the northwest, in the direction of Rosthern, and in the southeast near the Quill Lakes. The area of German settlement thus does not entirely overlap with the diocesan boundaries of St. Peter's Abbey [see Appendix, Map 4]. The latter includes townships in which Scandinavians, Irish, English and non-German immigrants from the Habsburg monarchy predominate.[51]

After the war several hundred new families immigrated from Banat, Hungary and Germany and settled mainly near St. Gregor. Through the purchase of farms the second generation of colonists has been extending the colony further to the east where, for instance, German settlers are gradually displacing French-Canadian settlers near Beauchamp.

The Census of 1931 shows about nine thousand German Catholics living in St. Peter's colony. To these must be added about six hundred

St. Peters Kolonie, Saskatchewan.

Gez. O. Lehmann 1931

///////// diocesan boundary of the German Benedictine Abbey
(*Abbatia Nullius*)

—.—.—.— borders of townships with numerical
German majorities in 1911

to seven hundred German Lutherans, who have been forming small congregations in Bruno, in Cudworth (eighty parishioners from Lodz in Poland) since 1903, and in Middle Lake, with two hundred parishioners from the United States and Germany since 1907.

The ministry of the German Catholics is exclusively in the hands of German Benedictines, fifteen of whom were active in the monastery of Muenster and sixteen as local clergy in the colony in 1936. The small monastery which had been moved from Cluny, Illinois, to Muenster, assumed in 1904 the duty and the right to minister in perpetuity to the Catholics of the fifty townships, in a charter confirmed by the Pope. The monastery grew with the colony and in 1911 was promoted to the status of an abbey. In 1921 its rank was elevated again to that of an *abbatia nullius* which conferred upon the German abbot in his diocese the rights of a bishop. The priors and abbots whose names are closely associated with the history of St. Peter's colony are Prior Alfred Meyer (until 1906), Prior and later Abbot Bruno Dörfler (until 1919) who had selected the spot for St. Peter's colony, Abbot Michael Ott (until 1926) and thereafter, Abbot Severin Gertken.

In 1911 the Sisters of Elisabeth from Klagenfurt (Austria) arrived at the colony to take over the operation of a newly founded hospital in Humboldt. In 1913 Ursuline Sisters arrived from Hanover and set up an academy for girls with boarding facilities in Bruno and later in Annaheim as well. The Benedictines run a college for boys in the monastery.

ii. St. Joseph's Colony

The second, even more extensive but less homogeneous, district of German Catholic settlement is St. Joseph's colony. It extends along each side of Tramping Lake over an area including seventy-seven townships or 7,185 square kilometers. None of the major railway lines pass directly through the colony. As a result it did not experience the expected economic development and failed to produce a dominant commercial center like Humboldt in St. Peter's colony. As for St. Peter's colony, we have an anniversary publication of 1930 for St. Joseph's colony[52] which contains a good description of the geographical conditions, the colonization (with a list of the names of the first settlers) and history of the parishes, as well as the aforementioned sociological study by Dawson.

The initiator of the settlements in St. Joseph's colony as in St. Peter's colony has been Mr. F. Lange. The main reason for the foundation of a new colony before the first was barely even settled was the dissatisfaction of the German immigrants from South Russia, the Volga and from the northwestern United States with the partially forested parkland of St. Peter's colony. They had been used to the open steppe and would have preferred to settle on the open prairie plains which were even better suited for exclusive wheat growing. In search of land meeting these requirements, Lange scouted the prairies west of Saskatoon at the end of July 1904. He intended at first to found a colony which would later comprise not only the seventy-seven townships of what became St. Joseph's colony, but beyond that the entire area as far as Spring Lake in Alberta, with Sullivan Lake as its southern boundary.[53] In other words he envisaged an area of settlement three to four times the size of St. Joseph's colony. Such a large German and Catholic settlement was of course not acceptable to the British and Protestant-oriented government. But the rapid and successful settlement of St. Peter's colony had made such a favorable impression that in August 1904 Lange was promised assistance for the foundation of his second colony. Its final size of seventy-seven townships was still enormous.[54]

Lange's work again was crowned with great success.[55] For the new colony he organized another settlement company, the Catholic Colonization Association. Under his leadership it carried out an advertising campaign in the United States and in Russia. A land company which would immediately purchase, as it had for the founding of St. Peter's colony, a large part of the odd-numbered sections in order to secure the entire district for a closed German settlement, was, not however, formed this time. Due to Lange's thorough and speedy work the stream of immigrants soon became so large that the major part of the planned colony nevertheless became a virtually closed German settlement. Besides Lange, Mr. W. Bentz (later on in Primate, Saskatchewan) deserves much credit for the colonization. While Lange was in charge of soliciting immigrants, Bentz welcomed the settlers at Battleford, procured the homesteads and looked after local development. Here the spiritual leadership and ministry was not in the hands of the Benedictines, but of the German Oblates of Mary Immaculate from Hünfeld who had been active as missionaries among the Germans and Indians of western Canada for quite some time. They were permanently entrusted with the ministry in the seventy-seven townships of St. Joseph's colony by Bishop Pascal of Prince Albert, who had the jurisdiction over this area. Its boundaries are thus ecclesiastical in nature. A glance at the map of lands occupied by Germans in St. Joseph's colony, published by Dawson and reproduced in the Appendix shows that these did not necessarily become ethnic boundaries. While the area around Tramping Lake, where the settlement began, is homogeneously German, the German element decreases noticeably towards the west and especially towards the periphery of the colony. Nonetheless Germans constituted the majority in fifty-five of the seventy-seven townships in 1911.[56] This is a surprising result in view of the fact that in those years of heaviest immigration the colony was, in principle, open to all immigrants.

May 12, 1905 is considered to be the birthday of the colony. On this day the first group of settlers from Saskatoon, led by Father Schweers, arrived at Tramping Lake. The name of Father Schweers, who was an exemplary minister to the colonists in his readiness to share all the hardships of the pioneer period, is as closely associated with the origins of the colony as the names of Fathers Laufer, Krist and Schwebius.[57]

Before the railway came to the district in 1908, the settlers could only reach their homesteads either via Saskatoon (about 190 kilometers away) or North Battleford (one hundred kilometers away) on two old trails across the prairie. Most of the settlers came from South Russia and from the Volga. Many of them had been in the United States for several years before they finally took up their land here. Second generation German Americans were also numerous. In addition, there were immigrants from Germany, Swabians from Banat and Germans from the rest of Austria-Hungary. Leipzig, for example, the oldest district, was settled by approximately equal numbers of Germans from Germany, Russia and Hungary. The first small group of immigrants led by Father Schweers was typical of the future colorful composition of the German element of the colony. It consisted of the priest from Essen, Germany, two Germans from Russia, one Austrian and one German American. Settlement began around the long Tramping Lake. In 1906-07 a very large number of settlers from the United States came to this site. They had some money and settled east of the lake as well as west of it as far as the present communities of Revenue and Tramping Lake.[58]

During 1908-1910, German immigrants from Russia, who were mostly poor, predominated. They settled particularly in the west of the colony as far as Macklin, Primate and Grosswerder. Only the war brought colonization to a halt.

At the beginning of 1907 there were 581 German families at Tramping

Lake. In the census year of 1911 the German population of the colony, which began to spread in the south and particularly in the west beyond the boundary of Alberta, was as high as 5,300. By 1912 all the homesteads had been taken up. Yet the purchase of railway land by the newcomers enabled the colony to grow until 1916. Since the war only a few newcomers have been added. The younger generation, on the other hand, has extended the boundaries of the colony even further through the purchase of farms. In March 1930, St. Joseph's colony numbered 1,186 German Catholic families.[59] There were nine thousand to ten thousand parishioners. According to the 1931 Census 10,099 persons declared themselves to be German by origin in Census Division No. 13.

The settlers formed the following Catholic parishes (the year of foundation is in parentheses) which are ministered by a total of eleven German Oblate priests:

> Leipzig (1905).
> Handel (1905-06): substation, Karmelheim (own church, 1906).
> Revenue (1907).
> Tramping Lake (1908): substations, St. Francis (1908) and Broadacres (1928).
> Scott (1909): substations, Unity, Wilkie, Rutland.
> Kerrobert (1909): substations, Ermine and Luseland (with own church), Major and Dodsland.
> Salvador, Church of the Holy Rosary (1913): substations, town of Salvador (own church) and Azor.
> Denzil (1911): substation, St. John's Church (1910).
> Grosswerder (1907); Primate (own church, 1924).
> St. Peter (Post Office Macklin) (1916): substation, St. Donatus (own church, 1915).
> Macklin (1916): substation, Evesham.

In Macklin there is a hospital operated by the Sisters of Elisabeth from Klagenfurt (Austria) with a German physician in charge. German-speaking Sisters of Notre Dame, known as *Arme Schulschwestern*, have been teaching in the high schools of Leipzig, Revenue, Tramping Lake and Macklin. There are also a few hundred Lutheran families of Germans from Russia, especially in Luseland, living among the large German Catholic majority. At present there are two Lutheran pastors in Luseland and one pastor in Wilkie.

Until recently the economic conditions of St. Joseph's colony have been quite satisfactory. Used to the steppe, the German colonists from South Russia and from the Volga, from Hungary and from the northwestern United States, could be happy with their choice of land. For the lack of scenic beauty in St. Joseph's colony the immigrants were compensated abundantly by the excellent economic opportunities. For miles and miles there was nothing but prairie land with fertile, dark, chocolate brown, loamy soils, completely treeless, so that without prior clearing the ground could be cultivated immediately. The terrain was almost completely level, so that cultivation with machines on a large scale was much easier than in St. Peter's colony, for instance. It was, to sum up, an excellent site for exclusive wheat growing. Only wood was completely absent and in the early years had to be hauled from Battleford over a distance of one hundred kilometers. Therefore all houses and stables had to be built from sod at the beginning. "The colonists were certainly not spared any hardship when they founded the colony. Only bog water to drink, only cereal foods to eat, only dry prairie grass for heating, no home, no shelter for wife and child: those were the first beginnings, beginnings full of troubles."[60] The winter of 1906-07 is still remembered by all the old settlers as a particularly severe one. For months it was bitterly cold, with constant blizzards. If the Mounted Police had not come to the rescue with food, many a settler would have perished miserably in his little sod house. In the years 1907, 1910 and 1911, the crops also suffered heavily from frost. But finally the perseverance of the settlers paid off. The war and postwar years brought good crops to the wheat farmers, with the bumper crop of 1915 averaging 35 to 37 bushels per acre, and high prices. As a result, prosperity came to St. Joseph's colony, and by 1917 the land of most of the settlers was free from mortgages. Exclusive wheat farming, however, carried with it the temptation to enlarge the farms and to add new land after every good harvest, often more than one could pay for from the proceeds of the crop. The farms, consequently, are much larger on the average than those in St. Peter's colony, but so are the debts, with one-half to three-quarters of the property mortgaged. Price slumps and droughts, therefore, had more disastrous effects here, especially since the scaling-down of the cultivation of wheat necessitated by the general economic development, and the conversion to mixed farming is practically impossible due to the lack of pastureland. The result was that some left for the forest belt in the north of the province, as well as for places in British Columbia, such as Kelowna, beginning in 1930.

iii. The Remaining German Catholic Settlements

The oldest district of German Catholic settlement in Saskatchewan is situated east of the capital, Regina, and comprises the colonies of Josephstal, near Balgonie; South Qu'Appelle; St. Peter's parish, consisting of the colonies of Katharinenthal, Rastatt and Speyer between the stations of Kronau and Davin; St. Paul's parish in Vibank, Odessa, Kendal and Sedley. In 1911 Germans formed the majority in two townships at the Qu'Appelle River as well as in seventeen adjoining townships to the south of it.[61]

This settlement started in 1886 near Balgonie on the C.P.R. main line with the colony of Josephstal. It, as well as the entire district described here, was settled exclusively by German Catholic families from the Odessa region.[62] In 1888 another smaller colony was founded east of it near South Qu'Appelle.[63] In 1890 some of the new immigrants founded the colony of St. Peter, south of Balgonie at Many Bone Creek, not far from the present station of Davin. Here they built, especially after they had received considerable reinforcements in 1891, 1893 and 1899, three small villages at some distance from each other and named them after some of the settlers' native villages in South Russia: Katharinental, Rastatt and Speyer.[64] Southeast of the farm district of St. Peter, starting in 1891, St. Paul's parish, later known as Vibank, developed at Many Bone Creek. After 1892 Josephstal, St. Peter and St. Paul received numerous new settlers year after year. Balgonie was for some time "the center of the largest German settlement in the entire Northwest."[65] During 1890-91 the first settlers came to Davin and to present-day Kronau, also named after a village in South Russia.

From the latter 1890s the immigrants from South Russia were joined by increasing numbers of Banat Swabians. Around the turn of the century the area of German Catholic settlement extended beyond Vibank further eastward and southward. To the east the colonies of Odessa and Kendal sprang up, the latter named for the village of Kandel in South Russia, while to the south new immigrants took up land close to the sites of what were to become the stations of Sedley and Francis.

The development of Vibank, as described by pharmacist Paul Abele on the occasion of the twenty-fifth anniversary of this German district, exemplifies the burgeoning economic development of this open prairie region, which is ideally suited for wheat growing.[66] The first hard times since the early years were experienced only during the last decade, when several harvests were destroyed by droughts.

The approximately five thousand German Catholics of this district have formed seven parishes, all served by secular priests: Balgonie (St. Joseph), Qu'Appelle, Kronau (St. Peter), Vibank (St. Paul), Odessa, Kendal and Sedley.

A number of German Lutheran families, who are also mostly from Russia (Kuchebe, Kherson), form small congregations in Kronau (founded in 1891), Davin (founded in 1890) and Vibank.

The colony of Vibank was founded by immigrants from the Odessa district and from Zichydorf in Banat, as well as by some Germans from Bukovina. By 1910 the colony had grown to 120 families, by 1929 to 180 families. After 1895, six school districts, whose school boards and teachers have almost always been German, eventually formed. There is also a high school in Vibank. The major turning point in the history of the colony was the completion of the railway in 1907, and the opening of Vibank station, around which a town sprang up immediately. The post office, the church which had already been built on the prairie, and one of the schools were transferred to the town, which became the center of the entire farm district. In 1923 an Ursuline convent was built in the town for German teaching sisters, who staff the high school and tutor private students in the convent. The long-time member of the provincial legislature for the constituency of South Qu'Appelle, Anton Huck, came from the colony of Vibank.

Kendal received its first settlers in 1901.[67] Almost all of the immigrants had lived in North America for some time before they finally settled here. Some had lived in the United States for up to thirteen years, some came from other colonies of western Canada or from Ontario where, for example, an immigrant family from Germany with several grown sons and their families had spent twelve years, from 1890-1902, before they moved on to the West. The European areas from which the German Catholic immigrants to Kendal came were primarily the area around Odessa in South Russia, Galicia, Banat, Bukovina, the Volga region, Germany, Austria and Romania. Their common language and denomination enabled them to grow together in a new community in spite of their different places of origin.

Besides Josephstal near Balgonie, the German Catholic colony of Landshut close to Langenburg traces its origins back to the 1880s. It was settled by Bavarians and Germans from South Russia. The parish has a German priest.

The origins of Mariahilf south of the present stations of Killaley and Grayson also date back to the 1890s. The first Germans arrived here in 1892. [68] The four townships, however, were not fully occupied until between 1898 to 1904. The settlers were German Catholics, most of whom came from Rosch, Moladia, Derelui and Cuszur Mare, suburbs of the city of Czernowitz in Bukovina.[69] By as early as 1904 all homesteads had been taken up and most of the friends and relatives of the first settlers who came later moved on to Spring Valley and Bayard. The Qu'Appelle River forms the southern boundary of the colony of Mariahilf; in the west it adjoins the German Lutheran farm district of Neudorf; in the north it extends to Township 21, Range 6 and in the east, German settlement reaches as far as the farm district of Dubuc. In the once exclusively English Dubuc, sons of Mariahilf farmers lease more and more land, gradually giving Dubuc a German character. In 1905 Mariahilf had one hundred families comprising five hundred persons.[70] Today there are about 250 families with about one thousand individuals. Most immigrants arrived almost penniless, and had a very difficult beginning until the C.P.R. Kirkella-Bulyea line was built in 1904. Until then the closest station was Grenfell, thirty-five to forty-five kilometers away. Now, however, the settlers only have to haul their wheat to the nearby stations of Killaley and Grayson. The colony, situated in the parkland, has groves of poplars and sloughs. It is suited for mixed farming. The soil is not first-class, but farmers can count with some certainty on good average crops and they have not yet suffered from drought. As early as 1902 the first small church was built on the prairie, to be followed by churches in the small towns of Killaley and Grayson which sprang up by the railway stations. The priest, an Oblate, lives in Grayson. Some of the farmers in the west of the colony are served by the priest residing in Lemberg.

In the southeast of the province northwest of Alameda station near what would later be the station of Steelman, Banat Swabians from Gross-Zsam founded the colony of Maryland in 1900. It soon received a new influx of Germans from South Russia (community of Landau), Bukovina, Romania, Bavaria, Ontario and Wisconsin. Twelve kilometers distant, a second smaller colony by the name of Landau was formed. In 1904 Maryland got its own church, whose German priest also ministers to parishioners in Landau. A few more German families arrived after the war. There were about seventy German Catholic families numbering 525 souls in Maryland in 1932.

In 1902 the colony of Marienthal got underway right on the American border. Its settlers came from the Black Sea, from Romania, Germany, Ontario and North Dakota. Germans also took up numerous farms in the adjoining townships, especially to the west in the direction of Mount Green and Graham Hill, where the community of Jakobsberg was founded in 1916. The 1911 Census showed the German element predominant in this district in nine adjoining townships. There are also Germans in the nearby small railway junction of Estevan, numbering 232 in 1931, and predominantly of the Catholic faith. Today there are about one hundred families comprising seven hundred people in Marienthal and Jakobsberg, served by a German priest. While the ministry here is still exclusively German and the bond of unity is quite strong, the same can no longer be said of the daughter colony of Bergfeld, situated about ninety kilometers further to the west. Bergfeld had sixty-two German Catholic families in 1932, including eighteen each from Russia and Romania, nine from Germany, six from Bulgaria, five each from Austria and Hungary, and one in Poland, for a total of 289 people. To these should be added 158 persons in the neighboring small town of Minton who had come mainly from the United States and from Hungary.[71] The colony, which was founded in 1911, suffered from the fact that the closest railway station, Ceylon, is about forty kilometers away. The colony therefore remained small and was never granted its own German priest. Since the death of its old German sacristan and teacher, German lessons have ceased. So has German church service since the place of worship burnt down in 1925. The complete assimilation of the young generation is the inevitable consequence.

In 1904 the colony of Claybank was founded in the south of the province on the C.N.R. branch line to Gravelbourg.[72] The immigrants came from the Low German colonies on the Sea of Azov, and from the suburbs of Czernowitz in Bukovina. After the war a few more families came from Bavaria and East Prussia, and one family from Russia. In 1932 there were ninety German-speaking families (six hundred persons) in Claybank. Except in dry years, the crops have repeatedly been excellent here on the open prairie. The school is run by two German Ursuline Sisters who have lived in the community since 1932. A somewhat smaller settlement was founded by German Catholics from Bukovina a few miles away in Spring Valley, where sixty-two German families were counted in 1932. In both districts there is also a German Lutheran minority.

At the same time a German Catholic colony northwest of Regina came into existence in four townships, all of which had German majorities in 1911. The first post office in the colony, and consequently the colony itself, was named Fröhlich after the postmaster. Later, however, the post office and the district were given the name of the railway station, Holdfast.[73] Colonization was undertaken between 1904 to 1908 by Catholic Germans from the Black Sea, who were joined by a number of Banat Swabians. The two men who laid the foundation of the colony were Andreas Bengert and Ignaz Selinger. In 1910 the first church was built. In 1920-21 the second one was built, near the railway station. In 1932 the Catholic parish consisted of about 170 families comprising one thousand parishioners. In addition, there is also a small German Lutheran congregation. The district of predominantly German settlers extends to the south as far as the station of Chamberlain, which is twelve miles away and also has a German Catholic parish.

In 1904 the foundation was laid for the predominantly German Catholic area of settlement of Quinton and Raymore on what was later the C.N.R. Saskatoon-Melville line. At that time, thirty-five families arrived from Banat and had three townships put aside for them, but reinforcements from the communities of their homeland did not arrive.[74] The townships were therefore opened up again for general settlement in 1905. They were nevertheless settled mainly by Germans from Germany, a smaller number from the Habsburg Monarchy, and, as everywhere else, by Germans from many other places. Almost all of them had spent some time in Winnipeg. There the Catholics were members of St. Joseph's parish, and were viewed as an offshoot of that colony. The new settlement's first name was Wolfsheim, after the immigration agent Johann Wolf, who brought the immigrants to this site and took up a homestead in the colony himself.[75] The main immigration took place in 1905 and 1906. In 1908 the railway line was built right through the center of the settlement, and the stations of Raymore and Quinton were opened. Today the German farm district extends almost to the station of Punichy, and the small town of Quinton became the center. The land is fertile and slightly hilly, partly covered with bush and suited for mixed farming. Getting started was extremely difficult, as the settlers had to travel almost two hundred kilometers to the next railway station, but the railway brought rapid development. The colony now has about 180 German families (1,100 people), 70 per cent of whom are Catholics (in Raymore and Quinton) and 30 per cent Lutherans (in Quinton). The names of the six school districts are Quinton, Schiller, Wallenstein, Mission Lake, Torontal (after a district in Banat) and Ravensberg. All the school board members and most of the teachers are Germans. Two German Catholic Sisters of Notre

Dame are teaching in Quinton.

On the prairies southeast of Saskatoon, another German Catholic colony to the south and southwest of the present railway station of Allan traces its beginnings to the year 1903. Most immigrants came in 1904 and 1905. By 1910 all available homesteads had been taken up. All the immigrants came from South Russia, some after many years in the United States. Today one essentially distinguishes between the two farm districts of Allan and Seltz (named after the South Russian native village of some of the immigrants) as follows: Allan has more than 150 German families, Seltz slightly less. The credit for organizing the church belongs to the Oblate Fathers Krist and Brabender, and especially to Father Schweers, who has almost twenty years of service in the colony. The economic growth is in no small way reflected in the fact that, in rapid succession, three churches, nine schools, two community halls and one Ursuline convent (whose sisters are in charge of a local high school) were built.[76]

By 1905, furthermore, the German Catholic settlements of St. Pius, Kronsberg and Arat had appeared. St. Pius colony, also called Stoetzel Colony, comprises the area on which the railway stations Kaiser (renamed Peebles during the war), Windthorst, Carlsberg and Dalzell were later built.[77] The colony was founded by German immigrants from the United States.[78] Later quite a number of families from Germany joined them. Today the parish of Windthorst has about five hundred members of German descent. The colony of Kronsberg developed south of what later became the station of Dysart, on the Bulyea-Kirkella railway line to the Qu'Appelle River in the south. It was settled mostly by Germans from Galicia. Today more than one hundred German Catholic families live there. German Catholics from Galicia and Bukovina settled in the colony of Arat, where there is a church eight kilometers from Edenwold.

After 1908, when immigrants were also directed to the dry belt. numerous German Catholic families settled in so-called Happy Land in the extreme southwest of the Province of Saskatchewan which, however, did not prove to be a "happy land" at all.[79] German immigrants who poured into the newly-surveyed district settled at a distance of sixty to one hundred kilometers from the closest station at the time, Maple Creek, west of the Great Sand Hills, and in the north over a large territory as far as the Saskatchewan River. They came mostly from South Russia, as the names of their new settlements indicate, and many of them had lived for years in the Romanian Dobrudja without putting down roots there. The Oblate Fathers Riedinger, Hermandung and Rapp founded the following parishes: Prelate, with its daughter parishes Leader (called Prussia until the war) and Lancer; Krasna (founded by Germans from Bessarabia) with its daughter parishes of Josephstal and New London; Rosenthal, with Rastatt and Richmond; Blumenfeld (Germans from Dobrudja), with Speyer and Liebenthal.[80] A few years ago a total of more than five hundred German Catholic families were reported to have lived there. South of Prelate, German Lutherans and Baptists are also to be found, although in smaller numbers. But the area has been afflicted by constant crop failures since 1930, and many German families have been among those leaving. At first the district seemed superbly suited for wheat production on a large scale. In rainy summers, bumper crops were harvested, averaging fifty to sixty bushels of wheat per acre which could make a farmer rich overnight. This was the case in 1915 and 1916, 1927, 1928 and 1929. In the intervening years, however, there was a series of very mediocre crops or even total crop failures. Since 1930 the temporary prosperity of the farmers has turned again into total impoverishment. Had the government not provided emergency assistance, the "Happy Land" would have been completely deserted by now.

After 1908 an even larger area of German settlement developed within the dry belt south of the Swift Current-Herbert-Morse railway line. Germans, mostly Protestant, were in the majority here in forty-five very thinly populated townships in 1911. German Catholics can be found west of the Neidpath-St. Boswells-Gravelbourg railway line near Hodgeville, Gooding and St. Boswells, then further to the south near Billimun and Mankota and near Rockglen, also north of Shaunavon near Swift Current Creek.

St. Joseph's parish in Hodgeville and the German congregations near Gooding (St. Mathias) and St. Boswells (St. Elisabeth), which are served by the German priest of St. Joseph's, were the result of new immigrations in the years 1909 to 1912. The ministry was organized by Father Wilhelm in 1912-1913.[81] The immigrants in Hodgeville are mostly from the United States (second generation), particularly from Perham, Minnesota, from which the oldest settler, Jakob Grismer, came. At first the colony was named Grismersville after him. A number of its families which had previously lived in Lemberg, Saskatchewan, had come from Bukovina, Galicia and Hungary. The German farmers in Gooding also came from these areas. The first settlers of the St. Elisabeth parish of St. Boswells were almost exclusively Banat Swabians from Zichydorf and the surrounding area. One family from Banat had temporarily settled in Bulgaria before coming here. The total number of German Catholic families in the three colonies is one hundred to 120, comprising about six hundred people. The economic development is the same here as in Happy Land. The railway reached the settlers only after some time. At first they had to travel eighty to ninety kilometers to the station at Morse; after 1912 it was still thirty to forty kilometers to Vanguard, and only recently has the construction of the Gravelbourg-Neidpath and Vanguard-Meyronne lines opened up the settlement to communication. Since the coming of the railway, however, conditions of continuous drought have left the settlers barely any crops to be freighted away.

German Catholics from the Odessa district in South Russia, who during the years 1910 to 1912 founded the colony of Billimun, initially had to cover a distance of 130 kilometers from Morse to their homesteads and, after 1912, still a distance of 55 kilometers to Aneroid or Hazenmore. The railway was not close to them until a few years ago (Mankota station).[82] After the most basic shelters had been erected, the men had to earn money in Regina, Balgonie, Holdfast, and so on during the winter and leave their families behind, 130 kilometers away from the closest railway station on the still wild prairie. In 1914 they built their first little church, but they were not granted their first German minister until 1925. In the years of bumper crops a large influx of German farmers from other parts of western Canada settled in the surrounding districts.[83] On the other hand, in bad years, as in recent times, many families left. In 1932 about eighty German families lived in Billimun. Since 1930, they are again dependent on assistance despite a period of bumper crops, just as in the prewar years when the new settlers still depended on subsidies of seed grain, livestock feed and groceries from the more developed farm districts. These days, only the Russian thistle seems to thrive on the prairies.

Even further southward, a German Catholic settlement developed near Rockglen, where during 1910 to 1915 about sixty-five families settled in five adjoining townships. They came from Germany, Austria and Hungary in about equal numbers, with the addition of a few Germans from Russia. They had all previously lived in Winnipeg and called their new colony Little Winnipeg. When in 1910 the first Germans from Hungary took up their land, the distance to Moose Jaw as well as to Rouleau on the Soo line was about three hundred kilometers. From 1913 to 1926 the settlers still had to cover a distance of sixty-five kilometers to the closest railway station, which was Verwood or Assiniboia, and only since then have conditions with regard to communication been tolerable. At Rockglen station a small town sprang up in which quite a number of German families from the surrounding farm districts have settled.

Finally a settlement somewhat further northeast near Horizon on the Weyburn-Assiniboia railway line should be mentioned, where Banat Swabians settled from 1906 onwards, a total of about seventy families (320 persons). Similar small German colonies, mostly Catholic, developed along the same railway line near Pangman, Khedive, Amulet, Viceroy, Govenlock and Senate. To Senate, in the far southwest of the province, a number of German families came in 1909 from South Russia, some from Wisconsin, North Dakota and from older settlements in western Canada like Sedley, Weyburn and Regina. Today the local St. Stephan's parish comprises thirty families with 160 members. Yet, as in many of these isolated communities, there are no German church services and language instruction and no German activities of any kind.

Almost all the postwar immigrants were directed to already existing colonies. All the community reports refer to a few new immigrant families after 1923. The only newly-founded area of settlement, St. Boniface colony north of St. Walburg, was not ethnically homogeneous. It comprised the homesteads of several hundred Catholic families at Loon Lake, Loon River and Beaver River. There, immigrants from Bavaria, Westphalia and Austria settled with families from the older colonies in Saskatchewan (St. Peter's and St. Joseph's colonies, Killaley, Allan, etc.).[84] The terrain consists of scenic bush, yet the soil is not particularly fertile. The lack of a railway, above all, has made a profitable sale of grain and livestock impossible, in view of the low prices and high marketing costs. Only the hunting and fishing opportunities of the area, and berrypicking in the summer, have enabled the homesteader to hold out for the time being on the basis of complete self-sufficiency. A German priest from St. Walburg, where a German colony had been formed as early as 1908 to 1910, ministers to the settlers.

c. *The Rural German Protestant Settlements*

The three oldest Protestant German settlements in Saskatchewan, which date back to 1885, are Strassburg, Edenwold and Langenburg.

In Strassburg (now Strasbourg), at the southern slope of the Last Mountains more than seventy kilometers north of Regina, since 1905 situated on the Bulyea-Lanigan railway line, the first homesteads were issued to German immigrants as early as 1884.[85] Colonization was directed by the German immigration agent of the C.P.R., D.W. Riedle, who brought out immigrants, mostly from Germany, to the new colony in 1885 and 1886. It was initially named Neu-Elsass (New Alsace). The colony had been founded in the expectation that the Regina-Prince Albert railway line would pass through there. However, the line was laid on the other side of Last Mountain Lake, then known as Long Lake, so that the closest railway station, Lumsden, was fifty kilometers away and Craven remained the nearest market. This severely hampered development of the colony, and caused some of the settlers to give up their homesteads in 1890 and resettle closer to the railway at Longlake-ton, east of the present Silton station. Apart from the lack of good communications, the farmers in Strassburg had no reason to complain. The colony is situated in the park belt, with medium heavy prairie soil that is partly covered with groves of poplars and willows and dotted with small ponds. It is well suited to mixed farming, but also to exclusive wheat growing.

Quite early and to a much stronger degree than in settlements of Germans from Russia, an active social life developed among these immigrants from Germany, with annual German *Volksfest* celebrations, with picnics in the summer and dancing in the winter. An athletic club, a glee club and a literary club were formed. Strassburg was therefore known as the "merry colony"[86] and was in fact the colony with the most social clubs. It was also the only place in which the local group of the *Deutsch-Canadischer Verband von Saskatchewan* was not closed during the war.

Until the turn of the century, however, the colony remained quite small.[87] Many of the farmers from Germany gradually moved to Regina as businessman. As a result, by 1904 only nine of the original thirty-two settlers remained, although in many cases their sons had taken over the farms.[88] After 1902, though, many Germans from Russia, and German Americans, settled all over the district. They had been attracted by the extensive propaganda of the Saskatchewan Valley Land Company. By 1907 the Strassburg district was completely occupied. Today there are about 350 German-speaking persons in a wide radius around Strassburg. In the north it adjoins Duval colony, in the south Bulyea and Earl Grey. Here, too, one finds numerous German families since 1905. Strassburg, Duval and Earl Grey have resident German Lutheran pastors.

The second oldest German Protestant settlement is Edenwold (originally Edenwald), about forty kilometers northeast of Regina on the C.N.R. Regina-Melville line, which has existed since 1911. There, within the westerly bend of the upper Qu'Appelle River, is a very fertile area of rare scenic beauty which is interspersed with groves of poplars and small ponds. Here in 1885 the first Germans, consisting of a few Baptists from Tulcea in Dobrudja under the direction of the Seiboldt brothers, arrived. They named their new colony Neu-Tulcea.[89]

They had intended to settle in the colony of Neu-Elsass (Strassburg) but had been deterred by the long distance from there to Regina, still village-like and primitive, capital of the Northwest Territories. They therefore founded their own colony further south. They took up their homesteads close to each other for mutual protection and assistance. Due to a special agreement the railway and the government gave them the land free of charge. They acquired draft animals and the rest of the inventory on credit. Their first shelters were mud huts, of which only a bit of the walls and the sod-covered roofs were visible above the ground. Meat was obtainable in the bush in the form of rabbit and quail. All the other provisions, such as flour, sugar, tea, tobacco, etc., were bartered in Regina in exchange for hay, wood and stone. The closest station was Balgonie. From 1886 on the German Catholics proceeded from there south to Josephstal, St. Peter and St. Paul, the Protestants went across the Qu'Appelle north to Edenwald. In 1888 Edenwald had its first bumper crop, with forty or more bushels of wheat per acre, so that overnight the homesteaders could repay their debts to the C.P.R.[90] The land-hungry farmers from southeastern Europe could not have wished for better land. No wonder that letter after letter of praise for the new soil went to friends in the old country. Among the recipients was Philipp Mang from Satulmare in Bukovina, who together with a few other Germans from his village and from Itzkani, took off for Edenwald in faraway western Canada in 1889, and in the following years drew more and more Bukovina-Germans after him. These German Lutherans from the Swabian villages of Bukovina henceforth formed the vast majority of the German settlers. The size of the homestead and the quality of the soil made such a great impression on the Bukovina-Germans after their small holdings and conditions of oppression at home, that they wasted no time advising their relatives and friends in the old homeland to emigrate and in many cases sent them tickets for the passage right away.[91]

German Baptists from Dobrudja founded a Baptist congregation in the first year of their settlement. They were visited from time to time by Preacher Petereit, but for the time being could only hold their services in the mud shack of a farmer. Following their example, Lutheran immigrants from Bukovina also immediately formed a congregation. Pastor Schmieder, the first German Lutheran pastor of western Canada, took up a homestead in the Edenwald farm district in 1889, and held regular services in the German school, which was built as early as 1888 and also served the Baptists as a meeting-place.[92] The first Lutheran church was built in 1883. It was the first German Lutheran church on the entire western Canadian prairies, and although it was only built of clay, its official dedication on July 17, 1893 was attended by four hundred to five hundred guests who came across the wild prairie from Strassburg, Longlaketon and Langenburg. The preacher of the day, Pastor Ruccius, even came from Winnipeg.[93]

In 1889 the colony got its first post office, Edenwald, which then replaced the original name of Neu-Tulcea. At that time Edenwald was already regarded as one of the most successful settlements in all of western Canada.[94] However, a series of bad crops after 1892 and a total crop failure in 1894 resulted in a certain setback. Many left the district at that time to try their luck in Dakota or in Texas. Yet most of them returned. In 1896 there were 265 German families with about twelve hundred persons in the Edenwald farm district.[95] Around the turn of the century, immigration to the Edenwald district resumed in larger numbers than around 1890. It was no longer confined to Bukovina-Germans, but also included families from Germany, South Russia, Poland and Galicia.[96] Shortly after 1900 the land in Edenwald had mostly been taken up. However, immigration of relatives and friends of the Germans living there, continued. The new arrivals had to look for land in new farm districts, but tended to spend some time in Edenwald in order to gather experience and earn some money. Edenwald thus became a stopover for a continuous stream of new immigrants, and a parent colony for several new settlements like Kennell, Southey, Earl Grey, Elbourne, Serath and even Vibank (as far as its Lutheran settlers are concerned). In nearby Kennell, which originally belonged to Craven, twenty German families from Bukovina settled in 1902, and an additional seventeen families between 1903 and 1905. Southey and Earl Grey were opened up starting in 1906. Even the Swiss German who founded Elbourne had earlier lived in Edenwald. In Serath, not far from Quinton and Raymore, about twenty German Baptist families from Dobrudja settled. After the war new homesteads north of

Zehner station and as far as the Qu'Appelle River were taken up by settlers from Edenwald.

In 1911 Germans in and around Edenwald were in the majority in seven adjoining townships on whose territory the stations of Edenwald, Frankslake and Zehner (a misspelling of the German surname Zebener) were built. In 1930 about 120 German families with about 750 persons lived in Edenwald, or about one thousand persons, if the surrounding districts with Frankslake and Zehner are included. Besides wheat growing, a large role is played by dairying, with its nearby market in Regina.

The small town of Edenwold—the incorrect English spelling of the station's name which has come into use—which grew around the new railway station after 1911, became the center of the entire district. It has a beautiful town hall, a cooperative association, an agricultural society which erected exhibition grounds and a exhibition hall (completed in the spring of 1929), also an athletic club, a mixed choir, a library and German clubs (see chapter VII). With regard to churches, the Lutherans have one congregation in the district (St. John's, since 1890) and one in town (St. Paul's, since 1916). The Baptists have one congregation, with a church, in the district and one meeting-place in town. The Catholics belong to the parish of Arat whose church, built of stone in 1902, is situated eight kilometers southwest of the town of Edenwold. In addition there has been an Adventist church since 1913 six kilometers to the north, and a Pentecostal congregation in the town itself. German is still the prevailing language in church services and religious instruction. The clergy give German language instruction on Saturdays and Sundays. In 1932 five of the ten teachers in the five schools of the district were of German descent and spoke German fluently. From the beginning most members of the school boards have been Germans. In other branches of the administration of the rural district and in town, the leading positions have been and are in the hands of Germans. Among the mayors of the town P.M. Bredt, the founder of the German newspaper *Der Courier* in Regina, should be mentioned. In the administration of the rural district the name of Philipp Mang stands out especially. Among the university graduates of the colony, the physician Dr. Sauer in Regina, and Dr. Mang, who has been a member in the provincial legislature since 1934, may be singled out. Both are sons of Bukovina-Germans.

The colony of Edenwold scored its greatest visible success in 1930 when it won first prize in the competition, inaugurated by the Canadian National Railways, among the non-British settlements in the

Province of Saskatchewan (see chapter V, part 4). The prize of one thousand dollars was applied to the completion of a new town hall with stage facilities, to replace the one destroyed by fire in 1928. Not only among the German, but among all the western Canadian settlements, Edenwold is no doubt the most thriving settlement, economically and culturally.

The third German settlement in Saskatchewan whose foundation dates back to the year 1885 is Langenburg, near the border of Manitoba. Like Edenwold, it is situated in the park belt and has fertile humus-rich soils. The same C.P.R. agent Riedle who founded Strassburg was instrumental here in the settlement of immigrants from Germany as well. The colony, which at first could only be reached from Solsgirth station in Manitoba eighty kilometers away, was named after Prince Hermann von Hohenlohe-Langenburg, who had travelled through western Canada two years before. The colony was given the name of Hohenlohe and the railway station, which was opened in 1887, the name of Langenburg. This name was soon thereafter transferred to the settlement. When the colony was founded, a large influx of immigrants from Germany was expected which, however, did not materialize. When the railway reached Langenburg in 1887 the settlement had only twenty-seven homesteaders.[97] Only when German immigrants from eastern Europe began to arrive in larger numbers around 1890 did Langenburg colony begin to fill up, and five additional settlements even had to be founded in the vicinity. These included Landshut in 1889, settled by Germans from Lower Bavaria and the Black Sea, Hoffnungstal by Germans from Bessarabia and Galicia, and Beresina by Germans from Bessarabia, Volhynia and Courland. In 1890 Landestreu was founded by Germans from the Galician village of Landestreu, and also Riversdale, primarily by Germans from Galicia.[98] In 1894 Langenburg and the above-mentioned sister colonies had a total of 890 Germans. After two years, however, their number had diminished to 868 in spite of new arrivals.[99] Crop failures, frost damage and millions of gophers that endangered every crop, but especially the lack of a market, forced many settlers to abandon their homesteads between 1892 and 1896 and to try their luck again in southern Manitoba or North Dakota. Many stayed only because they had no funds to move on. They had a hard time keeping afloat with work as farmhands in Manitoba.[100] Only the general economic revival after 1897 brought better times to the Langenburg district.[101] Immigration resumed from the old homeland, from Germany as well as from eastern Europe, and many of the previous settlers who had left in disappointment returned. *Der Nordwesten* of January 1899, a special issue featuring the German colonies, contained the following interesting justification for the temporary departure of some of the Langenburg settlers:

> From 1889 to 1891 immigration (to the Langenburg district) was particularly heavy, in part because a loan arrangement approved by the government granted the new settlers an advance of up to five hundred dollars. This advance, however, became the ruin of the colony for years to come. The way in which it was granted, the exorbitantly high prices for draft animals, cows, tools, as well as the carelessness and ignorance of the settlers, compounded by bad crops in the first years, primarily however the lack of interest in the homestead and the mobile assets which were acquired too easily and remained the property of the company until the debts were repaid, induced many settlers to abandon everything after one or two years and to disperse in all directions. Many even went to the United States. The remaining colonists were quite success-ful after the first unpleasant experiences, so that many of the defec-tors returned. Today all are quite prosperous farmers on the average, who keep good livestock and are satisfied in every respect.

With the beginning of the new century the Langenburg district passed the crisis. With increasing cultivation of the soil, the number of frosts and gophers diminished, the farmers bought more and more machines, they formed school districts, built churches, improved the roads and extended the entire area of German settlement further to the north in the direction of McNutt, where the sons of the settlers took up their own homesteads. In 1904 Zorra, another new colony near McNutt, was founded by new German immigrants from Galicia and Bessarabia. By 1911 Germans had a majority in a bloc of eight townships.

The economic growth of the area is demonstrated by the develop-ment of the small town of Langenburg. In the 1890s it consisted of a station, a store and the school. By 1932 it had a dozen businesses, two hotels, two blacksmith shops, one horse rental, one building sup-ply dealer, a physician, two butchers, a high school, an amusement hall, a sports arena and an ice rink. Among its 330 inhabitants, the 1931 Census identified 213 as German by origin.

Langenburg and Churchbridge municipalities had a total of 2,031 persons of German descent in 1931. Except for the Catholic settlers of Landshut, the Germans in Langenburg district are Protestant. Three German Lutheran pastors minister in Langenburg, one in Churchbridge and one in McNutt.

A large German settlement arose a few miles north of Yorkton. The first settlers arrived there in 1887.[102] As early as 1888-89 the settlement began to spread over the adjoining townships. The immigrants were largely German Baptists from Russia (Volhynia, Volga district), who called their new colony Ebenezer. Situated in the park belt, it had a thriving development from the beginning because the nearby small town of Yorkton provided the market. Ebenezer kept growing, due to an annual influx of immigrants, in a northwesterly direction. This resulted in 1893 in the establishment of the adjoining Langenau colony (north of the Whitesand River) whose first settlers were the Barschel family from Görlitz. The post office and railway station of the settlement were later named after their hometown. In 1889 there were as many as one hundred German families in the area. Their livestock was noteworthy and their crops were excellent.[103] A few years later the traveller Bach was particularly struck by their prosperity.[104] Ebenezer-Langenau-Gorlitz, like all the other successful colonies, became a stopover for many new immigrants until 1914, and thus a parent colony for a series of new colonies in the surrounding area, particularly of Rhein and Stornoway. In Yorkton a large German daughter colony of Ebenezer-Görlitz developed, with 675 persons by 1931. In 1911 Germans were in a majority in only four townships of Ebenezer-Görlitz. Today about fifteen hundred persons of German origin live there. In the surrounding area (Census Division No.9), which includes the colonies of Runnymede and Togo on the Dauphin-Kamsack line, 5,237 persons declared themselves German and 1,365 Austrian by origin. Runnymede with its thirty-eight families was founded in 1904, Togo with its thirty-one families in 1919. These families had left their homes on the Volga as early as 1902-03 and migrated to the United States or to Winnipeg, before they took up farming in Runnymede and Togo after the war.

The German clergy consists of two Lutheran pastors in Yorkton, who also serve parishioners in Ebenezer and Görlitz, as well as one each in Rhein (also for Stornoway) and Runnymede (also for Togo). In addition, there is one Baptist preacher in Ebenezer and one in Yorkton.

The district of Lemberg and Neudorf was opened up mainly by Protestant Germans from Galicia in 1890. Two years earlier the first German immigrants from eastern Galicia, some of whom were Lutheran, some Reformed, settled in two colonies by the name of Josephsberg, one near Dunmore in southern Alberta, and one twenty-two kilometers north of Grenfell station in Saskatchewan. When the colonists near Dunmore experienced a complete crop failure and were to make a new start near Stony Plain and near Fort Saskatchewan, they were invited by their countrymen to come to their obviously much more productive area near Grenfell. In 1890 some families arrived from Dunmore but settled north of the Qu'Appelle and became the founders of Neudorf. The new settlement, which like Josephsberg (south of the Qu'Appelle and north of Grenfell) was named after one of the German villages in Galicia, continued to receive an annually increasing influx of emigrants from the old homeland, particularly in 1893 and 1894. In this way Neudorf soon became the largest colony of Germans from Galicia, and the stopover of almost all later German immigrants from there. By 1896 as many as twelve hundred German settlers had spread over an area of twelve townships in the Neudorf district, whereas only thirty farming families had settled south of the river in Josephsberg.

In the Neudorf farm district most of the land had been taken up by 1900. New immigrants now proceeded somewhat further east where Lemberg colony after 1896, and south of it Hill Farm colony after 1900, were developing. The first colonists of Lemberg, incidentally, were German Catholics from Weissenberg near Hartfeld in Galicia. Today there are still twenty-five to thirty German Catholic families in Lemberg. In addition, German Lutherans from Poland, Volhynia, the Volga and northeastern Germany settled in Lemberg and especially in Hill Farm. Most of the settlers, however, just as in Neudorf, were Protestant Germans from Galicia. Germans of the Reformed Church from Galicia settled mainly in the northeastern part of Neudorf, where they founded Hartfeld colony near Duff. Until 1904, the farmers had to travel fifty to sixty-five kilometers by oxcart to Wolseley or Grenfell station. The construction of the Bulyea-Kirkella railway through the center of the colony in 1904 gave rise to the usual townlike developments at the new Lemberg and Neudorf stations, which became the focal points of the farm district. In Neudorf the land had been taken up by 1900, in Lemberg by 1907. The new arrivals went even further west to Abernethy or, after a few years of gaining experience in Lemberg-Neudorf, moved on to southwestern Saskatchewan (Herbert, Morse, St. Boswells, etc.), which also became the destination of the younger generation of Lemberg-Neudorf settlers.

In 1898, Neudorf Lutherans formed Zion congregation, which today is still regarded as the "mother congregation." Due to the long distances, the farmers in Lemberg and Hill Farm formed their own church. By 1906 they founded Trinity congregation in Lemberg, and later, St. Stephan's congregation in Hill Farm. Today Neudorf—town and rural district—has three German Lutheran pastors, and Lemberg and Grenfell one each. Grenfell, Wolseley and Duff (for Hartfeld) have one Reformed pastor each, in Neudorf there is a preacher of the Evangelical Association and in Lemberg a German Catholic priest.

The Lemberg-Neudorf district has a German population of 2,500 to three thousand persons. According to the 1931 Census, 1,374 persons reported themselves as German and 920 as Austrian by origin in the district of McLeod, 233 as German and one as Austrian by origin in the town of Lemberg, seventy-nine as German and 235 as Austrian by origin in the town of Neudorf, for a total of 1,686 persons of German and 1,156 persons of Austrian origin. To these should be added several hundred Germans in immediately adjoining townships. Especially in the Lemberg-Neudorf district it becomes obvious that the 'Austrian origin' classification consists mainly of Germans. Of the more or less closely related Germans in Lemberg and Neudorf, some called themselves Germans, some Austrians. This may be due to the questions asked by the local census official. We made the same observation in other places, where some of the Germans from Galicia and Bukovina did not report themselves as German but as Austrian by origin.

As everywhere in the park belt the economic development has been favorable here. At the Qu'Appelle River, there is a five to twelve kilometer-wide tract of open grass-steppe which produces excellent crops of up to fifty bushels of wheat per acre. Yet the danger of frost is also greater here. Lemberg and part of Neudorf, however, are situated in the bush zone which only yields crops averaging twenty to twenty-two bushels per acre. Here, however, except for 1931, the settlers have experienced no crop failures. Besides wheat, much rye, oats and barley are grown. The availability of pastureland makes some ranching possible for most settlers. As everywhere, the small farmer here seems to do better at present than the large farmer, for with the size of the land grows the size of the debts, which have been a heavy burden on the farmers since the price slump.

In the rural schools of Neudorf, four of which have teachers of German descent, half an hour of German is still being taught daily. Not so in Lemberg, unfortunately, due to the large number of English-speaking children in the school. The clergy assist with German lessons on Saturdays and Sundays. There is a very active community life. The two colonies have produced quite a few teachers as well as eight Lutheran pastors.

The park belt in the center of the eastern half of the province, in which all the colonies mentioned in this section are situated, gave rise to a few more German Protestant settlements in the decade before the World War.

In 1904, under the leadership of their teacher Popp, the first Germans came to Melville from Strembeni in Bessarabia. By 1906, as many as eighty-five German families lived in the Melville farm district: sixty from Bessarabia, twenty from Galicia and five from Germany. In the following years, until about 1912, Melville and the surrounding area as far as Waldron, Fenwood and Duff became a predominantly German district which merged with the settlement districts of Mariahilf-Killaley-Grayson and Neudorf-Lemberg. In 1911 German majorities were noted in a compact bloc of sixteen townships. In the rapidly growing town of Melville itself, two German Lutheran congregations, one German Catholic parish and one congregation of the Evangelical Association were formed. In addition to the clergy of these congregations, the Melville district is served today by one German Lutheran pastor in each of Duff, Hubbard and Melville, serving parishioners in nearby congregations of Goodeve, Waldron, Colmer and Zeneta, and there is a German Baptist preacher in Fenwood. In Melville, which has become a town of 3,891 inhabitants, there are about two hundred German families today. The Census of 1931 identified these as 1,119 persons of German and fifty-nine persons of Austrian origin. About seventeen hundred settlers of German descent live in the surrounding districts (Cana and Stanley).

West of Lemberg along the Bulyea-Kirkella railway line (since 1904-05) between Lipton and Earl Grey, a number of German colonies sprang up. In Lipton, where settlers identified by the census as of Jewish origin had originally been granted land, all of whom have since become businessmen in the town, German families from the Luzk district in Volhynia settled in 1907. Between 1912 and 1920, fifty more families came from Volhynia, Poland and Galicia. West of it is the German Catholic colony of Kronsberg near Dysart. It borders in the west on the German Lutheran colony near Cupar as well as the Markinch settlement. There, south of the railway line, German Lutherans from Bukovina, Germans from Germany, Russia, Galicia, Hungary and Romania, coming via Edenwald, settled between 1901 and 1904. Between 1904 and 1906 Markinch began to spread beyond the railway to the north, where mostly Lutheran, but some German Catholic, families settled. Markinch borders in the west on Southey and Earl Grey, which have been settled since 1906. At the same time Strassburg and Duval became fully occupied. A total of about thirty-six hundred German settlers live between Lipton and Earl Grey. The German clergy consists of one Catholic priest in Southey (with daughter parish in Markinch), three Lutheran pastors in Lipton, two in Markinch, one in Southey and one in Earl Grey (with substation in Fairy Hill) as well as a Baptist preacher in Southey.

Numerous smaller German Protestant colonies have developed between Big Quill Lake and the South Saskatchewan River near Saskatoon. In 1905, in the townships west of Big Quill Lake, Germans from Volhynia founded Gartenland colony near the present Jansen station, Germans from the Volga founded Prairie Rose colony (post office Dafoe) and Germans from Volhynia founded a colony on the southern shore of the lake, near Kandahar. All three colonies are served by the German Lutheran pastor in Jansen. In 1932 the congregation in Jansen numbered about 350, in Prairie Rose sixty and in Kandahar seventy members. At the same time German Lutherans from the State of Illinois settled near Esk and Lanigan, the latter numbering 120 persons today. Further south near Nokomis, German-American Baptists formed a colony somewhat earlier, which has about 180 settlers today.[105] East of Young at Manitou Lake and opposite Watrous, German Lutherans from South Russia (Kherson Government) founded Eigenheim colony in 1905. It had twenty-two families with 160 persons in 1932. At the same time the German Catholic colonies of Allan and Seltz were established a little further west. West of these again, Dundurn colony was founded in April 1902 by German Americans from Minnesota, North Dakota, Wisconsin, Iowa and Indiana as the first settlement in a wide area. The founder of Dundurn is supposed to be a certain Mr. Meilicke from Windom, Minnesota, a former senator of that state. He bought seven sections of land in 1901, set up a large farming operation and advertised the settlement in the States. Most of the German Americans who came, some of whom were born in Germany, later moved on and only about forty families remained. Dundurn had already lost its exclusive German character when about forty German Mennonite families from Soviet Russia settled there between 1924 and 1928 and restored it. Today about four hundred persons of German descent live in Dundurn. Finally, German Lutheran settlements were founded north and south of Dundurn on the C.N.R. Saskatoon-Regina line near Haultain and Kenaston. Besides serving in Jansen, German Lutheran pastors serve in Esk, Lanigan (with substations in Viscount, Guernsey,

Lockwood, Spalding) and Young-Eigenheim (with branches in Renown, Holdfast, Quinton). There is a Baptist preacher in Nokomis. A few small groups of German settlers have not formed congregations of their own. The German Americans in Dundurn, for instance, have joined the United Church of Canada.

In our account of the Mennonite settlements and Catholic St. Peter's colony we referred to their scattered German Lutheran congregations. At this point we also want to mention the formation of the Lutheran Luseland congregation within the boundaries of St. Joseph's colony. After sending out scouts in 1907 under the leadership of their pastor Sterzer, the first immigrants arrived from Campbell, Hastings and Blue Hill in Nebraska in April 1908. They came in a special train directly from Campbell. Some of them were born German Americans, some were born in Hanover and Westphalia or in Kolb on the Volga. The immigration from Nebraska continued until the war, and even after the war there were a few more newcomers so that more than one hundred German Lutheran families live in Luseland today. Germans occupy all the official positions on the town council, on the jury and on the school board, and the ministry is exclusively in German.[106] Every Saturday German school is held from ten in the morning until three in the afternoon. There is a German church choir and a brass band. The settlers who grew flax in the beginning later changed successfully to exclusive large-scale wheat farming.

Northeast of St. Peter's colony in the forest belt a few small settlements emerged as well. At the latitude of Prince Albert we find Mennonites near Lost River (forty-five families) and Teddington, Lutherans near Spooner (120 people) and Nipawin. Near Runciman, Germans from Poland and farmers' sons from Luseland colony have been settling since 1924. In 1932 these numbered 26 families, or 130 persons. Northwest of the large district of Mennonite settlement around Rosthern, the two German Lutheran congregations in Silver Grove and Brightholme at the western bank of the North Saskatchewan should be mentioned, with about 120 and 240 Germans respectively today.

Silver Grove's first settlers came from Germany. After having spent some time in Ontario, they arrived in 1904. The majority immigrated in 1911 and 1912 from South Russia, Volhynia and Central Poland. Sixteen additional families arrived from there after the war. The German colonists, who are scattered over a wide surrounding area, are served by a Lutheran itinerant pastor in Shellbrook.

Finally, a German settlement northwest of North Battleford in the area around St. Walburg was started in 1908 by Catholics and Lutherans. It was systematically developed, however, only after the war.

A few German Protestant settlements were also formed on the prairies in the extreme southeast corner of the province. The oldest of them developed in the period from 1897 to 1905 between Alameda and Arcola, as a result of the immigration of Germans from the State of Michigan. Their leader was former mayor Richert from Detroit.[107] At the same time Germans from Germany and from Russia joined them.[108] By 1902 four different colonies had been founded: Curt Hill or Dalesboro in 1897, with settlers from Wyandotte, Michigan, a Lutheran church since 1901, and twenty families with 110 persons in 1904; Douglaston, the so-called Detroit settlement, in 1897, with ten German families in 1904; Neu-Norka in 1899 with Germans from the Volga and elsewhere, with twenty families in 1904; and South Willcox in 1902, with eight families by 1904.[109] Several hundred German families live in this very fertile prairie district today. They are served by Lutheran pastors in Frobisher and Wordsworth. The pastor in Stoughton also ministers to the congregation in Arcola.

Around the turn of the century additional German Lutheran congregations were founded in and around Lampman and Estevan, which are in the vicinity of the Maryland-Landau and Marienthal-Jakobsberg Catholic colonies. Around the same time German Lutheran settlements sprang up on the North Portal-Moose Jaw railway line near Yellow Grass and Lang and an urban congregation in the small railway junction of Weyburn. Yellow Grass was founded by Germans from Volhynia. The first four families came in 1900, eight more in 1901, and a large number in 1905, but the majority between 1913 and 1918. After the war six more families arrived from Germany and Volhynia. Today Yellow Grass numbers eighty families or about six hundred persons. In 1915 the church congregation was formed. Its pastor teaches German to children during summer vacations in July-August for eight weeks, five days a week and also every Saturday from Easter to Christmas, as is done in many other settlements.[110] Verwood, a daughter settlement of Yellow Grass, is on the Weyburn-Assiniboia railway line. Its resident German pastor visits scattered German settlers in Lakenheath (twelve families), McEachern and Viceroy. These are situated in the dry belt and direct our attention to the other Protestant German settlements in this zone.

In the dry belt most of the Germans are to be found south of the C.P.R. Morse-Herbert-Swift Current main line. In the large wheat-growing region which is bounded by Chaplin Lake, Wood Mountain River, the Meyronne-Swift Current railway line and the Swift Current-Morse-Chaplin main line, most of the townships have German majorities. Lutherans, who make up the bulk of the German settlers here, have concentrated in Flowing Well, Neidpath-Scottsburg, Kelstern, St. Boswells and Bateman. The first six Lutheran families from the Volga came to Flowing Well in 1906 after having lived in South Dakota and Beauséjour, Manitoba. By 1914, thirty more German families had arrived from the Volga. Today the Lutheran congregation consists of about forty families (240 people) and the Mennonite congregation, which has also existed in the farm district since 1906, of an equal number of families. Besides these there is a congregation of the Evangelical Association. Since 1910, Protestant Germans from the Volga and Mennonites have also settled south and southeast of Flowing Well near the stations of Volga and Kelstern. Besides these Mennonite and Lutheran congregations of 250 and one hundred souls respectively, there is also an exclusively German Adventist congregation numbering ninety parishoners. Near Neidpath and Scottsburg stations, Kramer colony was founded in 1910. Most of its settlers came from the Caucasus, with some families from Germany and South Dakota. In addition to Mennonites, Lutherans and Catholics, the Adventists, the Evangelical Association and the Holy Rollers are represented. Near St. Boswells and Bateman, Germans from Dobrudja, the Volga, Germany, Bessarabia, central Poland and Volhynia settled from 1908 to 1910. Today 180 families live in St. Boswells and 130 families in Bateman. They have formed two Lutheran congregations and one congregation of the Evangelical Association, and engage eagerly in German-oriented activities. The *Deutsch-Canadischer Verband von Saskatchewan* and church congregations together established a German school for students fifteen to eighteen years of age. It does not content itself merely with the teaching of reading and writing in German, but has German conversation as its objective and a speaking competition for its final examination. The school inspector is the very active Pastor Hülsemann.

The entire region has heavy loamy soils which repeatedly have produced bumper crops. The large, roomy houses attest to the prosperous times which prevailed here until a few years ago. Now, however, the area has been suffering heavily from the drought of the last six years. Farmers and clergy alike have become dependent on government relief. Many have left for Vancouver to work in factories. Assistance in the form of donations of oats, potatoes, fruit and clothing which other Germans such as the *Deutsch-Canadischer Verband* have extended to their suffering fellow Germans in the dry belt have very much strengthened the feeling of community among the German element.

Along the C.P.R. main line near Rush Lake west of Herbert, Germans from the Volga and Poland have been settling since 1905, with the majority arriving between 1908 and 1910. Of the total of about one hundred families, only about forty belong to the Lutheran congregation, whereas the others have joined the Evangelical Association and the sects. Since 1912 a German Lutheran congregation has also been forming in the town of Herbert, composed of parishioners coming from Rush Lake and immigrants from Germany and Poland. The church was founded in 1917. Here, as in many other places, Mennonites and Lutherans have been living side by side in harmony. The Mennonites, for example, send their children to the German Lutheran Pastor Hoever for German lessons. German community life is very active, the German choir has seventy voices, and the elementary school has two teachers of German descent. In the high school, German is the most frequently chosen elective. For their children who have graduated from school, the Mennonites have maintained a Bible school since 1916.

Finally, east of Herbert near Morse station, a German colony was founded in 1909, composed of immigrants from Volhynia, the Volga and Dobrudja. Most of the settlers came during 1911-12. The Evangelical Association has about one hundred members. There are also some Lutheran families. In the southwest of the province there are still a few more small German Protestant groups, but these were seldom large enough to form church congregations. Some thirty families from Ontario and the United States have settled since 1907 near Gull Lake along the C.P.R. main line between Swift Current and Maple Creek. Their German Lutheran pastor also serves German parishioners near Carmichael, Success, Shackleton and Chambery. In Happy Land there are German Lutheran congregations at Leader, Mendham, Westerham, Burstall and Fox Valley. A number of church congregations in Happy Land have folded as a result of emigration caused by the drought, and defections to sects, which thrive in this region full of changes and economic uncertainties. Cornfeld colony at Eatonia station was founded in 1912 by settlers from Neudorf and Melville, forty to forty-five kilometers north of Leader and on the opposite side of the South Saskatchewan River. They were later joined by immigrants from Germany, Bessarabia, Poland and Romania. In Cornfeld-Eatonia and next to it at Laporte station, there are seventy-five German Lutheran families or four hundred souls.

Almost all the German Protestant immigrants of the postwar years, unless they had been invited by established relatives and friends into the colonies where they had settled, were directed to already existing settlements by the immigration boards. As far as we know, new settlements were founded only at Wapella on the C.P.R. main line, by Germans from Poland and Germany, at Whitewood, mainly by immigrants from Hanover and some from Danzig, and at Oakshela, by Germans from Galicia and Volhynia. New settlements were also formed in the northern bush country, particularly north of St. Walburg at Loon Lake and Loon River. The Catholics call this area St. Boniface colony, although at least as many Lutherans as Catholics, particularly from Germany, settled there on homesteads. In 1929 the so-called Thuringian settlement was established at Loon River. It consisted of seventeen families, most of whom came from Berka in Thuringia, and some from East Prussia, Brandenburg, Mecklenburg, Hanover and the Baltic region. They developed an active community life in spite of their economic plight.

d. Urban German Element

In the two largest cities of the Province of Saskatchewan, Regina (population 53,209) and Saskatoon (population 43,391), German colonies also formed due to migration from the surrounding rural German settlements.

When as the capital of the province, Regina experienced its first major growth in the first decade of our century (population in 1901: 2,249; in 1911: 30,213), the flourishing German settlements of Balgonie, Josephstal, Kronau, St. Peter, Vibank, Edenwald, Strassburg, Lemberg-Neudorf, etc. were already well established in the immediate vicinity. From these many a settler who had become tired of the hard farmer's existence of the pioneer period, and who hoped to do even better in the nearby small capital, moved to Regina which already had more than five hundred Germans by 1904.[111] Most of the Germans here were also from Russia, Galicia and Bukovina or were Banat Swabians, although the proportion of immigrants from Germany was higher than in the rural districts. Today, 7,500 of Regina's citizens are of German descent, or 14 per cent of her population. According to the 1931 Census, 7,160 reported themselves to be German and 468 Austrian by origin. Most of the Germans are workers, tradesmen and businessmen. There are also several large German businesses in town, such as a pharmacy, a hotel and a department store. The majority of the Germans are Catholics. St. Mary's parish is composed of eight hundred German Catholic families and is under the ministry of the Oblates. A smaller number form St. Therese's parish. Trinity Lutheran Congregation, which since 1906 has been a member of the American Lutheran Church, numbers 160 families. It has a beautiful, large church. Some thirty families belong to Grace Lutheran congregation (Missouri Synod) and sixty families to the German Baptist congregation. All the German church congregations have thriving clubs (relief, women's, young men's and young women's associations) and the Catholic parishes as well as the large Lutheran congregations each operate a small German school. Germans associate in a number of secular clubs (see chapter VII). Several of these, such as the *Oesterreichisch-Ungarischer Verein* (Austro-Hungarian Club, since 1910), trace their origins to the prewar period.

Regina may be characterized as the hub of the German element of western Canada, inasmuch as here in the capital of the province with the largest German population, a number of secular and spiritual organizations have their administrative center. These include the headquarters of the secular associations mentioned in chapter VII (part 2, section b) as well as the presidential seat of the American Lutheran Church (Canada District) and the western Canadian seat of the Prior of the Oblates of Mary Immaculate, a German Catholic order. Luther College, furthermore, the only college maintained by the American Lutheran Church in western Canada, is located in Regina. The German newspaper *Der Courier*, which started publication in the city in 1907, has spread its circulation to the entire West. Regina's role as the hub of German life is demonstrated most clearly during the German Days which are celebrated here on a large scale, and with greater participation than in the other provinces.

Saskatoon has a German population of a mere three thousand, i.e., 2,598 persons of German and 462 persons of Austrian origin as of 1931, who are not as well organized. Most are Lutherans. The presence of five hundred Mennonites in Saskatoon may be explained by the proximity of their large settlements in the north of the city. The German Catholics, on the other hand, have not yet formed a parish of their own. The Manitoba Synod of the United Lutheran Church of North America maintains its only college, which is connected with a theological seminary, in Saskatoon. The *Deutscher-Tag-Komitee* is the top German organization in the city. It is in charge of organizing this city's demonstration of the ethnic and cultural community of all the Saskatchewan Germans, which alternates every two years with Regina, and is a very impressive event here as well.

3. Alberta

a. The Mennonite Settlements

Before the war the Mennonites were almost exclusively confined to Manitoba and Saskatchewan. In Alberta sizable numbers of them have settled only in the wider area around Didsbury. As early as 1893, the first Mennonites from Waterloo County in Ontario settled near Didsbury, which is on the Calgary-Red Deer railway line, and near Carstairs.[112] Beginning around 1900, Mennonites from Ontario and the United States moved into the area of Knee Hills, east of Didsbury. This area is suited almost exclusively to ranching and therefore is very thinly populated. Sunnyslope, Swalwell, Acme and Beiseker may be considered as their main colonies there. The Census of 1911 recorded 504 in the Calgary District and 643 in Red Deer District (including Didsbury), for a total of 1,147 Mennonites.

The postwar years brought the immigration of about 3,500 Mennonites from Soviet Russia. Originally only about two thousand had gone to Alberta, but by and by an additional one thousand to fifteen hundred moved westward to the neighboring province from Saskatchewan, where the immigrants had settled at first. By 1935, 904 families of Mennonite postwar immigrants, consisting of three thousand to 3,500 individuals, were counted in Alberta.

Alberta has also become the refuge of a large number of Hutterites from the United States who in 1918 established twelve communal farms. Eight of these are situated between Lethbridge and Cardston: three located at Richards, East Cardston and Raly belong to the congregation of the *Dariusleut*; the other five at Old Elm Spring, New Elm Spring, Rockport, Milford and Big Bend to the congregation of the *Lehrerleut*. Three additional communal farms of the *Dariusleut*, namely Hinds, Spring Valley and Rosebud, are situated at Rockyford, about eighty kilometers east of Calgary. Finally, the Standoff communal farm of the *Dariusleut* was founded twenty-eight kilometers south of MacLeod.[114] In the meantime some new communal farms have appeared that are daughter colonies. The main line of business of the Hutterites, as is to be expected in southern Alberta, is cattle raising. After difficult early years, they quickly reached their usual level of prosperity here as well. Unlike the other settlers they did not suffer as much from the economic crisis because of their principle of communal work and ownership. There appears to be a total of fifteen hundred to eighteen hundred Hutterites in Alberta today. The 1931 Census showed a total of 8,289 Mennonites and Hutterites in the province.

b. The German Catholic Settlements

German Catholics chose to settle almost exclusively in Saskatchewan. Alberta has only a few more German Catholic settlements than Manitoba.

In 1896, second-generation German Catholic immigrants from the United States began to settle in Pincher Creek along the C.P.R. line in the southwest corner of the province, only thirty kilometers from the Rocky Mountains. They originally came from Westphalia. By 1906 their number had increased to forty families, who formed St. Henry's congregation.[115]

A large German Catholic colony emerged at Spring Lake. The first Germans settled in this fertile and scenic district of the park belt in 1902. Most came from Minnesota and the Dakotas, some from Germany and the Austrian Burgenland.[116] In 1903 and 1904 the entire district was occupied by Catholic Germans from the States. In order to get to their homesteads, the first settlers had to travel eighty to one hundred kilometers by oxcart from Wetaskiwin across the prairie. But the C.P.R. Wetaskiwin-Saskatoon line was soon put within reach (Daysland station, fourteen kilometers north of Spring Lake) and finally the C.N.R. even built a line right through the colony and opened Rosalind, Ankerton and Heisler stations within it. In 1906, about one hundred German Catholic families and thirty single young men for a total of six hundred people from the wide radius around Spring Lake, belonged to the parish founded in 1903 by Oblate Father B. Schulte.[117] By 1932 there were three churches, all of them with stately edifices that reflected the prosperity of the war and postwar years: Spring Lake had fifty-six families (353 people), St. Peter thirty-seven families (270 people), Heisler sixty families (440 people) and Wanda twenty-seven families (180 people). Spring Lake and St. Peter have a German priest and a ministry in German to this day, Heisler and Wanda only English-speaking clergy. Five of the thirteen teachers in the schools of the settlement, which extends over several townships, are of German descent. The colonists engage in mixed farming. Potatoes grow well (up to 350 bushels per acre), also wheat, oats, barley and rye. Horses, cattle, sheep and pigs can be found on every farm, also vegetable gardens and poultry.

Rosenheim colony (fourteen kilometers south of Provost station) has to be regarded as an extension of the large German Catholic St. Joseph's colony in Saskatchewan. In 1911 ten Alberta townships directly bordering on St. Joseph's colony recorded German majorities. Today more than one thousand German Catholics live in a wide radius around Rosenheim.

Fair numbers of German Catholics are to be found also near Beiseker, northeast of Calgary,[118] near Lethbridge[119] and near Morinville, northeast of Edmonton.[120]

In the Peace River district German Catholics from the Rhine and Black Sea live in Friedensthal near Fairview,[121] others in Berwyn and some in the settlement founded at Battle River in 1928 (North Star, Notikewin).

Few traces are left of the small Catholic colonies of Black Sea Germans, founded near Grassy Lake in 1908: Mariahilf parish (two hundred souls), Sacred Heart parish and St. Anthony's parish. They were never able to get a German priest, and have no more German parochial life.

The 1931 Census records 13,180 Catholics of German origin in Alberta.

c. *The German Protestant Settlements*

The Lutherans predominate among Alberta's Germans, as do the Mennonites among the Manitoba Germans and the Catholics among the Saskatchewan Germans. A description of the German Protestant settlements therefore provides the best review of the history of the German community in Alberta in general.

The reputation of having been the first German settlers in the province belongs to Gustav Neumann and Carl Schoening. They entered Canada from the United States, and having reached Ontario, had their belongings shipped to Medicine Hat, Alberta, at that time the most western point of the C.P.R. Then they went from Ontario to Poplar Point in Manitoba and from there to Alberta. After having retrieved their belongings, they hauled them by oxcart to Pincher Creek, 240 kilometers away in the southwestern corner of Alberta in 1882. In 1884 more German Lutheran colonists joined them. In 1896 German Catholics, also from the United States, settled not far from them.

In 1889, 630 Germans, mostly from Galicia, founded a colony south of Dunmore. Their scouts had been fooled by the mild climate in the previous fall and the quality of the soil, which led them to believe that they could even grow fruit and tobacco.[122] But neither the colonists nor the immigration agents had considered the hot winds and the unusual paucity of precipitation, which made farming without systematic irrigation in this area virtually impossible.

Full of hope, they had undertaken the first arduous cultivation of the prairie soil and the erection of their buildings, for which they had to procure the lumber from the Cypress Hills forty to fifty kilometers away. Then a complete crop failure was their reward. Livestock, feed, and food supplies for the winter had to be hauled by the cartload from Dunmore and Medicine Hat, which were also forty to fifty kilometers away.[123] Their starting capital which had amounted to 3,500 to 5,000 Marks ($890 to $1,250) on the average, and would normally have fully sufficed for the establishment of a healthy farming operation, was completely exhausted in the process. When in 1890 and 1891, drought again destroyed the entire crop, the newly founded Josephsberg and Rosenthal colonies south of Dunmore and the colony east of Seven Persons were almost totally abandoned. Only the misfortune of the German farmers, who had thoughtlessly been settled there, led to a proper assessment of the climatic difficulties within the dry belt, and to the realization that the C.P.R. had built its main line too far south. After 1891 only two families, who made their way economically by raising cattle, remained in Josephsberg near Dunmore. Around 1900 some German families from the United States again joined them.

Some of the settlers, who left southern Alberta disappointed and impoverished, moved to northern Alberta, some to Neudorf in Saskatchewan. The Lutherans from Galicia, under the guidance of their pastor Pempeit who had accompanied them earlier from Winnipeg, founded Hoffnungsau and Rosenthal colonies (Stony Plain), the Reformed Germans from Galicia founded Josephsberg near Fort Saskatchewan, and the Germans from Russia founded Heimthal colony in the Rabbit Hills. In these new colonies, which were all situated in the park belt, the immigrants were soon compensated for their first years of crisis near Dunmore by a healthy economic growth, even though they had a difficult start.

Hoffnungsau and Rosenthal colonies are better known by the name of Stony Plain, which was later given to the post office and the railway station.[124] The name of Hoffnungsau has gone out of use entirely, while Rosenthal is still the name for the western part of the colony. The first forty families who founded Hoffnungsau came up from Dunmore in 1891. The railway then went as far as Red Deer. From there they had to continue by oxcart. South of Edmonton they camped for awhile. When they arrived at their destination about thirty miles west of Edmonton, they were the only settlers for a considerable distance. Their first crop was a very promising beginning, and the colony consequently attracted new immigrants, primarily from Galicia, but also from Volhynia and the rest of Russia, each year until 1897. By 1892 there was no more land available in the original colony, and newcomers had to take up homesteads to the southwest. By 1897 all homesteads in the surrounding area were occupied, the first shacks had been replaced by stately new buildings, each farmer owned ten to twenty head of cattle and had harvested several crops of wheat, averaging thirty-five to forty bushels per acre.[126] Soon a few German families from Ontario settled nearby, and starting in 1893, German immigrants from the United States (Chicago) also began arriving. Between 1898 and 1900 Germans of the Reformed faith settled five kilometers to the north. After 1901, immigrants from Galicia established Golden Spike colony ten to twelve kilometers to the south, where around 1910, German families from Russia also settled. By 1911, three townships had German majorities and three neighboring townships had sizable German minorities. Today close to two thousand persons of German descent live in Stony Plain, Spruce Grove, Golden Spike and the areas in a wide radius around them. They are under the spiritual care of a German Lutheran pastor in Stony Plain and one in Golden Spike. The oldest ministry is that of Pastor Eberhardt, who has been associated with the German congregation in Stony Plain since 1897. In Onoway, a few miles north, there are a German Lutheran pastor and a Baptist preacher.

Economically this area is one of the most flourishing farm districts in all of western Canada. It is excellently suited for mixed farming, which was predominant until the war. The opportunities for profit presented by the war and postwar years, however, have led to complete conversion to wheat production. This is making a return to mixed farming difficult, even though it has become desirable since the onset of the Depression.

Of the Reformed families from Galicia, who had suffered so severely near Dunmore, twenty-four settled near the Beaver Hills northeast of Edmonton and launched the second Josephsberg colony near Fort

Saskatchewan. In 1897 there were more than forty families in the colony. With initial crops yielding up to sixty bushels of wheat per acre, as in 1897, its economic development appeared even better than that of Stony Plain. More recently, the railway station near Fort Saskatchewan adopted the German name of the settlement which otherwise might easily have fallen into obscurity. Its spelling, however, became slightly altered to Josephsburg. The Reformed congregation has always had pastors from Germany, and has so far retained its German identity well.

Only slightly further northeast, Germans from Volhynia settled in 1894 under the guidance of their pastor Lilge. They belonged to the church of the Moravian Brethren, and named their settlement Brüderheim.[127] During the first two years the entire colony was supported by German Mennonites in Manitoba, who thus have extended their assistance not only to their own coreligionists.[128] Soon, however, the farmers experienced healthy economic conditions here as well. Numerous German Lutherans from Germany and Russia settled near the Moravian Brethren, and formed their own church congregation in Brüderheim. The 1911 Census showed the Germans in a majority in eight townships, with the North Saskatchewan River forming the northwestern boundary. Today about twelve hundred Germans live in Josephsburg, Brüderheim and the surrounding area. They are divided into Reformed, Moravians and Lutherans in about equal numbers. The area is unusually fertile and has had no crop failure to date.

The third and largest district of German settlement developed south of Edmonton on both sides of the C.P.R. (Calgary–Red Deer—Wetaskiwin–Edmonton line). The Lutheran Germans from Russia, who had participated in the disastrous beginnings of Dunmore, were the first settlers in that district. In 1891 they founded Heimthal colony near the Rabbit Hills west of the present Nisku station.[129] To the north of it, in 1892-93, Germans from Volhynia founded Lutherhort congregation (five kilometers east of the later Ellerslie station). Today both colonies jointly form the Ellerslie Lutheran congregation. In 1893, the first German Baptists from Volhynia, under the guidance of their pastor Müller, settled in Leduc farm district. By 1904 as many as one hundred German families had settled there, almost all from Volhynia and mostly Baptists, with a few Lutheran families among them.[130] West of Wetaskiwin the first fifteen to eighteen German Lutheran families from Russia had settled in 1892.[131] This settlement continued to grow as a result of a steady influx of Lutherans and Baptists from Volhynia so that by 1897, it numbered fifty-five families and the German Baptist congregation was able to dedicate a church.[132] In 1894 the Moravian founders of Brüderheim also founded Brüderfeld colony, between South Edmonton and Ellerslie. Some of them also settled near the already existing Heimthal colony. Moravian Brethren were also the founders of Neu-Sarepta colony which, however, soon contained primarily Lutheran and Baptist settlers as did all the other German farm districts of the area. In 1894 the first settlers coming from Wetaskiwin took up land in the area beyond Bittern Lake, west of what later became Camrose station. Immigration to the area south of Edmonton was particularly strong during the decade 1895 to 1905. The economic success of the first settlers in this area, so ideally suited for mixed farming, attracted more and more friends and neighbors from the old homeland. This was the chief destination of Germans from Volhynia immigrating to western Canada. But besides these, there were also numerous German families from central Poland, Germany, and the United States.

Canadian immigration propaganda made particular efforts to solicit German immigrants in the United States. The German Americans settling at Red Deer, Wetaskiwin, Leduc, etc., from 1893 were in fact among the very first immigrants from the United States settling in western Canada.[133]

The result of immigration was that the Edmonton-Wetaskiwin-Camrose triangle was settled almost exclusively by Germans. After the turn of the century, however, more Scandinavians, British and Ukrainians immigrated there than Germans. Nevertheless, in 1911 Germans had a majority in eleven adjoining townships on both sides of the Wetaskiwin-Edmonton railway line, with the North Saskatchewan River as the northwestern boundary. East of it they were predominant at Neu-Sarepta, Hay Lake and at Bittern Lake (Camrose). Today seven thousand persons of German descent live in this area. They are under the spiritual care of two Lutheran pastors each in Leduc and Wetaskiwin, one Lutheran pastor in each of Ellerslie, Neu-Sarepta, Brightview and Patience (west of Wetaskiwin); furthermore, of two Baptist preachers in Leduc and Camrose and one in Wetaskiwin.

Southeast of Wetaskiwin a few more isolated German settlements have sprung up at New Norway, Bashaw and Stettler. It is worth noting that in Bashaw colony, as many as twenty-six to twenty-eight of the families coming from Volhynia are named Schulz, and so it is also referred to simply as the "Schulz settlement." German Swiss founded Blumenau colony near present-day Stettler in 1903. Later the post office, the railway station and finally the settlement itself were named after their leader Carl Stettler.[134] Originally a much larger colony, which was to extend over an area of forty-six townships, had been planned. Yet Blumenau-Stettler colony remained the way it was.[135] These German Swiss took up dairy farming from the beginning, and opened a cheese factory in their very first year. Shortly thereafter German Lutherans settled southeast of the German Catholic Spring Lake colony, which was established in 1903, near what were later Forestburg and Galahad stations, and further south at Tinchebroy. By 1911 six townships in the area had majorities of Germans. Finally, we find German Lutherans further south near Castor. German Lutheran pastors serve in Bashaw, Stettler, Forestburg and Castor.

Southwest of Wetaskiwin there are German Lutheran colonies near Hobbema (along the C.P.R. line) and near Bismarck.[136]

The first German settlements in the north, northwest and west of Edmonton were established in the last years before the outbreak of the war. In 1913 immigrants from Germany, mainly Württembergers, settled near Westlock, Dapp and Fawcett (on the railway line to Peace River), Newbrook (on the railway line to McMurray), Styal, Junkins and Speers (on the C.N.R. line to Edson-Jasper). Near Duffield, about ten miles west of Stony Plain, a small settlement was launched in 1897 by Volga-Germans of the Reformed faith from Norka. In 1934 it had twenty-one families. There are also German settlers thirty to forty-five kilometers west of Duffield at Little Volga and Tomahawk. In a northwesterly direction, in dense bush country, German Mennonites from South Russia first settled in Mellowdale in 1908, immigrants from Germany in Düsseldorf (in 1916 renamed Freedom) and in Barrhead (from 1909).

The area in the direction of Barrhead was systematically colonized only in the postwar years. Most of the Germans, who today make up about half the population there, did not come to settle until after 1927 in Westlock, Stettin, Freedom, Mellowdale, Manola, Mystery Lake, Bloomsbury and in Barrhead itself where the new railway and highway end. There are also fair numbers of them near Meadowview, Rochfort Bridge and Mayerthorpe (on the C.N.R. line to Whitecourt). All these settlers came primarily from Germany and Poland, with some from the United States and the southern part of the prairies. In 1927 a small settlement also emerged east and southwest of Flatbush station along the C.P.R. Edmonton-Peace River line. As early as 1914, Germans from Volhynia had taken up the first homesteads there, but not until the late 1920s did new immigrants arrive from Danzig (seven families), Germany, Austria, Hungary, Poland and Russia. Numerous post-war immigrants have settled near Edson, Rosevear and Pinedale on the C.N.R. line to Jasper, where the forest provides a convenient hunting ground during the winter. They have also settled forty kilometers west of Leduc, near Thorsby and Sunnybrook and near Warburg. Thorsby has about 150 Germans, Warburg seventy-five to one hundred, three-quarters of them from Germany, and the rest from eastern Europe. There are an athletic and a glee club in Warburg since an active social life here, as in other settlements inhabited by immigrants from Germany, helps the suffering homesteaders get over the worst.

In all of these new settlements Germans have cleared the dense bush with stubborn perserverance, and eked out a modest existence for themselves. Social clubs and church congregations which have formed almost everywhere demonstrate their bonds of unity. German Lutheran pastors serve among new settlers at Barrhead, Mellowdale, Meadowview, Rochfort Bridge, Waldheim, Flatbush, Newbrook, Thorsby, Tomahawk and Rosevear.

All the above-mentioned German Protestant colonies are situated in the park belt or in the forest, in the northern half of the colonized part of Alberta within a sixty-kilometer radius of the provincial capital of Edmonton. In the Census Division No. 11 alone, which comprises the area within a radius of forty kilometers around Edmonton, eleven thousand to 11,500 persons of German origin were counted, not including those in Edmonton.

The drier, more elevated southern part of the province, which is more suited to ranching, has been neglected by German immigrants. We mentioned the Mennonite settlements near Didsbury and Swalwell, for example, and those of the Hutterites. On the whole, between 1900 and 1914, especially from the United States, the south of Alberta had no shortage of German immigrants, who were scattered over the land as ranchers. It makes even less sense, of course, than elsewhere in western Canada, to speak of closed settlements in the ranching regions, and for that reason hardly any congregations were formed in the south. The accelerated process of anglicization of German Americans settling here in isolation is revealed by the constant reduction of the number of German clergy serving during the last decade. The only closed district of German settlement developed south of the Walsh (on the provincial border with Saskatchewan)-Irvine-Dunmore-Medicine Hat C.P.R. main line where in 1911 Germans had a majority in a bloc of thirty townships. Most of its German settlers came from Bessarabia and the United States. The German colony near Walsh was established between 1906 and 1911, and numbers fifty families today who, however, have no pastoral care, no clubs and no German language instruction. South of Irvine a colony of about two hundred German families (one thousand souls) emerged between 1890 and 1910. The colony stretched southward to the Cypress Hills and followed the hills towards the west. As a result there are German settlers in such farm districts as Robinson, Newburg (formerly Josephsberg), Elkwater, Thelma, Growan, Gros Ventre, Little Plume and Wisdom. This is the same area in which, between 1889 and 1891, Germans from Galicia had made their first futile attempt to settle. As ranchers, however, they were able to make a living after they had gathered the necessary experience and learned how to gather what little water there was in dams on the individual settlements. The climate is ideally suited for ranching.

With its risky farming conditions and abrupt ups and downs in external living conditions, this region is typical of the entire dry belt. Congregations of traditional denominations, who had proven their vitality in other regions, could barely survive here and had to make room for the most diverse sects. Besides Catholics, Lutherans and Baptists here one can find Congregationalists, the Evangelical Association, Adventists, Christadelphians, Nazarenes, Sabbatarians, Jehovah's Witnesses, Russellites, Holy Rollers, etc. Followers of the original Lutheran faith have become so few that they are only occasionally visited by German clergy from nearby Medicine Hat. The forty German families from South Russia in Schuler (founded in 1910), who had originally been Catholics, had also become converts to these same sects. Finally, there is a large German settlement in Hilda, where one Lutheran and one Baptist minister are serving to this day.

Besides these above-mentioned settlements in Happy Land, there is to our knowledge only one more German Lutheran pastor serving in a farm district of the south, namely in Claresholm, close to the foothills of the Rocky Mountains. From there he probably visits various groups of German settlers. One congregation of about twenty German Lutheran families in Loyalist receives its pastoral care from Luseland in Saskatchewan.

The Peace River district, Alberta's youngest area of settlement, which was, for the most part, settled only after the railway was built in 1916, today has a population of thirty thousand to 35,000 of whom 3,500 to four thousand are German.

The Peace River district, which is separated from the rest of Alberta by a wide belt of swampland, has proven quite suitable for grain production, as Hermann Trelle's wheat-growing achievements demonstrated, in spite of its location between the 55th and 59th parallels.[137] The area, abundant in lakes and swamps, is full of scenic beauty, with prairie-like lowlands, only sparsely wooded and with good soils. The elevations are more densely forested and have lighter soils. Colonization therefore began in the lowlands. In between the cultivable acreage suitable for settlement there are wide stretches of uncultivable land and small lakes which impede communications between individual settlements. The climate is pleasant. Spring arrives suddenly at the end of April. Summer with its very long days lasts until the end of August. The first snow does not fall until the middle of November, and only the months from November to February are very cold, with moderate snowfall. The cold period is at times interrupted by chinooks from the Rocky Mountains. As favorable as the natural conditions are for mixed farming in the north, economic growth is severely hampered by great distances from markets. It takes twenty to twenty-four hours by train just to reach Edmonton. The freight costs alone have made any profitable sale of wheat and livestock impossible since the price slump. Railway connections and an outlet to the Pacific coast are awaited impatiently. Meanwhile, however, many settlers have moved back to the south.

The first German colony in the Peace River district traces its origins to 1916. The founders were German Americans who settled in Waterhole, four miles south of the present community of Fairview near the Peace River itself. The first German Lutheran congregation with a resident pastor was formed as early as 1920. In addition to Waterhole colony, he had to serve farmers who in the meantime had settled 130 kilometers further south near Sexsmith. Most immigrants did not arrive until 1926. North of the river and west of the small town of Peace River, small German colonies appeared near Grimshaw, Berwyn (forty families), Whitelaw, Bluesky, Fairview-Friedensthal, Waterhole, Hines Creek (forty families, since 1928), Clear Prairie, and in the far north on the Battle River in Deadwood, North Star and Notikewin (about 150 souls). South of the Peace River, Germans live on the Spirit River; on both sides of the Burnt River in Northmark (since 1928, about eighty souls who are exclusively North Germans, hence the name); in Sexsmith (twenty-five families, from the farm districts west of Wetaskiwin, Alberta); Grande Prairie; Wembley (since 1925, about sixty families from Galicia, central Poland and Germany, also from Golden Spike and Stony Plain, Alberta); Hythe, Wanham, Hart Valley, Peoria, La Glace, Clairmont and River Top. In Wembley, Hythe, Beaverlodge, La Glace and Peoria, German Mennonites have settled as well. Germans can also be found in that part of the Peace River district which belongs to British Columbia, namely in the area of Rolla, Pouce Coupée and Tupper Creek. Germans are thus scattered all over this wide area of settlement. The spiritual care of the German colonists is in the hands of nine Lutheran pastors: two in Hines Creek and one each in Clear Prairie, Berwyn, Spirit River, Northmark, Sexsmith, Wembley, Alberta, and Tupper, B.C. The Lutheran Missouri Synod particularly is very active in this new mission field and has already set up four private parochial schools (in Wembley, Sexsmith, Hines Creek and Clear Prairie) where, in addition to the officially prescribed curriculum, time is set aside for instruction in the German language and in religion. German Catholics in Friedensthal and Berwyn are served by two German priests.

In conclusion, note should be made of a small group of young Germans who have settled halfway between Edmonton and Peace River at Lesser Slave Lake. They live by fishing and hunting, more or less as trappers, and produce on their homesteads only the most necessary items for their own needs. A devastating flood in 1935 forced many in this area to abandon their homesteads.

d. The Urban German Element

With the numerous rural settlements surrounding it, no wonder Germans put down roots early in the provincial capital of Edmonton as well. The first German church congregations in Edmonton and in Strathcona-South Edmonton were formed in the first years of our century. In 1911 there were 1,650 Germans in Edmonton among an urban population of 31,064 persons. Of the 79,197 inhabitants in 1931, 4,983 identified themselves as German and 313 as Austrian by origin. The German element from Germany is relatively strong. As in Regina, several large businesses are operated by Germans, such as Abele's German pharmacy and Springer's hotel, and some Germans are managers in large firms. Most of them, however, earn their living as workers, craftsmen and owners of small stores. In South Edmonton many farm and work in factories as well.

In Edmonton, more than in other prairie cities, Germans are continuously on the defense against the anti-foreign bias adopted by the socialist-oriented majority of the population. Solidarity among Germans, however, is not as strong as might be expected under the circumstances, even though the social club *Edelweiss* (with a large membership) has existed since 1905. Well attended German Days have been celebrated annually since 1928.

The German clergy consists of five Lutheran pastors and one minister each to the Baptists, the Moravian Brethren and the Evangelical Association. Since 1921 the Lutheran Missouri Synod has maintained Concordia College in a beautiful location on the bank of the river a short distance outside the city. It is a junior college and an institution preparing candidates for the theological seminaries of the Synod in the U.S.A. It has professors of German descent and puts great emphasis on the German language in its curriculum.

The German community in Calgary is only slightly less numerous. Here, in a total population of 83,761, those reporting themselves as German and 471 as Austrian by origin numbered 3,751. Most of the 1,028 Russians by origin are probably even Germans from Russia, since many of the Germans came from the Volga communities of Jagodnaja Poljana, Schilling, Alexanderdorf, Norka, and others. The first arrivals from Jagodnaja Poljana settled in Calgary in 1893, yet it was not until after 1900 that the German colony grew noticeably. These German immigrants, who earned their living as workers in factories, and breweries for example, and wanted to raise some livestock on the side, were settled south of the Bow River, opposite the city proper, in the suburb of Bowville which English Canadians called "Germantown." In 1904, when the Riverside congregation of Lutherans was founded, eighty families were living there.[138] New immigrations from the States and from eastern Europe increased the number of Germans gradually. German spiritual care in the city is in the hands of five Lutheran pastors, plus one preacher each for the German Baptists and the Moravian Brethren.

A small German colony also emerged in Lethbridge. Among an urban population of 13,489 there were 545 Germans and 615 Austrians. The relatively largest German element is found among the population of Medicine Hat, which is the market for the German settlers in Happy Land, north of the Cypress Hills. The 1931 Census counted 1,477 Germans by origin and eighty-nine Austrians among a population of 10,300. The German ministry in Lethbridge consists of two German Lutheran pastors and one German Baptist preacher.

4. British Columbia

In British Columbia the German population has remained numerically insignificant. Germans from the United States and from Germany predominate over immigrants from eastern Europe. The German element is strongly represented in the urban areas. In all these aspects the German community of the most western province differs strongly from its counterparts in the Prairie provinces examined previously, although during the past six years more and more Germans have been resettling from there to British Columbia. This might make its German element more like that of the Prairie provinces.

In British Columbia, too, individual German settlers can be found early. The first mill in the Okanagan Valley, for instance, which for a long time was the only grain mill in the vast area between the Columbia and Thompson Rivers, belonged to a German by the name of Fred Berndt, from Baden. Since 1865 he had been farming and cutting logs at Duck Lake (near the present community of Oyama). In 1871 he erected his mill at the stream near Lake Okanagan.[139] Large numbers of German immigrants, however, from such states as Washington, Oregon, California, Montana, did not arrive until 1890.[140] The German settlers took up fruit and vegetable growing, at first mainly in the Columbia River Valley, especially at Lower Arrow Lake and in the West Kootenay district (Edgewood, Nelson, Trail, etc.). Living there were 1,940 of the 5,807 persons of German origin in British Columbia in 1901. In the first decade of this century, German immigrants moved primarily into the Okanagan Valley (Kelowna, Penticton, Vernon, etc.) but also into the Fraser Valley east of Vancouver and New Westminster, and finally to the thriving port city of Vancouver itself. By 1911, 11,880 persons of German descent lived in the province; 3,506 of these in Vancouver, 1,779 in New Westminster and the Fraser Valley, 2,293 in the Yale-Cariboo district (Okanagan Valley) and 2,044 in the West Kootenay district (Upper and Lower Arrow Lake, Columbia Valley). The rest were scattered over the entire province. During the war years the Germans, particularly those from Germany, suffered severely in this most British of all the provinces, much more than, for instance, in the Prairie provinces. Due to emigration to the United States, and deportation, or refusal to acknowledge their German descent under the impact of the war psychosis, their numbers dropped to 7,273 in the 1921 Census.

After 1926, however, German immigration resumed. The Mennonite Board of Colonization in Rosthern settled close to three hundred families of refugees from Soviet Russia, for whom it had assumed responsibility, in the lower Fraser Valley. The 1931 Census registered 1,085 Mennonites. In 1935, 319 of the postwar Mennonite immigrants lived in the province: 129 in Yarrow, eighty-seven in Sardis, thirty-five in Abbotsford-Huntingdon, twenty in Oyster River, ten in Langley Prairie, eight in Agassiz, seven in Pitt Meadows and twenty-three in the city of Vancouver.[141] The German Lutheran and German Catholic immigration boards, as well, directed a number of immigrants for whom they had assumed responsibility, into the fruit-and vegetable-growing districts of the Fraser and Okanagan Valleys. By 1931 the number of Germans had again increased considerably and in the Census, 16,986 acknowledged their German, and 3,891 their Austrian, descent. In the meantime, immigration from poverty-stricken regions of Saskatchewan and Alberta has been growing every year, and we estimate the size of British Columbia's German population to comprise about thirty thousand to forty thousand today. Most of the Germans who arrived before the war have been more or less assimilated because they did not develop enough closed colonies, but settled randomly among the non-German population. British Columbia also never made concessions in the school question.

In the Fraser Valley we find besides the above-mentioned Mennonites, German Lutherans in Chilliwack, Rosedale, Abbotsford, Aldergrove, Cloverdale, Albion, Mission City, Pitt Meadows, etc. They are served by pastors in Chilliwack and New Westminster. In the city of New Westminster itself there are three hundred to 350 Germans.

Relatively speaking, the most homogeneous German colonies developed at Lake Okanagan. There are eight hundred to nine hundred Germans in Kelowna, and its suburb of Rutland eight kilometers away is predominantly German. They have formed one Catholic, one Lutheran and one Baptist congregation. The Catholic parish in Kelowna, whose priest was born in Cologne, Germany, has a membership of fifty to sixty German families, and the one in Rutland has eighty German families, most of whom came from St. Joseph's colony and from Claybank in Saskatchewan.[142] The German Lutheran congregation in Kelowna-Rutland numbered 132 souls in 1933. Its pastor also ministered to colonists in Oliver, near the American border. A similar-sized colony in and around Vernon has its own German Lutheran pastor. At the southern end of the lake about 150 Germans live in Penticton. Here a few young Germans who had belonged to the Youth Movement in Germany and were vegetarians, wanted to set up a fruit farm on a cooperative basis in 1927-28. They bought orchards with an elegant farm house for $20,000 with the help of a mortgage that was to be repaid in the form of half the gross yield of their harvest. The terms of this deal and internal difficulties, however, forced the idealistic German fruit growers to abandon their farms in 1929 and to work at first as day laborers on other farms, and even as construction laborers, until they could make a modest new beginning on their own land.[143]

In spite of the beautiful scenery, the fertility of the land, the suitability of the climate for the growing of choice fruit (such as peaches, apricots, tropical fruits), melons and tobacco, etc., and in spite of the Prairie farmers' hope of finding in British Columbia a refuge from total ruin, no one can deny that the economic conditions have become very difficult here as well. In 1936 a farmer in Osoyoos who had emigrated from Germany ten years before described the situation as follows:[144]

> The conditions for the farmers of the northern Okanagan Valley have not improved in years. The prices for farm products are kept so low that they hardly cover the production costs, and there is no hope of making headway. If anyone is fortunate enough to accumulate some savings he is an exception. Most live from hand to mouth. I had a bit of luck with raising chickens, and was able to lay aside a few hundred dollars so that I could move to the new Osoyoos settlement district on the American border and purchase some land. It is all Crown land here, partitioned into ten and twenty acre lots with extensive irrigation. The prices for virgin land range from seventy to 125 dollars, with a 20 per cent down payment and a 20-year mortgage at 6 per cent interest. Irrigation is $6 per acre for land which is now for sale. It will be $6 for the first three years, $9 for the second three and $12 after six years. The soil is light sandy loam, in places full of rocks, and much artificial and green fertilizing is needed. Rotation between crops (one year produce, one year sweet clover) is the rule. Early tomatoes, cucumbers, cantaloupes and watermelons, some early cabbage, carrots and lettuce are grown. The climate is hot and dry. There are other immigrants from Germany in this new settlement. We German nationals are treated by the English no worse than so-called New Canadians. I have been here for five years and I am still a German citizen and I have never had any difficulties because of that. In spite of this many of us Germans, including myself, would return to Germany tomorrow if there were a possibility of starting a new future there.

The same economic difficulties are prevalent in the entire province. They have had the severest effects on postwar immigrants who wanted to build a new existence for themselves when the economic crisis struck.

The Germans in the mountain valleys of the southeastern corner of the province are served by one Lutheran missionary in each of Nelson, Trail and Creston. In addition, the pastor in Creston (on the Kootenay River) ministers to about thirty German families (150 souls) in Camp Lister twice a month. Camp Lister settlement was originally set up for war veterans, but had to be abandoned due to lack of water. In 1930, however, irrigation systems were installed and Germans, who engaged in mixed farming in the bush, including fruit and vegetable growing, poultry farming and apiculture, settled there. The installation of some smelting furnaces in Trail is attributed to Germans.

Smaller German colonies scattered in the central and northern parts of the province are served by Lutheran pastors in Kamloops and Prince George, and a Baptist preacher in Fort George. Colonists in British Columbia's Peace River bloc (Rolla, Pouce Coupée, Tupper Creek) were already dealt with in the context of the larger Peace River district in Alberta. On Vancouver Island, we find German Lutherans, for instance near Duncan and in the Courtenay district. They are served by the German pastor in the provincial capital of Victoria (population 39,082) which never had a large number of Germans (457 in 1931).

In the large port city of Vancouver (population 246,593), however, Germans played a certain role in the business community before the war, and a German newspaper was even published temporarily in the city (see chapter VII). The World War, however, destroyed all that. Since 1925 the German community has been growing again. Most of the newcomers were job-seekers from the Prairie provinces who, just as in Winnipeg, hoped to make a living here in the metropolis during the winter months. Gradually they began to form a resident German community of factory workers, craftsmen and businessmen. The German colony continues to grow due to the influx of people from Saskatchewan and Alberta, since the port of Vancouver is thriving in spite of the temporary crisis. In 1931, persons of German descent and of Austrian descent in Vancouver numbered 4,371 and 904 respectively. Today it appears that a few thousand more Germans are in the city. A number of Germans have done quite well in Vancouver business, and such firms as the Capilano Brewery, the Café Deutschland, the Grandview Hotel and the Ziegler chocolate factory are operated by Germans. Many Germans are in leading positions, or are employees in all kinds of commercial and industrial enterprises.

There are four German church congregations: two Lutheran, one

Baptist and one Mennonite congregation. Since 1935 Vancouver has
had a German consulate.

CHAPTER VII

Religious, Secular and Cultural Life

1. The Church Congregation as the Mainstay of Ethnicity

As it had been among the German ethnic groups in eastern Europe, religious creed has been the strongest influence on community formation, also among their sons and daughters who emigrated to Canada. Secular associations were formed only where at least some of the emigrants in the settlement had come directly from Germany. In settlements that consist exclusively of Germans from eastern Europe, however, the church congregation is the only form of organizational association even today. It has to satisfy religious as well as social needs. The German farmer from Russia, Galicia, and other parts of eastern Europe clings to his religious heritage as the strongest, often the only, intellectual-spiritual need. It takes him away from the arduous daily routine of his pioneer existence for a while and gives some meaning to his life. The words of Theodore Roosevelt, the former President of the United States, also apply to the German settlements in western Canada: "No American settlement has ever succeeded without a church."[1]

From the outset the immigrants settled everywhere, as we saw, primarily in accordance with denominational considerations. The bond of religious unity protected them from the isolation which would have entailed the immediate loss of their inherited ethnic identity. They had barely settled down on their new homesteads when they began to meet on Sundays and holidays for regular gatherings, during which the most literate among them held a short worship service. Each one of them had, of course, brought a hymnal and prayer book from the old homeland.

A church ministry, however, was not long in coming. The Mennonites almost always emigrated under the guidance of their elders and preachers, who could immediately take charge of the formation of the parish or congregation in the new land. Most of the German Baptists from Russia and the Moravian Brethren also brought their clergy with them, who often even have to be considered as the initiators and leaders of the emigration. Among Lutherans and Catholics, however, this was not the case. Yet here, too, the respective denominational agencies which considered western Canada as their missionary field soon showed up, such as the German Lutheran synods of the United States, the German-American Benedictines, and the German priests of the Oblate Order, who had already been active in western Canada as missionaries among the Indians.

In America, membership in a church and its financial support have always been left up to the individual. The churches were therefore eager to follow the new settlers, to establish their influence in the settlement and to have the immigrants settle in groups or direct them to places where the prerequisites for the foundation of a parish existed. Church ministry would thus not be precluded at the outset by excessive distances between homesteads. We noted earlier how successfully the Catholic clergy directed the German immigrants into a few large areas of settlement in Saskatchewan by means of settlement companies. Lutheran pastors, too, had been in touch from the beginning with official agencies responsible for immigration and settlement. By counselling newcomers who were of their faith, they promoted group settlement as much as possible. After the war the economic interests of the railways, and the ecclesiastical interests of the individual churches in immigration, led to a close organizational cooperation and the creation of denominational immigration boards.

In new settlements, the organization of a church tended to take place in three stages. First the settlers were visited occasionally by an itinerant preacher. Then a congregation was formed, and a permanent clergyman appointed who by and large was still financially maintained by his church. Finally the parish was created, which supported its own pastor. The work of the itinerant preacher was very important in the creation of congregations and the formation of ethnically homogeneous German settlements. He usually had to serve a huge area and led a life full of hardship, barely less arduous than those of the settlers themselves. In 1907 Father Schweers, for instance, the first priest of St. Joseph's colony, was in charge of two fully established parishes west of Tramping Lake, and in addition on weekdays had to serve parishioners in five smaller preaching stations within a radius of sixty kilometers.[2] In any kind of weather the itinerant preacher had to visit the widely separated settlements, at first with horse and buggy, then with an old car. Telephone poles and wheel ruts frequently served as his only signposts. In the beginning, neighbors within a wide radius gathered in the cabin of a settler on a certain Sunday of the month. Here, if necessary, baptisms and confirmations were performed. As soon as homesteaders of a new district were past the worst, they proceeded with the building of a church. If there was a railway station within reach, the church was built near it. Otherwise the center of the settlement was selected as the site. Thus it could happen that the church was erected in the middle of the prairies without a house being anywhere in the vicinity. In the prewar era it did not take long for a real congregation to be formed, which after a few good harvests made it a point of honor to assume responsibility for the minister's salary and for related expenses such as the debts for the building of the church and the parsonage. Within the parish a church choir and a whole series of associations were formed. In the summer the parish celebrated with outdoor picnics and organized social evenings. In remote pioneer districts, church services, which tend to be followed by an informal gathering of neighbors, may have been possible only every four weeks. This may have been the only social event at all in long weeks of lonely life on the homestead.

The parish or church congregation therefore constituted the first and most important, frequently even the only, form of organization of the rural German element. The significance of the German clergy for the preservation of the German ethnic heritage of their parishes is therefore quite obvious. Among these church-oriented Germans, where even laymen compete for the honor of holding an office in the parish or congregation and in the institutions of the church, the clergy still enjoy a special appreciation. Their willingness from the outset to share the settlers' rough life in the pioneer years as the sole beacons of spiritual values is well remembered. Their example, their basic attitude with regard to the preservation of ethnic identity, thus influences the entire congregation.

In general the clergy of all denominations have proven to be the intellectual leaders of the rural German element. Where their influence was absent, a far-reaching loss of German ethnic identity has already occurred. Even though they usually do not attain the level of theological training and the general education of the clergy in Germany, they have tried almost everywhere as leaders of their congregations to promote cohesion among German settlers, and to preserve their ethnic heritage to the best of their abilities. The German language and religious instruction which these clergymen and their families provide on Saturdays and Sundays and during the summer vacations to the children of their parishes, have been virtually the only form of German instruction for children in the rural areas since the war. The conditions are, of course, most favorable where the clergy themselves come from Germany. Among the Catholic clergy most of the Oblates, but only a small number of the Benedictines, are from Germany. The Lutheran Manitoba Synod has received most of its current pastors from the Theological Seminary at Kropp in Holstein. Many of the pastors of the American Lutheran Church serving in western Canada are still from Germany too. The pastors of the Missouri Synod, on the other hand, are all born and raised in America, and full of religious and political prejudice against Germany. Also virtually the entire new generation of ministers of the other two synods mentioned was born in Canada and the United States and trained in its seminaries. The younger priests and pastors can therefore only in exceptional cases be expected to value the retention of the ethnic heritage, and to assume the responsibility for the preservation of the German character of their parishes to the best of their abilities.

On the other hand, only a minority among the younger clergy have become outspoken pioneers in the anglicization of their parishes. For these clergy the simplification of preaching duties in a situation of increasing bilingualism in the parish tended to be the occasion for dropping the German language in favor of English, before the congregation requested it. On the whole, even the pastors and priests trained in America and Canada are still showing at least an interest in the cultivation of the German language, in the use of German songs and hymns, which is the chief criterion distinguishing their parishes from the neighboring parishes which follow English tradition. The Lutheran Missouri Synod, especially, urges its pastors to promote the institution of parochial schools with German language instruction and to cultivate German-language traditions in the church service. As orthodox Lutherans, they have good reasons for preserving among their congregations the ability to understand Luther's German Bible. There is another reason for the careful attention given to the German language in church service and in religious instruction. It is the growing awareness that the rapid loss of ethnic identity, an all-too-sudden absorption in the ethnic mass of American-Canadian uniformity, would entail for the second generation not only the renunciation of traditional modes of thinking, but also the danger of moral uprooting. Above all, the fear of the churches is not unjustified that together with their ethnic identity, the youth of their parishes would give up the allegiance to the denomination of their ancestors.

The conversion to a denomination which is part of British tradition, and linguistic and spiritual assimilation by the politically dominant British population, frequently tend to go hand in hand. It may well appear that for some time after the transition to English-language church services many of the young assimilated generation in the parish will retain the inherited denomination. Frequently it is even assumed that a timely transition to English-language church services would be the only way to keep the youth in the parish. The conversion to the dominant denominations of the British population, however, is only a small step following anglicization, as is proven by Nova Scotia's example. There, according to the Census of 1931, among the estimated forty-five thousand inhabitants of German descent, only 5,731 souls have remained with the inherited Lutheran faith, while the majority of Germans by descent belong to the churches of British tradition today: Anglican, United Church of Canada, Baptist and Presbyterian.[3] In Canada, as everywhere among rural German communities overseas, church and ethnic group support each other.

Today the ranks of clergy who grew up in Germany and are imbued with German culture are thinning. The impact of the clergy on the retention of the German identity of their congregations is declining more and more. For the time being, however, the overwhelming majority of the German congregations and parishes of all the denominations are holding their services, religious instruction and Sunday schools in the German language, and the clergy give private German language lessons.

The strong denominational spirit which on the one hand prevented the spatial dispersal of the German settlers, on the other hand also affected the preservation of ethnic identity unfavorably. It caused denominational barriers to stand in the way of an organizational union of the entire German community to this day. Individual denominations and their clergy, to be sure, coexist peacefully. But any form of organizational cooperation for the purpose of defending cultural interests is being approached only reluctantly and with strong reservations, especially on the part of the Mennonites.

a. The Mennonites

The Mennonites originated from the Anabaptist movement of the Reformation and trace their beginnings to the Dutchman Menno Simons. They differ from the major Protestant denominations by more rigorous pietistic conduct, the refusal to take oaths and the principle of unconditional Christian non-resistance (conscientious objection). Intolerance drove them early to emigration. Since 1683, Mennonites from western Germany have migrated to Pennsylvania, and since 1790, Mennonites have migrated from the delta of the Vistula to South Russia. In Germany a mere ten thousand Mennonites are left in a closed settlement in the delta of the Vistula. In the German communities in other countries, however, they play a much more significant role. About ninety thousand live in Canada alone, of these more than seventy thousand in the western provinces. While the Mennonites of Ontario are descendants of immigrants from Pennsylvania, with a Palatine-southwest German accent, the Mennonites in western Canada are from South Russia, and speak a West Prussian-Low German dialect.

The Mennonites (and the denominationally related Hutterites) have the strongest cohesion of all the German groups. It is founded on their faith. This spirit of community does not so much apply to the Mennonite denomination in its entirety, but rather to its religious sub-groups which have developed, partly in Russia, partly in North America. It is in the very nature of Protestantism with its extreme individualism to split into ever smaller groups, just as in the case of the free churches of the English Congregationalists.

The Mennonites immigrating in the 1870s to Manitoba belonged to three specific sub-groups, each of which emigrated as a unit under the leadership of its elders and preachers: the Old Colony, the Bergthaler and the Kleine Gemeinde. When in the early 1890s the question of introducing public schools arose, the Bergthaler group in the West Reserve split. The conservative three-quarters of the Bergthalers reorganized themselves around Elder Doerksen in Sommerfeld and henceforth called themselves Sommerfelders, while the progressive part, which was sympathetic to the new schools, kept the name Bergthaler.

They still have that name today, but in the meantime have joined the group of General Conference Mennonites. The Bergthalers who remained in the East Reserve later changed their name to *Chortitzer Gemeinde* (known as Chortitzer Church). Some of the Mennonites immigrating after 1890 belonged to the *Mennonitische Brüdergemeinde* (Mennonite Brethren Church) which was founded in Russia in 1860. It soon formed numerous congregations in western Canada. A small closely related group is the *Krimer Brüdergemeinde* (Krimmer Mennonite Brethren). In Rosenort near Laird, Saskatchewan, the so-called *Rosenorter Gemeinde* (Rosenort Mennonite Church) was formed in 1896. Its founder and long serving elder, Peter Regier (who died in 1925), came from Für-stenau near Tiegenhof in West Prussia.[4] They were joined by immigrants from Germany, South Russia and Manitoba. Various divisions that originated in the United States have also found followers in western Canada, such as the group of the Holdemanites, or Church of God in Christ, that was formed in Ohio (Wayne County) in 1858, the *Brüderthaler Gemeinde* (Bruderthaler Church) founded in Mountain Lake, Minnesota, in 1888, and finally the Old Mennonites, who trace their origins to the first immigrants in Pennsylvania and hold their church services in English.

Such splintering into smaller and smaller church groups was bound to dimish the influence of the Mennonites in their efforts to win acceptance of their cultural-political objectives. A certain movement towards unification manifested itself in the foundation of a General Conference, but so far only one-quarter to one-third of all Mennonites have become General Conference Mennonites, while the remaining groups continue to exist outside of it. A discussion of the relatively extraneous differences would go too far in this context. The most conservative groups are the Old Colony, the Sommerfelders, the Kleine Gemeinde and the Holdemanites. Among the Old Colony group, for instance, four-part singing and musical instruments in the church, white collars for men, automobiles and telephones are taboo. Their church building is entirely plain, with sackcloth covering the windows. Only the pulpit, the doors and the windows are painted, with grey paint. The benches are backless, so that people have to rest their heads on their hands. Preaching and singing during the Sunday service lasts for several hours. Since ad-lib preaching is frowned upon, sermons are first read in High German and certain passages are re-emphasized in Low German. All preachers wear long black coats and their pantlegs are tucked into high-topped boots. They cling to the exclusive use of the

German language in church and community life, and put up the longest and most stubborn fight against the closing of their German private schools. Old Colony and Sommerfelder groups were the ones who emigrated in 1922 to Mexico, and in 1926 to Paraguay, because they could not adjust to English-language public schools as did the more liberal groups. The Old Colony and Sommerfelder groups have held on longest, some until this day, to their original village community government. Besides their spiritual leaders or elders, they have had a leader in secular affairs in the person of the *Oberschulze*, or chief magistrate, who was in charge of settling minor disputes within the community.

The General Conference, the Mennonite Brethren and the Rosenorter congregation are more progressive and more accessible to the influences of the environment. The Mennonite postwar immigrants have joined these congregations. The Mennonite Brethren display certain Methodist features in the importance they attach to the visible conversion of the individual. These groups more strongly approximate the other Protestant denominations. In contrast to the traditionally unsteepled prayer houses, some of their newer churches, for instance in Rosthern, already have steeples, and here and there English-language church services are considered necessary as well as German ones. While they do not seclude themselves as much from English influences as their conservative brethren, they are more open-minded about efforts to achieve greater unity among all German groups.

Even more prominent than all the differences in the details of religious conviction, are the features which are common to all Mennonites. The spirit of community which has proven itself a thousand times in Mennonite families and within the congregations from the days of their first settlement cannot be surpassed anywhere. The principle that "the public weal comes first" has always been realized among the Mennonites. To it they owe their obvious economic successes. Following the example proven successful in Russia, they established two so-called Waisenamts in southern Manitoba (with headquarters in Altona, Manitoba) which originally administered the assets of orphans and developed into regular banks for savings deposits and the issue of credit on a non-profit basis. In 1932 they administered combined deposits of about one million dollars.[5] Since 1911 they also have a life insurance plan with some five hundred members in Manitoba and Saskatchewan. Its simple organization is run by a storekeeper in Gretna, who receives a small fee for taking care of current business. On the same non-profit basis a fire and hail insurance plan has been organized. The fire insurance, which bases the amount of its levies on actual expenditures, insures only Mennonites, since unscrupulous men of other beliefs might set fire to their own buildings. The hail insurance, however, is open to all, since God alone can send hail. Finally there are also consumers' cooperatives such as the one in Altona, Manitoba.

The most significant collective accomplishment of the Mennonites of western Canada, however, has been the creation of the Board of Colonization in Rosthern, which made possible the immigration and settlement of the more than twenty thousand postwar immigrants. It is turning increasingly into an all-embracing economic-cultural organization for all the Mennonites of western Canada, regardless of the congregation to which they belong. A few years ago the *Zentrales Mennonitisches Immigrantenkomitee* (Central Mennonite Immigrant Committee, since 1923), the chief organization of the new immigrants, merged with it. The resolutions of the conferences of Hague and Winkler in 1923 restructured the Board of Colonization in Rosthern, under the leadership of the popular elder David Toews, into five departments: (1) the executive committee, (2) the finance committee, whose duty it was to collect the travel debts (*Reiseschuld*) of the postwar immigrants and pass on the money to creditors, (3) the settlement committee, (4) the committee for cultural affairs, and (5) the welfare committee, among whose objectives is providing assistance to those Mennonites who remained in Russia. The annual conferences held in Manitoba and Saskatchewan offer the opportunity of discussing matters concerning all Mennonites. The postwar immigrants have organized themselves systematically into local groups (with locally elected district men), districts and provincial associations. Among the outstanding non-profit institutions founded by the postwar immigrants are Concordia Hospital in Winnipeg and homes for girls in Winnipeg, Saskatoon, Lethbridge and Vancouver.

The highly developed community spirit is especially conducive to the cultivation of the inherited German language and mentality. Almost every community has its weekly singing and prayer hours, a youth club, a sewing club for women and girls and a Sunday school. Annual singing festivals, oratorio evenings, and so on bring singers from different regions together. From the outset the Mennonites devoted special attention to the education of youth. Finally, there is no German group in western Canada which has developed a press and a body of literature that is anywhere even near to being as noteworthy as theirs. In cultural respects the postwar immigrants have aroused the old-established Mennonites to new activities.

Above all there has been an awakening of a German ethnic and cultural consciousness as a result of the war and postwar troubles which the brethren had to endure in Russia, which had not existed among Mennonites before. The old generation may well fear a dilution of religious principles after the removal of denominational barriers, and will never abandon the idea of non-resistance which has always characterized Mennonite conduct. Yet the younger generation of the postwar immigrants, who had fought with arms in self-defence against Bolsheviks and plundering gangs of *Makhno*, cannot be confined within the narrow limits of the traditional creed. These Mennonites desire contact with western Canada's entire German community.

b. The Catholics

Among German Catholics the denominational bond of unity and the clergy's organizational abilities proved to be particularly successful in colonization. The immigrants were deliberately directed to Saskatchewan, where the diocese of Prince Albert was in French hands, and where until this day the francophone influence is predominant among the Catholic high clergy. Here the chances for an accommodation of German aspirations were better than in the neighboring province of Alberta, where the Anglo-Irish high clergy refused to get German priests for the few German Catholics of their dioceses. In Saskatchewan, however, the number of Germans among the Catholic population has become so large that they have good reason to demand that, for a change, a German priest be invested as one of the bishops of the province.

The German Catholic clergy, Oblates as well as Benedictines and secular clergy, have succeeded in drawing the lives of their believers entirely into the orbit of the church. In each parish there are numerous associations (clubs for men, women, young men and young women, etc.) which claim all the spare time of the individual members of the parish. In American fashion, there are club rooms, usually a small library, billiard tables, bowling alleys and lunch counters in the church building.

Besides German priests there are also German nuns serving in the parish. These are Ursuline Sisters and Sisters of Notre Dame (*Arme Schulschwestern*) as teachers and Sisters of Elisabeth from Klagenfurt, Austria, as nurses (for example in Humboldt).

The *Volksverein deutsch-canadischer Katholiken* (People's Association of German-Canadian Catholics) has served as the comprehensive organization of German Catholics. It was founded on July 14-15, 1909, in St. Joseph's Church in Winnipeg after the model of the *Volksverein für das katholische Deutschland* (People's Association for Catholic Germany).[6] It has local branches in almost all the large German colonies. In 1915 it had 55, today 36 local groups with a total membership of four thousand to five thousand. The *Volksverein* was to serve as a means of gaining political influence, in order to promote Catholic interests and the cultivation of the German mother tongue. Politically the *Volksverein*, therefore, opposed the Conservative Party as the party of Anglo-Canadian nationalism and Protestantism. The existence of a local group of the *Volksverein*, the equivalent of the German Center Party, thus obviated the foundation of a caucus of the Liberal Party in the same place. More recently a reorganization of the *Volksverein* has been attempted that was to eliminate its partisan political character, and restore its religious and exclusively cultural-political objectives. Its annual conventions have been turned into general Catholic Day rallies (*Katholikentage*). In the postwar years the *Volksverein* had its greatest tangible successes in the area of aid to immigrants, which was organized by Oblate Father Kierdorf. In the matter of German language instruction in the schools, the *Volksverein* has made its demands known from time to time, but so far without success, not even with the Liberal Party, to which it had delivered votes in elections.

c. The Lutherans

Neither the Evangelical Lutheran state churches in Germany nor the churches of the east European ethnic groups thought of ministering to German emigrants going to western Canada. Therefore the Lutheran synods that were formed in the United States claimed western Canada as their missionary field as well. This precluded any organizational ties with the church in the German motherland and only individual missionaries from Germany entered the service of the Manitoba Synod (United Lutheran Church) and the American Lutheran Church (formerly Ohio Synod). Even a brief training in Germany of the new generation of theologians would be hard to imagine, since there is no Protestant theological seminary in Germany orthodox enough for the American-Canadian synods.

All three large Lutheran churches of North America look after the

German Lutherans of western Canada.[7] The Manitoba Synod, as a part of the United Lutheran Church of North America, numbered fifty-four pastors and 18,287 baptized members in the three Prairie provinces in 1935, the Canada District of the American-Lutheran Church seventy-two pastors and 24,135 members in the same year, and the Missouri Synod ninety pastors and 24,888 members in 1936. This means that the total of sixty-seven thousand registered members of the congregations of these churches represents only three-quarters of the 89,504 Germans by origin who reported themselves as Lutherans in the Census of 1931. The considerable difference between the registered number of church members and the actual number is due to various reasons. First, the Lutherans chose closed settlements relatively infrequently, so that many could not join a congregation. Furthermore, there were financial considerations and the mistrust of postwar immigrants, who immigrated without any ecclesiastical ties and at times objected to the orthodox attitude of the average pastor. Finally, there was displeasure with the sometimes embarrassing competition among the three synods.

The General Council, from which the present-day United Lutheran Church evolved, sent its first pastors to western Canada in the 1880s. In 1889 Pastor H. C. Schmieder was able to found Trinity congregation in Winnipeg, still flourishing today, as the first German Lutheran congregation in western Canada. Soon thereafter he transferred his ministry to Edenwold, Saskatchewan, from where he also at times served parishioners in a large number of developing German Lutheran colonies. In October 1897, the six pastors of the General Council who were serving in western Canada constituted themselves as the Manitoba Synod. They were pastors Ruccius in Winnipeg, Berthold in Gretna, Hermann in Wolseley, Willing in Edenwold, Bredlow in Wetaskiwin and Pempeit in Stony Plain.[8] The Manitoba Synod was thus active in all three Prairie provinces from the beginning. In British Columbia, four pastors of German descent serve today as representatives of the Pacific Synod, a sister synod within the United Lutheran Church. Two of these pastors are in Vancouver, one each in Victoria and Prince Rupert.

The Missouri Synod (i.e., its Minnesota District) had sent ninety-two itinerant preachers to western Canada as early as 1879, and in the years from 1890 to 1892. Yet their first permanent minister, Pastor Eberhardt, did not officiate until 1894, starting as an itinerant preacher in Alberta, and since 1895, as a pastor in Stony Plain, where his ministry still is today.[9] Later on, the increasing activity of the Missouri Synod in western Canada has to be attributed particularly to Pastor C.F. Walther, the long-serving director of the mission in the West. The youth organization of the church, the Walther League, was named after him. In 1921 and 1922, the Missouri Synod was able to form two districts of its own for the four western Canadian provinces. In 1921, the year of its foundation, the Alberta-British Columbia District had twenty-seven pastors, twenty-four synodal congregations, twenty-two not-yet-affiliated congregations and sixty preaching stations with a total of 6,939 souls. The Manitoba-Saskatchewan District had forty-three pastors, forty-one synodal congregations, thirty-four not-yet-affiliated congregations and sixty-nine preaching stations with a total of 10,700 souls in 1922.[10]

The Ohio Synod did not begin its operation in western Canada until 1905 but, thanks to the activity of its presidents Gehrke, Tank and Hertz, has nevertheless been the most successful of the three churches. Since 1930, when the Ohio, Buffalo and Iowa Synods united to become the American Lutheran Church, the pastors serving in western Canada have formed its Canada District.

The competition among the three synods has often been harmful. Disputes within existing congregations were at times exploited by the competing synod to split them and launch a congregation of its own. Thus discord often was sown instead of love, and the interests of the German heritage were renounced. From a financial standpoint, too, the competition of the three churches was unpleasant. According to the above statistics there were three pastors for every one thousand German Lutherans. This is a ratio that is very hard on churches and congregations in good years, but is impossible to maintain in bad years. As a result, congregations are pressuring the various synods all over North America to bring about unification. Congregations simply do not care about the minor differences between the truly orthodox and moderately orthodox synods, and are not able to carry their financial debts. In spite of this, unification has not progressed beyond initial negotiations for years. The situation of the pastors, most of whom obtain a B.A. degree, attend a theological seminary for three years and spend one year as an assistant preacher, is often pitiful. Many have to survive these days with their families on three hundred to five hundred dollars a year. In some congregations they are on relief, just like the settlers. This is bound to weaken even further their already questionable dedication to the cause of promoting the preservation of the German heritage and of conscious German identity among their congregations.

Worship services, religious instruction and Sunday school are held predominantly in German to this day. On Saturday evenings, Sundays and during vacations, pastors make great personal sacrifices to give German lessons. The most recent statistics, however, show that the loss of German identity has already set in. In 1935, the Canada District of the American Lutheran Church counted 5,074 German and 908 English church services. Of the 158 Sunday schools, 101 were held exclusively in German, thirty-seven in German and English, and twenty exclusively in English.[11] Since the number of those attending German church services is still much higher than those attending English ones, a comparison of the mere number of church services would give the wrong impression. Yet it is worth noting that more than one out of every seven church services is already being held in English. In the Missouri Synod the situation is even less favorable, as disclosed by the following statistics:[12]

Table VII.1

Manitoba-Saskatchewan District			
language used in service	percentage of German used	number of congregations and preaching stations	number of church members
exclusively German	100	53	4,523
predominantly German	75	21	3,689
half German, half English	50	24	2,354
predominantly English	25	6	525
exclusively English	0	60	1,540
Alberta-British Columbia District			
exclusively German	100	46	2,661
predominantly German	75	11	2,567
half German, half English	50	36	3,478
predominantly English	25	9	1,065
exclusively English	0	68	2,486

According to calculations by the Synod, the proportion of German-language church services in the Manitoba-Saskatchewan District is only 65 per cent, and in the Alberta-British Columbia District it is 54 per cent. The impression which these figures convey is particularly unfavorable, because the number of those attending the various church services is not indicated here either. Also, the Missouri Synod formed some congregations among Scandinavian and other non-German Lutherans, which raise the number of the exclusively English church services in the statistics. However, there is no doubt that some German congregations have switched entirely to English services in the meantime, for instance, Nisku, Leduc, Golden Spike, Spruce Grove, Brightview in Alberta and Zion's congregation in Langenburg.[13] This switch was largely due to the Missouri pastor's ability to win over English and other non-German speaking members, for whose benefit the transition to English-language services has on occasion been accelerated. A good, but rarely implemented, alternative is that of Pastor Wetzstein in Regina who, for the sake of retaining its ethnic identity, did not merge his German congregation of more than 430 souls with his smaller English congregation, but formed two organizationally separate congregations.

The increasing anglicization of German congregations manifests itself, in any event, in the rapid decline of the proportion, computed by the above methods, of German church services since the end of the war, even though the above-mentioned circumstances make the computed percentage appear too low in each instance:[14]

Table VII.2

	1922	1926	1930	1934	1936
Manitoba-Saskatchewan District	82%	77%	73%	70%	65%
Alberta and British Columbia District	77%	64%	56%	57%	54%

In the Missouri Synod the transition to English language services is taking place most rapidly. All its pastors were born in North America, and feel practically no allegiance to the German fatherland and its cultural heritage which, from their orthodox old-Lutheran viewpoint, they even mistrust and condemn as heretical. In the light of this it is of little import that, for missionary reasons, the Synod maintains fourteen full-day private parochial schools which provide German instruction as well as the English curriculum.

Each of the three synods maintains one higher institution of learning. The Luther College of the Manitoba Synod in Saskatoon even operates a full-fledged theological seminary, while new generations of pastors of the other two synods have to complete their training in the United States. Each of the synods has its own youth organization (the Luther League of the American Lutheran Church and the Manitoba Synod, the Walther League of the Missouri Synod) and issue their own synodal newsletters, for example the *Synodal Bote* of the Manitoba Synod and the *Canadisch-Lutherisches Kirchenblatt* of the Missouri Synod. The American Lutheran Church runs a senior citizens' home and an orphanage in Melville, in which nineteen senior citizens and seven orphans respectively were accommodated in 1934.

d. The Remaining Protestants

Among the smaller German Protestant denominations the Baptists, with about 4,800 members, take first place in terms of numbers. Most of them are from Russia. However, Edenwold, their oldest congregation (1886), was founded by immigrants from Tulcea in Romania. Their forty-seven congregations in western Canada are organized into the Northern Conference of the German Baptist Congregations of North America. So far their preachers have conducted their services and children's lessons exclusively in German.

The Methodist-oriented Evangelical Association, which has recently adopted the name Evangelical Church and whose followers are also known as Albrights (*Albrechtsbrüder*), has barely three thousand members in western Canada, primarily in Alberta. The so-called Northwest Canada Conference of this church is still predominantly German. This also applies to the congregations of the Moravian Brethren (about fifteen hundred members) and the few congregations of the Reformed Church.[15]

The Hutterites deserve special attention because of their many eccentricities. Like the Mennonites, they trace their origins back to the Anabaptist movement of the sixteenth century. They differ from these only by the joint ownership of property on their communal farms (*Bruderhöfe*). They found their communism on Acts, chapter II, verses 44-45: "And all that believe were together and had all things in common. And sold their possessions and goods, and parted them to all men, as every man had need." No other group of the Anabaptist movement demonstrated the original principles and life of this movement as clearly as the Hutterites. The history of their migrations is sketched in chapter V. They have preserved their German ethnic heritage and South German dialect with a Tyrolean accent by their sectarian seclusion, in spite of their centuries of life in exile.

Each communal farm forms a complete living community. Its head is the preacher as spiritual leader and the *Wirt* or "boss" is general manager of all material needs. Five elders act as their advisors. The *Wirt*, who administers all the money and all the other possessions and assigns the work, is assisted in the supervision of the work by individual stewards who are responsible for various types of economic activities (agriculture, apiculture, smithy, etc.). In their economic methods the Hutterites are distinctly progressive. Most of their technological equipment is first class. Money is only used as a means of exchange with the outside world. Although there is no personal property on the individual communal farm, there is also no joint ownership of property among the various communal farms. Their economic community under the strict direction of the *Wirt*, who is chosen for life, has proven very successful. In spite of the young age of their communal farms in western Canada, the Hutterites have experienced virtually none of the effects of the Depression and unemployment. All profit is ultimately invested in new land, acquired for the purpose of outfitting a new communal farm. Following the pattern of bees, a partition of a communal farm takes place when it reaches the size of 120 to 140 souls. In this manner various new communal farms have been founded in western Canada in the last number of years.

A communal farm is usually situated in a river valley. The long houses, containing living rooms and bedrooms, are usually built along a sort of main street of the community. The largest house contains the kitchen and the communal dining hall. The school house also serves as a place of worship. Everything is as plain as possible. There are no bells and musical instruments. Singing is only for one voice as a matter of principle.

Clothing, like everything else in Hutterite society, is subject to the strictest regulation. The men wear grey overalls and round black hats, the women black dresses and white dotted kerchiefs. Great importance is placed on the school, for which for many generations the Hutterites have prepared their children with nursery and preschools (*Kindergärten*). Each boy has to learn a trade. Higher learning is rejected, since it takes man away from the superior moral value of manual work. How small was the number of people who lived in the seclusion of the Hutterite community for centuries is shown by the fact that only very few family names exist. In the Rosedale communal farm near Elie, Manitoba, which I visited, there were only four different names: Gross, Hofer, Mandel and Wallner.

There are thirty to fifty thousand persons of German descent who are either not members of any church or have joined denominations of English origin. Most of the latter belong to the United Church of Canada, which was formed in 1925 by a union of Methodists, Congregationalists and some Presbyterians. It also has a few exclusively German congregations and German-speaking pastors. Finally, numerous sects such as the Adventists, the Jehovah's Witnesses, the Sabbatarians, etc. have sprung up in the dry belt with its extremely variable economic conditions. These have also found followers among the Germans.

2. German Secular Clubs

For German rural immigrants from eastern Europe the church congregation or parish was in the beginning, as we saw, the only form of association. Secular clubs and associations, which in time might become mouthpieces for the cultural-political aspirations of the German ethnic group, originated in the cities, and there primarily among immigrants from Germany. If social clubs came into being in the rural areas, it was only where there was also, as in the case of Strassburg, a large number of immigrants from Germany in the settlement. Not until shortly before the outbreak of the World War were associations created that might assume the role of leading organizations of the German element, representing its interests with regard to the provincial government. In a 1914 leaflet entitled *The Germans, Canada's Cultural Fertilizer?*, we read:

> In the last year the development of German club life in Canada has made great strides. The *Deutsch-Kanadischer Nationalbund* has come into being and following on its heels was the *Deutsch-Kanadischer Provinzial-Verband für Saskatchewan* and the *Bund der Deutschen in Alberta*. The most qualified people are making an effort to organize the German element. In Winnipeg there exists the *Bund Deutscher Vereine* embracing Germans from Germany, Switzerland, Russia and Austria-Hungary. In Calgary—thanks to the efforts of Editor Hensen—the *deutscher Verein* has come to life again. In Edmonton the *Edelweiss* club has had its own home for years, and today represents a value of at least thirty thousand Marks. Flourish-

ing German clubs exist also in Vancouver and Victoria, B.C. As the last link in the chain of German efforts in Canada, Editor H. Becker in Edmonton, Alberta, has set up a *Deutsch-Kanadisches Presse-Bureau* which sets itself the task of looking after the interests of the German element everywhere, of initiating regular coverage of German news items in the English-Canadian press, as well as supplying reliable reports about the economic development of Canada to the press in Germany.

These organizational beginnings were quashed by the World War. To be sure, immigrants from Germany and Austria-Hungary were promised at the outbreak of the war that life would not be made difficult for them.[16] As a matter of fact, Germans in western Canada were left in peace as long as they kept quiet and continued to make "voluntary" contributions to the Red Cross, meaning the war bonds. When, however, the question of the introduction of universal conscription was raised, they were disenfranchised, not only the former citizens of the Central Powers naturalized after March 31, 1902, but all Canadian citizens of German descent in general. Any kind of organizational activity of the German community was out of the question. The clubs disbanded, and Germans concealed their identity. Of the highly promising German-Canadian Association of Saskatchewan, for instance, only the local group in Strassburg survived.

The German weeklies were censored. However, they had to suspend publication only temporarily at the end of the war and were soon back in circulation. The newspapers, led by *Der Nordwesten*, were therefore the ones to suggest and make possible the first organizational achievement of Germans in Canada after the war, i.e., financial assistance to suffering fellow Germans in Germany, the succession states of the Habsburg Monarchy and Soviet Russia. Thousands of dollars have been donated to relief organizations such as *Deutsche Kinder in Not* (German Children in Distress), and the *Ruhrhilfe* (Ruhr Relief), by German Canadians who had become prosperous. A part of this relief was organized by various denominational agencies which were also instrumental in implementing the second great postwar accomplishment, namely aid for new German immigrants with the help of the aforementioned immigration boards.

It was not until 1926, after an interval of more than a decade, that club life gradually began to flourish again. In that year Professor Rehwinkel of Concordia College in Edmonton founded the *Deutsch-Canadischer National-Verband* (German-Canadian National Association).[17] However it did not get off the ground to the extent he had planned. After the collapse of German associational life, the time for a new comprehensive organization of Germans in Canada was far from ripe. But at least local clubs, unions of fellow countrymen, glee clubs, gymnastic, sports and shooting clubs, card-playing and bowling clubs, aid societies, reading circles and literary clubs enjoyed a resurgence. However, the situation, especially in cultural-political respects, had now become much less favorable for the German community, compared to the prewar era. Now they were forced to send their children to the unilingual English school. In order to defend themselves against these manifestations of Anglo-Canadian nationalism, the Germans were virtually compelled to unite in more comprehensive organizations. As a result, large regional associations were soon formed in every province.

a. Manitoba

In Winnipeg, where various German clubs had existed before the war, only the *Deutsche Vereinigung* survived, but club life revived with the arrival of new immigrants. In 1930 the *Deutsch-Kanadischer Bund von Manitoba* (German-Canadian Union of Manitoba) was formed as the leading organization of the German element. Its corporate members were the following associations and—this was very important—church congregations: the *Deutsche Vereinigung*, the *Deutsch-Kanadischer Kranken-Unterstützungsverein*, (German-Canadian Fund for the Sick), the *Deutscher Hilfsverein* (German Aid Society), the *Deutsche Sportvereinigung* (German Sports Association), the Catholic *St. Josephsverein* (St. Joseph's Club), the Lutheran Cross, Christ and Trinity congregations in Winnipeg and the congregation in Newton-Siding, the *Siebenbürger Sachsen-Verein* (Transylvania Saxons Club) and the *Westfälischer Schützenverein von Little Britain* (Westphalian Riflemen's Club of Little Britain).[18] The number has increased since. The Winnipeg local group of the *Deutscher Bund Canada* formed in 1934 also belongs to the *Deutsch-Kanadischer Bund von Manitoba*. Its main tasks are the preparation of the *Deutsche Tage* (German Day celebrations), the arranging of German private instruction, the procuring of work and the representation of the interests of the provincial German element in general.

b. Saskatchewan

In Saskatchewan, the province with the strongest German element, there is the *Volksverein deutsch-canadischer Katholiken* with its thirty-

six local groups (see chapter VII, part 1.c.). The next largest association is the *Deutsch-Canadischer Verband von Saskatchewan* (German-
Canadian Association of Saskatchewan) which was revived in 1928.
In 1934 it comprised twenty-eight local groups in such places as Edenwold, Estevan, Fiske, Gull Lake, Herschel, Kelstern, Langenburg, Maple
Creek, Medicine Hat, Medstead, Middle Lake, Quinton, Regina (three
local groups), Rosthern, Saskatoon, St. Boswells, Strassburg, Waldeck
and Weyburn. Its main aim, according to its proclamation of 1930, is
the preservation of the German mother tongue in the family and congregation on a non-partisan, non-denominational basis. It therefore
wants to promote private instruction in the German language, German singing, German music, German libraries and the German press.
Besides providing private instruction and maintaining travelling libraries,
the association promotes the creation of local libraries, and awards prizes
for the highest achievements in the German language at the following
five private institutions of higher learning: the Luther Colleges in Regina
and Saskatoon (Lutheran), the *Deutsch-Englische Akademie* in Rosthern
(Mennonite), St. Peter's College in Muenster and Campion College
in Regina (Catholic).

Besides these two provincial associations there were local mergers
in Regina and Saskatoon. In Regina the *Deutsch-Kanadisches Zentral-
Komitee* was founded in the fall of 1929, to which the following
individual organizations belonged in 1934: two German Catholic parishes, two German Lutheran congregations, one German Baptist congregation, three local groups of the *Deutsch-canadischer Verband von
Saskatchewan*, one local group of the *Deutscher Bund Canada* (since 1934),
the *Deutsch-Canadischer Club* (since 1922), the *Deutsch-Canadischer
Unterstützungsverein* (since 1922), the *Deutsches Haus* (Germans from
Galicia, since 1928), the *Deutscher Verein Germania* (since 1932), the
Deutscher Club Teutonia (since 1933). Here, as in Winnipeg, church congregations and secular associations cooperate harmoniously in the
interest of the German ethnic cause. In Saskatoon, too, a central agency
of local clubs was created, the *Deutscher-Tag-Komitee*, explicitly for the
purpose of preparing German Day celebrations for Saskatchewan, held
alternately in Regina and Saskatoon every two years.

In 1934 one further step was taken. Following a suggestion by the
energetic editor Bernhard Bott, who was then still working for *Der Courier* in Regina, the *Deutsche Arbeitsgemeinschaft Saskatchewan* (German
Coordinating Committee of Saskatchewan) was founded as an umbrella
organization during the German Day celebrations in Saskatoon on June

30, 1934. It is supposed to serve all major secular and religious associations of the German community as a clearing house, and represent the general interests of Saskatchewan's German element. The following associations jointly constituted the *Deutsche Arbeitsgemeinschaft*, and could delegate three representatives each to the *Deutscher Volksrat* (German Ethnic Council), the actual working body in the *Arbeitsgemeinschaft*:[19]

1. the *Volksverein deutsch-canadischer Katholiken* (since 1908, with thirty-six local groups);
2. the *Deutsch-canadischer Verband von Saskatchewan* (since 1913, with twenty-eight local groups);
3. the *Mennonitisches Provinzialkomitee* (since 1923, with stewards in the individual localities);
4. the *Deutsch-Kanadisches Zentralkomitee* as urban association for Regina;
5. the *Saskatoon-Deutscher-Tag-Komitee*;
6. the Saskatchewan district of the *Deutscher Bund*.

The idea of uniting, in the form of an *Arbeitsgemeinschaft*, all German organizations of one province under one hat to give them more influence in of matters of common interest is a very good one. Meanwhile, following Saskatchewan's example, this idea has also been realized in the greater Montreal area and in the Provinces of Ontario and Alberta. In Manitoba, as pointed out above, the *Deutsch-Kanadischer Bund* takes the place of the *Arbeitsgemeinschaft*. The *Deutsche Arbeitsgemeinschaft* for Alberta (founded in Edmonton), however, resembles the *Deutsch-Kanadisches Zentralkomitee* of Regina. It is a local association for the purpose of organizing German Day celebrations.

c. Alberta

Organizational consolidation of Alberta's German ethnic group proved more difficult. Professor Rehwinkel's *Deutsch-canadischer National-Verband*, founded in 1926, folded the following year. The idea of uniting had, nevertheless, made enough of an impression to make possible the celebration of the first German Day for Alberta in Edmonton in 1928. It was the first major postwar demonstration of the German element of western Canada. In 1932 Rehwinkel's plan was resurrected with the foundation of the *Deutsch-Kanadische Zentralstelle für die Provinz Alberta* (German-Canadian Central Agency for the Province of Alberta), which assumed the former name *Deutsch-canadischer National-Verband* in May 1933. The objectives were good, but there was a lack of people to carry them out.[20] As early as 1934, the new *National-Verband* survived only as a local relief society in South Edmonton-Strathcona. In Edmonton itself most of its members constituted themselves in 1934 as a local group of the *Deutscher Bund Canada*. Additional clubs in Edmonton are: the *Edelweiss* club, founded before 1905, with its large club house,[21] the *Deutsch-Canadische Vereinigung von 1930* and the *Turn- und Sportverein Jahn* (since 1931); in Calgary the *Vergissmeinnicht-Club* (since 1930) and the *Harmonie* club (since 1932) and a local group of the *Deutscher Bund*; also here and there a few smaller clubs such as the *Deutsche Arbeitsgemeinschaft* in Dapp.

d. British Columbia

In British Columbia too the German element has recently better organized itself. In Vancouver there is a local group of the *Deutscher Bund Canada*, a *Deutscher Schulverein*, the *Deutsche Frauenschaft* and the more socially oriented *Alpenvereinigung*. As in Montreal, Germans in Vancouver are in the fortunate situation of being in constant personal contact with events back in the old homeland through the German ships visiting the harbor. These contacts are also the reason for the existence of a branch of the NSDAP (National Socialist German Workers' Party) and the *Deutsche Arbeitsfront* (German Labor Front). In the spring of 1938 all the German associations joined to form the *Arbeitsgemeinschaft Deutsches Haus* and have opened a "German Home" (*Deutsches Heim*). The celebration of a German Day according to the model of the other provinces is imminent.

Besides Vancouver, there are local groups of the *Deutscher Bund* in Kelowna, Osoyoos and Summerland. In Kelowna there is also a *Verein der Deutschsprechenden* and the *Deutsch-canadische Liberale Vereinigung*.

The aforementioned *Deutscher Bund Canada* wants to create a more sympathetic understanding for the new Germany among Canadian citizens of German descent. It wants to have the effect of a leaven among the world of German-Canadian associations, although it has barely five hundred members in western Canada to date. It has local groups in such places as Winnipeg and North Winnipeg (Manitoba); Regina, Saskatoon, Melville, Grayson, Edenwold, St. Walburg, Paradise Hill, Loon River (Saskatchewan); Edmonton and Calgary (Alberta); Vancouver, Kelowna, Osoyoos and Summerland (British Columbia); and footholds in a large number of settlements (Vibank, Wapella, Mossbank, etc.). Not only the idea of cultural, but also of economic self-help among the German Canadians, has been advocated successfully by the *Deutscher Bund* as well as by some of the older associations. Following the example of Germany a small *Winterhilfswerk* (Winter Relief Program) for the benefit of numerous needy Germans has been set up over here in recent years.

The number of German citizens residing in western Canada is minimal, therefore there are no local groups of the NSDAP or the German Labor Front outside Vancouver. Germany has been represented by a professional consul in Winnipeg since before the war, and by an honorary consul in Vancouver since 1935.

There is also a Communist German association in western Canada, the *Deutscher Farmer- und Arbeiter-Verband* (German Farmers' and Workers' Association) founded in 1930, and renamed in the summer of 1937 the *Deutsch-Kanadischer Volksbund* (German-Canadian People's Alliance). It is unlikely that it can increase the small number of its followers.

All in all, the past decade has been one of self-reflection and organizational growth for German Canadians. It is to be hoped that a nationwide organization of the German element as the superstructure still lacking above the provincial *Arbeitsgemeinschaften* (Coordinating Committees) will become a reality soon in some form. Such a consolidation would be absolutely necessary to accomplish the many cultural tasks that have not yet been tackled.

Unfortunately there is a widespread shortage of dedicated local leaders. It has to be borne in mind that Germans, who have brought with them quite different levels of education and different cultural backgrounds from different places of origin, are much more difficult to bring together as neighbors in everyday life than is made possible by the resolutions of the festive German Day celebrations. A lot of prejudice among the denominationally-divided German element has to be overcome. Petty disputes and the ambitions of *Vereinsmeier* (club fanatics) often turn away the quiet types who have leadership abilities from German club life. This is particularly the case in a situation where a dedicated engagement in the service of the German-Canadian cause often cannot be reconciled with the hard economic struggle for survival of the settler or urban businessman, clerk or worker. On the other hand, experience has shown that the unemployed, who have time to be active in organizations, frequently find it difficult to be accepted as leaders of the German cause. Consequently there is danger of a sudden collapse of organizational structure, not so much among the larger associations as on the level of individual clubs and local groups, and of the cessation of all club life in the respective locality when the personality who represents the driving force departs.

3. The German Day Celebrations

The events of the German Day celebrations convey the most vivid impression of the life of western Canada's German element these days. They are held on a weekend in the capital of each of the three Prairie provinces every summer between seeding and harvest. In Saskatchewan, Regina and Saskatoon take turns as host cities. Lately smaller German Regional Days (*Deutsche Gautage*) are being celebrated in St. Walburg or Barrhead, for homesteaders in the north of Saskatchewan and Alberta. The large German Day celebrations which have been held in Manitoba and Alberta since 1928 and in Saskatchewan since 1930, are attended by an average of four thousand to five thousand ethnic Germans. As celebrations representative of all segments of the German-Canadian community, they have already developed a definite pattern. They open in a stadium or a large festival hall, with an official ceremony during which keynote addresses and important resolutions are presented. This is followed by competitions of singing clubs, athletic competitions, performances of costume and folk dance groups, the awarding of prizes for the best academic achievements in German resulting from competition among pupils, etc. Simultaneously, small exhibitions of arts and crafts made in the long winter months by German Canadians, often with great artistic skill, are held.

German Day celebrations, and especially the resolutions adopted on these occasions, give an excellent picture of the cultural life and political aspirations of the German ethnic group. The resolutions show quite clearly that its leaders envisage three major challenges:

First and foremost, to alert the German element, to keep reminding it emphatically of the rights and duties arising from its ethnic heritage, and to challenge it to look after its interests in school and local administrations. The feeling among Canadian Germans of belonging together, and the awareness of the need to preserve one's ethnic heritage as a most valuable asset handed down for the benefit of the young generation, has in fact been strengthened considerably through

German Days.

Secondly, to remind the provincial governments, every year if possible, by impressive demonstrations of the legitimate demands of the German ethnic group for the restoration of German language instruction in the public schools of school districts with a German majority. All the attempts to restore the prewar conditions in the school question have unfortunately been unsuccessful so far. At least German Canadians are realizing more and more the overriding significance of the school question for the preservation of the cultural identity of the German ethnic group.

Thirdly, to refute with information, and by protest in Canada, the dissemination of false and biased information about the German fatherland as well as about the German element in Canada. Forming an integral part of this are the efforts to inform Canadian public opinion about the great foreign political questions affecting the German people and to call for an understanding, tolerant attitude towards Germany. In this regard as well, there is tangible progress. The German Day celebrations together with the German press, have attracted widespread attention in Anglo-Canadian circles, and have brought to light the reporting bias in Canadian daily newspapers.

4. The German Element in Canadian Politics

The political influence of the German element has been virtually nil so far. Only a comprehensive and effective organization of the German vote could change that. This, however, has never been attempted for the entire Dominion, and even on the provincial level it is still more a hope than a reality. Yet there is no lack of participation in political issues of the day at election time. But the number of German-Canadian deputies elected to the provincial and federal parliaments bears no relationship to the size of the German-Canadian community. The relatively low level of education of the majority of German immigrants, the language difficulties in the new country, plus a strong prejudice against any political activity among the Mennonites, have kept Canada's citizens of German descent away from politics to their own detriment. Individual German Canadians have played a certain role in public life, though without really being able to utilize their influence in the interest of the non-organized German element.

Among German Canadians who attained a special position in the public life of western Canada, the physician Dr. Christian Schultz from Ontario (1840-1896) must be mentioned first. Even before 1870 he had taken up residence at the Red River, where he organized the opposition of the settlers against the Hudson's Bay Company with his newspaper *The Nor'Wester* and demanded the incorporation of Manitoba into the Dominion of Canada set up in 1867. From 1888 to 1895, that is, during the critical years of Canada-wide commotion over the Manitoba school dispute, he headed the administration of Manitoba as its Lieutenant-Governor. In the early years of Manitoba, a certain Wilhelm Hespeler also stood out. Born in Württemberg, he had emigrated as a young man to Ontario. In 1870 he went to Manitoba, where he won much recognition for his efforts to settle the Mennonites in southern Manitoba. For many years he remained the elected member of the predominantly Mennonite constituency of Rosenfeld in the provincial legislature of Manitoba. In 1900 he even became its speaker, a position rarely attained by any German in a parliamentary body within the British Empire. Valentin Winkler, an Ontario-born German Canadian, like Hespeler made his way as an immigration agent. The small town of Winkler in southern Manitoba is named after him. He was the member for the constituency of Rhineland for a long time. For several years he occupied the position of Minister of Agriculture of Manitoba. The foundation and construction of the agricultural college in Winnipeg must be attributed largely to his efforts. In addition, the following German-Canadian members were elected in western Canada: In the legislature of the Northwest Territories (so named until 1905) A.S. Rosenroll for Wetaskiwin (since 1903) who continued to sit in the legislature of Alberta after 1905. In the legislature of Saskatchewan: Gerhard Ens (from 1905), long-serving member for the Mennonite constituency of Rosthern; Dr. J.M. Uhrich, a Catholic, for the same constituency since 1921; H.N. Therres, a Catholic, for the constituency of Humboldt (St. Peter's colony) from 1921 to 1934; Anton Huck, a Catholic from Vibank, for the constituency of South Qu'Appelle until 1934; since 1934, as well as Dr. Uhrich, the members Dr. H.P. Mang from Edenwold for the constituency of Lumsden, J.J. Mildenberger for the constituency of Maple Creek and G.H. Hummel for the constituency of Last Mountain. In the legislature of Alberta, besides Rosenroll, the members Hiebert for the constituency of Rosebud (from 1905) and F. Hennig for the constituency of Fort Saskatchewan (until 1934). For several years a Mennonite has been a member of the legislature of Manitoba. In the Dominion parliament in Ottawa, the German Canadian A.F. Totzke was a member for the constituency of Humboldt, Saskatchewan, for some time after the war. Presently the only German-Canadian cabinet minister in western Canada is Dr. Uhrich, born in 1877 in Formosa, Ontario, Minister of Public Health in Saskatchewan from 1922 to 1929, and since 1934. His attitude towards the acute ethno-political questions of the German community in western Canada is quite positive, as his address to the 1934 German Day celebrations shows (see end of chapter VIII). As long as he has no organized German element behind him, however, he cannot accomplish anything in matters like the school question.

In general, western Canada's Germans have so far supported the Liberal Party. One reason for this was its promotion of non-British immigration, in particular under Sir Wilfrid Laurier and Clifford Sifton. Another reason is the disenfranchisement of virtually all German-speaking Canadians and former citizens of the Central Powers by the Conservative government of Sir Robert Borden in 1917. In none of the provinces, however, have the postwar Liberal governments again relaxed the Anglo-Canadian nationalist school policies in the interest of non-British ethnic groups. It is therefore quite possible that German Canadians might renounce their support of the Liberal Party and cast their votes together with other ethnic groups for a change according to cultural-political criteria, such as the program of school instruction in the mother tongue. On the basis of the number of their votes, Germans, French Canadians and Ukrainians could dominate the legislatures of Manitoba and Saskatchewan, perhaps also of Alberta. Such an alliance, however, would be difficult to form. The French Canadians do not feel themselves at all on the same political level as the younger ethnic groups of immigrants. As Canada's oldest ethnic group they refer to themselves rather proudly as the embodiment of "Les Canadiens" and claim full equality with the British as one of the two charter groups. They know full well that they have great influence in the Province of Quebec, and therefore also with the federal government in Ottawa, and that they have good prospects of asserting themselves. They would be inclined rather to sacrifice the interests of the Germans, Ukrainians, et cetera, in return for concessions received. The last word about this has, of course, not yet been spoken, considering the recent formation on behalf of French Canadians of a more nationalist-authoritarian type of government in Quebec, and its growing dissociation from the Anglo-Canadian element in methods of government as well.

5. Cultural Level and the Preservation of the German Heritage

Our observations indicated that the rural German element in western Canada, just like the young rural German ethnic groups in eastern Europe, is still largely at a level that Kuhn characterizes as religious culture.[22]

The economic development of the settlements, the level of education and thus ethnic resistance to assimilation increase in the following order, observed among rural German groups everywhere outside Germany: from Catholics, to Protestants, and finally to Protestant sects (Mennonites).[23] The low level of education of Catholics is, among other factors, due to the cultural handicap of their ancestors in South Russia, on the Volga, in Galicia, etc., where the German Catholic colonists were dependent for a long time on Polish clergy, thus becoming leaderless and developing only second-class schools.[24] The very much higher level of education of the Mennonites, on the other hand, proves that all culture is created by a living community and must be maintained by it. Even though the German Mennonites in Russia had no acute consciousness of their German identity, their tightly-knit community led by such men as Johann Cornies was still able to develop gradually an efficiently functioning system of schooling and education, which cultivated the legacy of German cultural values. The head start they had gained in Russia has not been lost in western Canada, where the Mennonites developed the best school system among all the German-Canadian groups. Overall, they have a higher average education, more intellectual leaders, a richer body of literature and more newspapers, as well as especially great economic successes. The postwar Mennonite immigrants particularly have a very high level of education on average, since they attended Mennonite elementary and higher schools in Russia which had been continuously improved since the 1870s.

As may be expected for this level of "religious culture," the German identity of most of the colonists is based solely on the natural, unconscious retention of their ethnic heritage.

In material respects, German ethnic traditions have best been preserved among the Mennonites. Reference has already been made to the layout of their villages and fields in the *Gewannflur* tradition, as well as to the numerous place names that have been adopted from their South Russian and in part even from their West Prussian homelands. The house and barnyard were also set up in accordance with the pattern proven successful in South Russia.[25] Living quarters, kitchen, stable and barn were originally all accommodated under one roof with the gable end facing the street. The house has at least three large rooms. The *grosse Stube* is the general living room. In it are the big linen chest, the wall clock, the *Ziegelofen* (ceramic tile stove) fed from the kitchen, and the generous coffee mill; in the kitchen, highly polished copper kettles and platters are in profusion. Everything is in good old German fashion, which also was well tested in Russia. Among the Mennonites and the German immigrants from Russia generally, one could frequently find a so-called summer kitchen, a separate building with one or two rooms as prescribed by fire regulations in Russia. The summer kitchen is for cooking and eating, and the house, which in the summer is used only for sleeping, is thus kept cool and free of flies. Somewhat apart from the house is the free-standing baking oven. The desire of German colonists to plant trees around the house (maple, ash, willow) is also manifest everywhere. The broad main streets of the Mennonite villages, even those now abandoned in favor of single farm settlements, are recognizable from far across the prairie. The Old Colony Mennonite villages were characterized as follows:[26]

> One has the feeling of being taken back to the Mennonite villages at the Dnieper near Alexandrovsk: the same building style, the same picket fences, the same long barns—everything just as in Chortitza or Neuendorf. Even the interior decoration of the houses has remained the same. A *Sommerstow* is in every house. It appears that decades of modern civilization, especially of the English and American kind, have passed by the Old Colony settlements without a trace and unnoticed.

Among Lutherans and Catholics, but also in young Mennonite settlements, adaptation to the customs of the new country has been greater not only in acceptance of the single farm settlement, but also in the layout of the house and barnyard. Like all the other immigrants they first used sods and poplar wood as building materials. Churches and houses built later show certain frequently recurring forms. At first glance these appear to be manifestations of specific stylistic traditions, but upon closer examination turn out to be borrowed from one of the many catalogues of American building firms, who supplied to the farmer all of the finished building materials available in the catalogue. Only in interior decoration was the old flavor preserved, with here and there a few pieces of furniture which had been brought along from the homeland. Traditional costumes are put on only on festive holidays. Only the Hutterites continue to wear their special attire regularly, as briefly described in chapter VII, part 1(d). Otherwise practical American overalls have displaced traditional clothes as working clothes. Occasionally a genuine Russian sheepskin can still be seen among the Germans from Russia, the typical short pipe and peaked cap among the Volga Germans, and the kerchief usually is worn by the older wives of German farmers. Their attitude towards food was most conservative. The menu still contains many traditional dishes; the baking recipes are handed down, and hog butchering and sausage making are still special events in a German farming family.

Among religious and other holidays, Christmas especially is celebrated in traditional fashion, if possible with a Christmas tree and candles, and with carols and gifts for the children. At no time is homesickness and one's German origins felt more strongly than on this German family festival. In other respects picnics have to some extent replaced the traditional forms of celebrating.

Long-held customs and folklore have unfortunately fallen into general disuse. To be sure, one may occasionally see the old farmer's wife at the spinning wheel brought along from the old country. Among the young generation, however, the sewing machine has almost entirely replaced traditional embroidering and handiwork. Life on individual farms and the resulting absence of village community life has led to a widespread loss of old customs and sayings, stories, funny anecdotes, nursery rhymes and folk songs. These used to be handed down in the village spinning rooms, now extinct, or during gatherings of male village youth. This is bound to result in psychic impoverishment and the loss of German identity.

The dialects brought over to Canada are still spoken in their original forms. The Mennonites speak the Low German of West Prussia in their homes, while among Lutherans and Catholics the southwest German, Hessian and Palatine Rhenish-Franconian dialects predominate. Although German settlers from a greater variety of places of origin came together in individual colonies, there is no reason to expect the development of any mixed dialects at this point. The degeneration of the German language due to words borrowed from English, however, is in full swing, as one would expect.

6. The German Press

The German press of western Canada is almost as old as western settlement. Except for the Mennonite immigrants in southern Manitoba, German immigration did not set in until the second half of the 1880s, and as early as 1889 the first weekly began to appear in Winnipeg. It was *Der Nordwesten*, which still exists today. At first it had four pages, after 1891 eight pages, and later twelve to sixteen pages. For a long time it was the best and most widely-read German weekly of western Canada. It enjoyed great popularity, even among the Mennonites, two thousand of whom are still subscribing to it today in spite of various newspapers of their own. In accordance with the different origins of the German immigrants, it reported as much, and often more, about the scattered German settlements in Russia and in the old Habsburg Monarchy than about Germany, and became an outspoken advocate of the German ethnic cause as early as the 1890s. Time and again the example of such groups as the Transylvania-Germans and the German colonists in Russia was pointed out to the new immigrants, in order to encourage them to settle in closed German colonies, and to urge them to fight for German language instruction in the schools and the cultivation of inherited cultural traditions in German church congregations and associations. The names of the first editors—Brügmann, Harbs, Körmann, Carstens, Bach, Liebermann and above all, Gotthard Maron (1912 to 1920)—are closely associated with *Der Nordwesten* in its heyday. Immediately after the war, Maron and *Der Nordwesten* managed to raise considerable amounts of money from Canadian Germans for the relief project *Deutsche Kinder in Not* (German Children in Distress) and for the *Ruhrhilfe* (Ruhr Relief). In the past twelve years, however, *Der Nordwesten* allowed itself to be surpassed by the younger paper *Der Courier* in Regina. In 1934 *Der Nordwesten* had a circulation of about nine thousand. Its editor is W. Hensen.

Der Courier was launched in 1907 in Regina as the *Saskatchewan Courier* by P.M. Bredt from Edenwold, with the support of the ruling Liberal Party. It promoted immigration, and hoped that this paper would become another means of soliciting German immigrants. Since Saskatchewan was the main destination of German immigration, the foundation of a German newspaper in its capital of Regina proved to be a good idea. Under its editor, Konrad Eymann (1912-1920), *Der Courier*, judged by its contents and circulation, soon acquired a respectable reputation. During the World War it remained unchallenged, and continued so until the end of August 1918. For fifteen months it had to appear in English, until it resumed in its old form on New Year's Day 1920. The circles associated with the *Volksverein deutsch-canadischer Katholiken* and the Oblates, whose Winnipeg paper *Westkanada* had definitely folded for good, now acquired the decisive influence on the editorial board. Not until Bott became editor-in-chief (1923-1934) did the unilateral Catholic bias gradually give way to an inter-denominational, non-partisan, distinctly German ethnic attitude. As the mouthpiece of particular Catholic interests, the bi-monthly *Der Katholik* (1924-1931, circulation 3,200) appeared now in the same pub-lishing house. With *Der Courier*, Bott succeeded in reviving the German-Canadian movement which had completely collapsed under the con-sequences of the World War, in establishing "German Days" as the annual demonstration of the German population of the province, and in preparing the organizational consolidation of the German element in Saskatchewan. *Der Courier* became the most widely read German newspaper in Canada, with a circulation of close to twelve thousand. Bott's resignation from the editorial board and his founding of the *Deutsche Zeitung für Canada* in Winnipeg has since hurt *Der Courier*.

The *Mennonitische Rundschau* has appeared in Winnipeg from about 1909. It had been launched as early as 1877 for German emigrants from Russia to the United States and Canada. It was first published as *Nebraska-Ansiedler* at Elkhart, Indiana, then in 1908 moved for a short time to Scottsdale, Pennsylvania, but very soon began to appear in Win-nipeg.[27] Today the *Mennonitische Rundschau*, which forms a bridge to the Brethren in Russia, and which is read in western Canada as well as in the United States, has a circulation of about five thousand. It is edited by H. Neufeld. The same publishing house and the same editorial board also issue the *Christlicher Jugendfreund* and *Werden und Wachsen* as religious Sunday school and family papers. In 1933 they had a combined circulation of 3,500 to four thousand. Between 1924 and 1928, furthermore, the religious weekly *Zeugnis der Schrift*, with a circulation of twelve hundred, appeared from the same publishing house.

In 1913 another Mennonite weekly, *Der Volksbote*, was launched in Steinbach, Manitoba, by J.S. Friesen. It was issued later as *Steinbach Post* and *Steinbacher Post*, and appears today under the name of *Die Post*, with a circulation of about fifteen hundred (the owner is A.P. Dyck).

Since 1904, German Benedictines in Muenster, Saskatchewan, have been editing the *St. Peters-Bote* as a distinctly Catholic weekly for the settlers of St. Peter's colony. It had a circulation of twelve hundred in 1934 but, since the end of the war also has an English-language off-shoot, *The Prairie Messenger.*

In addition to the above-mentioned newspapers, all of which survived the World War, the launching of a whole series of weeklies can be noted during the years of heaviest German immigration between 1912 and 1914. After more or less brief lifespans these folded again, or had to cease publication during the war. In Winkler, in the Mennonite West Reserve in southern Manitoba, the *Volkszeitung* appeared for a brief period of time around 1902.[28] In Winnipeg the *Germania* was issued from 1904. In contrast to *Der Nordwesten*, with its Protestant and politically Liberal orientation at the time, it represented Catholic and Conservative tendencies. In spite of this it was merged with *Der Nordwesten* in 1911. Another distinctly Catholic paper was *Westkanada*, which appeared in Winnipeg from 1907 to the end of the war. It was the organ of the German Oblates and had a circulation of eight thousand around 1912. From the beginning of 1901 the *Rundschau* appeared in Regina. It was a purely local paper, which was absorbed by the newly founded *Saskatchewan Courier* in 1907. For the Germans who had settled after 1909 in Happy Land in the dry belt of southwestern Saskatchewan, the German-English paper *Enterprise*, the present day *Leader*, appeared for some time in Prussia, Saskatchewan. Around the same time *Der Deutsch-Canadier* was launched in Calgary, Alberta, and the *Alberta Herold* (founder: Körmann) in Edmonton. The former folded before the war, the latter when the war broke out. In Vancouver, British Columbia, the *Westliche Canadische Post* and the bilingual *Vancouver German Press* appeared.[29]

When immigration resumed after the war, new German papers were founded. Between 1928 and 1931 the initially well-edited *Herold* appeared in Edmonton, the capital of Alberta. However it could not survive economically, and eventually merged with *Der Courier*. The attempt to revive it in November 1931 under the name of *Alberta Herold*, once again in Edmonton, also failed. In 1931 the *Deutsche Arbeiterzeitung* was launched in Winnipeg as the organ of the Red *Deutscher Arbeiter- und Farmerverband in Kanada*. It turned into an anti-German, Communist propaganda sheet, especially after 1933. Fortunately it never found many readers.

More successful were the two newspapers launched by Mennonite postwar immigrants. Since 1923 Dietrich Epp has been editing the weekly *Der Bote*, with a circulation of more than two thousand. Since

1935 the *Mennonitische Volkswarte* (editor A. B. Dyck) has been appearing as a monthly publication in Steinbach, Manitoba. It serves as a mouthpiece of the postwar immigrants, containing their poetry and memories of the war and postwar experiences in Russia.

Finally, in response to the National Socialist revolution in Germany, Editor Bott launched in Winnipeg the *Deutsche Zeitung für Canada*. It wants to be the proponent of aspirations for unification and cultural self-help among Canadian Germans.

There are therefore in western Canada today three non-denominational papers, the *Deutsche Zeitung für Canada* and *Der Nordwesten* in Winnipeg, and *Der Courier* in Regina. These are read not only in the Prairie provinces and in British Columbia, but also in Ontario and Montreal, and have a combined circulation of about twenty-five thousand. *Der Nordwesten* and *Der Courier* every year distribute almanacs which are among the German farmers' favorite readings. To these should be added the denominationally-oriented weeklies, the *Mennonitische Rundschau* in Winnipeg, *Die Post* in Steinbach, *Der Bote* in Rosthern and the Catholic *St. Peters-Bote* in Muenster, as well as the *Mennonitische Volkswarte* in Steinbach, the only magazine so far.

The Lutherans have several church papers. Since 1929 the Manitoba Synod has been publishing the *Synodalbote* (edited by D. Ruccius in Winnipeg) which was an offshoot of the *College-Freund*, published in Saskatoon since 1914. Recently the Missouri Synod has been issuing, for both of its western Canadian districts, the *Canadisch-Lutherisches Kirchenblatt* (its editor is College Director Prof. Schwermann in Edmonton). It was preceded, from 1924 to 1933, by a separate paper for each of the two districts, namely *Unsere Kirche* of the Alberta-British Columbia District, and *Der Lutherische Missionar* (later *Der Lutherische Herold*) of the Manitoba-Saskatchewan District. The paper *Der Mitarbeiter*, published at the Mennonite college in Gretna, folded with the death of its editor, the director of the college, H.H. Ewert, in 1934.

Dr. Moellmann, author of the book *Das Deutschtum in Montreal* (1937) kindly made available to me his analysis of the contents of German-Canadian newspapers as of 1933 (in percentages of the total space of the newspapers—see Table VII.3).[30]

According to this analysis, more than half the space in each of the two non-denominational papers is devoted to news, and of this more than half again to news from Germany and the other places of origin of Canadian Germans, while Canadian news items trail behind. Among the religiously-oriented papers, news reporting is far from being as impor-

Table VII.3

Analysis of the Contents of German-Canadian
Newspapers, 1933

Contents:	*Der Nordwesten* and *Der Courier*	Mennonite papers	Catholic paper
Editorial	1.8%	—	—
News: (1) Germany and European places of origin of German immigrants (2) Canada and U.S.A.	27.8% 23.2%	15.2% 31.2%	16.8% 13.2%
Total News	51.0%	46.4%	30.0%
Agricultural	6.3%	1.0%	1.1%
Cultural: Family Religious Literary Group	2.9% 2.2% 15.8% —	— 6.2% 18.5% 8.4%	13.9% 24.6% 10.8% 4.5%
Total Cultural	20.9%	33.1%	53.8%
Advertising	15.2%	15.7%	7.7%
Miscellaneous (science, sports, theater, radio, etc.)	4.8%	3.8%	7.4%

tant. The fact that the Catholic *St. Peters-Bote* devotes only 30 per cent of its space to general news items and 10.8 per cent to literary subjects, against 24.6 per cent to church and 13.9 per cent to family news, is further proof for our contention that Catholics have adhered most firmly to their religious culture.

The relatively numerous German newspapers have an avid circle of readers, who provide their own input into the papers in the form of letters to the editor. The demand of Canadian Germans for news is, in fact, still almost entirely met by the German papers. The major English-language newspapers that appear in Winnipeg, Regina, Saskatoon and Edmonton, as well as the English local press, have so far found few subscribers among Germans. Only English illustrated magazines and specialized agricultural journals such as the *Free Press Prairie Farmer, The Nor'-West Farmer, The Country Guide,* are read relatively widely.

7. The Beginnings of a Canadian German Literature and Other Artistic Activity

The Mennonites, who produce the largest number of newspapers, have so far also been the only ones to develop a German-language literature of their own. In this regard the higher level of their culture was already noticeable in their South Russian homeland.

Unpretentious and impressively dramatized chronicles of the destiny of the Mennonites in southern Manitoba from the 1870s are the portrayals in *Kanadische Mennoniten,* edited by Dietrich Neufeld (Novokampus) on the occasion of the anniversary of the colonies in 1924. Most of their poets and writers are to be found among the postwar immigrants. The first to be mentioned is Jacob H. Janzen. Born in 1878 in Steinbach in South Russia, Janzen was a teacher at the early age of sixteen, and in 1906 he became a preacher as well. In 1908 he passed his qualifying examination for the rank of *Oberlehrer* (senior level teacher), attended university summer school courses in Germany 1913-1914, became an army chaplain in the German volunteer battalion in the White Army under General Wrangel, and came to Canada in November 1924. From his home in Waterloo, Ontario, he has been active as an elder and missionary preacher of the Mennonite Brethren Church in western Canada. Besides some religious writings, devotional booklets for the home and a hymnal, he has published memoirs, poems in High German and Low German, and a small play called *Utwaundre* (emigrants).[31] In his poetry, Janzen combines deep religious feeling with a sincere German ethnic consciousness.

For all the Mennonite postwar immigrants, the source of their literary creativity is the memory of the terrible years of misery in Russia during the war and revolution. This is characteristic of the literary works of Johann Wiens (former teacher in Alexanderfeld in South Russia), G.A. Peters, Gerhard Toews (Georg de Brecht), Johann Peter Klassen and D. Neufeld.[32] The most productive writer is Peter J. Klassen in Superb, Saskatchewan. He has published, often under a pseudonym, his rather lengthy, somewhat detailed, but still lively narrations in various western Canadian German papers, such as *Der Nordwesten*, *Mennonitische Rundschau*, *Der Courier*, *Volkswarte* and *Der Herold*.

Poems by postwar immigrants can be found regularly, for instance in *Mennonitische Volkswarte*, which has appeared since 1935. Some of these poems by H. Görtz, Fritz Senn, N. Unruh and J. Peetasch (Peters) are reproduced in the anthology by Kloss selected for *Der Auslanddeutsche* (1936). The fairy tales by Mrs. Maria Penner should also be mentioned.

To compare with this Mennonite literature, the Lutherans and Catholics have only a few small historical tracts about their settlements and churches, of the kind we used as sources in chapter VI. But the Catholic hymnal and prayer book *Salve Regina*, edited in 1913 by Oblate Father Riedinger in Regina for use in western Canada, is worth mentioning, as well as the tract by Oblate Father Joh. Schultz, *Muttersprache* (St. Paul, Minnesota, Wanderer Publishing House, around 1920) which exhorts German parents to cultivate the mother tongue. The collection of German folksongs of Russian Germans in America, *Sammlung deutscher Volkslieder der Russlanddeutschen in Amerika* (Bismarck, North Dakota, 1929) edited by Brendel, almost exclusively contains songs from Germany as well as some that were added in Russia, but none that might have originated in western Canada.

There are church choirs in the larger parishes, and congregations of all denominations which cultivate German choral music, and who occasionally even try their hands at large oratorios. The few choral groups which were formed almost solely by immigrants from Germany sing religious songs as well as merry folksongs. German orchestral associations have come into existence in Regina and Saskatoon. In some urban areas, Germans have formed amateur theatres and folkdancing groups. In a few Catholic parishes, religious plays (nativity plays, etc.) are staged on holy days. The painter Imhoff in St. Walburg has become some-what known in the fine arts. He has decorated numerous churches in Catholic colonies. Quite respectable achievements in arts and crafts are displayed in the exhibitions of German Day celebrations. In general, the German Days with their theatre and musicial performances, their exhibitions, and so on, provide the best survey of cultural life, and incentives for even higher achievements.

CHAPTER VIII

Language Loyalty
and Ethnic Retention

1. Measuring Ethnic Retention in
Western Canada

Since 1871 the Canadian Census, which is taken every decade, has been asking for the so-called 'racial origin.' The racial origin of the population, which is defined as descent in the male line, is ascertained by subjective declaration. Every Canadian citizen has to acknowledge a specific European (or Asian) origin. Canada or the United States may not be reported as countries of origin. Since in the past, however, the notion of ethnicity has been more difficult to comprehend than that of citizenship, the question of racial origin was widely understood to apply to the country of origin of the immigrant or his ancestors rather than to his ethnic identity. Only where ethnic identity and citizenship coincide, as for the British, the Germans from Germany, the Danes, Swedes, Norwegians, and so on, are statistics on racial origin really reliable. Where this, however, is not the case, as for example with the large numbers of immigrants from eastern and southeastern Europe, statistics on racial origin are inaccurate. It is, above all, important to realize that acknowledgement of non-British descent does not necessarily presuppose an objective retention of the respective original linguistic and cultural heritage, but frequently goes hand in hand with complete adaptation to the Anglo-Saxon community.

Much more revealing about ethnic retention are the statistics on 'mother tongue' published for the first time in 1921. Mother tongue is defined as the "language of customary speech employed by the person." For children under five years of age, the 1931 Census takes the language of the parents. In connection with statistics on the mother tongue, valuable information can be derived from the statistics on racial origin.

If we examine the tables listing side by side the statistics on racial origin and mother tongue in the 1931 Census (see Appendix, Table 2), we note that in the colorful mixture of peoples of the Prairie provinces, those of British descent make up only 50.8 per cent of the population. In the most densely populated Province of Saskatchewan they represent a mere 47 per cent, and among that province's rural population no more than 40 per cent. The mother tongue statistics, however, indicate that the British have already begun to assimilate the smaller ethnic groups of immigrants linguistically and culturally. The number of persons employing English as their language of customary speech is larger by almost one-fifth than those of British descent. Among all the other ethnic groups, a proportionately smaller number of persons speak their native language than the racial origin statistics suggest. It looks as if only the Germans and Ukrainians are exceptions. But we shall see that the census figures reporting more persons with a German mother tongue than of German racial origin are due to various errors in the racial origin statistics. The same applies to the Ukrainians who frequently replied to the question on racial origin with "Russian," "Austrian" or "Polish," thus confusing their ethnic identity with their former citizenship. On the whole, linguistic anglicization has made the greatest inroads among ethnic groups of the Germanic family of languages, and of course among the very small and spatially-dispersed ethnic groups of immigrants. It has made the fewest inroads among Asians and Jews. It is striking that virtually all Jewish immigrants from eastern Europe acknowledge their own Yiddish linguistic community, and thus only a minimal number of Jews may be assumed among the German-speaking category.

The best measurement of the retention of German ethnicity is, of course, statistics on the mother tongue. It shows, first of all, that of the entire Canadian population, the German element is definitely concentrated in the Prairie provinces of western Canada. There 71.2 per cent of all the German-speaking people in Canada live today. They comprise 11.2 per cent of the total population of these three provinces, and as much as 15.2 per cent of the Province of Saskatchewan.

The figure of 275,660 German-speaking persons given for western Canada is, no doubt, the minimum number. English was adopted frequently, especially among the youth, as the language of customary speech according to the testimony of German Canadians, after the use of English in the school had weaned them, possibly only temporarily, from German spoken in the home. It must also be assumed that with regard to the second generation, statistical errors occurred in favor of English and to the detriment of the German language of the home. The number of persons actually speaking German, i.e., the ethnic Germans, should be between 275,000 and 300,000.

In the discussion of statistics on racial origin the confusion between former citizenship and ethnic identity as a major source of errors has already been indicated. The racial origin statistics prove unsatisfactory, especially for the Germans, nine-tenths of whom did not come directly to western Canada from Germany, but as the citizens of one of the east or southeast European countries, or even of the United States. Without thorough corrections these statistics should not be used to determine numerical strength.

The considerably lower figures of the racial origin statistics compared to those on the mother tongue for Manitoba and Saskatchewan, and thence for all of western Canada, have above all to be attributed to the fact that, among the total of 72,064 unquestionably German-speaking Mennonites of western Canada, only one-third actually acknowledged their German ethnic identity, while 47,282 reported their racial origin to be "Dutch" or "Russian." According to Bulletin XXXV of the 1931 Census, which classifies religious denominations by racial origin, there were:[1]

Table VIII.1

In:	Mennonites of Dutch descent	Mennonites of Russian descent
Manitoba	19,047	4,738
Saskatchewan	14,266	4,608
Alberta	2,060	1,675
British Columbia	761	127
Western Canada	36,134	11,148

When designating themselves as "Russian" they were confusing country of origin with ethnic identity. This mistake was also made by other German immigrants from areas outside Germany, and even more frequently by their descendants, when answering questions asked by census enumerators. There are stronger reasons for the designation of "Dutch." The Mennonites know that Menno Simons was Dutch and consequently the origin of their religious denomination is Dutch. They also know that in the seventeenth century, Dutch Mennonites immigrated into the lowlands of Danzig. Several of the recurring Mennonite family names such as Friesen, Klassen, Dyck, are Dutch Friesian, even though these Dutch Mennonites had become germanized by the time they continued their migration from the delta of the Vistula near Danzig to South Russia. They had adopted the Low German dialect of West Prussia. The sectarian separation of the Mennonites in Russia drove home to them constantly the history of their faith. But it also considerably weakened their sense of community with the rest of the German element, to the point where they began to feel in part a separate people who considered the Netherlands as their country of origin. After the World War, when they were persecuted as pacifists, many Mennonites in western Canada found it more opportune not to identify with the people who were the enemy in the World War but to declare themselves neutrally as "Dutch" in the 1921 Census. This was made easier by the obvious similarity between the English word "Dutch" and the German term "Deutsch." In the 1931 Census it largely remained that way.

Furthermore, about five-sixths of those who reported themselves as Austrian by origin in the Census should be considered Germans. This is justified not only by the fact that all the remaining nationalities of the Habsburg Monarchy are listed separately, but also by the statement that all "Austrians not otherwise specified" were counted predominantly in the farm districts which were settled by German farmers from the formerly Austrian regions of Galicia and Bukovina. Among these districts were Neudorf, Grayson, Edenwold, Longlaketon, South Qu'Appelle, the Yorkton District, Ituna, Pincher Creek, etc. as well as the larger cities (Winnipeg, Regina, Saskatoon and Edmonton) in all of which Germans from Galicia and Bukovina are to be found. Partly responsible for the designation "Austrian" is, of course, the absence of a notion of German ethnicity and the confusion with the country of birth. Partly responsible is also the assumption that the English would consider Austrians as more harmless and not view them as suspiciously as Germans. This partial camouflage in the first postwar census was repeated in the 1931 Census as well. The total number of persons who reported themselves as Austrian by origin in 1931 were:

Table VIII.2

In	Persons
Manitoba	8,858
Saskatchewan	17,061
Alberta	6,737
British Columbia	3,891
Yukon and Northwest Territories	16
Total	**36,563**

We know that a large number of Ukrainians from Galicia errone-ously reported themselves as Austrians, which is primarily revealed by the indication that 10 per cent of the Austrians belonged to the Orthodox Church.[2] In spite of this, about thirty thousand of the above-mentioned 36,563 Austrians by origin may be considered to be Germans.

Furthermore, we have a right to assume that besides those 11,148 Mennonites mentioned, an equal number of Lutheran and Catholic Germans from Russia reported their former Russian citizenship (country of origin) instead of their German ethnic identity. The majority of Germans from areas outside Germany, though, avoided this mistake. The 1931 Census recorded:

Table VIII.3

Russian by origin		mother tongue Russian
Manitoba	11,573	3,746
Saskatchewan	35,421	17,085
Alberta	16,381	7,344
British Columbia	10,398	9,052
Yukon and Northwest Territories	28	21
Total	74,801	37,248

Difference	37,553
Minus Mennonites of Russian origin	11,148
Remaining number	26,405

Even if we want to assume that among these 26,405 Russians whose mother tongue was not Russian there are several thousand genuine Russians who have already been assimilated linguistically, and divide the remaining number equally into Ukrainians and Germans from Russia who erroneously designated themselves as Russians, we may conclude without exaggerating that, apart from the aforementioned Mennonites, an additional twelve thousand Protestant and Catholic Germans from Russia were classified by the census as Russian by origin.

Finally, a number of Germans appear to be contained in the Hungarian, Romanian, Polish and Yugoslavian classifications due to the confusion of ethnic identity and former citizenship. An additional large number of descendants of ethnic German immigrants from the United States probably reported a British origin. I doubt then whether we exaggerate in estimating the number of those persons of German origin erroneously classified in the census as British, Hungarian, Romanian, Polish, and so on to number twelve thousand as well, although the census does not clearly establish that.

We add the following:

Table VIII.4

258,883	Germans by origin according to the census
47,282	German Mennonites classified as Dutch or Russian by origin
30,000	Austrians by origin
12,000	Catholic and Lutheran Germans from Russia who reported themselves as Russian by origin
12,000	persons of German origin erroneously reporting a British, Hungarian, Romanian, Yugoslavian, Polish origin etc.
c.360,000	persons altogether of German origin in western Canada

These Germans by origin are distributed among the individual provinces, according to our estimates, as follows:

Table VIII.5

In	persons of German origin
Manitoba	70,000
Saskatchewan	173,000
Alberta	95,000
British Columbia	21,800
Yukon and Northwest Territories	200
Total	**360,000**

Contrary to the figures of the 1931 Census, which reported only 258,883 Germans by origin in western Canada, our estimate of the number of persons of German origin according to the criteria of the Canadian census statistics is higher by about one hundred thousand.

Our estimates are confirmed by the recent publication of the racial origin statistics of the 1936 quinquennial Census of the three Prairie provinces.[3] The educational effort within the German ethnic group and perhaps also the clarification of the questions by the official census enumerators has considerably increased the number of those who acknowledged their German origin in the Prairie provinces in 1936 as compared to 1931, although there was no German immigration at all but rather emigration to British Columbia, eastern Canada and back to Germany instead. While in the 1936 Census the number of Germans by origin — and by the way also of Ukrainians by origin — came much closer to the actual number than in the 1931 Census (not to speak of the 1921 Census), the number of Austrians, Russians and Poles by origin declined in proportion. In Saskatchewan the number of Dutch by origin declined by 5,000 as compared to 1931, while in Manitoba it remained about the same. This means that the same number of Manitoba Mennonites — 19,047 in 1931 — still identify with their Dutch origin. No data on mother tongue are available from the 1936 quinquennial Census.

The data of the 1931 Census and 1936 Census with regard to the number of Germans and Austrians by origin in the three Prairie provinces are reproduced in Table 5 of the Appendix.

The actual proportion of western Canada's German ethnic stock, however, is lower after all. Racial origin is determined by descent through the father. Among German immigrants the proportion of males always predominated. Of the 271,372 persons with German as the mother tongue in 1931, 145,241 or 53.5 per cent were males, and 126,131 or 46.5 per cent were females. This indicates a low surplus of males and points to the character of German immigration as a family migration. Yet this male surplus results in a higher number of mixed marriages between German males and non-German females whose children are classified in the census as German by origin, than of mixed marriages between German females and non-German males whose children are classified according to the non-German descent of the father. Demonstrating the number of married German males are the following statistics on the "racial origin of mothers of children having German fathers."[4]

Table VIII.6

Births, Exclusive of Stillbirths, Classified According to the Racial Origin of Mothers of Children Having German Fathers

Racial Origin of mother	Prairie Provinces	total percentage	British Columbia	total percentage
German	5,947		149	
"Austrian" and "Dutch"[5]	72	80.8	5	52.2
British	870	11.7	97	32.9
French	103	1.4	7	2.4
Scandinavian	145	1.9	15	5.1
Slavic	216	2.9	14	4.7
Other	97	1.3	8	2.7
Total	7,450	100.0	295	100.0

According to these statistics, four-fifths of all German males in the Prairie provinces marry German females, but among the smaller German population of British Columbia only half of them do. There almost one-third of the German males marry females of British origin. The proportion of the German ethnic stock is therefore certainly lower than the figure of 360,000 Germans by origin, computed by us according to the criteria of the Canadian census, would suggest at first hand. Mixed marriages and the almost self-evident loss of German identity of children born to these explain to a large extent the difference between Germans by origin (360,000) and those with German mother tongue (275,000 to 300,000). This difference also shows the beginning of assimilation of the second and third generations due to the Anglo-American environment. Although it has begun only recently, it has already assumed tangible proportions. Anyway, this is the impression one gets on the spot.

The percentage of agriculturists attached to the soil is not only considerably higher among Germans than among the British (72.3 per cent versus 48 per cent), as shown in Table 4 of the Appendix, but it is also higher than among most of the remaining ethnic groups.[6] The areas colonized by German settlers are today among the most densely-populated farm districts, such as the Mennonite settlements in southern Manitoba and northern Saskatchewan, and most of the smaller German Lutheran and German Catholic settlements. More intensive cultivation—preference of mixed farming with emphasis on the raising of hogs and small livestock —and a high birthrate are typical of areas settled by Germans. Vital statistics prove Germans of western Canada to be extraordinarily healthy; marriages are entered into early, and the death rate is low. German families in rural areas have an average of four to six children although we cannot statistically verify this estimate. The German element thus grows much faster than the ruling Anglo-Canadian one and would catch up with it in the foreseeable future if cultural assimilation by the Anglo-Canadian environment were not to offset the advantage of the birthrate, and probably soon even reverse it.

2. Revitalization of German Ethnicity in Eastern Canada

The German community in eastern Canada has by now nearly become a part of history. In the nineteenth century the German-Canadian farmer and craftsman clung to his German language and mores, if at all, not out of a live consciousness of German identity but due to the staying power of the inherited customs and for religious reasons. Only very few tried to rise socially, which would have led them mostly to the anglophone upper class. The stream of the educated emigrants from Germany, who after 1848 went to the United States where they became leaders of the German community, passed by the Canadian provinces with the result that Canada's Germans always lacked intellectual leaders within their ranks. The German element was therefore bound to be absorbed by the culturally dominant English element, as long as its ethnic consciousness was not aroused by the new glamour of the German reputation after 1871. When towards the end of the nineteenth century the question of nationality, which was everywhere in the air, also became increasingly relevant to Canada, and in 1890 led to far-reaching changes in school legislation in favor of English as a language of instruction, the Germans of eastern Canada became conscious of their identity as an ethnic minority only in Waterloo County, and here and there in Perth, Grey, Bruce and Renfrew. Yet even here they did not take up the challenge to fight for cultural autonomy. The World War, finally, appeared to have dealt the death blow to the desire of the German element in eastern Canada to survive as an organized ethnic community with a press, clubs and private schools of its own.

It would therefore be wrong to assume that even as far back as the turn of the century, a quarter million eastern Canadians had retained a German identity, as the data on racial origin suggest in the 1901 Census:

Table VIII.7

In	Germans by origin
Ontario	203,319
Ouebec	6,923
Nova Scotia	41,020
New Brunswick	3,816
Prince Edward Island	709
Eastern Canada	255,787

Since the census takers have always asked for the name of a European country, never Canada or the United States, as the country of origin, the data thus collected do not provide us with conclusive evidence about the true identity of the individual. Many thus declared themselves "German by origin," simply taking their name as a cue, although their old family tradition may have been completely anglicized. In the three Maritime provinces of Nova Scotia, New Brunswick and Prince Edward Island, there were at that time hardly any ethnic Germans left in our sense of the word, i.e., ethnic Germans retaining German as a mother tongue and German cultural aspirations. In the

Province of Quebec there were perhaps still three thousand to four thousand of them, including up to two thousand German businessmen and craftsmen in Montreal who had immigrated from Germany. In the Province of Ontario an estimated 120,000 to 150,000 Germans may have retained their ethnic identity. They lived in the cities of Toronto, Hamilton, London and in the almost exclusively German twin towns of Berlin and Waterloo; primarily, however, they lived in the relatively closed colonies of farmers scattered over wide parts of the province, especially in Waterloo, Perth, Wellington, Bruce and Grey Counties in the southwest of the province, as well as in Renfrew at the upper Ottawa.

In the meantime a new generation has grown up. In the wake of the violent destruction of the German press and the closure of the German private schools under the impact of systematic British war propaganda, this generation often abandoned their German heritage more hastily than the natural course of assimilation would probably have accomplished. Among the descendants of those Germans who came with the great nineteenth-century tide of migration to Ontario, perhaps sixty thousand to seventy thousand might be characterized today as ethnic Germans in the sense that, by cultivating their German dialect in the home besides the English used for business and school, they want to pass on their German traditions to future generations as well. These ethnic Germans are to be found primarily among the members of the religious communities of specifically German origin, such as the Mennonites and Lutherans, but also among the descendants of closed German Catholic colonies. Here, as everywhere, faith and ethnic tradition have reinforced each other.

Even this group should actually be designated as no more than potentially ethnic German. It would probably soon have become assimilated as well, had not over twenty thousand of the more than seventy thousand immigrants of German descent who came to Canada between 1923 and 1930, found their new homes in the East. The great majority of the postwar immigrants went to Manitoba, Saskatchewan and Alberta where the opportunities for wheat growing seemed unlimited, particularly in the boom years 1925-1929. Only about thirteen thousand German immigrants gave eastern Canada in advance as their destination, according to Canadian statistics. The generous, but in the final analysis unscrupulous, promotion of western Canada by the two large Canadian railway companies was bound to bring the severest disappointment to innumerable immigrants. Particularly since 1929, many Germans have therefore turned their backs on western Canada. Having become completely destitute, they travelled eastward and, hoping to be able to return to Europe, frequently ended up as farmhands and craftsmen in the villages and towns of the East, especially Montreal and Toronto. Such re-migrants from the West, who have started again from scratch under immensely difficult circumstances, can be found everywhere in the East.

We estimate for eastern Canada therefore, or rather for the Province of Ontario and the city of Montreal, a total of eighty thousand to ninety thousand ethnic Germans, i.e., sixty thousand to seventy thousand prewar residents, plus twenty thousand postwar immigrants.

This is also in agreement with the census data on the number of those still using German as a mother tongue, most of them probably speaking it besides English as the language of everyday life. For 1931, their numbers were:

Table VIII.8

Ontario	82,089
Greater Montreal	6,068
the rest of the Province of Quebec	1,227
the three Maritime provinces	1,255
Total	**90,639**

Compared to these figures, the 'German by origin' statistics are meaningless, as we noted above. However, the increase between 1921, when as a result of the war psychosis a mere 164,217 persons in eastern Canada acknowledged their German descent, and 1931, when again 214,661 were counted in the same area, is interesting. Not counting the twenty thousand new immigrants, about thirty thousand persons appear to have recovered a certain pride in their German descent.

The 1931 Census data on birthplace reveal the consistently low proportion of Canadian Germans born in Germany:

Table VIII.9

Ontario	10,662
Greater Montreal	2,254
Province of Quebec	535
Maritime Provinces	531
Total	**13,982**

According to Canadian statistics, 53 per cent of Canadian immigrants born in Germany were still German citizens in 1931. By now the five-year waiting period for naturalization in Canada has passed for the immigrants of the years 1926-1929. On the other hand, the economic difficulties in Canada and, above all, the impact of the National Socialist revolution in Germany, may have considerably reduced the urge to give up German citizenship at the earliest possible moment, even though its renunciation would be necessary for the acquisition of a homestead as well as for applying for a better job. Thus we are estimating about five thousand of the 13,982 born in Germany still to be German citizens.

The German immigrants of the postwar years did not come in large closed groups to Canada, but individually and at their own risk. The only exceptions were the twenty thousand German Mennonite refugees whose emigration from Soviet Russia to Canada after 1923 was organized by a central agency, the Mennonite Immigration Board in Rosthern, Saskatchewan, under the direction of their highly deserving elder (bishop), David Toews. About two thousand to 2,300 of these are living in Ontario today. Following the precedent of their forebears, the German postwar immigrants from all parts of Europe could be found in urban and rural areas primarily in places where German colonies already existed from earlier times. The German-Canadian clergy of all denominations, acting as agents of the railway companies, helped to make sure that this would happen. They directed most of the German immigrants who came from eastern and southeastern Europe.

In the long run this proved to be quite advantageous for the revitalization of the German community, intimidated by the ordeals they had suffered during the war. There was no better way to reawaken the aspirations for an ethnic German cultural self-assertion than by the presence of young Germans from Europe among them. The latter, having become sensitive to ethnic questions as a result of the consequences of the collapse of the Central Powers, appeared to the intimidated German Canadians almost as their own conscience. At first, however, it made the gulf between the old and the new element even more manifest. The feelings of certain of the old-time settlers were of affection and nostalgia towards their ancestral homeland, precisely because of their bitter wartime experiences. They despised the type of greedy expatriate who was unfortunately no exception among the postwar immigrants from Germany. With the neo-nationalististic immigrants, on the other hand, who had been psychologically transformed by the war and tended early to sympathize with National Socialism, they felt they had little in common. Unfortunately the newcomers were frequently exploited and were ridiculed as "greenhorns" while claiming to know more about everything, so that it was difficult to develop mutual understanding and common goals between the two groups. The new arrivals, due to their experience at the front, did indeed have a better understanding of the commonality of fate among all the many German ethnic groups in the world. Yet they had no influence with the old-established Germans, due to their sheer inability to build for themselves a free and secure existence in the country during the years of severe economic crisis. The two groups have come closer together only in the most recent past.

The postwar immigrants had to find out for themselves that it had become very difficult to gain a footing even in Ontario. Ontario's relatively high degree of industrialization guarantees a good local market to a highly developed agriculture whose most important branches today are no longer grain growing, but dairying and cattle ranching, fruit and vegetable cultivation and, in particularly favorable spots, even vineyards. Despite a significant drop in prices, therefore, there is still a certain stability in the marketplace. Yet in spite of the best farming experience, the immigrant arriving with only limited means is bound to find the beginning much more difficult in such a highly developed agricultural economy, than on the prairies with its comparatively simple wheat-growing economy. Many a postwar German immigrant who rented or purchased a farm from his savings therefore unfortunately was forced to give up his land in order to make his living as an industrial worker in the city, with no hope of putting something aside for himself in the foreseeable future.

The more than two thousand Mennonites who immigrated to Ontario from the Ukraine and the Crimea between 1923 and 1927 appear to have been relatively the most successful. The largest group of more than one thousand have settled near Kingsville and Leamington in Essex County. Besides fruit and vegetables, they grow tobacco, which is not without irony, since smoking is taboo in their community. Five hundred have settled in the area around the twin towns of Berlin (Kitchener)-Waterloo which they supply with vegetables, tomatoes, cucumbers, etc., and the same number near Vineland at Lake Ontario in the vicinity of St. Catherines not far from Niagara Falls, where they grow grapes in accordance with tradition. In both areas, they have settled on historic ground, where in 1800 (Berlin) or even earlier in 1786 (Vineland) the first Pennsylvania-German Mennonites wrested their farms from the virgin forest. The descendants of the latter, by now strongly anglicized but still adhering to the Mennonite faith, helped their coreligionists who were seeking refuge from Soviet Russia to acquire their own farms or, at least, to find work as farmhands. Even among these Mennonites there are a few who, as wealthy landowners in Russia, had owned automobiles long before the war, but whose circumstances have now been reduced so that they have become ordinary industrial workers. Despite the economic difficulties in Canada, and the lingering homesickness of these Mennonites for South Russia, the new immigrants would happily adopt Ontario as their new home after their dreadful experiences under the Soviets, were it not for their fears that their descendants would forfeit their German identity.

The apprehensions about the prospects of preserving their German heritage is bound to be a matter of some importance to the postwar German ethnic groups from Germany and from other countries. It may indeed worry them more than their momentary economic distress. What was possible for the German ethnic groups in eastern Europe (for instance the Mennonites in South Russia), namely to create their own first-class German school system, appears to be impossible in Ontario. The need for a private German school and adult education system (touring libraries, films, travelling theatres, lectures) is recognized among all Germans in Canada today. The awareness of how closely the destiny of their ethnic heritage is tied up with the High German language is demonstrated by the Mennonites, who are coming to the conclusion that they cannot retain High German as their literary and church language and their West Prussian dialect of Low German, as well as the English language. A large number of families are therefore teaching their children High German instead of the cherished old Low German.

In the prewar years it was primarily the German clergy who in real self-sacrifice conducted German private classes in their various congregations in Ontario. It appears that in the future, organizations which are primarily secular and are beginning to recognize their cultural responsibilities more clearly, will have to take charge of German instruction. This also becomes necessary because young bilingual clergy (including Catholics, Lutherans, preachers of the Evangelical Association, etc.) who are being sent to serve in German-Canadian congregations, now are frequently no longer willing to do so. Born in the United States or Canada and trained in a theological college, they often no longer appreciate the values of an ethnic tradition. At best, they comply with the desire of the older members of the congregation for German services, but dispense with German lessons to the children, thereby facilitating anglicization. The Canada Synod for instance, which is the Ontario branch of the United Lutheran Church of North America, and whose clergy have been a bulwark of German culture to the older generation, has, under the influence of the younger generation, changed over to English as conference language on their annual synods of ministers, without being able to justify such a change on the basis of the language spoken in the congregations.

The requirement that children take private lessons in German, and that people come together to assist each other when sickness or death strikes, have therefore frequently been the reason for the founding of new German clubs. A number of local clubs have assumed responsibility for these two tasks. Such local clubs cannot, of course, meet the larger cultural challenges which the German community of Ontario faces.

A decisive development for Ontario's German community was the first German Day celebration of Ontario held on September 1-3, 1934, in Toronto and attended by over 3,000 ethnic Germans. Following the precedent of the German Days in the three Prairie provinces, where they have become increasingly impressive avowals of the German cause, the young and active Franz Straubinger from Straubing, Germany, organized the first large rally of Ontario-Germans, which was succeeded by German Day rallies held in Kitchener in the following years. The most important accomplishment in this context was the foundation of a so-called *Deutsche Arbeitsgemeinschaft von Ontario* (German Coordinating Committee of Ontario). The large number of clubs which have joined it provide a certain measure of the composition and local distribution of the German element:

> From Toronto:
> The *Deutscher Verein Harmonie* (founded in 1921, since 1933 in an impressive new building, with departments for singing, sports, theatre, women's group, schools, and culture); The *Deutscher Kulturverband* (German school, singing, theatre and women's group); the *Deutsche Gesellschaft*; the local group of the *Deutscher Bund*; the *Deutsch-Katholischer Verein*(founded in 1929 by Father Stroh, sports department and choir); the *Deutsch-Lutherische Gemeinde* (since 1932, Pastor Lewerenz); the local group of the *Stahlhelm*.
>
> From Kitchener-Waterloo: The *Siebenbürger Sachsen und Schwaben Krankenunterstützungsverein* (since 1928); the *Deutsch-Schwäbischer Krankenunterstützungsverein* (which split off from the first one, since 1931); the *Concordia Club* with two theatre clubs; the local group

of the *Deutscher Bund*.

From Ottawa: The *Liederkranz* and the *Deutscher Club*.

From Hamilton: The *Verein Deutsches Heim* (since 1929; German school and mixed choir).

From London: The *Deutsch-kanadischer Verein* (since 1933, German school, over one hundred members).

From Woodstock: The *Deutscher Club* (since February 1934).

From Windsor: The *Deutscher Verein Teutonia*[7] and the *Erster Siebenbürger Sachsen Krankenunterstützungsverein*.

From Kingsville: The *Deutscher Verein Frohsinn*[8] (since 1931, singing club, sixty members).

In Quebec, according to the 1931 Census, close to one thousand persons speak the German language at the upper Ottawa in Labelle and Pontiac Counties. Here a few tracts of land had been opened up by German farmers, beginning in the 1860s, in conjunction with the development of German colonies on the opposite bank of the Ottawa in Renfrew County (Ontario). A more active German life developed only in the metropolis of Montreal, today the largest city in all of Canada.

From the early nineteenth century, Montreal—at some distance behind New York—has been the most important gateway for European immigration to North America, a gateway not only for Canada, but above all for the American Midwest. No wonder a German colony developed early in the city, and that as early as the spring of 1835 a German aid society came into existence for the protection and support of German immigrants in need. The immediate cause for the foundation of this German Society, or *Deutsche Gesellschaft*, was the arrival of several hundred German immigrants who had just been shipwrecked. To this day, the *Deutsche Gesellschaft* has been working around the clock. At all times distress and misery have been the companions of German immigration. The voluntary charity of the German craftsmen and businessmen in Montreal has, therefore, always found its field of action until the most recent times, when the society has been supporting unemployed postwar German immigrants in Montreal with daily meals, the collection of clothes, etc.

Before the outbreak of the war about two thousand Germans lived in Montreal. They have had their own German Lutheran congregation (St. John's) since 1853, and organized their social life in the *Deutscher*

Verein Teutonia (since 1882) and the *Deutscher Verein Harmonia* (since 1911). To the *Harmonia* belonged the Germans of the poorer classes, while the educated and wealthier ones gathered in the *Teutonia*. Even today this old social distinction is still quite apparent. An important factor in the social life of the German community of Montreal has been the presence of the German Consul General, who had been the only German professional diplomat in Canada until shortly before the World War, when the first professional consul was appointed for Winnipeg.

After the war the composition of the German community in Montreal became much more colorful and diverse. Numerically it increased to more than six thousand persons, of whom, according to the 1931 Census, about 2,250 were born in Germany, while the majority of the German postwar immigrants are from Banat, Transylvania and Hungary. When the onset of the Depression in 1929 resulted in large-scale unemployment in western Canada, Montreal, as Canada's largest port of transshipment for grain overseas, was also very severely economically affected by export difficulties. To the many postwar German immigrants who at that time turned their backs on western Canada, the prospects for employment still appeared relatively better in a city of a million people. Therefore, Montreal received a particularly high percentage of the re-migrants from the West.

The immigrants from Germany, mostly clerks and highly-skilled workers, are scattered over the entire city, with perhaps some concentration in the southern suburb of Verdun on the St. Lawrence. On the other hand, the German immigrants from southeastern Europe who earn their living as craftsmen, or predominantly even as unskilled workers, live in the poor residential sector east of St. Laurent between Sherbrooke and Duluth Streets, or, to be exact, between St. Dominique, Colonial, De Bullion Streets and City Hall. Banat Swabians, who immigrated between 1928 and 1930, form the largest group among them. They are mostly young people in their early thirties who came over with very few resources. It is worth noting that most of the men speak German, Hungarian and Romanian, while most of the women can only speak German.

Due to the large number of German immigrants from Banat and Hungary, the majority of Montreal's German population is Catholic today. A flourishing German Catholic parish has developed under Father Debelt. The Lutherans have three congregations: St. John's (Pastor Lamartine), St. Paul's (Pastor D. Klaehn, since 1931) and Christ congregation (Pastor Mueller). Half of the members of the latter congregation are immigrants from the wholly Lutheran village of Liebling in Banat, while most of the rest are from Transylvania. The pastor preaches in Verdun to a second congregation of immigrants from Germany.

Today there are, besides the *Harmonia* (300 members), the *Teutonia* (50 members) and the *Deutsche Gesellschaft*, the *Deutsch-Schwäbischer Verein* (120 members from Banat) founded in 1929, the *Verein der Deutsch-Ungarn* (80-100 members) which split off from the latter in 1931, the *Edelweissverein der Deutsch-Schweizer* and the *Sportklub Kickers* (50 members) which was founded in 1932 as a branch of the socialist-oriented *Deutscher Arbeiter- und Farmerverband von Kanada*, but purged its Red members in 1933. All these clubs enjoy a very active life today. They agree on the common objective of deliberately cultivating German traditions.

3. Language Loyalty and the Question of German-Language Instruction

Numerous newspapers and the first signs of an indigenous literature augur well for the cultural maturity of the western Canadian Germans. The likelihood that the next generation may no longer be able to read German newspapers and German-language literature is nonetheless great, and perhaps inevitable. The unilingual English school system by which Canadian authorities deliberately hasten assimilation, seriously endangers the retention of the German ethnic heritage.

Even though the significance of the school vis-à-vis the influence of the family should not be overrated in a rural population, the unilingual English public school and the compulsory bilingualism of German-speaking youth raises the specter of a wedge being driven between parents and children linguistically, intellectually and psychologically. It loosens the natural bonds of family unity which alone are capable of resisting the influences of the school. Even in the rural districts the English-language public school, by undermining the family, is thus the most effective means of assimilation.

Legislation in matters of education is the preserve of the Canadian provinces, not of the federal government. This was written into the British North America Act of 1867 because full cultural autonomy had to be granted to the French Canadians in the Province of Quebec. The school question therefore developed differently in the various provinces of western Canada. There is, however, uniformity in the administration of schools. They are strongly decentralized. Each school is under the authority of its own school board. For the establishment of a rural school district, three persons have to be elected as trustees, who form the school board. They must be literate, and are elected for three years. In villages and towns, due to the larger population, the school board has more than three members, who are elected for two-year terms. Each school board makes its own decisions regarding school expenditures, hires its teachers and also has a limited influence on the way the school is run.

Rural schools all over western Canada even have the same external appearance. They are all one-room schools. Else Giese gives the following description:[9]

> The children ride to school on reliable horses, who instinctively know the way to school as they make this trip year after year, sometimes one, sometimes two or three children per horse. In winter they often sit on a horse-drawn wagon, which is heated by a small stove. Near every school building there is a horse barn where the horses are kept during classes. As the children have to stay in school at noontime, they bring their simple lunches in a dish. Each school makes arrangements, often in a very primitive fashion, for pupils to have lunch.

Strong decentralization of administration following the English model, allows the farmers at least a limited influence on the school in their district. It is therefore a thorn in the side of Anglo-Canadian nationalists. They aim at a more centralized school administration which would take away from local school boards the right to select their teachers.

Until the World War, as long as western Canada was still clearly in the pioneer stage, non-British immigrants had no reason to be dissatisfied with legislation regulating school education, and even less with the actual conditions under which the schools operated.

In Manitoba it was possible, according to the School Act of 1897, to establish bilingual public schools until 1916. This legislation has its own history. Until 1890 the so-called separate school had been the rule in Manitoba. It was a state-supported, church-supervised denominational public school, modelled according to the French-Canadian Catholic pattern of the Province of Quebec, because initially Catholic French Canadians also played a special role in Manitoba. In 1890, however, the new Liberal provincial government in Manitoba replaced these denominationally-oriented separate schools with a system of non-sectarian public schools such as existed in anglophone Protestant Ontario. The Catholic Church thereupon induced the Conservative federal government in Ottawa to exert pressure on Manitoba and to make the provincial government withdraw its new legislation. The school conflict in Manitoba touched on all the controversies existing in Canada, those between Catholics and Protestants, francophones and anglophones, Conservatives and Liberals, federal and provincial governments. As a result, the federal election campaign in 1896 was fought over this one issue in the entire country. Under the slogan 'No coercion for Manitoba,' it was won by the Liberals, and introduced the fifteen-year term of the Laurier cabinet (1896-1911). As a French Canadian, the new Liberal Prime Minister Wilfrid Laurier was quickly able to agree on a compromise with the provincial government of Manitoba, which resulted in the School Act of 1897. The suspension of the separate school and the limitation of religious instruction to the last half-hour of the school day was confirmed. The wishes of the francophones, however, were met to the extent that in all school districts with a Catholic majority, only Catholic teachers were to be hired and French could be retained as a language of instruction as far as possible. The School Act of 1897 regulated this with the provision that in all schools where ten or more students speak French or any language other than English as their native language, this language would be granted equal status as language of instruction besides English.[10] Based on this, not only French Canadians, but also Germans, Ukrainians and Poles established bilingual schools in Manitoba until the beginning of the World War.

According to the Department of Education, German bilingual schools were judged to be the best. Shortly before they were abolished, there were sixty-one German school districts with seventy-three teachers and 2,814 students, according to a report of February 1, 1916.[11] In the first school years, German was the language of instruction and English was taught as a subject. In the later years, English became the language of instruction and German was confined to language lessons and religious instruction. According to the above-mentioned departmental report, the results were quite encouraging. It was an advantage that the bilingual teacher was always a member of the respective German, French, Ukrainian or Polish ethnic group, and so was able to establish a better rapport with the children than the young female anglophone teacher who was usually in charge of a rural school in western Canada. To procure such bilingual German and English-speaking teachers was quite difficult in the early years of colonization when a new generation had not yet graduated. This explains why the bilingual school existed among the Mennonites who had been resident since 1874, but rarely among the German Lutheran settlements that had been established around the turn of the century in Manitoba. Up to that time the Mennonites were the only group to produce a supply of bilingual teachers from within their own ranks. For this purpose they had founded two teacher training institutes, one in 1891 in Gretna by the Bergthaler congregation which survives until this day, the other in 1907 by the Sommerfelders in Altona. The latter burned down in 1924 and was never rebuilt. In the establishment of a viable bilingual school system for all of Canada's German groups, the accomplishments of the Mennonites were exemplary, and were fully acknowledged by Canadian authorities and by experts.

The establishment of public bilingual schools among the Mennonites is all the more worth noting, since in 1873 in Manitoba they had been granted the privilege of educating their children in independent private schools. For certain groups of Mennonites emigrating from South Russia, recognition of the right to their own school system had been the most important prerequisite for choosing Manitoba instead of, perhaps, Kansas or Nebraska as their new homeland.[12]

The Mennonites in Manitoba admittedly took less time setting up schools than any other ethnic group in western Canada, including British settlers. The children learned to read and write, to do math and to sing in German. The German Bible formed their main reading material.[13]

Only the two most conservative Mennonite religious groups, the Old Colony and the Sommerfelders, have as a matter of principle retained the purely private school system, which is entirely under the supervision of the elders of these Mennonite congregations. These two combined constituted more than half of the Mennonites in southern Manitoba.

The less conservative Mennonites attempted as early as the 1880s, when the denominational, church-supervised school was still the rule, to open their first eight public schools. They thereby secured government subsidies for themselves, especially important in the first years of struggle, without, however, having to make concessions regarding the internal structure of the schools. From 1891 to 1903, Professor H.H. Ewert, (who was in charge of the Collegiate Institute in Gretna until his death in 1934), successfully promoted the establishment of public

schools among the Mennonites in his official capacity as a school inspector, first for the denominational separate schools, and after 1897 for
the bilingual schools. In 1891 there were eight, in 1893 twenty, and
around 1900 as many as forty, public schools in Mennonite settlements.[14] Altogether in 1897 there were fifty German-English schools
in Manitoba based on the Act of 1897, forty-nine among the Mennonites and one in the German Lutheran settlement of Hiebert. These
schools were located in the following communities and farm districts:[15]

> Rhineland Municipality:
> Strassburg, Houston, Halbstadt, Edenthal, Edenburg,
> Altona, Kleinstadt, Langevin, Amsterdam, Hoffnungsthal,
> Rosenfeld, Weidfeld, Steinfeld, St. Peter, Plum
> Coulée, Neu-Kronsthal (x), Grossweide, Grünfarm,
> Schantzenfeld, Kronsthal, Blumenfeld.
> Stanley Municipality:
> Winkler, Edward, Rosenbach, Burwalde, Rosewell,
> Queen Centre, Blumstein, Zion, Valleyfield, Wakeham.
> Morris Municipality:
> Whitehaven, Lowe Farm, Rosenhof (x), Rosenort (x),
> Leabank, Poersch, Brunkild, Hiebert (Lutheran).
> Hanover Municipality:
> Steinbach (x), Blumenort (x), Blumenhof (x),
> Neuanlage (x), Grünland (x), Hochstadt (x), Grünfeld (x),
> Glen Cross.

When the raising of the English flag became mandatory in 1907
for all public schools, which the Mennonites rejected as a military
gesture, a number of congregations began to revert to private schools
until the government made some concessions in the question of flag
raising.[16] By 1912 the number of German-English public schools had
risen again to sixty, and by the beginning of the war they existed, as
mentioned before, in sixty-one school districts, with seventy-three
teachers and 2,814 students.

Just as the Old Colony and the Sommerfelders contented themselves with their private schools, so the few German Lutheran congregations of the province tended to develop denominational private
schools of the type to be found especially in Saskatchewan and Alberta.
Some German Lutheran farm districts also set up public bilingual
schools which, however, were short of teachers. Some were satisfied
with the unilingual English school, that could do little harm to their
ethnic heritage in the period before the World War, when school attendance was very irregular anyway in the pioneer stage of the settlements.

In contrast to Manitoba, bilingual schools for minority groups never existed in the two provinces of Saskatchewan and Alberta, both of which were created in 1905. Soon after their creation, when their provincial legislatures debated school legislation, the domestic political situation in the Dominion enabled Catholic French Canadians to regain the right to set up denominational separate schools which had been denied them in Manitoba in 1897. In return for this, and for the privilege of being allowed to offer instruction in French at the primary level in school districts with a francophone majority they gave up the bilingual school. Due to their powerful position in the Province of Quebec, attention would have been paid to francophone demands for bilingual education in the West as well. In 1905, however, the bilingual school was no longer acceptable to the anglophone majority, when the large immigration from all parts of eastern and southeastern Europe had begun.

In spite of this, school conditions were satisfactory for the German-speaking population in Saskatchewan and Alberta, because private schools could be set up. The English principles—that public school attendance is compulsory only as the parents wish it, and that children do not have to attend public schools if the parents make alternate arrangements for satisfactory education—had been adopted in the new school legislation. It would allow religious sects such as Russian Doukhobors and German Mennonites, who in Manitoba had school privileges which were not recognized in Saskatchewan and Alberta, the establishment of their own schools.[17] Large numbers of private schools were founded particularly by German Mennonites and Lutherans, but also by Catholics.[18]

The desire to set up schools for their children was one of the first priorities of German immigrants, even if they had little schooling themselves. They barely had roofs over their heads when regular lessons were started. Looking back, the reporter of a Catholic colony in Saskatchewan, settled primarily by Germans from Russia, writes of these days. (The bad grammar and spelling that is characteristic of many of these community reporters, incidentally, cannot be rendered into English.)

> The majority of these people have shown great eagerness to have their children educated and taught, have first and foremost cared to set up schools, formed school districts, wherever possible hired good teachers, sent their children to school in stormy and cold weather, often drove them themselves, put them into higher grades, so that today we have hired students from our own dis-

trict as well-trained teachers who give German instruction.

As soon as the German clergyman arrived in the newly-formed farm district, he gathered together the children for reading, writing and religious instruction.[19] In numerous settlements and with the backing of their churches, clergymen gradually established fully-equipped private schools with classes five days a week. Lutherans of the Missouri Synod, especially, made efforts to establish private parochial schools, such as Christian Day Schools. Before the war, the Synod made it a duty for all its missionaries to set up such private schools in newly-founded congregations. Thus, in Alberta, private schools supported by the Missouri Synod were opened in Stony Plain, Edmonton, Beaver Hills, Wetaskiwin, Didsbury, Calgary, Pincher Creek and a few other places.[20] The other Lutheran synods also promoted the establishment of private schools among their congregations. Sometimes trained teachers, sometimes theology students, sometimes the missionaries themselves were in charge of these schools. They enjoyed a peaceful life and were not bothered by the government.

German Catholics had the opportunity of setting up separate schools supported by the public school tax. Only Catholics turned out to be actually eligible to set up these separate schools, since only the minority of ratepayers in any district, whether Protestant or Catholic, could apply for them. Yet since everyone was considered Protestant who was not Catholic, there were virtually no Protestant minorities anywhere.[21] In 1928 there were only twenty-three Catholic and eight Protestant separate schools in the whole of Saskatchewan.[22]

Since the government-supported separate school had to put up with a certain amount of supervision by the Department of Education, German Catholics tended to prefer more expensive but fully autonomous private schools to separate schools, as for example in St. Peter's colony in Bruno, Muenster, Marysburg, Lake Lenore, Leofeld and other places.

The parents' financial ability, of course, limited the establishment of private schools. Since no one who wanted to send his child to a private school was exempted from the general school taxes for that reason, such an expensive school could only be opened if no people speaking other languages lived in the farm district, thus making the maintenance of a public school superfluous. It also needed the support of the respective church.

Private schools were virtually free to determine their curriculum. Besides sufficient instruction in the German language and in religion, fairly extensive English-language instruction was provided everywhere as well, except among the strictly conservative Mennonite groups. German settlers insisted on this for economic reasons. Where no private schools were set up, i.e., especially in areas where Germans were not the only settlers in the school district and where therefore a public school had been opened and the maintenance of an additional private school was too costly, German children had to attend the unilingual English public school even before the war. In both provinces, as earlier in the Northwest Territories (which was their name before 1905), instruction in the mother tongue was permitted only twice weekly for half an hour, if the majority of members of the school board demanded it. Attempts were made to circumvent even this small concession by withholding official approval for German schoolbooks.

In spite of this, there was barely any danger of losing one's German identity through the schools before the war. Until 1914, Saskatchewan and Alberta were still too sparsely settled for such statutes to be enforced. To begin with, there were barely any English-speaking teachers for non-British farm districts, since there was a general shortage of teachers and those few preferred to teach in Anglo-Canadian farm districts. Above all, however, school was usually held only during the few summer months and, even if English was the main subject, this foreign language tended to be forgotten again by non-British children during the many school-free months.[23] In those days the school had barely any impact compared to the overwhelming influence of the home. This also holds true for British Columbia where, by the way, school legislation never made any concessions to non-British immigrants.

When the World War began, western Canada was just about to leave the pioneer stage behind. In the rural districts there was the first tangible progress in the establishment of schools and in school attendance. At this point, the World War and the national passions it aroused provided Anglo-Canadians with the welcome opportunity to strike the decisive blow in the school question not only against the German element, but also against all other non-British ethnic groups, by forcing the unilingual English public school on them.

In Manitoba the public bilingual schools were abolished in 1916 and all German private schools, especially the numerous Mennonite schools, were prohibited. Section 258 of the School Act of 1897, providing for bilingualism, was rescinded and even the Mennonite privilege was contested. The war sentiment against anything German made it impossible for settlers of German descent to put up political resistance to the imposition of the English public school. The Mennonites, however, challenged the new laws of 1916 on the basis of the privilege granted to them in writing in 1873, and took the matter as far as the highest court of law of the British Empire, the Judicial Committee of the Privy Council in London. Its verdict of July 30, 1930, concurring with the decisions of the lower courts, definitively rejected their claims.[24] The verdict was based on the words "as provided by law" which the Dominion Government in Ottawa had inserted after the word "schools" in the text of the privilege (compare the text in Chapter VIII, footnote 12) when it ratified the agreement of the provincial government of Manitoba by an Order-in-Council of August 13, 1873. In opposition to the verdicts of the Canadian and British high courts, the Mennonites and many others, including the French-Canadian Curé Sabourin,[25] argue that this insertion was merely supposed to mean that the Dominion Government had no intention of ever encroaching on this right granted by the Government of Manitoba. The decisions of the courts, while endorsing a school policy serving the purpose of assimilation, appeared from a strictly legal point of view to be miscarriages of justice.

Many Mennonites and other German Canadians had no choice but to put up with the enforced closing of their German private schools and the opening of English public schools. A large number of the conservative Old Colony and Sommerfelders, however, resisted the closing of their private schools, and refused to send their children to the newly set up public schools. The government had to appoint its own school boards for the new schools because the Mennonites refused to serve. As conscientious objectors, they especially resented the fact that since 1918 the government had sent a number of discharged soldiers as teachers to their villages. They continued to operate their prohibited private schools, and some public schools had hardly any children. Only heavy fines gradually broke their resistance. Even this only partially succeeded. The persecutions and violations of their rights and religious convictions embittered the Mennonites to the extent that a large number of the Old Colony and Sommerfelders saw emigration to Mexico (1922) and Paraguay (1926) as their only way out (see Chapter V). In Canada they had been very successful economically. The threat to their religious principles and their ethnic identity, however, made them once again take upon themselves all the hardships and uncertainties of emigration.

In Saskatchewan and Alberta as in Manitoba, the general agitation and political paralysis of immigrants from Central Europe during the war was utilized to launch a systematic attack against private schools in German and other non-British settlements. In contrast to Manitoba, bilingual public schools, which could have been dissolved, did not even exist here. The strike against the private schools came with the sudden demand that their curricula be coordinated with those of the public schools. This could be accomplished simply by an Order-in-Council, since nothing was said in the School Act about the form of the private school. An additional requirement was the establishment of an English public school in all school districts where hitherto only a German private school had existed. This was to make financial support of the private school even more difficult, if not entirely impossible. The adjustment of the curriculum to that of the public school, however, removed any incentive for assuming the costs of a private school. With very few exceptions, such as some German Catholic parishes of St. Peter's colony, all German private schools in Saskatchewan and Alberta eventually folded.

One of the most vociferous spokesmen in the struggle for unilingual English schools and against the cultural autonomy of the non-British population was public school teacher J.T.M. Anderson, who was to become Premier of Saskatchewan from 1929 to 1934. His book *The Education of the New Canadian* which appeared towards the end of the war, contained many unjustified attacks against German private schools supported by church congregations and against their teachers.[26] There he plainly stated his conviction that it was the primary objective of the public school to attempt to deprive non-British immigrants of their ethnic identity. Robert England, too, views the public school as the chief means of eliminating non-British ethnicity. In several studies, in which he discussed the problem of assimilation from the Anglo-Canadian perspective, he shows no overt partiality, but rather acknowledges repeatedly the accomplishments of non-British immigrants in the opening of western Canada. His book *The Central European Immigrant* (1929) aims at convincing his fellow countrymen of the great importance of rural schools in particular for a successful policy of assimilation. The thesis of his whole book is summed up in his statement that "because the non-English settler is bound by the custom and habit of Old Country life, we must start our work with the children."[27] The report of a rural school teacher about his teaching experience at the school of a German farm district in southern Saskatchewan proves that the Anglo-Canadian teacher has fully grasped the role assigned to him:[28]

> In a district like this, children would naturally tend to relapse
> into German out of school hours, or when in the play-field, so
> I had to make it a point of honour with them to practice speaking
> English as much as they possibly could, and in this the co-operation
> of the senior pupils was invaluable. . . . In fact, among the new
> generation of "new Canadians" that is springing up, the teacher
> becomes veritably an ambassador of Empire. He has to help with
> the "acclimatization" . . .

German Canadians were deceiving themselves when they began to
believe that after the emotions roused by the war had abated, the prewar
state of affairs with regard to the school question would be restored.
In reality, the World War had only provided the opportunity of accelerating a development in school policy which would have taken place
anyway after the passing of the pioneer stage. The cultural offensive
against the non-British population was thus in no way abandoned, but
rather intensified.

In the public school, which is now common in the German settlements, no German is spoken, not even on the playground. Only in
isolated instances is daily religious instruction still given in German
during the last half hour of the schoolday in Alberta today. The laws
specify no particular language of instruction for this subject, which
makes possible, at least indirectly, some German language instruction
in the public school. But this can be done only in districts where the
majority of the school board is German, where the teachers themselves
can speak German or where a German clergyman whose congregation
tends to comprise three, four or more school districts, lives close enough
to the school in order to be able to teach regularly. Even that became
impossible in Saskatchewan, the province with the greatest proportion
of residents of German descent, when Anderson, as leader of the Conservatives, became Premier. In December 1929, he decreed that religious instruction was to be given in the English language only.[29] In
1930 he even abolished French as a language of instruction on the
primary level. Even in francophone communities, French is permitted
only as a subject.[30] English has become the exclusive language of
instruction for a child's entire school period. If the language of the home
can still form a certain counterbalance at all, it is only thanks to the
fact that rural schools frequently have to close for three to four months
in the winter due to the weather, and the number of school days is
left to some degree to the discretion of school boards.[31] "Thirty per
cent of the rural children seldom attend school for more than fifty days

a year."[32]

Legally there is, however, another possibility of giving additional German language instruction which is barely taken advantage of. Provided the parents defray the costs, some German instruction may be given, according to the School Act, in classrooms and even occasionally during regular school hours unless—and this is the critical point—such instruction interferes in the teacher's opinion with the other work.[33] As matters stand, the school day is already too long for the children, from 8 a.m. till 3:30 p.m. with a brief lunch break, and the present curriculum is much too extensive, as it is, for any additional instruction to appear commendable from a pedagogical point of view. Under these circumstances the Anglo-Canadian teacher, of course, opposes the introduction of additional German language instruction.

Many prerequisites are necessary to offer any German language instruction on such a basis. In the school district, Germans would need to have a majority on the school board and would need to hire only teachers conscious of their ethnic descent even though, of course, bilingual teachers are more expensive. Such teachers can also not be found easily, since many of the young German men or women do not remain sufficiently conscious of their ethnic background when attending normal schools for training. Even if a teacher with these qualifications has been found who besides all her other duties would be willing to offer extra German lessons, only little would be accomplished in such a lesson, since the children are already tired out and extra lessons are never popular with children.

Such additional German instruction can only be successful where the sense of community is highly developed, as for instance among the Mennonites and Hutterites. They have availed themselves of this opportunity, which means that their children have to sit in school almost all day. For their future supply of teachers the Mennonites instituted teachers' conferences in 1929 for the continued training of their German language skills.[34] Today there are public schools almost everywhere in the closed Mennonite settlements, which are almost exclusively staffed by Mennonite teachers providing additional German language and religious instruction. It was a fortunate coincidence that a large number of Mennonite postwar immigrants came from Russia already trained as teachers, or at least with higher education. After a certain period of preparation at the colleges in Gretna or Rosthern, they could acquire the official Canadian teacher's certificate and assume teaching positions in Mennonite settlements.

This, unfortunately, is only rarely possible in smaller settlements of postwar Mennonite immigrants. The following complaint of the Mennonite H.P. Lohrenz in Whitewater near Boissevain, Manitoba is typical:

> The children in our settlement receive their schooling in six different district schools. Almost everywhere the teachers are of non-German descent. The parents are happy if the female teachers maintain at least some discipline among the students . . . How long the German language will be understood and used by the younger generation, only the future will tell. As matters are now we will lose the German language in the course of time. Every Sunday, to be sure, the children have religious lessons in German, and programs in German are being prepared for Christmas. A group of children has received German lessons every Saturday for several winters, another group for one month during two summer holidays. As a result of these exercises the children understand German, but they will not be able to master it. To achieve this, a systematic German instruction which only a school can provide is needed. Our own mother tongue is Low German. In order to acquaint the children with the language of German literature High German is spoken now in many homes . . .

German Catholics operate public schools and separate schools, as well as a few five-day private schools. "In some cases it was possible to employ German-speaking nuns as teachers in public schools. Thus in St. Joseph's colony, German Sisters of Notre Dame (*Arme Schulschwestern*) from Munich teach at the public schools in Leipzig and Tramping Lake. Recently they have opened their own Canadian home for mothers in Waterdown near Hamilton, Ontario. Sisters of the Ursuline Order from Haselüne near Osnabrück, Germany, teach at the public school in Annaheim (St. Peter). They also work at the separate schools in Humboldt and Watson. In 1927 a total of a forty-six Ursulines from Haselüne taught about one thousand children in eight parishes. Today they have as many as twenty German Canadians, mostly former students of the Ursulines who are competent in the German language, among their teaching sisters."[35] In the public schools as well as in separate schools, the official curriculum must be strictly adhered to in the English language of instruction. The nuns may well be allowed to teach in the Catholic spirit. This, however, is of little use for the preservation of the German heritage among the young generation, even though the nuns or other German-speaking teachers may offer additional German language and religious instruction. One of the nuns remarked: "It is very difficult to get the children of Russian-German or American-German parents to speak German."[36]

Private schools offer still more freedom in the operation of the school, and more possibilities to teach German. Their high costs, however, make them feasible only in large, wealthy communities that are willing to make sacrifices. "Here instruction in English would be given in the first grade only after children can read German. In the German Catholic parochial schools in Bruno, Muenster, Lake Lenore, Marysburg and Leofeld (St. Peter's colony) German Ursuline sisters from Haselüne near Osnabrück are the teachers . . . The Oblates have established similar parochial schools in their German parishes in Manitoba and Saskatchewan. Next to the German Catholic church in Regina, for instance, there is a stately parochial school in which nuns are teaching, similarly in Winnipeg."[37] German Ursuline sisters also teach in schools at Vibank, Kendal, Odessa, Claybank, Raymore, Allan, Prelate, Blumenheim and Mendham in Saskatchewan.[38]

Among the Lutherans and smaller Protestant groups there are public schools almost everywhere today, with all their disadvantages for retaining German identity among the youth. Only in a few parishes, full-time (five-day) private schools have been reinstituted after the war with the help of the synods. Besides the official curriculum, they are able to offer additional German language and religious instruction.

New private schools, of which as we saw there were a considerable number before the war, could, however, only be opened with the greatest difficulty after the war. In 1921 the Missouri Synod in Stony Plain, Alberta, attempted to reopen its former private school as the first one after the war. Its principal was to be a clergyman who had obtained the official Canadian teacher's certificate. Its curriculum was entirely in accord with that of the public schools, and merely provided additional German language and religious instructions during one-fifth of the school hours. The Government of Alberta immediately thwarted this modest step towards reopening German private schools. Since private schools were not officially prohibited, they were closed on the grounds of "inefficiency," i.e., as unsatisfactory from a pedagogical point of view. Parents who took their children out of the public school which opened during the war and sent them to private school were penalized. Considerations of principle motivated the Missouri Synod to have them sue the government. They went through all the stages of appeal up to the Supreme Court of Canada in Ottawa. When it dismissed the action of the German parents, scouts of the parish, headed by the old pioneer pastor Eberhardt himself, went to Mexico to investigate the possibilities of emigration. This step, and even more, the threat of moving Concordia College of the Missouri Synod from Edmonton, the capital of Alberta, brought about a change of mind by the Alberta government in April 1923. The school in Stony Plain was declared as "efficient" and attendance was permitted. A precedent had thus been created.

It was, however, impossible to get the government to define the meaning of "efficiency" once and for all. The Alberta School Attendance Act states that a child can be exempted from attending a public school only if, in the opinion of a school inspector, fully equivalent alternative instruction is provided.[39] Professor Rehwinkel, who was then teaching at Concordia College in Edmonton, asked the Alberta government in a memorandum to replace this flexible regulation with specific guidelines for what would be considered to constitute fully equivalent alternative private instruction. He proposed as conditions that: (1) instruction in such an officially recognized private school should only be given by teachers with an official teacher's certificate, (2) instruction should be provided in all the basic subjects of the public school, and (3) the school day should be organized as in the public schools.

Not even the concession of clear guidelines has been made, so that closure due to "inefficiency" continues to hang like a Sword of Damocles over such private schools. On the other hand, no western Canadian provincial government has since prevented the establishment of such private schools with their special German-language instruction as long as they have fully adhered to the curriculum of the public school, i.e., the use of English as the language of instruction in the remaining subjects. In 1931 the Missouri Synod explicitly encouraged its ministers to set up private schools in their parishes. As a result, a number of new schools have been opened since 1932. In 1936 the Missouri Synod again had fourteen private schools in German-speaking parishes of western Canada (see Table VIII.10).[40]

It is typical of these schools that several of them are situated in the young pioneer districts of northwestern Saskatchewan and in the Peace River district (Loon Lake, Hines Creek, Wembley, Sexsmith), where for fiscal reasons the government has refrained from the establishment of public schools. These schools closely resemble the prewar private schools when all of western Canada was still in the pioneer stage.

Since the war, German Canadians in the West have, generally speaking, accepted the fact that they can no longer count on any German

Table VIII.10

Inventory of German Parochial Schools Maintained by Lutheran Church, Missouri Synod, in Western Canada, 1936

Alberta-British Columbia District:	
1. Stony Plain, Alberta	40 students, 2 teachers
2. Brightview	31 students, pastor as teacher
3. Hines Creek	31 students, pastor as teacher
4. Edmonton, St. Peter's	24 students, pastor as teacher
5. Lavesta.....................	19 students, pastor as teacher
6. Wembley	38 students, pastor as teacher
7. Sexsmith	20 students, pastor as teacher
8. Prince George, B.C............	12 students, pastor as teacher
9. Nelson	7 students, 1 teacher
Manitoba-Saskatchewan District	
10. Winnipeg, Holy Cross..........	68 students, 1 teacher, 1 theology student
11. Winnipeg, Emmanuel	23 students, 1 teacher
12. Spring Valley	79 students, 1 teacher and pastor
13. Loon Lake..................	27 students, pastor as teacher
14. Leader	12 students, pastor as teacher

instruction in public schools, that there would be no point in reopening costly five-day private schools which would not offer a much more advantageous curriculum, and that they must rely on private instruction outside the school and regular school hours. For instituting such private German reading and writing lessons on Saturdays (which are always public school holidays), on Sundays in connection with Sunday school and during long summer vacations, credit has to be given to the clergy of all denominations, and to the members of the families in their respective parishes. Many a brave colonist has even discovered his talent for teaching, and gathered the children of surrounding farms for instruction. The results, of course, vary greatly but are seldom very encouraging. In closed German settlements with a very active community life such irregular instructions on Saturdays, Sundays and during vacations may suffice in order to retain among the younger generation the ability to communicate in their mother tongue as well as in English. Generally speaking, however, the goal of such private lessons can be no more than the comprehension of uncomplicated German readings and the writing of a German letter. In no way can it be a satisfactory counterbalance against the influences of the English school which imperceptibly educates them to think in English, often enough makes them resent the mother tongue which is not being used during the day, and thus alienates parents and children from each other. An additional impediment to the success of the all-too-rare German lessons is the dialect of the parents, and the small German vocabulary of colonists who immigrated from eastern Europe. They still speak the language which their forefathers took with them from eighteenth century Germany. Modern concepts are missing and are substituted by their English equivalents, which makes the mother tongue appear inferior to the children. There is no time to read good, modern German books which means that their ability to express themselves in German remains limited. Writing in High German, finally, is made difficult by the dialect spoken at home and by the English spelling and syntax learned in school.

Under the impact of the numerous German postwar immigrants, even local groups of German clubs such as the *Deutscher Bund Canada* and the *Deutsch-Kanadische Vereinigung von Saskatchewan* have recently begun to organize some German instruction on Saturday afternoons and during school vacations. In 1936 in Winnipeg a committee of German teachers was formed who want to review the overall situation regarding private instruction in German and who intend to publish a standard German textbook for German instruction all over Canada. Gratifying and absolutely necessary as this German private instruction may be, which is organized for school-age youth in urban and in rural areas by German-speaking clergy as well as by German clubs, its significance for the preservation of the German identity should not be overrated.

To accomplish this a more comprehensive and free system of education is needed, which familiarizes the youth of German descent with the great achievements of the German spirit and the emotions and values of the German psyche, and which ties them with strong emotional bonds to their German heritage. This requires the existence of good German libraries in all the larger municipalities, travelling libraries for rural Germans, a travelling German theatre, travelling costume and folk art groups, art exhibitions during German Days to stimulate German handicrafts, German film shows, lectures in the form of adult training courses, and direct contact with the intellectual life of the people in Germany by way of radio and short-wave broadcasting. A beginning for all this has been made, yet much work remains to be done in order to achieve lasting results.

Private instruction in German for school children is merely one step in this direction, and is only the absolutely indispensable prerequisite. Equally important, and according to past experiences even more successful, is the teaching of the youth of German descent before and after school age. In Winnipeg, Regina, Rosthern, etc., nursery schools and kindergartens have been organized. The little ones are exposed to the rich world of German fairy tales, and their young souls receive impressions that accompany them for the rest of their lives, and which they will always remember as a part of the traditions of their old homeland. In addition there is the possibility of teaching them to read and write some German before they enter the English school. The introduction of such pre-schooling in all towns and large German rural settlements would be desirable.

The Mennonite Bible schools address those that are past school age. Even though their first concern is religious education and the training of their lay preachers, they also reinforce among their students the awareness of their German heritage, since almost all the classes are taught in German. In courses extending over a period of three or four years, the participants are taught church doctrine, Bible study, the history of the church, homiletics and exegesis. In addition they receive thorough German language instruction with exercises in dictation and composition as well as musical training. In western Canada, Mennonite Bible schools have become firmly established only by postwar Mennonite immigrants from Russia, who had developed this special form of adult education in their old homeland. However, the oldest Bible school in Herbert, Saskatchewan, goes back to the year 1916 with an enrollment of five hundred to six hundred students. Courses usually start on November 1 and end on March 31. Some schools begin as early as October 1, others finish only on May 1. As a rule they are boarding schools, except for the one in Winnipeg. In the winter of 1933-34 there were Bible schools in the following places: in Herbert, Sask. (since 1916, 25 students); Winkler, Man. (since 1925, 75 students); Hepburn (since 1927, 72 students), Dalmeny (since 1928, 34 students), Aberdeen, Sask. (since 1930, 6 students); Yarrow, B.C. (since 1930, 10 students); Rosthern, Sask. (since 1932, 12 students); Rosemary, Alta. (since 1932, one student); Swift Current (since 1933, 14 students); Gem, Alta. (since 1933, 10 students); Coaldale, Alta. (since 1933, 56 students) and two schools in Winnipeg (since 1929, with 56 students, and 1933, with 38 students). In addition, German Baptists have a Bible school in Alberta.[41] It would be very desirable if similar adult training schools existed among all segments of the German-speaking population. They could take the external structure and teaching method of these Bible schools as their model. However, they should not merely serve a specific denomination, but should be founded on the more comprehensive objective of introducing their students into the rich German intellectual life by means of a thorough instruction in the German language.

One of the rules of order of the Bible school in Herbert states: "High German must be used in the school yard. Low German may not be spoken." The provincial conference of the postwar Mennonite immigrants in Saskatchewan makes a similar recommendation to individual families to de-emphasize their inherited Low German in favor of High German when raising their children.[42] They realized, with good reason, that under existing school conditions in Canada it was impossible to keep alive among the young generation the High German as well as the Low German language, in addition to English. They deliberately renounced their cherished Low German because they understood the necessity of saving the language of German literature for the sake of preserving their German ethnic identity. The dialect, which is not much good for either reading or writing, is doomed among Germans in other lands in the age of highly-developed school systems. Only those who through the literary language keep in constant touch with the living stream of German culture can pass on their German ethnic identity to their children. This, however, is what they want. The postwar Mennonite immigrants from Soviet Russia particularly, have manifested a distinct German national consciousness as a result of their experiences during the World War and Bolshevik rule. The earlier-quoted letter of the Mennonite Lohrenz from Whitewater, Manitoba, is an example of their deep concern for the fate of the school and language questions. Also commendable, by the way, are the efforts of Mennonite institutes for girls in Saskatoon, Lethbridge and Vancouver. They "have excellent leaders who spare no pains to practice German in word and song during the get-togethers of German girls."[43]

Just as the German language has been eliminated from grade schools, it has also almost entirely disappeared from public high schools. Foreign languages are elective subjects. According to the latest Canadian statistics, French is chosen as an elective by 68.6 per cent of students in Manitoba, by 87 per cent in Saskatchewan, by 66.6 per cent in Alberta and by 68.4 per cent in British Columbia. German, however, is taken by a mere 4 per cent of all students. This figure is valid for all Canada, while more exact figures for the western provinces are not available.[44] It is highly regrettable and outright ironic that, especially in Saskatchewan where the German-speaking population is far more numerous than any other non-British ethnic group, 87 per cent of high school students choose to learn French, even though this language is of no practical value for them, while German is neglected. The relatively small number of German farmers' sons who attend high school at all, are of course not to be found in public schools but in one of the private institutions of higher learning operated by one of the German-Canadian churches.

These schools primarily serve the training of the new generation of clergy of the respective denomination. In addition, however, they are open to all members of that church who want to become teachers or enter any academic profession. The Mennonites have two such institutions, one in Gretna, Manitoba, which was founded as early as 1891 and until recently was headed by the previously-mentioned Professor H.H. Ewert, the other one called the German-English Academy, in Rosthern, Saskatchewan, which owes its reputation especially to Elder Toews. One of the schools has fifty, the other about sixty students. In addition, each of the Lutheran churches operated a school of this type. In 1912 the Manitoba Synod founded Luther College in Saskatoon with a full-fledged theological seminary affiliated with it. It is the only one of its kind in all of North America in which all lectures are given exclusively in German. The American Lutheran Church has its Luther College in Regina. It was originally founded in 1913, in Melville, Saskatchewan. Concordia College of the Missouri Synod is in Edmonton. The two latter institutions have about fifty, the first one somewhat fewer students. The Catholics have eight private institutions of higher learning besides the small college of the Oblates in Battleford. Three of these, Campion College in Regina, and St. Paul's and St. John's colleges in Winnipeg, no longer show any distinct German Catholic influences. The remaining five consist of the college in Muenster run by German Benedictines, and four higher girls' schools supervised by German Ursulines and Sisters of Notre Dame in Bruno, Vibank, Leipzig and Prelate, all in Saskatchewan.

All these schools teach German only as a subject. They have a total of no more than two thousand students. In order to be officially recognized as high schools (ninth to twelfth grade) or as colleges (first and second academic year) they have to adapt their requirements to the general Canadian standards, which include English as the language of instruction. A somewhat larger scope is, however, left to the study of German than in other higher Canadian schools, by making German language and German literature compulsory subjects, and by always giving religious instruction in German. At Concordia College in Edmonton even classical languages are taught in German. At Luther College in Regina, the language of instruction in the first, fourth and fifth years is exclusively German. The two colleges of the Mennonites in Gretna and Rosthern are reported to "get as far as Schiller, Lessing, Goethe in the two higher grades...German is also used outside the school on literary evenings, in the school theatre, in folk and classical songs and by means of a library donated by the VDA. The schools even performed such German oratorios as St. Paul's, Christ [sic] and the Messiah."[45] All the schools have three to five grades. They are boarding schools, and are becoming very costly for the congregations that fund them, since the children of German settlers can afford to pay only low tuition fees.

Commendable as the efforts may be for the education of an intellectual leadership, made under great financial sacrifices, these already partly-anglicized private higher schools of German religious communities can in no way compensate for the lack of any systematic instruction at the elementary level. The fate of the German language and of German ethnicity is decided in the public school. It impairs ethnic retention by the mere fact that the subjects which it teaches are those of Anglo-American urban civilization, which threaten to draw away the youth from rural areas. Even well-informed English Canadians like R. England have repeatedly pointed that out.[46] Of the greatest impact is the fact that the English language of instruction endangers not only the German mother tongue, but severely inhibits the intellectual development of German-speaking youth. The unfortunate consequences of enforced bilingualism have frequently been the subject of thorough investigations, so that we need not raise them here in detail. It is significant that even R. England, who endorses the unilingual English public school as the inevitable prerequisite for the assimilation of the non-British in western Canada, admits its detrimental influence on the intellectual development of the children of foreign descent, when he writes:[47]

> In most non-English schools it will be found that the reading by the junior grades and the composition of the senior grades should be taken in the morning. These are subjects with which the non-English child has difficulty. The manual subjects, such as writing and art, a memory subject such as spelling, and, curiously enough, arithmetic, give little trouble. But reading and composition, with their training in interpretation and expression, tax the non-English child's mental powers as do few other subjects.

England unfortunately does not draw the only possible conclusion from this observation, namely to recommend the use of the mother tongue of the children as the language of instruction.

The greatest disadvantage of the unilingual English public school, as pointed out at the beginning of this chapter, however, lies in the fact that it opens a deep gulf between the old and the young within the non-British families. Thus the difficulties of the generation gap are intensified by enforced linguistic alienation during adolescence. This means that the young Canadian German who has no strong family ties is bound to lose his ethnic identity all the more easily.

4. The Prospects of Ethnic Retention

Canadian school policies are almost the sole visible indication of the deliberate intention of the Anglo-Canadian majority to assimilate the non-British as fast as possible. However, they make no effort to conceal this objective and, since the war, have shown their determination to pursue it even more obstinately and frantically. They have obviously realized that among the plurality of nationalities that have poured into the country since 1900, the anglophones constitute only 50.8 per cent of the population of the Prairie provinces, and a mere 47 per cent in Saskatchewan with the prospect of falling more and more behind the non-British numerically as a result of their low birth rate. Under present school conditions, upward social mobility of the non-British is, in fact, almost unthinkable without a far-reaching loss of ethnic identity. Even the private elementary and high schools established by German-speaking religious communities are, in spite of the ample attention they still give to the German language, bound to promote Canadianization and the disappearance of the German heritage among the young generation, by the mere fact that the subjects taught are structured according to Anglo-Canadian ideas, and by the way these are presented.

Apart from the school, however, no constraints of any kind are imposed on the non-British population. The non-British are not denied access to Anglo-Canadian political, economic and social organizations; their membership, on the contrary, is even solicited, and they barely experience any discrimination in everyday life. This is born out of the realization that pressure would only result in national counterpressure from among the ethnic groups of the immigrants. The generation of new immigrants is even encouraged outright to cultivate their inherited culture within certain limits, in order to accelerate their adjustment to the new country. This idea is, for instance, the basis for the competitions organized by the Canadian National Railway among non-British settlements. It is assumed that the second and third generations will become Anglo-Canadians all the more easily, trusting that the influences of school and environment will do the job.

Environment, as in the neighboring United States, is one of the strongest equalizing and assimilating forces. Sports, movies, radio, dancing, picnics and the whole Anglo-American urban civilization, which result in the extinction of the old social culture and inherited traditions, have their attractions even in remote small prairie towns and among the youth of German descent, who often are only too eager to discard their ethnic background along with the external lifestyle of the older generation. Anglo-Canadian economic, social and youth organizations are most effective in this respect. Among the organizations operating with an assimilating effect in the small towns of the Mennonite settlements of southern Manitoba, Dawson mentions the

Boy Scouts, Girl Guides, Tuxis, Canadian Girls in Training, the Junior Red Cross, the Women's Institute, the Manitoba Teachers' Federation, the Manitoba Consumers' Cooperative Association, the Seed Growers' Club and the Agricultural Society.[48] Even in the remotest rural districts, membership in such associations promotes the linguistic assimilation begun by the schools, as do English-language movies, radio, farm journals and illustrated magazines, although such assimilation may not be necessary for occupational and economic reasons.

The decisive point, however, is that the all-pervasive spiritual climate, the individualism and liberalism of North America, is in principle hostile to the retention of ethnicity. Only the individual and his accomplishments are recognized. Inner tensions are not regarded as providing any valuable experiences, but are eschewed at all costs. "To take things easy" is the supreme maxim. Therefore allegiances of the individual to the ethnic community are often misunderstood, and the desire to transmit inherited ethnic traditions to the children is frequently ridiculed.

The influences of the environment which are imperceptibly eroding German ethnicity are, on the whole, much more harmful than Anglo-Canadian school policies, which deliberately and directly aim at linguistic change. Von Loesch observed correctly "that among all peoples, linguistic change is only one part of the process of losing one's ethnic identity, and that the decisive criterion lies perhaps in another area, namely the acceptance of different political ideals, the shifting of the frame of reference and the adoption of a foreign way of life."[49] Today even in closed areas of German settlement in western Canada it is already noticeable that young people hardly differ from English-Canadian youth in their outlook on life, their clothes, sports activities and amusements, and tend to reject outright any parental guidance in the choice of their careers and marital partners. Dawson believes that even among the German Mennonites in southern Manitoba, living in uniquely homogeneous bloc settlements, complete absorption is only a matter of time:[50]

> Through many channels the world is insinuating itself into the community life and breaking down the distinguishing characteristics of a "peculiar people." Whether this assimilation will be complete fifty years hence, a hundred years, or more, it is impossible at present to predict. Nor does it greatly matter, for in the interim the group will have become an integral part of the larger Canadian community and there will be no more talk of "the Mennonite problem."

Are there any chances for a survival of a German identity in Canada beyond the second and third generations, in view of the tremendous forces of assimilation facing it in the form of the school and the environment? Until a few years ago this question would undoubtedly have been answered in thè negative due to the incipient weakness of any adequate countervailing forces within the German ethnic group.

A great handicap for the preservation of German ethnicity has always been the low level of education and weak ethnic consciousness of German-speaking immigrants. They belonged almost exclusively to the class of small farmers and agricultural workers, who have a far less developed sense of ethnic identity than the urban middle and upper classes. This situation was aggravated by the fact that more than 85 per cent of these immigrants did not come directly from Germany, but from the rural linguistic enclaves in eastern Europe. They had therefore not been able to participate fully in the cultural life of the German homeland but, culturally speaking, had to lead a poorer colonial existence. Kuhn argued convincingly that each emigration and reconstitution of a linguistic enclave reduces an ethnic culture to its innermost core, namely its folkways and religion.[51] The emigration of German colonists from their east European settlements has entailed a repetition and intensification of the process of cultural impoverishment.

Overseas emigration particularly, of course, endangers German cultural life which is merely vegetating due to the rigorous spiritual and psychological separation from the old homeland. The immense spatial distance gives rise to the feeling that there is no going back. This leads to a greater willingness to accept the new country, to take root in it as quickly as possible and to adapt to it in every respect. Among German groups overseas, therefore, the less developed was the ethnic consciousness of the immigrants, the faster it was displaced by the affirmation of the new country. In our case, the feeling of allegiance, at first confined to the land, the pride in the economic prosperity and the vast expanses of Canada, ultimately assumes the character of a true loyalty to Canada itself. It is significant that the second generation do not want to refer to themselves as *Kanadadeutsche* (i.e. Germans of Canada or Canadian Germans) with the emphasis on German ethnicity, as is the case among the German ethnic groups in Europe such as the so-called *Russlanddeutsche* (i.e., Germans of Russia), *Galiziendeutsche* (Germans of Galicia), etc., but rather as German Canadians, with the emphasis on the new citizenship in line with German Americans, German Chileans, German Australians. This unconscious abandonment of ethnic identity simply by affirmation of the new country, is acknowledged as a major reason for the loss of German ethnicity overseas.[52]

> They view the renunciation of their identity not as assimilation by a foreign ethnic community conscious of its own identity, but as casting off the customs of the "old world." They believe they are following the example of the other ethnic elements of the new country's population and, in concert with them, form a truly new people composed of ethnic groups of different descent. They do not realize that a European motherland is shaping these newcomers, including them. They believe that they are assuming a truly new ethnic identity as "Americans," "Canadians," or "Australians," when in reality they are merely being anglicized imperceptibly.

The Germans in western Canada are, as we know, apart from several thousand people of the lower middle class in the prairie towns, a purely agricultural population. According to Gottschick, however, a linguistic enclave's chances of survival increases in proportion to the level and vitality of its cultural life.[53] The low level of education and the lifestyle of German agricultural immigrants from eastern Europe, which reflects the cultural level of the end of the eighteenth century, has not only impeded interaction with the people of Germany, it has also lowered the political and social prestige of the German ethnic group in the eyes of the Anglo-Canadian host people. It therefore facilitated the assimilation of the upward socially mobile among the youth of German descent. The gap appeared to be too wide between the tradition-bound lifestyle and outlook of the immigrating generation and the British culture to which the youth are exposed in school and public life. Without having any notion of the actual greatness of German culture, German youth, with their aspirations of upward social mobility, are often ashamed of their inherited language and culture simply because their native dialect, which was brought over by their parents and which reflects the conceptual level of the late eighteenth century, does not appear suited for modern life. All the higher concepts must be borrowed from English. Here lies the root of the inferiority complex, which is always the prerequisite for the abandonment of the inherited ethnic identity. Such inferiority complexes are more frequent among German girls who want to become teachers than among young men. This is most regrettable, because of the important role of the mother in the retention of the ethnic identity by the family.

The chief threat to the survival of German ethnicity in the young

English-speaking countries overseas thus seems to have its deepest roots in the absence of any cultural intelligentsia among the immigrants themselves. The natural process of maturation of the German ethnic group, which extends over a period of several generations, and the development of a richer cultural life from within it, could not come to its conclusion. Already, in the pioneer stage, an aggressive school policy and the attractions of a distinctly articulate and highly-developed culture is beginning to a large extent to assimilate the youth with its rising social and cultural expectations. The ethnic group remains exclusively rural in character, and produces virtually no spiritual leaders, until after three or four generations it too is absorbed, because of its lack of leadership and cultural narrowness. This is aggravated by the distance from the German homeland across the ocean, by the extensive geographical dispersal in western Canada, by the variety of places of origin and by the division into three large and several small denominations.

Weakest in their resistance to assimilation among the Germans of western Canada have been native German Americans and Germans from Ontario. These groups have, of course, been living for two or three generations in the British environment and are therefore ahead of the remaining Germans in the alienation of their ethnic identity by one or two generations. Until the postwar era the higher level of education of immigrants from Germany was compensated for by their greater ability and desire to adapt rapidly to the Anglo-Canadian environment. Even they were only rarely inspired by a living ethnic consciousness. Our above reflections on the ethnic situation applied primarily to the Germans who immigrated from eastern Europe. Among these, however, the Mennonites hold a special position. Their consciousness of a German identity was even less developed than that of the remaining German immigrants from eastern Europe.

The Mennonites owe the relatively high degree to which they have been able to preserve their ethnic heritage primarily to their sectarian desire for seclusion from the Anglo-Canadian environment, and their strongly developed sense of community. They have persisted in their traditions and customs, not with the intention of remaining German, but in order to prevent absorption by the Anglo-Canadian host society. Even long ago when the Mennonites emigrated from West Prussia to South Russia, they had a much less developed consciousness of German identity than other Germans emigrating simultaneously. This was due to their religious separation, their special political and economic status as a "tolerated" group, even in West Prussia, and finally the uncertainties of their geographical origin (Friesian or Dutch?). For these reasons, in faraway South Russia the Mennonites were even less able to develop a sense of community with the remaining German colonists and began to feel like a separate people, simply like Mennonites. This designation combined ethnic and religious identity. The Mennonites emigrating to western Canada in the 1870s brought this fundamental attitude with them. The more conservatively and the more stubbornly they clung to their religious convictions, the more unequivocal this attitude. A German-Canadian Mennonite made this comment about the Old Colony Mennonites: "Not only have they closed their doors to the English language but they have also cut off all sources that could revitalize their German. This method of remaining German is not acceptable to the majority of our people here."[54] Only the tragic fate of the German element in Russia during the war and postwar era, which the Mennonites had to share with the rest of the Germans in Russia, has awakened them to a new German ethnic and cultural consciousness, even in western Canada, where it has been newly revived especially by the postwar immigrants from Russia. The new attitude becomes noticeable in the reflections of the teacher Rempel on the future of the German language among the Mennonites of western Canada:[55]

> If German is retained only for the reading of the Bible, then the next obvious step is the replacement of the German Bible by the English Bible. These are logical steps which most of the Mennonite congregations in the United States have made long ago. As long as our German is confined to this narrow usage it cannot last. There is also little point retaining it for this purpose.

> If we want to remain German we have to widen our horizon and draw from the wealth of the German heritage. We were always more or less strangers to the idea of the German national state, and want to remain that way. But we have to cling to the German heritage with its great men in the realm of art and science, and above all German literature,... The gracious song born from the soul of the German people should take root, especially among our youth. To the maturer youth, particularly the student generation, the treasures of German poetry and literature should be made accessible.

Also indicative of the new ethnic and cultural consciousness of the Mennonites are the remarks of the provincial representative of the postwar immigrants in Saskatchewan, Mr. Gerhard Toews in Herschel:[56]

> Previous efforts to preserve German traditions tried to do without a sense of German identity. Where was it supposed to come from?

Today it is cultivated by the German homeland. The help from
there should also assist the newly-immigrated Germans, who have
been living in other lands for four generations, in their efforts to
retain their German heritage. It must not be forgotten that without
a consciousness of German identity, it will not be possible in the
long run to resist the influence of anglicization.

Here it has been clearly recognized by one of the leaders that even
the prospects of survival of Mennonite culture are closely connected
with their identification as a part of the wider German ethnic community.

The Mennonites are perhaps the best example of the revival of a
subjective sense of German identity through the impact of external
events, at least as long as objectively German traditions and the German language have been retained. This is the great, but also the only,
prospect that we can hold out for the preservation of German ethnicity in Canada in the face of all the forces of assimilation which we
attempted to take account of above. There is no doubt that as a result
of the experience of the World War, and the sufferings which the German ethnic groups in East and Southeast Europe had to endure since
the end of the war, a new German ethnic consciousness has begun
to sprout among Germans in western Canada. The influence of the
postwar immigrants who had experienced the World War in Europe
has reinforced this development.

Everything depends on whether it is possible to improve cultural
contacts with the parent community even more than before, to prevent the customary assimilation of the socially upwardly mobile, and
to educate German Canadians of the second and third generations who
speak German as a second colloquial language as fluently as they speak
English, and not only as a foreign language learned in school. They
must readily accept the tensions between their allegiance to the ethnic
community and the country of their citizenship in order to preserve
the inherited traditions of their German background for the benefit
of their new homeland, Canada. Only if German Canadians of the
second and third generations guide the German community in this
spirit is there hope for its survival beyond the third generation.

Western Canada's Germans, as a matter of fact, have to rely entirely
on their own strength. New immigrations from Europe that repeatedly,
until recently, kept infusing fresh vitality into the overseas ethnic groups
can no longer be expected. It would also be wrong to believe that the
future of the German community in western Canada could be firmly

secured by tactics of political collaboration with other non-British ethnic groups. Such an approach, whose chances we examined earlier, might bring about at best certain changes in school policies.

Such changes in school policies, incidentally, as unlikely as it would seem to appear at the moment, might also be introduced by Anglo-Canadians themselves. Here and there the realization seems to dawn that previous efforts at assimilation have been very much to the detriment of Canada. By depriving the children of German and other non-British immigrants of the firm foundations of the ethnic traditions of their ancestors, they left them with nothing but the chaff of Anglo-American civilization as a replacement. A starting point for the renunciation of the previous policy of assimilation could be Robert England's remarkable admission:[57]

> In the sense in which it is applied by many, there is no such thing as assimilation. If it be taken to mean sufficient similarity of mental outlook to make cooperation feasible, that is about all we can do. We can never make a German an Anglo-Saxon any more than we can make Englishmen Irish.

As gratifying as an about-face in the previous policy of assimilation might be, we still have to admit that the survival of German ethnicity would not be saved by this act alone. Everything depends on the quality of leadership that will be offered to the German community, and on the community's desire to uphold the faith in the value of its own ethnic heritage. "Only if the German immigrants in Canada believe that the preservation of their ethnic heritage is of benefit to Canada as well as to the German people, will they muster the necessary strength to fulfill their mission. Many a German has become a Canadian because he could not be a German Canadian. He can only be a German Canadian who manages to do justice to the claims of allegiance of both the ethnic community and the state."[58]

May the Germans in Canada always heed the words with which one of their own, Saskatchewan cabinet minister Dr. Uhrich, addressed them on the occasion of the Saskatchewan German Day in Saskatoon on July 1, 1934, words that are both a confession and an exhortation:[59]

> We Germans in other lands are the outposts of German language and culture. We have to carry out the apostolic duty of the German idea in the world. Our fellow Germans in Canada form the bridge, culturally and economically, to the various peoples who

have established a new home here.

There are some who see the salvation of Canada only in a rapid amalgamation of all the various nationalities in one uniform Canadian nation. Nothing would be as wrong as that. The more cultural and spiritual freedom within the framework of general legislation one concedes to the immigrants and their descendants, the more will their good qualities abound and flourish for the benefit of their country.

It is the duty of each one of us to cultivate the German language, the German folksong, German choral singing and German music to the best of our abilities.

I want to call upon each one of you:

Support the German press which defends, enlightens and educates us! Each German family should have one German-language newspaper. Support existing German organizations or found new ones.

Our chief duty should be to do honor to our German descent as law-abiding, honorable, honest and industrious Canadian citizens in the future as in the past. Everyone should speak of us with respect.

It should be our ambition to be counted among the best Canadian citizens, without in turn forgetting our mother tongue and the magnificent traditions of our people.

In order to do these tasks we want to unite more closely and more firmly, and together declare:

We know and do our duty, we want peace, freedom and tolerance for ourselves and for all the other fellow citizens in our dear, great and beautiful Canada.

APPENDIX

APPENDIX TABLE 1

1931 Census Data on the German Element in Canada

Area	Total Population	Mother Tongue German	Mother Tongue Austrian	Mother Tongue Total	German by Origin	Birthplace Germany
Nova Scotia	512,846	989	52	1,041	27,098	397
New Brunswick	408,219	243	19	262	2,659	122
Prince Edward Island	88,038	23	—	23	282	12
Quebec	2,874,255	7,295	437	7,732	10,616	2,789
Ontario	3,431,683	82,089	2,046	84,135	174,006	10,662
Eastern Canada	7,315,041	90,639	2,554	93,193	214,661	13,982
Manitoba	700,139	57,312	907	58,219	38,078	3,561
Saskatchewan	921,785	138,499	1,510	140,009	129,232	9,832
Alberta	731,605	63,410	1,001	64,411	74,450	8,121
British Columbia	694,263	12,066	866	12,932	16,986	3,626
Yukon & Northwest Territories	13,953	85	4	89	137	41
Western Canada	3,061,745	271,372	4,288	275,660	258,883	25,181
Canada	10,376,786	362,011	6,842	368,853	473,544	39,163

Source: Heinz Lehmann, *Das Deutschtum in Westkanada* (Berlin, 1939), 134.

APPENDIX TABLE 2

Ethnic Composition of Western Canada's Population, 1931

Mother Tongue / Racial Origin	Prairie Provinces		B.C.(incl.Yukon & N.W. Terr.)	
	Mother Tongue	Racial Origin	Mother Tongue	Racial Origin
English (British origin)	1,377,564	1,195,084	528,977	492,287
by country of origin:				
England		566,967		273,622
Scotland		344,531		135,829
Ireland		261,633		72,008
Other		21,953		10,828
German	262,639[1]	241,760	13,021[1]	17,123
Austrian	—	32,656	—	3,907
Dutch	19,581	63,317	1,686	6,266
Flemish	8,589	13,507[2]	792	1,616[2]
Norwegian	49,853	72,378	9,954	13,070
Swedish	35,595	51,735	13,440	16,248
Danish	13,191	21,268	2,489	3,998
Icelandic	15,314	18,161	506	859
French	112,927	136,416	8,252	15,493
Italian	6,654	8,185	10,666	12,277
Spanish	195	?	317	?
Ukrainian	213,719	192,878	3,191	2,586
Polish	66,247	87,361	3,410	4,615

Russian	28,175	63,375	9,073	10,426
Finnish	5,719	6,644	5,168	6,896
Hungarian	18,877	20,820	1,084	1,321
Romanian	9,828	16,329	568	1,162
Slovak	8,387	13,856	2,899	2,769
Czech	4,200		594	
Serbian, Croat	1,728	3,312	2,066	2,936
Lithuanian	1,422	1,577	226	247
Greek	984	1,430	716	980
Bulgarian	175	308	58	78
Hebrew	27,822	28,179	2,631	2,749
Chinese	9,763	9,108	49,243	27,140
Japanese	1,102	817		22,258
Syrian and Arabic		?	183	?
Negro	?	1,799	?	541
Indian	?	45,934	?	30,188
Eskimo	?	65	?	4,755
Miscellaneous	53,279		37,006	
from Europe		2,107		791
from Asia		1,678		1,618
Unspecified		1,785		1,016

Source: Seventh Census of Canada, 1931, vol. II, as quoted by Heinz Lehmann, Das Deutschtum in Westkanada (Berlin, 1939), 132.

[1] Included in this number are 3,418 persons in the Prairie provinces and 870 in British Columbia who claimed Austrian as their mother tongue. According to a note in the Seventh Census of Canada, 1931 (vol. II, 814) these people should be considered as German-speaking.

[2] Their country of origin is Belgium.

APPENDIX TABLE 3

Proportion of German-speaking to Total Population
of Prairie Provinces, 1931

	mother tongue German	total population	percentage of German to total population
Manitoba	58,219	700,139	8.3
Saskatchewan	140,009	921,785	15.2
Alberta	64,411	731,605	8.8
Prairie Provinces	262,639	2,353,529	11.2

Source: *Seventh Census of Canada, 1931*, vol. II, as quoted by Heinz Lehmann, "Zur Karte des Deutschtums in der kanadischen Prärieprovinzen," *Deutsches Archiv für Landes-und Volksforschung*, II: 4 (1938), 863.

Note to Table 3:

The 1931 Census shows 259,221 persons reporting German and 3,418 persons reporting "Austrian" as mother tongue. A note in the *Seventh Census of Canada, 1931* (vol.II, 814) indicates that these are to be considered of German mother tongue as well.

APPENDIX TABLE 4

Distribution of Germans (and British) Among
Rural and Urban Localities, 1931

	Rural		Urban Localities	
	farm districts	under 1,000 population	1,000 population to 30,000	30,000 population and over
Manitoba	21,698 (175,288)	1,182 (14,890)	1,989 (45,456)	13,209 (132,376)
Saskatchewan	99,452 (251,221)	12,431 (59,278)	7,591 (60,128)	9,758 (67,209)
Alberta	56,710 (195,365)	4,658 (29,225)	4,348 (43,532)	8,734 (121,116)
British Columbia	9,238 (187,518)	315 (7,206)	2,605 (72,607)	4,828 (222,592)
Yukon and Northwest Territories	103 (1,502)	34 (862)		
Western Canada	187,201 (810,894)	17,620 (111,461)	16,533 (221,723)	36,529 (543,293)
Percentages	72.3 (48.0)	7.2 (6.6)	6.4 (13.2)	14.1 (32.2)

Source: *Seventh Census of Canada, 1931*, vol. II, 501.

Note: If data were available for all the Germans by origin, i.e., if the missing Mennonites and Germans from Russia as well as from Austria etc. were included, the proportion of the German rural population would be even higher. The figures for British by origin are given in brackets.

APPENDIX TABLE 5

Comparison of 1931 German Mother Tongue Data
With 1931 and 1936 German and Austrian Origin Data

	mother tongue German 1931	German by origin 1931	Austrian by origin 1931	German by origin 1936	Austrian by origin 1936
Manitoba	58,219	38,078	8,858	52,450	3,414
Saskatchewan	140,009	129,232	17,061	165,516	6,976
Alberta	64,411	74,450	6,737	90,961	6,363
Prairie Provinces	262,639	241,760	32,656	308,927	16,753

Source: "Racial Origins of the Populations of the Prairie Provinces 1826, 1931, and 1936,"
Canada Year Book 1937, 149f, as quoted by Heinz Lehmann, *Das Deutschtum in Westkanada*
(Berlin, 1939), 139f, 144.

APPENDIX TABLE 6

Religious Denomination of Canada's German Population by Province, 1931

	Roman Cath. by German Origin	Lutherans by German Origin	Mennonites	Evang. Assoc.	German Baptists 1933	Moravians 1921	German Reformed 1921	Hutterites 1931
Nova Scotia	994	4,637	1	1	–	–	–	–
New Brunswick	378	57	2	–	–	–	–	–
Quebec	4,920	2,464	8	111	–	–	–	–
Ontario	31,980	50,628	17,661	10,592	–	–	–	–
Manitoba	5,445	16,379	30,352	164	1,080	–	111	1,443
Sask.	47,121	41,059	31,338	1,308	1,499	–	374	–
Alberta	13,180	27,551	8,289	1,240	2,165	648	781	1,180
British Columbia	3,841	4,470	1,085	25	35	97	77	–
Yukon and Northwest Territories	41	45	–	1	–	–	–	–
Western Canada	69,628	89,504	71,064	2,737	4,779	741	1,343	2,623
Canada	107,940	147,290	88,736	13,441	4,779	741	1,343	2,623

Note on sources: The data for Roman Catholics, Lutherans, Mennonites and Evangelical Association are derived from the *Seventh Census of Canada, 1931*, Bulletin XXXV (No. 69), those for the remaining religious groups from their own private publications. The figures for New Brunswick include those for P.E.I. See Heinz Lehmann, "Das evangelische Deutschtum in Kanada" (No. 259), 38.

Resolution Adopted by the
First German Day Celebrations for Saskatchewan,
Held in Regina on August 9 and 10, 1930

On the occasion of the official opening ceremony of the first German Day celebration for Saskatchewan which was held in Regina, the more than four thousand German Canadians assembled adopted a resolution calling primarily on the German Canadians themselves in these words:

> As British subjects and Canadian citizens, we participants of the first German Day held in Regina on August 9 and 10, 1930, and we representatives of all German-speaking Canadians of the Province of Saskatchewan, renew our pledge of allegiance to His Majesty King George V and to the authorities of our country.
>
> German pioneers were among the vanguard of those who followed the call to open the previously wild Canadian West to civilization and culture. They readily accepted the invitation to come to Canada. Under conditions of unspeakable hardship and privations, they transformed the prairies and the bush into fertile agricultural land. They founded business and industrial enterprises and so have made the West and especially our beloved Province of Saskatchewan into a home for themselves and their children.
>
> German industry, German thriftiness, German family pride and German persistence are the conspicuous traits of pioneers of German descent. These good qualities have contributed in a large degree to the growth of Saskatchewan. Therefore our pioneers deserve a major share of the recognition for the development of the West. The flourishing German settlements in many parts of our province visibly attest to that.
>
> The German-speaking citizens of Saskatchewan have also proven to be valuable components of Canada by the faithful attendance to their civic duties and their active participation in the public life of their adopted homeland. As honest, self-confident and clear-thinking men and women they expect every level of government, provincial and federal, to concede to them full equality with the citizens of different ethnic origins, and grant them justice and freedom in the free country of Canada. They want to cultivate, freely and unhampered, the beautiful and great traditions of their people and entrust them as a precious legacy to the Canadian nation. May they contribute the treasures of German literature, German music, German art and German technology to the cultural develop-

ment of Canada in the firm conviction that they can provide a mighty stimulus to the intellectual life of this country. To every German-speaking Canadian, his mother tongue is one of his most precious assets. It is the language of a Goethe and Schiller, a Kant and Richard Wagner, a Mozart and Schubert. The beautiful German language could be heard in the German colonies of Russia and of former Austria-Hungary, Bukovina and Bessarabia, Yugoslavia and Romania, Volhynia and Bohemia, Poland and Switzerland for centuries. May its sounds continue to be heard here as well.

It is the natural right of every father and every mother to pass on their own language to their children. It is the sacred right of our German church congregations to proclaim the word of God in German, to sing German church hymns and to say German prayers. Where possible, instruction should be provided in the German language which ought to be supported most strongly by German-speaking parents. Cultivate also the German folksong, German choral singing and German music!

As German-speaking Canadian citizens we consider it an important duty to become active in church congregations, on school boards, in the municipalities, in town administrations, in co-operative associations as well as in all the non-profit organizations. We demand full equality in these corporations and organizations for us and our children. In public offices for which we pay our taxes, and in business and industrial enterprises which we support as good and reliable customers, our sons and daughters, who have successfully attended the schools of the country, should have the same employment opportunities as others. For this reason it is essential that talented children of German parents attend institutions of higher learning, such as colleges and universities. Special reference may be made in this context to our denominational institutions of learning.

Mapping German Settlement in the
Prairie Provinces

The map of the provinces of Manitoba, Saskatchewan and Alberta published by the Dominion Department of the Interior in Ottawa in 1928 forms the basis for our map. From it the township division was adopted. All the land in the prairies suitable for settlement was surveyed in a checkerboard pattern in townships of six miles by six miles. The position of each township is clearly determined by two coordinates. Townships are numbered northward from a base line on the American border, ranges of townships east and west. In order to keep the number of ranges low, six principal meridians have been adopted, each one as a starting point for counting the ranges in a westerly direction. Only from the first principal meridian, which runs through the center of Manitoba, ranges are numbered in an easterly as well as in a westerly direction. Thus Herbert, Saskatchewan, for example, is located in township 17, range 9 west of the third meridian, and Brüderheim, Alberta, in township 55, range 20 west of the fourth meridian. With the help of the township grid, therefore, every single settlement can be quickly located.

The boundaries of the zones of vegetation (semi-arid steppe or dry belt, semi-humid grass-steppe or prairie, forest steppe or park belt, forest or bush) have been drawn in accordance with the map of Hamilton and Freund.[1] The courses of the most important rivers and the railway lines provided a sufficient indication of the geographic background. But for a proper understanding of the location of the individual German settlements and their economic possibilities, the zones of vegetation were indispensable, because these are also settlement and economic zones.

The oldest—by far the most numerous and largest areas of German settlement—are to be found in the park belt. Those settling on the prairie came largely either from the United States, bringing with them the ideal of the "wheat miner," which undoubtedly could best be realized on the prairie, or they came from South Russia or the east bank of the Volga (*Wiesenseite*) where they had been used to the treeless steppe from the beginning. In the dry belt of southwestern Saskatchewan and southern Alberta, Germans have also settled, although not very many. The forest of the north—the bush—where lighter soils promised lower yields, and where in contrast to the prairie breaking ground required arduous effort to clear initially, has only in exceptional cases been the destination of immigrants, as long as there was still good cheap land available in the park belt and prairie.

The checkerboardlike survey of the Prairie provinces into townships containing thirty-six sections each, with each settler's homestead a quarter section equalling 160 acres, has led to the single farmstead as the form of settlement. Closed villages are exceptions. A settlement therefore actually consists of a larger or smaller, more or less uniformly-settled district of single farmsteads that are grouped around a gradually growing townlike center. A focal point is usually the railway station.

Under these circumstances a spatial projection of German settlements is possible only for the large, relatively homogeneously-settled German colonies of the Mennonites in southern Manitoba (East and West Reserves) and north of Saskatoon, as well as for the Catholic St. Peter's and St. Joseph's colonies (areas marked with marginal hatching). For the two Catholic colonies, the diocesan boundaries (i.e., those of the German Benedictine Abbey of Muenster and of the German Oblate mission) are shown. In general, however, only graphic symbols representing the absolute numbers of German-speaking people made sense. The various red circles, therefore, stand for 1,000, five hundred and one hundred Germans respectively who do not necessarily live in closed settlement, even though of course an accumulation of circles in a specific area is also indicative of the relative density and rather far-reaching homogeneity of German settlement in this area. More exactness in this respect might only be obtained by identifying the ethnic origin of the owners of each quarter section of a particular area. For western Canada's Germans this has been done so far only by C.A. Dawson's two maps of the Catholic St. Peter's and St. Joseph's colonies,[2] which are reproduced in the Appendix as Maps 4 and 5.

The map shows as few as a hundred Germans who settled in the same township. Only in that way does the fact of any German settlement for wide areas become visible at all, and the extensive scattering of the German population become really obvious.

The map thus shows the numerical strength of the German element; not, however, in relation to the remaining ethnic groups. Only a general map of the ethnic population of the Prairie provinces could accomplish that. To produce it with modern methods would be up to the Canadian Bureau of Statistics in Ottawa. It had already made an attempt in this direction in its *Atlas of Canada* of 1915. There, based on the racial origin statistics of the 1911 Census, it identified those ethnic groups by a distinct color for each township that formed the majority of the township's population (see Appendix, Map 3).[4] Reference should also be made to the maps of the rural population which are reproduced below (see Appendix, Map 2), of German (as well as of Austrian, Dutch, Polish and Russian) origin in the atlas *Agriculture, Climate and Population of the Prairie Provinces of Canada* of 1931 reproduced below. It illustrates by means of dots the results of the first postwar Census of 1921 which, however, is only of very limited usefulness as far as the data on the Germans are concerned.

In determining the size of the circles for 1,000, for five hundred and a hundred Germans, I took care that in each province the total area taken up by these circles is roughly in the same ratio to the total area settled as the proportion of the German ethnic group to the total population. Thus the impression, corresponding to the facts, is created that in the centrally located Province of Saskatchewan, the German element constitutes about 15 per cent, in the two other provinces about 8 to 9 per cent, of the total population (see Appendix, Table 3).

The square blocks representing the German element in the larger cities are not in proportion to the respective city's total population, whose number appears below the name of that city. These blocks are only proportional in size to each other and to the circles representing the rural German population. In this instance I thought it was more important to convey the proper proportion between the size of the urban and the rural German element in order for the map to show clearly that we are dealing with an ethnic group that is four-fifths rural in character.

An illustration of the denominational structure on the map was deemed expedient, because to this day the bond of unity is strongest within the individual denominational groups, and because a survey of the denominational structure is essential for understanding the obstacles to organizational association among the segments of the German ethnic groups. In the process of settlement, attention was paid from the beginning not only to a certain degree of ethnic consolidation, but also to denominational homogeneity, so that better spiritual care could be provided for the very church-oriented German immigrants. Thus here Lutherans joined Lutherans, there Catholics joined Catholics or Mennonites joined Mennonites, just as the German colonies in eastern Europe, from which almost 90 per cent of the German immigrants originated, had almost always been established on a homogeneous denominational basis. On the map the German Baptist congregations

(4,800 souls) and the few congregations of the Reformed and Moravian Churches have been added to the Lutherans, just as the Hutterites (near Elie west of Winnipeg, south of Lethbridge and near Beiseker in Alberta) have been added to their spiritual kin, the Mennonites. A special subdivision was chosen for those who converted to a church of British tradition (e.g. the United Church of Canada) and who have thereby made a very important step in the direction of abandoning their inherited ethnic identity, and also for those who joined such sects as the Adventists, Jehovah's Witnesses, Sabbatarians, the Holy Rollers, etc. that have found a following, particularly in the dry belt with its great economic instability.

To map the places of origin of the German immigrants, however, is not possible. The bond of unity among fellow-countrymen has not been preserved as closely as among coreligionists. Thus, for instance, German Lutherans from Galicia, Bukovina, Poland, Volhynia, northern Germany and the United States, and German Catholics from South Russia, Banat, the Volga, Bavaria and western Germany joined to form new homogeneous settlements.

Among the various sources used and evaluated, the most important ones are the racial origin statistics according to the 1931 Census, published in the *Seventh Census of Canada*, Ottawa 1933, vol. II. The data contained in it were analyzed and supplemented by the denominational statistics in the same census, as well as on the basis of 128 handwritten reports from various districts of German settlement and church congregations. These reports were initiated and collected by editor-in-chief Bott in Winnipeg in 1932-33. He made them available to me for evaluation. I was further aided by parish statistics of German-Canadian churches, and finally by my own inquiries and research during a study trip through the Prairie provinces from May to August 1934. Only the rather laborious processing of these materials based on private enumerations and computations, which have thus become accessible to scholarship for the first time, has made possible the verification and revision of the official statistics. This has given the map presented here a far-reaching precision, though not perfected in all points to the degree desirable.

To confine oneself exclusively to the illustration of the faulty Canadian racial origin statistics when drawing a map of the German element will not do. The map attached to the article "Alberta" in *Handwörterbuch des Grenz- und Auslanddeutschtums*[5] took into consideration besides the "Germans by origin", the German-speaking natives of Russia. The format combines the presentation of absolute numbers by means of dots, with the illustration of their ratio to the total population by way of hatching, a methodologically innovative approach. This map, which is reproduced in the Appendix, however, is unfortunately still based on the 1921 statistics on origin, which were collected when the effects of the war psychosis were still apparent. Even the 1931 statistics on origin are still sufficiently imprecise as a comparison with the 1931 data on mother tongue and the 1936 statistics on racial origin reveals (see Appendix, Table 5). The 1936 quinquennial census of the Prairie provinces produces a figure on Germans by origin which is higher by one-quarter, even though between 1931 and 1936 no immigration at all had taken place as a result of the effects of the economic crisis, but rather some emigration to British Columbia, eastern Canada and back to Germany. The mistake still made in 1931 by many German immigrants from eastern Europe and their descendants to report their or their father's previous citizenship, instead of their German ethnic descent, has obviously been avoided in 1936 to a large degree, though not entirely. Today's number of ethnic Germans in the prairie provinces lies between the numbers reported in 1931 for the mother tongue (262,639) and for the 1936 racial origin statistics (308,927).

Our map has to rely unfortunately on the 1931 data on racial origin, which are undoubtedly too low. Yet only these have been published in the required differentiation, while the results of the two other statistics are available only by province. In two instances, however, corrections were possible on the basis of the 1931 Census itself, namely in the case of the Mennonites and the "Austrians." Of the 69,979 Mennonites of unquestionably German descent in linguistic and cultural respects, 11,021 reported themselves as of Russian and 35,373 as of Dutch origin. In the first instance, we have a case of ethnic origin being confused with the country of origin; in the second instance, ethnic origin and origin of their denomination are confused. The designation "Dutch by origin," however, is also supported by the fact that some of their predecessors did in fact migrate from Holland and Friesland to the delta of the Vistula, where they became germanized before they continued their migration to South Russia. In 1936, by the way, the majority of the Mennonites again acknowledged their German descent. To correct the extremely low figures of 1931, I therefore relied on the 1931 denominational statistics for our mapping of areas of Mennonite settlement.

In 1931, furthermore, tens of thousands of Germans from Galicia and Bukovina, by confusing their homeland with their ethnic descent, reported themselves as Austrians, a mistake that they, too, largely avoided in 1936, as the decrease in the number of "Austrians not otherwise specified" from 32,656 (1931) to 16,753 (1936) and the simultaneous increase in the number of Germans by origin indicates. Since all other nationalities of the former Habsburg Monarchy are listed separately, and the Austrians of the 1931 Census are to be found in particular in the areas settled by German immigrants, I felt justified in adding to the number of Germans up to three-quarters of the total number of those Austrians living in the cities and in such areas as Edenwold, Lemberg, Neudorf, Grayson, Yorkton, etc., settled by German immigrants from Galicia and Bukovina.

Our map shows the township as the smallest spatial unit, but the 1931 racial origin statistics unfortunately make available only the figures for every nine townships (in squares of three by three townships). For the exact location of the places where Germans live, the abovementioned private reports from the settlements were invaluable. Where these failed, some inaccuracy was unavoidable, insofar as a certain circle perhaps might instead have been put into the adjoining township. Often, the mere mentioning by name of a German parish in one of the church statistics gave a clue. Then, for example, the respective circles within the space of the nine townships in question were moved close to the railway station of the same name (provided such a station existed). In cases where German settlers may have been widely scattered, no entry at all was made on the map, provided the Census reported no more than 250 Germans by origin within the unit of nine townships and other sources did not indicate a small German settlement of at least a hundred persons in this area. We proceeded as a matter of principle rather too cautiously, and always rounded off numbers to the next lower full hundreds. Therefore the map shows only about two hundred thousand Germans, while the racial origin statistics on which it is based identify, as mentioned, 241,750 Germans by origin. The actual number of ethnic Germans in the Prairie provinces is certain to be even higher, probably around 260,000 to three hundred thousand.

In order not to impair the readability of the map, only the names of German settlements best known and most important for orientation could be entered. The names of the remaining districts settled by German people had to be left out.

Footnotes

[1] Hamilton and Freund (No. 174), 413.

[2] Dawson (No. 103), 280-283.

[3] *Atlas of Canada* (No. 68), 25-26.

[4] *Agriculture, Climate and Population* (No. 203), 91, illustration: "Racial Origin of Rural Population, Rural Population of German, Origin, 1921."

[5] *Handwörterbuch des Grenz- und Auslanddeutschtums*, vol. I (Breslau, 1933), 85.

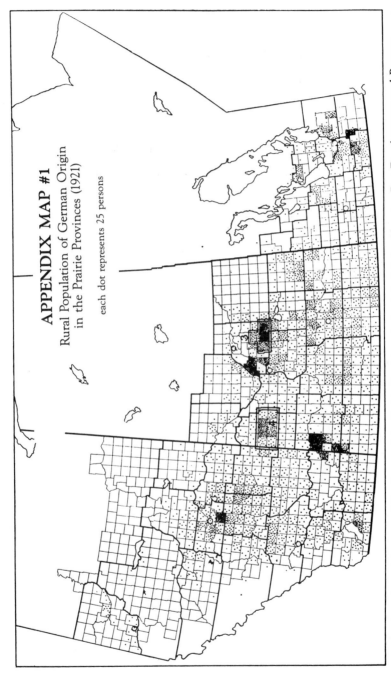

APPENDIX MAP #1

Rural Population of German Origin
in the Prairie Provinces (1921)

each dot represents 25 persons

Source: *Agriculture, Climate and Population of the Prairie Provinces. A Statistical Atlas Showing Past Development and Present Conditions* (Ottawa, 1931), p. 91.

APPENDIX MAP #2

Saskatchewan's Population of
Non-British Origin in 1911.

(SEE INSIDE FRONT COVER)

Based on the 1911 Census showing predominanting ethnic
origin in response to the question of paternal ancestry. An
undetermined number of Austrian and Russian respondents were
of German ethnic origin.

APPENDIX MAP #3

Alberta's Population of German Origin in 1921

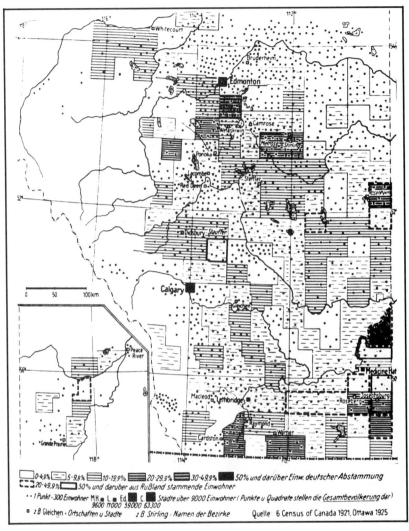

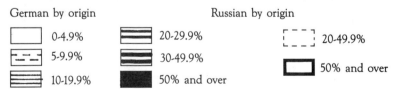

Proportion of Germans by origin among total population of Alberta by subdistricts, 1921. Source: H. Schwalm, in *Handwörterbuch des Grenz- und Auslanddeutschtums*, vol. I. (Breslau, 1933), 85

German by origin		Russian by origin
0-4.9%	20-29.9%	20-49.9%
5-9.9%	30-49.9%	50% and over
10-19.9%	50% and over	

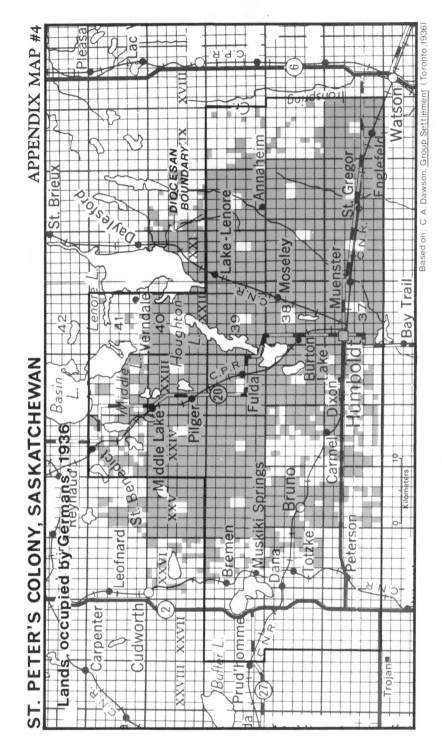

ST. PETER'S COLONY, SASKATCHEWAN

APPENDIX MAP #4

Lands occupied by Germans 1936

Based on: C. A. Dawson, Group Settlement (Toronto, 1936)

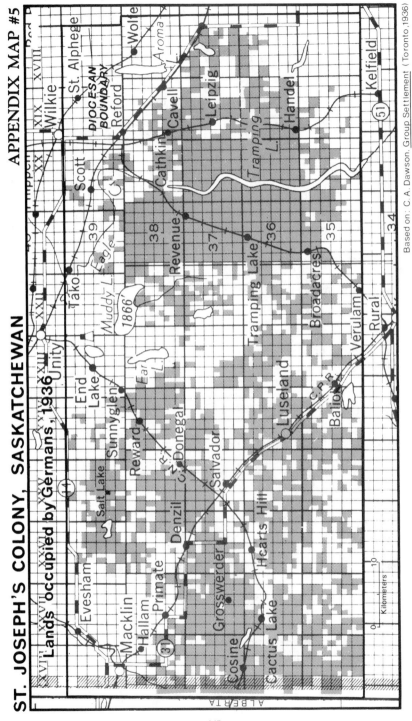

ST. JOSEPH'S COLONY, SASKATCHEWAN

APPENDIX MAP #5

Lands occupied by Germans, 1936

Based on: C. A. Dawson, Group Settlement (Toronto, 1936)

367

APPENDIX MAP #6

(SEE INSIDE BACK COVER)

Germans in Western Canada

By Heinz Lehmann

Scale 1 : 2,500,000

1,000 Germans ◯

500 Germans ◯

100 Germans ◯

1931 Population

Manitoba   700,139
Saskatchewan   921,785
Alberta   731,605

Provincial boundry —·—·—·—·

Main railway line ————————

Township with numbers [10 | 11]

Roman Catholics

Mennonites (including Hutterites)

Lutherans and smaller German Protestant groups, including Baptists

Members of small sects and Anglo-Saxon denominations

Germans in cities with 10,000 population or more ■

Northern boundary of zones of vegetation:

the park belt (parkland)   ————
the semi-humid grass steppe (prairie)   — — —
the semi-arid grass steppe (dry belt)   ··········

Heinz Lehmann, May 1985.

Elder David Toews and Heinz Lehmann at the Russlander Mennonite reunion in Herschel, Saskatchewan, 18 July, 1934.

Sod house, with German settlers, St. Joseph's colony, Saskatchewan, around 1900.

The first church in Bruderheim, Alberta, in the early 1890s. This picture was given to Lehmann in 1934 by settlers.

Heinz Lehmann Collection

Katherine Voelpel-Page

Farm of Johann and Margarete Voelpel in Kipling, Saskatchewan, 1914. In 1903 they homesteaded on a quarter section of Kipling and within a decade were able to build this impressive two-storey brick home and the surrounding farm buildings.

Katherine Voelpel-Page

Johann and Margarete Voelpel in Winnipeg, 1910. They grew up in different parts
of Russia, married in 1892 at the age of 23 and 22 in the West Russian province
of Volhynia and emigrated as day laborers to Winnipeg in 1894 with two
children. After working in Winnipeg and Pine Ridge, Manitoba for nine years,
they bought their own homestead in Kipling, Saskatchewan. By 1914 they had
become prosperous farmers with eight children.

German farmers from Volhynia threshing grain crop near Kipling, Sask., 1918.

Germans from Volhynia meet itinerant Lutheran minister Honebein (center) in the prairies near Kipling, Sask., 1924.

Katherine Voelpel-Page

German farmers from Volhynia in Kipling, Sask., 1918, cutting grain with four-horse teams.

Katherine Voelpel-Page

German Sunday school teachers in Kipling, Sask., in the early 1920s. They were the children of five German pioneer families from Russia (the Voelpels, Herters, Hirsekorns, Bachels and Montheys) who came to Canada in the mid-1890s and decided to homestead together in Kipling, Sask.

Katherine Voelpel-Page

A wedding party of second-generation Volhynia-Germans in front of the Lutheran church in Edenland near Kipling, Sask., 1925.

Father Krist in front of his rectory in St. Joseph's colony, Saskatchewan, in 1934.
Next to him, his new housekeeper who had just arrived from Essen, Germany.

Heinz Lehmann

Two of the pioneers of St. Joseph's colony, Sask., who were interviewed by Heinz Lehmann in 1934.

A German settler breaking virgin prairie sod in the Saskatchewan bush, spring 1934.

Heinz Lehmann

Heinz Lehmann

A German from Russia photographed in Saskatchewan in 1934 with her spinning wheel from her homeland.

Heinz Lehmann

Reunion of Russlander Mennonites near Herschel, Saskatchewan, July 17-18, 1934.

Heinz Lehmann

The reunion of these Mennonite refugees from Soviet Russia near Herschel, Sask., was held in tents on the farm of Abraham P. Klassen and was attended by entire families from far and wide.

Heinz Lehmann

A pioneer German homesteader in the Saskatchewan bush improving his first
dwelling, 1934.

Heinz Lehmann

The Hutterite communal farm at Elie, near Winnipeg, in 1934.

Heinz Lehmann

Heinz Lehmann

A farm near St. Peter's colony, Sask., 1934, belonging to post-World War I German immigrants from eastern Europe.

Heinz Lehmann

Post-World War I German immigrants farming near St. Peter's colony, Sask., 1934.

Heinz Lehmann

The Abraham P. Klassen family, post-World War I German Mennonite immigrants from Russia, in front of their farmhouse near Herschel, Sask., July 1934.

Heinz Lehmann

A Russlander Mennonite family attending the reunion near Herschel,
Sask., July 1934.

Heinz Lehmann

Three generations of the Hermann Lenzmann family in 1934. These Russlander
Mennonites fled the Russian Revolution and settled near Herschel in
Saskatchewan in the 1920s.

German Day rally in Winnipeg, 1931, with the German Consul, Dr. Heinrich Seelheim (left) and Bernhard Bott, editor of *Der Courier*, on the podium.

A scene from the German Day rally in Winnipeg, 1931.

Motorcade in Winnipeg on the occasion of German Day celebrations, 1931.

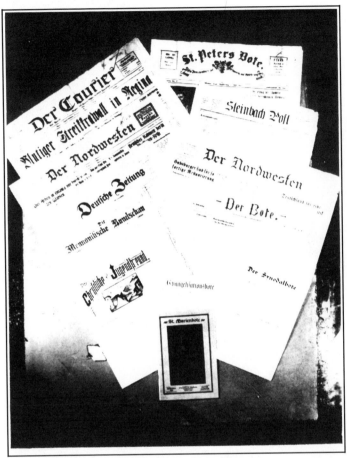

German-language papers in western Canada, 1934.

Elder Jacob H. Janzen, one of the leading Russlander Mennonite writers, celebrating the tenth anniversary of his immigration to Canada at his home in Waterloo, Ont., 1934.

NOTES

NOTES TO CHAPTER I

Editor's note: Parts 1 to 5 of this chapter represent the "I. Kapitel" of *Zur Geschichte des Deutschtums in Kanada. Band I: Das Deutschtum in Ostkanada*. Part 6 is taken from *Das Deutschtum in Westkanada*, 21-22, 41-47. The number (in parentheses) immediately following the author's name always denotes the consecutive number under which the source is cited in the bibliography.

[1] Kapp (No. 225), 98 ff.

[2] See *ibid.*, 107:

> When in the summer the colony of New York furnished its quota for the expedition to Canada — which later failed ignominiously — it was decided "to add 300 Palatines to the 350 Christians and 150 Indians of Long Island." The Palatines supplied the desired number immediately . . . For the first time in the history of the colony Germans and Indians served in the same regiment, that of Colonel Schuyler. They never received any payment for their services. After their return, Governor Hunter even had them disarmed for fear they might become a threat to him, in spite of their prowess and willingness to serve.

See also Benton (No. 26), 36, who lists the names of some twenty Palatine soldiers. The 300 Palatines, by the way, were not, as a note by Pierce (No. 324), 294, suggests, on board the unlucky fleet, but were a part of the overland army that was supposed to march under the leadership of Colonel Nicholson past Lake Champlain to Montreal. It was recalled after the fleet began to return.

[3] Kingsford (No 238), vol. II, 444-473, gives a detailed account.

[4] Bittinger (No. 32), 130-134.

[5] Mönckmeier (No. 295), 10, and Faust (No. 137), vol. I, 249-252. According to Faust, forty families came in 1740, and 150-160 persons in 1742 to Waldoburg in Maine, almost all of whom participated in the campaign against Louisbourg in 1745.

[6] Zuberbühler reappears later in Lunenburg, N.S. See DesBrisay (No. 108).

[7] Faust, *ibid.*; Le Conte (No. 255), 112, and Burrage (No. 63), 86f.

[8] See Bittinger (No. 32), 206f. The regiment was led by Colonel (later General) Bouquet who came from Berne. The Swiss-born Haldimand, who later became Governor of Canada, was also an officer in this regiment. See Kingsford (No. 238), vol. VI, 471.

[9] See beginning of chapter II.

[10] See chapter II, part 1.

[11] See the address of Franklin to the English Parliament before the outbreak of the war, quoted in Beidelman (No. 25), 90, and Faust (No. 137), vol. I, 291. See also the blacklist of the Loyalists in Pennsylvania which includes barely any German names: Sherk (No. 387), 109 ff.

[12] Faust (No. 137), vol. I, 287.

[13] Flick (No. 139), 182, concludes that about half of all the inhabitants of New York State remained loyal to the English cause.

[14] Casselman (No. 83), 61, indicates that "the Palatines were divided in their opinions, but the majority was loyal." See also Bittinger (No. 32), 240: "In the midst of the patriotic ardour, they [the Pennsylvania Germans] are shocked to learn that the Germans of Tryon County [New York] and of North Carolina 'appear to be unfriendly to the common cause'."

[15] Benton (No. 26), 122, and Cruikshank (No. 99), 8. Her maiden name was Katharina Weissenburg.

[16] Benton, 66 ff.

[17] See Canniff (No. 76), 67f. and 666; Faust (No. 137), vol. I, 305, and Cruikshank (No. 99), 8.

[18] Canniff, 68; Benton (No. 26), 73, and Cruikshank (No. 99), 30f.

[19] See chapter II, part 6.

[20] See the accounts of the battles in Kapp (No. 225), and Faust (No. 137), vol. I, 310 ff., as well as the note in Pierce (No. 324), 295.

[21] Reprinted in Benton (No. 26), 120.

[22] According to Simms (No. 394), 529, and Kapp (No. 225), 274f. At the Schoharie the Revolution caused the bitterest disputes. Brother stood against brother. Simms (No. 394), 206 ff. gives interesting details. At the Mohawk matters seemed to have taken a quieter course. According to Benton (No. 26), 120, the estate of only one German appeared to have been declared confiscated. He was Johann Jost Herckheimer, a relative of the general fighting on the American side. In 1783 he settled in Kingston Township at the Bay of Quinte. See chapter II, part 6.

[23] Pierce (No. 324), 295.

[24] See chapter II, parts 3 to 7.

[25] Schlözer (No. 361), 521.

[26] Thus Beidelman (No. 25), 100, with whose cautious estimates I concur. Eelking (No. 125), vol. II, 225, on the other hand, estimates the total number of casualties to be a mere 1,800 men.

[27] Particularly indicative of this appears to be a decree of the Duke of Brunswick dated February 8, 1783, which is reprinted in Eelking, *ibid.*, 253-255. For each of their soldiers who did not return home, the English government had to pay a high capitation to the Duke. The fewer who returned, therefore, the greater the profit.

[28] Eelking (No. 125), vol. II, 230.

[29] *Ibid.*

[30] Beidelman (No. 25), 100.

[31] One indication of their number is a note by Loeher in Stricker's *Germania* (No. 417), vol. II, 492. According to this, a German regiment appears to have been stationed in Montreal at the end of the war and from its ranks "around 1,000 persons settled in Canada, some also staying in Sorel as invalids." There is also the remark in Monarque (No. 294), 153, that as many as 1,200 Brunswick and several hundreds of Hanau and Anhalt-Zerbst troops had remained in Canada.

[32] See chapter II, parts 3 to 6.

[33] The division into Upper and Lower Canada was retained until 1841 and corresponds to the present one between Ontario and Quebec.

[34] Thus, e.g., Canniff (No. 76), 616.

[35] See chapter III, part 1.

[36] For the following Cassel (No. 82), 63ff. and Bittinger (No. 32), 93.

[37] In the 19th century the Canadian census for a long time had only one common classification for Mennonites and Tunkers without distinguishing between them.

[38] That this reasoning was typical of the farmers, taking into account the needs of their children and children's children, and was, in fact, the main reason for the emigration, is told by Mabel Dunham with particular affection in her novel *The Trail of the Conestoga*. It is based on the existing source materials and has as its subject the Mennonite immigration to Ontario.

[39] See chapter III, part 1.

[40] See chapter III, parts 1, 2 and 5.

[41] See chapter III, part 2.

[42] A reference in Benton (No. 26), 117, seems to suggest a larger emigration of Germans from New York State to Ontario. The Palatine settlements at the Mohawk and Schoharie had experienced severe difficulties due to the constant crop failures from 1816 to 1820. The completion of the Erie Canal on top of that, which made grain from the western states more cheaply available, deprived them of their hitherto secure markets, such as Albany. "The Herkimer County recovered slowly from its depressed and embarrassed condition. It lost, however, very considerably of its German population between 1818 and 1830." For the Germans from the upper Hudson, Ontario was the closest area where cheap and good land for settlement could still be obtained.

[43] See chapter III, part 1.

[44] The three exceptions of the eighteenth century were the two thousand German emigrants of 1750-1752 who were settled in Lunenburg and Halifax (see chapter II, part 1), the approximately six hundred emigrants who came to Nova Scotia after the Seven Years' War (see chapter II, part 1), and the 350 Lutherans who after a stopover in New York State settled in York County, Ontario, in 1794 (see chapter III part 5).

[45] See chapter III, footnote 49.

[46] Sartorius (No. 352), 93f. For a systematic analysis see List (No. 267), 14 ff.

[47] Lord Durham's Report (No. 272), vol. II, 212f.

[48] As early as 1826, the parliament of Upper Canada passed a law according to which unoccupied land, i.e. Crown land, was to be sold at low rates or given away free in return for certain obligations. See *Canada* (No. 71), 78-86. It was supposed to prevent land speculation and enable the true colonist to settle even with limited means. It became, therefore, the precursor of the Dominion Land

Act of 1872 which is still valid today as the homestead law in western Canada. Concerning the stipulations of the Canada Land Company on whose territory many Germans settled, see chapter III, footnote 116.

[49] Loeher (No. 268), 276, and *Canada and Its Provinces* (No. 388), vol. XI, 51.

[50] About the declining immigration of the Mennonites, who appear to have come over in scattered numbers until the American Civil War, see chapter III, part 2.

[51] In the 19th century Quebec was as important as a port of immigration for the American West as for the Provinces of Quebec and Ontario. According to the Reports on Immigration, an average of one-third of all the immigrants, including the British ones, continued on to the United States. See Cowan (No. 91), 236f.

[52] Western Ontario suffered from a chronic shortage of labor. In 1830 it was decided to encourage an immigration of American agricultural laborers by all possible means. See Cowan (No. 91), 238.

[53] As early as 1836, A.C. Buchanan, the Chief Emigration Agent for Canada, summarized the reasons for the neglect of the Canadian route as follows in his Reports on Immigration (Great Britain *Parliamentary Papers*, hereafter cited as P.P., 1837, XLII):

> The superior accommodation and less crowded state of the American vessels, which generally perform the voyage in a shorter space of time, offer sufficient inducement to those who can afford it, to give the preference to that [the New York] route; while the many facilities which they meet on arrival, smoothing the way, as it were, to the Province Line and the borders of Lake Ontario and Erie, have obtained for the transit by way of New York a large share of popular favour. It is gratifying, however, to recall to mind that Upper Canada receives every year by this route a valuable accession of prudent and steady settlers whose means and capital enable them at once to become permanent occupiers of the land.

[54] Nor did any German immigrants arrive on English boats in Quebec prior to 1846. Only a single large shipment was reported before this date. The Report on Immigration for 1836 (P.P., 1836, XLII, 17) states: "From the continent of Europe 483 immigrants have arrived during the season, chiefly Swiss and Bavarians who sailed from Hâvre du Grace. Part of the latter proceeded to join their countrymen on the Ohio, and about 200 have settled in the Eastern Townships (Prov. Quebec)."

[55] See e.g. the complaints in the Report on Immigration for 1850 (P.P., 1851, XL).

[56] See e.g. Schmidt (No. 364) and *Canada* (No. 72).

[57] As published in Mönckmeier (No. 295), 192.

⁵⁸ At that time on the average more than 2 per cent of the German emigrants died on this fifty-day-long voyage and at the quarantine station.

⁵⁹ See the computations in the Canadian Reports on Immigration.

⁶⁰ See e.g. the Reports on Immigration for 1852 and 1853. In 1854, the record year of German immigration via Quebec, distress and poverty reached a climax even though the immigration of a number of wealthy Germans to Ontario is documented (P.P., 1854-55, XXXIX, 125). Cholera took a much higher toll among the Germans than among the other immigrants (p. 126).

Particular reference is made to a shipment of 422 community paupers from Baden (*ibid.*, 117) who had been provided jointly by the Baden government and by their communities with a free passage to Quebec and with a minimal sum of ten Gulden upon their arrival there. Because of the more expensive passage to New York and the capitation duty which the United States imposed on each arrival to prevent the immigration of paupers, Baden disposed of them via Quebec. They disembarked as late as October, much too late for Canadian conditions. Destitute, with nowhere to go, old, sick, and weak, they became a charge on the Canadian government for the winter.

In 1855, again, the same type of emigrant was to be found, although under somewhat more fortunate circumstances (P.P., 1857, X, 904). The German immigrants sent to the Ottawa Valley in 1858, too, arrived destitute, and depended for the first two years on the mercy of their neighbors (P.P., 1859, Sess. 2, XXII, Appendix 9). Initially, by the way, the German emigration via Quebec was not characterized by particular poverty. On the contrary, in 1847 it is reported: "The Germans were, as a class, well provided with means. Some were wealthy, and all possessed an ample stock of clothing, suitable tools and implements, and even furniture." After 1860 references appear again which even point to the wealth of most of the German immigrants.

⁶¹ That the Germans were primarily farmers and wanted to remain in Canada is explicitly confirmed in the Reports on Immigration. In 1858 it is noted (P.P., 1859, Sess. 2, XXII): "A larger portion of the people who emigrate from North Germany is composed of farmers as distinguished from labourers, than is the case in the emigration from the British Isles; and they more generally seek for land for immediate settlement than the English or Irish families."

⁶² *Census of Canada, 1871*, vol. IV. See chapter III, footnotes 19, 54, and chapter III, part 3. An immigration checkpoint at the Canadian-American border did not yet exist. German immigration from this side was nonetheless noticed by the Canadian authorities. In a report to London ("Reports made for the year 1848 to the Secretary of State for the Colonies," P.P., 1849, XXXIV, 16) the percentages of the foreign-born according to the two census reports of the Province of Upper Canada (Ontario) of 1842 and 1848 are compared and commented on as follows: "The increase of Germans (and Dutch) has been very great, while the decrease in natives of the United States is rather singular, when it is known that large numbers come annually from the Union into Canada, the inference is that no influx of native Americans takes place." The Dutch are only mentioned

because in the early Canadian census reports they were listed together with "Germans" and "Prussians" in one classification. There had been, as a matter of fact, no Dutch immigration to Canada, so that in the 1871 Census no specific mention is made of the Dutch. In the Canadian Reports on Immigration of those years that deal exclusively with the immigration via Quebec, there is only one pertinent reference in the Report for 1846 (P.P., 1847, XXXIX):

> Among the immigrants who have come into the province by the route of the United States were a party of Germans, 500 in number, who arrived at Hamilton in November. They were represented as having but limited means on arrival, but they were proceeding to their friends and countrymen in the townships of Waterloo and Wilmot, who are competent to afford them the most efficient aid in their establishment. This party, with German immigrants who have arrived by the route of St. Lawrence, of whom 200 have settled in the same section of the province, will prove a valuable addition to our population. They are generally hardy and industrious and from their extreme thriftiness, usually make successful settlers. The townships in the Wellington District, established by the Pennsylvanians of German origin, are amongst the finest and most thriving settlements in the province, and they have served as nucleus around which a very extensive and now populous district has grown up.

[63] The geographer Traugott Bromme (No. 52), who travelled in Canada in the 1830s, estimated for good reason the number of Germans in Ontario to be 20,000 at that time (*ibid.*, 265). By 1848 they had probably doubled in number. According to rough estimates there appear to have been in Waterloo and Perth 4,000 to 5,000 Mennonites and other German Americans, besides the 12,000 immigrants from Germany. In the Niagara district there were approximately as many, and scattered over the remaining districts of western Ontario an additional 5,000 German Americans. In eastern Ontario, where the German Loyalist settlements in Dundas-Stormont and in the area around the Bay of Quinte from Frontenac to East Northumberland County date back as far as 1784, and where in 1871 far more than 30,000 persons of German descent were counted, there must have been 12,000 to 15,000 persons of German descent living at that time. To these would have to be added several hundred German-American farmers scattered over almost all the counties.

[64] The disappointment that, even after the opening of the direct route from Hamburg-Bremen to Quebec, the Germans continued to come largely via New York, is noticeable in every Report on Immigration by the Canadian authorities in the 1850s.

[65] For the years 1872 and 1885-1888 the total of the numbers in the last three columns (areas of destination) is not equal to the total number of immigrants.

[66] For the years 1862 and 1867, for which we have no figures, a German immigration approximately equal in volume to those of the remaining years of this decade may be assumed.

[67] See particularly Bryce (No. 57), 157 ff.

[68] Willson (No. 460), vol. II, 182 ff.

[69] Martin (No. 282), 116; also Bryce (No. 58), 241.

[70] Von Grafenried (No. 159).

[71] *Ibid.*, 94 ff.

[72] See the report of farmer Polson in Bryce (No. 57), 163.

[73] *Maria Immaculata*, XVI (1908-09), 82f. Also Armstrong (No. 19), 250.

[74] "Die Schweizer Kolonisten . . . " (No. 381), X, 436 ff., 489 ff., and XI, 12 ff.

[75] Ross (No. 341), 57 ff., and Bryce (No. 58), 350.

[76] See "Die Schweizer Kolonisten . . . " (No. 381), XI, 15 ff., as well as Faust (No. 137), vol. I, 482 ff.

[77] Reprinted in *Census of Canada, 1871*, vol. IV, 175.

[78] According to information from Prof. Hennings, Freiburg, Germany.

NOTES TO CHAPTER II

[1] About the political reasons for this see chapter I, part 2.

[2] The proclamation to the German Protestants which Dick had published at Rotterdam and other towns in Germany by order of the English government is reprinted in English translation as Appendix I to Raymond (No. 330).

[3] After the end of the War of the Austrian Succession the desire to emigrate was temporarily quite strong again. As an example of the false pretenses that succeeded in inciting thousands of Germans to emigrate at the time, a few passages shall be cited from this prospectus (No. 194), 198 and 206f.:

> . . . Governor Cornwallis arrived with 2,000 persons in the company of two preachers and two teachers who had brought sufficient provisions and other utensils in order to establish themselves there. In addition to these, discharged soldiers who had served in New England, and others in Nova Scotia would be gladly and willingly accepted and food and lands to cultivate would be allotted to them. In response to this most gracious royal disposition more than fifteen ships of German families had arrived in Nova Scotia during the months of August, September and October. [That was an outright lie! H.L.]
>
> Because Nova Scotia is situated in such a blessed and fertile region and the government is so admirably organized that each, if he so desires, can live according to his station, quietly, happily and blissfully . . . one should not wonder that so many persons leave Germany annually and come in large numbers to this blessed and happy land. For how can the poor subjects of the Old World find fault with a gift of thirty-four acres of land, which he can cultivate

and use for his benefit for ten years, without having to pay the government the least amount in taxes and other duties, whereas in Europe he owned barely a few acres of land and had to live off these in poverty and indigence, in want and misery, and even with the hardest and most onerous effort could barely earn enough to meet the demands that many a prince made upon him. Here not only can he eat his bread by himself with his family, but he can also live without worries during the first year, because he with his entire family will be fed and looked after by His Royal Majesty. Here he does not have to fear that his grain or fruits which he had sown and planted in the sweat of his brow, and with great difficulty, would be consumed by game. Instead, when harvest time comes he can gather the produce that God had given him as a present without bother. In the woods he can find enough deer, and in the rivers and lakes enough fish, to appease his hunger and delight his appetite without having to worry that he would be punished for this, since no prince has yet seized the woods and rivers and made them his property. How happy, therefore, are the inhabitants of Nova Scotia, who not only can enjoy peacefully and quietly all that which nature produces for sustenance as well as amusement of human life, but who also are able to rejoice in a complete freedom of their consciences and an undisturbed practice of their religion.

For the response to this prospectus we quote *Der Deutsche Pionier* (No. 113), XIV (1882), 150:

Due to this account, and since Köhler had employed several sub-agents in the towns along the Rhine who had to recruit emigrants for him, numerous Germans were, in fact, persuaded to emigrate to Nova Scotia instead, as hitherto, to Pennsylvania and the Carolinas. The enterprise benefited from the particular advantage that it was able to pretend to be authorized by the King and Parliament, whereas the promotions for Pennsylvania, Virginia, Carolina, etc. were all private affairs. Dick, or rather his commissioner Köhler, also received from the Reichstag in Regensburg the Imperial authority to undertake such solicitations in those German lands of the Empire whose princes would grant their subjects the right to emigrate. It was, therefore, a legal undertaking.

[4] For the following see *Canada and Its Provinces* (No. 388), vol. XIII, 83-85. Hill (No. 191), 8, dates the arrival of the first transport in the month of September. Partridge (No. 320), VI, 138, however, says about the arrival of the first Germans: "The actual number was 312, who arrived in Halifax in safety on July 13th, 1750, in the ship *Ann*."

[5] Partridge , *ibid*., VI, 138.

[6] *Ibid*., 137: "Mr. Dick, it appears, had engaged to send over 1,000 foreign Protestants on condition of being paid one guinea for each person." Hence he only cared to have as large a number as possible. Several of them appear to have been more than eighty years old (see p. 124). After a detailed account of their situation (*ibid*., 138 ff.), Partridge (p. 124) continues:

There can be little doubt, that many of the German colonists were poor, though not all. But the miseries of their condition were to a great extent caused by others; they had in the first place been deceived by the Government Agent Dick, as to the condition in the new settlement. They doubtless expected the land cleared at least, and anticipated no difficulty with the aborigines, and even Mr. Dick could hardly have supposed that a government which held out so great inducements to emigrants, would make no provision for tools and implements, whereby they might build themselves a shelter from the elements.

[7] *Canada and Its Provinces* (No. 388), vol. XIII, 83. Hill (No. 191), 8, states the exact number of 958 for 1751 and about one thousand for 1752; so does Bryce (No. 59), 245.

[8] See DesBrisay (No. 108), 22, and Bourinot (No. 41), 17. Also Lucas (No. 271), vol. III, 51. The assumption that a brigade of Brunswick-Lunenburg troops belonged to those English troops who founded Halifax in 1749, appears to be based on a misunderstanding of the author of the article in *Der Deutsche Pionier* (No. 113), XIV, 150. Faust (No. 137), vol. I, 256, attributes it to this incorrect source.

[9] Lucas (No 271), vol. I, 221.

[10] Partridge (No. 320). VI, 140.

[11] *Ibid.*, 144: "They had been compelled, however their wives and families might suffer from want of proper dwellings, to work out every penny of their passage money."

As an interesting example, Agnes Creighton in her article "A Plea of Remembrance" (No. 92) publishes the shipping contract, by which those eighty-three Germans who came over with their families on the *Pearl*, had to bind themselves to work off their passage in Nova Scotia. By 1907 an original copy of this contract had still been preserved by a Lunenburg family, and reads as follows:

> We, the undersigned passengers on board the ship named the *Pearl*, bound from here out of Rotterdam, overseas to Halifax situated in the Province of Nova Scotia or New Scotland in North America, witness and acknowledge hereby: — That we are bound to Mr. John Dick, Agent of his British Majesty for the Province of Nova Scotia aforesaid, to pay the same in Dutch currency in an honourable, faithful and legal manner. Which different sums we collectively and individually, and each man for him and his, vow and solemnly promise most truly to pay and discharge to Mr. John Dick as soon as God shall give us a prosperous arrival at our above-mentioned Nova Scotia. This we shall do by the work of our hands in all and every manner in which the Governor there shall demand or find for us; at the payment for our work of eighteen Pence Sterling per day, for so long until our debts according to agreement for every one of us shall be paid and discharged.

> In witness whereto, and for our own confirmation whereof have we made of this obligation three copies of the same tenour, of which when one is fulfilled the other two shall be of no weight or value.

> Signed and sealed with our own hands at Rotterdam,
> June 30th, 1751. [*Translation as cited in* Creighton, *ibid.*, 5].

[12] *Canada and Its Provinces* (No. 388), vol. XIII, 84.

[13] *Ibid.*, 84f. DesBrisay (No. 108), 27f., etc.

[14] See Raymond (No. 330), 25 ff. Of the approximately 10,000 Acadians about 6,000 to 7,000 were forcibly deported in 1755 and an additional one thousand somewhat later. The remainder fled or were left scattered in the interior of the country. See *ibid.*, 35: "The expulsion of the Acadians from the territory which they and their forefathers had possessed for nearly a century and a half, left Nova Scotia with a European population practically confined to the to the town of Halifax and the German settlement of Lunenburg."

[15] *Ibid.*, 53-54, and DesBrisay (No. 108), 53.

[16] The Census of 1766-67 showed the population of Nova Scotia to be already as high as 11,779 and that of New Brunswick to be 1,196. A peculiar feature of the immigration from the New England colonies is its eastward direction, whereas the other North American migrations were always characterized by their westward direction.

[17] Raymond, *ibid.*, 85-86. The German Society in Philadelphia had applied for a total grant of one hundred thousand acres of land for settlement in the Maritime Provinces at that time. In 1764 the promotional campaign for it had begun among the Pennsylvania-Germans. "Colonel McNutt arrived at Philadelphia in September 1764, and at once found a field for his energies among the Germans and Quakers of Pennsylvania." His report, anticipating a large influx of Germans, is immediately passed on by the Governor of Nova Scotia to his superiors, the Lords of Trade, in a letter dated April 30, 1765, which states according to Raymond, 86:

> . . . the proposed settlements are to be undertaken by people of very sufficient and able circumstances and . . . the establishment of so many German families will serve to divert the annual current of German immigration from the colonies to Nova Scotia, which will materially be strengthened by the acquisition of these "frugal, laborious and industrious people," who will not only improve and enrich their property, but, if need be, "pertinaciously defend it."

[18] These figures are computed on the basis of the original statistical data as published by Allison (No. 11), 57 ff. In the *Census of Canada*, 1871, vol. IV, the data of 1766-1767 were converted to the new Census divisions, resulting in some inaccuracies. Only the total number of Germans—1,946 for greater Nova Scotia—has remained as high as before.

[19] One indication of this may be the following remark in Raymond, 95: "In 1766 McNutt had ceased to be a middleman between the German immigrants of Pennsylvania and the Nova Scotia government." McNutt may no longer have been the middleman, but German immigration continued.

[20] The English government itself, by the way, prohibited any further immigration from the Continent in 1753. See Faust (No. 137), vol. I, 257.

[21] The particulars are unfortunately not clear. See, however, E. Lehmann (No.

256), 16: "If we finally mention one last unsuccessful emigration attempt in 1765 whose remnants united to settle in Nova Scotia, then we have reached the most northerly point to which German settlements extended in North America during the previous century." According to Bleichröder (No. 34), 16, Officer Stümel led six hundred Palatines and Swabians to Nova Scotia, where they settled in Halifax and Annapolis. Mönckmeier (No. 295), 12, mentions Officer Strümpel and the year 1769. The Census of 1766-67 takes no account of these German immigrants, so that Mönckmeier's date seems to be more plausible.

[22] See chapter I, part 3, and chapter II, parts 3 and 4.

[23] See e.g. the position of Pastor Hausihl in the German colony in Halifax (chapter II, part 3).

[24] According to Lucas (No. 271), vol. III, 67, all of Nova Scotia was in a state of stagnation from that time on: "Nova Scotia was fairly complete in 1830 . . . A man might walk from end to end of Cape Breton Island and Nova Scotia, using Haliburton's *History* (1829) as guide-book and without finding anything except what he expected to find."

[25] DesBrisay (No. 108), 27f.

[26] Editor's note: this information is taken from IV.*Kapitel*, footnote 5, and H. Lehmann (No. 259), 4-5, footnote 2.

[27] For the following see *Canada and Its Provinces* (No. 388), vol. XIII, 84 ff.

[28] DesBrisay (No. 108), 49, quotes the following excerpt from the "Minutes of H.M. Council at Halifax":

> A return of the settlers at Lunenburg, with the alterations from the 28th of May 1753, being the time of embarkations, to the 22nd of January 1758:
>
> | | |
> |---|---:|
> | Original number | 1,453 |
> | Dead | 152 |
> | Discharged | 854 |
> | Deserted | 19 |
> | Born | 440 |
> | Entered and Re-entered | 506 |
> | Remaining at Lunenburg | 1,374 |
>
> (Signed) D. Christopher Jessen.

[29] According to Lucas (No. 271), vol. III, 51, Lunenburg produced as much as 13,000 bushels of rye and barley in 1767, when no other settlement on the coast of Nova Scotia, except for Chester, harvested even one thousand bushels of grain.

[30] According to the Census of 1766-67 the total Lunenburg population was barely larger than in 1753. Only 51 of the 1,468 inhabitants, by the way, were British. These were Scottish Protestants, or English officials and soldiers. See Faust (No. 137), vol. I, 256.

[31] Lucas (No. 271), vol. III, 51f. Among these Germans there were apparently also emigrants from those colonies founded by Palatines in Ireland in 1710. See chapter II, footnote 92. The particulars concerning Pernette and the boundaries of his land grant are in DesBrisay (No. 108), 181ff.

[32] Reprinted in DesBrisay (No. 108), 69-72.

[33] According to the Census of 1766-67 as published by Allison (No.,11), there were only twenty-three Germans among the 107 inhabitants of New Dublin, and only eleven Germans among the 231 inhabitants of Chester. About the Germans from Lunenburg as of 1891, we learn that (*ibid.*, 61):

> . . . a few families had moved out into the adjacent townships of Dublin and Chester, places where now the German element largely predominates, but which were originally settled under other auspices. In the course of the ensuing quarter of a century, this element had entered quite an extensive migration along the Atlantic shore in both easterly and westerly directions.

For the spreading of German colonists to the northeast see also Bouchette (No. 39,) 15: "St. Margaret's Bay . . . was settled by the descendants of some German and French families in 1783."

[34] DesBrisay (No. 108), 252.

[35] For example Wentzel's Lake (Lunenburg Tp.), Schmidtville (Halifax), Meyer's Creek—which was the name of Belleville, Ont. from 1790 to 1816 according to Canniff (No. 76), 495 and 499—Glen Becker (Dundas County, Ontario) and Mayerthorpe (Alberta).

[36] DesBrisay (No. 108), 145. Among the first settlers around 1780, we find the same names as in the land patent for the township of Lunenburg. "Zwicker, Ernst, Rooder, Loy, Ham, Mader, Smeltzer, Swinehammer, Moser, Eisenhauer, Lantz, Keiser, Vienot and Hyson were among the first settlers on the west side of the bay."

[37] In Bridgewater the first real house was built around 1812 (DesBrisay, 191 ff.). New Germany was founded around 1805, according to Lucas (No. 271), vol. III, 52. See also DesBrisay, 156: "New Germany is one of the most thriving agricultural districts in the County . . . First settlement . . . by persons from La Have, principally of German origin, between eighty and ninety years ago." (written in 1895!)

[38] The settlement of Riversdale at the La Have, for instance, not far from Wentzel's Lake between Bridgewater and New Germany, was founded as late as about 1845 by German settlers from Kingsburg (New Dublin Tp.), according to DesBrisay, 154.

[39] *Ibid.*, 193:

"People used to walk from the country outside what is now Bridgewater to Lunenburg to attend divine service Sunday after Sunday and return in the evening. There were no churches nearer home, and no school buildings. The children were instructed by itinerant teachers in private houses." In Mahone Bay the first church was built in 1832 and was used by Lutherans, Presbyterians, Baptists and Methodists together in harmony (*Ibid.*, 148). There were no national conflicts among the various denominations. Their members were all more or less of the same German descent. See e.g. the Board of Trustees of the church in Mahone Bay, on which Valentin Zwicker represented the Presbyterians, Peter Strum the Lutherans and Friedrich Mader the Methodists. In general the Germans in the whole county did not remain confined to the Lutheran congregations. Their acceptance of the forms of the originally sectarian English churches did not automatically entail the loss of their ethnic identity. The Methodists in Lunenburg, for instance, at first had a purely German worship service. They have had their own church since 1813 and George Roth was their first preacher (DesBrisay, 102).

[40] For the following see *Jubiläums-Büchlein* (No. 219), 5-8.

[41] The Anglican preacher P. Bryzelius, previously a Lutheran pastor, had been commissioned by the Bishop of London with the ministry of the Germans in Lunenburg. According to *Canada and its Provinces* (No. 388), vol. XI, 204, he served from 1766 to 1773 and held church services three times each Sunday, in German, English and French. His successor De la Roche, too, was apparently soon able to preach in three languages. At Easter 1775 his candidates for confirmation are reported to have consisted of 120 Germans, fifty French and thirty English (DesBrisay, 83f.).

[42] *Jubiläums-Büchlein, ibid.*

[43] DesBrisay, 95 ff., and *Jubiläums-Büchlein*, 8.

[44] See DesBrisay, 98, where the following is said about Pastor Cossmann: "He has preached regularly twice every Sunday, in one place or other. In the early days of his ministry he travelled annually about 4,000 miles, the most part in the saddle." In Halifax he preached occasionally in German until 1892 (*ibid.*, 97).

[45] See Loeher (No. 268), 344, writing in 1846: "Nova Scotia still has its vigorous German population which has spread over the entire province and, cut off from all communication with Germans, has gradually blended its Lower Saxon language with the English one."

[46] See *Jubiläums-Büchlein*, 8. See also the remark in DesBrisay, 99, about the celebration of the 350th anniversary of the Augsburg Confession in the church of Lunenburg in 1880. Pastor Cossmann read the confession in German. "Although many in the audience could not understand the German tongue, yet the older people and the better educated could, and a respectful hearing was obtained to the cause."

[47] The relationship between the 'Germans by origin' and the total population, according to the census, developed as follows:

	1871	1881	1901	1911	1921
total population	23,834	28,583	32,389	33,260	33,742
German by origin	16,612	20,102	22,709	22,837	17,867

(The 1891 Census did not ask for the "racial origin.")

[48] Hill (No. 191), 8, and Oppel (No. 317), 31.

[49] Partridge (No. 320), VI, 150.

[50] *Jubiläums-Büchlein* (No. 219), 3. According to Partridge (No. 320), VI, 151, the teacher's name was Torpel. For a fee of £ 10 annually he apparently had to read the prayers and to preach every Sunday "until the congregation should be able to procure and maintain the services of an ordained minister."

[51] *Jubiläums-Büchlein*, 3f. Particulars in Partridge (No. 320), VI, 145 ff.

[52] Partridge, *ibid.*, VI, 151 ff. On p. 154 the names of those confirmed are listed:

Joh. Aug. Peitsch	Phil. Haass
Caspar Hann	Regina Kühn
Wilhelm Dennemann	Elisabeth Hann
Michael Silber	Doroth. Schmidt
Phil. Fullmer	Sophie Schmidt
Math. Saur	Elis. Messer
Caspar Köller	Elis. Röchl
And. Baur	Cather. Borgeld
Christopher Schmidt	

[53] *Jubiläums-Büchlein*, 3f. The Protestant German state churches did not show the least interest in the spiritual care of those who had emigrated.

[54] Partridge (No 320), VI, 147 and VII, 73 ff. The first German church service held by an ordained minister among the Lutherans was conducted by the Anglican military chaplain Slater on Pentecost 1758. Later Dr. Breynton, the rector of St. Paul's, used to consider St. George's congregation a sub-group of St. Paul's congregation.

[55] *Ibid.*, VI, 148, and VII, 77f.

[56] Partridge, VII, 78:

> The history of the church of St. George continues with uneventful smoothness during the years 1762 to 1784. The schoolmaster officiated on Sundays when no clergyman was present, and good and energetic Mr. Breynton gave what services he could, baptising, marrying and burying their dead. The German congregation, however, did not consider themselves a part of St. Paul's.

For the schoolmaster's name see *ibid.* 79. Breynton used to preach mostly in English but apparently had the liturgy read in German (*ibid.*, VI, 147).

[57] The 1767 Census (No. 11) reports the number 264. See also Partridge, VII, 77-78: "In February 1763, the number of parishioners in Halifax is returned by Mr. Breynton as being about 1300, of whom 250 were Germans (and French), who continued the worship in the German Church in the north suburbs."

It appears that in 1753 the number of Germans remaining in Halifax was larger. It could be that in the meantime some of them moved on to the northeast, where in the area of Halifax County in three locations near the coast there were sizable German settlements in the 19th century (see chapter II, footnote 69).

[58] According to his diary Seume appears to have spent the entire time of the war in Halifax.

[59] See Brown (No 54), 75:

> There were many Hessians here who had served in the army in the American Revolutionary War, some of whom lived in the second quarter of this [19th] century. One was well known, the parish clerk in St. George's Church, who gave the responses with a peculiar intonation . . . His name was Jahn Jacob Myrah, and he had been a surgeon in Knyphausen's Division and fought at the battle of Brandywine.

[60] For this and the following, *Jubiläums-Büchlein*, and Partridge, VII, 82-87.

[61] Partridge, VII, 86: "They were a poor and struggling community, though they had a few men of means amongst them."

[62] *Ibid.*, VII, 86, 81. Conflicts about property between St. Paul's and the German St. George's congregation had, by the way, taken place before. In 1779 a certain Melchior had left his estate to "the congregation", meaning of course his German congregation. Yet St. Paul's, according to English law the only congregation in Halifax, claimed the inheritance for itself. A compromise was reached at the time, according to which in return for a sizable payment the German congregation was to have the usufruct. (See *ibid.*, VII, 79f.) All such questions of property were radically solved in 1800 when St. George's congregation was declared a part of the Church of England. Compare also the actions of the Anglican state church against the German Lutherans in Williamsburg, Dundas County, Ontario (chapter II, part 6). In both cases the Germans were deprived at the most opportune moment of the best prop of their ethnicity.

[63] Hill (No. 191), 7-16. The name Schmidtville should also be mentioned. Until the end of the 19th century it was the designation for a large complex of land and houses in Halifax and is also a reminder of its original German occupants.

[64] See Kloss (No. 245).

[65] Calnek and Savary (No. 66), 197-200. See also the 1767 Census (No. 11), 57.

[66] See chapter II, footnote 21 above.

[67] See Calnek and Savary (No. 66), 243f.

> These settlements [Waldeck Line and Hessian Line] are formed on lines parallel
> to each other and two miles apart, their direction being nearly east and west,
> and are still, in part, cultivated by their descendants, who, at this day, are
> scarcely distinguishable from the other inhabitants by any peculiarity of lan-
> guage or custom, a fact that may be accounted for by another, namely, that
> the English tongue only has been taught in the schools there, while intermar-
> riages with the settlers of British origin have been constant and common. In
> the lists of original grantees' names . . . a considerable portion are English,
> Irish or Scotch, so that, from the beginning, the element of such a fusion existed
> and began to operate, and the results referred to have been gradually though
> certainly produced.

The name "Waldeck Line" still exists. Hessian Line is now called Clementsvale.
The original number of settlers is reported to be 240. See also Bouchette (No.
39), vol. II, 37, about Clements Tp.: "It was settled in 1784 by some disbanded
Hessian and American Loyalists."

[68] Lucas (No. 271), vol. III, 67.

[69] In Halifax County there are three small places at the Moser River (name!),
near Ship Harbour and Seaforth, where Germans appear to have settled at a
very early time (see chapter II, footnote 57 above).

[70] *Census of Canada, 1921*, vol. II, 520.

[71] Concerning these German settlements in present-day Albert County see
Raymond (No. 330), 90, 91:

> To one of these townships (originally called Monckton, now Hillsborough)
> there came a little colony from Pennsylvania in 1765, which introduced the
> well-known names of Steeves, Lutes and Somers. Another township at
> Shepody, called Hopewell was established about the same time by an associa-
> tion from Philadelphia which sent a ship with 25 families, placed them on
> their lands, furnished them with stock, materials for building and farming,
> and supported them for a time until they were able to do for themselves.

See also chapter II, footnote 17 above.

[72] Ganong (No. 147), 134: "Germantown—former temporary settlement
formed in 1765 or 1766 about the mouth of German Creek by Pennsylvania
Germans, tenants of the company which received the grant of Hopewell Tp. in
1765 . . . It is locally said they joined their fellow countrymen at Hillsborough,
but this is doubtful."

See also *ibid.*, 172. Later Germantown adopted its old name Shepody again. The
Germans in Shepody-Germantown are mentioned in a letter to Haldimand, later
to be Governor, as early as February 7, 1766 (Brymner, "Report on Canadian
Archives 1886." Sess. Pap., 1887, No. 12b, XI, 488): "The Germans want
experience and must be supported."

[73] See Ganong (No. 147), 151: "Moncton—early township . . . granted in
1765 to a company which in that year brought some dozen families of Pennsyl-

vania Germans as tenants and settled them on the present site of Moncton City, some of whom soon removed to Hillsborough."

In and around Moncton, the third largest city in New Brunswick today, a part of the population reported themselves as German by origin as late as the twentieth century. See also Burpee (No. 62), map
73, where the area around Moncton is identified as an area of German settlement.

[74] See Ganong, 126: "Coverdale—settled opposite Moncton by some of the Pennsylvania-German settlers in 1765 and along the Petitcodiac by an expansion from the last mentioned settlements (Hillsborough, Moncton) . . . Later the descendants of these settlers extended up Turtle Creek and Little River, and to the back lands."

[75] Ganong, 134 and 139. This settlement seems by and large to be a daughter colony of Moncton. See also chapter II, footnote 73 above. The first settlers were the Pennsylvania-Germans Heinrich Steeves and his six sons. Later some Germans from Germantown seem to have joined them. (See chapter II, footnote 72 above.)

[76] Ganong, 170. Founded by settlers from Moncton and Hillsborough.

[77] *Ibid.*, 159.

[78] *Ibid.*

[79] *Ibid.*, 146. Lutz Mountain was founded as a daughter colony of Moncton, whose population appears to have had a German element that was still growing at that time. Memel was founded in 1830 by settlers from Shepody-Germantown (Ganong, 149) where Germans were also still identifiable by that time.

[80] Loeher (No. 268), 344. "During that year [1783] no less than 14,000 loyal exiles, chiefly from the old colonies of Massachusetts, Connecticut, New York, New Jersey and Pennsylvania came to settle on the River St. John." *New Brunswick Historical Society* (No. 305), XII, 314. The settlement of Saint John itself, only an insignificant hamlet up to that time, suddenly numbered 5,000 inhabitants (*ibid.*, X, 88).

[81] Monarque (No 294), 154f.

[82] All references to the German part of the population are missing. The curious fact, however, should be mentioned that the oldest tombstone in the churchyard in Saint John undoubtedly belonged to a German. "The oldest stone is that of Conradt Hendricks, 1784, and his, if not the first, is the first known interment." (New Brunswick Historical Society, X, 98.)

[83] See Lucas (No 271), vol. III, 83: "There were hardly any foreigners and the only foreigners were from the United States . . . The movement towards New Brunswick was intensely national."

[84] In Carleton and York Counties the small German villages are perhaps as old as at the lower St. John. Northampton and Pennfield (Carleton) and Southampton (York), for instance, were founded by a Loyalist regiment from Pennsylvania, part of which almost certainly consisted of farmers of German descent. Names such as Francfort and Manzer (York County) and Newburg (Carleton) point definitely to the existence of German settlers. The place name Newburg (without an "h"), which is not too rarely found in North America, can mostly be traced to Pennsylvania-Germans of Palatine descent who thereby honored the memory of their old ruling dynasty.

[85] See chapter I, part 3.

[86] Monarque (No. 194), 153.

[87] See chapter I, part 3.

[88] Loeher (No. 268), 344, refers in 1846 to the German element in Lower Canada in these words: "Many of the top English and French families are of German or mixed German descent, since German soldiers came often enough into this area." See also Loeher's remark in Stricker's *Germania* (No. 417), 482 (compare chapter I, footnote 31). About the German family names which we encounter here and there, Monarque (No. 294), 153f., makes the following comments:

> Parcourez ces mêmes paroisses aujourd'hui et vous rencontrerez les mêmes noms qui apparaissaient sur la liste de Sieur Godecke, paie-maître général des Brunswickers, décédé à Sorel le jour de Noel 1782. Plasse, Aussant (Aussem), Matte, Koenig, Globenky, Blumhart, Bender, Pratte, Piuze, Kimber, Trestler, Glackmeyer, Besner, Arnoldi, Klein, Eberts, Heynemand, Grothé et nombres d'autres, autant de noms dont les ans ont quelquefois trahi l'orthographe, mais qui n'en ont pas moins gardé leur marque d'origine.

Compare in this context also Dionne's fat volume on *Les Canadiens-Francais. Origines des familles . . . et signification de leurs noms* (No. 116). Quite a few of the French-Canadian families listed there have the same German names, which surely can also be traced to the troops of mercenaries in the War of Independence. Dionne, however, does not have the slightest notion of this background and instead invents the most daring etymologies, such as:

> *Bender*, Ville de Bessarabie, ou de Benderen, dans la Basse-Alsace.
> *Haussmann*, D'Haussimont commune du dép. de la Marne.
> *Hecker*, D'Esquay, commune du Calvados.

In a similarly ingenious manner Dionne explains such names as Hégeman, Heineman, Hermant, Hertel, Hesse, Hirschbach, Koch, Koenig, Kratz, Schappert, Schmidt, Stein, Stengell and Wexler. Jonathan Würtele (1828-1904), finance minister of Quebec and son of a seigneur at the David River, was apparently also the descendant of a "Hessian", according to an article in the *Milwaukee Sonntagspost* of April 1, 1928.

[89] Bryce (No 59), 211.

[90] See in particular Siebert (No. 389), 32 ff. See also Bradley (No. 44), 150: "Along the good wheatlands by the Richelieu and around the indented foot of Lake Champlain, numbers of refugees both German and English, soldiers and civilians, found homes."

[91] See Day (No. 105), 313f.:

> The first permanent settlement made in St. Armand was in the autumn of 1784 [should read 1783], when a party of United Empire Loyalists, most of whom had been in the British service during the Revolutionary war, chose locations near Missisquoi Bay. Many of them were of German origin, and had left their homes on the Hudson or elsewhere, to share the fortunes of the Royal cause. Their land was purchased of Mr. Dunn on very favorable terms. The distance to St. Johns was 20 miles through the wilderness or over 50 miles around by the lake and river, and before they could raise enough grain for their families they had often to go this distance, or to Burlington, Vt., for the necessaries of life.

> The names of the first party of settlers were John Ruiter, Alex Taylor, Christjohn Wehr, Harmonas Best, Adam Deal, Lewis Streit, Christjohn Hayner, Conrad Best, Alexander Hyatt, John Saxe, Gilbert Hyatt, Jacob Barr, John Mock, Philipp Luke, Joseph Smith, Garret Sixby, James Anderson, Frederick Hayner, and Peter Miller . . . Many of them located permanently near the Bay, at which point the settlement increased rapidly. The locality soon assumed the appearance and characteristics of a village, while the aspect of the surrounding country was fast changing from a solitary wilderness to cultivated fields and green pastures.

The German character of most of the names mentioned is quite obvious from the family name or given name. Even Taylor, Smith and Miller could be the Americanized forms of Schneider, Schmidt and Müller.

[92] Noyes in his article "The Missisquoi German or Dutch," (No. 311) leaves no doubt that these were Germans who came from New York State. Even though the colonists were generally called "Dutch", the label "Dutch" was in fact the collective designation for all the German immigrants in North America until the nineteenth century. They could not have been Dutch in the present-day narrower sense, namely people from the Netherlands, for the simple reason that not a single name can be found on the lists of the Loyalist free corps identifying a person as coming from Holland. On the other hand "included in one or the other of these corps were the Germans of Dutchess County and the Hudson Valley, from which came most, if not all, of those who settled later in Missisquoi Bay." (*Ibid.*, 24). Could it be, by the way, that Dutchess County originally was called "Deutsches" County?

Tucker (No. 432) in his book on the Camden Colony, which should more appropriately be entitled "German-Irish Families in Canada," states that a considerable number of the Missisquoi settlers had Irish names although by language and mores they were Germans. They were the descendants of Palatines who had been settled in Ireland in 1710 from where they emigrated in 1760 and 1765 to New York State, to the area around Camden in Oneida County. See also the note of the editor of Noyes (No. 310). 106:

Irish names of Savage, Mitchell etc. in Missisquoi and Shefford appearing among the German early settlers . . . no wonder! It is a fair and reasonable presumption that it was through intermarriages with the Irish during the sojourn in Ireland that the Germans mentioned came into possession of distinctive Irish names. But on arrival here, they were Germans in speech, habits, thrift and manners.

Tucker traces individual Irish-German families from their original domiciles in Ireland all the way to Canada. He shows the presence of Irish Germans not only at Missisquoi Bay, but also among the Loyalists on the Napanee at the Bay of Quinte, Ontario. Some Palatines from Ireland, finally, also apparently came directly to Canada in 1765 and were settled by Pernette on his estates on the La Have in Lunenburg County. (See chapter II, part 2 above.) Tucker states on p. 97:

> . . . it seems like a strange coincidence that the Palatines should always locate on the hills by the water courses, as if the sounds of old Germany were still ringing in their ears and hearts. The Napanee in Ontario, and the La Have in Nova Scotia like the picturesque shores of Missisquoi Bay, afforded splendid opportunity for the play of this dominant mountaineering spirit.

[93] Published by Noyes, "The Canadian Loyalists and Early Settlers in the District of Bedford," (No. 310), 101 ff., as well as in his publication with the same title (No. 309). The petition, according to *ibid.*, 17, is the only document from the early years of the colony at the Missisquoi Bay which contains any names at all. It appears to prove that all the signatories had participated in actual combat.

[94] Day (No. 105) relates various names of the first occupants of farmsteads in the early years, among them the following German ones:

1796	in Dunham Tp. (Missisquoi County): Joseph Buck, John and Jacob Heliker, David and Jeremiah Reychart, Jacob Best and Philipp Ruiter (Day, 293),
1797	in St. Armand East Tp.: Abram Freligh and Elijah Kemp (p. 319)
1801	in Stanbridge Tp.: Jacob Bomhower, Peter Rosenburgh, Peter Kraus, Philip Kruller and Frederick Kemmermann (p. 305), and
1803	in Roxton Tp. (Shefford County): 7 Ruiter families, 6 Kerr families, 4 Platt families, John Kobatch and William Wehr jun (p. 341).

There are also scattered German names in other townships.

[95] For the immigration from Germany we have only a single clue. Of the nearly five hundred Bavarians and Swiss who in 1836 entered the country with the only shipload of emigrants that came via Quebec before the opening of the direct emigrants' route, Hamburg-Quebec in 1846, about two hundred settled in the Eastern Townships (see chapter I, footnote 54).

[96] Loeher (No. 268), 344.

[97]

In	1871	1881	1901
Missisquoi County	1,950	1,475	423
Brome County	462	732	115
Stanstead County	408	87	70
Shefford County	147	114	58
Totals	2,967	2,408	666

[98] See chapter II, part 7.

[99] Bromme (No. 53), 187, almost certainly influenced by the Canadian immigration authorities, recommends this area most warmly in his *Rathgeber für Auswanderer* as early as 1846.

[100] In the special report about German immigration for 1861, P.P. (No. 4a), 1862, XXXVI, 402, the following is stated:

> In August last, the nucleus of a new settlement was formed in the township of Bowman between the rivers Gatineau and Lièvre; there are already from 200 to 300 persons there, and a large addition may be expected from this year's emigration. Many of the settlers are in easy circumstances, having 5,000 or 6,000 dollars in money amongst them. In the vicinity more than 15,000 acres of very good land can be purchased 40 per cent cheaper than the land on the Upper Canada side.

[101] In his "Report on German Colonisation in the Ottawa District," Sess. Pap. (No. 4b), 1888, No. 4, 218f., the following observations are of interest:

> I first visited the German settlements in the townships of Bowman, Villeneuve and Portland, going by rail to Buckingham, thence by boat up the Lièvre River . . . Generally I found all in good circumstances and prosperous, although their locality has been somewhat deficient in the facilities for marketing their products, but is at present much improved in that respect, owing to the development of the mining industry of those and the adjoining townships which is proving advantage and benefit to the settlements along the Lièvre R. I am pleased to report that in many instances German settlers have successfully maintained themselves and families, and are doing well where settlers of other nationalities have failed to make a living. The reason they assign for their success is that they do not follow other pursuits such as lumbering and milling, but devote their whole time to their farms and keep out of debt.
>
> As indisputable proof of their industry and frugality the Germans in these tps. maintain their own schools, in which is taught English during one half of the day and German in the other half.
>
> Next I proceeded to the tps. of Mulgrave and Derry, which are about 50 miles from travelable road, and visited the majority of the German families settled in these tps., nearly all of whom I found fairly prosperous, maintaining their schools and other institutions in much the same way as those in Bowman, Villeneuve and Portland, but they have not the advantage of as good markets, having to depend to a great extent for the sale of their products on the lumbering firms there not being any mining carried on in that locality.

[102] This assumption is supported by a table in the *Census of Canada, 1921,* vol. II, 520, according to which as many as 1,652 of the over-ten-year-old Germans in Quebec still spoke their German mother tongue in addition to French or English and only twenty-six spoke German exclusively. All of these are to be found in Labelle and Pontiac Counties, and especially in Montreal.

[103] This township was not named, as is often maintained, after the city of Thorn in West Prussia, although apparently only East and West Prussian agriculturists settled there. This name appears on a map as early as 1854 when the township was only a surveyor's mark.

[104] Report on Immigration 1865, in Sess. Pap., 1866, No. 5, 38.

[105] Report on Immigration 1868, in *ibid.*, 1869, No. 76, 8.

[106] Karl Müller-Grote (No. 297), 254 ff., tells in a funny way how, in an improvised election rally among the Germans in Pontiac County in 1890, he created propaganada for an anti-prohibitionist conservative candidate. It did not take the 120 upright East Prussians in attendance very long to side with good German jokes against going dry. According to this they appeared to have lost little of their East Prussian heritage up to that time!

[107] The list of pastors until 1911 can be found in *Jubiläums-Büchlein* (No. 219), 39, and *Der Nordwesten-Kalender* for 1927.

[108] Bromme (No. 53), 189: "The seigniories Aubert de l'Isle and Aubert Gallion (Beauce County) are the property of a German, Jacob Pozer, who drew many of his fellow countrymen there in order to settle them. The situation is excellent; the estates are traversed by the Chaudière."

[109] Reports on Immigration after 1846.

[110] Loeher (No. 268), 344.

[111] *Jubiläums-Büchlein* (No. 219), 57, and *Der Nordwesten-Kalender* for 1929. Concerning the Canada Synod see chapter II, part 7.

[112] See chapter II, part 5.

[113] Bryce (No. 59), 211 f.

[114] Croil (No 94), 129, and Canniff (No. 76), 441.

[115] See chapter I, part 3. Also Croil (No. 94), 128: "Johnson's Regiment was 800 strong . . . chiefly composed of Germans, with a few Scotch, the former mostly of the Lutheran, the latter of the Presbyterian faith." See also Bryce (No. 59), 212: "Almost all of the first battalion of the 'Royal Greens' were of German origin."

[116] See Casselman (No. 83), 66: "I have included the two former townships (Cornwall, Osnabrück), because the greater number of the first settlers in them were German. Williamsburg and Matilda were wholly German."

Osnabrück, by the way, did not receive its name from its German population but was named in honor of the second son of George III, Frederick, who from 1764 to 1803 was titular Bishop of Osnabrück in Westphalia. Many German place names and other designations in the early years of Canada's history owe their origins not to German influences, but simply to the Guelph dynastic connections of the English royal house. Thus, for example, Governor General Lord Dorchester in 1788 divided the newly settled territory of Ontario into four administrative districts which he named Hesse, Nassau, Mecklenburg and Lunenburg. When Ontario was elevated to the status of an independent province in 1791, they were given the good English names of Western, Home, Midland and Eastern by the first bill of the new provincial parliament.

[117] Published in Casselman, *ibid.* He adds this comment: "That in the short space of three months these early settlers had built habitation for themselves and cleared, as we see from the returns, about two-thirds of an acre for each man is a remarkable record of their energy, activity and earnestness."

[118] See Croil (No. 94), 130:

> Each soldier was entitled to draw one hundred acres on the river front, besides 200 acres at a distance remote from the river. This was the soldier's bounty. If married and with a family, or if at any future time he should marry, he was entitled to 50 acres more for his wife, and 50 for every child. This was his family land. Besides all this, each son and daughter, on coming of age or at marriage, was entitled to a further grant of 200 acres. The greater part of Mountain and Winchester Tp. was thus drawn by children of the U.E. Loyalists.

[119] *Jubiläums-Büchlein* (No. 219), 8. According to Croil (No. 94), 250, it was a frame building of about 18 meters by 12 meters.

[120] The first minister of the Reformed faith among the Germans in Dundas County had the name Broeffle: see *Canada and Its Provinces* (No. 388), vol. XI, 266. It appeared that the Reformed later adopted the Scottish variant of Calvinism. Croil, 258, in any case, seems to confuse them with the Presbyterians:

> The first Presbyterians in Dundas were all U.E. Loyalists, chiefly Germans, and Mr. Broeffle officiated to them in the German language exclusively. Preaching in Matilda, Williamsburg and Osnabrück, he resided in Williamsburg . . . Living on terms of good fellowship with the Lutherans, they were permitted by them to occupy their pulpits alternately.

[121] *Jubiläums-Büchlein* (No. 219), 8.

[122] *Ibid,* 9. See also chapter II, part 6 below.

[123] See *ibid.*

[124] See Canniff (No. 76), 271f., especially the following:

> He seems to have been inadequately supported by the people, and yielding to inducements, too tempting for most men to resist, he, in 1811, secretly joined the Church of England, and was reordained by Bishop Mountain in Quebec. Upon his return, he pretended still to be a Lutheran minister, and preached, as usual, in German exclusively. Suspicions, however, soon arose that all was not right, for he began to use the English Book of Common Prayer, and occasionally to wear the surplice, practices which gave such offence to his former friends, that they declared they would no longer go to hear a man who proclaimed to them in his shirt sleeves.

See also the interesting remark in Croil (No. 94), 252: "It was in vain he [Wiegand] tried to convince them that there was really no difference, that it was only substituting English for German." See also *Jubiläums-Büchlein* (No. 219), 9-10.

[125] See chapter II, part 3.

[126] Canniff (No. 76), 271f.

[127] *Ibid.*

[128] The conflict about the church property continued, according to Croil (No. 94), 254f., until it was finally awarded to the Anglican Church in 1833. In 1846, however, the Lutheran congregation was paid a belated compensation. It received two thousand dollars and 37½ acres of its parish property was returned. See also *Jubiläums-Büchlein* (No. 219), 9-10.

[129] Croil (No. 94), 255. Canniff (No. 76), 272. *Jubiläums-Büchlein*, 10.

[130] Not an English word was spoken in the church service up to that time (see footnote 124 above). We also know that in these early years only German teachers were employed. They moved from place to place and offered instruction to the children from the surrounding farms for two weeks at a time (Croil, 141). In time, however, a number of English teachers seem to have been called, due to the lack of suitable German teachers and in the desire to procure for the children the advantages of knowing the language of the country. These were bound to accelerate the anglicization of the youth in the absence of the countervailing force of a German pastor.

[131] Croil (No. 94), 255: "During the first years of his ministry, he officiated in German and English alternately, and having quietly brought them through the difficult transition state from one language to another, restricted himself to the English."

[132] *Ibid.*, 256.

[133] According to the list of the German clergy in *Der Nordwesten-Kalender* of 1929 (No. 306). About the Protestant Synods see chapter II, part 7.

[134] In:	total population	German by origin				
	1871	1871	1881	1901	1911	1921
Dundas County	18,777	5,563	6,996	5,393	2,605	597
Stormont County	18,987	3,125	2,798	4,015	1,772	443
	37,764	8,688	9,794	9,409	4,377	1,040

(The 1871 and 1881 data for Stormont County include Cornwall County)

[135] Canniff (No. 76), 419 ff.

[136] *Ibid.*, 425f., the following names are mentioned: Colonel Hanjost Herkimer (Herckheimer), Lawrence and Nicholas Herkimer, Captain Jost Hartmann, Lieut. Ellerbeck, Land Surveyor Lieut. Kotte, Captain Harkman, the "Irish Palatinec" H. Detlor (see footnote 92 above), various Wartmanns and a John Frelick or Freeligh (Fröhlich). Colonel Hanjost Herkimer, whose estates were at the upper Mohawk in the so-called "German Flats" (see chapter I, part 3), did not belong to the group led by Grass. According to Canniff he may have come as early as 1783 (i.e., before all the others), to the Bay of Quinte.

[137] Canniff, 440.

[138] Casselman (No. 83), 63, and Pierce (No. 324), 295.

[139] Gourlay (No. 158), vol. I, 129.

[140] See Chapter II, end of part 6.

[141] Gourlay, *ibid.*

[142] For this and the following see "Lutheran Church Record 1793-1832" (No. 274), 136-167.

[143] See below.

[144] Edited with notes under the above-mentioned title "Lutheran Church Record 1792-1832" (No. 274).

[145] In the baptismal registers dating from 1794 to 1850 German names prevail for the early years and still predominate in the later years. The marriage registers are complete only for the period 1827 to 1833. As can be expected, mixed marriages between the two national groups were quite common. While the names of the brides were in most cases clearly German, those of the bridegrooms are often Scottish or English. In the reverse case the German bridegroom would join the church of his English bride. The lists of the communicants are available for the period 1796 to 1839, but only a few of them have been published. In 1806 the Ebenezer congregation had 46 members. Among these the male heads of families and unmarried adults had the following names: Pastor John G. Wigant, Gerhard

van De Berg, John Keller, George Simmons, Wm. Rambach, George Smith, Martin Fralig, Iacob Fralig, Iacob Fratz, Iacob Schmith, Peter Fralig, Christpr. Fralig, Philip Schmith, Frederick Keller, Peter Hofmann, Wm. Kochnant, Adam Vant, Wm. Keller, Jacob Johnson, Nicholas Brunk, Catharina Shriber, Elisabeth McCarty, Elizabeth Zicker, Mary Pickle, Daniel Overacker.

For decades thereafter the Ebenezer congregation in Fredericksburg remained the same size, as proven, for example, by an entry into the church book of 1832, when Pastor Killmer administered Holy Communion to fifty-one members of the congregation.

[146] See below.

[147] Canniff (No 76), 271. See also Chapter II, part 6 above.

[148] Canniff, *ibid.*, 272, reprints the following advertisement from the *Kingston Gazette*: "Married. In Ernesttown, 29th. Jan., 1816, the Rev. William McCarty, Minister of the Lutheran congregation to Miss Clarissa Fralick." Pastor McCarty, who married a German here, was certainly bilingual, since German must have still been the language of the church among the Lutherans at the Bay of Quinte at that time. He may very well have been Scottish in name only, but by language and denomination a Palatine.

[149] According to "Lutheran Church Record" (No. 274).

[150] According to statistical data of 1848 in the "Report made for 1848 to the Secretary of State for the Colonies," P.P., 1849, XXXIV, 13, there were in Midland district (Frontenac and Lennox and Addington Counties) at that time no more than 548 Lutherans. The number of Germans by origin, therefore, must have been much larger. The "Lutheran Church Record" states: "In the forties the membership had become gradually absorbed in the Methodist classes, and the last two or three ministers joined the Methodist ministry, there being too few members to support a minister."

[151] According to "Lutheran Church Record."

[152] Canniff (No. 76), 449.

[153] Among the names of the original settlers listed in Canniff, *ibid.*, 453-455, the following are probably Germans: Philip Flagler, Paul and Salomon Huff, Isaac Bern, John Huyck, Gilbert and Abraham Bogart, Joseph and Benjamin Clapp, Nicholaus Hagerman, Henry Redner, and Andrew Huffmann. A certain Christopher A. Hagerman (1792-1847) from Adolphustown later became one of the pillars of the Tory party in Ontario, and Solicitor General.

[154] Bryce (No. 59), 213. Also Canniff, 459: "By referring to the oldest map of the township in the Crown Lands Department it is found that while most of the land was allotted to the Hessians, a considerable portion was taken up by commissioned and non-commissioned officers of the 84th Regiment."

[155] Among these Loyalists was the unquestionably German Schmidt family, whose first domicile gave Smith Bay its name and on whose land stood the small German church. See Canniff, 463, and Smith (No. 397), 259 ff.

[156] See the detailed account of the ordeal of the Hessians in Canniff, 461f. According to Canniff the Hessians numbered forty. Did this include the families? Probably there were a lot more of them.

[157] See Canniff, 462.

[158] Ibid., 463.

[159] Canniff, 462:

> As a general thing, they had not the means of removing. But there were a few who managed to extricate themselves and who returned to the old country. One John Crogle went to Kingston, mortgaged his farm for £ 6 to Rev. Mr. Stuart, and took his departure for the fatherland. Another mortgaged his lot to Captain Allan and left, leaving his wife, and never returned.

See also Smith (No. 397)

[160] Whether the "Hessians" in their much more extensive settlements in Nova Scotia and New Brunswick had to endure equally difficult early years is an open question. We know nothing about the quality of the land that they found there. We know, however, that the German soldiers settled by Selkirk at the Red River, after they had been discharged in 1816, were not able to endure farming life and moved on to the last man (see chapter I, part 6).

[161] Canniff, 271.

[162] Hunter (No. 202), 186, states explicitly: "U.E. Loyalists (Germans!) settled in 1784 and succeeding years in Sophiasburgh, Hallowell and Ameliasburgh."

[163] The 1911 Census records in the aforementioned counties a mere 8,826 Germans by origin among a total population of 135,210.

[164] Canniff, 316, mentions "a considerable number of Moravian Loyalists who had settled upon the Bay of Quinte."

[165] Canniff, 314-317. He was the son of the first Moravian preacher in New York, Abraham Bininger. German Moravians have cared for the Indians in other parts of Canada as well. A good example is their activity since 1792 among the Delawares in Kent County (see chapter III, part 6). See also Bromme (No. 52), 283: "Herrnhuter, often called Moravians, have spread considerably in the Union, in the West Indies and in Upper Canada."

Until recently the Moravians have been active in Canada as missionaries. See *Handbuch des Deutschtums im Auslande* (No. 176), 289: "Only one German Protestant missionary society, that of the Moravian Brethren, is active in Canada. They operate in Labrador from six stations (1903: 21 missionaries, 1,261 Christians) and also in Alaska among the Eskimos". The coastal station Hopedale (Labrador) was originally founded by the German Moravians under the name of Hoffenthal.

[166] Report on Immigration for 1858, in P.P., 1859, S. 2, XXII, 918.

[167] According to a detailed statement in the Report on Immigration for 1860 (P.P., 1861, XL, 505f.) which also contains all the names of the settlers.

[168] Estimate of the Immigration Agent Sinn—the author of the statement mentioned in footnote 167 above—in his letter to the Lutheran Canada Synod of the winter of 1860-1861 in which he draws their attention to their new missionary field. See *Jubiläums-Büchlein* (No. 219), 14f. There were possibly up to four hundred Kashubs—he calls them Prussian Poles—among the nine hundred immigrants from Germany. Sinn's figures cannot be corroborated since the Ottawa Immigration Agency, which probably never registered all the immigrants, reported particularly unsatisfactory data for those first years.

[169] See the statement of 1860 mentioned in footnote 167 above and Sinn's letter in *Jubiläums-Büchlein*, 14-15.

[170] According to the annual reports of the Ottawa Immigration Agency. Kashubs are no longer mentioned.

[171] Canada in general, in contrast to the United States, had few promotional publications printed in the German language. Yet a good number about the Ottawa Valley were distributed in Germany, including: Eby, *Auf nach West-kanada (1854)*; *Canada, Darstellung der natürlichen, sozialen und Verkehrsverhältnisse dieses Landes* (1858); Wagner, *Canada ein Land für deutsche Auswanderung* (1861); *Canada, mit bes. Rücksicht auf Colonisation* (1864). In all these publications the district at the upper Ottawa is particularly recommended. For promotional reasons Meidinger contends in his *Canadas rasches Aufblühen* of 1858 (No. 268), 29, that there already existed at that time "British settlements intermingled with some Germans" at the Ottawa.

[172] Among the very first Germans and Kashubs who immigrated in 1858 there were quite a few who had encountered difficulties and distress. See the Report on Immigration 1858, P.P., 1859, S. 2, XXII, 917. In the German-Kashub colony at the Opeongo which was formed in 1859-1860, the situation also soon looked bad. Some of the lots there turned out to be completely worthless. See Sinn's long comment in the statement of 1860.

[173] See Sess. Pap., 1866, No. 5, 38. For this purpose even a report of five German colonists of Sebastopol Tp. is included (*ibid.* 66c) in which all responsibility for the failures is attributed to the incompetence of the settlers themselves. It cannot however, refute the general impression that the Germans in Renfrew had to struggle at first with unusually bad circumstances.

[174] Thus an article about the "Deutschtum in Canada" in *Der Deutsche Pionier*

(No. 113), II, 189, stated in 1870: "Germans are to be found as far as the rugged regions in Renfrew County. They migrate there, deceived and seduced by unscrupulous persons, even so-called Crown Land agents. The laments from these regions are often heart-rending". And even as late as 1884 Jung (No. 220), 10, wrote: "The reputation of Canada was harmed particularly by the immigration of Germans into the rugged County of Renfrew in northeastern Ontario. It was the work of unscrupulous persons. Bitter adversity and grief awaited the disappointed ones there."

[175] See the remark of the Ottawa Immigration Agent in his Report for 1878 (Sess. Pap., 1879, Nr. 9, 20): "My impression is that for years to come large numbers will annually go from here to the North-West, and the vacancy thus created will afford room for newly arrived immigrants to fill their place". In 1882 he finally wrote (Sess. Pap., 1883, No. 14, 198): "I am happy to state that the Germans in the Ottawa district have sent me a larger sum of money than during any former period to defray the passage of their friends. This shows the enormous importance of making fresh nuclei of Germans, no matter at what expense".

[176] The *Atlas* shows the people of English, Scottish and Irish origin separately. This is why Redcliffe and Raglan Tps. show a German majority when, in fact the people of German origin, who only settled there after 1880, are in a minority with regard to the entire British population. Starting from the north with McKay Tp. the Germans had an absolute majority in Petawawa, Alice, Fraser, Wilberforce, Algona, Sebastopol and Lynedoch Townships according to the 1911 Census.

[177] See Maron in *Der Nordwesten-Kalender* for 1914 (No. 306), 107.

[178] See "Report on German Colonisation in the Ottawa District," Sess. Pap., 1888, Nr. 4, 218.

[179] The beginnings of the foundation of the congregation date back to 1861 See Report on Immigration 1861 (P.P., 1862, XXXVI, 401 ff.):

> The [German] settlements in Alice, Wilberforce, Algona and the other townships in the County of Renfrew are making steady progress. Three congregations of the Canada Evangelical Lutheran Synod have been established. The larger commune, near Pembroke, has received a free grant of 15 acres as a site for a church, school, and burial ground; the other two congregations have also made application to Government for a like grant.

[180] About the various Synods see *The Concordia Cyclopedia* (No. 88). The Evangelical Church advocates an extreme liberalism, unitarianism and rationalism in rejecting all dogmas which are beyond reason.

[181] According to the list of the clergy in *Der Nordwesten-Kalender* for 1929.

[182] See Report on Immigration 1872 (Sess. Pap., 1873, No. 26, 25): "The German residents of this city have formed recently a national society composed

already of upwards of 80 members, and it bids fair to be of much service to them."

It was still active in the 1880s. See *Mitteilungen* (No. 292).

[183] See *Der Nordwesten-Kalender* for 1929 and the *Statistical Year Book* of the Missouri Synod (No. 409), 179 ff.

[184] It was not until the 1850s that this area became accessible as a result of the construction of the Addington Road. From then on the Canadian Government promoted its settlement and referred explicitly to this newly opened area in the German-language promotional literature: see e.g., *Canada* (No. 72), 30. In 1858 the first two German families, Neumann and John from Silesia, arrived in Denbigh in response to such a publication. See Stein (No. 413), 14 ff. By 1866 so many Germans had moved into their vicinity that a public school was established in the "German settlement" in Denbigh. (*Ibid.*, 19.)

All of Clarendon Tp. with up to sixty thousand acres had been reserved until 1862 for settlement by Germans. When Agent Telgmann, however, only managed to bring over fifteen German families by 1864 because of the remoteness of the area, the contract was revoked. See the report of the Kingston Agent in Sess. Pap., 1863, No. 4, and 1865, No. 6. Although a few more German families were added in the following years, all German immigration ceased thereafter. By 1911 the number of Germans in the two townships had increased to 204 and 220 respectively.

In Denbigh the German Lutherans built a parsonage, and in 1886 a church. Since 1884 they have always had a German pastor who also serves the German Lutherans in Clarendon Tp. (in the community of Plewna), in Raglan Tp. (Renfrew) and in Maynooth (in the north of Hastings County). For this see Stein (No. 413), 18; *Der Nordwesten-Kalender* for 1929, and *Jubiläums-Büchlein* (No. 219), 63.

NOTES TO CHAPTER III

[1] Casselman (No. 83), 63: "Butler's Rangers, Jessup's Rangers and Roger's Rangers also contained not a few Palatines." Also Pierce (No. 324), 295: "There were many Palatines too in Butler's Rangers."

[2] Cruikshank (No. 99), 88 ff., and Siebert (No. 389), 90 ff.

[3] Cruikshank (No. 100), Appendix B mentions their names, among them: Bernhard Frey, Andrew Bradt, Jacob Ball, Peter Ball, Jacob Benner, George Raneier, Samuel Lutz, Philip Bender, Henry Volleck, and Joseph Petrey (spelled Hansjost Petrie in *ibid.*, 22).

[4] Cruikshank, *ibid.*, provides in Appendix C "A List of the Persons who have subscribed their names in order to settle and cultivate the Crownland opposite to Niagara. July 20th, 1884." His sources are the *Canadian Archives*, Series B,

Vol. 168, p. 38. There we find in addition to the above-mentioned German names the following: Lieutenants John Bradt and Michael Rosenkrantz; Corporals Benjamin Frelick, Arnold Hogerman, Frederick Schram and Peter Wintermute; Disbanded Rangers: Fr. Berger, Bowman (three times), Minardt Bradt, Matthew Friedenburg, John Gallinger, Lodwick Hornbeck, John Jacobs, Van Alstine Schram, Frederick Segar, Jacob Segar, Frederick Shoulitz, John Snider, Richard Springer, Caspar Springsteen, William Stedmann, Hendick Windecker. About their discharge see Cruikshank (No. 99), 110 ff.

[5] Cruikshank (No. 100), Appendix C.

[6] Canniff (No. 76), 440.

[7] Cassel (No. 82), 247; *Canada and Its Provinces* (No. 388), vol. XVII, 47, and Breithaupt (No. 46), 9. There we read:

> In Col. W.W.H. Davis' History of Bucks County, Pennsylvania, there is an account of what appears to have been the beginning of (Mennonite) emigration to Upper Canada. The movement began in 1786, when John Dilman, Jacob and Stoffel Kulp (also spelled Kolb), Franklin Albright and Frederick Hahn and their families left the country to seek new homes in Canada. Favourable accounts from the pioneers induced many of their old friends and neighbours to follow. Most of the emigrants were of Bucks County and from the Tps. of Plumstead, Hillborn, Bedminster and Tinicum in that county.

[8] P. Campbell in his *Travels in the Interior Inhabited Parts of North America in the Years 1791 and 1792* (Edinburgh, 1793) makes the following observation which is reprinted in Cruikshank (No. 97):

> In the neighbourhood (of the Niagara Falls) live a set of religionists [who are frequently confused with the Mennonites] with long beards, orginally from Germany. They are a very innocent, inoffensive, industrious people that have many peculiarities in their manner of worship and mode of living. They are as yet not above a score of them in this neighbourhood, but many more are expected. I have heard several people say they would like them well as neighbours, and the Quakers are particularly fond of them, on account of their mild and inoffensive dispositions.

[9] Cruikshank (No. 97), 30, and Siebert (No. 389), 107.

[10] See the letter of the two agents to the British Consul in Philadelphia who passed it on to Simcoe. *Simcoe Papers* (No. 95), vol. III, 296:

> From Edmund Milne and John Musser to Phineas Bond. Philadelphia, Febr. 13th, 1795.
> Sir, Being desirous of obtaining a Grant from the Government of Upper Canada, and having it in our power, to procure a number of Germans, industrious and of good moral character, chiefly of Lancaster County, who will go forward and settle on such lands, and not doubting in the least to engage a sufficient number by the time a Grant may be made to us and our Associates, at which time we shall be ready to perform on our part the usual stipulations with Government, we intend petitioning His Excellency the Lieutenant

Governor of the Province of Upper Canada for a Grant, and having the honor
of being personally known to you, beg the favour of your recommending us
and our Petition to the notice of Government, not doubting we shall have
it in our power fully to comply with the stipulations to Government.

We have the honor to be Edmund Milne
John Musser.

In two letters to Simcoe of February 16 and 19 (*ibid.*, 299) the Consul recommended the project only half-heartedly. He admitted that Musser had great
influence in Lancaster County, Pa., among the Germans whom he calls Moravians (which is the same mistaken identification as Campbell's in footnote 8
above) and recommended the coastal districts at Lake Erie if the plan was
accepted. He wondered, however, whether it would be politically advisable to
turn such large coherent tracts of land over to foreigners. It would certainly
delay settlement if such a large area would be reserved for one group which
could presumably fill it only after a long time. Simcoe did not then pursue the
matter any further.

[11] According to *Canada and Its Provinces* (No. 388), vol. XVII, 47, Mennonites
settled soon after the end of the American war of Independence and before
1800, as is evident from the context, not only at Twenty Mile Creek (Louth,
Clinton) but also at Black Creek, i.e. in Bertie and Willoughby Tps.

[12] See Breithaupt (No. 46), 10:

> There are many Pennsylvania German descendants in Bertie, Humberstone
> and Wainfleet Tps. Many of the lands were originally held in larger grants
> by U.E.L. officers. When some of these lands were broken up and sold, from
> 1796 on, we find the registration to Pennsylvanians and others. In Humber-
> stone Jacob Gander, John and Peter Neave, George Schuman and Christian
> Sturm received patents in 1797. Abraham Neave, Jacob Neave and Christian
> Sevitz in 1798. In Wainfleet we find Jacob Sevitz Jr. in 1796, Jacob, Samuel
> and Henry Sevitz in 1797. Jacob Misner Sr., Jacob Misner Jr. and Christian
> Sevitz in 1799. Other names are Bauer, Bitner, Bucher, Barnhardt, Buerger,
> Critz, Eberle, Hahn, Heximer, Kunz, Koebel, Loeffler, Pitzinger, Shisler,
> Snetzinger, Woehl, Zimmerman, Reinhardt, Weiss. Some, if not most, came
> from Pennsylvania, and some probably from central New York. A noted family
> with descendants still in the original location at the frontier are the Boehms,
> descendants of Jacob Boehm who came from Pennsylvania about 1792. A later
> form of the name is Beam, the town of Beamsville so getting its name.

In Willoughby Tp. there were a few German farmers even before 1796. See Breithaupt,
ibid.: "Michael Gander (later Gonder) came to Upper Canada from Pa. in 1789. In
1796 he settled on the Niagara River six miles above Chippawa, on a farm which
is still owned and occupied by some of his descendants."

See also Carnochan (No. 78), 222. According to their digest from the *Book of
Records* for Willoughby, there were three Germans among the ten officers of the
congregation in 1796: Michael Gander (Paymaster), Matthew Buchner and
Abraham Beam (Church or Town Wardens). In 1797 the names of Henry
Wierhuhm and Christian Boughner are among them.

[13] See Breithaupt (No. 46), continuation of quote in footnote 7 above:

The party . . . in 1799 . . . consisted of Rev. Jacob Moyer, Amos Albright, Valentine Kratz, Dilman Moyer, John Hunsberger, George Althouser, and Moses Fretz. In 1800 came John Fretz, Lawrence Hipple, Abraham Grob, Michael Rittenhouse, Manassah Fretz, Daniel Hoch Jr., Samuel Moyer, David Moyer, Jacob Hoch, Jacob Hausser, John Wismer, Jacob Frey, Isaac Kulp, Philip Hoch, Christian Hunsberger, and Abraham Hunsberger; and in 1802, Isaac Wismer. The Bucks County families generally settled in the Twenty Mile Creek district, in the vicinity of Vineland and Campden of the present day.

Before this contingent arrived, Jacob Moyer with Amos Albright and Abraham Moyer coming by foot from Hilltown Township, Pennsylvania, had selected the land in the summer of 1799 and purchased an area of 1,100 acres for a down payment of forty dollars. (*Ibid.*)

[14] See chapter III, part 2.

[15] See the account in M. Dunham's novel *The Trail of the Conestoga*, (no. 123).

[16] Gourlay (No. 158), vol. I, 456.

[17] Breithaupt (No. 46), 10.

[18] *Ibid.*, 13. At that time the Mennonite colonies in the Niagara district were probably stronger than the two sister colonies in Waterloo and York Counties, with whom they united in 1820 under the leadership of their bishop, Moyer, as the Canada Conference district.

[19] According to the 1848 Census there were 1,085 natives of Germany in the Niagara district. By 1861 these had increased to 2,301 (see *Census of Canada*, 1871, vol. IV, 166 and 259). If we take into consideration the deaths over a period of thirty years, not to speak of the later departure of some of the Germans for Waterloo, Grey and Bruce Counties — as Spetz (No. 404), 44, 203, pointed out — then we have to assume that between 2,500 and 3,000 Germans from Germany had immigrated by 1860.

[20] About the early German Catholic settlers in Bertie, Rainham, Cayuga, etc., see Spetz, *ibid.*, 4, 203, 228, and 238. For the numbers pertaining to the individual denominations see the Canadian Census for 1848, 1860 and 1871 ff.

[21] Loeher (No. 268), 342f.

[22] The 1870-71 Census shows:

In	German by origin	total population
Welland County	5,916	20,572
Monck County	5,628	15,130
Haldimand County	3,357	20,091
Lincoln County	4,844	20,672
Niagara Town	414	3,693
Totals	20,159	80,158

[23] The natives of Germany, as the statistical data on the birthplace reveal, settled almost exclusively in those townships that had absolute German majorities, as well as in the towns of Chippawa and St. Catherines. In Gainsborough they manifested their allegiance to developments in Germany, even in later years, by naming their main community Bismarck.

[24] Spetz (No. 404), 203, 228 and 238.

[25] The sister colonies of the Mennonites in Waterloo and York Counties experienced the same development. The main difference was that in the predominantly German Waterloo County the renunciation of the Mennonite faith was far from entailing the loss of German ethnicity, while in York County, due to the lack of any German immigration, the total assimilation of the descendants of the Mennonites occurred as early as the period between 1870 and 1880 (see chapter III, part 5). For the Mennonites in the Niagara district, the development appears to have been between these two extremes.

[26] This is the total of Germans by origin in the three newly delimited counties of Lincoln, Welland and Haldimand.

[27] According to the 1911 Census. See also the *Atlas of Canada* (No. 20), map 24.

[28] As early as 1820, a German school is explicitly mentioned in Humberstone as well as the English one. See Gourlay (No. 158), vol. I, 407. The Mennonites clung to their own schools here as well. The Catholics maintained, wherever possible, German private schools, as in Rainham from 1848 to 1864; see Spetz (No. 404), 238. For the Lutherans there is no documentary evidence of such schools under the direction of the clergy, but they probably existed.

[29] See the last section of Chapter III, part.

[30] According to Joest (No. 212), published in 1888. Oppel (No. 316), published in 1906, no longer mentions it.

[31] Their distribution was as follows:

Welland	6,091
Haldimand County	2,472
Lincoln County	1,527
Total	10,090

[32] According to *Der Nordwesten-Kalender* for 1929.

[33] Waterloo Historical Society, founded shortly before the World War and endeavoring to keep awake the memory of the colonizing achievements of the German ancestors in Waterloo County among fellow German Canadians in spite of their irreversible anglicization, erected a tower near Doon on the Grand River on August 28, 1926. It is dedicated to the memory of "The first settlers in

Waterloo County, German Mennonites from Pennsylvania, and also to the German pioneers who followed in Waterloo as well as in adjoining counties of southwestern Ontario." See *Waterloo Historical Society* (No. 450), XIV, 185.

The Historic Sites and Monuments Board donated a memorial plaque for the tower, thereby recognizing the significance of these first German settlements for all of Ontario, with the following inscription (*Ibid.*, XIV, 203):

> In the Spring of 1800 Joseph Schoerg and Samuel Betzner Jr., brothers-in-law, Mennonites, from Franklin County, Pa., began the first two farms in the county of Waterloo; Schoerg on land adjoining this farm, Betzner on the west bank of the river three miles down-stream. In the same year came Samuel Betzner Sr., who took up a farm including this site. Other settlers followed and in 1805 a company formed in Pennsylvania purchased sixty thousand acres, the German Company Tract, comprising the greater part of Block 2, Grand River Indian Land, now Waterloo Township. This constituted the first larger settlement in the then far interior of Upper Canada.

[34] Thus he offered, for instance, in 1795, the huge territory of the present-day townships of North and South Dumfries (Waterloo and Brant Counties) to the German Loyalist Philipp Stedman, who had fought under Butler and had settled in Queenstown (see footnote 4 above), for a relatively small sum. The sales contract between Stedman and the Indian chiefs has been preserved and is published in *ibid.*, II, 203. He did not keep his land very long.

[35] See for the following the extensive publication of documents by Cruikshank, "The Reserve of the Six Nations on the Grand River and the Mennonite Purchase of Block No. 2" (No. 98).

[36] *Ibid.*, 321, and Breithaupt (No. 48), 44.

[37] Cassel (No. 82), 239; Breithaupt (No. 48), 44, and *Waterloo Historical Society* (No. 450), III, 14.

[38] According to Breithaupt (No. 47), 15, Joseph Schoerg and Samuel Betzner (see footnote 33 above) came with three additional families from Lancaster County, Pa.: Samuel Betzner, the father, and Johann and Christian Reichert. In 1801 the Gingerich, Bechtel, Kinsey, Rosenberger, Brickers and Baer families came from the counties of Lancaster, Montgomery and York, Pa., plus a few additional families in 1802 from Cumberland, Montgomery and other counties.

[39] See Mabel Dunham's account (No. 123).

[40] The sales contract is published in (No. 450), VII, 87.

[41] According to *ibid.*, VII, 60: "Bucks, Montgomery, Chester, Berks, Lancaster, York, Cumberland and Franklin Counties supplied the bulk of the Upper Canada settlers of Pennsylvania orgin."

[42] According to Spetz (No. 404), 197, it comprised 45,195 acres for which they paid £16,364. See also Cassel (No. 82), 243.

⁴³ See Breithaupt (No. 47), 16:

> By 1823, most of the lands in Waterloo and Woolwich townships had been
> taken up by Mennonites from Pa., who, however, continued to come until
> about 1835, and some stragglers later, up to the beginning of the American
> Civil War. Common names among their descendants to this day are Betzner,
> Brubacher, Baumann (Bowman), Bechtel, Bean, Bergay, Bingemann, Burk-
> holder, Cressmann, Detweiler, Eby, Erb, Gingerich, Graff, Hallmann, Hagey,
> Hunsberger, Hoffmann, Kinsey, Kolb, Martin, Moyer, Musselmann, Reichert,
> Schneider (Snyder, Snider); Stauffer, Shantz, Weber (Weaver), Witmer and
> others.

⁴⁴ Sherk (No. 387), 103, and Breithaupt (No. 48), 44.

⁴⁵ See *Waterloo Historical Society* (No. 450), XI, 47.

⁴⁶ Cassel (No. 82), 256. Even the highest spiritual offices are held as honorary
posts. Their preachers have to earn their living in a practical occupation. They
are therefore mostly farmers as well.

⁴⁷ The immediate cause for the change of name can not be determined, but it
is probably attributable to the influence of Prussians who had immigrated in the
meantime. See *Waterloo Historical Society* (No. 450), I, 14.

⁴⁸ According to Gourlay (No. 158), vol. I, 382 and 402. At that time there
were three grain mills and five sawmills; three schools whose teachers received
an annual salary of 60 shillings each; two preachers but still no doctor, in
Waterloo. In addition to agriculture the Mennonites raised sheep and produced
three thousand pounds of wool annually. Bad roads and a shortage of people
held back the development of the township, according to the report written by
Mennonites themselves in Gourlay, *ibid.*

⁴⁹ See Breithaupt (No. 47), 17: "From about 1820, Germans and others
directly from Europe began to come to Waterloo Tp., mostly to Berlin and
Waterloo, also to Preston."

⁵⁰ See Loeher (No. 268), 257; Smith (No. 402), Vol. II, 122; Teuscher (No.
423), 8; Cassel (No. 82), 247f.; Smith (No. 399); Spetz (No. 404), 188; and Oppel
(No. 317), 125f.

⁵¹ See their report to Gourlay (footnote 48 above).

⁵² See chapter III, part 3.

⁵³ Wellesley, which was officially surveyed only in 1842, was invaded by squat-
ters as early as ten years before that date. See Spetz (No. 404), 74f.

⁵⁴ According to the 1848 Census (see *Census of Canada, 1871*, vol. IV, 166)
3,075 inhabitants of the Wellington district (later Waterloo and Wellington
Counties) reported Germany, and the unusual number of 6,623 inhabitants

reported "other countries," as their place of birth, although all the remaining countries in question were listed separately. Under the classification "other countries" nothing less than the states of the Germanic Confederation (Baden, Württemberg, Bavaria, etc.) are hidden, and possibly France which the Alsatians reported as their place of birth. Only a minority of the German immigrants reported Germany as their homeland, the majority mentioned their respective states. The Canadian authorities, however, were not able to combine these under one classification.

Since Wellington County had only a few hundred Germans—according to the 1851 Census (*ibid.*, 183) when Waterloo and Wellington were already separated there were 335—we may safely assume a number exceeding nine thousand Germans for Waterloo County at that time. A mere 1,594 mentioned the U.S.A. as their place of birth in 1848.

[55] Concerning the history of the German Catholic settlements, see particularly Spetz (No. 404), 186. New Germany was the largest and most homogeneous colony. What Spetz wrote (*ibid.*, 50) about their early years, also sheds, in part, some light on the general social conditions:

> The first Catholic immigrants came from Europe in about 1826 or 1827. Being poor, they first remained for some years among the older and wealthier Mennonites, and worked for them until they became acquainted with the conditions of this new country and earned a little money to begin farming for themselves . . . As the German Catholic population increased and occupied all the land in Waterloo Tp., they overflowed north into Woolwich and Pilkington Tps . . .

The bulk of the Germans in New Germany came from Baden and the Alsace, some of them also from Württemberg, Bavaria, Hesse and the Rhineland (*ibid.*, 50 and 212f.). The prevailing dialect was thus Alemannic while everywhere else in Waterloo the Palatine dialect, which was spoken by the original Mennonites, predominated. See Spetz, *ibid.*, ix and 50:

> Many of the settlers had a trade and practiced it for many years, at least in part, after they had secured farms . . . The newcomers from Europe, having scanty means and being quite inexperienced in bush life, obtained valuable advice, employment and credit from their better situated Mennonite neighbours. These were uniformly kind, neighbourly and hospitable to a degree. In fact, without this helpful disposition of the Mennonites the European settlers could scarcely have remained in the wilderness. Even with these kind neighbours most of the immigrants from Europe had a hard enough task to get on in the new world. Almost everyone of them could tell of many instances of getting help in distress and great need.

According to the statistics of the first German Catholic itinerant preacher, in 1837 there were 307 Catholics in Rottenburg, as New Germany was called at that time (Spetz, 4). By 1838 this number had increased to 446 (p. 54). As a result of immigration the parish continued to grow quickly and passed the two thousand mark around 1850. In 1866 it still counted 1,645 members in spite of the verifiable emigration to Grey and Bruce Counties. Of this number 836 lived in Waterloo Tp., 462 in Woolwich Tp., 279 in Pilkington Tp. and 68 in Guelph Tp. (Wellington County), since in the meantime the colony had spread beyond the boundaries of the county and into four adjoining townships (*ibid.*, 65). About the beginnings of the second, predominantly Catholic area of settlement, (St. Agatha, etc.,) Spetz, 2f., notes:

> The first Catholic settler from Europe seems to have been Theobald Spetz, who came from Upper Alsace, about 1827 . . . Through correspondence with friends in Alsace, others came in. The earlier ones located west of Waterloo Town on the Upper Road, as it was formerly called, and called the little settlement Rummelhart after one of the principal early immigrants. Frieburger, Schwartz, and others bought land here from the Mennonites. Carl Schaefer, a shoemaker from Baden, began the first tavern here, and kept it till his death, making and mending shoes at the same time . . . The next immigrants, mostly Alsatians, went across the boundary into Wilmot Tp. and settled on Crown lands along the Upper Road for about two miles, to St. Agatha. As the farms along Erb's Road were all taken, mostly by Catholics, later ones betook themselves to the concessions further north, in time up to the northern line of the township and beyond and also northwest of St. Agatha. The Upper Alsatians were the first and remained the most numerous, but others from Baden, Württemberg, Bavaria, the Rhine Province, Hessia, and other parts of Germany settled among them . . . These German immigrants were, almost without exception, splendid acquisitions, and soon hewed for themselves excellent farms out of the virgin forest, although most of them came with little or no means.

In 1837 there were twenty-one German Catholic families numbering 112 souls, and one school for Catholics and Lutherans combined in St. Agatha (Spetz, 4 and 42). In the mid-1850s the Catholic priest of St. Agatha served all the villages in a wide radius. Spetz, 26, states:

> The parish included the villages of Waterloo, Berlin, Strassburg, Williamsburg, Mannheim, New Dundee, Shingleton, Petersburg, Baden, New Hamburg, Philipsburg, Bamberg, Erbsville and Rummelhart. New Prussia and South East Hope were dependent missions. All through this large territory Catholics were scattered more or less numerously. They must have made a population of 600 families and more.

[56] See *Jubiläums-Büchlein* (No. 219). 40-64. The first two Lutheran congregations were founded in Preston and New Hamburg in 1834. In Waterloo the first Lutheran church was built in 1838. In 1843 Philippsburg obtains its first Lutheran pastor. In Heidelberg the Lutherans form a congregation in 1845 and in Mannheim around 1846.

[57] Eby (No. 124) in 1854 estimated the number of Germans between Lake Ontario and Lake Huron (i.e., particularly Waterloo and Perth Counties) to be 12,000-15,000 which was probably still too low.

[58] See chapter II, part 7. It is interesting to note that by the end of the 1850s even old-established settlers of Waterloo turn to Renfrew in the hope of finding a better future there (see Report on Immigration for 1859, P.P., 1860, XLIV, 405).

[59] Spetz (No. 404), 93 and 150.

[60] According to Smith (No. 402), vol. II, 117-121, who also describes the German settlements at the Grand River in his very carefully written handbook of 1850. Preston with its population of 1,100 was the largest German settlement at that time. In Berlin, with a population of 750, there were five small churches, one for each of the following denominations: Mennonites, Lutherans, German Methodists (Albrights?), the Wesleyans and the New Jerusalem Church. Enough British, therefore, seem to have lived in the settlement for two small British sects to be able to build chapels. According to Smith, *ibid.*, German Methodists could be found in Waterloo and New Aberdeen. In each of these places, they as well as the Lutherans maintained a church of their own at a time when Waterloo had only 250, and New Aberdeen 120, predominantly German inhabitants. New Hamburg was at that time an elongated village with a population of five hundred.

[61] See Spetz (No. 404), 24, who states:

> Almost at every cross road there were a few houses occupied by labourers and craftsmen. The latter, especially the tailor and the shoemaker, came to the settler's house to make clothes and shoes for the whole family . . . Beside the saw mill of every village, there were a distillery, a blacksmith and wagoner, often a potter and an ashery and many other little customs factories, all working on small scale for the neighbourhood and giving employment to many.

[62] See Spetz, 107, whose observations applied to all denominations:

> The "Saugeen Fever" began in the later fifties. Many of the rural Catholics had only a few acres of land and plied a trade or worked in the woods or in the farmers' field for a living. With the advent of farm machinery and the clearing of the forest there remained little employment for this class. Others with large families had to look elsewhere for cheap land to settle on. Some of the older farmers died and their children sought farms where they could get cheap land. All these found what they wanted in "Saugeen", the counties of Bruce and Grey, then newly opened for settlement. Most of the land was good and cheap there, though still covered with virgin forests. Father Ebner and other priests endeavoured to stem this emigration, but in vain. This movement and later the emigration to the States continued. There was a succession of poor crops, and in towns and villages this was felt by the business people. Many of these failed or made only a precarious living. The towns were nearly all at a standstill or going backwards.

And *ibid.*, 25: "The rural population was gradually reduced to at least one-half. A number of schools had to close for want of children, others had their pupils greatly reduced."

[63] See the statistics of the Hamilton Agency in chapter I, part 5.

[64] Of these four only Wellesley had a larger percentage of British settlers from the beginning. See Breithaupt (No. 47), 17.

65

In	German by origin	total population
Waterloo, Woolwich, Wellesley, Wilmot	21,620	32,473
North Dumfries, Galt	430	7,778
Waterloo County	22,050	40,251

66

In	German by origin	total population
Waterloo, Woolwich, Wellesley, Wilmot	22,541	33,706
North Dumfries, Galt	829	9,034
Waterloo County	23,370	42,740

[67] See also Spetz, footnote 62 above.

[68] According to the 1901 Census there were:

In	German by origin	total population
Waterloo, Woolwich, Wellesley, Wilmot	31,424	41,737
North Dumfries, Galt, Ayr	1,238	10,857
Waterloo County	32,662	52,594

[69] Minister of Agriculture Martin was nevertheless able to celebrate Waterloo as the most flourishing agricultural district and one of the foremost industrial districts of Ontario, when in 1926 he dedicated the Memorial Tower in honor of the first German settlers (compare footnote 33 above). See (No. 450), XIV, 217 ff.

[70] See Wallace (No. 448). About his work see also *Canada and Its Provinces* (No. 388), vol. XVII, 237, and XVIII, 479. In particular see the article on him in *Waterloo Historical Society* (No. 450), XIII, 159-166.

[71] These are the:

Common School Act of 1850 (13-14 Victoria, Cap. 48, Clause 19);
Separate School Act of 1851 (14-15 Victoria, Cap. 111, Cl. 4);
Supplementary School Act of 1853 (16 Victoria, Cap. 185, Cl. 4).

All three are published in *Law* . . . (No. 371a).

[72] Clause 8 of the resolution of the Council of Public Instruction of April 25, 1851, concerning the training of teachers, states: "In regard to teachers of French or German, that a knowledge of French or German grammar be substituted for a knowledge of English grammar, and that the certificate of the teacher be expressly limited accordingly."

See Sissons (No. 359), 20 ff.

[73] Johnston (No. 217), 80.

[74] Sissons (No. 359), 22.

[75] Martin Rudolph, the Local Superintendent of Waterloo County, wrote in 1854 (*ibid.*, 28f): "A great drawback for our schools, too, is that our children have to learn two languages, the German and the English, and well qualified teachers in both languages are few, seeing that they can earn more in any other vocation than that of school teaching."

[76] Sissons, *ibid.*, 31f.

[77] *Ibid.*, Dr. Ryerson, the Chief Superintendent of Education in Ontario, believed with good reason that at that time all German teachers could at least read English, and that English was taught in all German schools.

[78] According to Sissons, 67f., the pertinent clauses of the amendment to the school law of 1890, passed by the Conservative government, read:

Clause 1.

1. In school sections where the French or German language prevails, the trustees, with the approval of the inspector may in addition to the course of study prescribed for the public schools require instruction to be given in French or German reading, grammar or composition to such pupils, as are desired by their parents or guardians to study either of these languages, and in all such cases the authorised textbooks in French or German shall be used.

2. It shall be the duty of the teacher, to conduct every exercise and recitation from the textbooks prescribed for the public schools in the English language, and all communication between teacher and pupil in regard to matters of discipline and in the management of the school shall be in English, except so far as this is impracticable by reason of the pupil not understanding English. Recitations in French or German may be conducted in the language of the textbook.

[79] The report of the Commission on the German schools submitted in 1889, which was to justify the school law about to be introduced, and therefore exaggerates somewhat, stated (according to Sissons, 32f.):

As the surrounding districts became occupied by English-speaking people the German language gradually gave way to the English, so that now the schools, though attended by German children and making some use of German, are practically English schools, and the German language is no longer used as a medium of instruction in any of them, except in so far as it may be necessary to give explanations to those pupils who on coming to school know but little English . . . There are others in which German is sometimes taught and sometimes omitted, according to the prevailing desire of the people. There are also many schools, especially in Waterloo County, in which large numbers of German pupils are found, but in which the German language is not taught.

[80] Karl Müller-Grote who lived in Waterloo intermittently from 1872 to 1910, wrote (No. 297), 272f.:

> The English side had always been working against the German instruction sometimes openly, sometimes secretly and with such success that finally in Berlin barely 100 children attended the German classes. When thanks to the activity of the *Schulverein* the number of students had risen to 400, German lesson was moved to a time before the beginning of the regular school period. That meant that the child learning German had to get up one hour earlier. When in spite of this, the number of students increased considerably, I succeeded also in bringing into existence a *Verein* in nearby Waterloo. — We organized special festivities for the German students, distributed German books as prizes and I had a large number of the beautiful Vogtlander stone prints sent from Leipzig. When I left Berlin in 1910, there were approximately 1,000 children attending German classes.

[81] As late as the middle of the World War, Sissons (No. 359), 33, wrote:

> German is still taught in many school sections where the majority of the ratepayers speak that language, but to an extent which interferes little, if at all, with the general work of the school. In most of the elementary schools of Waterloo County a half hour each day is given to the study of the vernacular, but in Berlin, now Kitchener, even that has been abandoned as interfering unduly with the general work and organisation of the large city schools. A large number of students of German origin have found their way through the high schools and universities. Indeed, the language difficulty in German districts in Ontario was solved twenty-five years ago.

[82] According to the 1911 Census there were

In	German by origin	total population
Waterloo, Woolwich, Wellesley, Wilmot	35,312	49,390
North Dumfries with Galt and Ayr	1,255	12,217
Waterloo County	36,567	61,607

[83] See Müller-Grote (No. 297), 272f.: "Even after the Kaiser memorial had been destroyed by an angry military mob, after the last German language newspaper had suspended publication and the club rooms of Concordia had been turned into a heap of ruins, the *Schulverein* . . . still existed."

But the school could not be saved either. "In 1918 the school board suddenly inquired, in a manner that was unmistakable to the English teachers, which of the subjects might be dispensed with in order to accelerate the progress of the children. The response from 29 teachers was that German stood as an obstacle in the way."

See also footnote 81 above. The memorial to Kaiser Wilhelm I mentioned by Müller-Grote was unveiled in 1897 on the occasion of the last choral festival of all the German-Canadian singing clubs. These had played a role similar to that played among the German community in the United States. See Maron in *Der*

Nordwesten-Kalender for 1914 (No. 306), 106f.

[84] On the occasion of the dedication of the Memorial Tower in honor of the first German pioneers of Waterloo County, the President of the Waterloo Historical Society, W.H. Breithaupt, did not consider it beneath his dignity to remind his audience of this fact with the following words, as quoted in *Waterloo Historical Society* (No. 450). XIV, 221:

> In the Great War, enlistments from Waterloo County totalled approximately 4,000, and of this number about 10 per cent, about 400, were killed in action or died of wounds or disease. A very large proportion were descendants of German and Pennsylvania settlers, neither Germans nor Canadian-Germans, but Canadians; and most of them volunteer enlistments, embued with love of their country. Worthy of mention here is that the first Waterloo County man to fall in action in the war, March 20th, 1915, at Neuve-Chapelle, was Alexander Ralph Eby, direct descendant in line of oldest sons, Isaac E., Menno E., Alexander E. and then Alex. Ralph Eby from Bishop Benjamin Eby . . . "

See also Breithaupt's speech of 1915 to the Waterloo Historical Society (No. 450), IV, 7.

[85] According to the 1921 Census there were

In	German by origin	total population
Waterloo, Woolwich, Wellesley, Wilmot	33,627	59,127
North Dumfries (incl. Galt and Ayr)	1,010	16,139
Waterloo County	34,637	75,266

[86] In the once overwhelmingly German community of Kitchener (Berlin) a mere 9,728 of those over ten years old, among a population of more than fifteen thousand, still reported their origin to be German. Of these, however, only ninety-six spoke German as their only language, 5,255 spoke German and English, and 4,377 declared English to be their only language. For all of Ontario the respective proportions are even worse (see *Census of Canada, 1921*, vol. II, 530), although those figures are not to be taken absolutely, since the Austrians and Swiss are not included in them. Of the 103,738 Germans by origin over ten years of age, a mere 475 spoke only German, 53,289 spoke German and English (or French), but 49,032 were unilingually English.

[87] Pietsch (No. 325), 78.

[88] *Ibid.*, 78. The new paper was already noticed by Mrs. Jameson in her *Winterstudien und Sommerstreifereien* of 1837-38. In (No. 210), vol. II, 89 she writes: "In Berlin the Germans have a printing press and they publish a newspaper in their own language which circulates among fellow Germans in the entire province."

[89] See Sherk (No. 387), 107.

[90] Pietsch (No. 325), 78.

[91] *Ibid.*

[92] *Ibid.*

[93] According to *Der Deutsche Pionier* (No. 113), VIII (1876), 319.

[94] See Müller-Grote (No. 297), 276.

[95] *Der Deutsche Pionier*, VIII (1876), 319. Lemcke (No. 264) still mentions it in 1887, but Joest (No. 212) no longer does in 1888.

[96] Müller-Grote (No. 297), 275f.

[97] According to the article "Zeitungen und Zeitschriften" in *Deutsch-Amerikanisches Konversations-Lexicon* (No. 357), edited by Prof. Schem as cited by Kloss (No. 245). It is no longer mentioned in *Der Deutsche Pionier*, VIII (1876).

[98] Joest (No. 212) mentions it in 1888, Oppel (No. 316) no longer does in 1906. Around 1895 the *Lutherisches Volksblatt* was no longer published in Berlin, but in Sebringville, Perth County (see footnote 157 below).

[99] Joest, *ibid.*

[100] Oppel (No. 316).

[101] According to Joest as of 1888, Lenker (No. 265) as of 1896, and Oppel as of 1906. In addition to these local parish papers the bi-monthly *Kirchenblatt der Ev.-Luth. Synode von Canada*, published in Toronto, was read since 1868 (see Lenker, *ibid.*). In 1910 it amalgamated with *Der Deutsche Lutheraner* of the General Council. See *Jubiläums-Büchlein* (No. 219), 19.

[102] About the beginnings of the *Berliner Journal* and the interest of its subscribers, Müller-Grote (No. 297), 275f. reports:

> At that time there were neither postal nor railway communications and when the small paper printed with the hand press was ready, the printer got on his horse, rode into the countryside and distributed the newspapers to the subscribers living far apart on scattered farms. The poor devil of a printer often had to swim through the high tides of the Grand River or the Conestoga with his horse and in the winter he was sometimes near freezing to death . . . The *Journal* always maintained the standards of its meticulously clean print and its punctual appearance. When war broke out in 1870, some of the faraway subscribers were not satisfied with this punctuality. They came from distances of over ten English miles, by foot or by carriage, this is how passionate was their interest in the events at the theater of war.

[103] See chapter III, beginning of part 2.

[104] See Mabel Dunham's second Mennonite novel *Toward Sodom* (No. 122),

whose plot refers to the 1860s and the turning away of the young generation from the faith and traditions of the fathers. The census reports show the number of Mennonites to be 4,767 for 1871, 5,097 for 1881 and 3,004 (?) for 1901.

[105] According to the 1921 Census. In 1911 there were 6,456.

[106] According to the 1921 Census there were 13,645 Mennonites in all of Ontario.

[107] According to the census there were 2,025 Lutherans in 1848, 5,628 in 1851 and 10,290 in 1861. Most of the congregations, therefore, trace their origins to the 1850s. See *Jubiläums-Büchlein* (No. 219), 40-65.

[108] According to the census there were 10,290 in 1861; 10,013 in 1871; 11,252 in 1881 and a mere 9,745 in 1901.

[109] It appears not at all unlikely that the church services of these sects were held in German (see chapter II, footnote 39). Müller-Grote (No. 297), 274, reports that in the 1870s Berlin had three different Lutheran congregations "and in addition there was a German Baptist congregation, a so-called Evangelical and a Mennonite congregation, and in the churches of some sects the sermon was even given in German."

[110] Chapter II, end of part 7.

[111] According to *Der Nordwesten-Kalender* of 1929.

[112] See *Jubiläums-Büchlein* of 1911 (No. 219), and Neve (No. 304).

[113] *Jubiläums-Büchlein*, 44.

[114] We recall that in 1921, of the total number of the Germans by origin in Ontario, only slightly more than half acknowledged that they were able to speak German in addition to English (see footnote 86). But of Waterloo's 34,637 Germans by origin, especially in the rural districts, at least two-thirds must be considered to have been capable of retaining the German language. That would roughly correspond to the above number.

[115] See Spetz (No. 404), 30. The priests were recruited not only from Germany, but later also from the sons of German-Canadian farmers. Like Spetz, they received their first training in the St. Agatha seminary, founded in 1865; and moved to Berlin in 1866 (St. Jerome's College).

[116] The amount of purchase, as a rule, did not have to be paid until ten years later, then however with a surcharge of 2.5 per cent. Until that time the farmer had to clear four acres annually, and pay rent in the amount of 6 per cent of the purchase price. For an estate of 100 acres valued at one dollar per acre, thus, six dollars rent had to be paid. With thriftiness and hard work he would have been able to save the amount of purchase after ten years. The land was worth at least a small mortgage after it had been cleared. The Land Company

thus worked with the only capital that the settler had, namely his labor. See Johnston (No. 217), 25f.

[117] According to the Census of 1840, published in *Statement . . .* (No. 408), 5, and the Census of 1848 and 1851 (*Census of Canada, 1871*, vol. IV, 164 and 180).

[118] Johnston (No. 217), 35, finds the following high-flown words for him:

> As a stream of water welling from a spring on the mountain side increases in volume as it pursues its onward way, so does the history of Perth County begin in December of 1829 at that lonely shanty of Sebastian Fryfogle in South Easthope . . . In this German we have the keynote or starting point of our history. He it was who bore the banner of our civilisation aloft into the forest and was a veritable voice crying in the wilderness: "Prepare ye the way, the conqueror is close at hand."

[119] *Ibid.*, 259f. Freyvogel was born in the Canton of Bern, emigrated to Pennsylvania in 1806, came to Waterloo in 1827 and to South Easthope two years later. I am sure many Germans in the Huron Tract came by way of similar stages. For a long time Freyvogel played the leading role in South Easthope (see also Spetz, 45). When in 1850 Perth was constituted as a county, Freyvogel, who was the district delegate for South Easthope, was made the first Warden of the County Council (see Johnston, 40f.). In general, the Germans in Perth appear to have been quite active in public life as mayors, chairmen of community councils, etc., as Johnston's detailed history of the county reveals.

[120] Spetz, 45.

[121] Johnston (No. 217), 261 and 264. This was the very first formation of a church group in Perth. As far as we could ascertain, the Lutheran congregation in what later became Sebastopol is older than any of its sister congregations in Waterloo County (see footnote 56 above).

[122] Spetz, 45f. Although they built a small church in South Easthope, German Catholics most of the time went to the church service in New Hamburg. In a list of the members of the early congregation the following names can be found: Arnold, Berger, Buckel, Bunes, Dantzer, Denfridi, Doehlen, Greib, Gfroerer, Grewey, Huetlin, Hartleib, Rudolph, Schmidt, Schlatermann, Scherer, Selzer, Spitzig and Weiss.

[123] Spetz, 45.

[124] Johnston, 258.

[125] See the statistics in *Statement . . .* (No. 408).

[126] See Johnston, 80 and 260.

[127] See Johnston, 261. Tavistock, now after Stratford the largest community

on the border of South Easthope which has grown together with the larger town of Sebastopol, was founded in 1848 under the name of Freiburg. During the Crimean War Freiburg was first renamed Inkerman (1854) and later (1857) Tavistock.

[128] Johnston (No. 217), 305. Individual Germans could be found here as early as the 1830s. According to Spetz (No. 404), 4, the above-mentioned itinerant preacher, P. Wiriath, appears to have visited nine German Catholic families comprising forty-six souls here even before 1837.

[129] Johnston, 312, and *Jubiläums-Büchlein* (No. 219), 40.

[130] Johnston, 286.

[131] *Ibid.*, 279: "In this Township the trend of settlement was from the Huron Road northward, and excepting a portion around Kinkora and a section near Stratford composed of North of Ireland people, all are German."

[132] *Ibid.*, 284, and *Jubiläums-Büchlein*, 41.

[133] See Johnston, 281:

> In sections entirely composed of Germans, farm buildings are often found more pretentious than such accommodations amongst English speaking people. A number of palatial dwellings, erected on farms in these northern municipalities by Germans, indicate a lavish expenditure of money, which one could think inconsistent with profit to an average farmer and with that cautious and economical rule of conduct attributed to their German owners.

[134] See *ibid.*, 324:

> Logan has a mixed population of English, Irish, Scotch and German. In certain sections either one or other of these nationalities predominate. In the district surrounding Brodhagen all are German. At this point were located such families as Schultz, Puschelburg, Hildebricht, Kraukopf, Brodhagen, Rock, Jacob and Eckmire.

In 1858 a German congregation was founded in Mitchell by Pastor Hengerer (*ibid.*, 327 and 492).

[135] The first Germans came to Mornington as true squatters even before 1835. They were Andreas Bissinger and Georg Stemmler with their families, from Rottenburg on the Neckar. In the 1840s, together with newly immigrated fellow Germans they founded the settlement of Hesson which they wanted to name at first "Habenichts," [i.e. Have-Nothing], according to Spetz (No. 404), 204f. Soon a German Catholic congregation formed there which maintained a school of its own from 1859 on. The Lutheran congregation in Hesson was formed in 1863, according to *Jubiläums-Büchlein* (No. 219), 63. In the south of the township Germans had settled primarily around Milverton, where two Lutheran congregations were formed in 1872 and 1873. In later years these maintained thriving Saturday

and Sunday schools for German children with one hundred students and sixty students respectively in 1902.

[136] About Downie, Johnston (No. 217), 179, says: "North, along the Goderich Road, are Germans, and we have such names as Seebach, Kastner, Sebring, Pfrimmer, Arbogast, Schelleberger, Klein, Göttler, Goetz and Schweitzer. The settlement of Kasterville should be mentioned. For Fullarton and Hibbert see Johnston, 199 and 242."

[137] Johnston, 219f.

[138] *Ibid.*, 220.

[139] See *Census of Canada, 1871*, vol. IV, 183. According to the Census of 1848 there were at that time 1,501 natives of Germany in the Huron Tract (*ibid.*, 166).

[140] According to *Der Deutsche Pionier*, XI, 18. See also chapter I, part 6.

[141] *Jubiläums-Büchlein* (No. 219), 43, states: "Around 1850 Germans of the Lutheran and Reformed faiths settled in Hay Tp. (Huron)." The German immigrants must, in fact, have arrived in 1850 and in the years immediately following, since in 1851 the total number of Germans in Huron County is reported to be still 230, and an immigration after 1855 was very unlikely. In 1871 in Hay Tp. and the adjoining Stephen Tp. alone 2,737 Germans were recorded by the census. Of these, 934 belonged to the Evangelical Association, 829 were Lutherans and 279 Mennonites. The remainder were probably Catholics or belonged to the smaller English sects. In 1861 the first "Lutheran and Reformed" congregation was founded in Zurich with a daughter congregation in Dashwood (Stephen). See *Jubiläums-Büchlein*, 43.

[142] Only a few Germans came to Elma. Not until 1889 did they found a Protestant church there in the community of Monckton. Its pastor was also in charge of a German Saturday school which according to Johnston (No. 217), 354, numbered fifty students in 1902. Considerably more Germans settled in Wallace Tp. For this township furthest to the north of Perth, which was settled between 1855 and 1861, we find a strong immigration from Waterloo expressly confirmed (Johnston, 392). In the community of Wallace there were three German Lutheran churches in 1902. According to *Jubiläums-Büchlein*, 53, the church of the Missouri Synod dates back to 1860, and that of the Evangelical Church to 1875, while the church of the Canada Synod was younger. The first two had Sabbath schools of forty-four and 165 students respectively in 1902. In Listowel there were two Lutheran churches (Canada Synod and Evangelical Association), each with Saturday schools (*ibid.*, 394f., 444). In Kurtzville (name!) too, the German Lutherans formed a congregation in 1874, according to *Jubiläums-Büchlein*, 53. For the lists of clergy see *Der Nordwestern-Kalender.*

[143] As early as 1856, school inspector John Eckford of Bruce commented on the German Catholic schools, as cited by Sissons (No. 395), 29: "I may in a few

words notice the Roman Catholic Separate Schools in Carrick. German is the only language taught or spoken." *Jubiläums-Büchlein*, 38, states: "During the years 1850-1855 the area of Normanby and Carrick was opened for settlers. Among them were many German Lutherans."

[144] In 1881 the distribution of the Germans was as follows:

In	German by origin	total population
Carrick	4,317	5,909
Brant	1,263	5,423
Culross	1,045	3,807
Remaining Townships	3,002	49,635
Total	9,627	64,774
Normanby	3,105	6,140
Bentinck	1,291	5,472
Sullivan	724	4,143
Remaining Townships	1,872	58,374
Total	6,992	74,129

The ethnic German proportion of the total population has remained the same to this day.

[145] See *Canada* (No. 168), 9. In this publication a certain Dr. Schreiner, who travelled through western Ontario in 1881 and, among other places, visited the entire German area from Mildmay to Neustadt and Carlsruhe by carriage, wrote: "The Germans living in Grey County, mostly from Baden and the Alsace, are on the whole well off. Many of them have even become very prosperous. One farm next to the other, one more beautiful than the other, with cattle-breeding, cheese-making, orchards and a beautiful stand of forest."

[146] German place names, in addition to those mentioned above, are Carlsruhe, Moltke and Holstein.

[147] At that time North and South Easthope belonged to Oxford County, Wallace to Wellington County. Their numbers are, however, included above.

[148] The 1,365 Germans in Stephen Tp., which was at that time part of Middlesex County, are included above.

[149] The county seat of Stratford, where from 1863 on the most important German newspaper in Perth was published (see footnote 152 below), numbered only very few Germans for a long time. In 1881 there were no more than 436 among a population of 8,239. Around 1890, however, immigration from the German rural districts began in earnest and by 1911 there were as many as 1,714 Germans among a total population of 12,946. Today their number is estimated to be 3,500 among a population of about 18,000. The oldest Lutheran congregation dates back to 1859 (Johnston, 493; *Jubiläums-Büchlein*, 58). Today there are three

of them.

[150] About the beginnings of church life among the Germans in Perth, see footnote 121 and the following above. In Bruce and Grey Counties the oldest Catholic parishes date back to the mid-1850s, as the creation of separate schools attests (see footnote 143 above). Father Laufhuber from Berlin (Waterloo) had been active there as one of the first German priests since 1860 (Spetz, 102). During his time the Catholic parishes in Riverdale, Neustadt, Ayton, Carlsruhe, etc. were founded (*ibid.*, 226 ff.). At the same time the Lutherans, too, formed their first congregations, e.g. in the very northerly situated Sullivan Tp., as early as 1862. See *Jubiläums-Büchlein*, 42: "German Lutherans from West Prussia and Mecklenburg had settled in Sullivan Tp, where P. Behrens from Normanby was the first to organize them into one congregation in 1862."

[151] See Hunter (No. 202), 193.

[152] See Johnston (No. 217), 487.

[153] Pietsch (No. 325), 78.

[154] *Der Deutsche Pionier*, VIII (1876), 319.

[155] According to the article, "Kanada,", in *Deutsch-Amerikanisches Konversations-Lexicon* (No. 357), as cited by Kloss (No. 245).

[156] Lemcke (No. 264), and Pietsch (No. 325), 79.

[157] Lenker (No 265), 770.

[158] *Der Deutsche Pionier*, VIII (1876), 319.

[159] Pietsch (No. 325), 78.

[160] It is mentioned in all the surveys of the German press in Canada (*Der Deutsche Pionier*, 1876; Lemcke, 1887; Joest, 1888; Oppel, 1906).

[161] Pietsch, 78.

[162] *Ibid.*, 79.

[163] Loeher (No. 268), 342.

[164] According to the 1871 Census there were:

	Germans by origin	Lutherans	Mennonites	Evang. Association
East Zorra	1,307	500	254	105
Blenheim	1,341	238	208	194

The rest were Catholic or had converted to the Baptists, Methodists, etc. In East Zorra the first Lutheran church was dedicated in 1852 (*Jubiläums-Büchlein*, 65). To this day the Evangelical Association maintains a pastor of German descent in Plattsville (*Der Nordwesten-Kalender*, 1929). About the Amish see the article "East Zorra" in *Mennonitisches Lexikon* (No. 182).

[165] The only German place name in East Zorra Tp. is Cassel. In Oxford County, furthermore, a river is called Spittler's Creek after a German by the name of Joseph Spittler who allegedly settled there in 1808. See Wintemberg (No. 464), 294. The place name of Erbtown and the designation "German Creek" for the present Cole's Creek have disappeared (*ibid.*, 271, 289).

[166] In 1871 the rural districts of Brant numbered a mere 1,766 Germans among a population of about thirty-two thousand. By 1911 there were still 1,431 and by 1921, 1,316 Germans by origin in this area.

[167] Gourlay (No. 158), vol. I, 371, noted in 1822: "The Tunkers [of West Flamboro' and Beverly Township] have divine service regularly performed." Hunter (No. 202), 190, claims to know that German ("late") Loyalists settled in Ancaster and Beverly Tps. For East Flamboro' and Glanford Tps. he reports Germans from the United States as settlers who, in fact, had spread over all the townships of the county and were most densely settled in Ancaster (see 1871 Census). From Waterloo Township, whose surplus population went to nearby Puslinch Tp. from the early days, a few Germans appeared to have come only to the furthest northwest, to Beverly and West Flamboro', as settlers. The adherence of a part of the Germans there to the Lutheran faith points to a connection with the Waterloo Germans (see 1871 Census).

[168] See the preceding page.

[169] In 1881 as many as 5,127 reported themselves as German by origin in Wentworth, not including Hamilton. In 1911 there were only 3,856, and in 1921 no more than 1,192 Germans by origin.

[170] See the statistical data of the Hamilton Agency in chapter I, part 5.

[171] The Report on Immigration for 1852 (P.P., 1852-53, LXVIII) states: "Of the Germans, about 2,000 are estimated as having remained in the province. They all proceeded to Hamilton, where a large number found profitable employment." Similar references can be found in almost all the annual reports at that time.

[172] *Jubiläums-Büchlein*, 46.

[173] Pietsch (No. 325), 79.

[174] These are mentioned in the article "Zeitungen und Zeitschriften" in *Deutsch-Amerikanisches Konversations-Lexicon* (No. 357), vol. II (1874) as cited in Kloss (No. 245). They are, however, no longer contained in the survey of *Der*

Deutsche Pionier, VIII (1876), 319.

[175] See the list of the German clergy in *Der Nordwesten-Kalender* of 1927. The Evangelical Association is identical with the Evangelical Church mentioned in chapter II, footnote 180.

[176] As early as 1837 P. Wiriath, the first German Catholic priest in Waterloo, visited fourteen German families comprising 65 souls in Guelph (Spetz, 4). About the first Germans in Puslinch and Peel, see Spetz, 160 and 169. About the expansion of New Germany across the border into Guelph and Pilkington Townships, see footnote 55.

[177] See the 1871 Census. In *Canada* (No. 168), 9, Dr. Schreiner reports about a trip by carriage from Arthur "through a number of German settlements to Mount Forest" (Arthur Tp.).

[178] See 1871 Census. In Garafraxa Tp. we find the place names of Spier (must refer to Speyer!) and Metz side by side. The name of Luther Tp. as well as the nearby Melanchthon Tp. in Dufferin County do not necessarily point to German settlers. Most townships received their names when they were surveyed and long before they were settled. This is also true for the townships of Osnabrück (Dundas), Thorne and Bowman (Labelle and Pontiac Counties). Their names were incorrectly attributed to the later settlement of Germans there.

[179] The numbers of Germans by origin were as follows:

	1871	1881	1901	1911	1921
Wellington area	2,969	3,696	4,250	3,674	3,139
Guelph City	145	501	929	1,277	774

[180] See *Der Nordwesten-Kalender* for 1929.

[181] See about him in *Dictionary of Canadian Biography* (No. 448).

[182] Lucas (No. 272), vol. III, 161. Kingsford (No. 238). vol. VII, 221. *Canada and Its Provinces* (No. 388), vol. XVII, 50f. Bryce (No. 59), 226f. *Jubiläums-Büchlein* (No. 219), 11.

[183] Breithaupt (No. 47), 14.

[184] See *History of Toronto* (No. 195), vol. I, 115: "He made a wagon track from York to the southern portion of Markham, which, winding in and out among the trees, marked the beginning of Yonge Street."

See also Teefy (No. 422), 53:

> "In effecting this first lodgment of a considerable body of colonists in a region entirely new," says the Rev. Dr. Scadding in 'Toronto of old,' "Mr. Berczy necessarily cut out by the aid of his party and such other help as he could obtain, some kind of track through the forest. It was along the line of this track Governor Simcoe determined to build Yonge Street."

[185] An example of such a treaty between Berczy and an emigrant is published in Häberle (No. 167), 17f.

[186] See the following document in *Simcoe Papers* (No. 95), vol. III, 192:

> Letter from a gentleman to his friend descriptive of the different settlements in the Province of Upper Canada. New York, 20th Nov. 1794. . . these Germans came in this summer, furnished with everything to make their situation comfortable and enable them to improve their land to advantage, and no doubt in a short time will make a fine settlement; they are supported by a company, who have liberally supplied them with teams, farming utensils and provisions, sent them a clergyman of their own country and are about to build them mills, a church, and a school house.

[187] In the *History of Toronto* (No. 195), vol. I, 116, Berczy's losses are estimated at £30,000. When his capital was used up, Berczy left Markham in 1799 and first went to Montreal and then to New York, where he died destitute in 1813. See also Bryce (No. 59), 226f:

> . . . Berczy was a man of cultivation and energy . . . He became involved for the benefit of his colony in erecting the expensive "German mills" in Markham, and from the complications thus arising he was only extricated by his death in New York in 1813.

[188] See the opinion of Gourlay (No. 158), vol. I, 460.

[189] See Bryce (No. 59), 227. Concerning the further development of Markham see *History of Toronto* (No. 195), vol. I, 114 ff.: "The mills formed for long the nucleus of early settlement, the road lying between this point and Yonge Street being a well travelled thoroughfare." For biographical information about the families of the German settlers see *ibid.*, vol. II, 285 ff.

[190] See Breithaupt (No. 46), 12f.

[191] See chapter III, beginning of part 2.

[192] See Cassel (No. 82), 242.

[193] See Breithaupt (No. 46), 13.

[194] In Whitchurch, where at first a Baron von Hoen, officer with the Hessians and "great friend of the Baldwin family" (?), had a large estate and where about eighteen hundred Quakers from Pennsylvania had settled, the same famous Mennonite families (Betzner, Bechtel, etc.) as in Markham turn out to be the owners of the land patents since 1803. See *History of Toronto* (No. 195), vol. I, 145 ff.

[195] In Vaughan two Germans are among the first four owners of land patents in 1797: W. Peters and Samuel Kiener (*ibid.*, vol. I, 124). At that time the former Hessian officer, Stegmann or Steichmann, settled with his family in Vaughan near the Pine Grove (*ibid.*, vol. I, 126). As a land surveyor in Canadian services after 1783, he played a leading role in the laying out of the townships

on the St. Lawrence (Dundas) and at the Bay of Quinte, according to Canniff (No. 76), 441. There were also German Loyalists here and there in the county. See e.g. *History of Toronto* (No. 195), vol. I, 90:

> About Eglinton (York Tp.?) the name of Snider is prevalent, the family being of old U.E. Loyalist stock, of German ancestry; Martin Snider was one of the Loyalist refugees who emigrated to Nova Scotia. He afterwards settled on Yonge St.

The tide of emigrants after 1800 brought not only Mennonites to Markham and Whitchurch, but also other Germans who, according to Hunter (No. 202), 189, settled in York and Vaughan Tps. and even as far north as King Tp. There an old village by the name of Schomberg can be found, just as in Vaughan the village of Kleinburg, as noted in the *History of Toronto* (No. 195), vol. I, 141 and 132. In general the characterization of Markham, Whitchurch and surroundings in 1822 by Gourlay (No. 158), vol. I, 460, applied:

> . . . simple and unsuspecting Germans — Tunkers and
> Mennonites — have been thinly stuck in by the knowing
> ones among their precious blocks and reserves, by whose plodding labours
> the value of their sinecure property may be increased.

[196] There were hardly any German Catholics in York. In his survey of 1837 the itinerant preacher Wiriath mentioned only one family of ten for Markham. See Spetz (No. 404), 5.

[197] See footnote 186 above.

[198] For this and the following see *Jubiläums-Büchlein* (No. 219), 10 ff.

[199] See chapter II, parts 3 and 6.

[200] About Mayerhoffer we read in *Jubiläums-Büchlein*, 12:

> He preached to the German Lutherans alternating between German and English, and on the whole conducted his ministry to the German congregations entirely in the spirit and according to the wishes of the Episcopal Church. By means of various machinations he brought a part of the German church property and a number of Lutherans into the Anglican state church.

[201] The Canada Synod split off from the Pittsburg Synod in 1861.

[202] *Jubiläums-Büchlein* (No. 219), 13, states:

> Diehl was a German pastor, but he knew enough English in order to be able to officiate in his new congregation in English which had become necessary in the meantime.

[203] See *History of Toronto* (No. 195), vol. I, 148:

> The great majority are thoroughly Canadianized by this time, and have little more than their names and family traditions to mark their foreign extraction.

[204] The census showed the following numbers of Germans by origin:

In	1871	1881	1911	1921
Markham	1,910	1,836	899	113
Whitchurch	1,172	811	273	42
Vaughan	1,084	993	471	46
Remaining Townships	1,637	1,940	2,534	660

[205] See Loeher (No. 268), 343, in 1846: "In the towns at Lake Ontario there are a few Germans everywhere, in Toronto about twenty families."

[206] See *Jubiläums-Büuchlein* (No. 219), 54. Meidinger (No. 286), 62, mentions the German church in Toronto as early as 1858. Even today there is still one pastor for the Lutheran Canada Synod and one for the Evangelical Church serving in Toronto, according to the list of the German clergy in *Der Nordwesten-Kalender* of 1929.

[207] The number of Germans by origin in Toronto was:

1871	1881	1901	1911	1921
985	2,049	4,728	8,766	4,689

[208] See Hammann (No. 175), 501 ff.:

> Apart from craftsmen and workers, there appears to have been only one branch of industry in which the German element [in Canada] was leading. That is the manufacturing of musical instruments and a number of accessories. The center of this industry is in Toronto. Here almost all the large business firms have been founded by Germans and are, in large part, still owned by Germans. In the brewing industry, on the other hand, it is striking that Germans have not been playing the role as, for example, in the United States where they have a monopoly in this industry, so to speak.

Among the larger German business firms in Toronto before the war there was the piano factory by Nordheimer & Heintzmann, also the firms of Nerlich and Co.; Peters, Summers and Co.; Graef, Bredt and Co.; A. Schnaufer, Finsterer and Ruhe. See Maron (No. 281), 26.

[209] See Hunter (No. 202), 188. That these were Mennonites is attested to by the fact that by 1871 as many as 261 still acknowledged this faith.

[210] According to the census the number of Germans by origin in Ontario County was:

1871	1881	1901	1911	1921
1,723	2,582	3,259	1,076	336

[211] See footnote 210 above.

[212] See Hunter (No. 202), 189.

[213] Of the 1,718 Germans of the entire County, 585 lived in Nottawasaga Tp. and 202 in its center of Collingwood. Together they constituted almost half of

all the Germans in Simcoe. At that time there were still 246 Mennonites in Nottawasaga and Collingwood, but only twenty-eight Lutherans.

[214] According to the census the following reported themselves as "German by origin" in Simcoe County:

In	1871	1881	1901	1911	1921
Nottawasaga and Collingwood	787	619(?)	712	627	
Remaining Tps.	931	1,876	2,090	1,574	
Simcoe County	1,718	2,495	2,802	2,201	940

In 1871 a mere 148, in 1881 a mere 153 reported Germany as their birthplace. In the 1870s the German immigrants appear to have come predominantly from York County.—How Kempenfeldt Bay of Lake Simcoe near Barrie got its name cannot be determined. It had already that name before 1850.

[215] In Peel County, part of which appears in the 1871 and 1881 Census as Cardwell County, the following numbers reported themselves as German by origin:

1871	1881	1901	1911	1921
642	397	219	255	128

[216] Germans by origin, according to the census, in Halton County numbered as follows:

In	1871	1881	1901	1911	1921
Nelson, Trafalgar		838	926		297
Remaining Tps.	444	643		381	
Total	1,282	1,569	888	678	277

The place names of Zimmermann (Nelson Tp.) and Snider (Trafalgar Tp.) point to the role of Germans when they were founded.

[217] In 1871 there were nineteen Lutherans in Halton and two in Peel, and only one Mennonite for both townships together.

[218] The first U.E. Loyalist in Norfolk was a German, Lucas Dedrick, who settled in Walsingham Tp., two kilometers west of Port Rowan, according to Tasker (No. 421), 70:

> The creek which flows into the Lake just west of Port Rowan is called Dedrick's Creek. Over it Mr. Dedrick built a rude, but substantial bridge, the earliest engineering structure in this country.

Since 1801 two German Loyalist families by the name of Buchner from New Jer-

sey had been living in Windham Tp. Before that time they had already been in
the Niagara district for five years (*ibid.*, 68). M. Smith (No. 400), 182, states
about Walsingham Tp. in 1813: "The greater part of the inhabitants are Dutch."
By 1871 Germans had settled by the hundreds in all the townships which had
been taken up by immigrants from the U.S.A. in the first decades of the century, as many as 1,114 in Charlotteville alone.

[219] Before 1837, itinerant preacher Wiriath also visited some German Catholic
families in Norfolk, fifty-three persons altogether, who may have been among the
first immigrants from Germany, according to Spetz (No. 404), 4. The number of
those who acknowledged Germany as their birthplace indicate, however, that,
except for Middleton Tp., the immigration from Germany was negligible (452 in
1861, 393 in 1871, 350 in 1881). The place names of Marburg and Rhineland
point to settlers from Germany.

[220] See Hunter (No. 202), 195. In 1871, 343 claimed to be Lutherans in Middleton, in the rest of the county, however, there were only seventy-seven. A
total of 904 persons reported themselves as German by origin in Middleton at
that time. Until the war the Missouri Synod maintained one Lutheran pastor of
German descent in Rhineland and one in Delhi (Middleton Tp.). See *Der
Nordwesten-Kalender* for 1914. Today only one of them still serves in Delhi.

[221] In Norfolk the number of Germans by origin was as follows:

1871	1881	1901	1911	1921
5,384	5,124	4,965	3,902	1,453

In the figure for 1901, the Germans of Walpole, Dereham and Tillsonburg Tps.
are not included, since they belonged to different counties in the other enumerations.

[222] The following reported Germany as their place of birth:

In	1851	1861	1871	1881
Elgin	43	168	308	351
Middlesex	43	78	121	150

[223] In Aldborough 235 of the 573 Germans by origin claimed to be Lutherans
in 1871, and forty-seven were Mennonites, while in the rest of Elgin and Middlesex there were no more than 159 Lutherans and ninety-six Mennonites.

[224] German by origin:

In	1871	1881	1901	1911	1921
Elgin	4,650	4,726	5,069	3,413	1,549
Middlesex (Land)	2,610	2,790	3,089	1,977	611
London	278	406	756	1,561	1,234

[225] See footnote 224. In London a Lutheran pastor of the Missouri Synod serves to this day (*Der Nordwesten-Kalender* for 1929).

[226] See Smith (No. 402), vol. I, 29. Ever since Count Zinzendorf, during his visit to North America around 1740, directed his followers to the mission among the Indians, the Moravians were not deterred by any of the many dangers in their new field of activity. Among these dangers was not only the process of conversion itself, but in particular also the attacks by other tribes against their Christianized neighbors. Our tribe of the Delawares was led for decades by the missionary David Zeisberger — his name is verified by Canniff (No. 76), 316 — who moved with them first to Ohio and then to Ontario. Gourlay (No. 158), vol. I, 294-296, reprints a report of 1822 by Christian Friedrich Denke, who was a missionary at the time. According to it, 167 Delawares and Iroquois who professed to be Moravians lived in Moraviantown. According to Bouchette (No. 39), vol. I, 94, it appears that besides the Indians and their missionaries, there were also a small number of white Moravians in Moraviantown. The number of Germans by origin which is later reported for Orford Tp., would support this assumption.

[227] See Smith (No. 402), vol. I, 29, and A.B. Jameson (No. 210), vol. II, 209 ff.

[228] Loeher (No. 268), 342, writes about the Germans in Ontario: "They have settled most thinly in the western district which has only small settlements, as well as new homesteaders in the towns of Malden, Amherstburg, Sandwich, Ft. Edward and Chatham."

[229] The numbers of those who in the census acknowledged their German origin, were as follows:

In	1871	1881	1901	1911	1921
Kent District	1,407	2,170	1,569	2,649	1,285
Bothwell Dist.	1,663	1,843	1,627	—	—
Lambton District	1,342	2,173	1,987	2,253	928
Kent and Lambton Co.	4,412	6,186	5,183	4,902	2,213
Essex County	2,156	3,476	4,746	4,894	3,626
Western District	6,568	9,662	9,929	9,796	5,839

[230] In Camden and Chatham Tp. we find the place names of Dresden, which Smith (No. 402) characterized as a young settlement, and Eberts. Both of these were almost certainly founded by Germans.

[231] In Sombra Tp. the place name of Becher suggests its founding by Germans, while in Wallaceburg, according to Lemcke (No. 264) the German newspaper *Das Echo* appeared in the 1880s. This was probably the only German-language paper ever published in southwestern Ontario.

[232] Following Hunter (No. 202) Muskoka and Parry Sound are included as part of New Ontario. For the figures see the census reports. German place names in Muskoka are Falkenburg and Germania.

[233] See the census reports from 1881 on. Hunter (No. 202), 197, mentions Catholic natives from Germany, and Swiss in Gurd, Nipissing and Himsworth. The presence of German Protestants is proven by the activity of two of their pastors in Arnstein and Magnetawan (see below). Besides Arnstein the place names of Loring and Alsace appear to suggest German settlers.

[234] The second group of towns appears to have had an early population of Germans. Among them in 1816 was the justice of the peace, Ermatinger, in Sault Ste.Marie who had immigrated from the U.S.A. in 1759, according to Bryce (No. 58), 242.

[235] The numbers of Germans in New Ontario were as follows:

Table III.2

Counties	1871	1881	1901	1911	total population 1921	1911
Haliburton	—	—	—	—	192	—
Muskoka	321	1,681	2,535	1,171	585	21,333
Parry Sound	29			2,167	1,451	26,547
Nipissing	267	—	998	2,105	525	74,130
Timiskaming	—	—	—	—	837	—
Sudbury	—	—	—	—	678	—
Algoma	58	409	2,050	2,357	793	73,380
Thunder Bay	—	—	—	2,043	664	67,249
Rainy River	—	—	—		416	
Manitoulin Isl.	1	—	—	—	101	—
Total	76	2,090	5,583	9,843	6,242	262,639

[236] See e.g. the comment on Massey in footnote 238 below.

[237] Karl Karger was such a teacher for a long time. He describes with much bitterness his teaching experience in Waldhof (Thunder Bay) in his book *Zehn Jahre unter Engländern* (Breslau, 1926).

[238] According to the list of German clergy in *Der Nordwesten-Kalender* for 1914, 1927 and 1929. The pastors in Sault Ste. Marie and Massey were supplied by the Canada Synod. About the beginnings of the congregation in Massey we read in *Jubiläums-Büchlein* (No. 219), 52: "Around 1900 the first German Lutheran farmer, Ed. Maass, settled three miles from Massey. Others followed in the years thereafter, especially from the area of Ladysmith (Pontiac County) and Pembroke. In 1904 a church was built two miles from Massey on the south side of Spanish River."

As an itinerant preacher, the pastor of Massey also had to serve other German Lutheran congregations in Mattawa, Latchford, Cache Bay (Nipissing County), Haileybury, New Liskeard, Mattheson, Cochrane (Timiskaming County) and Copper Cliff near Sudbury. The minister of the Missouri Synod in North Cobalt also served in North Bay (Nipissing), Krügersdorf, Sesekinika, Cochrane, Porcupine, Kelso (Timiskaming County), Mond and Bisco (Sudbury County). Besides Krügersdorf we find the following German place names in the far north: Schumacher, Buskegau, Brander (Timiskaming County), Elsass (Sudbury County), Tondern, Bertram, Franz, Wartz Lake (Algoma County), Schreiber, Jacobs and Waldhof (Thunder Bay). The settlement of Schreiber (Thunder Bay County) was named after one of the leading engineers of the C.P.R., according to the *Milwaukee Sonntagspost* of April 1, 1928.

NOTES TO CHAPTER IV

Editor's note: The first part of this chapter is excerpted from the general introduction to *Das Deutschtum* in Westkanada, pp. (48), 23-28. This introduction (1. Kapitel) is entitled "The Western Canadian Space, its Settlement and its Economic Development." It was intended to provide a general background for the reader in Germany. It deals only marginally with German immigration and settlement.

The second and third part of this chapter represent the 3. Kapitel and 4. Kapitel of *Das Deutschtum in Westkanada*, pp. 48-93.

[1] R. England (No. 134), 81.

[2] *Ibid.*, 72.

[3] *Ibid.*, 70. Sallet (No. 351), 22.

[4] Dafoe (No. 102), 131, characterized the situation around 1897 as follows: "The first thing to do was to settle the empty West with producing farmers; this was also the second, third, fourth and fifth thing to do. Solve the problem of how to get people of the right kind into the West and keep them there, and the problem of national development was also solved; if the West remained empty, every expedient to restore prosperity would be futile."

[5] *Ibid.*, 132f.

[6] *Ibid.*, 320, footnote 1.

[7] *Ibid.*, 319f.

[8] According to Dafoe, *ibid.*, 322, he said in a speech in 1922: "The policy was completely and perfectly successful while it lasted. There was not one-half of one per cent of the people we got from Hamburg who were not actual agriculturists. Almost without exception they went on farms, and practically without exception they are on their farms yet if they are alive."

[9] Immigration Act, *Revised Statutes of Canada 1927*, Cap. 93, Section 37 (b).

[10] According to this the government is authorized;

> to prohibit, or limit in number for a stated period or permanently, the land-
> ing in Canada or the landing at any specified port or ports of entry in Canada,
> of immigrants belonging to any nationality or race or of immigrants of any
> specified class or occupation, by reason of any economic, industrial or other
> condition temporarily existing in Canada or because such immigrants are
> deemed unsuitable having regard to the climatic, industrial, social, educational,
> labour or other conditions or requirements of Canada or because such
> immigrants are deemed undesirable owing to their peculiar customs, habits,
> modes of life and methods of holding property, and because of their probable
> inability to become readily assimilated or to assume the duties and responsi-
> bilities of Canadian citizenship within a reasonable time after their entry.

[11] Included among these were, according to Section 3 of the Immigration Act,
the insane and feeble-minded; persons afflicted with tuberculosis and with other
contagious diseases; deaf, blind, and otherwise physically defective persons unless
they had sufficient money or support by a third party; persons who had been
convicted of any crime; prostitutes, pimps, beggars and persons whose passage
had been paid by charitable organizations; illiterate people who were unable to
pass a reading test in their mother tongue; alcoholics, as well as persons who
wanted to overthrow the system of government and were opposed to private
property (anarchists, communists).

[12] Neufeld (No. 302), 17.

[13] England (No. 134), 91-115, reports on the activities of the railway companies in the area of immigration and settlement. For years he had occupied a
leading position with the C.N.R.

[14] Angus (No. 18), 83.

[15] For a survey of the phases of settlement see Stumpp (No. 418), 30-34, and
Malinowsky (No. 278), 24-30. Both works have a good map.

[16] Schmid (No. 362), 40f.

[17] Stumpp (No. 410), 36, provides the following table for 1911:

Table IV.2

Government	Protestant	Catholic	Mennonites	Total
Bessarabia	57,931	4,914	—	62,845
Kherson	66,663	99,072	3,578	169,313
Tauria	56,581	27,050	50,293	133,924
Ekaterinoslav	26,811	48,109	48,240	123,160
Don area	13,927	13,879	540	28,346
Kharkov	2,367	2,617	1,719	6,703
Total	224,280	195,641	104,370	524,291

Stumpp adds: "The actual number is considerably higher than the total of
524,291. The numbers for the Don area and for Kharkov especially are incredi-
bly low. If the German tenants and small farmers who live scattered among the
Russians, the factory workers and the urban German colonies of this region,
were added, the total would undoubtedly reach 600,000."

[18] Schmid (No. 362), 44.

[19] Traeger (No. 43l). 21-23.

[20] Kuhn (No. 247), 251.

[21] Traeger (No. 431), 25.

[22] Leibbrandt (No. 262).

[23] Malinowsky (No. 277), 20.

[24] Concerning the property laws, see Stumpp (No. 410), 40 ff.

[25] Schmid (No. 363), 28.

[26] *Ibid.*

[27] Some of the Mennonites who came to western Canada from 1891 on were
not without means. About the first group the Report on Immigration for 1891
(Sess. Pap., 1892, No. 7, 105) states that all of them were wealthy and some had
as much as four thousand dollars with them. The Report continues:

> These Mennonites, numbering about 300 souls, were induced to come to
> Manitoba from reports of their countrymen's success and especially through
> the efforts of Mr. Klaus Peters, a very successful farmer who went as return
> man last year with the very flattering result as above mentioned. They are
> for the most part settled about Gretna and Morris. In addition to these, about
> 600 Mennonites have arrived and have been distributed to different points
> throughout Manitoba and the North West Territories.

[28] Metzger (No. 289), 10.

[29] For the purpose of German-Canadian genealogical research it should be
pointed out that the work by Keller (No. 234) contains lists of the settlers of the
Odessa Catholic colonies with references to their origins in Germany. This
might enable many a German Catholic family in Canada to trace their roots
back to their original native community in Germany.

[30] Busch (No. 65), as cited in Eichler (No. 128), 72.

[31] Karasek and Lück (No. 228), 28f.

[32] *Der Nordwesten*, November 28, 1890.

[33] Karasek and Lück (No. 228), 30, and Ehrt (No. 136), 179-181.

[34] Bonwetsch (No. 36), 110f.

[35] Schmid (No. 362), 11.

[36] The number and impact of such letters was quite significant. Bonwetsch (No. 36), 117, reports that as early as 1877 there were instances when a single mail bag in Norka brought fifty letters from North America.

[37] Kuhn (No. 251), 126.

[38] *Ibid.*, 123, 127.

[39] Kaindl (No. 221), 171, 169-177.

[40] Zöckler (No. 472), 64.

[41] From the same districts by the way, came those 120 unfortunate Germans who, due to the unavailability of land, left for Dobrudja in 1866, and whose fates are described in Kaindl (No. 221), 149, and Traeger (No. 431), 75. On the way they came down with cholera. Only 79 reached their destination where, on top of that, they did not even receive the land promised to them, so that most were forced to return.

[42] For those Canadian Germans whose families came from Josephsberg and who are interested in their genealogy, attention is drawn to the article by Kuhn (No. 249). In it the native communities of the Josephsberg settlers are listed with detailed comments.

[43] "Bukowina" (No. 60).

[44] Kaindl (No. 221), 373-377.

[45] *Ibid.*, 277.

[46] See the resigned comments about our ignorance in the article "Banat" (No. 22).

[47] Letter of Peter Kleckner from Vibank, Sask., to B. Bott, editor of *Der Courier* in Regina. It was written in 1932. Bott kindly made it available to me. It was intended for publication in the newspaper's section "Letters to the Editor."

[48] The statistics in Rüdiger (No. 347), 128, show that in Zichydorf, the population with German as mother tongue grew from 2,337 in 1880 to 2,464 in 1910 and 2,900 — which is 92.9 per cent of the total population of Zichydorf — in 1921. The emigrant's statement must therefore be exaggerated. Yet it is understandable, in view of the fact that almost the entire surplus population appears to have emigrated.

[49] Rieth (No. 339), 73f.

[50] Teutsch (No. 424), 186.

[51] See the methodologically exemplary study by Traeger (No. 431). On the emigration of the Germans from Russia see Chapter IV, part 3(a), above.

[52] Traeger (No. 431), 101f.

[53] *Ibid.*, 136f.

[54] *Ibid.*, 104f.

[55] Kaindl (No. 221), 422.

[56] *Statistik des Deutschen Reiches* (No. 411), 116.

[57] Reports of this kind about western Canada, part of which belonged clearly to the category of promotional literature, were the following: Wiedersheim (No. 457), Hahn (No. 168), *Mitteilungen über Manitoba* (No. 292), Lemcke (No. 264), *Manitoba und das Nordwest-Territorium* (No. 279), as well as three reports by a Walter Abel from Berlin, which appeared as part of the official Canadian Reports on Immigration (Sess. Pap., 1886, 10, 133 ff.; 1887, 12, 151f., and 1889, 5, 98).

[58] It is published in the official Report on Immigration for 1884 (Sess. Pap. 1885, 8, 160), as well as in the promotional booklets by Lemcke (No. 264), 1, and *Manitoba* (No. 279). The relevant paragraph reads:

> When I am asked by Germans who want to emigrate, and who cannot be kept at home, where they are to go, I advise them to turn their steps to Canada, as I am convinced that nowhere in America, except when Germany is lucky enough to possess colonies, will our peasants and workingmen feel more comfortable, or get on better and surer, than in the land where I had been received last year by everybody with so much amiability and kindness. I hope it will be possible, by and by, to convince our emigrants that a settlement in Canada is far more promising than in the United States.

[59] Lemcke (No. 264), 66.

[60] Miller (291). Editor's note: This speech is quoted according to a publication of the Parliament of Canada, the *Official Report of the Debates of the House of Commons* (No. 73), 6834.

[61] The first year with a substantial immigration from the United States was 1891: among 2,266 immigrants there were as many as 309 German Americans. The Winnipeg Immigration Agent reported at that time (Sess. Pap., 1892, 7, 108f.): "I am now in receipt of letters from nearly every portion of the United States, being particularly from British subjects and Germans, and I look forward to a large and continuous influx from the American side."

[62] As cited in Sallet (No. 351), 22.

[63] Kennedy (No. 237), 146.

[64] *Census of Canada, 1921*, vol. I, 564.

[65] See the report of 1915 by Canada's chief immigration agent in the United States (Sess. Pap., 1916, 25, II, 87):

> Before war was declared, several large colonies of Americans of German and Austrian extraction, had selected their location, some in Manitoba, some in Saskatchewan, some in Alberta and others in British Columbia. They had given up their farms in the States, had made arrangements for the sale of some of their effects, and were all ready to move. The declaration of war accompanied by the report of conscription placed a sudden check upon this movement. A fair estimate of the number thus effected might be placed at 8,000. They were all farmers, good farmers too.

[66] See chapter II, part 7, and chapter III, part 2.

[67] Meyer (No. 290), 116.

[68] Burkholder (No. 61). Chapter V of this book deals with the emigration of the Mennonites from Ontario to western Canada and mentions many names of emigrating families.

[69] See the travel account of Mr. Hauswirth and Dr. Meyer in the Report on Immigration for 1886 (Sess. Pap., 1887, 12, 87-92), as well as the reference to the colony in Lemcke (No. 264), 66.

[70] Census of Canada, 1921, vol. II, 582.

[71] In 1896 it is reported (Sess. Pap., 1897, 13, IV, 118 ff.) that sixty-three Germans from South America passed through Winnipeg. *Ibid.*, I, 12, states: "German immigration from Chile and Brazil continues, though slowly, in consequence of the expenses of the journey, and the loss in exchange owing to depreciated currency."

NOTES TO CHAPTER V

[1] C. Henry Smith (No. 398) recorded in English the emigration of the Mennonites from South Russia to North America for their Americanized descendants. See also Leibbrandt (No. 262).

[2] About Hespeler the person see chapter VII, part 4.

[3] This document, containing 15 points, is published in Smith (No. 398), 67 ff.

[4] On the role that Shantz played in the immigration of the German Mennonites from Russia, see the article by Bowman (No. 42).

nonites from Russia, see the article by Bowman (No. 42).

[5] The Mennonites had asked for bloc settlements and educational autonomy in the U.S.A. as well, and had submitted a petition to the Senate and the House of Representatives in Washington to this effect. However, their request was turned down after a long debate, out of considerations of principle that were hostile to the preservation of foreign ethnicity. See Leibbrandt (No. 262).

[6] Friesen (No. 143), 69f. Also Peters (No. 321), 45.

[7] Sess. Pap., 1875, 40; 1876, 8; 1877, 8; 1878, 9; 1879, 9; 1880, 10.

[8] According to the unpublished M.A. thesis of J.J. Friesen (No. 142).

[9] P.M. Friesen (No. 143), 54.

[10] Here only two of the most significant historical works on Canada may be mentioned. In *Canada and Its Provinces* (No. 388), vol. XX, 295, we read: "It was not until the coming of the Mennonites that the possibilities of the prairie were demonstrated." In vol. VI of the *Cambridge History of the British Empire* (No. 67), 527, it is stated:

> An advance guard of German-speaking Mennonites — the first Europeans to settle in the prairies after confederation — came from Russia to Manitoba as early as 1874 with a promise of their own schools on the part of the Dominion Government. By 1875 they had established an extensive community of 6,000 in Manitoba. They demonstrated the possibilities of open prairie farming and the feasibility of growing flax.

[11] According to the *Cambridge History*, ibid., 526f., the first nine Ukrainian families did not arrive until 1894, and there was no noticeable Ukrainian immigration until 1897.

[12] See United States, *House Documents* (No. 4c and 436), Reports of the Bureau of Immigration, table VIII a: "Emigrant Aliens departed, by countries of intended future residence and races or peoples." (Germans going to British North America.)

[13] Sess. Pap., 1897, No. 13, 124f.: "Summary Statement showing location of German and Slavic colonies in Manitoba and the North West Territories with approximate number of settlers, acreage under cultivation, and number of stock owned by them, 31st October, 1896."

[14] The survey of townships of western Canada and the method of locating a settlement are explained in the note on cartography (see Appendix). The following abbreviations are used: Tp. for Township, Rg. for Range, W. for West, E. for East, and M. for Meridian.

[15] The data for the Provinces of Saskatchewan and Alberta are converted from those collected for the Northwest Territories at the time.

[16] United States, *House Documents* (No. 4c and 436), Reports of the Bureau of Immigration, table VIII: "Immigrant Aliens admitted by countries of last permanent residence and races of peoples," gives the following figures:

1908-09:	3,031	1909-10:	3,082
1910-11:	3,898	1911-12:	4,041
1912-13:	5,406	1913-14:	6,287
1914-15:	5,679	1915-16:	6,180
1916-17:	5,917	1917-18:	1,209

[17] See e.g. in the novel by A. Geissler (No. 149) the account of the conditions in and around Winnipeg, and the march of the unemployed Germans to Emerson at the American border. Due to their destitution only a very small number of them were admitted to the United States.

[18] Sess. Pap., 1900: Nr. 13, II, 136. The impressive economic setup of this *Bruderhof* was especially stressed in the Report on Immigration. At that time a major influx from the Hutterite colonies in South Dakota was expected in Canada. In 1898 these had sent five delegates on a tour of inspection through the Canadian West (*ibid.*, 131). But the immigration did not materialize.

[19] See the chapter "Keeping the Faith" in Smith (No. 398).

[20] J.J. Hildebrand (No. 190).

[21] See e.g. Neusatz and Erka (No. 303).

[22] *Mennonitische Rundschau*, March 19, 1930.

[23] Iden-Zeller (No. 207), 215-216.

[24] C.F. Klassen (Winnipeg), the former vice-president of the General Mennonite Agricultural Association in Soviet Russia, in his speech on the situation of the Russian Mennonite congregations since 1920, presented to the Mennonite World Conference in Danzig in 1930. See Neff (No. 300), 55.

[25] According to the speech of Elder Toews'(Rosthern) on "The Emigration from Russia to Western Canada," *ibid.*, 73-79.

[26] England (No. 134), 103.

[27] *Der Auslanddeutsche*, VII (1924), 22.

[28] Weber (No. 457), 51.

[29] According to Toew's speech at the Mennonite World Conference (No. 300), 96.

[30] Winkler (No. 461), 287.

[31] According to the official Canadian Reports on Immigration.

[32] Winkler (No 461), 173.

[33] *Ibid.*, 284.

[34] *Nachrichtenblatt der Reichsstelle für das Auswanderungswesen*, 1933, 224.

[35] For the figures through 1925 see *Canada Year Book 1926* (No. 6); for the figures after 1926 see "Racial Origin of Immigrants into Canada, Calendar Years 1926-35," *Canada Year Book 1937*, 196.

[36] *Deutsch-Canadischer Herold*, May 1929, 160. [Editor's note: this is a retranslation of the German translation. The original English source could not be found.]

[37] According to the article "Auslandsprotestantische Rundschau" in *Der Reichsbote* (Berlin) of May 10, 1930, 10,750 Lutheran immigrants are supposed to have come to Canada since 1923. This figure, however, is too low. It is highly likely that among the Protestant immigrants a considerable number were not registered by the immigration boards.

[38] Hermann Trelle was born in Ontario of Westphalian parents. About his role in the opening up of the Peace River district, the most recent scholarly work by Dawson and Murchie (No. 104), 45, states:

> At the very moment when the settlement recession threatened to become serious, the Peace River Country produced a Wheat King, Hermann Trelle. Indeed he was a King of wheat, oats, peas, and other agricultural products. Trelle became interested in pure seed strains particularly suitable to the Peace River region. With a keen mind and by dint of hard work he got to the point where he was ready to exhibit his seed strains in provincial competition. He began winning prizes back in 1922. Since that time he has received so many major prize awards for his grains and other seed strains in provincial, national and international competitions that the name of Hermann Trelle has become deservedly famous. The stories of his achievements made excellent news copy in Canada and other countries. While he had brought agricultural distinction to Canada in general, it must not be forgotten that his prize grains were grown on his Wembley farm in the Peace River Country. His fame drew further attention to its agricultural possibilities which were described in glowing terms by the daily press.

[39] According to Friesen (No. 142). See also Quiring (No. 329), 218 ff.

[40] Unruh (No. 437), 213 ff.

[41] *Deutsche Zeitung für Canada*, October 7, 1936.

[42] "Die Deutschen in Canada" (No. 380).

[43] *Nachrichtenblatt der Reichsstelle für das Auswanderungswesen*, 1935, 69.

[44] Dawson and Murchie (No. 104), 240 ff.

[45] Dawson (No. 103), 313-317.

[46] England (No. 134), 168-170 and 179 ff.

[47] According to the *Nachrichtenblatt der Reichsstelle für das Auswanderungswesen*, 1936, 126, the average wages for agricultural laborers in Western Canada in 1935 were as follows (in dollars):

Monthly Wages (Summer)	Man.	Sask.	Alta.	B.C.
Men	17	18	21	26
Women	9	9	11	14
Annual Wages				
Men	160	173	189	242
Women	92	96	115	160

[48] Excerpts of the diary were edited by Mrs. Ilse Schreiber (No. 373), 16, 39.

[49] *Ibid.*, 65.

[50] *Ibid.*, 64.

[51] *Ibid.*, 65.

[52] *Ibid.*, 91.

[53] See her lecture "Deutschland in Canada" (No. 374).

NOTES TO CHAPTER VI

[1] Sess. Pap., 1878, No. 9, 72 ff., and 131.

[2] *Ibid.*, 1879, No. 9, 65.

[3] See Hespeler's report for 1880 (Sess. Pap., 1881, No. 12, 57): "Through the exceptionally wet seasons this Province has experienced during the last four years, some 300 families of Mennonites were obliged to move from the eastern and somewhat low reserve to the southern and higher located one, leaving 400 families still residing on the former reserve."

In the spring they occupied their new land. The immigration agent in Emerson wrote in 1881 (Sess. Pap., 1882, No. 11, 108): "The Mennonite settlement of Southern Manitoba is rapidly progressing. From three to four hundred families have removed this season from the Rat River Settlement to this Reserve."

[4] See, e.g., the first of the very vivid historical scenes composed by D. Neufeld (Novokampus) under the title *Kanadische Mennoniten* (No. 307) on the occasion of the fiftieth anniversary of the settlements in 1924.

[5] C.H. Smith (No. 398), 179, quotes a homesick settler writing in his first year. [editor's translation]:

> With sorrow I look at the stead,
> Which for my home I took,
> No house, no stove, no chair, no bed,
> No horse, no cow, no food to cook,
> No dish, no spoon, how poor am I,
> Left lonely in this world to cry.

[6] It is adopted from the work by C.A. Dawson, *Group Settlement* (No. 103), 111.

[7] There is a detailed statement about the level of development reached by these oldest German Mennonite villages in Western Canada in the third year of their existence in the official Report on Immigration for 1877 (Sess. Pap., 1878, No. 9, 131).

[8] Sess. Pap., 1890, No. 6, 146 ff.

[9] According to J.J. Friesen (No. 142).

[10] *Der Nordwesten*, special issue, January 1898.

[11] In 1889 the commissioner for settlement, Jacobsen, who was sent to the Mennonites, gave a report about the reasons for their dissatisfaction (Sess. Pap., 1890, No. 6, 146-148), which states:

> The greatest grievance [in the East Reserve] is that they have not land enough for their increasing families in their Reserve here, and that even some of the land they possess, is in many places too stony and sandy for proper and advantageous cultivation. This I especially observed to be the case near the villages of Gnadenfeld, Grünthal and Bergfeld . . . .
> In the western or southern reserve round Morris, Plum Couleé, Morden, Gretna, etc. the trouble is greater. The western reserve is much larger, contains a great many more young men, who are also more enlightened, numbers of them knowing the English language thoroughly. These wish to spread out, and unless good inducements are held out to retain them on this side of the boundary line they may do a good deal of harm.

[12] In a speech in Winnipeg, Lord Dufferin referred to his visit in the following enthusiastic words, cited according to C.H. Smith (No. 398), 185:

> Although I have witnessed many sights to give me pleasure during my various progresses through the Dominion, seldom have I beheld any spectacle more pregnant with prophecy, more fraught with promise of an astonishing future than the Mennonite settlement (Great applause). When I visited these interesting people they had been only two years in the Province, and yet in a long ride I took across the prairie which but yesterday was absolutely bare,

desolate and untenanted, and the home of the wolf, the badger and the eagle,
I passed village after village, homestead after homestead, furnished with all
the conveniences and incidents of European comfort and a scientific agriculture; while on the other side of the road were cornfields already ripe for harvest, and pastures populous with herds of cattle stretching away to the horizon
(Great cheering). Even on this continent, the peculiar theatre of rapid change
and progress, there has nowhere, I imagine, taken place so marvellous a t⁻ans-
formation (renewed cheering).

[13] *Der Nordwesten*, January 12, 1896.

[14] *Ibid.*, special issue, January 1899.

[15] Pietsch (No 325), 48.

[16] According to the "List of Immigrated Mennonite Settlers and District
Men," of 1935 (No. 75) they settled in the following districts (with the number
of families indicated in parentheses): Altona (47); Arnaud-Dominion City (85);
Alexander (25); Austin-Sidney (5); Blumenfeld-Eichenfeld (9); Barkfield (18);
Blumenort (25); Beauséjour, Brokenhead and Lowland (9); Burwalde (15);
Brockdale-Moorepark (13); Beulah (2); Brandon (9); Boissevain (32); Dallas (1);
Crystal City (16); Chortitz, West Reserve (14); Chortitz, East Reserve (53); Car-
man (8); Culross, Elm Creek and Fannystelle (31); Carroll-Hayfield (5); Elie (11);
Elkhorn (5); Foxwarren (25); Fork River-Winnipegosis (36); Gretna (4); Graysville
(3); Gnadenthal (34); Gruenthal (43); Glenlea (24); Gnadenfeld (17); Gimli and
Winnipeg Beach (3); Headingly (9); Horndean (9); Hochfeld (19); Holmfield (15);
Kleefeld (4); Killarney (10); Kelwood (1); Lena (29); La Salle-Domain (34); Lowe
Farm (8); Margaret and Dunrea (16); Minnedosa (5); Manitou (59); McCreary
(8); McAuley (23); Morden (49); Marquette (14); Meadows (7); Melita, Elva and
Pierson (14); Myrtle-Kronsgart (14); Morris (16); Mather (9); Neuenburg (6); Neu-
horst (2); Ningu (3); Niverville (72); Newton Siding (26); North Kildonan (79);
Osterwick (9); Osborne (11); Oak Bluff (13); Oak Lake-Griswold-Kenton (35);
Portage la Prairie (11); Pigeon Lake (19); Plum Coulée (11); Reinland (17); Rein-
feld (13); Rivers (13); Rapid City (11); Rosenort (12); Rosenfeld (13); Rosengart
(21); St. Elisabeth (31); Springstein (25); Schoenwiese (11); Ste. Anne (17); Stein-
bach (61); Sperling (18); Stuartburn-Gardenton (8); Swan River (3); Spenser (13);
Stonewall-Balmoral (10); Starbuck (16); Ste. Rose du Lac (3); Whitewater (48);
Winkler (124); Winnipeg (280); Westbourne (2).

[17] Dawson, (No. 103), 163.

[18] *Ibid.* 125.

[19] According to C.H. Smith (No. 398), 211f., the following names were listed,
with the number after the name indicating its frequency: Reimer (47), Penner
(23), Toews (23), Friesen (18), Barkman (15), Plett (15), Loewen (10), Giesbrecht
(9), Wiebe (8), Goosen (6), Unger (7), Kroeker (5), Cornelson (5), Brand (5),
Dyck (4), Koop (4), Wohlgemuth (4), Bartel (3), Klaassen (3), Regier (3), Enns (2),
Thiessen (2), Funk (2). The following names appeared once: Duerksen, Eidse,
Esau, Fast, Kliewer, Klippenstein, Neufeld, Schellenberq, Suderman, Warkentin,

Peter, Froese, Goertzen, Janzen, Janz, Regehr, Sawatzki, Schultz, Weidemann.

[20] Clark (No. 85), 358.

[21] According to information from Pastor Voss in Tenby, Manitoba.

[22] "Cosmopolitan Winnipeg" (No. 90).

[23] Sess. Pap., 1885, No. 8, 44.

[24] "Cosmopolitan Winnipeg" (No. 90).

[25] *Der Nordwesten*, November 28, 1890.

[26] About the history of the congregation see *Gedenkblatt* (No. 148), which contains a list of the members of the congregation as of July 1, 1910.

[27] *Maria Immaculata* (No. 280), 1907-08, 422.

[28] "Cosmopolitan Winnipeg" (No. 90).

[29] *Der Nordwesten*, February 2, 1927.

[30] *Ibid.*, special issue, January 1899. [Editor's note: The German text referred to the "Rosenorter" erroneously as "Rosengarter" Mennonite congregation.]

[31] In 1893 the immigration agent in Prince Albert reported (Sess. Pap., 1894, No. 13, III, 146): "The only colony we have in this district is that of the Mennonites. They are steadily coming, some from Manitoba, others directly from Russia. They occupy a stretch of country south of Duck Lake, between the two Saskatchewan Rivers in the Townships 40-44, Ranges 2-5 west 3rd Meridian."

[32] Sess. Pap., 1897, No. 13, 125.

[33] *Der Nordwesten*, special issue, January 1899.

[34] In Sess. Pap., 1901, No. 13, II, 153, detailed lists of the immigrants' names are given.

[35] Sess. Pap., 1900, No. 13, II, 172, and Sess. Pap., 1902, No. 25, II, 131.

[36] Friesen (No. 142), 74.

[37] According to the *Atlas of Canada* of 1915 (No. 20) which maps the 1911 Census.

[38] As early as 1901-1902 the official Report on Immigration stated explicitly (Sess. Pap., 1903, 25, II, 118): "The German Colonies between the two branches of the Saskatchewan Rivers are flourishing in the most gratifying manner."

[39] Dörfler (No. 119).

[40] Oliver (No. 314), 75.

[41] *Der Nordwesten*, December 14, 1905.

[42] See Kennedy (No. 237), 197: "A remarkable feature of the immigration to the Swift Current district in the last year or two has been the predominance of Mennonites, who have deliberately given up their farms in Manitoba to settle in this drier region."

[43] Oliver (No. 314), 75.

[44] According to the "List of Immigrated Mennonite Settlers" (No. 75), they settled in the following places (with the respective number of families in parentheses) as of 1935: Aberdeen (36), Beharm (2), Beechy (38), Beverly (2), Blumenhof (30), Borden-Great Deer (15), Braddock (13), Balgonie-Pilot Butte (3), Bournemouth (23), Carrot River (13), Carnduff (6), Colonsay (14), Cactus Lake (2), Central Butte (8), Cabri (11), Carmel-Hillsley (3), Duff (8), Dundurn (51), Dalmeny (27), Drake (79), Davidson (3), Eyebrow-Tugaske (14), Eyebrow (3), Evesham-Macklin (6), Eastbrook (15), Elbow (15), Fiske (20), Flowing Well (9), Fleming (7), Foam Lake (8), Fairholme (27), Guernsey (26), Gilroy (12), Glenbush (63), Gull Lake (19), Glidden-Madison-Kindersley (16), Gouldtown (13), Govan (3), Hague-Osler District (115), Humboldt (12), Hanley (44), Hepburn (47), Herschel (45), Herbert (66), Harris-Ardath (9), Indian Head (8), Jansen (8), Khedive (13), Kelstern (6), Laird (56), Langham (29), Lockwood (9), Lost River (19), Luseland (2), Lanigan (9), Main Centre (25), Mayfair (34), Mullinger (24), Moose Jaw (6), McMahon (14), Meadow Lake (5), Neville (4), Osage (3), Parkerview (29), Parry (2), Rosthern (93), Rush Lake (21), Rudell (2), Rabbit Lake (59), Regina (20), Sheho (12), Scottsburg (4), Saskatoon (70), Swift Current (24), Swift Current-Sykes Farm (17), Springwater (15), Superb (13), Sonningdale (14), Schoenfeld (5), St. Boswells (6), Swan Plain (3), Tomskins-Stone-Carmichael (4), Truax (16), Tessier (2), Viscount (2), Waldheim (56), Wymark (13), Watrous (38), Wishart (4), Wingard (3).
In the area of Hague and Osler the new immigrants settled in the following villages or farm districts: Schoenwiese (36 families), Grünfeld (17), Hoehfeld (18), Hague (20) and Neuanlage (24).

[45] *Zum Andenken an das Silberne Jubiläum der St. Peters-Kolonie* (No. 15).

[46] Dawson (No. 103), 275-332. Dawson's main collaborator with regard to this German Catholic colony was the Canadian German Dr. Albert Moellmann, who is now at Waterloo College, Ontario.

[47] Dawson (No. 103), 286.

[48] *Canada and Its Provinces* (No. 388), vol. XIX, 1, 178-179.

[49] Humboldt, by the way, was not named by its first German immigrants.

According to Bryce (No. 57), 311, there was a telegraph station at this location as early as 1880: "At Humboldt in a telegraph station of the Canadian telegraph, some 500 miles west of Winnipeg, in the open prairie, and 100 miles from the nearest settlement, two young women have in perfect safety kept the office for the past two years."

About the present status of Humboldt as the economic center of the colony, see Dawson (No. 103), 294-295:

> Today Humboldt stands out as the undisputed centre of dominance in the colony. It has a population of 1,899 persons and ranks fifth among the towns of Saskatchewan. An imposing town hall, a new $15,000 skating rink, 3 schools, 4 churches, a large hospital, and a courthouse are the outstanding buildings in the community. Seventy-five business units draw trade within a radius of 20 miles. The flour mill has a capacity of 100 barrels a day and the creamery of 10,000 to 12,000 pounds of butter per week. Work on the railway normally provides employment for upwards of 100 men. Four ministers, 4 lawyers, 16 teachers, 34 nurses, 3 doctors, 2 dentists, and 2 bankers provide the town and the surrounding district with professional services. Numerous lodges, farmers, organizations, political organizations, sports clubs, and societies have their headquarters here. In short, Humboldt's secular influences have reached the far corners of the whole colony.

[50] Dawson (No. 103), 303, writes:

> The field survey made in Humboldt during the summer of 1932 showed that 18 out of 75 business units in the town were operated by Germans. Other German business and professional leaders included a doctor, a dentist, the rural municipal secretary, and the local agent of the German American Land Company. This information . . . suggests that the Germans are making a bid for the urban leadership of St. Peter's colony.

[51] According to the *Atlas of Canada*, 1915 (No. 20).

[52] *Bilder und Blätter* (No. 30). Compiled and edited by the Oblate Fathers in the colony. The author is Father Schulte.

[53] *Ibid.*, 24.

[54] The Chief Agent of Immigration, Mr. Speers, even maintained that he suggested to Lange the founding of the second colony (Sess. Pap., 1906, No. 25, II, 114):

> In August 1904 I recommended a new location for the German people, who had placed one thousand families on the Quill Plains. Mr. F. J. Lange, who had settled this district, inspected the new territory on my request, which proved highly satisfactory, and he has already placed a large number of German families in the new district, being from Tps. 37 to 39, inclusive. Ranges 18 to 25 inclusive w. 3.M.

[55] Pietsch (No. 325), 58, says about Lange: "He is not your commonplace fellow. In his younger years he studied classical languages at the University of Muenster and he is still preoccupied with the plan of a new world language. He has suffered many reverses, has helped many a person to wealth and a secure

position in life, and has remained poor himself."

[56] *Atlas of Canada*, 1915 (No. 20).

[57]   Father Schweers wrote a vivid account about the beginnings of the colony in the periodical *Maria Immaculata* (No. 380), 312-315, 344-349, 380-385.

[58] Sess. Pap., 1906, No. 25, II, 107. See also Dawson (No. 103), 288.

[59] *Bilder und Blätter* (No. 30), 125.

[60] P. Schweers (No. 380), 346.

[61] *Atlas of Canada*, 1915 (No. 20).

[62] Josephstal is mentioned for the first time in the Report on Immigration for 1886 (Sess. Pap., 1887, No. 12, 75): "This colony has a population of 95 souls; with the exception of one Russian family, they are all Germans and speak the German language."

[63] South Qu'Appelle was characterized in 1906 (Sess. Pap., 1907, No. 25, II, 82) as follows: "This colony was started in 1888, and has steadily increased on account of nearness to a railway station. There are probably of 300 families, 1,800 souls, in the district. Five schools have been established, and the district is generally successful, many of them increasing their holdings in land by purchase."

[64] According to Metzger (No. 289). Attached to this brief account is a complete list of the families of the settlers with their places of origin.

[65] *Der Nordwesten*, July 28, 1893.

[66] *Festschrift* (No. 7).

[67] The information about Kendal is taken from the report (No. 1) of Mathias Eisler.

[68] Sess. Pap., 1907, No. 25, II, 82.

[69] According to my own inquiries in the colony, the following families came from Rosch: Hubenick and Hack; from Moladia: Ottenbreit, Rieger, Flegel, Baer and Hicke; from Derelui: Gelowitz and Lipinski; from Cuszur Mare: Stradetzki, Batzer and Lesko.

[70] Sess. Pap., 1907, 25, II, 82.

[71] According to the report (No. 1) of Franz Klein in Bergfeld.

[72] According to the report (No. 1) of the local minister, P. Andreas Zimmer-

mann, formerly the pastor of Klosterdorf and Speyer in South Russia, and Canon of the Tiraspol Chapter in Saratov on the Volga. He has been in western Canada since 1921.

[73] The information about Holdfast is based on the report (No. 1) by Johann Dielschneider.

[74] According to the report (No. 1) of Carl Deutsch in Quinton.

[75] The earliest report is by Father Funke in *Maria Immaculata* (No. 280), 1907-1908, 270 ff.

[76] See *Bilder und Blätter* (No. 30), 114f. It contains a list of names of the first settlers.

[77] The earliest report about the colony by Father Hilland is in *Maria Immaculata* (No. 280), 1907-1908, 274-277.

[78] See Sess. Pap., 1905, No. 25, II, 83: "Special mention must be made of the Stoetzel Colony, containing about 100 families of German-Americans, who came from Dakota, Minnesota, Wisconsin, Iowa and Illinois, whose progress has been very rapid and satisfactory."

See also *Canada and Its Provinces* (No. 388), vol. XIX, 178.

[79] The name is not related to the adjective "happy" but is derived from an Indian word.

[80] Pietsch (No. 325), 55. In Prelate an Ursuline convent was established, with thirty to thirty-five nuns from Cologne, Germany, some of whom serve as teachers in Prelate, Rosenthal and Blumenfeld.

[81] The information about Hodgeville is derived from the report (No. 1) of the local priest, Father Fehrenbach, the information about St. Elisabeth parish from Mr. F. Kratzer.

[82] The information about Billimun and vicinity is taken from the report (No. 1) of Joseph Herbach.

[83] In 1917, for instance, nine German Catholic families from the U.S.A. settled twenty-seven kilometers southeast of Billimun. Others founded the colony of St. Marcel (post office Glentworth, thirty-two kilometers east of Billimun) and the settlement of Rosefield (seventy kilometers west of Billimun).

[84] Father Schultz (No. 377), 237 ff.

[85] In the Report on Immigration for 1884 (Sess. Pap., 1885, No. 8, 143) we read:

> German colony established at Long Lake . . . 22 homesteads are already taken

up, and from 60 to 100 families are expected to arrive during the months of May and June next. This colony is called New Elsass, and will be under the care of the German Immigration Society, lately formed in Winnipeg, which, if successful, will form a strong nucleus for German immigration to the North-West.

The Report for 1885 stated (Sess. Pap., 1886, No. 10, 68): "There is every reason to believe that the greater portion of the country north of Regina will, ere long, be filled with a population that will not only reflect great credit upon the 'Vaterland,' but be a great boon and blessing to the land of their adoption. These expectations did, however, not materialize."

[86] *Der Nordwesten,* July 21, 1893, as well as the special issues of January 1899 and May 1904.

[87] According to the handwritten church book of the Lutheran congregation of Edenwald, whose minister also served the Strassburg congregation, its membership consisted of only forty-two adults and thirty-six children on October 1, 1898.

[88] *Der Nordwesten,* special issue of May 1904.

[89] A report about Edenwold from the pen of Mr. E.H. Zarek was published by Dr. C.E. Hennings (No. 470). Our account is essentially based on it. It contains complete lists of the names of the immigrants until 1892.

[90] Sess. Pap., 1889, No. 5, 55.

[91] Sess. Pap., 1890, No. 6, 109.

[92] In his early years as an itinerant preacher, Pastor Schmieder also had to serve the German Lutherans in Strassburg, Longlaketon, Kronau, Davin and Neudorf. Like all the ministers in homestead areas, he had to travel enormous distances, mostly on horseback, week after week.

[93] According to the church book of St. John's Lutheran Congregation in Edenwald district.

[94] In the detailed official "Report on German Colonists" of 1890 (Sess. Pap., 1891, No. 6, 98), Edenwald is characterized already as "one of the best and most prosperous of the foreign colonies which we have in the North-West Territories." At that time there was already a shortage of free government land, so that the settlers bought C.P.R. land for their friends whom they expected from their old homeland. Each Sunday they had a church service and the school was attended by as many as fifty children.

[95] Sess. Pap., 1897, No. 13, 125.

[96] The marriage register in the church book of St. John's Lutheran congregation in Edenwald, which has been kept since 1898, gives a survey of the places

of origin of the settlers. The married couples registered the following places of birth:

> **Germany**: Altengamme near Hamburg, Posilge in West Prussia, Emilienthal in West Prussia, Husum, Hannover, Eimsbüttel-Hamburg, Parchim, Carlsburg in Saxony, Gross-Klinsch in West Prussia.
>
> **Russia**: Eigenfeld, Ebenfeld, Hoffnungsort, Hamburg in South Russia, Neuenburg, Cainmitz in Poland, Pereiaslav.
>
> **Bukovina**: All the "Swabian villages."
>
> **Galicia**: Alt-Jazow, Kamionka, Karalufka.
>
> **Romania**: Ciucurova.
>
> **Austria**: Vienna.
>
> **Ontario**: Arnprior.

[97] The official Report on Immigration for 1887 (Sess. Pap., 1888, No. 4, 156f.) gives an exact statement on the homesteaders, their inventory and their still quite modest beginnings on the farm.

[98] Sess. Pap., 1894, No. 13, 14-15.

[99] Sess. Pap., 1895, No. 13, 17f., and Sess. Pap., 1897, No. 13, 124f.

[100] According to the report (No. 1) of farmer Johann Betz in Langenburg.

[101] Farmer Betz reports about the changes after 1897 from memory:

> The old Laurier knew how to bring business enterprises and life to the West. Markets were created for the products, cream factories were built, grain elevators, etc., all the products could be sold and there were big changes in the country. Fortunately the taxes were also not high in those years, with the result that many of the German families who had left came back from the States and started farming again from scratch.

[102] Sess. Pap., 1888, No. 4, 118.

[103] *Der Nordwesten*, special issue, January 1899.

[104] Bach (No. 21).

[105] The earliest reference to Nokomis dates from 1900 (Sess. Pap., 1901, No. 25, II, 154): "We lately had some delegates from Kentucky. These are German Baptists, and are well pleased with the country, climate and people. They represent 200 families of that state, who all intend to move over to Canada next spring."

[106] Until 1924 the ministry was in the hands of the pioneer-pastor Sterzer, who has since then ministered to the mother congregation in Neudorf. We owe him all the above information about Luseland.

[107] Here the official notes about the formation of the settlement will be reproduced since they reveal how the immigration from the States proceeded. In

1897 the Canadian immigration agent for Detroit and the surrounding area reported (Sess. Pap., 1898, No. 13, IV, 70):

> I succeeded in planting a German colony in the south-eastern part of Assiniboia which has been named the Alameda German settlement. A German delegation which I sent out last spring, chose this point for a settlement, and nearly every week has added a few to the Alameda district, which will receive an accession of hundreds of Germans with the first excursion in spring. They are of an exceptionally desirable class, and a German town will be started in the locality. A number of Germans from Cleveland, Ohio, has gone west this fall, and not less than fifty families will follow them as soon as the winter is over. A large number of first-class Germans from Wyandotte, Saginaw and Mount Pleasant will start with their families early next spring. East Detroit will add another fifty or seventy-five families.

See also his correspondence with individual German farmers, who as delegates from Michigan went to western Canada in search of land, published *ibid.*, 72-76. In 1898 he wrote in his report (Sess. Pap., 1899, 13, II, 269): "The German colony which I started in the Alameda district in 1897, fully realized my expectations, 374 homesteads having been entered there as against 107 the previous year, an increase of nearly 300%."

In 1899 about two hundred Germans arrived from Detroit and Wyandotte (Michigan), the first group under the leadership of their former mayor, W. Richert of Detroit. They settled in Tps. 5 and 6, Rg. 3 (Sess. Pap., 1900, 13, II, 151 and 180). In April 1900 an additional 119 Germans came under the personal leadership of Richert, who now became the organizer of the German emigration from the Detroit area (Sess. Pap., 1901, 25, II, 170).

For 1901-1902 we read (Sess. Pap., 1903, 25, II, 131): "Mr. W. Richert, the prime mover in the enterprise, was several times in Detroit during the year . . . A large number of well-to-do settlers went back with him each time." For 1902-1903 the agent in Detroit reported again (Sess. Pap., 1904, 25, II, 128): "Residents have principally gone from Trenton, Wyandotte, Ecorse and other suburban towns of Detroit, and not a few from the city itself . . . Many active Germans have joined this colony during the year, and many are preparing to follow."

Similar references to new German reinforcements for the colony at Alameda can also be found in the Reports of the following years.

[108] See Bach (No. 21), and *Handbuch* (No. 176), 287f

[109] *Der Nordwesten*, special issue, May 1904.

[110] The information about Yellow Grass is from the report (No. 1) of Pastor A. Fricke.

[111] Oppel (No. 318), 216.

[112] Burkholder (No. 61), chapter V.

[113] According to the list of the Canadian Mennonite Board of Colonization

(No. 75) these settled in the following districts and towns (with number of families): Acme (13), Beaverlodge (26), Blue Ridge (9), Coaldale (231), Crowfoot (20), Chinook (7), Carstairs (19), Castor (17), Coronation (4), Calgary (27), Countess (33), Didsbury-Burns Ranch (14), Didsbury (town) (10), Duchess (10), Edmonton (3), Grassy Lake, Tabor and Purple Springs (22), Gem (51), Glenwoodville (11), Hussar (10), Irma (8), Lacombe (9), La Glace (34), Lymburn (15), Munson and Drumheller (12), MacLeod (5), New Brigden (18), Namaka (19), Olds (13), Provost (18), Paradise Valley (2), Peoria (1), Pincher Station (4), Rosemary (67), Rimbey (2), Sunny Slope (19), Swalwell (15), Springridge (13), Tofield (38), Vauxhall (14), Wembley (31), Willow Creek, Rosedale and East Coulée (10).

[114] Clark (No. 85), 359.

[115] Sess. Pap., 1897, No. 13, IV, 122. Also *Maria Immaculata* (No. 280), 1907-08, 124f.

[116] According to the report (No. 1) of Michael Leeb from Spring Lake.

[117] *Maria Immaculata*, 1907-08, 420.

[118] Grösser (No. 163), 94.

[119] Pietsch (No 325), 65.

[120] *Der Nordwesten* of July 15, 1892, mentions German Catholic families in Tp. 56, Rg. 26 W. 4th M. In May 1904 the special issue of *Der Nordwesten* refers to the German Catholic colony near Morinville as the "Westphalia settlement." See also the information about Egg Lake in the table of 1896, reproduced in chapter V, part 1 (see chapter V, footnote 13 for identification).

[121] Dawson and Murchie (No. 104), 67.

[122] See the reports of the immigration agent in Medicine Hat in 1888 and 1889 (Sess. Pap., 1889, 5, 67, and Sess. Pap., 1890, 6, 113).

[123] Sess. Pap., 1891, No. 6, 99 ff.

[124] "Stony Plain" does not mean a plain that is stony, just as "Happy Land" does not mean a happy land. Too much do the realities of nature—here the flourishing fertile Stony Plain, there the drought ridden Happy Land—contradict these names. Stony and Happy are rather the names of Indian tribes which are spelled like the similar-sounding English adjectives.

[125] *Der Nordwesten* July 8, 1892.

[126] *Der Nordwesten*, January 20, 1898.

[127] Sess. Pap., 1895, No. 13, I, 6. According to the handwritten church book

of Brüderheim, the Moravian congregation comprised the following families (some names recur frequently): Sampert, Schwanke, Selinsky, Schulz, Jadeschke, Werner, Henkelmann, Arndt, Prochnau, Dey, Otto, Hennig, Kulitz, Schneider, Hauer, Bartz.

[128] According to the author's interview with Mr. Oberthür in Brüderheim.

[129] *Der Nordwesten*, July 8, 1892.

[130] Sess. Pap., 1894, Nr. 13, III, 144, and *Der Nordwesten*, special issue, May 1904.

[131] *Der Nordwesten*, July 8, 1892. The first two families of settlers came from Alt-Schwedendorf, Kherson Government, South Russia.

[132] *Der Nordwesten*, July 15, 1897, especially the report of the immigration agent, Hugo Carstens.

[133] The result of a mass meeting in Chicago, organized by Canadian agents and attended predominantly by Germans, is described in 1893 as follows (Sess. Pap., 1894, 13, III, 150): "Some twenty heads of families left Chicago in June and took up homesteads on the line of the Calgary and Edmonton Railroad. They took with them sums of money averaging about 500 Dollars per family. Some of them have since sent for their families and all have been self-supporting." It is reported (*Ibid.*, 156) that a group of farmers from Michigan including the names Schlichter, Wisner, Hunsberger, Engelhardt, Crysler and Hartwick who acted as trusted agents for their neighbors, had inspected the land at the railway line to Edmonton with the greatest interest. About another group from Michigan the following is stated (*ibid.*, 157):

> Seven of the best farmers went west, to spy out the country, with the result that they entered for 17 homesteads, and a whole settlement of about 60 families will move west in the early spring of 1894. These people are principally Pennsylvania-Germans or their descendants, and are progressive and prosperous and are not excelled by any class of settlers.

[134] Sess. Pap, 1904, No. 25, II, 107.

[135] *Der Nordwesten*, January 1, 1904.

[136] A.E. Johann (No. 215), 164f., tells the following story about the founding and naming of Bismarck:

> All by himself did the old Rathjens live on his small farm in the wide bound-less bush. When he had set out to clear the bush with the younger Bürssen from Friedrichskoog forty years ago there was nothing but wilderness and "civili-zation" was far away. Bürssen made headway rapidly, many children helped him. His grown-up sons, strong as the Enacim, have already cut new farms of their own out of the bush. Rathjens had bad luck. His wife died too early. She could not endure the extreme winters—and the many reverses of the begin-ning: frost, even snow, in the middle of July, hail destroying the crops for three years in a row, cyclones which destroyed the barely framed house! The

man was left behind alone. While all the others who arrived in the beginning and later, have taken root a long time ago, he is still to this very day dreaming of returning to his homeland which his wife was also never able to forget.

When more and more settlers took up land around the two pioneers they were finally granted a small post office of their own. This put them before the question of giving their settlement a name. Some proposed "Bear Creek" because before the land had belonged to the bears alone and they had been more numerous here than anywhere else. But Rathjens, whose mind was constantly preoccupied with Germany, proposed "Bismarck." Thus, it came to be "Bismarck," even during the World War, when everywhere in North America German names were replaced by English ones.

[137] See chapter V, end of part 2, above.

[138] *Der Nordwesten*, May 26, 1904.

[139] According to the report (No. 1) on Kelowna by Mr. J. Brendel.

[140] In 1890 the official Report on Immigration (Sess. Pap., 1891, No. 6, 137) stated: "Most prominent among the settlers for British Columbia being immigrants from Ontario, England and Scotland, and quite a number of Germans and Scandinavians, very few of whom were unprovided with means."

[141] According to the list of the Canadian Mennonite Board of Colonization (No. 75).

[142] The information about Kelowna and Rutland is taken from the report (No. 1) of Mr. J. Brendel in Kelowna, written in 1933.

[143] *Der Auslanddeutsche*, 1931, 45.

[144] *Nachrichtenblatt der Reichsstelle für das Auswanderungswesen*, 1936, 211.

NOTES TO CHAPTER VII

[1] As cited in Bowman (No. 43), 18.

[2] *Maria Immaculata* (No. 280), 1907/08, 384.

[3] *Seventh Census of Canada, 1931* (No. 69).

[4] See the article by Mrs. P. Regier (No. 331).

[5] Dawson (No. 103), 168.

[6] See Bour (No. 40).

[7] According to *The American Yearbook* (No. 13), 642, the Lutherans in North

America are divided mainly into three groups:
1. United Lutheran Church,
2. the American Lutheran Conference, consisting of the American Lutheran Church, the Evangelical Lutheran Augustana Synod of North America, the Norwegian Lutheran Church of America, the Lutheran Free Church and the United Danish Evangelical Lutheran Church in America, and
3. the Evangelical Lutheran Synodical Conference, of which the leading group is the Synod of Missouri.

[8] *Der Nordwesten*, October 14, 1897.

[9] Meyer (No. 290), 116 ff.

[10] *Ibid.*, 130.

[11] *Wartburg-Kalender* (No. 449), 75.

[12] *Statistical Year-Book* (No. 410), 144 and 151.

[13] *Ibid.*, 17 ff. and 63 ff.

[14] *Ibid.*, 151.

[15] About the formation of the individual Reformed congregations in western Canada see *Kanada* (No. 223).

[16] *The Cambridge History of the British Empire* (No. 67), 743, reports that in the session of the Dominion Parliament in Ottawa after the outbreak of the war Sir Robert Borden wholeheartedly agreed with Sir Wilfrid Laurier that "nearly half a million of the very best citizens of Canada are of German origin" and promised that no Austrians or Germans would be molested "unless they gave aid to the enemy or tried to leave Canada for enemy parts . . ."

[17] Prof. Rehwinkel's *Statuten* (No. 332).

[18] *Pressekorrespondenz des DAI*, July 2, 1930.

[19] According to *Der Courier* of July 11, 1934, the guidelines of the *Arbeitsgemeinschaft* declared the following eligible for membership:
1. All church associations whose scope of activity goes beyond that of a local congregation.
2. All organizations of a religious or secular kind which have at least a provincial character.
3. All municipal associations whose practical operation (by way of participating in German Day celebrations or joint actions, etc.) transcends the scope of their town and who have already proven that in the past.

[20] According to *Der Courier* of November 23 and 30, 1932, the goals of the new *Zentralstelle* were formulated as follows:

1. cultivation of the German language;
2. cultivation of German literature (libraries), music, songs, science and physical exercise;
3. promotion of associational activities;
4. celebration of the "German Days";
5. protection of the interests of German Canadians at the municipal and higher levels of government, as well as in the press and in public;
6. creation of social welfare agencies;
7. establishment of an archive for the history of the German Canadians in the Province of Alberta.

[21] The *Edelweiss* club in Edmonton is the oldest extant German social club in western Canada. On the occasion of a celebration in 1931 its president at the time, Hermann Carl, told the following impressive story (according to *Der Auslanddeutsche*, March 1932):

> At the time the club was founded the Province of Alberta did not yet exist. The city of Edmonton and the area around it belonged to the Northwest Territories. The legislature of Alberta was not created until 1905. The celebrations held on the occasion of the founding of the province were attended by Sir Wilfrid Laurier, the Prime Minister of Canada. Among other things a parade was organized in which, of course besides other Germans from Edmonton and the surrounding area, our club was represented. One of us, Mr. Bruno Brandt, high on horseback with a saber in his hand, led the club. The club members marched in step with such discipline and order that after the parade the Premier enquired who these men were. A *Germania* on a float was also part of the train, a genuine German one, whose appearance reflected great credit on her country of origin. The English-language press, however, referred to her as *Helvetia*. In the first session of the legislature the request for incorporation of the club was submitted and approved without any objections.

[22] W. Kuhn (No. 247), 382-383.

[23] *Ibid.*, 327 ff.

[24] Concerning the cultural handicap of the German Catholics in Russia and Galicia see Malinowsky (No. 278), 63 ff.; Bonwetsch (No. 36), 83-84; Kaindl (No. 221), 169 ff., and Zöckler (No. 472), 22.

[25] Smith (No. 398), chapter X: "Transplanting a Bit of Russia."

[26] Staff (No. 407), 51.

[27] Kloss (No 245), 384.

[28] Mentioned in Oppel (No. 31), 33.

[29] Mentioned by Maron in *Der Nordwesten-Kalender für 1914*, 107.

[30] These percentages are of course only rough estimates, but they make a point nevertheless. Moellmann based his analysis on one issue of *Der Courier*

and one of *Der Nordwesten* in the summer of 1933; three issues of *Mennonitische Rundschau*, one issue from each of the months of April, May, June 1934; four numbers each of *Die Post* and *Der Bote* of 1933, and four numbers of *St. Peter's Bote* of January, April, July, October 1933.

[31] *Zenian. Denn meine Augen haben den Heiland gesehen* (1910). *Durch Wind und Wellen. Gedichte* (Waterloo, 1928). *Aus meinem Leben. Erinnerungen* (Rosthern). *Die Biblischen Geschichten als Hausandachten für jeden Tag des Jahres angeordnet* (Waterloo, 1929). *Die Praxis der mennonitischen Kirchengemeinden und die Heilige Schrift* (Waterloo, 1929). *Choralbuch. Melodien zum neuen Gesangbuch* (Waterloo, 1930). *Abraham. Innere Wandlungen zur Zeit der Geschichte des Alten Bundes, zum Vortragen auf Jugendvereinsfesten in 15 Gesängen dargestellt* (Waterloo, 1931). *Utwaundre. Stimmungsbild in 2 Aufzügen* (Waterloo, 1931). For poems see Emil Maxis, ed., *Volk auf fremder Erde. Das Schicksalsbuch der Auslanddeutschen* (Breslau, 1933) and *Der Auslanddeutsche*, 1936, 827.

[32] Johann Wiens, *Eine Hilfe in der grossen Not* (Winnipeg, 1925). G.A. Peters, *Gedichte* (2 volumes), *Wehrlos?* and *Die Hungersnot in den mennonitischen Kolonien in Südrussland, mit besonderer Berücksichtigung der Molotschna-Kolonie* (1923). Gerhard Toews (Georg de Brecht), *Die Heimat in Flammen*. Johann Peter Klassen, *Dunkle Tage* (Winnipeg, 1923), *Reiseskizzen über die Auswanderung im Jahre 1932*, and several volumes of poems: *Brocken* (1923), *Krümlein, Wegeblumen*. In *Der Auslanddeutsche*, 1936, 817, Kloss erroneously ascribes these to Peter J. Klassen in Superb, Saskatchewan. D. Neufeld wrote *Tagebuch aus dem Reiche des Totentanzes*.

NOTES TO CHAPTER VIII

Editor's note: the composition of the contents of this chapter is explained in the Editor-Translator's Note at the beginning of the book.

[1] *Seventh Census of Canada 1931, Bulletin XXXV* (No. 69).

[2] *1931 Census Monograph No. 4* (No. 206), 285.

[3] "Racial Origins of the Populations of the Prairie Provinces 1926, 1931 and 1936," *Canada Year Book 1937*, 149f.

[4] Canada, Dominion Bureau of Statistics, *Vital Statistics 1931* (No. 70), Table 27.

[5] These are also to be considered of German origin, as pointed out above.

[6] See Appendix, Table 4. *Canada Year Book 1937*,142 states: "The Germans and Austrians who have come to Canada are well represented in agriculture, over 50% of their number being employed in farming occupations, while only about 25% of the Central European Immigrants of such races as Czech and Slo-

vak were engaged in agricultural occupations in 1931."

[7] Editor's note: This was substituted for the original "Deutsch-Kanadischer Verband" in accordance with information from Franz Straubinger, Montreal.

[8] Editor's note: This was substituted for the original "Deutsch-Kanadischer Verband Frohsinn" in accordance with information from Franz Straubinger, Montreal.

[9] Giese (No. 153), 134.

[10] Section 258 of the School Act states: "When ten of the pupils in any school speak the French language, or any language other than English, as their native language, the teaching of such pupils shall be conducted in French, or such other language, and English, upon the bilingual system."

[11] The report was published by the Ministry of Education under the title "Special Report on Bi-lingual Schools in Manitoba." It is cited in Sissons (No. 395), 140f.

[12] Article No. 10 of the document, which contained all the privileges and exemptions granted to the Mennonites, and which was handed to the Mennonite delegates on July 23, 1873, was worded as follows, as cited in Smith (No. 398), 68: "The fullest privilege of exercising their religious principle is by law afforded the Mennonites, without any kind of molestation or restriction whatever; and the same privilege extends to the education of their children in schools."

[13] Kuhn (No. 247), 379, characterized this type of school as "pre-state" by "its primitivity, the poor training or complete lack of it and the low social position of its teachers, its frequently very short school year and its predominantly religious orientation."

[14] *Canada and Its Provinces* (No. 388), vol. XX, 435.

[15] According to a report in the *Winnipeg Free Press* of November 26, 1910. The (x) after a place name means that, due to the flag dispute, an existing bilingual public school had reverted to a private school, permitted by the chartered privileges granted to the Mennonites.

[16] Friesen (No. 143), 71.

[17] In the Saskatchewan School Attendance Act the Section permitting private schools reads as follows: "4. A parent, guardian or other person shall not be liable to any penalty imposed by this Act in respect of a child . . . if the child is under efficient instruction at home or elsewhere."

[18] See also Sissons (No. 395), 164: "As a matter of fact, many German com-

munities established private schools rather than public schools. Thus they were able to teach German as much as they liked in their schools and otherwise escape irksome regulations."

[19] See the report of Father Schweers about his first year in St. Joseph's colony at the Tramping Lake, in *Maria Immaculata* (No. 380), 344 ff.

[20] According to information from Prof. Baepler, formerly in Edmonton.

[21] The pertinent sections 39 and 44 in the Saskatchewan School Act, which are identical to sections 22 and 26 of the Alberta School Act, read:

> The minority of the ratepayers, in any district, whether Protestant or Roman Catholic, may establish a separate school therein; and in such case the ratepayers . . . shall be liable only to assessments of such rates as they impose upon themselves in respect thereof . . .

> After the establishment of a separate school district under the provisions of this Act, such separate school district and the board thereof shall possess and exercise the rights, powers and privileges and be subject to the same liabilities and method of government as is herein provided in respect of public school districts.

[22] England (No. 133), 106.

[23] See, e.g., Elston (No. 132), 425-432.

[24] Weir (No. 452), 106-107.

[25] Sabourin (No. 350), 230 ff.:

> En 1873 . . . ni le gouvernement de Londres ni celui d'Ottawa ne pouvaient d'eux-mêmes faire des promesses restreignant les pouvoirs du gouvernement manitobain. C'est pour cette raison que le gouvernement d'Ottawa, pour confirmer les promesses de M. John Lowe, avait ajouté ces mots en 1873; selon qu'il y sera pourvu par la loi.

[26] Anderson (No. 16), 74 ff., 96 ff., 201f.

[27] England (No. 133), 170.

[28] Saunders (No. 354), 174-176.

[29] *Der Katholik* (Regina) of December 21, 1929, as cited in *Der Auslanddeutsche*, February 1930. Up to that time religious instruction in the mother tongue of the child was permitted on the basis that, according to Section 179 of the School Act, it was not part of the regular school curriculum. Now Anderson fell back on Section 178 of the same Act which, except for French, prescribed English as the only language of instruction in all the schools, and prohibited the teaching of any language other than English during school hours.

[30] Weir (No. 452), 113.

[31] England (No. 133), 107.

[32] Giese (No. 153), 134.

[33] Section 177 (2) of the Saskatchewan School Act and Section 184 (2) of the Alberta School Act state:

> The board of any district may, subject to the regulations of the Department, employ one or more competent persons to give instruction in any language other than English in the school of the district to all pupils whose parents or guardians have signified a willingness that they should receive the same, but such course of instruction shall not supersede or in any way interfere with the instruction by the teacher in charge of the school as required by the regulations of the department and by this act.

[34] Eid (No. 131), 347.

[35] Giese (No. 153), 140.

[36] Eid (No. 131), 348.

[37] Giese (No. 153), 138-139.

[38] On the activity of the Ursuline sisters from the convents of Cologne, Haselüne near Osnabrück, Dorsten in Westphalia and Schweidnitz in Silesia as teaching nuns in Canada, see also Kleinschmidt (No. 241), 376-377.

[39] The pertinent Section 5 of the Alberta School Attendance Act states: "(5.) No parent, guardian or other person shall be liable to any penalty, imposed by this Act in respect of a child if . . . in the opinion of a school inspector, given by a writing dated within one year prior to the date of the complaint, the child is under efficient instruction at home or elsewhere."

[40] According to the *Statistical Year-Book* (No. 410), 17 ff. and 63 ff.

[41] Eid (No. 131), 349.

[42] See *Der Auslanddeutsche, October 1929*.

[43] Thielmann (No. 425), 16.

[44] *Deutsche Zeitung für Canada*, November 24, 1937.

[45] Eid (No. 131), 348.

[46] See England (No. 133), 201 and 207, as well as England (No. 134), 133, 166 and 184.

[47] England (No. 133), 125.

[48] Dawson (No. 103), 139.

[49] Loesch (No. 269), 233.

[50] Dawson (No. 103), 171.

[51] Kuhn (No. 247), 240-241.

[52] Pfeffer (No. 322), 66.

[53] Gottschick (No. 157), 391.

[54] Rempel (No 334), 108.

[55] *Ibid.*, 108 and 109.

[56] Toews (No. 429).

[57] England (No. 133), 203.

[58] Moellmann (No. 293), 85.

[59] According to *Der Courier* (Regina) of July 11, 1934, 7.

BIBLIOGRAPHY

Editor's note: This bibliography contains all the sources used by Heinz Lehmann listed in the footnotes and bibliographies of the publications on which this edition is based. If the form of a bibliographic citation in the original German publication was found to be incomplete or incorrect, the entry was corrected. In instances where an editor or author not listed in Lehmann's citation could be ascertained, Lehmann's as well as the corrected citation was entered in the alphabetically appropriate places, however with one number serving as a cross reference for all entries of the same item. Individual volumes in a multi-volume set are distinguished from the volumes of a periodical by the abbreviation "vol." instead of merely the Roman numeral.

A. The Main Primary Sources

1. 128 handwritten reports on individual German settlements in western Canada, initiated and collected by Editor B. Bott in Winnipeg, mainly in the years 1932 and 1933. Added to these are a few handwritten parish registers, such as the ones for St. John's Lutheran congregation in Edenwold, Saskatchewan.

2. The German-language press in Canada (see chapter III, parts 2-4, and chapter VII, part 6), in particular the following weekly papers:
   a. *Der Nordwesten* (Winnipeg), since 1889. A complete run of all the volumes was available to me in Winnipeg, as well as *Der Nordwesten-Kalender*, appearing annually.
   b. *Der Courier* (Regina). The volumes from 1907 on were unfortunately

destroyed by a fire in the Regina editorial office. An almost complete run of the paper was available only from the end of the war. In addition I used this paper's almanac which appeared once a year as *Deutsch-canadischer Hausfreund.*

c. *Deutsche Zeitung für Canada* (Winnipeg), since May 12, 1935.

3. Among periodicals published in Germany, the following report about ethnic Germans overseas:
    a. *Der Auslanddeutsche* (Stuttgart), since 1917, now appearing under the title *Das Deutschtum im Ausland.*
    b. *Nachrichtenblatt der Reichsstelle für das Auswanderungswesen* (Berlin), since 1919.
    c. *Archiv für Wanderungswesen* [und Auslandkunde] (Leipzig), since 1928.
    d. *Die Getreuen. Zeitschrift für die Katholiken deutscher Zunge in aller Welt* (Berlin, Regensburg and Vienna), 1924-1935.
    e. *Der Reichsbote* (Berlin).

4. The official Reports on Immigration:
    a. Great Britain, *Parliamentary Papers*, abbreviated as P. P., containing the reports of the Canadian immigration agents for the years 1831 through 1861.
    b. Canada, *Sessional Papers*, abbreviated as Sess. Pap., containing the official Canadian immigration reports from 1862 to 1891 as an appendix to the "Annual Reports of the Ministry of Agriculture," from 1892 to 1917 as Part III of the "Annual Report of the Ministry of the Interior," from 1917-18 to 1923-24 as "Annual Reports of the Department of Immigration and Colonisation," and since 1924-25 as part of the "Annual Departmental Reports."
    c. For the migration of German Americans to Canada and of German Canadians to the United States since 1905-06 the "Annual Reports of the Commissioner-General of Immigration to the Secretary of Labor," Department of Labor Reports, 1906 ff., United States *House Documents*, were consulted. The earlier reports are not relevant for this migration. Editor's note: See also No. 436.

5. The official Canadian population statistics, based on the decennial enumeration (from 1871 to 1931) by the Dominion Bureau of Statistics in Ottawa and published under the title *Census of Canada.* For the three Prairie provinces the quinquennial *Census of Prairie Provinces* of 1906, 1916, 1926 and 1936 was also available. The first census of the new Dominion of Canada, published in 1871, contains in vol. IV a digest of all the earlier enumerations from the beginning of settlement.
    Supplementary publications by the Dominion Bureau of Statistics that were used, such as bulletins and monographs based on the census data, are listed separately in the following compilation of the literature on the German element in Canada.

6.   The official Canadian *Year Book*, published under the following names:
     from 1867 to 1879 as *Yearbook and Almanac of British North America*,
     from 1886 to 1888 as *Statistical Abstract and Record of Canada*,
     from 1889 to 1904 as *Statistical Yearbook of Canada*,
     since 1905 as the *Canada Year Book*.

B. The Literature on the German Element in Canada

7.   Abele, Paul.   *Festschrift zur 25jährigen Jubiläumsfeier der Gründung der St. Pauls-Kirchengemeinde in Vibank, Sask., 12. Juni 1929*. Regina, 1929.

(203.) *Agriculture, Climate and Population of the Prairie Provinces. A Statistical Atlas Showing Past Development and Present Conditions*. Prepared under the direction of W. Burton Hurd and T.W. Grindley. Ottawa, 1931.

8.   Akins, Thomas B.   "History of Halifax City," *Collections of the Nova Scotia Historical Society*, VIII (1895), 3-272.

9.   "Alberta," *Handwörterbuch des Grenz- und Auslanddeutschtums*, vol. I. Breslau, 1933, 83-85.

10. Alleweldt.   "Der kanadische Westen als Ziel deutscher Auswanderung," *Nachrichtenblatt der Reichsstelle für das Auswanderungswesen*, 1930, 164, 174f.

(176.) Allgemeiner Deutscher Schulverein zur Erhaltung des Deutschtums im Auslande, ed. *Handbuch des Deutschtums im Auslande*. 2nd ed., Berlin, 1906.

11. Allison, D.   "Notes on a general return of the several townships in the province of Nova Scotia for the first day of January, 1767," *Collections of the Nova Scotia Historical Society*, VII (1889-1891), 45-71

12. Althausen, Ernst.   *Zersplitterung oder Verbindung? Bilder aus dem Leben der Deutschen in Canada und Wolhynien*. Berlin, 1922.

13. *The American Yearbook: Record of Events and Progress, Year 1933*. Editor: A.B. Hart. New York, 1934.

14. *Amerikanischer Kalender für deutsche Lutheraner auf das Jahr 1937*. [Missouri Synod] St. Louis, Mo., n.d.

15. *Zum Andenken an das Silberne Jubiläum der St. Peters-Kolonie, 1903-28*. Muenster, Sask., 1928.

16.   Anderson, J.T.M.   *The Education of the New Canadian. A Treatise on Canada's greatest educational problem.* London and Toronto, 1918.

17.   Andree, Karl.   *Nord-Amerika.* Braunschweig, 1854.

18.   Angus, H.P.   "Canadian Immigration: The Law and its Administration," *American Journal of International Law*, XXVIII (1934), 74-89.

(458.)   *Ansiedlungen in den Urwäldern von Canada. Von einer Emigrantin.* Translated by Dr. A. Wiese. Leipzig, 1838.

19.   Armstrong, George H.   *The Origin and Meaning of Place Names in Canada.* Toronto, 1930.

20.   *Atlas of Canada.* Revised and enlarged edition. Prepared under the direction of J.E. Chalifour, Chief Geographer, Department of the Interior, Canada. Ottawa, 1915.

(3e.)   "Auslandsprotestantische Rundschau," *Der Reichsbote* (Berlin), May 10, 1930.

21.   Bach, R.   *Eine Reise durch das westliche Kanada im Sommer 1902.* Montreal, 1902.

22.   "Banat,"   *Handwörterbuch des Grenz- und Auslanddeutschtums*, vol. I, Breslau, 1933, 207-286.

23.   Baumgartner, F.W.   "Central European Immigration," *Queen's Quarterly*, XXXVII (1930), 183-192.

24.   Begg, Alexander.   *History of the North-West.* 3 vols. Toronto, 1894-1895.

25.   Beidelman, William.   *The Story of the Pennsylvania-Germans, embracing an account of their origin, their history and their dialect.* Easton, Pa., 1898.

26.   Benton, Nathaniel Soley.   *A History of Herkimer County, including the upper Mohawk Valley, from the earlier period to the present time, with a brief notice of the Iroquois Indians, the early German tribes, the Palatine immigrations . . .* Albany, N.Y., 1856.

27.   *Bericht über die 31. Allgemeine Konferenz der Mennoniten in Canada, vom 26.-28. 6. 1933 in Gnadenthal bei Plum Coulee, Manitoba.* Rosthern, Saskatchewan, n.d.

28. *Reise Seiner Hoheit des Herzogs Bernhard zu Sachsen-Weimar-Eisenach durch Nordamerika in den Jahren 1825 und 1826.* Edited in 2 parts by H. Luden. Weimar, 1828.

29. "Bessarabien," *Handwörterbuch des Grenz- und Auslanddeutschtums,* vol. I, Breslau, 1933, 390-422.

30. *Bilder und Blätter zum Silbernen Jubiläum der St. Josephs-Kolonie.* Compiled by Oblate Fathers in the colony. Regina, Sask., 1930. [Author: Father Schulte?]

31. "The Bilingual Schools of Manitoba," [a series of essays in] *Winnipeg Free Press,* January and February 1913.

32. Bittinger, Lucy F. *The Germans in Colonial Times.* Philadelphia and London, 1901.

33. Black, N.F. *History of Saskatchewan and the old North West.* Regina, 1913.

34. von Bleichröder, Hanns. "Die Ziele der Deutschen Auswanderung bis zum Kriege 1914." Ph.D. dissertation, University of Heidelberg, 1915.

35. Boam, H.J. *The Prairie Provinces of Canada.* London, 1914.

36. Bonwetsch, Gerhard. *Geschichte der deutschen Kolonien an der Wolga.* Schriften des *Deutschen Ausland-Instituts Stuttgart,* series A. vol. 2, Stuttgart, 1919.

37. Borchardt, Alfred. "Deutschrussische Rückwanderung," *Preussische Jahrbücher.* CLXII.

38. Bott, Bernhard. "Ein Beitrag zur deutschen Siedlungsgeschichte Westkanadas," *Die Getreuen,* XII (1935), 156-158.

39. Bouchette, Joseph. *The British Dominions in North-America.* 2 vols. London, 1832.

40. Bour, P. "Deutsche Katholikenversammlung in Winnipeg," *Maria Immaculata,* XVI (1908-09), 413 ff.

41. Bourinot, Sir John G. "Builders of Nova Scotia," *Proceedings and Transactions of the Royal Society of Canada,* 2nd Series, vol. V (May 1899), sec. 2, 1-198.

42.   Bowman, H.M.   "Jac. Y. Shantz, Pioneer of the Russian Mennonite Immigration to Manitoba," *Waterloo Historical Society, Annual Reports*, XII (1924), 85-100.

43.   Bowman, Isaiah.   *The Pioneer Fringe.* American Geographical Society, Special Publication No. 13. New York, 1931.

44.   Bradley, A.G.   *The Making of Canada.* London, 1908.

45.   Brady, Alexander.   *Canada.* The Modern World Series. London, 1932.

46.   Breithaupt, W.H.   "First Settlements of Pennsylvania Mennonites in Upper Canada," *Ontario Historical Society, Papers and Records*, XXIII (1926), 8-14.

47.   Breithaupt, W.H.   "The Settlement of Waterloo County," *Ontario Historical Society, Papers and Records*, XXII (1925), 14-17.

48.   Breithaupt, W.H.   "Waterloo County History," *Ontario Historical Society, Papers and Records*, XVII (1919), 43-47.

49.   Brendel, John.   *Sammlung deutscher Volkslieder der Russlanddeutschen in Amerika im nordwestlichen Teil der Vereinigten Staaten und Kanada.* 1. Teil. Bismarck, N.D., 1929.

50.   "Britisch-Kolumbien,"   *Handwörterbuch des Grenz-und Auslanddeutschtums*, vol. I. Breslau, 1933, 545f.

51.   Bromme, Traugott.   *Neuestes, vollständiges Hand- und Reisebuch für Auswanderer, aus allen Klassen und jedem Stande . . . nach Nordamerika.* Bayreuth, 1846.

52.   Bromme, Traugott.   *Nordamerikas Bewohner, Schönheiten und Naturschätze im allgemeinen und die der britischen Besitzungen im besonderen.* Stuttgart, 1839.

53.   Bromme, Traugott.   *Rathgeber für Auswanderungslustige. Eine umfassende Beleuchtung der bisherigen deutschen Auswanderung und aller deutschen Ansiedelungspläne . . .* Stuttgart, 1846

54.   Bromme, Traugott.   *Reisen durch die Vereinigten Staaten und Oberkanada.* Baltimore, 1834.

55. Brown, W.M. "Recollections of Old Halifax," *Collections of the Nova Scotia Historical Society*, XIII (1908), 75-101.

56. Brumbaugh, Martin G. *A History of the German Baptist Brethren in Europe and America*. 2nd ed., Elgin, Ill., 1907.

57. Bryce, George. *Manitoba: Its Infancy, Growth and Present Condition*. London, 1882.

58. Bryce, George. *The Remarkable History of the Hudson's Bay Company*. 3rd ed., London, 1910.

59. Bryce, George. *A Short History of the Canadian People*. 2nd ed., London, 1914.

(4b.) Brymner, Douglas. "Report on Canadian Archives 1886 (Being an Appendix to Report of the Minister of Agriculture)," Canada *Sessional Papers*, 1887, No. 12b, XI.

60. "Bukowina," *Handwörterbuch des Grenz- uud Auslanddeutschtums*, vol. I. Breslau, 1933, 611-644.

61. Burkholder, L.J. *A Brief History of the Mennonites in Ontario*. Toronto, 1935.

62. Burpee, Lawrence J., ed. *An Historical Atlas of Canada*. Toronto, 1927.

63. Burrage, Henry. *Maine at Louisbourg in 1745*. Augusta, Me., 1910.

64. Bürzle, A. "Volkstreue Jugend in Canada," *Muttersprache* (Berlin), 5 (May, 1936).

65. Busch, E.H. *Beiträge zur Geschichte und Statistik des Kirchen-und Schulwesens der Evangelischen Augsburgischen Gemeinden im Königreich Polen*. Leipzig, 1867.

66. Calnek, W.A. and A.W. Savary. *History of the County of Annapolis*. Toronto and London, 1897.

67. *The Cambridge History of the British Empire*. Edited by J. H. Rose, A. P. Newton, E. A. Benians. *Vol. VI: Canada and Newfoundland*. Cambridge, 1930.

68.   Campbell, P.   *Travels in the Interior Inhabited Parts of North America in the Years 1791 and 1792.* Edinburgh, 1793.

(20.)   Canada, Department of the Interior. *Atlas of Canada.* Revised and enlarged edition. Prepared under the direction of J.E. Chalifour, Chief Geographer. Ottawa, 1915.

(168.)   *Canada. Die Berichte der vier deutschen Delegierten über ihre Reise nach Canada im Herbst 1881.* Edited and introduced by Dr. Otto Hahn, Reutlingen. 2nd ed., Reutlingen, 1883.

69.   Canada, Dominion Bureau of Statistics. "Religious Denominations by Racial Origins," *Bulletin XXXV. Seventh Census of Canada, 1931.* Ottawa, 1933.

70.   Canada, Dominion Bureau of Statistics. *Vital Statistics 1931.* Eleventh Annual Report. Ottawa, 1933.

71.   *Canada.* Eine Darstellung der natürlichen, sozialen und Verkehrs verhältnisse dieses Landes. Mit besonderer Rücksicht auf die Ansiedlung. Berlin, 1858.

72.   *Canada. Mit besonderer Rüksicht auf dessen Kolonisation nach den gegenwärtigen Verhältnissen geschildert.* Leipzig, 1864.

73.   Canada, Parliament. *Official Report of the Debates of the House of Commons of the Dominion of Canada.* Fourth Session, Tenth Parliament, 1907-8, vol. LXXXV. Ottawa, 1907-8.

74.   *Canada 1938. The Official Handbook of Present Conditions and Recent Progress.* Ottawa, 1938.

(388.)   *Canada and Its Provinces. A History of the Canadian People and Their Institutions.* Edited by A. Shortt and A.G. Doughty. 23 vols. Toronto, 1913-1917.

(6.)   *Canada Year Book.*

75.   Canadian Mennonite Board of Colonization. *Liste der eingewanderten mennonitischen Siedler und Distriktmänner.* Rosthern, Sask., July 29, 1935.

76.   Canniff, W.   *History of the Settlement of Upper Canada (Ontario), with special reference to the Bay of Quinte.* Toronto, 1869.

77. Canstatt, Oscar. *Die deutsche Auswanderung. Auswandererfürsorge und Auswandererziele.* Berlin-Schöneberg, 1904.

78. Carnochan, Janet. "Early Churches in the Niagara Peninsula, Stamford and Chippewa with Marriage Records of Thomas and James Cummings, J. P., and Extracts from the Cummings Papers," *Ontario Historical Society, Papers and Records,* VIII (1907), 149-225.

79. Carnochan, Janet. *Inscriptions and Graves in the Niagara Peninsula.* Niagara Historical Society Publications, No. 19. 2nd ed., Welland, 1910.

80. Carnochan, Janet. *Names Only But Much More.* Niagara Historical Society Publications, No. 27. Welland, 1915.

81. Caro, L. *Auswanderung und Auswanderungspolitik in Oesterreich.* Schriften des *Vereins für Sozialpolitik,* vol. 131. Leipzig, 1909.

82. Cassel, Daniel K. *Geschichte der Mennoniten.* Philadelphia, 1890.

83. Casselman, Alexander C. "The German U. E. Loyalists of the County of Dundas, Ontario." *United Empire Loyalists' Association of Ontario, Transactions,* III (1900), 53-76.

(5.) *Census of Canada,* 1871, 1881, 1891, 1901, 1911, 1921, 1931, and 1936.

84. *Centennial of the Settlement of Upper Canada by the U. E. Loyalists, 1784-1884 . . . With an appendix, containing a copy of the U. E. List, preserved in the Crown Lands Department at Toronto.* Toronto, 1885.

85. Clark, Bertha W. "The Hutterian Communities," *The Journal of Political Economy,* XXXII (1924), 357-374, 468-486.

86. Coats, R.H. "The Immigration Problem of Canada," in L.J. Dublin, ed., *Population Problems in the United States and Canada.* Boston and New York, 1926, 176-194.

(305.) *Collections of the New Brunswick Historical Society.* 12 vols. 1894-1928.

87. Colonus. "Eine neue deutsche Kolonie in Westkanada [i.e., the Schneider colony near Winnipeg]," *Die Getreuen,* IV (1927), 67-69.

88. *The Concordia Cyclopedia. A Handbook of Religious Information.* St. Louis, Mo., 1927.

89.   Correll, Ernst.   "Mennonite Immigration into Manitoba: Sources and Documents, 1872, 1873, 1874," *Mennonite Quarterly Review*, XI (July-October 1937), 196-227, 267-283.

90.   "Cosmopolitan Winnipeg. Part III: The Germans," *Winnipeg Free Press*, December 7, 1912.

91.   Cowan, Helen I.   *British Emigration to British North America, 1783-1837*. Toronto, 1928.

92.   Cowan, Helen I.   "Early Canadian Emigration to the United States," *Dalhousie Review*, VIII:1 (1928).

93.   Creighton, Agnes.   "A Plea for Remembrance," *Acadiensis*, VII:1 (January 1907), 3-8.

94.   Croil, James.   *Dundas*. Montreal, 1861.

95.   Cruikshank, E. A., ed.   *The Correspondence of Lieut. Gov. John Graves Simcoe, with allied documents relating to his administration of the Government of Upper Canada*. 5 vols. Toronto, 1923-1931.

96.   Cruikshank, E. A.   "The Loyalists of New York," United Empire Loyalists' Association of Ontario, *Transactions*, I (1898), 49-62.

97.   Cruikshank, E. A.   *Notes on the History of the District of Niagara 1791-1793*. Niagara Historical Society Publications, No. 26. Welland, 1914.

98.   Cruikshank, E. A.   "The Reserve of the Six Nations on the Grand River and the Mennonite Purchase of Block No. 2," *Waterloo Historical Society*, Annual Reports, XV (1927), 303-350.

99.   Cruikshank, E. A.   *The Story of Butler's Rangers and the Settlement of Niagara*. Lundy's Lane Historical Society. Welland, Ont., 1893.

100.   Cruikshank, E. A.   *Ten Years of the Colony of Niagara, 1780-1790*. Niagara Historical Society Publications, No. 17. Welland, 1908.

101.   Cumberland, R. W.   "The United Empire Loyalist Settlements Between Kingston and Adolphustown," *Queen's Quarterly*, XXX (April–June 1923), 395-419.

102.   Dafoe, John W.   *Clifford Sifton in Relation to His Times*. Toronto, 1931.

103. Dawson, C.A. *Group Settlement: Ethnic Communities in Western Canada.* Canadian Frontiers of Settlement, vol. VII. Toronto, 1936.

104. Dawson, C.A. and R.W. Murchie. *The Settlement of the Peace River Country: A Study of a Pioneer Area.* Canadian Frontiers of Settlement, vol. VI. Toronto, 1934.

105. Day, C.M. *History of the Eastern Townships, Province of Quebec.* Montreal, 1869.

106. Deckert, Emil. *Die neue Welt. Reiseskizzen aus dem Norden und Süden der Vereinigten Staaten, sowie aus Kanada und Mexiko.* Berlin, 1892.

107. *Denkschrift zum Silber-Jubiläum der Evangelisch-lutherischen Synode von Manitoba und anderen Provinzen, 1897-1922.* Winnipeg, 1922.

108. DesBrisay, M.B. *History of the County of Lunenburg.* 2nd ed., Toronto, 1895.

(357.) *Deutsch-Amerikanisches Konversations-Lexikon.* Edited by Prof. A.J. Schem. 11 vols. New York, 1869-1874.

109. *Der Deutsch-Kanadische Herold* [since July 1929 renamed *Der Kanadische Herold*]: *Illustrierte Zeitschrift über Landwirtschaft, Handel, Industrie, Touristik und Sport in Kanada* (Berlin-Wilmersdorf), 1929-1930.

110. *Deutsch-canadischer Hausfreund. Kalender.* 1924, 1925, 1927. Regina, Sask.

111. *Deutsche Erde. Beiträge zur Kenntnis deutschen Volksthums Allerorten und Allerzeiten.* Edited by Prof. Paul Langhans, Gotha. Vols. I-XII (1902-1914).

112. "Deutsche Katholiken in Kanada," *Deutsche Auslandseelsorge,* V (1931), 169-173.

113. *Der Deutsche Pionier. Monatsschrift für Erinnerungen aus dem deutschen Pionierleben in den Vereinigten Staaten* (Cincinnati). Vols. I-XIV. (1869-1882).

114. *Die Deutschen: Kanadas Kulturdünger?* Flugschrift. N.p., 1914.

115. Dietrich, B. "Britisch-Nordamerika," in Klute, ed. *Handbuch der Geographischen Wissenschaft.* Volume: *Nord- und Mittelamerika.* Potsdam, 1933, 57-185.

116. Dionne, N.E. *Les Canadiens-Francais. Origine des familles . . . et signification*

de leur noms. Quebec, 1914.

117. "Dobrudscha," *Handwörterbuch des Grenz-und Auslanddeutschtums*, vol. II, 278-290.

118. "The Dominion of Canada. Special Review," *The Economist* (London), January 18, 1936.

119. Dörfler, Bruno. "Through Western Canada," *The Prairie Messenger* (Muenster, Sask.), June 29 to October 17, 1928. [This article was originally written and published in 1903].

120. Droonberg, Emil. *Die Ansiedler in Canada. Roman.* Leipzig, 1930.

121. Duncan, Hannibal Gerald. *Immigration and Assimilation.* Boston and New York, 1933.

122. Dunham, Mabel. *Toward Sodom.* Toronto, 1927.

123. Dunham, Mabel. *The Trail of the Conestoga.* Toronto, 1924.

(272.) *Lord Durham's Report on the Affairs of British North America* (1839). Edited by C.P. Lucas. 3 vols. Oxford, 1912.

124. Eby, Peter. *Auf nach Westkanada! Regierungsbericht über die Zustände Canadas, nebst einem Anhang, die deutsche Einwanderung betreffend.* Berlin, 1854. [Editor's note: This bibliographic entry could not be verified but Staadt (No. 405), 32, cites the following similar item: Peter Eby. *Auf nach West-Canada! Regierungsbericht über die Kronländereien im Township Waterloo.* Berlin, 1854].

125. von Eelking, Max. *Die deutschen Hülfstruppen in Nordamerika im Befreiungskriege, 1776-1783.* 2 vols. Hanover, 1863.

126. Ehrt, Adolf. "Die deutschen Wolhynier in Uebersee," *Deutsche Post aus dem Osten*, III (1928), 179-181.

127. Ehrt, Adolf. *Das Mennonitentum in Russland von seiner Einwanderung bis zur Gegenwart.* Langensalza, 1932.

128. Eichler, Adolf. *Das Deutschtum in Kongresspolen.* Schriften des Deutschen Ausland-Institut Stuttgart, series A, vol. 4. Stuttgart, 1921.

129. Eichmeier, Max. "Die kanadische Prärie als Wirtschaftsraum," in *Amerikanische Landschaft*. Berlin and Leipzig, 1936, 131-229.

130. Eid, Ludwig. "Die deutsche Sprache an den Schulen in Kanada," *Der Auslanddeutsche*, XIV (October 1931).

131. Eid, Ludwig. "Der deutschsprachige Unterricht in Kanada," *Mitteilungen der Deutschen Akademie*. München, 1930, 333-355.

132. Elston, Miriam. "English Schools for Foreigners in Alberta," *The Westminster*, XXIX, 425-432.

133. England, Robert. *The Central European Immigrant in Canada*. Toronto, 1929.

134. England, Robert. *The Colonization of Western Canada: A Study of Contemporary Land Settlement (1896-1934)*. London, 1936.

135. "Der erste Seelsorger in der deutschen St. Josephs-Kolonie in Kanada," *Deutsche Auslandseelsorge*, V (1931), 102-111.

136. von Eyern, Gert. "Die Bedeutung der weltwirtschaftlichen Krise für Kanada," *Vierteljahreshefte zur Statistik des Deutschen Reichs*. Berlin, 1935, 121-136.

137. Faust, Albert B. *The German Element in the United States, with Special Reference to its Political, Moral, Social, and Educational Influence*. 2 vols. Boston and New York, 1909.

(7.) *Festschrift zur 25jährigen Jubiläumsfeier der Gründung der St. Pauls Kirchengemeinde in Vibank, Saskatchewan, 12. Juni 1929*. Regina, 1929.

138. Fisher, Peter. *History of New Brunswick, as Originally Printed in 1825*. Saint John, N.B., 1921.

139. Flick, Alexander C. *Loyalism in New York during the American Revolution*. Studies in History, Economics and Public Law, vol. XIV, 1. New York, 1901.

140. Freitag, K. W. *Denkschrift zum 30jährigen Gemeinde-Jubiläum der Evangelisch-lutherischen Dreieinigkeitsgemeinde zu Strathcona* (South Edmonton). N.p., 1931.

141. Fricke, Arnold.   *Geschichtlicher Ueberblick des zwanzigjährigen Bestehens des Canada-Distrikts der Evangelisch-lutherischen Synode von Ohio und anderen Staaten.* Regina, 1928.

142. Friesen, J.J.   "The Mennonites of Western Canada, With Special Reference to Education." Unpublished M.Ed. thesis, University of Saskatchewan, 1934.

143. Friesen, P.M.   *Die Alt-Evangelische mennonitische Brüderschaft in Russland 1789-1910 im Rahmen der mennonitischen Gesamtgeschichte.* Halbstadt, 1911.

144. Fritz, J.   *Festschrift und Gottesdienstordnung zum 25. Jubiläum der evangelisch-lutherischen Dreieinigkeitsgemeinde zu Regina, Saskatchewan.* Regina, 1931.

145. Fuller, Basil.   *Canada To-day and To-morrow.* London, 1935.

146. Gaebler, Ernst W.J.   "Die Statistik der deutschen Auswanderung," O. Hübner's *Jahrbuch für Volkswirtschaft und Statistik,* I (1852), 263-275.

147. Ganong, W.F.   "A Monograph of the Origins of Settlement in the Province of New Brunswick," *Proceedings and Transactions of the Royal Society of Canada,* 2nd Series, vol. X (1904), sec. 2, 3-186.

148. *Gedenkblatt zum 25jährigen Jubiläum der deutschen evangelisch-lutherischen Dreieinigkeitsgemeinde in Winnipeg, Manitoba, 1888-1913.* Winnipeg, 1913.

149. Geissler, A.   *Das Land ohne Gnade. Roman der Amerika-Deutschen.* Berlin, 1933.

150. Geissler, Bruno.   "Aus den Sprachenfragen der Diaspora," in *Evangelische Diaspora und Gustav-Adolf-Verein. Franz-Rendtdorff-Festschrift.* Leipzig, 1930, 76-95.

151. Geissler, Bruno.   "Die evangelische Kirche bei den Auslanddeutschen," *Staat und Volkstum 1926.* Bücher des Deutschtums, vol. II, 568-628.

152. Gerhard, Karl.   "Erwachendes Deutschtum in Kanada," in *Wir Deutschen und die Welt.* Berlin, 1935, 75-84.

153. Giese, Else.   "Das Erziehungs- und Schulwesen in den deutschen Siedlungen Kanadas," *Jahrbuch des Reichsverbandes für die katholischen Auslanddeutschen* (Muenster i.W.), III (1929-30), 129-142.

154. Gleiss, Friedrich.   "Das Deutschtum in Kanada," *Deutsche Welt*. Berlin, 1928, 69-74.

155. Glynn, Ward H.   *The Glamour of British Columbia*. London, 1926.

156. Gockel, Anton.   *Die Landwirtschaft in den Prärieprovinzen Westkanadas.* Berlin, 1928.

157. Gottschick, H.   "Die bevölkerungsbiologische Lage und Bedeutung auslanddeutscher Siedlungsgruppen," *Archiv für Bevölkerungswissenschaft und Bevölkerungspolitik*, 1935, 387-399.

158. Gourlay, Robert.   *Statistical Account of Upper Canada, compiled with a view to a Grand System of Emigration*. 2 vols. London, 1822.

159. von Grafenried, Friedrich.   "Sechs Jahre in Canada, 1813-1819. Aus dem Tagebuche und den Reiseerinnerungen des Lieutenants Friedrich von Graffenried," *Jahresberichte der Geographischen Gesellschaft in Bern*, X (1890), 73-143.

160. Grentrup, Theodor.   "Entnationalisierung der Jugend und Familienethos," *Jahrbuch des Reichsverbandes für die katholischen Auslanddeutschen*, III (1929-30), 21-43.

161. Grentrup, Theodor.   "Grundsätzliches zum muttersprachlichen Religionsunterricht der Kinder," *Jahrbuch des Reichsverbandes für die katholischen Auslanddeutschen*, IV (1930-31), 42-50.

162. Griffin, A.P.C.   *A List of Works relating to the Germans in the United States, contained in the Library of Congress*. Washington, 1904.

163. Grösser, Max.   "Deutsche Prärie," *Die Getreuen*, I (1924), 89-94.

164. Grothe, Hugo.   "Die Entwicklung des Deutschtums in Kanada, 1901-1931," *Archiv für Wanderungswesen und Auslandkunde*, VII (1935), 58-60.

165. Grothe, Hugo.   "Glaubensbrüderliche Hilfsgemeinschaft: Auslanddeutsche Mennoniten in Kanada," *Kölnische Zeitung*, December 29, 1929.

166. Grothe, Hugo, ed.   *Jahrbuch des Vereins für das Deutschtum im Auslande für 1922*. Berlin, 1921.

167. Häberle, Daniel.   *Auswanderung und Koloniegründungen der Pfälzer im 18. Jahrhundert*. Kaiserslautern, 1909.

168. Hahn, Otto, ed. *Canada. Die Berichte der vier deutschen Delegierten über ihre Reise nach Canada im Herbst 1881.* 2nd ed., Reutlingen, 1883.

169. Hahn, Dr. "Die Entwicklung von Canada," *Deutsche Kolonialzeitung,* 1888.

170. Haliburton, T.C. *An Historical and Statistical Account of Nova Scotia.* 2 vols. Halifax, 1829.

171. Haller, Johannes. "Das Deutschtum in Russland," Süddeutsche Monatshefte, July 1915. Reprinted in Johannes Haller, *Reden und Aufsätze zur Geschichte und Politik.* Stuttgart and Berlin, 1934, 244-256.

172. Hamilton, Louis. "Die Deutschen in Kanada," *Zeitschrift für Politik* (Berlin), 1930, 773-785.

173. Hamilton, Louis. *Deutschland und Kanada.* Berlin, 1927.

174. Hamilton, L. and R. Freund. "Weizenwirtschaft und Agrarkrise in Westkanada," *Berichte über Landwirtschaft,* XIX (1934), 411-441.

175. Hamann, Dr. "Vom Deutschtum in Kanada. Reisebeobachtungen und - erfahrungen," *Das Deutschtum im Auslande* (Berlin), 1911, 501-508.

176. *Handbuch des Deutschtums im Auslande.* Edited by Allgemeiner Deutscher Schulverein zur Erhaltung des Deutschtums im Auslande. 2nd ed., Berlin, 1906.

177. *Handwörterbuch des Grenz-und Auslanddeutschtums. Unter Mitwirkung von etwa 800 Mitarbeitern und in Verbindung mit Prof. Dr. H. Aubin et al. Edited by Carl Petersen and Otto Scheel.* Vols. I-III. Breslau, 1933-1938.

178. Harms, J.F. *Geschichte der Mennoniten Brüdergemeinde.* Hillsboro, 1925.

179. Hartzler, J.E. *Education Among the Mennonites of America.* Danvers, Ill., 1925.

180. Heberle, Rudolf. *Auslandvolkstum. Soziologische Betrachtungen zum Studium des Deutschtums im Auslande.* Archiv für Bevölkerungswissenschaft und Bevölkerungspolitik, Vol. VI, 2. Beiheft. Leipzig, 1936.

181. Heck, Karl. "Minderheitenschulwesen in Kanada in der neueren Rechtsprechung des Privy Council," *Zeitschrift für ausländisches öffentliches Recht und Völkerrecht,* I (1929), 550-595.

182. Hege, Christian and D. Christian Neff, eds. *Mennonitisches Lexikon.* [3 vols.] Frankfurt a.M., 1913, [1937, 1940]

183. Hennings, C.R. "Vom Deutschtum in Kanada," *Der Auslanddeutsche*, XVII (1934), 142-148.

184. Henns, W. "Die Zweisprachigkeit als pädagogisches Problem." *Ethnopolitischer Almanach* (Vienna), 1931, 47-55.

185. Herkenrath, August. "Kanada und die Hudson's Bay Company." Unpublished Ph.D. thesis, University of Bonn, 1904.

186. Herold, Otto. *Kanada. Gegenwart und Zukunft.* Hamburg, 1928.

187. Herrington, Walter. "Pioneer Life on the Bay of Quinte," *Lennox and Addington Historical Society, Papers and Records*, VI (1915), 7 ff.

188. Herzog-Hauck, ed. *Realenzyklopadie für protestantische Theologie und Kirche.*

189. Heyne, Bodo. "Siedlung und Kirche in Kanada," *Die innere Mission im evangelischen Deutschland*, XXV (1930), 97-102.

190. Hildebrand, J.J. "Russlanddeutsche in Uebersee," *Deutsche Zeitung für Canada*, November 3, 1937.

191. Hill, G.M. "Nomenclature of the Streets of Halifax," *Collections of the Nova Scotia Historical Society*, XV (1911), 1-22.

192. Hill, R.B. *Manitoba: History of its early settlement, development and resources.* Toronto, [1890] 1927.

193. Hilland, P. "Die katholische Einwandererfürsorge in Kanada," *Die Getreuen*, XI (1934), 4-6.

194. *Historische und geographische Beschreibung von Neuschottland, darinnen von der Lage, Grösse, Beschaffenheit, Fruchtbarkeit und besonderen Eigenschaften des Landes, wie auch von den Sitten und Gewohnheiten der Indianer, und von den merckwürdigsten Begebenheiten so sich zwischen denen Cronen Franckreich und England seit deren Besitznahmung zugetragen, hinlängliche Nachricht ertheilt wird. Auf Befehl Seiner Grossbrittannischen Majestät Georg II und des Parlements in Englischer Sprache verfasset, Nunmehro ins Teutsche übersetzet.* Frankfurt and Leipzig, 1750.

195. *History of Toronto and the County of York, Ontario.* 2 vols. Toronto, 1885.

196. Horsch, John.   *The Hutterian Brethren, 1528-1931: A Story of Martyrdom and Loyalty.* Studies in Anabaptist and Mennonite History. Goshen, Ind., 1931.

197. Howison, John.   "Skizzen von Oberkanada in häuslicher, örtlicher und volkstümlicher Hinsicht, nebst einigen praktischen Belehrungen für Auswanderer aller Klassen," *Ethnographisches Archiv* (Jena), XIX (1822), 185-356.

198. Huber, Arnim O.   *Auf wilden Pfaden im neuen Kanada.* Stuttgart, 1932.

199. Huber, Arnim O.   *Bei roten und weissen Abenteurern in Kanada.* 2nd ed., Stuttgart, 1932.

200. Huber, Arnim O.   *Helga und der Hermelin. Roman einer kanadischen Liebe.* Berlin, 1937.

201. Huber, Arnim O.   *Karussel Amerika.* Berlin, 1936.

202. Hunter, A. F.   "The Ethnographical Elements of Ontario," *Ontario Historical Society, Papers and Records,* III (1901), 180-199.

203. Hurd, W. B. and T. W. Grindley.   *Agriculture, Climate and Population of the Prairie Provinces. A Statistical Atlas Showing Past Development and Present Conditions.* Ottawa, 1931.

204. Hurd, W. B.   "Is there a Canadian Race?" *Queen's Quarterly,* XXXV (1928), 615-627.

205. Hurd, W. B.   *Origin, Birthplace, Nationality and Language of the Canadian People: A Census Study Based on the Census of 1921 and Supplementary Data.* 1921 Census Monograph. Ottawa, 1929.

206. Hurd, W. B.   *Racial Origins and Nativity of the Canadian People.* 1931 Census Monograph No. 4. Reprinted from *Seventh Census of Canada, 1931,* vol. XII. Ottawa, 1938.

207. Iden-Zeller, Anita. "Die grosse Wanderung aus Russland nach Kanada," *Reclams Universum,* 46 (1929), 215f.

208. Immigration Act of 1927. *Revised Statutes of Canada,* 1927, Cap. 93.

209. Innis, Harold. *A History of the Canadian Pacific Railway*. London and Toronto, 1923.

210. Jameson, Anna B. *Winterstudien und Sommerstreifereien in Kanada*. 3 vols. Braunschweig, 1839.

211. Janzen, J. H. "Die Belletristik der canadischen russlanddeutschen Mennoniten," *Christlicher Gemeinde-Kalender für das Jahr 1938* (Iberstein bei Worms), 47 (1938).

212. Joest, Wilhelm. *Die aussereuropäische deutsche Presse*. Cologne, 1888.

213. Johann, A. E. [pseudonym for Alfred Wollschläger]. *Amerika. Untergang und Ueberfluss*. Berlin, 1932.

214. Johann, A. E. *Mit 20 Dollar in den wilden Westen. Schicksale aus Urwald, Steppe, Busch und Stadt*. N.p., 1928.

215. Johann, A. E. *Pelzjäger, Prärien und Präsidenten. Fahrten und Erlebnisse zwischen New York und Alaska*. Berlin, 1937.

216. Johnson, Stanley C. *A History of Emigration from the United Kingdom to North America, 1763-1912*. London, 1913.

217. Johnston, William. *History of Perth County, 1825-1902*. Stratford, Ont., 1903.

218. Jones, L. Rodwell. "Some Physical Controls in the Economic Development of the Prairie Provinces," *Geography*, XIV (1927-28), 284-302.

219. *Jubiläums-Büchlein. Festschrift zur Feier des 50-jährigen Jubiläums der evangelisch-lutherischen Synode von Canada*. N.p., 1911.

220. Jung, Karl E. *Deutsche Kolonien. Ein Beitrag zur bessern Kenntnis des Lebens und Wirkens unserer Landsleute in allen Erdteilen*. Leipzig and Prague, 1884.

221. Kaindl, Raimund F. *Geschichte der Deutschen in den Karpathenländern*.Vol. III: *Geschichte der Deutschen in Galizien, Ungarn, der Bukowina und Rumänien seit etwa 1770 bis zur Gegenwart*. Gotha, 1911.

222. *Kalender der Reformierten Kirche in den Vereinigten Staaten*. Cleveland, Ohio, 1935.

223. *Kanada. Geschichte der Deutschen Manitoba-Klassis der Synode des Nordwestens der Reformierten Kirche.* Cleveland, Ohio, 1924.

224. "Kanada und das Deutschtum in Kanada," *Nachrichtenblatt der Reichsstelle für das Auswanderungswesen* (Berlin), 1933, 142-148.

225. Kapp, Friedrich. *Geschichte der Deutschen im Staate New York bis zum Anfange des neunzehnten Jahrhunderts.* Geschichte der deutschen Einwanderung in Amerika, vol. I. [New York, 1867], Leipzig, 1868.

226. Kapp, Friedrich. *Der Soldatenhandel deutscher Fürsten nach Amerika. Ein Beitrag zur Kulturgeschichte des 18ten Jahrhunderts.* 2nd ed., Berlin, 1874.

227. Karasek-Langer, Alfred. "Die Bewohner der jungen deutschen Sprachinseln im Ostraum," in Wähler, ed., *Der deutsche Volkscharakter.* Jena, 1937, 486-513.

228. Karasek-[Langer, Alfred and Kurt] Lück. *Die deutschen Siedlungen in Wolhynien. Geschichte, Volkskunde. Lebensfragen.* Plauen i.V., 1931.

229. Karger, Karl. "Aus der Schule—für die Schule." A lecture given to the *Deutsch-canadischer Provinzialverband von Saskatchewan,* founded on March 27, 1913, on the occasion of its first conference in Regina on March 26, 1914.

230. Karger, Karl. *Zehn Jahre unter Engländern. Ein Auswandererschicksal.* Breslau, 1926.

231. *Katalog der Mennonitischen Deutsch-Englischen Lehranstalt zu Rosthern, Saskatchewan, 1926-27.*

232. "Katholisches Deutschtum in Westkanada. Von einem stillen Beobachter." *Kölnische Volkszeitung,* November 15, 1929.

233. Keiter, Friedrich. *Russlanddeutsche Bauern und ihre Stammesgenossen in Deutschland.* Schriftenreihe Deutsche Rassenkunde, No. 12. Jena, 1934.

234. Keller, C. *Die deutschen Kolonien in Südrussland.* Vol. I. Odessa, 1905.

235. Kempff, Ludwig. *Kanada und seine Probleme.* Stuttgart, 1926.

236. Kennedy, Howard A. *The Book of the West.* Toronto, 1925.

237.   Kennedy, Howard A.   *New Canada and the New Canadians*. London, 1907.

238.   Kingsford, William.   *The History of Canada (1608-1841)*. 12 vols. London 1890 ff.

239.   Klassen, Cornelius F.   "The Mennonites in Russia, 1917-1928," *Mennonite Quarterly Review*, VI:2 (1932), 69-80.

240.   Klaus, A.   *Unsere Kolonien. Studien und Materialien zur Geschichte und Statistik der ausländischen Kolonisation in Russland*. Odessa, 1887.

241.   Kleinschmidt, Beda.   *Das Auslanddeutschtum in Uebersee und die katholische Missionsbewegung*. Deutschtum und Ausland, No. 2-4. Muenster i.W., 1926.

242.   Klopp-Vogelsang, E. A.   "Die Entwicklung der katholischen Kirche in Kanada," *Die Getreuen*, VIII (1931), 112-117.

243.   Kloss, Heinz.   "Deutschkanadische Dichtung," *Der Auslanddeutsche*, XIX (1936), 815-834.

244.   Kloss, Heinz.   "Die Eigenständiggkeit des Ueberseedeutschtums als Erbe und Aufgabe," *Mitteilungen der Deutschen Akademie*. Munich, 1934, 1-34.

245.   Kloss, Heinz.   "Materialien zur Geschichte der deutschkanadischen Presse," *Der Auslanddeutsche*, XI (1929), 384 ff.

246.   Kohl, J. G.   *Reisen in Canada und durch die Staaten von New York und Pennsylvanien*. Stuttgart und Augsburg, 1856.

247.   Kuhn, Walter.   *Deutsche Sprachinselforschung: Geschichte, Aufgaben, Verfahren*. Plauen i.V., 1934.

248.   Kuhn, Walter.   "Die deutschen Siedlungsräume im Südosten," *Deutsches Archiv für Landes- und Volksforschung*, I (1937), 808-827.

249.   Kuhn, Walter.   "Die Herkunft der Josephsberger Ansiedler," *Ostdeutsches Volksblatt*, VII (1928), Folge 47 and 48.

250.   Kuhn, Walter.   "Die Herkunft der Wolhyniendeutschen," *Wolhynischer Volkskalender für das Jahr 1937*, 161-167.

251.   Kuhn, Walter.   *Die jungen deutschen Sprachinseln in Galizien*. Deutschtum

und Ausland, No. 26-27. Muenster i.W., 1930.

252. Kuhn, Walter. "Die Siedlungsräume des bäuerlichen Deutschtums in Polen," *Deutsche Monatshefte in Polen*, II (1935-36), 34-48.

253. Lambert, John. *Travels through Lower Canada and the United States of North America in the Years 1806, 1807, and 1808.* [3 vols. London, 1810] Vol. I: *Canada.* 2nd ed., London, 1814.

254. Lamprecht, Karl. *Deutsche Geschichte.* 2. Ergänzungsband. Berlin, 1903-1904.

255. Le Conte, René. "L'Emigration allemande au Canada," *Mouvement geographique* (Bruxelles), 1920, 424 ff.

256. Lehmann, Emil. *Die deutsche Auswanderung.* Berlin, 1861.

257. Lehmann, Heinz. "Aus der Frühzeit Westkanadas: Deutsch-Schweizer Soldaten als Siedler," *Deutsche Arbeit* (Berlin), 35 (1935), 652-654.

258. Lehmann, Heinz. "Deutsche Zeitung für Canada: Zur Geschichte der deutschkanadischen Presse," *Deutsche Arbeit* (Berlin), 35 (1935), 482-487.

259. Lehmann, Heinz. "Das evangelische Deutschtum in Kanada," in D. Dr. Schubert, ed., *Auslanddeutschtum und evangelische Kirche*, Jahrbuch 1935. München, 1935, 218-252.

260. Lehmann, Heinz. "Der Kampf um die deutsche Schule in Westkanada," *Deutsche Arbeit* (Berlin), 36 (1936), 26-31, 72-78.

261. Lehmann, Heinz. *Kanada.* Volksdeutsche Abende, No. 8. Berlin, 1936.

262. Leibbrandt, Georg. "The Emigration of the German Mennonites from Russia to the United States and Canada, 1873-1880," *Mennonite Quarterly Review.* VI (October 1932), 205-226, and VII (January 1933), 3-41.

263. Leichner, Georg. *Abenteuerliches Kanada. Reiseerlebnisse.* Leipzig, 1933.

264. Lemcke, Heinrich. *Canada, das Land und seine Leute.* Leipzig, 1887.

265. Lenker, J.N. *Lutherans in All Lands; the Wonderful Works of God.* 5th ed., Milwaukee, 1896.

266. Lindeman, Karl. *Von den deutschen Kolonisten in Russland. Ergebnisse einer Studienreise 1919-1921.* Schriften des Deutschen Ausland-Instituts Stuttgart, series A, vol. 14. Stuttgart, 1924.

267. List, Friedrich. *Die Ackerverfassung, die Zwergwirtschaft und die Auswanderung.* Stuttgart and Tübingen, 1842.

(75.) *Liste der eingewanderten mennonitischen Siedler und Distriktmänner.* Edited by Canadian Mennonite Board of Colonization. Rosthern, Saskatchewan, July 29, 1935.

268. von Loeher, Franz. *Geschichte und Zustände der Deutschen in Amerika.* Cincinnati and Leipzig, 1847.

269. von Loesch, Karl C. "Eingedeutschte, Entdeutschte und Renegaten," in *Volk unter Völkern.* Breslau, 1925, 213-244.

270. Lowell, E. J. *Die Hessen und die andern deutschen Hülfstruppen im Kriege Grossbritanniens gegen Amerika, 1776-1783.* Uebersetzt von O. C. Frhr. von Verschuer. Braunschweig and Leipzig, 1902.

271. Lucas, C. P. *A Historical Geography of the British Colonies.* [7 vols. London, 1905-192-5] Vol. V: *Canada.* Oxford, 1923.

272. Lucas, C. P., ed. *Lord Durham's Report on the Affairs of British North America.* 3 vols. Oxford, 1912.

(28.) Luden, H., ed. *Reise Seiner Hoheit des Herzogs Bernhard zu Sachsen-Weimar-Eisenach durch Nordamerika in den Jahren 1825 und 1826.* 2 parts. Weimar, 1828.

273. Luther College, Regina. *Prospect 1933-34.*

274. "Lutheran Church Record 1793-1832," *Ontario Historical Society, Papers and Records,* VI (1905), 136-167.

275. Mackintosh, W. A. *Prairie Settlement: The Geographical Setting. Canadian Frontiers of Settlement,* vol. I. Toronto, 1934.

276. *Makers of Canada.* 12 vols. Oxford, n.d. [Edited by Duncan C. Scott, et al., 20 vols. Toronto, 1903-1908].

277. Malinowsky, Josef Aloys. *Die deutschen katholischen Kolonien am Schwarzen*

Meer. Schriften des Deutschen Ausland-Instituts Stuttgart, series C. vol. 2. Stuttgart, 1927.

278.   Malinowsky, Josef Aloys.   *Die Planerkolonien am Asowschen Meere.* Schriften des Deutschen Ausland-Instituts Stuttgart, series A, vol. 22. Stuttgart, 1928.

279.   *Manitoba und das Nordwest-Territorium. Ein Bericht über Klima, Boden, Ernteergebnisse und Erwerbsquellen für Capitalisten, Landwirthe, Handwerker, Arbeiter, Dienstboten etc. unter besonderer Berücksichtigung für beabsichtigende Ansiedler.* London, 1890.

280.   *Maria Immaculata. Monatsblätter der Missionare Oblaten der Unbefleckten Jungfrau Maria.* Organ des Marianischen Missionsvereins (Fulda). Vols. I (1893-94)- XXV (1917-18).

281.   Maron, Gotthard L.   *Facts About the Germans in Canada.* Winnipeg, [1914?]

282.   Martin, Chester B.   *Lord Selkirk's Work in Canada.* Oxford, 1916.

283.   McArthur, D. A.   "Immigration and Colonization in Canada, 1900-1930," in *Pioneer Settlement: Co-operative Studies by Twenty-Six Authors.* American Geographical Society Special Publication No. 14. New York, 1932.

284.   McGibbon, Duncan A.   *The Canadian Grain Trade.* Toronto, 1932.

285.   McWilliams, Margaret.   *Manitoba Milestones.* Toronto and London, 1928.

286.   Meidinger, H.   *Canadas rasches Aufblühen, besonders als Ackerbau treibender Staat, und seine Wichtigkeit für Auswanderer in Bezug auf Arbeit, Landerwerb, gesundes Klima und bürgerliche Freiheit.* Frankfurt a.M., 1858.

287.   "The Mennonites in Manitoba," *Free Press News Bulletin* (Winnipeg), November 26, 1910.

288.   "Die Mennoniten Kolonien in Manitoba," *Der Deutsche Pionier* (Cincinnati), IX (1878), 29-37.

289.   Metzger, H.   *Geschichtlicher Abriss über die St. Peters-Pfarrei und Anlegung der Kolonien Rastadt, Katharinenthal und Speyer.* Verfasst von Hochw. Pater H. Metzger bei Gelegenheit des 40-jährigen Jubiläums der ersten Ansiedler, 3. Juni 1930. [Regina, 1930].

290. Meyer, H. *Pflanzungsgeschichte des Minnesota-Distrikts der Evangelisch Lutherischen Synode von Minneapolis. Minnesota.* N.p., 1932.

291. Miller, H. H. "Die Deutschen in Canada," *Deutsch-Amerikanische Geschichtsblätter* (Chicago), VIII (1908), 118-124.

292. *Mitteilungen über Manitoba und das Nordwest-Territorium (Nordamerika) für Capitalisten, Landwirthe, Handwerker, gewöhnliche Arbeiter, Dienstboten etc. unter besonderer Berücksichtigung der deutschen Ansiedler.* Liverpool, 1883.

293. Möllmann, Albert. *Das Deutschtum in Montreal.* Schriften des Instituts für Grenz- und Auslanddeutschtum an der Universität Marburg, Heft 11. Jena, 1937. [Editor's note: This is the German translation of the first part of his study "The Germans in Canada: Occupational and Social Adjustments of German Immigrants in Canada," Ph.D. thesis, McGill University, 1934. The second part was published by C.A. Dawson in *Group Settlement* (No. 103), 275-332, 389-390].

294. Monarque, Georges. *Un Général allemand au Canada. Le baron Friedrich Adolphus von Riedesel.* Montreal, 1927 [2nd ed., Montreal, 1946].

295. Mönckmeier, Wilhelm. *Die deutsche überseeische Auswanderung. Ein Beitrag zur deutschen Wanderungsgeschichte.* Jena, 1912.

296. Monro, A. *History, Geography and Statistics of British North America.* Montreal, 1864.

297. Müller-Grote, Karl. *Onkel Karl. Deutsch-Kanadische Lebensbilder.* Bremen, 1924.

298. *Nachrichten von den Vereinigten Deutschen Evangelisch Lutherischen Gemeinden in Nordamerika.* Halle, 1787.

299. Nederkorn, Wilhelm. "Die Entdeckungs-, Besiedlungs- und Entwicklungsgeschichte Canadas und seiner Grenzgebiete," *Deutsche Geographische Blätter*, XXII (1899).

300. Neff, D. Christian, ed. *Bericht über die Mennonitische Welthilfskonferenz vom 31. August bis 3. September 1930 in Danzig.* Karlsruhe, 1931.

301. Nelson, Helge. "The Interior Colonization in Canada at the Present Day and its Natural Conditions," *Geografiska Annaler* (Stockholm), V (1923), 244-308.

302. Neufeld, Gerda.   "Einwanderung in Kanada nach dem Kriege."
Unpublished Ph.D. thesis, University of Berlin, 1931.

303. Neusatz, H. and D. Erka.   *Ein deutscher Todesweg. Authentische Dokumente
der wirtschaftlichen, kulturellen und seelischen Vernichtung des Deutschtums in
der Sowjetunion.* Berlin, 1930.

304. Neve, J. L.   *Kurz gefasste Geschichte der lutherischen Kirche Amerikas.*
Burlington, Iowa, 1904.

305. *Collections of the New Brunswick Historical Society.* Vols. I-XII, 1894-1928.

306. *Der Nordwesten-Kalender* for 1914 and 1925 through 1930. Winnipeg.

307. Novokampus (pseudonym for Dietrich Neufeld). *Kanadische Mennoniten.
Bunte Bilder aus dem 50jährigen Siedlerleben. Zum Jubiläumsjahr 1924.*
Winnipeg, 1925.

308. N. [Noyes, Ino P.?].   "The Camden Colony: A Story of the United
Empire Loyalists," *Missisquoi County Historical Society Reports,* III (1908),
108-109.

309. Noyes, Ino P.   *The Canadian Loyalists and Early Settlers in the District of
Bedford.* St. Johns, Quebec, 1900.

310. Noyes, Ino P.   "The Canadian Loyalists and Early Settlers in the District
of Bedford," *Missisquoi County Historical Society Reports,* III (1908), 90-107.

311. Noyes, Ino P.   "The Missisquoi German or Dutch," *Missisquoi County
Historical Society Reports,* II (1907), 31-35.

312. Oliver, E. H.   *The County School in Non-English-Speaking Communities in
Saskatchewan.* Regina, 1916.

313. Oliver, E. H.   "Saskatchewan and Alberta, General History 1870-1912," in
A. Shortt and A. G. Doughty, eds.   *Canada and Its Provinces,* vol. XIX.
Toronto, 1914, 147-280.

314. Oliver, E. H.   "The Settlement of Saskatchewan to 1914," *Proceedings and
Transactions of the Royal Society of Canada,* 3rd Series, vol. XX (1926), sec. 2,
63-88.

315. Oliver, E. H.   "The Settlement of the Prairies, 1867-1914," in *Cambridge*

History of the British Empire, vol. VI. Cambridge, 1930, 528-547.

316. Oppel, Alwin. "Das Deutschtum in Kanada," Deutsche Erde (Gotha), V (1906), 47-54.

317. Oppel, Alwin. Kanada und die Deutschen. Das Deutschtum im Auslande, vol. III. Dresden, 1916.

318. Oppel, Alwin. "Reise in den Prärien und Seengebieten von Nordamerika," Deutsche Geographische Blätter (Bremen), XXVIII (1905), 155-248.

319. Ott, Adolf. Der Führer nach Amerika. Basel, 1882.

320. Partridge, Francis. "Notes on the Early History of St. George's Church, Halifax," Collections of the Nova Scotia Historical Society, VI (1888), 137-154, and VII (1891), 73-87.

321. Peters, Klaas. Die Bergthaler Mennoniten und deren Auswanderung aus Russland und Einwanderung in Manitoba. Hillsboro, Kansas, 1924.

322. Pfeffer, Karl Heinz. "Deutsche Volksgruppe und angelsächsische bürgerliche Gesellschaft," Auslanddeutsche Volksforschung (Stuttgart), I (1937), 65-70.

323. Pfister, Albert. Die Amerikanische Revolution, 1775-83. Entwickelungsgeschichte der Grundlage zum Freistaat wie zum Weltreich, unter Hervorhebung des deutschen Anteils. 2 vols. Stuttgart and Berlin, 1904.

324. Pierce, Lorne A. "The German Loyalist in Upper Canada," The Canadian Magazine [of Politics, Science, Art and Literature], LV:4 (August, 1920) 290-296.

325. Pietsch, Johannes. Bei den Deutschen in Westkanada. Hünfeld, 1928.

326. Pietsch, Johannes. "Das katholische Deutschtum in Westkanada," Jahrbuch des Reichsverbandes der katholischen Auslanddeutschen (Muenster i.W.), 1926, 211-217.

327. Pioneer Settlement: Co-operative Studies by Twenty-Six Authors. American Geographical Society Special Publication No. 14. New York, 1932.

328. Quiring, Walter. "The Canadian Mennonite Immigration into the

Paraguayan Chaco 1926-27," *Mennonite Quarterly Review,* VIII:1 (1934).

329.   Quiring, Walter,   "Weltweite Wanderung. Ein Beitrag zur Geschichte der Mennonitenwanderungen in der Nachkriegszeit," *Der Auslanddeutsche,* XVII (1934), 218-228.

330.   Raymond, W.O.   "Colonel Alexander McNutt and the Pre-Loyalist Settlements of Nova Scotia," *Proceedings and Transactions of the Royal Society of Canada,* 3rd Series, vol. V (May 1911), sec. 2, 23-115.

331.   Regier, Mrs. P.   "Ueber die Entstehung der Rosenorter Gemeinde," *Christlicher Bundesbote* (Newton, Kansas), November 10, 1931.

332.   Rehwinkel.   *Statuten des Deutsch-canadischen Nationalverbandes. Ein Aufruf an das Deutschtum Canadas.* Edmonton, Alta., 1926.

333.   Reisinger, G.   "Die Schulen der deutschen Kirchenverbände in Kanada," *Die deutsche Schule im Auslande* (Wolfenbüttel), 22 (1930), 93f.

334.   Rempel, J.   "Die russlanddeutschen Mennoniten in Canada und die deutsche Sprache," *Deutsche Post aus dem Osten,* II (1927), 107 ff.

335.   *Report of the Saskatchewan Royal Commission on Immigration and Settlement.* Regina, 1930.

(4.)   Reports on Immigration.

336.   Rethwisch, J.   *Die Deutschen im Auslande. Beiträge zur Kolonial-und Auswanderungspolitik.* Berlin, 1889.

337.   *Review of Historical Publications Relating to Canada.* Toronto, 1896-1919

338.   von Riedesel, Friederike Charlotte Louise, Freifrau, ed.   *Briefe und Berichte des Generals und der Generalin von Riedesel während des nordamerikanischen Krieges, 1776 bis 1783.* Freiburg i.B., 1881.

339.   Rieth, Adolf.   *Die geographische Verbreitung des Deutschtums in Rumpf-Ungarn in Vergangenheit und Gegenwart.* Schriften des Deutschen Ausland-Instituts Stuttgart, series A, vol. 18. Stuttgart, 1927.

340.   Rosengarten, J.G.   *Der deutsche Soldat in den Kriegen der Vereinigten Staaten von Nordamerika.* Kassel, 1890.

341.   Ross, Alexander.   *The Red River Settlement: Its Rise, Progress and Present State.* London, 1856.

342.   Ross, Colin.   *Zwischen U.S.A. und dem Pol. Durch Kanada, Neufundland, Labrador, Arktis.* Leipzig, 1934.

343.   Ross, Edward A.   *The Old World in the New.* New York, 1914.

344.   *Royal Bank of Canada Letters.* Montreal, n.d.

345.   Ruccius, M.   "Deutsch-Evangelische Arbeit in Kanada," *Der Auslanddeutsche*, XIII (1930), 647-649.

346.   Ruccius, M.   "Deutsche Schulen in Kanada," *Auslandswarte.* IX (1929), 329f.

347.   Rüdiger, Hermann.   *Die Donauschwaben in der südslawischen Batschka.* Schriften des Deutschen Ausland-Instituts Stuttgart, series A, vol. 28. Stuttgart, 1931.

348.   Rusticus, J.   "Aus der Josephskolonie und den Nachbargebieten in Saskatchewan," *Die Getreuen*, II (1925), 10-14.

349.   Sabine, Lorenzo.   *The American Loyalists, or biographical sketches of adherents to the British Crown in the War of the Revolution.* Boston, 1847.

350.   Sabourin, J. A.   "Nos Mennonites: leur immigration et leur émigration, *Action française* (Montreal), XVIII (1927), 230-233.

351.   Sallet, Richard.   "Russlanddeutsche Siedlungen in den Vereinigten Staatcn von Amerika," *Deutsch-Amerikanische Geschichtsblätter*, Jahrbuch der Deutsch-Amerikanischen Historischen Gesellschaft von Illinois, XXXI (1931), 1-126.

352.   Sartorius von Waltershausen, August. "Auswanderung," *Handwörterbuch der Staatswissenschaften*, vol. II, 4th ed., Jena, 1924, 60-115.

353.   *Saskatchewan Year Book*, 1927 and 1928. Regina.

354.   Saunders, F. W. J.   "The Prairie Teacher," *Commonwealth and Empire Review*, 1932, 174-177.

355.   Sax, Karl.   *Der Auswanderer. Roman.* Zürich, 1931.

356.   Schäfer, Hans.   *Die deutsch-kanadischen Wirtschaftsbeziehungen seit Beendigung des Weltkriegs unter besonderer Berücksichtigung der kanadischen Wirtschaftsentwicklung.* Euskirchen, 1934.

357.   Schem, Alexander J., ed.   *Deutsch-Amerikanisches Konversations-Lexicon.* 11 vols., New York, 1869-1874.

358.   Schenk, Ernst.   *Kanada. Anleitung zur praktischen Landwirtschaft und Siedlung.* Berlin, 1930.

359.   Schirmunski, Viktor.   *Die deutschen Kolonien in der Ukraine. Geschichte, Mundart, Volkslied, Volkskunde.* Moscow, 1928.

360.   von Schilling, Edith.   "Ein Besuch bei den Deutschen in Loon River, Saskatchewan, *Der Auslanddeutsche,* XIX (1936), 478-480.

361.   Schlözer, August Ludwig.   *Staats-Anzeigen* (Göttingen), VI:24 (1784).

362.   Schmid, Edmund.   *Die deutschen Bauern in Südrussland. Berlin, 1917.*

363.   *Schmid, Edmund.   Die deutschen Kolonien im Schwarzmeergebiet Südrusslands.* Berlin, 1919.

364.   Schmidt, Carl.   *Dies Buch gehört dem Deutschen Auswanderer. Eine geographisch-statistische und geschichtliche Beschreibung der Vereinigten Staaten von Nord-Amerika mit besonderer Rücksichtnahm auf Auswanderung und Colonisation. Ein vollständiger Rathgeber für Auswanderer nach und durch Nord-Amerika, Canada, Texas, Californien etc . . .* Leipzig, 1855.

365.   Schmidt-Rohr, Georg.   *Muttersprache. Vom Amt der Sprache bei der Volkwerdung.* Schriften der Deutschen Akademie, No. 12. 2nd ed. Jena, 1933.

366.   Schmidt-Rohr, Georg.   "Sprachenkampf im Völkerleben," *Der Volksspiegel,* I (1934), 75-82.

367.   Schmidt-Rohr, Georg.   "Stufen der Entfremdung. Ein Beitrag zur Frage der Assimilation von Sprachgruppen," *Der Volksspiegel,* I (1934), 75-82.

368.   Schmieder, O.   *Länderkunde Nordamerikas.* Leipzig and Wien, 1933.

369.   Schneider, Carl.   "Das Evangelium der deutschen Reformation im angelsächsischen Gewand," in *Evangelische Diaspora und Gustav-Adolf-Verein.*

Franz Rendtorff-Festschrift. Leipzig, 1930, 328-341.

370. Schneider, Fritz. "Ein Anfang deutscher Gemeinschaftssiedlung in Kanada," *Deutsche Bodensee-Zeitung,* November 21, 1927.

371. School Acts:
   a. Ontario. *Law of Separate Schools of Upper Canada, by the Roman Catholic Bishops and the Chief Superintendent of Schools, being the first part of the correspondence, ordered to be printed by the Legislative Assembly.* Toronto, 1855.
   b. Manitoba School Act, *Manitoba Revised Statutes,* 1913, vol. III, Cap. 165.
   c. Saskatchewan School Act, *Statutes of Saskatchewan,* 1915, Cap. 23.
   d. Saskatchewan School Attendance Act, *Statutes of Saskatchewan,* 1917, Cap. 197.
   e. Alberta School Act, *Revised Statutes of Alberta,* 1922, Cap. 51.
   f. Alberta School Attendance Act, *Revised Statutes of Alberta,* 1922 Cap. 55.

372. Schott, Carl. *Landnahme und Kolonisation in Canada am Beispiel Südontarios.* Schriften des Geographischen Instituts der Universität Kiel, vol. VI. Kiel, 1936.

373. Schreiber, Ilse. "Deutsche Siedler in Kanada. Ein Tatsachenbericht," *Gartenlaube,* 1934, 15-17, 39f., 64-66, 91.

374. Schreiber, Ilse. "Deutschland in Kanada," *Deutsche Zeitung für Canada,* September 15, 1937.

375. Schreiber, Ilse. *Die Schwestern aus Memel. Ein Kanada-Roman.* Berlin, 1936.

(30.) Schulte, P. *Bilder und Blätter zum silbernen Jubiläum der St. Josephs Kolonie.* Gesammelt von den Patres Oblaten in der Kolonie. Prince Albert, 1930.

376. Schultz, Johannes. *Die Muttersprache.* St. Paul, Minnesota, (ca. 1920).

377. Schultz, Johannes. "Erste Reise in die St. Bonifatius-Kolonie am Beaver Fluss," *Der Kanadische Herold* (Berlin-Wilmersdorf), 1930, 237 ff.

378. Schultze, Ernst. "Bevölkerungsbewegung im westlichen Kanada," *Zeitschrift für Sozialwissenschaft.* Neue Folge, I (1910), 515 ff.

379. Schwabe, H. "Mitteilungen über Kanada," *Zeitschrift für allgemeine Erdkunde,* Neue Folge, XVII (1864), 287-326.

380. Schweers, T., P. Funke, P. Hilland, et al. "Die Deutschen in Kanada," *Maria Immaculate* (Marburg), XV (1907-08), 239-246, 270-277, 312-315, 344-349, 380-385, 417-424.

381. "Die Schweizer Kolonisten an der Hudson's Bay," *Der Deutsche Pionier* (Cincinnati), X (1878), 436-442, 489-495, and XI (1879), 12-22.

382. Schwerla, C.B. *Kanada im Faltboot.* Berlin, 1930.

383. Sering, Max. "Die Einwanderung in die landwirtschaftlichen Distrikte Nordamerikas," *Verhandlungen des deutschen Kolonialkongresses 1905.* Berlin, 1906, 849 ff.

384. Sering, Max. *Die landwirtschaftliche Konkurrenz Nordamerikas in Gegenwart und Zukunft.* Leipzig, 1887.

385. "Sechzigjährige Jubiläumfeier der ersten Mennonitensiedlung in Manitoba," *Der Nordwesten-Kalender* (Winnipeg), 1935.

386. Seume, Johann Gottfried. "Mein Leben." [In J. G. Seume. *Prosaschriften.* With an introduction by Werner Kraft. Cologne, 1962, 53-154.]

387. Sherk, A.B. "The Pennsylvania Germans of Waterloo County, Ontario," *Ontario Historical Society, Papers and Records,* VII (1906), 98-109.

388. Shortt, Adam and Arthur G. Doughty, eds. *Canada and Its Provinces. A History of the Canadian People and their Institutions by One Hundred Associates.* 23 vols., Toronto, 1913-1917.

389. Siebert, W.H. "The American Loyalists in the Eastern Seigniories and Townships of the Province of Quebec," *Proceedings and Transactions of the Royal Society of Canada,* 3rd Series, vol. VII (1913), sec. 2, 3-42.

390. Siebert, W.H. "The Dispersion of the American Tories," *Mississippi Valley Historical Review,* I:2 (Sept. 1914), 185-197.

391. Siebert, W.H. "The Loyalists and the Six Nation Indians in the Niagara Peninsula," *Proceedings and Transactions of the Royal Society of Canada,* 3rd Series, Vol. IX (1915), sec. 2, 79-128.

392. Siegfried, André. *Le Canada, puissance internationale.* Paris, 1937.

393. Siegfried, André. *The Race Question in Canada.* London, 1907.

(95.) *Simcoe Papers.*

394. Simms, Jephta R.   *History of Schoharie County, and Border Wars of New York; containing also a sketch of the causes which led to the American Revolution, and interesting memoranda of the Mohawk Valley.* Albany, N.Y., 1845.

395. Sissons, C.B.   *Bi-Lingual Schools in Canada.* London, 1917.

396. Skelton, Oskar D.   *Life and Letters of Sir Wilfrid Laurier.* 2 vols. [Toronto, 1921] Oxford, 1922.

397. Smith, A.   "Some Hessians of the U. E. L. Settlements in Marysburgh," *Ontario Historical Society, Papers and Records,* XXI (1924), 259-261.

398. Smith, C. Henry.   *The Coming of the Russian Mennonites. An Episode in the Settling of the Last Frontier, 1874-1884.* Berne, Indiana, 1927.

399. Smith, G.   "The Amishman," *Ontario Historical Society, Papers and Records,* XVII (1919), 40-42.

400. Smith, Michael.   *A Geographical View of the Province of Upper Canada and promiscous remarks upon the government.* Hartford and New York, 1813.

401. Smith, W.G.   *A Study in Canadian Immigration.* Toronto, 1920.

402. Smith. W.H.   *Canada: Past, Present and Future, being a historical, geographical, geological and statistical account of Canada West.* 2 vols. Toronto, 1850.

403. von Soden, Carl Th.   *Des Auswanderers Schutz diesseits und jenseits des Ozeans. Wegweiser für Auswanderer.* Hamburg, 1853.

404. Spetz, Theobald.   *The Catholic Church in Waterloo County. Book 1: The Catholic Register and Extension.* N.P., 1916.

405. Staadt, Anne-Lise.   "Von der deutschen Auswanderung nach Canada und der Geschichte des dortigen Deutschtums," *Archiv für Wanderungswesen,* II: 1 (1929), 31-33.

406. Stach, Jakob.   *Die deutschen Kolonien in Südrussland. Kulturgeschichtliche Studien und Bilder über das erste Jahrhundert ihres Bestehens.* Prischib, 1904.

407.   Staff, A.   "Von den russlanddeutschen mennonitischen 'Altkoloniern' in Mexiko und Kanada," *Deutsche Post aus dem Osten*, I (1926), 51 ff.

408.   *Statement of the Satisfactory Results which have attended Immigration to Upper Canada from the Establishment of the Canada Company until the Present Period.* London, 1841.

409.   *Statistical Year Book of the Evangelical Lutheran Church of Missouri, Ohio and other States for 1927.* St. Louis, Mo., 1928. [Missouri Synod]

410.   *Statistical Year Book of the Evangelical Lutheran Church of Missouri, Ohio and other States for 1936.* St. Louis, Mo., 1937. [Missouri Synod]

411.   *Statistik des Deutschen Reiches*, vol. 336. Berlin, 1928.

412.   Stead, Robert J.C.   "The Old Prairie Homestead," *Canadian Geographical Journal*, VII (1933), 13-21.

413.   Stein, Paul.   "A Story of the Rear of Addington County," *Lennox and Addington Historical Society, Papers and Records*, II (1910), 14 ff.

414.   Strahlow, Theodor.   "St. Bonifatius. Neue deutsche Siedlung in Nord-Saskatchewan," *Der Kanadische Herold* (Berlin-Wilmersdorf), 1930, 139 ff.

415.   Stricker, Jacob.   *Erlebnisse eines Schweizers in Kanada.* Zürich and Leipzig, 1935.

416.   Stricker, Wilhelm.   *Die Verbreitung des deutschen Volkes über die Erde. Ein Versuch.* Leipzig, 1845.

417.   Stricker, Wilhelm, ed.   *Germania. Archiv zur Kenntniss des deutschen Elements in allen Ländern der Erde.* 3 vols. Frankfurt a.M., 1847-1850.

418.   Stumpp, Karl.   *Die deutschen Kolonien im Schwarzmeergebiet.* Schriften des Deutschen Ausland-Instituts Stuttgart, series A, vol. 7. Stuttgart, 1922.

419.   Sturz, John J.   *Plan for Securing to British North America a Larger Share than heretofore it has received of the Emigration from the United Kingdom as well as from Germany and also from other countries of Europe. Private and Confidential.* Berlin 1860.

420.   Switzer, E.   "The Switzers of the Bay of Quinte," *Ontario Historical Society, Papers and Records*, VI (1905), 95-96.

421. Tasker, L. H. "The United Empire Loyalist Settlement at Long Point, Lake Erie," *Ontario Historical Society, Papers and Records*, II (1900), 9-79.

422. Teefy, L. "Historical Notes on Yonge Street," *Ontario Historical Society, Papers and Records*, V (1904), 53-60.

423. Teuscher, Jakob. *Briefe über Westkanada*. Preston, Ont. and Basel, 1854.

434. Teutsch, Friedrich. *Geschichte der Siebenbürger Sachsen*. vol. IV: *1868-1919*. Hermannstadt, 1926.

425. Thielmann, G. G. "Zur kulturellen Lage der Deutschen in Kanada," *Deutsche Post aus dem Osten*, IX (1937), 16 f.

426. Timpe, G. "Ansiedlung in Kanada," *Der Auslanddeutsche*, X (1927), 176-179.

427. Timpe, G. "Vom Deutschtum in Kanada," *Die Getreuen*, IV (1927), 84-87.

428. Toews, David. "Mennonitische Einwanderung in der Zukunft," *Christlicher Bundesbote* (Berne, Indiana), October 31, 1929.

429. Toews, Gerhard. "Die seit 1923 aus Russland vertriebenen Mennoniten als Kulturfaktor im kanadischen Deutschtum," *Deutsche Zeitung für Canada*, February, 5, 12 and 19, 1936.

430. Tracy, Frank B. *Tercentenary History of Canada from Champlain to Laurier*. 3 vols. New York and Toronto, 1908, 1913.

431. Traeger, Paul. *Die Deutschen in der Dobrudscha, zugleich ein Beitrag zur Geschichte der deutschen Wanderungen in Osteuropa*. Schriften des Deutschen Ausland-Instituts Stuttgart, series A, vol. 6. Stuttgart, 1922.

432. Tucker, W. Bowman. *The Camden Colony, or the Seed of the Righteous. A Story of the United Empire Loyalists (U.E.L.) with geographical tables*. Montreal, 1908.

433. Tuckermann, Walther. "Das Deutschtum in Kanada," in *Aus Sozial- und Wirtschaftsgeschichte. Gedächtnisschrift für Georg von Below*. Stuttgart, 1928, 299-342.

434. Tuckermann, Walther. "Die ländlichen Siedlungen Kanadas," in Klute,

ed., *Die ländlichen Siedlungen in verschiedened Klimazonen.* Breslau, 1933, 161-170.

435.   "Die überseeische Aus- und Einwanderung in den Jahren 1925 und 1926 mit einem Ueberblick über die Entwicklung der deutschen und der internationalen Wanderungsbewegung," *Statistik des Deutschen Reiches,* vol. 336. Berlin, 1928, 95-140.

436.   United States Bureau of Immigration. *Annual Report of the Commissioner General of Immigration, 1906 to 1930.* Washington, 1906 to 1930. [Editor's note: For Lehmann's citation of the same source see No. 4c.]

437.   Unruh, Benjamin.   "Ansiedlung der deutsch-russischen Bauern in Canada, Brasilien und Paraguay," *Die Auslandswarte* (Berlin), XI (1931), 213-216.

438.   Unruh, Benjamin.   "Die Mennoniten in Russland," *Ostdeutsche Monatshefte,* V (March 1925), 1157-1167.

439.   Vasterling, Christian.   *Entdeutschungsgefahren im Reifealter. Zur Psychologie der Umvolkung Jugendlicher.* Berlin, 1936.

440.   *Verhandlungen der ersten Versammlung des Canada-Distrikts, Amerikanisch-Lutherische Kirche.* Regina, Sask., 1931.

441.   *Verhandlungen der 21. Versammlung des Canada Distrikts der Allgemeinen Evangelisch-Lutherischen Synode von Ohio und anderen Staaten* (July 4-10, 1929). Regina, Saskatchewan.

442.   *Verhandlungen der 24. Versammlung der Evangelisch-Lutherischen Synode von Manitoba und anderen Provinzen* (June 26-July 1, 1929). Saskatoon, Saskatchewan.

443.   *Verhandlungen der 29. Versammlung der Evangelisch-Lutherischen Synode von Manitoba und anderen Provinzen.* Winnipeg, 1936.

444.   *Vertrauliche Briefe aus Kanada und Neu-England vom Jahre 1777 und 1778.* Göttingen, 1779.

445.   Wagner, Hermann.   "Kanada und die deutsche Auswanderung," *Zeitwende* VI (1930), 385.395.

446.   Wagner, Hermann.   "Vom jungen Deutschtum in den Kanadischen

Prärieprovinzen," *Archiv für das gesamte Auslanddeutschtum* (Dresden), 1931, 144-148.

447.   Wagner, Hermann.   *Von Küste zu Küste.* Hamburg, 1929.

448.   Wallace, W. Stewart, ed.   *The Dictionary of Canadian Biography.* Toronto, 1926.

449.   *Wartburg-Kalender 1937.* Amerikanisch-Lutherische Kirche. Columbus, Ohio, and Chicago, Illinois.

450.   *Waterloo Historical Society, Annual Reports* (Berlin, i.e., Kitchener, Ontario). Vols. I-XV (1913-1927).

451.   Weber, Walter.   "Deutsche Neuansiedlungen in Kanada," *Die deutsche Schule im Auslande,* XVII (1925), 51-54.

452.   Weir, George M.   *The Separate School Question in Canada.* Toronto, 1934.

453.   von Weiss, Andreas.   "Zweisprachigkeit und Sprachtheorie," *Auslanddeutsche Volksforschung.* Stuttgart, 1937, 256-266.

454.   Whitton, Charlotte.   *The Immigration Problem for Canada.* Queen's University Publications No. 48. Kingston, 1924.

455.   Weld, Conrad.   *Reise durch die nordamerikanischen Freistaaten und durch Ober- und Nieder-Kanada in den Jahren 1795, 1796 und 1797.* Berlin, 1800.

456.   Wiebe, Gerhard.   *Ursachen und Geschichte der Auswanderung der Mennoniten aus Russland nach Amerika.* Winnipeg, n.d.

457.   Wiedersheim, Eduard.   *Kanada. Reisebeschreibung und Bericht über die dortigen land- und volkswirtschaftlichen Verhältnisse.* Stuttgart, 1882.

458.   Wiese, A., trans.   *Ansiedlungen in den Urwäldern von Canada. Von einer Emigrantin.* Leipzig, 1838.

459.   Willcox, Walter F., ed.   *International Migrations.* 2 vols. Demographic Monographs, vols. 7 and 8. New York, 1929 and 1931.

460.   Willson, Henry Beckles.   *The Great Company, 1667-1871.* 2 vols. London, 1900.

461. Winkler, Wilhelm. "Statistik der Wanderungen des deutschen Volkes," *Deutsche Hefte für Volks- und Kulturbodenforschung* (Langensalza), III (1932), 47 ff., 100 ff., 172 ff., 284 ff.

462. Winkler, Wilhelm, ed. *Statistisches Handbuch des gesamten Deutschtums.* Berlin, 1927.

463. Wintemberg, W. J. "German-Canadian Folk-lore," *Ontario Historical Society, Papers and Records*, III (1901), 86-96.

464. Wintemberg, W. J. "The Place and Stream Names of Oxford County," *Ontario Historical Society, Papers and Records*, XXII (1925), 259-295.

465. Wittke, Carl. *A History of Canada.* 2nd ed., New York, 1933.

466. Wood, Louis A. *The Red River Colony.* Toronto, 1915.

467. Woodsworth, James S. *Strangers Within Our Gates.* Toronto, 1908.

468. *Year Book of the United Lutheran Church in America.* Philadelphia, Pa. 1935.

469. Yeigh, Frank. *Through the Heart of Canada.* London, 1913.

470. Zarek, E. H. and C. R. Hennings. "Zur Geschichte der Siedlung Edenwold," *Der Auslanddeutsche*, XVII (1934), 148-156.

471. Ziehen, Eduard. "Canadianism. Zur Genesis der Kanadischen Nation," *Historische Zeitschrift, 149 (1934), 497-558.*

472. Zöckler, Theodor. *Das Deutschtum, in Galizien.* Dresden, 1915.

(15.) *Zum Andenken an das Silberne Jubiläum der St. Peters-Kolonie, 1903-28.* Muenster, Sask., 1928.

Index

abbatia nullius 208
Abbey, Benedictine (Muenster, Sask.) 357
Abbotsford (B.C.) 253
Abbotsford-Huntingdon (B.C.) 253
Abel, Walter 433 n.57
Abele's pharmacy 250
Abele, Paul 213
Aberdeen (Man.) 442 n.44
Aberdeen (Sask.) 332
Abernethy (Sask.) 229
Abinger Tp. 60
Acadia Valley (Alta.) 132
Acadian(s) 1, 9, 10, 32, 33, 42, 379 n. 14
accent 262
accent, Tyrolean 273
acclimatization (also see anglicization,
   assimilation) 324
Acme (Alta.) 239
Acts – Alberta School Attendance Act 328;
   Alberta School Act (Section 178–2) 457
   n.33; Alberta School Attendance Act
   (Section 5) 457 n.39; British North
   America Act of 1867 100; British North
   America Act of 1867 314; Common
   School Act of 1850 409 n.71; Dominion
   Land Act of 1872 373 n.48; Immigration
   Act 103; Immigration Act of 1927 430
   n.9, n.10; Imperial Public School Act of
   1869 (Reichsvolksschulgesetz) 119; Land
   Act 187; Land Act of 1872 97, 100;
   Quebec Act of 1774 45; Saskatchewan
   School Act and Alberta School Act 456
   n.21; Saskatchewan School Act (Section
   177–2) 457 n.33; Saskatchewan School
   Attendance Act (on private schools) 455
   n.17; School Act of 1890 75; School Act
   of 1897 316; School Act of 1897 321;
   School Act, Section 258 455 n.10;
   Separate School Act of 1851 409 n.71;
   Supplementary School Act of 1853 409
   n.71
assimilation 306
Addington Co. (Ont.) 49, 55, 60, 395 n.150
Addington Road (Denbigh Tp.) 399 n.184
Adolphustown (Ont.) 52, 54
Adventist(s) 118, 194, 195, 225, 235, 248,
   274, 359
Agassiz (B.C.) 253

agricultural college, Winnipeg 283
agricultural population (Germans in
   western Canada) 339
Agricultural Society 337
agriculture 273, 454 n.6
agriculturists, German, proportions of 304
Alameda (Sask.) 132, 144, 215, 234, 448
   n.107
Alaska 397 n.165
Albert Co. (N.B.) 33, 43, 44, 385 n.71
Albert Gallion (Beauce Co., Que.) 391
   n.108
Alberta 97, 99, 129, 132, 162, 164, 171, 173,
   211, 239-251, 241, 253, 272, 278, 283, 319,
   321, 322, 332, 333, 356, 453 n.21
Alberta Herold (Edmonton) 290
Alberta, as destination 434 n.65;
   Government of A. 327; northern A.
   242; Alberta-British Columbia District
   (Lutheran) 271; Alberta-British Columbia
   District (of the Missouri Synod) 269
Albion (B.C.) 253
Albrechts (see Albrights)
Albright, Amos 402 n.13
Albright, Franklin 400 n.7
Albrights 408 n.60
Alcester (Man.) 195
Aldborough (Ont.) 93, 426 n.223
Aldergrove (B.C.) 253
Aldersyde 132
Alexander 440 n.16
Alexander I, Tsar 108, 110
Alexander Street (Winnipeg) 197
Altona (Man.) 191
Alexanderdorf (Volga region) 118, 251
Alexanderfeld (S. Russia) 294
Algoma (see Sault Ste. Marie)
Algoma Co. (Ont.) 428 n.234
Algona Tp. (Ont.) 57, 59, 398 n.176, n.179
Alice Tp. (Ont.) 57, 59, 398 n.176, n.179
aliens, emigrant (term used in U.S. House
   documents) 435 n.11, 436 n.16
Allan (Sask.) 114, 144, 218, 221, 232, 327
Allan, Capt. 396 n.155
Allied Powers, Allies xxxiv, 98
Alpenvereinigung 279
Alsace (Eur.), Alsatian 28, 70, 71, 406 n.54,
   n.55, 407 n.55, 418 n.145

497

Catholic 64, 71, 72, 79, 81, 84, 86, 88, 105,
109, 112, 113, 114, 117, 119, 120, 121, 126,
144, 167, 195-149, 154, 161, 185, 191, 197,
206, 208, 211, 213-217, 219, 220, 221, 223,
225, 227, 229-234, 237, 238, 240-242,
246, 248, 250, 253, 258, 260, 266-7, 277,
285, 286, 289, 290, 292, 294, 300, 310,
313, 315, 319, 320, 323, 326, 334, 358,
359, 403 n.28, 406-407 n.55, 408 n.62,
415 n.122, 416 n.128, n.135, 417 n.141,
419 n.150, 420 n.164, 423 n.196, 426
n.219, 428 n.233, 430 n.17, 431 n.29, 442
n.46, 445 n.82, 449 n.120
Catholic – Church 316; C. colonies 357;
C., colonization policy of clergy 204; C.
Day rallies (Katholikentage) 267; C.
Settlement Society 204
Catskill, Catskills 8
cattle 28, 29, 242; c. breeding 418 n.145; c.
ranching 239, 240
Caucasia, Caucasus (region, Russia) 117,
152, 235
Cayuga Tp. (Ont.) 64, 402 n.20
Central Agency of German Mennonites
from Russia xxviii
Central Butte 442 n.44
Central Europe 322; C. European
immigrants 454 n.6
Central European Immigrant, The 323
Central Powers 103, 275, 284
Ceylon (Sask.) 216
Chaco (Paraguay) 163
Chamberlain (Sask.) 217
Chambery (Sask.) 236
Chaplin Lake (Sask.) 235
Chapman Tp. (Ont.) 94
charity 312
Charkov (see Kharkov)
Charlotteville (Ont.) 426 n.218
Chatham (Ont.) 93, 427 n.230
Chaudière R. (Que.) 391 n.108
cheese, cheese making 191, 246, 418 n.145
Chesley (Ont.) 83, 85
Chester (N. S.) 35, 36, 380 n.29, 381 n.33
Chester Co. (Pa.) 404 n.41
Chetlain 27
Chicago (Ill.) 97, 243, 450 n.133
Chicago Tribune 148
Chignecto Bay 33
Chihuahua (State) (Mexico) 163
Chile 434 n.71
Chilliwack (B.C.) 253
Chinese 192
chinook (warm air current) 249
Chinook (Alta.) 449 n.113
Chippawa (Upper Canada) 401 n.12, 403
n.23
cholera 151, 432 n.41

Chortitz (E. Res., Man.) 188, 440 n.16
Chortitz (Sask.) 202, 203
Chortitz (W. Res., Man.) 188, 440 n.16
Chortiz, Chortitza (Khortitza) 109, 286
Christ congregation (Montreal) 313;
(Winnipeg) 276
Christadelphians 248
Christian Day schools 320
Christlicher Jugendfreund(Winnipeg) 289
chronicles, of Mennonites in Manitoba
(*Kanadische Mennoniten*) 293
church – c., German, lack of 248; c.
decoration 295; c. in decline 236
Church of England (see also Anglican) 384
n.62; 393 n.124
church organizations 266
church service 270, 382 n.41, 446 n.94; c.
s., in English 264, 270, 271, 393 n.130,
423 n.202; bilingual c. s. 423 n.200; c. s.,
change to English language 261, 311; c.
s., German 260, 272; c. s., lack of 221
church, Catholic (in Arat, Sask.) 225
Churchbridge (Sask.) 227
church, churches 227, 240, 258; c., of
British tradition 261; c., establishment
of 169; c., Lutheran, first on prairies 224
Churchill, Winston xxxiv, 1 n.18
City Hall (Montreal) 313
Ciucurova (Dobrudja) 127
Clairmont (Alta.) 249
Clapp, Benjamin 395 n.153
Clapp, Joseph 395 n.153
Clarendon Tp. (Ont.) 60, 399 n.184
Claresholm (Alta.) 248
class, lower middle (in western Canada) 339
classification 159, Table V.12; c., census 301;
c., inaccurate 375 n.62
Claybank (Sask.) 114, 121, 253, 327
Clear Prairie (Alta.) 249, 250
Clements Tp. (N. S.) 40, 41, 385 n.67
Clementsport 41
Clementsvale (formerly Hessian Line, N.S.)
385 n.67
clergy – bilingual c. (German and English)
310; c., German 421 n.175; c., German,
all denominations teaching German 330;
c., German, language classes given by
310; c., German-Canadian 308; c.,
impact of on ethnic identity 261; c.,
itinerant, duties of 259; c., loss of ethnic
loyalty in 310; c., Mennonite 258;
c., Polish 285; c., secular 266
clergyman, activities of 320
Cleveland (Ohio) 448 n.107
Clinton Tp. (Ont.) 63, 64, 87, 401 n.11
clothing – manner of dress 263
clothing, Hutterite 273, 287
Cloverdale (B.C.) 253

origin (see racial origin, German by origin, and by nationalities and countries)
orphanage 272
Orthodox Church 112-3, 300
orthodoxy, inadequate 267
Osage 442 n.44
Osborne 440 n.16
Osler (Sask.) 442 n.44
Osnabrück (Dundas Co., Ont.) 49, 50, 392 n.116, n.120, 421 n.178
Osnabrück (Westphalia) 392 n.116
Osoyoos (B.C.) 254, 279
Osterreichisch-Ungarischer Verein (Austro-Hungarian Club) 238
Osterwick (Sask.) 202
Osterwick (W. Res., Man.) 188, 440 n.16
Ott, Michael, Abbott 208
Ottawa (city, county, district, river, valley) 19, 23, 47, 48, 56, 58, 59, 60, 84, 132, 151, 153, 284, 306, 312, 316, 327, 374 n.60, 390 n.100, 397 n.171, 398 n.175
Ottawa Immigration Agency 397 n.168, n.170
Ottawa Valley, upper 306, 312
Ottenbreit family 444 n.69
Ottenhausen (Galicia) 120
Otto family 450 n.127
Overacker 395 n.145
ownership, communal 240
oxcart(s) 165, 168, 240, 241, 243
Oxford (Co., Tp.) (Ont.) 16, 86, 418 n.147, 420 n.165
Oyama (B.C.) 252
Oyster River (B.C.) 253

pacifists (see also conscientious objection) 299
Palatinate, Palatine(s) xxvi, xl, 8, 11, 15, 16, 32, 40, 46, 49, 50, 53, 54, 61, 70, 77, 369 n.2, 370 n.14, 380 n.21, 387 n.84, 388-9 n.92, 395 n.148, 399 n.1; P. in Ireland 381 n.31; P. settlements 372 n.42
Pangman (Sask.) 221
von Papen, Chancellor xxx
Paradise Hill (Sask.) 279
Paradise Valley 449 n.113
Paraguay 154, 163, 192, 264, 322
Parchim (Germany) 447 n.96
parents, suit against Alberta government 327
parishes, list of 211
Parkerview (Sask.) 442 n.44
parochial schools (see schools, parochial)
Parry (Sask.) 442 n.44
Parry Sound (Co., Tp.) 94, 428 n.232, 428 n.234
Pascal, Bishop of Prince Albert (Sask.) 209

Paschetag, Friedrich 176
passage (see also immigration, railway, routes, oxcart, ship, train, wagon) – cheap p. 136
pastors, hardship suffered by 269
pasture, common (Allmende) 187, 192, 202
pastureland 191, 230
Patience (Alta.) 245
patriotism, Canadian, increasing as ethnicity decreases 338
Peace Hill (Alta.) 116
Peace R. 99, 249
Peace River (Alta.) 246, 249, 255
Peace River (B.C.) 250, 255
Peace River district 162, 175, 241, 248, 328, 437 n.38
Pearl (ship) 378 n.11
Peebles (formerly Kaiser, Sask.) 218
Peel (Co., Tp.) (Ont.) 88, 92, 421 n.176, 425 n.215, n.217
Peetasch (Peters), J. 294
Peitsch, Joh. 383 n.52
Pembina (Man.) 28
Pembroke (Ont.) 57, 59, 60, 398 n.179, 428 n.238
Pempeit, Pastor 242, 268
Penn, William 14
Penner 440 n.19
Penner's sawmill 199
Penner, Erdmann 203
Penner, Maria 294
Pennfield (Carleton Co., N.B.) 387 n.84
Pennsylvania 9-11, 13-16, 34, 38, 40, 46, 61, 63, 69, 70, 90, 93, 262, 263, 289, 370 n.11, 377 n.3, 379 n.19, 385 n.71, 386 n.80, 387 n.84, 404 n.33, n.41, 405 n.43, 412 n.84, 415 n.119, 422 n.194
Pennsylvania-German(s) xlii, 33, 42, 63, 64, 68, 92, 309, 370 n.14, 375 n.62, 379 n.17, 385-6 n.72, 386 n.75, 401 n.12, 450 n.133
Pennsylvania-Germans, of Palatine descent 387 n.84
Pentecostal 225
Penticton (B.C.) 252, 253
People's Conservatives of Treviranus xxx
Peoria (Alta.) 249, 250, 449 n.113
Pereiaslav (Russia) 447 n.96
Perham (Minn.) 219
Pernette, Joseph 35, 381 n.31, 389 n.92
persecution 299, 322
Perth (Co., Tp.) (Ont.) 22, 71, 74, 80, 81, 83-85, 305, 306, 375 n.63, 413 n.98, 415 n.118, n.119, n.121, 417 n.142, 419 n.150
Perth Volksfreund 86
Petawawa (Ont.) 59, 60, 398 n.176
Peter 441 n.19
Petereit, Preacher 224
Peters, G.A. 294

retention of German ethnicity (also see
ethnicity, retention of) 306
Revenue (Sask.) 210, 211
Revolution (American) 371 n.22
Revolution, Russian 149, 150
Reychart, David and Jeremiah 389 n.94
Rhein (Sask.) 228
Rheinfelden (nr. Basel) 28
Rheinland (Sask.) 202
Rhine (Germany) 28, 32, 241, 377 n.3
Rhine Province (see Rhineland, Germany)
Rhineland (Germany) 406 n.55, 407 n.55
Rhineland (Man.) 186, 283
Rhineland (Ont.) 426 n.219, n.220
Rhineland Municipality (list of German-
English schools) 318
Richards (Alta.) 239
Richelieu R. (Que.) 45, 388 n.90
Richert, W. (former mayor of Detroit) 234
Richmond (Sask.) 219
Richmond Tp. (Ont.) 53, 55
Ridgeville (Man.) 141
von Riedesel, Baron Friedrich xlii
Riedinger, Father (Oblate) 219, 294
Riedle, D. W. 222, 226
Rieger family 444 n.69
Riel, Louis 96
right of assembly of Germans, prohibited
in Russia 149
rights, violation of 322
Rimbey 449 n.113
Rindisbacher, Peter xli, 30
Rittenhouse, Michael 402 n.13
River St. John (see St. John River, N.B.)
River Top (Alta.) 250
Riverdale (Ont.) 140, 419 n.150
Rivers 440 n.16
Riversdale (N.S.) 381 n.38
Riversdale (Sask.) 226
Riverside congregation (Riverside, Alta.)
251
roads 227, 405 n.48; construction of
r. neglected 18
Robinson (Alta.) 248
Rochfort Bridge (Alta.) 246, 247
Röchl, Elis. 383 n.52
Rock 416 n.134
Rockglen (Sask.) 219, 220, 221
Rockport (Alta.) 239
Rocky Mountains, Rockies 25, 97, 240, 248,
249
Rockyford (Alta.) 239
Roger's Rangers 399 n.1
Rogers, Col. 52
Rolla (B.C.) 250, 255
Romania 107, 108, 120, 121, 125-127, 155,
159, 174, 195, 214, 215, 216, 218, 231,
236, 355

Romania, as origin 447 n.96
Romanian 301, 313
Rooder 381 n.36
Roosevelt, Theodore (former U.S. President)
148, 257
Rosalind (Alta.) 240
Rosch (Bukovina) 121, 215, 444 n.69
Rosebud (Alta.) 239
Rosedale (Alta.) 449 n.113
Rosedale (B.C.) 253
Rosedale (nr. Elie, Man.) 193, 274
Rosefield (Sask.) 445 n.83
Rosemary (Alta.) 332, 449 n.113
Rosenbach (Man.) 318
Rosenbach (Sask.) 203
Rosenberger family 404 n.38
Rosenburgh 389 n.94
Rosenfeld (Man.) 190, 191, 194, 283, 318
Rosenfeld (N.Sask.) 202
Rosenfeld (S. Sask.) 203
Rosenfeld (W. Res., Man.) 188, 440 n.16
Rosengart (nr. Plum Coulée, W. Res., Man.)
188, 193, 440 n.16
Rosenheim (Alta.) 241
Rosenhof (Man.) 186, 318
Rosenhof (Sask.) 203
Rosenhof-Rosenort (nr. Morris, Man.) 192,
193
Rosenkrantz, Michael, Lieut. 400 n.4
Rosenort (Man.) 186, 188, 318, 440 n.16
Rosenort (Sask.) 203, 263
Rosenort (nr. Tiegenhof, W. Prussia) 200
Rosenorter congregation 264
Rosenorter Gemeinde (Rosenort Mennonite
Church) 263
Rosenroll, A.S. 283
Rosenthal colony (Alta.) 242, 243
Rosenthal (Crimea) 114
Rosenthal (Sask.) 219, 445 n.80
Rosenthal (W. Res., Man.) 188
Rosenthal-Leduc (Alta.) 116
Rosevear (Alta.) 162, 247
Rosewell (Man.) 318
Rosthern (model district) 200
Rosthern (Sask.) xxxiii, 105, 116, 141, 144,
151, 152, 154, 163, 198, 199, 201, 206,
233, 252, 277, 283, 325, 331, 332, 442
n.44
Rosthern district (Sask.) 202, 205
Rostock (Ont.) 81
Rotermühl, Johann 29
Roth, Georg (George) 382 n.39
Rottenburg (see New Germany, Ont.)
Rotterdam 31, 376 n.2, 378 n.11
Rouleau (Sask.) 220
Rousseau (land speculator) 68